Islam and Dhimmitude
Where Civilizations Collide

By the Same Author

Les Juifs en Egypte, Geneva: Editions de l'Avenir, 1971.

Yehudai Mizrayim. Foreword by Hayyim Ze'ev Hirschberg. Revised and enlarged Hebrew edition of *Les Juifs en Egypte*. Translated from the French by Aharon Amir. Tel Aviv: Maariv, 1974.

Le Dhimmi. Profil de l'opprimé en Orient et en Afrique du Nord depuis la conquête arabe. Paris: Editions Anthropos, 1980.

The Dhimmi. Jews and Christians under Islam. Translated from the French by David Maisel, Paul Fenton and David Littman. With a preface by Jacques Ellul. Revised and enlarged English edition. Rutherford, NJ: Fairleigh Dickinson University Press/Associated University Presses, 1985 (Fifth printing, 2001).

Ha-Dimmim; B'nai Hasoot. Enlarged Hebrew edition of *The Dhimmi*. Translated by Aharon Amir. With a preface by Jacques Ellul and an introduction by Moshe Sharon. Jerusalem: Cana, 1986.

The Dhimmi. Jews and Christians under Islam. Russian edition, 2 vols. Jerusalem: Society for Research on Jewish Communities—"Aliya" library, 1992.

Les Chrétientés d'Orient entre Jihâd et Dhimmitude. VIIe–XXe siècle. With a preface by Jacques Ellul. Paris: Les Editions du Cerf, 1991.

The Decline of Eastern Christianity under Islam. From Jihad to Dhimmitude. Seventh-Twentieth Century. With a foreword by Jacques Ellul. Translated from the French by Miriam Kochan and David Littman. Madison/Teaneck, NJ: Fairleigh Dickinson University Press/Associated University Presses, 1996.

Juifs et Chrétiens sous l'Islam: les dhimmis face au défi intégriste. Paris: Berg International, 1994.

Islam and Dhimmitude

Where Civilizations Collide

Bat Ye'or

Translated from the French by
Miriam Kochan and David Littman

Madison • Teaneck
Fairleigh Dickinson University Press
Lancaster, UK: Gazelle Book Services Ltd.

Associated University Presses
2010 Eastpark Boulevard
Cranbury, NJ 08512

Associated University Presses
P.O. Box 338, Port Credit
Mississauga, Ontario
Canada L5G 4L8

Gazelle Book Services Limited
Falcon House, Queen Square
Lancaster LA1 1RN, England

The paper used in this publication meets the requirements of the American National Standard for Permanence of Paper for Printed Library Materials Z39.48-1984.

Library of Congress Cataloging-in-Publication Data

Bat Ye'or.
    Islam and Dhimmitude : where civilizations collide / Bat Ye'or ; translated from
  the French by Miriam Kochan and David Littman.
      p. cm.
    Includes bibliographical references (p.) and index.
    ISBN 0-8386-3942-9 (cloth) — ISBN 0-8386-3943-7 (pbk.)
    1. Dhimmis.   2. Islamic Empire—Ethnic relations.   3. Islamic countries—Ethnic relations.
  I. Title.
  DS36.9.D47 B395   2002
  808'.097671—dc21   2001040101

SECOND PRINTING 2003

PRINTED IN THE UNITED STATES OF AMERICA

A false balance is
abomination to the Lord.
                    —Proverbs 11:1

In the end, we will remember
not the words of our enemies,
but the silence of our friends.
                    —Martin Luther King Jr.

Contents

Contents

Abbreviations

Periodicals

AAM	*Afrique et l'Asie Modernes* (Paris)
AAS	*Asian and African Studies* (Haifa)
AIEO	*Annales de l'Institut d'Etudes Orientales* (Algiers)
ARABICA	*Revue d'Etudes Arabes* (Paris)
BAIU	*Bulletin, Alliance Israélite Universelle* (Paris)
BEO	*Bulletin d'Etudes Orientales* (Damascus)
BIJS	*Bulletin of the Institute of Jewish Studies* (London)
BJRL	*Bulletin of the John Rylands Library* (Manchester)
BSOAS	*Bulletin, School of Oriental and African Studies* (London)
BYZANTION	*International Journal of Byzantine Studies* (Brussels)
DOP	*Dumbarton Oaks Papers* (Washington, D.C.)
EI	*Encyclopaedia of Islam,* first edition
EI²	*Encyclopaedia of Islam,* second edition
EJ	*Encyclopaedia Judaica* (Jerusalem, 1971)
EO	*Echos d'Orient, Revue de Théologie, de Droit Canonique, de Liturgie, d'Archéologie, d'Histoire et de Géographie Orientales* (Paris)
FA	*Foreign Affairs* (New York)
HERODOTE	*Revue de géographie et de géopolitique* (Paris)
HESPERIS	*Institut des Hautes Etudes Marocaines* (Paris)
HGS	*Holocaust and Genocide Studies* (Oxford)
HI	*Hamard Islamicus, Journal of Studies and Research in Islam* (Karachi)
IOS	*Israel Oriental Studies* (Jerusalem)
ISLAMOCHRISTIANA	*Journal, Pontificio Instituto di Studi Arabi e d'Islamistica* (Vatican)
JA	*Journal Asiatique* (Paris)
JAOS	*Journal, American Oriental Society* (New Haven, CT)
JES	*Journal of Ecumenical Studies* (Philadelphia)
JESHO	*Journal, Economic and Social History of the Orient* (Leiden)
JHSE	*Jewish Historical Society of England* (London)

JIMMA	*Journal, Institute of Muslim Minority Affairs* (Jeddah)
JJS	*Journal of Jewish Studies* (London)
JOS	*Journal of Ottoman Studies* (Istanbul)
JPS	*Journal of Palestine Studies* (Beirut)
JQ	*Jerusalem Quarterly* (Jerusalem)
JRAS	*Journal of the Royal Asiatic Society* (London)
JSAI	*Jerusalem Studies in Arabic and Islam* (Jerusalem)
MEJ	*The Middle East Journal* (Washington)
MEQ	*Middle East Quarterly* (Philadelphia)
MER	*Middle East Review* (New York)
MES	*Middle Eastern Studies* (London)
Midstream	*A Monthly Jewish Review* (New York)
MW	*Muslim World* (Hertford, CT)
NC	*Nouveaux Cahiers* (Paris)
PAAJR	*Proceedings of the American Academy for Jewish Research* (New York)
PISAI	*Pontificio Instituto di Studi Arabi e d'Islamistica* (Vatican)
RAS	*Royal Asiatic Society* (London)
REI	*Revue des Etudes Islamiques* (Paris)
REJ	*Revue des Etudes Juives* (Paris)
REMMM	*Revue du Monde Musulman et de la Méditerranée* (Aix-en-Provence)
REP	*Revue des Etudes Palestiniennes* (Paris)
RFSE	*Revue de la Faculté des Sciences Economiques* (Istanbul)
RHR	*Revue d'Histoire des Religions* (Paris)
RMM	*Revue du Monde Musulman* (Paris)
ROC	*Revue de l'Orient Chrétien* (Paris)
RSPT	*Revue des Sciences Philosophiques et Théologiques* (Paris)
SENS	*Revue, Juifs et Chrétiens dans le monde aujourd'hui* (Paris)
SI	*Studia Islamica* (Paris)
Shofar	*An Interdisciplinary Journal of Jewish Studies* (West Lafayette, IN)
SPS	*Studies in Plural Societies* (The Hague)
TM	*Les Temps Modernes* (Paris)
WLB	*Wiener Library Bulletin* (London)
YOD	*Revue des Etudes Hébraïques et juives modernes et contemporaines* (Paris)
Zion	*A Quarterly for Research in Jewish History* (Jerusalem)

C.J.   *Codex Justinianus,* C.E. 529
C.Th.   *Codex Theodosianus,* C.E. 438

Archives

AE   Affaires Etrangères (Paris)
AIU   Alliance Israélite Universelle (Paris)
FO   Foreign Office (Public Record Office, London)
ISA   Israel State Archives (Jerusalem)
MAE   Ministère des Affaires Etrangères (Paris)
PP   Parliamentary Papers (London)
PRO   Public Records Office
SP   State Papers (London)
WJC   World Jewish Congress (Geneva)

AIU, LIBYE I.C.12	FO 195/2308	FO, SP 97–17
ISA R.G.2. 5/155	196–10	97–21
R.G.2. 10/244	141/710	97–40
	424/40	PP 1877 (C.1739)
	1520	PP 1877 (C.1806)

Press

AFP   *Agence France Presse* (Paris)
AP   *Associated Press* (New York)
IHT   *International Herald Tribune* (Paris)
JP   *Jerusalem Post* (Jerusalem)
MEMRI   *Middle East Media and Research Institute*
             (Washington)
NYT   *New York Times* (New York)
PM   World Jewish Congress (New York)
PMW   *Palestinian Media Watch* (Jerusalem)
Reuters   *Reuters* (London)

Author's Note

As in my previous publications, the general rule has been to omit diacritical points, with the exception of an apostrophe (') used indiscriminately for the *hamza* or the *ayin*, occurring in the middle of a word. Some accents have been kept in a few cases.

I have used Richard Bell's authoritative translation of *The Qur'an*. However, the more common English usage: "Koran" and "koranic" has been maintained throughout—except in quotations from Bell's work, and any other quotations in English where the word "Qur'an" was used by the author. Bell's usage of the Arabic term "Allah" has been retained, except where the word "God" for the divinity is found in English quotations.

All texts and quotations from English have been reproduced as originally printed, with the punctuation, syntax, and spelling left intact. Square brackets [containing clarifications, or "*sic*"] are by the author, whereas round parentheses were in the original text.

The word "antisemitism" is spelled throughout, following the preferred usage initiated by Dr. James Parkes in his remarkable work, *The Conflict of the Church and the Synagogue. A Study in the Origins of Antisemitism* (London, 1934).

The King James Authorized translation of the Bible was used.

Acknowledgments

The English translation of this work was made possible thanks to a grant from an American Foundation, to which I am grateful.

I wish to thank the Public Record Office (London) for permission to reproduce extracts from Foreign Office documents, particularly in appendix 1.

It is my privilege to express here my gratitude to David Littman, historian and experienced nongovernmental representative to the United Nations Commission on Human Rights (UNCHR) in Geneva, to whom I am indebted for all the UN documentation in this work; these numerous reports allowed me to examine a contemporary aspect related to my research, which is generally neglected by nonspecialists. He is also responsible for the English translations of the sources from the archives and publications of the Alliance Israélite Universelle in Paris, particularly the extracts from a letter by the school director in Iran to the AIU, describing the 1910 destruction of the Jewish quarter of Shiraz in Iran (appendix 2). Once again, he undertook the daunting task of preparing the comprehensive bibliography, covering all the reference notes.

I am deeply indebted to Dr. Gaspar Biro of the University of Budapest, who kindly acceded to my request at the end of his six-year mandate (1993–98) as the United Nations Special Rapporteur on Sudan, by providing me with valuable background information. His professional insight has enabled me to gain a broader understanding of this particular situation.

My thanks also to Professor Paul Fenton of the Sorbonne who provided me with erudite observations and reread the final proofs. René Wadlow—a former professor and Director of the Research Graduate Institute of Development Studies, University of Geneva—kindly read the manuscript and provided me with useful editorial suggestions.

As with my previous book in 1996, Miriam Kochan and David Littman have discharged with much competence and infinite patience a difficult task, with the manuscript being constantly reworked. My special thanks go to both of them for the fine quality of their joint translation.

To this work, I would like to associate my husband—constantly by my side during thirty years of research—whose unstinted assistance never flagged, and whose engagement has allowed me to develop and improve my efforts in this field.

Introduction

A reader unfamiliar with this area of history might consider some aspects of the following chapters as a repetition of my earlier writings. Indeed, the field of study under review is the same, but this time the aim was directed toward a synthesis between the *dhimmi* status and the concept of dhimmitude. The two fields can merge but they are not identical. The *dhimmi's* legal status is conditioned by a legal corpus; it is circumscribed and pre-scribed by what Islamic theologians consider to be divine laws; its compul-sory and repressive provisions are applied by government agents charged with supervising their execution. The *dhimmi* status is thus made up of emi-nently concrete and visible elements which constitute a field of study, easily classified because these essentials are integrated into everyday social life.

Dhimmitude, on the other hand, represents a domain which embraces the social, political, and religious *relations* of different human groups. Al-though these groups evolve in the same specific doctrinal context, they are subject to a variety of external and conflicting pressures. The range and intensity of these pressures are conditioned by durable or circumstantial factors, and it is precisely the identification of these: their origin, function, evolution, and their correlations, that compose the field of research on dhimmitude. Consequently, the realm of dhimmitude is lodged in evolu-tionary historical time—in contingencies and alterations—but within per-manent structures fixed by theology. This overlap between diverse factors—which are irreducible, but at the same time fluctuating —prompts the diversity of the manifestations of dhimmitude. Its contradictions, which are not merely superficial, express compromises between the injunctions of dogma, the modalities of interpretation, and the potential for their real-ization.

Dhimmitude embraces the condition of the *dhimmi*, which incorporates one of its stable elements, but any study of this status does not encompass the whole field of dhimmitude which evolves according to various factors. In fact, the concepts of both *dhimmi* and dhimmitude are equivalent to the notions of Jew and Judaism, of Christian and Christianity. Although these notions are linked, they still imply significant differences. The concept of dhimmitude restores the *dhimmis* to the context of relationships between groups and gives them the characteristics of a specific "civilization." It also

21

grants them the breadth and complexity of history's dynamic. Here the word "civilization" means a comprehensive system of laws, traditions, and culture, evolving in duration according to specific and structural parameters, which maintain its homogeniety, its behavioral patterns and their transmission. An Armenian *dhimmi*—whether in the Balkans, Mesopotamia, or Egypt—belongs to the civilization of dhimmitude, in the same way as any Jewish or Christian *dhimmi:* either Serb, Copt, Greek, or other.

As any methodological work requires precise and accurate definitions, the terms "religious minorities" and "Islamic tolerance" should be completely excluded from serious research in this field. In effect, after the Arab-Muslim conquest, the Christian *dhimmi* peoples remained for centuries ethnic majorities and, therefore, to define them as "religious minorities" locks them into demeaning and erroneous concepts which falsify the nature of their historical identity. Likewise, the ambiguity and subjectivity of the word "tolerance"—used to designate all the complexity of dhimmitude—make it inadequate as an area of study which requires precision and objectivity. This reservation does not contradict the principle of Islamic tolerance in respect of other religions, a tolerance which is actually inscribed in the Koran, although its interpretations by jurists and its application by the Islamic authorities display divergences. A search for more precise terminology circumscribes the limits of this tolerance and defines its criteria but it does not annul it. The expression "Islamic tolerance" is both too vague and too restricted to express all the contents of a comprehensive domain covering history, theology, and politics that extended over three continents. Furthermore, any objective analytical reasoning becomes specious if the material to be studied is defined at the outset—even before being analyzed—by a subjective notion, such as the term "tolerance." This practice reverses the rational order which involves examining the material before proceeding to a judgment. "Toleration" must be qualified in the context of the Koran, and not in a modern Western generalization, bearing in mind the diversity of its extension into the religious, legal, and historical spheres.

This study, therefore, attempts to define and examine that field of research which I have called dhimmitude: its various sectors and facets. The sheer extent of the geographical and historical multiformity defies the abstract organization of data which is an indispensable procedure for any methodology. Dhimmitude has two aspects: one formed by the body of relationships with non-Muslims, contracted at the historical, social, theological, and juridical levels of the Muslim world; the other is determined by the varied reactions of the *dhimmi* peoples.

As a pioneering work in a vast subject, this preliminary examination only represents a sounding line which will have to be corrected, completed, and amended by other, better-equipped researchers. Perhaps it will then be possible to evaluate the civilization of dhimmitude at a historical and cultural level, despite the dearth of sources in some sectors. This new approach was undertaken in a previous study,[1] but the present book develops it more fully.

I realize that my study of dhimmitude remains incomplete because it is limited to Jews and Christians. It should be supplemented by the dhimmitude of the Zoroastrians, located in an inferior category, and that of Buddhists and Hindus, considered as idolaters. A few books on this subject have recently been published in India. The picture they paint is similar to that of regions to the west of the Indian subcontinent. The contemporary historical negationism in India, with the collusion of Hindu politicians, is discussed in detail by Koenraad Elst in his book on this subject.[2]

Like a giant jigsaw puzzle scattered over the world, the different elements of the diversified *dhimmi* civilization should be collected to allow an evaluation and a comparative analysis of regional particularisms in order to produce a better knowledge of the whole. I have tried to gather the specific data of dhimmitude in different sectors of life. This analytical inventory throughout time and space may confuse the reader, but it is essential for framing the world of dhimmitude.

As the Islamic conquests extended over vast populations from Spain to India, the conquerors pragmatically adapted their rule to local circumstances. Although different aspects appear in the overall picture of dhimmitude, the condition of Jews and Christians was broadly identical, with a few regional differences, for instance, the *devshirme* practice of enslaving children which was limited to Christians in the European Ottoman provinces. Good relations between the caliphs and the Eastern patriarchs developed in the context of dhimmitude, that is, for as long as these Church leaders served Islamic interests, either by betrayal of their own peoples during battles, or by compliance and obedience to the caliph's designs. These good relations barely influenced the oppression of the population, as is still evident today in the *dhimmi* communities of Iraq, Syria, and Egypt where, for example, persecution of the Copts coexists with the patriarchate's alliance with the regime and the silence of notables.

A few critics have described my books as anti-Muslim. Such judgments of intent avoid discussion of the subject and aim to block all research which is not inscribed in advance within a conventional fictitious definition of "tolerance." Furthermore, my publications are in no way concerned with either theology or Islamic civilization as a whole.

They do not center on the founder of Islam's religion, and its policy in respect of Jews and Christians, but they do explore the different facets of these peoples' history in their Islamized countries. I have cited the juridical decisions of Muslim jurists and theologians concerning the subjected Christian and Jewish populations, with their koranic justifications, *as sup-*

plied by these jurists, themselves. This constitutes a specific domain of Muslim history which may seem unimportant today in view of the small size of these minorities; however, an enquirer does not measure the interest of a subject by its size. In addition, the populations ruled by Islamic military and administrative authority consisted of Christians, Jews, Zoroastrians in Persia, and Hindus and Buddhists. Governing all these peoples from Spain to India assumed primordial importance for the minority Arab power, whose ethnic center was situated in Arabia. It was, therefore, amidst the multitude of conquered peoples that the juridical and cultural fundamentals of Islamic civilization were formulated, with its manifold cultural and scientific manifestations.

My research only covers the specific and shared condition of Christians and Jews in Islamic societies. Texts elucidating this domain by the promulgation of laws, their objectives, and their justifications are amply cited. This area forms the historical and cultural heritage of the "People of the Book," Jews and Christians, since the sources mention them by name, usually together. Hence, dhimmitude concerns a joint Jewish and Christian civilization. It was not the Muslims who were the *dhimmis,* but Jews and Christians, and therefore they have the right and the duty to know and to study this history which concerns them directly, and which forms a part of their historical and cultural heritage. They must know their own history, examine it, reflect upon it, and form their opinion. These opinions can then be discussed, approved, or dismissed by critics.

They also have the right to criticize the prejudices and laws which, over the centuries, reduced them to a humiliating and subhuman condition. The self-appointed apologists for this oppressive system might themselves be taxed with anti-Jewish and anti-Christian racism or bias. Their scholarship can also be dubious if it serves to cover up this history. My research is not aimed at proving a theory, but it brings together and examines a considerable number of elements, which are frequently and deliberately ignored. Hence, it is the amorphous label of "tolerance" which provides a scholastic thesis and a dogmatic assertiveness.

I have attempted here to distinguish the varied components of a condition defined by legal texts specific to this subject. These regulations constitute a body of explicit laws, recognized by all four schools of Muslim law, clearly enunciating the rights and duties of the *dhimmis.* They prescribe the behavioral norms down to the smallest detail, even indicating the type of material allowed for clothing. Historical data complement the picture by exposing the modalities of these rules, their interpretation and application in different places, and the popular reactions and prejudices which they generated.

Another crucial element of this condition lies in the caliph's power to arbitrate and his conviction that, by applying Islamic laws, he is administering divine justice. Indeed, the continued existence of the tolerated religions on his territory depended solely on his protection. Some historical texts suggest an amicable relationship between *dhimmi* patriarchs and caliphs. Others report that the same patriarchs were tortured on the orders of the same caliphs on suspicion of concealing treasures. Obviously, to preserve an empire which was always threatened by disruptive forces within and external enemies required considerable, constantly replenished financial resources, coupled with pitiless harshness. The caliph's—or ruler's—policy, woven into the contingencies of historical events, and into the solution of immediate crucial problems, evolved as a function of these conjunctures. Personal factors, circumstantial developments, violence, fanaticism, and the cruelty of contemporary customs—common to every civilization—influenced the course of history.

Often the situation in the provinces was totally beyond the state's control. Nevertheless, one element in the attitude of the supreme Muslim authority remains constant and stands out among the disparate and fortuitous aspects of history: a conscientious determination to administer justice according to Islamic norms in deciding disputes between communities and to ensure the protection of vulnerable groups. Sometimes the Muslim authority, in order to save itself, had no option but to yield to violence. However, considering itself to be their guarantor and protector by virtue of the Prophet's law, the army was often sent to protect threatened communities. Clearly, the People of the Book would have totally disappeared were it not for this koranic recognition of the legality of the tolerated religions—a legality upheld by the caliphs, sometimes against extremist *ulema*—and the effective guarantee of their "protection" (*dhimma*). Consequently, this protection seems to be the basis of law and order against the forces of anarchy and destruction threatening society as a whole. Despite religious barriers, interaction between communities and personal relationships sometimes wove a network of human solidarity and friendship; evidence of this, emerging from the chronicles, casts a ray of hope on the picture of human baseness.

The study of dhimmitude involves different levels and the mastery of a large number of disciplines. Here, a few preliminary points of methodology are indicated.

The theological level would consist of examining the many references to Jews and Christians in the Koran, from the *hadiths* which explain it and complement its teaching, and in the biographies of the Prophet—a body of texts which forms the foundations of the normative sacred character of the *shari'a*. The origin, the foundation, and the justification of dhimmitude are to be found in this theological corpus. Examination of this material by Islamists, Orientalists, and Arabists exists but is dispersed in articles or general works. A first step would be to collect these various writings. A thorough study of the Jews mentioned in the *hadiths* exists since 1937.[3] A second stage would consist of examining the interpretations of these various texts by earlier Islamic theologians and jurists, and by contemporary scholars. Modern works of this type do exist.

A major example is the study by a leading European scholar on comparative religions and Middle East studies, Professor Emeritus Heribert Busse of the University of Kiel in Germany, whose book first appeared in German, translated in 1998 for the Princeton Series on the Middle East under the title: *Islam, Judaism, and Christianity: Theological and Historical Affiliations.*[4] The author examines the *suras* in the Koran, the *hadiths,* and the biographies of Muhammad, analyzing the evolution of his attitude regarding Jews and Christians—from early good-will, even admiration, to later hostility and war. Another study: *Judaism, Christianity and Islam. Interactions and Conflicts,* by Moshe Sharon—professor of Islamic history at the Hebrew University of Jerusalem—has a useful analysis of interaction between the three religions.[5]

These two scholarly works —and other studies—demonstrate the coexistence of numerous *suras* that extol an open dialogue and the acceptance of religious pluralism, alongside those *suras* which incite to hostility and war. Both authors provide a critical analysis of later sources (eighth to ninth centuries) that contain the prejudices and anachronistic justifications for earlier events.

Some Muslim theologians and jurists have tried to adapt the koranic message to modern times. This school of thought is exclusively concerned with the political structures of contemporary Muslim states and has not reassessed the fundamental concepts governing the relationship with non-Muslims. In fact this procedure is apparently regarded as pointless because of the preexisting presumed tolerance. What is more, the concealment of dhimmitude has prevented this tolerance from being evaluated in terms of theology, jurisdiction, and history. Consequently, it is imperative that Muslim theologians, armed with modern tools of exegesis, look at their own religious texts for means to render void the concepts of *jihad, harbi,* and *dhimmi* which were formulated twelve centuries ago.

According to Islamic doctrine, the Koran is uncreated. The Prophet's words and deeds related by the *hadiths* and biographers are believed to express the divine will. That is why the accusation of blasphemy is not limited to the name of Allah and to Muhammad, the messenger of Allah, but extends over all of Islam's sacred writings, including the *shari'a.*

Sacred texts justifying dhimmitude should be subjected to critical analysis by specialists, according to the deontological principles of historical exegesis as applied in the West, since the West itself is now directly concerned with this concept. In the absence of such a critical procedure, dhimmitude will continue to represent a perfect, well-tried, and unalterable divine schema. All these questions are linked to the nature of the Koran: whether created or uncreated; whether a part of the divine or human interpretation of a Revelation. The fundamental divergences between the two religions of the Bible and that of the Koran concern, *inter alia*, the mission of the prophets in general, and the interpretation and nature of prophecy.

On the historical plane different levels of investigation are possible. The first concerns the justification and rules of *jihad*, since it is *this* war which subsequently conditions the *dhimmis'* rights, as a function of the tactics leading to victory.

Within the *dhimmi* status, the differences between the "People of the Book" and Zoroastrians and Hindus should be noted. Likewise, within the category of People of the Book, the condition of Jews and Christians in Arabia is not identical with that of their coreligionists in all the conquered regions of the *dar al-harb*. Jews and Christians from Arabia were totally expelled from the Hijaz, and their temporary presence there is subject to specific conditions.

The study of the *dhimmi* status should record the diverse manifestations of this condition in the geographical extension of the *dar al-Islam*, and their accordance with Islamic laws. This classification of the available data would allow the possibility of assessing their common features or their differences, and their evolution as a function of circumstantial parameters.

Another section concerns the laws applicable prior to Islam, which were incorporated into Islamic jurisdiction after the conquest. Historians have pointed out the influence of pre-Islamic Arab customs, and the adoption by the Arab conquerors of fiscal methods employed by earlier Byzantine and Persian regimes. But, to my knowledge, no comparative study exists of the regulations decreed by the various Christian councils in respect of the Jews—including those introduced into the codes of Theodosius II and Justinian in the fifth and sixth centuries—and the later Islamic legislation concerning the *dhimmi*, which borrowed from them. This study would establish similarities, but would also point to the specific features and variations in their development within two different theological systems: that of the fallen deicide people, and that of the *harbi* infidels, conquered but equally demonized and excluded. It must be emphasized that the concept of collective downfall is applied to non-Muslims. Barred from divine love they are described as "enemies of Allah" and consequently must be combatted by "the party of Allah" (*Hizb Allah*). The theological and political contexts coalesce in the doctrine of *jihad*.

The area of dhimmitude also concerns intervention by Christian states in the form of political, commercial, and religious protection, and of the missiological movements—with their consequences for the various *dhimmi* groups. These aspects fall into the category of international policy and provide a rich body of documentation in diplomatic archives. Specialized monographs have already been published on this subject. However, the relationships between the various *dhimmi* groups in their interactions with the *umma*, the Muslim community, and with the Christian states still remain to be explored more fully. The same is true of the *dhimmi* peoples' liberation movements and the various possibilities for emancipation from the laws of dhimmitude: integration into a secular state, or territorial independence. An examination of the inter-*dhimmi* conflicts grafted onto these movements, and intervention by foreign powers, would shed light on wide historical areas which are still plunged in darkness. Lastly, a comparative study of the mentalities of dhimmitude and its various manifestations in geographical and historical space, constitutes a virgin area of research in the sector of social psychology.

It should be recalled that dhimmitude does not only cover the relationship between Islam and the People of the Book; it also includes the relationship between Christians and Jews. Christian dogma and legislation relating to Jews was integrated into dhimmitude. In the following chapters it will be shown that during the entire twentieth century the interactions of the three monotheistic religions developed according to traditional historical schemas, which maintained the same conflictual relationships. Only knowledge of their structures and mechanisms will permit their destructive malevolence to be contained in this new century.

In this study, I have examined Christian anti-Judaism only in the specific context of dhimmitude. Anti-Judaism was innate to the Eastern Churches, as expressed in the patristic literature and in numerous Canon laws—particularly by the persecution and humiliation of Palestinian Jewry from the Byzantine period on. For the contemporary period, I have endeavored to distinguish Christian anti-Jewish currents from the overall Judeo-Christian relationship. I strongly believe that anti-Judaism is not shared uniformly by all strands of Christianity, but derives either from a theological or a state policy, which is deliberately conceived and disseminated for strategic goals. Indeed, countless Christians have opposed anti-Judaism in modern times.

It is within the context of dhimmitude that certain links between the genocide of the Armenians and of European Jewry are revealed, whereby the Muslim world's influence—particularly its Arab component—effectively determined the policies of the Western powers during both World Wars, respectively toward the two groups of victims.

In pursuance of this research, I have examined the historical terrain common to Christians and Jews, as circumscribed and specified by Muslim jurists. This is the matter—both historical and human—that I have labeled dhimmitude and I have attempted to ascertain its sources, spheres, and development. Understanding of this domain requires an intellectual approach that complements the classification of long-term events. Shackled by silence and subjection, the *dhimmi* societies remained static, imprisoned in historical autism, albeit without ceasing to exist as organized human groups. It is this transhistorical human field, both materially and spiritually, that I have attempted to grasp and interpret within its sensibility and its wealth of significance. The linguistic, historical, even psychosocial skills needed to explore such a vast domain would require a comprehensive undertaking by multi-disciplinary teams, hence experts in various fields will certainly find omissions in my pioneering studies.

The mutual animosity of Jews and Christians—acting as repulsive magnetic fields—has impeded the comprehensive study of dhimmitude as a historical domain common to the two groups. *This is the basis of its negation.* Yet, a thoughtful approach to the subject can progressively eliminate prejudices and carefully hidden personal preconceptions, thus clearing the way for the rediscovery of the human being, within his universal dimension and his nothingness—which are the two areas of reconciliation.

I also believe that by analyzing the new hate-filled forms of substitution theology—"Palestinianism" replacing "Israel"—this study may assist those Christians opposed to such a theology of replacement, which will inevitably destroy the very essence of Christianity (see chapters 9 and 10 below, and the conclusion).

A comprehensive study of dhimmitude raises further acute questions fathoming the depths of our identity and the values of Western civilization. In a review of my previous book, *The Decline of Eastern Christianity. From Jihad to Dhimmitude*[6] Professor Emeritus James E. Biechler of La Salle University (Philadelphia, PA), rightly points out its ecumenical implications for relations with Islam.[7] These implications are even stronger in the case of Judeo-Christian relations, oscillating between destroying or strengthening the bond between Jews and Christians, which is ontological and primordial since the Church was born of the Synagogue, and the Hebrew Bible is the foundation of Christianity. Consequently, the destruction of the Judaic component within Christianity would destroy Christianity itself. This historical, cultural, and theological situation—which does not concern Buddhists, Hindus, and others—is totally rejected by Muslim immigrants in the West. Their opposition obliges us to examine the Judeo-Christian identity in depth, to evaluate it, and to decide whether or not it should be maintained in the twenty-first century. A choice is thus forced upon the fundamental values of Western civilization structured by the Bible. This inter-relationship problematic between Judaism and Christianity is not new. It has developed from the Christian New Testament, and over the centuries has engendered the diverse reformed and evangelical Churches integrated into the political, theological, and philosophical history of the West. It is important to know whether or not Jews and Christians wish to pursue this dialogue in order to overcome the prejudices which divide them, or if they are going to import into the West the self-destructive relationships of hatred nurtured by the world of dhimmitude, which are forced upon them by a third, external party. If Jews and Christians do not succeed in resolving together the Judeo-Christian antagonisms, they will also fail in their dialogue of reconciliation with Islam.

The history of dhimmitude represents a panorama of more than a millennium, spanning three continents. It still continues to appear today in new forms which drive out and renew the traditional ones. This history, so old and yet so modern, which is taking place before our eyes and unfolding on our television screens, when the media decide to cover it—this ever-camouflaged history, has no name. In this book I have tried to delineate and define it by the term: "dhimmitude." This is a painful history of hatred, suffering, death, heroism, betrayal and cowardice. Consequently, it is the history of mankind in all its diversity and all its components.

The approach to the world of dhimmitude first requires that one live among the *dhimmis*, who experience and actualize it. To gain entry into their closed and silent world necessitates dismantling its artifices, its lies, and its amnesia—antidotes to the violence, terror, and humiliation targeting them. This process, fraught with hazards and uncertainties, will lead the enquirer toward that large sick body, ashamed of its blisters yet moribund, which continues to survive, refusing treatment for fear of dying from it. Should one lift the veil, auscultate, and diagnose the illness? Can one brave the prohibitions and pull down the barriers to let light stream into the cesspools of history? In fact, dhimmitude is the central place where the three monotheistic religions collide, thus making it the requisite terrain for their reconciliation.

The Judeo-Christian rapprochement that began in the West—although bitterly opposed by the *dhimmi* Eastern Churches—constitutes a major advance and a model for the rapprochement of the two peoples of the Book with the Muslim world. The reconciliation of the two *dhimmi* religions—Christianity and Judaism—is an indispensable step toward embarking with Islam along the same path of mutual reflection on the dogmas and history of dhimmitude. In this respect, those individuals and their followers who initiated the Judeo-Christian rapprochement could contribute their experience in a domain which has required much courage, intellectual integrity, and frankness. Thus, this huge task, which has brought forth so many human qualities on both sides is not yet over, since it would be redeployed in evermore enriching and fertile perspectives for humanity's spiritual adventure in its approach toward the sacred.

Switzerland, April 2001

Islam and Dhimmitude
Where Civilizations Collide

1

The Orient on the Eve of Islam

From ancient times Jewish, and later Christian, religious currents had spread to all of Arabia, being disseminated along the spice and incense caravan routes. By the seventh century Christian Egypt teemed with religious fervor, while in the Fertile Crescent region multitudes of monks and pilgrims thronged around imposing monasteries. Babylonia (southern Iraq), where Christians and Jews formed the population's majority, became a brilliant center of Nestorianism, and of Talmudic studies. In southern Arabia, the destruction of the ephemeral Jewish kingdom of Yemen by Abyssinia in the sixth century had scattered the vanquished population among the oases of the peninsula, while Nestorian Christianity reached Bahrein and Oman. Thus, political events as well as Arab caravan and overseas trade were instrumental in transmitting and circulating religious ideas and preparing the way for the advent of "that religion for the Arabs," which pagan Arabs, who mixed with Jews and Christians, were vaguely expecting.

The Seventh-Century Religious Context

On the eve of the Arab-Muslim conquest, the clash of two great empires—Sassanian Persia and Byzantium—had spread war throughout Asia Minor, where Christianity was emerging from paganism by fire and sword. Five major patriarchates were consecrated as a result of the Christianization of the Roman Empire (324): Rome, Alexandria, Antioch, Constantinople, and Jerusalem. A century later, their dissensions drenched the Empire in blood. The conflicts concerned the hierarchical precedence of the patriarchal dioceses, their financial autonomy and, above all, dogmatic differences grafted onto ethnic characteristics. At the Council of Ephesus (431) and at the Council of Chalcedon (451), the Diophysite Church (Rome and Constantinople) condemned as heretical the Nestorian, and then the Monophysite (Jacobite) definitions of the nature of Christ.

Driven out of Antioch, the Nestorian Church took refuge in Persia. As its hostility to Byzantium earned it the favors of the Sassanian authorities, it gained ascendency over the Monophysites and supplanted them in Hira (southern Babylonia). Forming—with the Jews—the majority of the population of Babylonia, the Nestorians propagated Christianity to Arabia and as far afield as Asia. Meanwhile, Monophysitism, represented by the patriarchate of Alexandria, won over all the populations of Egypt (Coptic), Syria (Syriac rite), and in northern Mesopotamia (the Assyrians), Abyssinia, and the autocephalous Armenian Church. The Greek Church, determined to bring the dissident Churches back under its obedience, did its utmost to eradicate all "heresies." Schismatic bishops were hunted down and monks tortured, while their churches, convents, monasteries, and all their property were confiscated by the Greek Orthodox Melchite Church.

While the war of the patriarchs raged, the evangelization of the Orient progressed, accompanied by a virulent anti-Jewish policy.[1] From the fourth century, religious violence instigated by bishops and monks became a general phenomenon in the eastern provinces. Under ecclesiastical pressure, a considerable number of discriminations affecting Jews were introduced into Byzantine law. Jews were killed sporadically, and synagogues expropriated or burned down.[2]

In Visigoth Spain, after King Reccared converted from Arianism to Catholicism in 587, the state gave force of law to the anti-Jewish canons of the Councils of Toledo from 613 to 694. In 613, and again in 633 and 638, Jews were subject to expulsion or baptism. The Twelfth Council of Toledo (680) adopted King Erwige's decisions ordering that Jews renounce Judaism within a year, that forced baptism be administered on pain of confiscation of property, and that those resisting be punished by head-shaving, accompanied by a hundred strokes of the rod and exile.[3] This anti-Jewish policy, which was opposed by some members of the clergy and the nobility, pushed King Egica (687–702) to impose his authority by hardening his stance. The Sixteenth Council of Toledo (693) ordered that the property of Jews be confiscated and their taxes increased. A proclamation by the Seventeenth Council (694) ordered all Jews to be made slaves and dispersed over the kingdom; their families were to be broken up, and their children from the age of seven taken from them and brought up in the Christian faith.[4]

Persia's defeat of the Byzantines in 611 brought Antioch, Damascus, all of Syria, Palestine, and Egypt under Sassanian power (611–627). Nestorian Christianity, favored by the Persians, prevailed over the Monophysite and Melchite (Byzantine) Churches. At the battle of Nineveh in 627 the Byzantine emperor Heraclius expelled the Persian army and reconquered the eastern provinces of the empire. Weakened by Avar and Slav attacks on Constantinople (626), he adopted a policy of appeasement toward the Persians. To win the favor of the powerful Eastern Churches, which were collaborating with the Persians against the Greek Empire, Heraclius vainly tried to find some common theological ground by proposed changes in the new doctrine of Monothelitism.

Indoctrinated by the Palestinian clergy during his sojourn in Jerusalem, the Greek emperor (*basileus*) was apparently persuaded to attribute the destructions caused by the Persian occupation solely to the Jews. Jews certainly had served in the ranks of the Persian armies, but so had an even larger number of Zoroastrians, Nestorians, and Jacobites, equally motivated by their loathing of the Byzantines. Favored by the Persian victories, Copts, Syrians, and Nestorians had no scruples in taking their revenge on the Melchites, who had persecuted them cruelly for nearly two centuries. In Persia itself, the Nestorian clergy harried Monophysites—just as zealously as Melchite clergy hounded the other two Eastern Churches in the Byzantine lands. But since accusations leveled only at Jews would contribute to peace with the Persians and the unity of the Churches which Heraclius desired, the clergy of Palestine, particularly eager to destroy the local Jewry, declared them responsible for all the war's destructions. In fact, the Church was confronted in the Holy Land with the history of Israel and the people of Israel. Together with the Samaritans, Jews still formed the majority of the country's population at the time of the Arab conquest, despite Church persecutions.[5] Not satisfied with having banished all Jewish presence from Jerusalem since Constantine the Great in the first half of the fourth century, the Palestinian Church had converted the area of the destroyed Temple in Jerusalem into a dumpsite. On its orders, all the town's rubbish and dung was heaped there as a testimony to the downfall of Judaism.[6]

In 628, at the instigation of the Palestinian Church, Heraclius decreed the destruction or conversion of Jews throughout his Empire. A wave of persecution, pillage, and massacre befell the victims.[7] The failure of Monothelitism also rekindled persecution of the Jacobite Church, forcing it into clandestinity.[8] Arab caravaneers, who stopped in the towns lining the desert, picked up from anchorites or fugitives terrifying stories of the clash of empires. The echoes of religious fanaticism passed on by the numerous Christian Arab tribes—whether Monophysite or Nestorian—circulated throughout Arabia, varying according to distance from commercial routes and zones of political influence.

The Birth of the Islamic State

In Medina, where Muhammad, the Prophet of Islam, had taken refuge with a small number of loyal followers in 622, the population consisted of pagans and Jewish tribes of Arab stock or emigrants from an earlier period.[9] Farmers or craftsmen, these Jews paid a tribute in cash or kind to pagan Arab tribes charged with protecting them. The lack of any central power and state organization in Arabia rendered this protection an essential element governing relations between settled inhabitants of oases and warlike nomadic tribes. In fact, for the sedentary communities of peasants and artisans, protection or clientelism represented the sole guarantee of safety from nomadic depredations.[10] This custom derived from the right to retaliate and to conduct vendettas, a common tribal practice. It was the tribe which collectively ensured the security of each of its members and those it protected. The life and property of an individual deprived of protection were at the mercy of any passing nomad.

The Prophet organized the Muslim immigrants into a community, the *umma*. He preached a monotheistic religion and a moral code based on justice and the distinction between Good and Evil. He strove to encourage solidarity and charity, love, and equality between all Muslims. He enhanced their pride by bringing to the lawless Bedouins a Revelation inscribed in a book, similar to Judaism and Christianity. Illiterate Bedouins were very impressed by the assiduous study of the Torah by the Jews who were living among them. However, the opposition of the Meccan idolators to Muhammad led to the gradual elaboration of relationships with non-Muslims, which emerged from a strategy of hostilities and truces pursued in accordance with the requirements needed to assure a Muslim victory. Razzias in the cause of Allah, which inextricably mingled war and religion, inspired many verses regarding the holy war (*jihad*) and its twofold reward: booty and paradise.[11] According to his eighth-century biographer, Ibn Ishaq, Muhammad signed an agreement comprising forty-seven articles with the chiefs of the Medina tribes. Known as the Constitution of Medina, this document governed political and social relations between the various groups and allegedly incorporated the Jews of Medina on an equal footing.[12]

In Medina, where he lived until his death in 632, Muhammad assumed the functions of a war leader, politician, and legislator. These three activities determined the whole political and legal conception of the Islamic state. As Muhammad declared himself the last messenger conveying Allah's commands, and chosen to implement them on earth, all his words and deeds formed, for his followers, part of a divine pattern: "Whoever obeys the messenger, has obeyed Allah" (Koran 4:82).[13] Thus, not only the Koran but also episodes in the Prophet's life were recorded by traditionalists and chroniclers who lived one or two centuries later, and were claimed to be manifestations of Allah's will. Here it is interesting to note that this conception of prophecy, which sees the expression of the divine will in all the manifestations of the life of one man, is foreign to the Bible. In biblical Israel, the kingly function was separated from the priestly function, even if political ambitions could temporarily combine them in a single leader.

During his Medina period Muhammad undertook no less than thirty-eight raids.[14] At first these expeditions consisted of plundering the caravans which secured Syria's trade with Mecca; he would keep a fifth of the booty taken from the merchants, the remainder being shared among his companions. His successes earned him renown, which brought him more followers, thus improving his situation. He was henceforth able to neutralize the protectors of the principal Jewish tribes in Medina: the Banu Qaynuqa, Banu Nadhir, and Banu Qurayza. Muhammad was probably encouraged to rid himself of the Medina Jews by the growing weakness of their traditional protectors, the Persians, then confronting the Byzantines. The expulsion of the Medina Jewry (Banu Qaynuqa, Banu Nadhir),[15] or the massacre of all the men, accompanied by the enslavement of women and children of the Banu Qurayza,[16] formed part of a strategy of conflicts or alliances with the Arab tribes, aimed at unifying them under Muhammad's command. This policy, which strengthened the military potential of the *umma*, enabled him to launch raids on oases, mainly cultivated by Jewish and Christian peasants.

The only existing information on the many Jewish communities inhabiting Medina and the oases of Arabia comes from what can be gleaned from tendencious Muslim accounts. The complete lack of other sources undermines the veracity of accusations brought against them. Despite these reservations, such accounts depict the Jews as farmers, artisans, merchants, and poets. They assembled in synagogues to pray, studied the Bible, and were on good terms with the pagan Arabs among whom they lived, sometimes intermarrying with them.

The elimination of the Medina Jews between 624 and 627 enriched the *umma*. The property of the Banu Nadhir formed the Prophet's share of the war-treasure, while the booty taken from the other tribes was apportioned between the Muslim warriors, the Prophet receiving a fifth. In 628, benefiting from a nonaggression treaty (Hudaybiya) with the Meccans, Muhammad went on to besiege the oasis of Khaybar, 140 kilometers away, cultivated by Jewish peasants.[17] They surrendered after a siege lasting one and a half months. According to Muslim jurisconsults some centuries later, the agreement (*dhimma*) made between Muhammad and the Jews of Khaybar formed the basis of the *dhimmi* status. The Prophet allowed the Jews to farm their lands, but only as tenants; he demanded delivery of half their harvest and reserved the right to drive them out when he wished. On these conditions, he granted his *dhimma*, that is to say, his protection for their lives and safety.[18] Similar pacts were concluded in the same year with Jews living in other oases, Fadak and Wadi'l-Qura (628), Mu'ta (629), as well as with nomadic or sedentary Christianized tribes. These tribes preserved their religion on payment of a tribute (*jizya*), the symbol of their submission. In exchange, Muhammad undertook to respect their religion and to protect them from Bedouin razzias. Each community could keep its own religious jurisdiction.

The *dhimma* of Khaybar inspired the treaties which the Arab conquerors subsequently granted to the indigenous inhabitants of lands outside Arabia. Later treaties concluded with the People of the Book (Jews and Christians) were modeled on the letters of protection which Muhammad sent from Tabuk in 630 to the Jewish and Christian populations of Makna (north of the Hijaz, on the gulf of Eilat) and in south Palestine: Eilat, Jarba, and Adhruh.[19] The anarchy prevailing in the north of the Arabian peninsula permitted Muhammad to extend his hegemony over all Arabia and to prepare expeditions to Syria. In such propitious circumstances, it was not long before the razzias on south Palestinian oases inhabited by Jews and Christians turned into a total war of conquest. Contacts between Muslim military leaders and the various members of the clergy through the intermediary of nomadic Christian Arab tribes unquestionably facilitated conquests and betrayals.

These episodes in Muhammad's life determined the relationship between Muslims and infidels that became established through koranic revelations. The substance of this relationship was the strategy of warfare (*jihad*), the rights of conquest, the division of booty, and the fate of the vanquished, which included their protection. Land-expropriation of the vanquished is considered a divine right: tradition records that at the siege of Khaybar Muhammad said: "The land belongs to Allah and to his Messenger."[20] *Jihad* consisted first of inviting non-Muslims to convert to Islam, then, if they refused, to fight them until victory.

The caliph Umar Ibn al-Khattab cited the *dhimma* of Khaybar when he expelled the Jews and Christians from the Hijaz in 640: "the land belongs to Allah and his Messenger, the Messenger of Allah can annul his pact if he so wishes." Umar also referred to the Prophet's wish: "Two religions shall not remain together in the peninsula of the Arabs."[21]

Persia, weakened by dynastic struggles and the defection of some Arab-Christian tribes settled on its territory, was overwhelmed after its army was defeated at the battle of al-Qadisiyya (637). Egypt and Syria, torn apart by religious fanaticism, only offered feeble resistance, whereas the Byzantine army was disbanded, betrayed by Armenian and Christian Arab mercenaries. The stronghold of Babylon (Old Cairo) and Alexandria, commanded by Cyrus, the Greek governor-bishop, surrendered almost without a fight, while the Melchite governor of Damascus was won over to the Arab cause and collaborated in the town's surrender. In Jerusalem, the patriarch Sophronius, instigator of anti-Jewish persecution, allegedly surrendered the city to the caliph Umar Ibn al-Khattab, urging him to maintain the Church's decree excluding Jews from the city. The Jews had asked the caliph to allow two hundred families to return; Umar set the figure at seventy.[22]

Despite the apparent docility of the Coptic senior clergy and the treachery of men in positions of responsibility, the Islamic conquest of Egypt aroused popular resistance, records of which are preserved in rare extant documents.

Some historians have put forward the hypothesis of a collaboration between the Muslims and the Coptic Church, which had been banned by the Byzantines and had taken clandestine refuge in the desert. In any case, it is an established fact that the many Monophysite and Nestorian Christian Arab tribes in Arabia and the borderlands of the Greek and Sassanian Empires maintained close relations with the Muslims of Medina. Information on the political situation in neighboring countries reached Muhammad through Christian channels. According to one tradition, the bishop of Gaza visited the Prophet when he was in Tabuk (630) and gave him a sum of money;[23] in addition, Christians from Najran in Arabia promised to fight with the Muslims.[24] The Nestorian Chronicle recounts that the Catholicos Ishoyab II (elected in 628) sent Gabriel, bishop of Meisan, to bring Muhammad gifts and money. The bishop arrived in Medina after the Prophet's death and handed his offering to the caliph Abu-Bakr; he informed him of the situation in the Persian Empire and of the sufferings which the Muslim armies were inflicting on Christians. Hearing of this, King Yazdegerd reproached the Catholicos. Ishoyab claimed, in his defense, that the money was intended to assist Christians, forced by Muslims to convert or pay a capitation tax.[25]

The Chronicle of Seert (compilations of apocrypha until the eleventh century) reproduces a document supposedly discovered in 878–879, and allegedly a copy of the Pact and Edict given by the Prophet Muhammad to the Najran Christians and to all the Christians in the world.[26] Some salient points emerge from this forged document. The text, allegedly dictated by the Prophet himself, expressly confirms the Muslims' duty to love and protect Christians. This commandment purportedly emanated from the divine will, reflected a right which the Christians acquired by proving their devotion to Islam and contributing to its victory. The document contrasted Christian perfection with the perfidy of the Jews, who are pictured as harsh and cunning rogues, concealing the truth, and described as criminals and enemies of Allah and Islam—vices which justified their extermination in Medina and barred them from the protection granted to Christians, as was explained:

It is a fact that some trustworthy Christians who know the divine religion [Islam] helped us [Muhammad] to proclaim this religion and lent assistance to Allah and to his Apostle, in order to preach to men according to his wish and for the accomplishment of his mission.

The Sayyid,[27] 'Abdiso, Ibn Hejra, Abraham the monk, and Isa the bishop came to see me, accompanied by forty horsemen from Najran and other people who, like them, professed the Christian religion in regions of Arabia and in foreign regions. I informed them of my mission and I called on them to help to reinforce it, to proclaim it, and to assist it.[28]

The document goes on to indicate that the Christian emissaries returned to their coreligionists and "proved their devotion, and united to make war on the Jews," supporting and strengthening the cause of Islam in every country.[29]

This fabrication reveals the extreme vulnerability of the Christians who tried to protect themselves against the Muslims by bringing accusations against the Jews. The links that it describes between Muhammad and certain bishops, also mentioned by other sources, would explain the speed of the Islamic conquest and the defections among Christian Arab tribes. It was probably no coincidence that the massacre and expropriation of the Medina Jews and attempts to exterminate them in the Greek Empire at the instigation of the Jerusalem clergy occurred at roughly the same period. Koran 30:1–4 alludes to the Greek victories and the persecution of the Jews; likewise various Christological quarrels are often evoked in a few koranic verses.

Conquests

Many detailed accounts of Muhammad's life have been written. Only relevant to this study are those essential aspects which determined the *umma*'s relationship with the People of the Book. These were set in the context of a war whose laws, codified through theology after the Prophet's death, regulated the conditions of armistice and peace treaties, the strategy and tactics employed in battle, and the fate of prisoners of war. This legislation, which constituted the codification of *jihad*, was grounded in a few basic principles expressed in the Koran and in Muhammad's policy toward Jews and Christians as it emerged from three sources. These are the Koran, early biographies of Muhammad, and the corpus of *hadiths*—the words and deeds attributed to the Prophet and reported on the authority of a chain of transmitters (*isnads*). The latter two sources have been found unreliable by Western scholarship. The *hadiths* were compiled into a corpus of Traditions (*Sunna*) that were completed toward the end of the ninth century.[30] Different interpretations of the *Sunna* were codified by the four principal orthodox Muslim schools of law from the eighth century (Hanafi, Maliki, Shafi'i, and Hanbali).

The general basic principles according to the Koran are as follows: the pre-eminence of Islam over all other religions (9:33); Islam is the true religion of Allah (3:17) and it should reign over all mankind (34:27); the *umma* forms the party of Allah and is perfect (3:106), having been chosen above all peoples on earth[31] it alone is qualified to rule, and thus elected by Allah to guide the world (35:37). The pursuit of *jihad,* until this goal will be achieved, is an obligation (8:40). The religions of the Bible, and Zoroastrianism, are deemed inferior as their followers falsified the true Revelation which their respective prophets conveyed to them—this Revelation was considered to be Islam—before Muhammad's arrival. Albeit inferior, these peoples, each a beneficiary of Revelation, have the choice between war or submission to the *umma,* whereas idolators are forced to convert to Islam or be killed.

It is important at this point to mention three crucial concepts which were manifest in Muhammad's military activities and which later jurisconsults utilized to formulate the theory of *jihad.* The first concerns the position of the *harbi,* an individual beyond the rule of Islam, who was not party to any alliance with the Prophet. The second involves the very principle of the recognition of the right to life, property, and security, a right recognized solely on the authority of the Prophet, Allah's viceregent on earth. The third concept follows from the second and governs the requirements which qualify these rights. Either the individual or the tribe would convert to Islam, thus submitting to the Prophet's authority, or conversion was replaced by payment of a tribute to the Prophet. These three principles, which are integrated into the geographic and social context of pre-Islamic Arabia, are directly mentioned by Muhammad in the letters he sent to the Christian leaders and governors. He gave them the choice between conversion or tribute, failing which war was declared.[32]

A century after the Prophet's death, eighth century Muslim jurisconsults fixed the policy regarding the People of the Book on the basis of decisions decreed by Muhammad concerning the Jews of Arabia, which were followed by other protection pacts granted to Jews and Christians. These proceedings constituted the normative rules applicable to all peoples conquered by *jihad.* Likewise, the *dhimma* of Khaybar served the jurisconsults as a model for drawing up treaties with populations which submitted to Islamic domination. The *dhimmi* condition, a direct result of *jihad,* is linked to this "protection pact" which suspended the conqueror's initial right to kill or enslave followers of the tolerated religions, provided they submitted themselves to pay the tribute (*jizya*).

The first wave of Islamic conquest engulfed Christian lands up to Armenia in the northeast, and to North Africa and Spain as far as Poitiers, and in Italy up to the Alps. It also overwhelmed Sassanian Persia and reached the Indus. The Muslims were thus brought into close contact with the most prestigious civilizations.

Although it was now master of a vast empire, the invading Arab army was in a minority among the non-Muslim peoples, mainly Christians and

Zoroastrians, but also important Jewish communities. Circumstances dictated that the Byzantine and Persian administrations be maintained, but relations between Muslims and non-Muslims were regulated. Jurists used the Koran and the Traditions as a basis when they formulated the status of the *dhimmis,* non-Muslim indigenous inhabitants, subjected and protected by Islam. This body of rules is also known as the Covenant of Umar, being attributed by Arab chroniclers sometimes to Umar Ibn al-Khattab (634–44), or to Umar b. Abd al-Aziz (717–20).

All the regions conquered by *jihad* were governed by Islamic legislation. The mass of native inhabitants either converted or became *dhimmis,* that is: non-Muslim peoples protected from the *jihad* onslaught by the *dhimma,* the treaty of submission that ended the *jihad.* A new civilization slowly developed in these regions, that of the *dhimmis.* I have called this vast political, religious, and cultural domain the "civilization of dhimmitude." Only the Judeo-Christian sphere of this condition will be examined in this study.

The *dhimmi* status for Jews, Samaritans, Christians, Sabeans, and Zoroastrians varied with place and period. In traditionalist regions such as North Africa, it continued to exist until nineteenth-century European colonization abolished it; in Persia and Yemen it still remained into the twentieth century.

In the Ottoman Empire, pressure from the European powers forced Sultan Abd al-Majid (1839–61) to proclaim religious equality and abolish discrimination against the *dhimmis*—called *rayas* in the Ottoman Empire.[33] But emancipation was never fully implemented throughout the empire, although there were improvements.

Abundant information on the subject can be found at different periods in Muslim legal literature and in the writings of Arab and Turkish chroniclers, *dhimmis,* European consuls, and travelers.

Jihad

As already mentioned, *jihad* denotes the sacralization of the Bedouin razzia, a consequence of the sociological context in which Muhammad preached. The content of this preaching does, of course, go far beyond the concept of a holy war and, furthermore, it was not the Prophet but later jurisconsults who transformed *jihad* into a legal-theological theory. Besides, one can easily find in the Koran and *hadiths* enough moral exhortation to oppose the theory of *jihad.* But since this doctrine, as elaborated by Muslim jurists, established a single pattern for relations between Muslims and non-Muslims it, therefore, touches the very core of the subject of this study. The concept of *jihad* was, in fact, central to the relationship of Muslims to the People of the Book. This relationship was constructed within an ideology of territorial expansion and world domination. *Jihad* can thus be examined at three levels: in its dogma; in its institutions; and in its historical evolution.[34]

Dogma

The Muslim jurists formulated the doctrine of *jihad* on the basis of the Koran and *hadiths*. By reason of this origin which binds it to the words of the Prophet and consequently to Allah, this doctrine forms part of an eschatalogical vision of a war aiming to impose on mankind the will of Allah as expressed by his last messenger. Here, it is important to understand that these two terms are inseparable. The designs of Allah are only revealed by his Prophet Muhammad. Any Revelation other than Islam is false; Allah's religion is Islam (3:17). The doctrine teaches that the Koran is the uncreated, eternal word of Allah. As far as mankind is concerned, Muhammad declared that "the world belongs to Allah and to his messenger." The Islamic community (*umma*), recipient of this Revelation, is perfect. It is chosen by Allah above all other nations.

> Ye have become the best community ever produced for the people urging what is reputable and restraining from what is disreputable, and believing in Allah. If the People of the Book had believed, it would have been better for them; some of them are believers, but the most of them are the reprobate (3:106).

Its election creates for the Islamic community the duty to take possession of its heritage, the whole world, so that Allah's word, transmitted by Muhammad, will reign supreme. Assumption of this heritage, which belongs to it by divine right, justifies *jihad*. It is a compulsory command.

Jihad divides the peoples of the world into two irreconcilable groups: the Muslims—inhabitants of the *dar al-Islam*, regions subject to Islamic law; and infidels—inhabitants of the *dar al-harb* (*harbis*), the territory of war, destined to come under Islamic jurisdiction, either by the conversion of its inhabitants or by armed conflict. *Jihad* is the Muslim's permanent state of war or hostility by the *dar al-Islam* against the *dar al-harb*, until the infidels' conclusive submission and the absolute world supremacy of Islam. According to the Maliki school of jurisprudence:

> *Jihad* is a precept of Divine institution. Its performance by certain individuals may dispense others from it. We Malikis maintain that it is preferable not to begin hostilities with the enemy before having invited the latter to embrace the religion of Allah except when the enemy attacks first. They have the alternative of either converting to Islam or paying the poll tax (*jizya*), short of which war will be declared against them.[35]

The famous Hanbali jurist of the fourteenth century, Ibn Taymiya, states the principles of Muslim doctrine on *jihad*:[36]

> In ordering *jihad* Allah has said: "Fight them until there is no persecution and religion becomes Allah's". [2:189] (p.21)
> Allah has, in fact, repeated this obligation [to fight] and has glorified *jihad* in most of the Medina *suras*: he has stigmatized those who neglected to do so, and treated them as hypocrites and cowards. (p.123)
> It is impossible to count the number of times when *jihad* and its virtues are extolled in the Book and the *Sunna*. *Jihad* is the best form of voluntary service that man consecrates to Allah. (p.125)
> Therefore, since *jihad* is divinely instituted, and its goal is that religion reverts in its entirety to Allah and to make Allah's word triumph, whoever opposes the realization of this goal will be fought, according to the unanimous opinion of Muslims.
> Jews and Christians, as well as Zoroastrians (Magians), must be fought until they embrace Islam or pay the *jizya* without recriminations. Jurisconsults do not agree on the question of knowing if the *jizya* should be imposed on other categories of infidels; on the other hand, all consider that it should not be required of Arabs [hence they should convert to Islam or be killed or expelled]. (p.130)

Because the Islamic community is sanctified by possession of the only true religion, it is also the only legitimate beneficiary of the material wealth created by Allah. Thus *jihad*, which strives to "restore" to Muslims the possessions which the infidels illegally control, unfolds in accordance with the divine will. According to Ibn Taymiya, "thus is restored to a man the inheritance of which he was deprived, even if he had not yet taken possession of it."[37] That is why *jihad* legitimizes—even sanctifies—all acts of war in the *dar al-harb*, regions where illegality reigns, populated by unsubjected non-Muslims and, therefore, destined for conquest.[38] In the war, Muslims "had to fight with the object of upholding the religion of Allah and annihilating opposing religions."[39] The methods of conquest were governed by regulations:

> In the war against the infidels the law prohibits the killing of: minors, aliens, women, and hermaphrodites who do not in any way tend toward the male sex; but it is legitimate to kill: monks, mercenaries whom the infidels have taken into their service, the old and weak, blind or sickly persons, even when they have neither taken part in the battle nor given information to the enemy . When they have not been killed in the war, they must in any case be reduced to slavery. The wives of infidels must also be reduced to slavery and the possessions of infidels must be confiscated. It is lawful to besiege infidels in their towns and in their fortresses and to use flooding, fire and the machines of war against them, and to attack them unawares at night, all of this without regard for the presence in their midst of Muslim prisoners or merchants for whom these means of mass destruction are equally dangerous. It

is the teaching of our [Shafi'i] rite. On the basis of the same principle it is even permissible to shoot at women and children when the infidels continue to fight by hiding behind them; but one must refrain from such procedure if the infidels hide behind them solely for the purpose of saving their lives and if the nature of the military operations does not imperatively require resorting to these extreme measures. The same principles must also be followed in cases when the infidels hide behind Muslims [. . .]

It is lawful to destroy the dwellings and plantations of infidels, both because of military necessity and because this measure procures an easier victory; it is even good to resort to this measure in every instance when it is not expected that the dwellings and plantations will one day become our property. But when this eventuality is expected, it is preferable not to proceed with destruction.[40]

The law of war also regulated the fate of prisoners:

Infidels' women and minors, taken as war captives, must be reduced to slavery; and slaves, taken in their country, become our possession. As for free adults of the male sex, the sovereign can choose as he wishes between the following five measures, according to whichever seems to be the most advantageous for the Muslims. He can:

1. Put them to the sword.
2. Set them free unconditionally.
3. Exchange them for Muslims taken as prisoners of war.
4. Set them free on payment of some ransom.
5. Reduce them to slavery.

In cases when circumstances do not indicate which of these measures merits preference, the prisoners must be held until the circumstances have changed and clarified the measure to be taken. Some authors do not allow an idolator to be subjected to slavery, and only one jurist considers this measure unlawful in respect of a pagan Arab. The infidel, taken prisoner of war, who embraces the faith, has in any case saved his life and in his case the sovereign only has a choice between the above measures 2 to 5. According to others, however, such a prisoner must always be reduced to slavery. The conversion of an infidel before his defeat has the guaranteed effect of securing not only his life but, in addition, of safeguarding his property and his young children, although our faith does not extend this favor to his wife.[41]

According to the Hanbali rite:

Those, such as women, children, priests, the old, the blind, the infirm, etc.—who can not be considered "resisters" or "combatants"—will not be killed, according to generally acknowledged opinion, unless they have actually fought with either words or deeds. Certain jurisconsults maintain that it is permissible to kill them on the grounds that they are "infidels" (kuffar), with the exception, however, of women and children who become Muslim property. The first doctrine is the correct one. We must only fight those who fight

us, because we wish to make the religion of Allah triumph. The law imposes
the duty to fight the infidels (*kuffar*), but not to kill them when they have
been seized. When an infidel has been captured in war or in other circumstances, after a shipwreck for example, or a mistake on the road or an am-
bush, the head of state decides his fate in the way he thinks best: he can have
him put to death; reduce him to slavery, restore his freedom, or free him
against a ransom which can be paid in money or consist of the freeing of
Muslims. This doctrine, acknowledged by most jurisconsults, is in accordance with the Book [Koran] and the *Sunna*, although certain jurisconsults
maintain that the right to restore a prisoner's freedom or to free him for a
ransom has been annulled.[42]

This context of war required the presence of troops or volunteers
charged with defending the frontiers with the *dar al-harb* and of spreading
desolation and destruction by repeated razzias on the border regions. *Jihad*
also makes provision for military expeditions into enemy countries three
times a year. It is a permanent state of war which excludes the idea of
peace. Only provisional truces are permitted when required by the political
situation. These truces, limited to a maximum of ten years, can be unilaterally ended by the imam, after notifying the adversary. *Jihad* also regulated
the conditions of the treaties with the *dar al-harb*.

According to the jurisconsults:

The imam's representative is not allowed to agree to peace with the enemy
when he has superiority of forces over him [. . .] It is therefore for the imam
to make peace with the polytheists when it is advantageous to Islam and to
the religion, and when by so doing he hopes by gentleness to lead them to
convert.[43]

Furthermore, a treaty is only valid if its provisions are in accordance with
Islamic law. The conditions for an armistice are also laid down:

An armistice is only allowed when some advantage to Muslims ensues: for
example, if we are weak in numbers, or if we lack money or ammunition, or
even if there is hope that the infidels may convert or offer to surrender and
pay the capitation tax. An armistice which, although advantageous is not motivated by our weakness, can be concluded for four months or more, provided that the period always remains less than a year; but if we are the weaker
party, a maximum period of ten years can be stipulated. In cases when the
maximum period has passed, all the jurists regard the armistice as valid for
the legally stipulated period and only consider the extra period as unlawful;
but any armistice is invalidated when a precise period has not been stipulated or when an illegal clause has been stipulated. [. . .] On the other hand,
it is perfectly lawful for the sovereign, when he agrees to an armistice, to
reserve the right to recommence hostilities when it seems good to him. In
any case, the sovereign must refrain from committing acts of hostility while

the armistice is in force; he must only recommence the war after the legal expiry of the armistice.[44]

The freeing of prisoners or hostages is governed by the following regulations:

It is not fitting that the imam allow any of those who have been taken prisoner in an enemy country, and who have thus fallen into Muslim hands, to return there without demanding a ransom; on any condition other than ransom, this must not occur.

When a special unit has been sent by the imam and has attacked an enemy locality from where it has taken the inhabitants—men, women and children—to an Islamic country, in accordance with the imam's order so that the division [of booty] can take place; and when, following this, the imam has redeemed them and freed them all, if the men and women want to return to the enemy country, he must not allow them to do so, nor allow any of those who find themselves in this way in an Islamic country to return to an enemy country other than on condition of a ransom, as I have just said.[45]

The restitution of the corpses of prisoners is variously interpreted:

If a polytheist is killed by Muslims and the enemies wish to buy back the corpse, Abu Hanifa sees nothing wrong in this exchange, because, he says, Muslims can lawfully remove their [the polytheists] possessions by violence; therefore, when they offer to pay of their own accord, it is even more lawful and better. But, for my part, I [Abu Yusuf] disapprove and prohibit this procedure: Muslims can not sell wine, pork, corpses or blood to the enemies or others.[46]

Regarded by Islamic theologians as one of the pillars of the faith, *jihad* remains an obligation on all Muslims who have to assist according to their capacity: by their persons, their possessions, or their writings.[47]

Institutions

Lands having been conquered by force were often subjected to a regime of military occupation and administration; likewise, the fiscal system of the conquered peoples. The need to retain the gains of war and the obligation to pursue *jihad*, led to its codification. This determined the militarist nature of the political institutions of the Muslim state that applied to the Arab and Turkish conquests, both being built on the same foundations: the Koran, *jihad*, and *shari'a*.

The most important of these policies was the division of the conquered territory into military districts, and the organization and maintenance of militias consisting of slaves, who were mainly Christians. These slaves—

from Andalusia, the Maghreb, and the Ottoman Empire—were sometimes levied from among the conquered populations as in the Balkans (*devshirme*), or they formed a part of the booty from frontier wars or razzias, supplemented by contingents of purchased slaves. Other aspects of this policy involved disarming, deporting, and imposing obligations relating to the lodging and provisioning of Muslim troops on the subject peoples. On the financial level, the major part of the war effort was supplied from the tax systems of the conquered peoples and from a fund established to bribe personalities from the enemy's ranks—in religious, political, and military positions—who were likely to facilitate Islamic victories by their betrayal.[48]

The military organization of the conquered lands also embraced every aspect of Islamic colonization, notably the organization of massive emigration of Arab or Turkish tribes, the planning of their settlement in the conquered territories and their privileged status in military, religious, social, economic, and legal spheres at the expense of the non-Muslim native inhabitants, now reduced to the status of *dhimmis*.

Jihad in History

Jihad, or the Islamic war of conquest, unfolded for more than a millennium on three continents in the Christian lands bordering the Mediterranean and the hinterland—not to mention Buddhist and Hindu Asia. This explains the difficulty in understanding a process which was adapted to circumstances and to different terrains, combining persecutions and periods of respite, withdrawals, massive assaults, and destruction. Two violent waves of Islamization can be distinguished: the Arab wave (634–750) and the Turkish wave (c. 1021–1689).

The Arab conquest which developed in the context of betrayals, collaboration, and reprisals inherent in any war, was accompanied by tremendous destruction. Christian sources, but Muslim chronicles even more so, describe entire towns, innumerable villages given over to pillage and fire, to massacres, slavery, and the deportation of populations. Even towns provided with a treaty of protection in exchange for surrendering without resistance did not escape pillage by Arab tribes, fascinated by the immensity of the booty which the conquered territories and their inhabitants constituted. However, it must be emphasized that cruelties of war were perpetrated by armies at all times in history. Human barbarity was unleashed with equal violence by all warring ethnic or religious groups.

A war of skirmishes, raids, or military battles continued in Sicily, Italy, Syria, and Mesopotamia until the eleventh century, while a slow penetration of Islamized Turks via Iraq and Armenia destroyed the homogeneity of Byzantine Anatolia and prepared the way for its disintegration. This process was facilitated by dynastic rivalries, religious antagonisms between the Byzantine Church and the Eastern patriarchates, tactical alliances by the Christian princes with the Turkish power, and the flight of Christian populations terrorized by the Turks.[49] Rooted in the same military ideology, the two waves of *jihad*, separated by several centuries, are nonetheless remarkably homologous. The ethnic and religious changes they imposed were inscribed in the same political and juridico-religious structure—dhimmitude—a concept which will be examined in the next chapters.

2

Political and Economic
Aspects of Dhimmitude

Given the vast territories of Asia, Africa, and Europe conquered by the two waves of *jihad*, it is no easy task to clarify all aspects of the status imposed on the indigenous Christians, Jews, and Zoroastrians. Moreover, this status was in existence for periods ranging from one or two centuries to more than a millennium, depending on the region concerned. The subject can be examined at two levels: from the juridico-religious dogma, and through historical data. These do not always coincide, although the political, economic, and social realities of the conquest did influence and modify the legal regulations. This disparity between the dogma, its diverse interpretations, and the complex interaction of historical conjunctures accounts for the ambiguities in the *dhimmi* condition.

The four basic factors which dominated the history and fate of the *dhimmis* are the *dhimma* (a contract of submission), the *fay*, the *kharaj*, and the *jizya*. Legal and economic by nature, they derive from a religious war and form a functional dogmatic framework which is unalterable, being based on theology and, consequently, regarded as having established a model for a perfect society.

The *dhimma* concept embraces the other three categories and all the elements of the *dhimmi* condition, since it ratifies the terms of submission to Islamic law for the indigenous non-Muslims. However, in the course of a millennium of conquests over three continents, where vast regions were ravaged and populous cities often razed to the ground amid the violence of battles and religious hatreds, it is unlikely that treaties were invariably concluded. In Iraq, destruction and enslavement crushed all the populations at the beginning of the conquest, sparing neither the clergy nor their churches and monasteries. Despite collaboration by some Christians, "Arabs were lodged in churches and convents which they profaned horribly."[1] Nevertheless, the chronicler writes that numerous Muslims came and respected Christianity above any other religion. But elsewhere he notes: "For five years countries were thrown into confusion by the arrival of the Arabs, by uninterrupted wrongdoing and continual afflictions; and this continued until their rule was firmly consolidated." The passage ends by glorifying Arab rule, which rejoiced Christians hearts.[2]

According to Ibn al-Balkhi, a Muslim geographer living at the beginning of the fourteenth century:

> In the early days of Islam, after Fārs [Persia] had been conquered [by the Arabs], for a time there was nothing but massacre and pillage and all things were taken by force, but at length matters quieted down, and the ruin and disorder that had overspread the land began to be amended.[3]

In Egypt, the Muslims plundered a large number of towns on the borders of the Fayyum. Pushing further afield they devastated the region by their depredations, subjugating several villages and often abducting children.[4] In Palestine the conquest destroyed a considerable number of towns and villages. The conditions of surrender of places in Galilee required that half the number of houses be handed over to the Muslims in addition to payment of the *jizya* and tribute in kind. Insecurity, particularly in desert regions, led to the abandonment of urbanized areas at this period, as well as monasteries, churches, and synagogues.[5]

In this context of war, the *dhimma* constituted a protection pact granted by the conquerors, assuring the vanquished an institutional legal framework which would guarantee their religious freedom, rights, and duties. For the victors, it assured a political and economic supremacy. It should be stressed that this protection was ascribed to the Prophet, which means that it fulfilled the will of Allah. To transgress it represented a breach of religion—an important point because the non-Muslim's right to existence within the context of Islamic law no longer depended on the whim of a potentate but, henceforth, was rooted in a divine command.

The origin of the *fay* can be found in Koran 59:6–10, revealed to Muhammad at the time of his victory over the Jewish Banu Nadhir tribe.[6] The Shafi'i jurist, al-Mawardi specifies that "the property of the *fay* and the various sources of booty derive from the infidels or have been produced by the latter."[7] It represents the indivisible booty, administered in its totality by the caliph for the benefit of the *umma*.

The justification for the *kharaj* is based on the agreements made between Muhammad and the Jewish farmers of Khaybar, Fadak, Tayma, and Wadi'l Qura.[8] As for the *jizya*, it originated in Koran 9:29.

> Fight against those who do not believe in Allah nor in the Last Day, and do not make forbidden what Allah and His messenger have made forbidden, and do not practice the religion of truth, of those who have been given the Book, until they pay the jizya off-hand, being subdued.

It is important to emphasize here that among the different categories of *dhimmis*, Zoroastrians represented a demographic majority only in Persia, not including Mesopotamia (Iraq). This geographical localization means that documents which mention them are limited to Persia. On the other hand, there are many more references to Jews, and an even greater number to Christians, who together formed the only populations of the Near and Middle East, paganism having almost totally disappeared under Christianity. Furthermore, whereas the Zoroastrian population dwindled to small communities, Christian populations subjected to Islam were constantly growing, due to the continual expansion during a millennium of Muslim conquest of Christian lands in which large Jewish communities also lived from ancient times.

Another important element of the *dhimmi* status affecting the vanquished peoples is the unification of Jews and Christians under the same designation: the "People of the Book" (the Bible). In fact, the legal regulations of the *dhimma* applied uniformly to both groups with no differentiation, which was not the case for the Zoroastrians. Not only were Jews and Christians closely associated in the same status, but also in numerous verses of the Koran, for example:

> O ye who have believed, do not choose Jews and Christians as friends; they are friends to each other; whoever makes friends of them is one of them; verily Allah doth not guide the wrong-doing people. (5:56)

Thus, the relationship between the two religions had not escaped the Prophet during his long caravan tours of Syria and Palestine where he had probably encountered sects such as the Sabeans who still practiced a Judeo-Christian syncretism.[9] Integrated into the *shari'a*, the status of the "People of the Book" was theoretically the same throughout the Islamic Empire, but in practice their situation differed according to local customs, political circumstances, and the sociogeographic context.[10]

The Islamic concept of religious war institutionalized the elements of the *dhimmi* status into a theological structure. These elements covered three main spheres: political, economic, and socioreligious; the interactions and contradictions between these spheres determined the varying fate of the *dhimmi*. It should be noted that, under the Umayyads (661–750), Islamic legislation had not yet been formed into the homogeneous and definitive corpus that it assumed in later centuries when law schools were founded to educate judges. In fact, the Umayyad period represented a temporary phase of mutual adaptation between an Arab Muslim minority army of occupation and a vanquished Christian majority, possessing all the technology and prestige of a brilliant civilization. Released from Byzantine oppression, the Christian leaders could have seized political power and reestablished their independence. The scarcity of contemporary documents only permits conjecture on this point. The flight, death, or enslavement of the political elites would probably have made it easier for lay and religious officials who had collaborated with the Muslim leaders to achieve power. The traitors were rewarded with important positions, while high-ranking Monophysite and Nestorian clerics obtained privileges under Islam which the imperial Byzantine authority had denied them. The patriarch replaced the latter, henceforth assuming all the administrative, religious, and fiscal powers relating to his community, thus becoming its undisputed leader and representative to the caliph. Invested with such privileges, the patriarchs had no wish for a return to a restrictive Christian imperial power.

The major endeavor at this period still remained the extirpation of paganism which was corrupting the Church at its very heart. Fornication, simony, and magic among ecclesiastics and laymen alike were denounced and combated. The conceptual world, inspired by the Holy Scriptures, indulged in an aura of edifying stories and miracles. Theological treatises, the organization of the liturgy, church services, prayers, ecclesiastical discipline, and canon law were built up through conflicts and reciprocal anathemas. Nothing illustrates better the separation of the theological and political levels than the indifference to the Arab-Islamic conquest shown by the Eastern patriarchs, absorbed in their doctrinal struggles. Only their parochial interests, their religious rivalries, and their Judeophobic policy led them to become actively involved in inter- Muslim conflicts. Two impervious worlds seem to be superposed at that time, collaborating, although disconnected from each other. The invaders, their civil wars, their customs, their unknown religion, and their language which was incomprehensible for a long time, were regarded as manifestations of a separate and external world. Despite the conciliatory attitude of Christians in positions of responsibility, chroniclers were scandalized that Christians were designated as "enemies of God".[11] The battles between Umayyads and Abbasids which engulfed the Near East in bloody strife seemed like battles between foreigners. And the Coptic patriarch Michael I (744–68), whom the last Umayyad caliph Marwan dragged along with him when he fled, subjecting him to torture and brutality in order to extort gold, needed an interpreter because he did not know "their language."

As the election of the patriarch could only be validated by the caliph, any opposition to his policy of Islamization was mercilessly repelled from the bosom of the Church, which became the supreme tool of Islamic control over the Christian populace. The Syriac scholar Sebastian Brock mentions the excellent relations which existed between the Nestorian catholicos Ishoyab (d. 659) and Timothy I (d. 823) and the Arab authorities.[12] The fabulous sums raised in taxes by the Byzantine state were henceforth levied by the patriarch, collected from his flock, and handed over to the caliph. This source of enrichment and power for the *umma* conversely brought poverty and ruin to the Christian populations. The Church's privileged position established a zone of mutual interests between the caliphs and the patriarch. In the interminable, internal struggles surrounding the patriarch's election, or in the incessant conflicts between warring Churches related to the ownership of churches or monasteries, the patriarch did not hesitate to seek arbitration from the caliph or his representative.

This collaboration created a broad symbiosis between the administrative and economic domains controlled by Christians and the Islamic political and military authority. Recognition of the need to protect the vanquished peoples in order to prevent rebellions appears in *hadiths* advocating kindliness toward the tributaries. This period of symbiosis prepared the way for the transition to the Islamic state. It was then able to strengthen legislation and impose the distinctive patterns of a new civilization by assuming control of simoniacal patriarchates, and by disrupting the organization of the Christian peoples, often deported or swamped by the influx of foreign tribes, mainly from Arabia and later from central Asia.

The Political Domain

Many verses in the Koran counsel tolerance toward the religions of the Bible. Appeals to these verses averted the total destruction of the non-Muslim populations, victims of the wars, invasions, and oppression during conquests from one end of the *dar al-Islam* to the other: in Egypt, Mesopotamia, Iran, Armenia, Anatolia, the Maghreb, Spain, and in the Balkans. However, although the indigenous populations had totally disappeared from certain regions, these periodic excesses were not the major cause of their numerical decline, as will be seen later. But before pursuing this subject further, it is important to note that dhimmitude is in no way comparable with the position of Jews in Christendom. If Arab caliphs or Turkish sultans had decreed the expulsion of the *dhimmis*—as had some Christian rulers in the Middle Ages for the Jewish communities scattered on their lands—those countries would have lost their entire population. Religious violence took other channels, since the demographic and ideological context of dhimmitude was radically different from the relationship between Church and Synagogue—a necessary clarification in order to avoid the pitfalls of misleading comparisons.

The realm of dhimmitude is actually situated in a political ideology of permanent war which ruined entire regions, justified massacres, slavery, usurpation of land, and deportations. Consequently the concept of protection hinges on the concept of war.

Protection

The principle of protection alleviated and modified the laws of war which annulled the rights of the individual.[13] This was effectively the position of the *harbi,* the non-Muslim living in an area which was not subject to Islam and consequently considered a land of war. According to the Muslim jurisconsults the *harbi* has no rights: his blood and his property being licit prey to any Muslim:[14]

> The infidel, not subject to Muslim authority, and the apostate, are outlaws [from the *lex talionis*] and can be killed with impunity [. . .] (p.116)
> One is not responsible for mortally wounding an infidel not subject to Muslim authority, or an apostate, even when one or the other should repent from his errors before dying. (p.123)

This situation applies even in the case of accidents. If polytheist castaways coming from enemy lands are washed up on the shores of a Muslim country, and state that they are bearing a gift for the imam on their king's behalf, these castaways must appear with their cargo before the imam:

> If their words do not accord with the truth, these people and their cargo constitute a *fay* for the benefit of the Muslim community, and the decision concerning them depends on the Imam, who is entitled either to allow them to live or to put them to death at his will. If the sailors claim to be merchants bringing goods to Muslim countries, their statement is not accepted, and they, and their cargo, constitute a *fay* for the Muslim community.[15]

Two conditions secure the safety of the non-Muslim: the *amân* which only concerns the *harbi;* and the *dhimma,* reserved for the *dhimmi:*

> Every adult Muslim, endowed with reason, can grant a safe-conduct or give quarter to one or several enemies, provided that their number is determined and that he acts of his own free will without any constraint [. . .] The safe-conduct or quarter can not be granted for a period exceeding four months; however, one author allows validity to extend to any period under one year. In addition, the law requires that the action is in no way prejudicial to Muslim interests, for example, it is forbidden to give a safe-conduct to a spy. On the other hand, the Sovereign must respect a properly obtained safe-conduct or quarter, as long as he does not fear some fraud or machination on the part of the infidel. The safe-conduct or quarter are purely personal, and can not revert to the family or the property of the infidel, whether they are still on enemy territory or whether the infidel has brought them with him.[16]

> The *amân* granted to the enemy by tributaries [*dhimmis*] whose cooperation Muslims have utilized to fight against him [the enemy], is non-existent, because an *amân* granted by tributaries to the detriment of Muslims is not allowed. If it is granted by one of the combatant slaves, it is valid on the basis of the *hadith* relating to this fact, and the least of them can grant the safe-conduct [. . .][17]

Hence, it is in this specific context of a total denial of the *harbi*'s rights that the protection accorded by the *dhimma* is granted. Provided certain conditions are fulfilled, it restores to the non-Muslims their rights—albeit restricted—forfeited by *jihad.*

The most important of these conditions is payment of a poll tax, which represents the sum given to buy back from the *umma* the non-Muslim's right to life. This poll tax has a compulsory, mandatory value because of its religious origin (Koran 9:29).[18] Refusal to pay it turns the *dhimmi* into a *harbi,* subjecting him to the rules of *jihad*—slavery or death. Certain jurists advocate expulsion from Islamic territory:

> When infidels do not observe the conditions which have been imposed on them, the agreement with them still remains intact, but they must hence-forth be forced to fulfill their obligations more scrupulously. Only when they make war on us or refuse, either to pay the poll tax or to submit to our laws, is the agreement rightfully broken and we, too, are freed from our obligations toward them.[19]

> The *wali* is not permitted to spare any Christian, Jew, Magian [Zoroastrian], Sabean or Samaritan from payment of the poll tax and no-one can obtain a partial reduction; it is illegal for one person to be exempt and another not, because their lives and their possessions are only protected by reason of payment of the poll tax, which plays the role of the *kharaj* relating to property.[20]

Disarming

Other constraints of a military nature were imposed on the *dhimmis,* such as the prohibition on carrying or possessing weapons.[21] Although rendered totally obsolete by their demographic decline, this prohibition remained in force up to the twentieth century in some Arab regions where desert conditions preserved their isolation and maintained ancient mores.

The prohibition preventing specific groups from bearing arms placed the indigenous masses in a state of permanent insecurity and humiliating inferiority to the allogenic populations, for whom the principle of war became a sacred obligation. The permanent anarchy which prevailed in the provinces of the *dar al-Islam,* and tribal invasions or rebellions, caused the endemic lack of safety on the highways. Those factors combined to erode considerably the demography of the disarmed populations, in spite of the efforts by the Muslim central power to maintain general security. This prohibition on bearing arms caused a wide movement toward Islamization (as with the Bosnian Serbs, or the exodus of their Christian nobles). At the psychological level, it constituted an essential element in the *dhimmi* syndrome which will be discussed later.

At the beginning of the Ottoman conquest of the Balkans in the fourteenth century, Christians were able to retain their fiefs and weapons on condition that they participated in Turkish military expeditions. In addition to these Christian *spahis*, garrisons made up of Christians and Muslims (*derbendjijas, martolosi*) ensured the defense of frontiers, the upkeep of fortresses and the safety of difficult routes. In return for these military services, the Christians enjoyed some fiscal relief. However, the number of Christians in these positions gradually declined.

In Kosovo in 1860, the disarming of Serbs was still compulsory:

> For a long time the province [of Skopje] has been a prey to brigandage [. . .] Christian churches and monasteries, towns and inhabitants, are not now pillaged, massacred, and burnt by Albanian hordes as used to be done ten years ago [. . .] They [the Christian peasants] are not allowed to carry arms. This, considering the want of a good police, exposes them all the more to attacks from brigands.[22]

In towns prone to Albanian violence and anarchy, the Serbian population did not dare to leave the town without an Albanian guard. According to the Serbian sociologist and geographer Jovan Cvijic, "one [a Christian] could not own fields, vines, houses, or shops of a certain importance; one could only wear wretched clothes." He shows that these Serbian Christians, who were relegated to lowly trades scorned by Turks and Albanians, represented until 1912 a population of pariahs who had fallen to the lowest social level.[23]

William Shaler, American consul in Algiers (1816–28), mentions the prohibition preventing Jews and Christians from bearing arms. The same prohibition applied to Jews in Yemen until the twentieth century.[24] The prohibition on bearing arms, linked to a religious dogma, was an innovation introduced by Islam and did not exist in the Roman, Byzantine, and Sassanian empires.

Deportations

The transfer and deportation of populations, although not mentioned in the *dhimma*, was nonetheless linked to the condition of the conquered peoples. Rebellions by *dhimmis* or security measures, such as the removal of Christians and Jews from frontier or strategic zones, motivated these displacements, particularly frequent under the Ottomans in Anatolia, the Balkans, Kosovo, and Armenia. The last massive deportation of Armenians was ordered by the Turks as part of the genocide of 1915. These deportations uprooted populations, hampered the cohesion of the social fabric, and broke down resistance. Replacement of the deportees by Muslim or other ethnic groups facilitated control of the vanquished by fragmenting them and developing ethnic antagonisms.[25] The deportations also responded to economic imperatives, such as revitalizing trade and reviving agriculture in regions totally ravaged by the wars.[26] It should be noted here that deportation was a general military strategy in earlier times: the Assyrians, Persians, Romans, and Byzantines deported or exchanged populations from whole regions.

Other obligations were imposed on the *dhimmis*, such as billeting and provisioning the army, both men and horses, and the duty to guide Muslims correctly on the road, while refraining from any collaboration with their enemies. As a consequence of a millennium of war between Islam and Christendom, this clause poisoned relationships between Christian *dhimmis* and *harbis* (Europeans). It forced the *dhimmi* to assume an ever-increasing hostility toward the *harbi* in order to forestall bloody reprisals by an ever-suspicious Muslim authority. In addition, the obligation to lodge soldiers in churches, synagogues, and in their homes subjected the *dhimmis* to a regime of extortions and humiliations, worsened by frequent pillaging and sometimes even the abduction of women.[27]

These clauses were laid down by the four juridical schools:

> Furthermore, the law recommends the Sovereign to require that infidels should, as far as possible, extend hospitality to Muslim travelers passing through their country, all without prejudice to the legal minimum poll tax. It is true that jurists maintain that this duty can be taken into account when one wishes to know if the infidels pay the minimum. In any case, however, the duty of hospitality can not be imposed on the poor, but only on the rich and those who enjoy a degree of prosperity. In requiring the exercise of hospitality, the Sovereign must mention the number of guests, men and horses, that each individual should lodge; the nature and quantity of foodstuffs, both staple foods and seasoning, due to each individual; and the fodder for animals. The guests must be accommodated in either the church or synagogue or the best house in the area; the length of their stay must be stipulated up to a maximum of three days.[28]

Muslim, Christian, and Jewish chronicles, as well as European travelers over the centuries, mention old churches and synagogues which had been converted into mosques, destroyed, abandoned, or turned into refuse dumps or stables.[29] In 1852, Turkish soldiers and Arabs from Nablus still stabled their donkeys and horses in a Tiberias synagogue.[30] In Suleymaniya (northern Iraq) in 1909, a traveler noticed that the soldiers were housed in a room in the synagogue and had made of it a shambles filled with filth.

Territorial Dispossession

Territorial expropriation added to these factors, being linked to the military relationship of a conquering army with the indigenous populations. It remained a permanent element inherent in the *dhimmi* condition.

All territory taken from infidels became the property (*fay*) of the state. It formed, henceforth, the *dar al-Islam,* land administered by Islamic law for the benefit of Muslims and their descendants.[31] This principle, established by the Arab conquest, introduced a political and legal dogma rooted in theology.

> These possessions received the name of *fay* since Allah had taken them away from the infidels in order to *restore* (*afa'a, radda*) them to the Muslims. In principle, Allah has created the things of this world only in order that they may contribute to serving him, since he created man only in order to be ministered to. Consequently, the infidels forfeit their persons and their belongings which they do not use in Allah's service to the faithful believers who serve Allah and unto whom Allah restitutes what is theirs; thus is restored to a man the inheritance of which he was deprived, even if he had never before gained possession of it.[32]

At the beginning of the Arab conquest claims by tribes to war booty, land, and peoples provoked internecine wars and revolts against the caliph's hegemonic power. These conflicts plagued the whole Umayyad Caliphate (661–750). In the Abbasid period (750–1258), jurists based themselves on the alleged methods of conquest from which had been formulated the land legislation, and attributed its origin to the second caliph, Umar Ibn al-Khattab.

Islamic law prohibited non-Muslims from owning land and transferred ownership to the Muslim treasury administered by the caliph. The latter delimited military districts which he granted as fiefs either temporarily or in perpetuity to members of his family, tribes, and military leaders, in return for equipping soldiers for their participation in battle.[33] This form of administrative military hierarchy still existed in the Ottoman Empire in the nineteenth century. In Bosnia, only Muslims could own "free" lands (*mulk*), the Ottoman state keeping all conquered lands (*miri* lands) for itself.[34]

However, *dhimmis* could retain possession of the soil, draw the usufruct from it, and inherit it. Nonetheless, the Islamic conquest did actually create a dramatic situation described in innumerable sources and with consequences, which, in the long run, culminated in the disappearance of the indigenous Christian and Jewish peasantry. In fact, even if Islamic legislation guaranteed a *dhimmi* possession of his land, this principle was often transgressed, particularly through transfers of populations forced to abandon their property, both land and personal possessions.

In the mid-nineteenth century, when the *dhimmis* were emancipated and Ottoman law was being modernized, the ulema forbade the sale of land to Christian Serbs. When the latter did manage to buy a plot, it could be taken from them "on one unjust pretext or another."[35] British consuls mention a similar situation affecting Jews and Christians in Palestine and Syria at the same period.[36]

Demography

This political context also included the huge Islamic immigration into the conquered lands, which altered the ethnoreligious composition of the populations. The demographic disparity between the vanquished and the Muslims after the conquest and during the ensuing centuries represented a considerable danger, threatening the permanence of Islamic power. A collection of measures—including deportations and transfers—were employed to reduce the ethnoreligious gap. The planned emigration and settlement of many waves of Arabs and Turks in the conquered territory was accompanied by forced conversions in frontier zones. This was supplemented by abductions of women and children—forbidden by law but endemic in certain regions[37]—and enslavement for insolvency.

Inability to pay taxes, offenses in respect of individuals or troops, razzias by rebels—there was scarcely a place or period when slavery did not claim its harvest of *dhimmis:* men, women, and children. This demographic dilution increased under the Ottomans with the *devshirme* institution, introduced by Sultan Orkhan (1326–59). It consisted of the regular conscription, as tribute, of one-fifth of Christian children from the conquered eastern and central European countries. The intervals between such levies varied depending on requirements. Some places, such as Jannina, Galata, and Rhodes, were exempted.

These children, aged between fourteen and twenty, forcibly converted to Islam, entered the corps of janissaries, military militias formed almost exclusively of Islamized Christians. The periodic levies, consisting of contingents of one thousand, subsequently became annual. The Christian children were conscripted from among the aristocracy of Greeks, Serbs, Bulgarians, Albanians, Armenians, and from the sons of Orthodox priests. At a fixed date every father had to appear in the town square with his sons. There, in the presence of the kadi, the recruiting agents, themselves janissaries, selected the handsomest and most robust. No father could avoid this child tribute on pain of severe punishment.[38]

Parallel with this recruitment system, another levy operated for children aged between six and ten (*ichoghlani*), destined for the sultans' seraglios. Confined in palaces in the care of eunuchs, they were subjected to exacting discipline and forced to perform arduous tasks for fourteen years. It was they who supplied the Ottoman state with its top hierarchy of officials. This specific and regular erosion of the vanquished peoples increased the Muslim population and correspondingly reduced the Christians. The *devshirme* system was theoretically abolished in 1656, but recruitment of *ichoghlani* lasted until the mid-eighteenth century. The slave system which determined the whole social, political, and military structure of the *dar al-Islam* permanently introduced Christian influence at every level. Placed in harems, in the army, and the government, or kept in the countryside, Islamized Christian slaves of both sexes formed a considerable population. The workforce they provided was essential to maintain Islamic domination, while it fed a constant current of Islamization. Children, adolescents and adults—these human waves endlessly renewed by razzias and wars—kept all the social wheels in motion. In the seventeenth century, the Chevalier Jean de Chardin described this process in Persia:

> He [Shah Abbas I, 1588–1629] attracted these Christian peoples by his favors and by promoting them. Those whom he placed in high positions were mainly his slaves, who had been sent to him as gifts or had been taken in war. He raised to office all those he found handsome and sturdy, men of spirit and courage. He did more, he established a corps of twelve thousand of them for war; and later, beginning to throw off the mask, he promoted them only to all commands of war and of political government, where it was not necessary to know the law and the [Muslim] canon law. (5:226)
>
> He transported settlements of twenty or thirty thousand souls at a time, two or three hundred leagues from their native land. Almost all of them were Georgian and Armenian Christians [. . .] It was in this way that the kings of Persia rose to that point of absolute power which I will show, and which they sustain [. . .] because as almost all the Georgians and Iberians [from South Caucasus] who are given the status to govern are slaves by origin, and genuine outsiders in the government, they have no contacts either in the kingdom or with one another; and as most of them know neither from where nor from whom they come, it happens that they are not driven by any desire for freedom on the one hand and are incapable of forming leagues or conspiracies on the other; because men who have no relationship among themselves do not rise in rebellion on behalf of each other, either to save their lives or to ascend the throne. (5:227–28)
>
> This name of *coular* [Turkish: *kullar*] means slave, not that these men are not as free as other Persians, but because they are natives of countries such as Georgia, Circassia, Iberia, and of Moscow, from where slaves are drawn. Thus they are of Christian origin. Some were sent to the king as a gift, being still young; others are descended from the peoples of these countries, who have become accustomed to Persia. As almost all of them embrace the Muhammadan religion, they are all renegades or the children of renegades. They can easily be compared with the famous Mamluks of Egypt, who were masters of that kingdom for almost three hundred years [. . .] because there are many similarities between the two: for example, these Mamluks [slaves of the monarch] were all Christian renegades; they alone were placed in offices; and they were introduced in order to counterbalance the power of the Arab troops who deposed the princes and ministers of Egypt at will and caused their death when they so pleased, as do the janissaries in the Ottoman government [. . .]. These troops of slaves are established on the same

basis as the children of tribute in Turkey; but these slaves are neither numerous, nor raised communally, nor so good. (5:306–8)[39]

Slavery constituted the most effective channel of Islamization. The European stream of slaves was supplemented by constantly renewed razzias against the Christian and animist populations of Africa, and from maritime piracy for ransom.

Rebellions

Rebellions by infidels were regarded as equivalent to breaking the protection treaty, and led to the slaughter of the rebels and the enslavement of women and children.

> Only when they combat us does the violation of their treaties by the tributaries permit them to be slain, their belongings to be pillaged, and their wives and children to be enslaved. Otherwise they are to be evicted from Muslim territory and afforded safe conduct until they reach their place of safety in the nearest polytheistic country. If they do not leave of their own will, then they are to be expelled by force.[40]

> The infidel who has broken the treaty by use of weapons must be beaten and killed immediately. The infidel who breaks the treaty in another way can not demand to be taken back to his country; but the Sovereign can have him put to death, reduced to slavery, pardoned or released on payment of a ransom, whichever seems to him the most advantageous. However, he can not be made a slave if he embraces Islam before the Sovereign has pronounced his fate. The loss of safe-conduct or quarter, granted an infidel, in no way extends to his wife and children. The infidel who renounces the treaty with us and asks to be regarded hereafter as an enemy can demand to be conducted in safety outside our frontiers.[41]

After the Arab conquest, the population of Persepolis in Persia which had revolted was massacred and the city destroyed.[42] Chroniclers mention revolts in Lebanon, Egypt, and Armenia. In Spain the *muwallads* (neo-converts) were in almost constant revolt against the Arab immigrants who had carved out large estates for themselves, farmed by Christian serfs or slaves. Fiscal extortions and expropriations lit the flames of continual rebellion by *muwallads* and *mozarabs* (Christian *dhimmis*) throughout the Hispanic peninsula. The leaders of the rebellions were crucified and the insurgents put to the sword. During the entire period of the Hispano-Umayyad emirate until the tenth century, these bloody conflicts fed endemic religious hatred. A letter from Louis the Pious to the Christians of Merida in 828 reflects their situation under Abd ar-Rahman II and during the preceding reign: usurpation of their property, unfair increase of the exacted tribute, removal of their freedom—which probably meant slavery—and oppression by "heavy and iniquitous taxes."[43] Ibn Hafsun (d. 918), leader of the *mu-wallad* rebellion in southern Andalusia, roused the peasants against the government which, he claimed, was taking their property and subjecting them to heavy tribute, and against the Arabs who were crushing them with humiliations and treating them as slaves.[44]

In the Maghreb, tribal wars which also decimated the Muslim populations were even crueler on the *dhimmis* living as they did under the protection of a monarch, whose assassination could cause their destruction. In Fez, for example, between five and six thousand Jews were reported massacred during revolts in 1032;[45] three thousand perished in an uprising of 1066 in Grenada (Andalusia).[46] Data on *dhimmis* are very incomplete; concerning Jews, rabbinic literature (*responsa*) and *genizah* documents indicate that Jewish peasants paying the *kharaj* lived in the neighborhood of Qairuan (Tunisia) in the tenth century. As for African Christendom, once so vigorous and aggressive, its decline was such that in 1076 it was impossible to find in Africa the three bishops indispensable for an episcopal ordination.[47] The destruction wrought by Bedouin tribes from Arabia when they entered Tripolitania and Ifriqiyya (May 1050) was described in detail by the reputable historian Ibn Khaldun in his *History of the Berbers;* the Andalusian geographer Al-Idrisi lamented the fate of Qairuan, once the most prestigious African city, now reduced to ruins where "every type of calamity" was rife. These events, related later by Muslim chroniclers, are confirmed by contemporary letters written by Jewish merchants and travelers.[48]

In the Maghreb, and earlier in Yemen, Christian *dhimmis* had completely disappeared. During periods of instability and a change in monarch, Jewish districts were plundered, men slaughtered or ransomed, and women and children abducted by tribes massed around the towns.[49]

The endemic unrest aggravated the *dhimmis'* situation, although they were not the direct targets of the conflicts. Thus, the removal of the Umayyads by the Abbasids in 750 created anarchy throughout the Empire. Marwan, the last Umayyad caliph in the East, operated a scorched earth policy when he fled from Abbasid troops. Towns, villages, and harvest were set alight and large numbers perished in the general exodus. The Coptic patriarch Michael, imprisoned in his camp together with a few priests, was tortured daily: he was beaten, his beard torn out, and he was subjected to other humiliations designed to extort money from him.[50]

The dynastic conflicts and tribal revolts brought the destruction of villages. Populations were ransomed by rebels who tortured notables, the clergy and monks, suspected of concealing treasures in churches and monasteries.[51] The authorities strove to protect the *dhimmis* by dispatching troops, if only to preserve the state's source of finance. *Dhimmis* were exploited and despoiled by all parties. They were used as economic tools in political struggles which did not concern them.

In Palestine in the early Middle Ages, all contemporary sources confirm the ravages which followed Arab tribal battles, resumed with the arrival of the Turkomans in 1071. In 1077 the Turkoman rebel Atsiz, after persecuting the inhabitants of Jerusalem for four years, slaughtered three thousand people there and decimated the population of Ramlah; Gaza was cleared of inhabitants; he left no more than three thousand survivors in Damascus. According to contemporary Arabic, Jewish, Coptic, Syriac, and Latin sources, Palestinian towns and villages were destroyed, their inhabitants taken prisoner, often tortured, or murdered; the countryside was plundered and set alight, and plantations razed to the ground. These events were reported by Christian refugees and pilgrims and were instrumental in provoking the first Crusade of 1096.[52]

In the Ottoman Empire the rules of *jihad* still applied in the nineteenth century. After the Serb revolt had been crushed in 1813, one thousand eight hundred women and children were sold in a single day in Belgrade.[53] The repeated revolts by the Greeks replenished the slave markets.

In 1821, the sultan Mahmud II ordered the Egyptian army that had been sent to subdue the Greek revolt to obey the *shari'a* which stipulated that "rebels be openly fought and put to the sword, that their property be plundered and their women and children treated as slaves."[54] But, in 1824, an edict confirmed the *amân* granted to rebels performing an act of submission and imposed a fine on those who molested them. An imperial decree based on three *fatwas* forbade Muslims to kill non-Muslims who had been granted the *amân* and were paying the *jizya,* or to plunder their property. It forbade soldiers to plunder their houses and, in accordance with the laws, prohibited, on pain of imprisonment, any act of violence against non-Muslims, loyal subjects of the sultan.[55] This is a clear example of the Islamic principle of the protection of subjected *dhimmis.* But this principle, which in the seventh century represented a restraint on the barbarism of war and acknowledged religious pluralism, no longer corresponded with modern nineteenth and twentieth century concepts. The legislation of *jihad* governing the methods of battles was strictly maintained at the time of the wars against the Serbs, Greeks, and Bulgarians during the whole nineteenth century, and against the Armenians in the massacres of 1894–96, and the genocide of 1915–17.[56]

Apart from the enslavement of rebels, there were episodic abductions of Christian and Jewish women and children by nomads in rural regions of Kurdistan, Mesopotamia, Iraq, Palestine, Syria, and the Maghreb. Although totally illegal according to Islamic law, this continued to be a regular practice during razzias and uprisings until the twentieth century.

Islamic dogma teaches that all children are born Muslim.[57] In Yemen the law decreed that Jewish orphans "revert" to Islam. Abrogated by the Turks in 1872 after their short occupation, it was reintroduced by the imam Yahya in 1922 and renewed in 1925. Precocious marriages arranged by parents of Jewish children was intended to prevent abduction of orphans.

The Economic Domain

Kharaj

Muslim chroniclers of the Abbasid period (750–1258), describing the period of the conquests, use the terms *kharaj* and *jizya* indiscriminately to designate the collective tribute levied by the conquerors on the indigenous *dhimmi* peoples. This tax, handed over to the Muslim authorities by representatives of the subjected peoples, corresponded to the fiscal practices of the Sassanian and Byzantine Empires. Although Muslim jurists do not always agree on the classification of lands, either as to their nature or their assessment, they all acknowledge the *dhimmi*'s obligation to pay the *kharaj* on the land he cultivates. The vastness of the conquered territory extending from Armenia to Spain, the scale of the destruction and the incessant inter-Muslim ethnic struggles developed different local situations which the lack of documents—attributable to these disorders—renders an evaluation difficult.[58]

Muslim and *dhimmi* sources provide information on the peasant condition in Armenia, Iraq, Syria, Palestine, and Egypt. In these regions, payment of the *kharaj* in cash and kind was incumbent on villages collectively, the peasants being jointly responsible to the tax collectors. Taxes, demanded in advance and levied several times over, were supplemented by additional taxes on orchards, livestock, pasturage rights, fishing, tolls, and certain commodities. Ruinous requisitions and corvées reduced the peasant to poverty.[59]

The basis of the tax varied according to a number of criteria, such as the quality of the land, its irrigation, and local traditions.[60] Payment was effected in cash and kind, the latter at three fixed dates. Collection was entrusted to tax collectors accompanied by soldiers, inspectors, surveyors, and money-changers paid, fed, and lodged for several days at the taxpayers' expense.

The tax-collectors used punishments and torture to carry out their task. These practices, theoretically prohibited, drove the *dhimmi* populations to take flight and abandon their lands.[61]

At the beginning of the conquest, when the peasantry was exclusively *dhimmi*, representatives of each community divided the taxes they had to pay the Muslim Treasury among their coreligionists. The farming out of taxes to these *dhimmi* leaders resulted in auctions among Christian clergy and Jewish notables who coveted this duty—the caliph or sultan granting it to the highest bidder. To alleviate the Treasury's empoverishment caused by the *dhimmis'* abandonment of lands or conversion to Islam, the *kharaj* soon became a tax attached to land, payable by the farmer regardless of his religion, on the principle that the yield from *fay* land constituted collective booty for Muslims in perpetuity.[62]

The concept of *fay*—collective booty reserved for the upkeep of the Islamic community—constituted the legal argument which preserved the religions of the conquered peoples. This economic burden, which devolved on the disarmed vanquished people to the benefit of a warlike community destined to conquer the world, is very clearly set out by the Muslim jurisconsults. However, the other specific aspect of the koranic revelation which teaches respect for the religions of the Book, and forbids religious constraint, also appears in the writings of these jurists, sometimes in the same discourse.[63]

Chroniclers of the period explain what it meant "to be a *fay* people." In Egypt in 702, for example, the governor Abdallah, son of the caliph Abd al-Malik, demanded three thousand dinars from the patriarch Alexander II, who was thrown into prison and humiliated at his command. The governor ordered men in their twenties to be brought from his country (Arabia) and these inflicted manifold afflictions on the Egyptians, slaughtering many of them. Branded on hands and forehead, the *dhimmis* were sent off to various places and none of them could be buried if he had not paid the poll tax. According to the chronicler, even someone who died of starvation could not be buried. Kurrah, the new governor, demanded gold from the patriarch, once again imprisoned. His residence and all his possessions were seized, the clergy were tortured, and all officials expropriated. Tyranny and extortions devastated the land, causing people to take flight. The next governor, Usamah, ordered monks to be mutilated and to wear iron bracelets bearing their name, their monastery or church, and the date. The *Chronicles of the Patriarchs* are explicit:

> For he [the governor] commanded that no one should lodge a stranger [a fugitive] in the churches or at the inns or on the wharfs, and the people were afraid of him and drove out the strangers that were in their houses. And he commanded the monks not to make monks of those who came to them. Then he mutilated the monks, and branded each one of them on his left hand, with a branding iron in the form of a ring, that he might be known; adding the name of his church and his monastery, without a cross, and with a date according to the era of Islam. Thus there was, in the year 96 [715] of the Hegira, trouble among the monks, and oppression of the faithful [Christians]. If they discovered a fugitive or one that had not been marked, they brought him to the Amir [Emir], who ordered that one of his limbs should

be cut off, so that he was lame for life; and the number could not be counted of those whom he maimed for this cause. And he shaved off the beards of many, and slew a great multitude, and put out the eyes of many without mercy, and killed many under punishment with scourges. And out of love for money he commanded the governors to put the people to death, and bring him their money; and he wrote to them, saying: "I have delivered up to you the lives of the people, therefore collect all the wealth that you can, from bishops or monks or churches or any of the people, and bring stuffs and money and cattle and all that you find belonging to them, and respect no one. And whatever place you visit, pillage it". Accordingly the officials laid the country waste, and carried off the columns and the woodwork, and sold what was worth ten dinars for one dinar [. . .][64]

The emir subsequently ordered that all the inhabitants be plundered and all their property confiscated, with the result that people sold their own children. Greeks found residing in Egypt were slaughtered, impaled, or their hands and feet mutilated. Monks discovered without a bracelet were executed or flogged to death, their churches closed, and a ransom of a thousand dinars demanded. Superiors of monasteries were rounded up, tortured, and threatened with the galleys if they did not pay one dinar each. When the new caliph Umar II took power in 717, he freed the monks and ecclesiastical property and restored prosperity by abolishing the new taxes. Then he gave Christians the choice between Islam and expulsion:

"Omar commands saying, Those who wish to remain as they are, and in their own country, must follow the religion of Muhammad as I do; but let those who do not wish to do so, go forth from my dominions." Then the Christians gave him all the money that they could, and trusted in God, and rendered service to the Muslims, and became an example to many. For the Christians were oppressed by the governors and the local authorities and the Muslims in every place, the old and the young, the rich and the poor among them; and Omar commanded that the poll-tax should be taken from all men who would not become Muslims, even in cases where it was not customary to take it.[65]

Dhimmi chronicles in Palestine, Syria, Mesopotamia, and Armenia present the same pictures of peasant life. Caliphs and sultans did, however, endeavor to protect the *dhimmi* peasantry against uncontrolled extortions by governors or local tyrants. Because of the economic importance of agriculture, landed property constituted the Muslim ruling classes' main source of wealth and power. The state drew its resources from the prosperity of the land which depended for its yield on compulsory work by an abundant workforce. Consequently, the Muslim jurists of the Abbasid period advocated moderation in levying taxes.[66] Despite these exhortations, the abandonment of cultivated land was an endemic phenomenon in the *dar al-Islam*, particularly in outlying provinces which escaped state control. The need to revitalize deserted lands was the motive behind a large number of deportations of *dhimmi* communities. The Armenian chronicler Ghevond describes this situation in Armenia during the reign of the first Abbasid caliph, al-Saffah (749–54):

> Barely had he arrived when he began to burden the population with taxes and exorbitant contributions. One saw the revival[67] of horrible scenes of every sort of torture; nor did he forget to tax the dead; the multitude of orphans and widows suffered the same cruelty; priests and ministers at the holy sanctuary were forced by the vile punishments of flogging and whipping to disclose the names of the dead and of their parents; in short, the whole population of the country, smitten with enormous taxes, after having paid large sums of *zuze* (silver coins), also had to wear a lead seal around their necks. [p.124]
>
> In the reign of Abdallah II [Abu Ja'far al-Mansur, 754–75] and on the orders of Yazid, Armenia was struck by extremely onerous taxation. The infernal avarice of the implacable enemy was not satisfied with devouring the flesh of the Christians, the flower of the country, nor with drinking their blood as we drink water; Armenia in its entirety suffered horribly from the absolute lack of money. Every individual, even by giving all he had, his clothes, his foodstuffs and prime necessities, did not succeed in paying his ransom and redeeming his person from torture. Gibbets, presses and gallows had been set up everywhere; nothing but fearful and continual torture was seen everywhere. [pp.130–131]
>
> [. . .] as for the lower class of the population, it had been exposed to different sorts of torture: some suffered flagellation for being unable to pay exorbitant taxes; others were hanged on gibbets, or crushed under presses; and others were stripped of their clothing and thrown into lakes in the depths of an extremely severe winter; and soldiers spaced out on the banks prevented them clambering ashore and forced them to perish wretchedly [. . .][68]

During the early Middle Ages, strict control of the whole village population, reinforced by severe penalties for those who took flight, was needed to keep the peasants on their lands. The parceling out of the *dar al-Islam,* and the chronic insecurity prevalent in the provinces, exposed the *dhimmis* to arbitrary extortions from the rebel nomad chiefs who terrorized their regions at various periods when the armies of the central authority were unable to protect them. The wealth-producing *dhimmi* communities became a coveted prize and plunder to warring political forces.[69]

Thus, the destruction of the *dhimmi* peasantry—representing the majority of the non-Muslim population at that period of agrarian and rural economy—resulted from a long-term overall situation combining the constant waves of immigration by allogenic peoples, the expropriation of the indigenous populations, insecurity, fiscal oppression, accompanied by brutality and enslavement, and the consequences of endemic wars.

A large number of Coptic, Armenian, Syriac, Jewish, and Serbian sources—letters and chronicles—describe the process whereby the *dhimmi* peasantry was expropriated. Crushed by taxation and forced into debt toward their Muslim creditors at exorbitant rates, Christian and Jewish peasants abandoned their mortgaged lands to the Muslim overlord and went into exile or became slaves. Abu Yusuf records a declaration by Umar II in which he stated that prices were low in his predecessors' time because "taxing the tributaries beyond their powers, the latter had inevitably sold what they possessed [. . .]"[70]

The Turkization of Armenia, Anatolia, and the Balkans from the eleventh century brought these countries under a military administration controlled by warrior chiefs endowed with fiefs (*timar*). Similar situations were created resulting in the uprooting of the *dhimmi* peasantry.[71]

Jizya

Verse 9:29 of the Koran links the obligation of *jihad* to the exaction of the *jizya*. The *jizya* was a poll tax assessed at three rates: 12, 24, and 48 *dirhams*, depending on the taxpayer's economic situation. Like the *kharaj*, the poll tax stemmed from a patron-client relationship between a population disarmed by the laws of war and a warrior caste which assumed its defense in return for a payment. The extension of the conquest transferred the politicoeconomic relationship, specific to Arabia, into other regions and simultaneously transposed it to an inter-religious context.

In theory, women, the poor, the sick, and the infirm were exempt from the poll tax; however, Armenian, Syriac, Serbian, and Jewish sources offer abundant proof that the *jizya* was demanded from children, widows, orphans, and even the dead. For the Shafi'ites:

> Our religion compels the poll tax to be paid by dying people, the old, even in a state of incapacity, the blind, monks, workers, and the poor, incapable of practising a trade. As for people who seem to be insolvent at the end of the year, the sum of the poll tax remains a debt to their account until they should become solvent.[72]

The Syriac *Apocalypse*, attributed to Methodius and written in the Sinjar region (Mesopotamia) in 690 or 691, mentions that even widows, orphans, and priests paid the poll tax.[73]

Anyone who left their homes without their receipt for the *jizya* or who had lost it incurred the greatest danger. In the Ottoman Empire the receipt had to be produced on pain of immediate imprisonment, at the demand of tax-collectors who stopped *dhimmis*—recognizable by their distinctive dress—in the street.[74]

Muslim jurisconsults determined the ceremonial for payment of the *jizya*. According to the Shafi'i rite, as described by an-Nawawi in the thirteenth century:

> The infidel who wishes to pay his poll tax must be treated with disdain by the collector: the collector remains seated and the infidel remains standing in front of him, his head bowed and his back bent. The infidel personally must place the money on the scales, while the collector holds him by his beard and strikes him on both cheeks. However, according to the majority of scholars, these practices are recommended but not, as some think, compulsory. The authors cited in the latter instance also prohibited an infidel from giving a Muslim the mandate to pay his poll tax, or from effecting payment through transfer of a credit on a Muslim, or a Muslim from standing bail for payment. However, most scholars acknowledge these practices.[75]

According to the Moroccan jurist al-Maghili (d.1504), whose preachings incited pillage of Jews and their slaughter in the Gurara and Tuat oases in the fifteenth century:

> On the day of payment they [the *dhimmis*] shall be assembled in a public place like the *suq*. They should be standing there waiting in the lowest and dirtiest place. The acting officials representing the Law shall be placed above them and shall adopt a threatening attitude so that it seems to them, as well as to the others, that our object is to degrade them by pretending to take their possessions. They will realize that we are doing them a favor (again) in accepting from them the *jizya* and letting them (thus) go free. Then they shall be dragged one by one (to the official responsible) for the exacting of payment. When paying, the *dhimmi* will receive a blow and will be thrust aside so that he will think that he has escaped the sword through this (insult). This is the way that the friends of the Lord, of the first and last generations, will act toward their infidel enemies, for might belongs to Allah, to His Apostle, and to the Believers.[76]

Two accounts of the collection of the *jizya* from the Jews of Mogador in 1825 by an American shipwrecked captain,[77] and the report quoted below from Marrakesh in 1894, confirm that these measures were implemented in Morocco until the end of the nineteenth century:

> [. . .] The kaid Uwida and the kadi Mawlay Mustafa had mounted their tent today near the Mellah gate and had summoned the Jews in order to collect from them the poll tax (*jizya*) which they are obliged to pay the sultan.
> They had me summoned also. I first inquired whether those who were European-protected subjects had to pay this tax. Having learned that a great many of them had already paid it, I wished to do likewise. After having remitted the amount of the tax to the two officials, I received from the kadi's guard two blows in the back of the neck. Addressing the kadi and the kaid, I said: "Know that I am an Italian-protected subject." Whereupon the kadi

said to his guard: "Remove the kerchief covering his head and strike him strongly; he can then go and complain wherever he wants."

The guards hastily obeyed and struck me once again more violently. This public mistreatment of a European-protected subject demonstrates to all the Arabs that they can, with impunity, mistreat the Jews.[78]

Traveling in central Asia in 1863, the Hungarian orientalist, Arminius Vàmbéry, noted:

The Jews in the Khanate are about 10,000 in number, dwelling for the most part in Bukhara, Samarcand, and Karshi, and occupying themselves rather with handicrafts than with commerce. In their origin they are Jews from Persia, and have wandered hither from Kazvin and Merv, about 150 years ago. They live here under the greatest oppression, and exposed to the greatest contempt. They only dare to show themselves on the threshold when they pay a visit to a "believer" [a Muslim]; and again when they receive visitors, they are bound in all haste to quit their own houses, and station themselves before their doors. In the city of Bokhara, they yield yearly 2,000 Tilla Djizie (tribute), which the chief of their whole community pays in, receiving as he does so, two slight blows on the cheek, prescribed by the Koran as a sign of submission. The rumor of the privileges accorded to the Jews in Turkey has attracted some to Damascus and other places in Syria; but this emigration can only occur secretly, otherwise they would have to atone for the very wish by confiscation or death.[79]

In the Ottoman Empire such proceedings were not implemented; the levy was collected directly by representatives of the heads of community.

Additional Taxes

All taxes on trade and transport paid by Muslims were generally doubled for *dhimmis*. In addition, the population—but particularly the *dhimmi* communities—were subject to ruinous extortions designed to cover the financing of incessant wars.

In regions where anarchy prevailed, rebel leaders demanded ransoms from *dhimmis* on pain of death or enslavement. Fiscal oppression in the form of *kharaj, jizya,* and ransoms was a primary cause of the disappearance of large numbers of *dhimmi* populations through conversion to Islam or flight. In Egypt the Coptic patriarch Michael I (d.766) informed the caliph Marwan II that his people had been ruined to the point of having to sell their children.[80] During the whole Umayyad period (661–750) the Copts suffered fiscal extortions, sometimes accompanied by torture and mutilation.

In their desperate calls for aid, the *dhimmi* populations often mentioned such situations in different periods and regions. Traveling in Persia in

1673–74, the Chevalier Jean de Chardin noticed that the suburb of Julfa (Isfahan), built under Shah Abbas I by Armenians he had deported there in 1604, "is now no more than heaps of ruins among which wander unhappy wretches overcome by poverty and inflictions."[81]

In Palestine Bedouin chiefs devastated the countryside and subjected the *dhimmis* to a regime of constant extortions. Eleventh-century Judeo-Palestinian documents mention the taxes imposed on the Jewish community on pain of severe reprisals: for entering Jerusalem, for the protection of pilgrims, for the right to pray on the Mount of Olives, and even for the right to pray aloud there.[82] All *dhimmi* chronicles throughout the centuries mention the excessive rates the Muslims charged in order to strip the community of its property. However, it was in Palestine, cradle of the Bible, that religious ransoming was most harshly and cruelly rampant. In 1813–14 the notables of the small Jewish community of Hebron were imprisoned and tortured until a ransom was paid to the Arab sheikhs by the Jewish communities of Germany, Holland, and England. In the Hebron region from the end of the 1830s till 1859 Abd al-Rahman Amr, the Arab leader of the Qays coalition, was waging war against another Arab tribe, the Yamans of Bethlehem. He terrorized the *dhimmis,* threatening to expel the Jews from Hebron as well as the handful of Christians who lived there if they did not pay him various ransoms and protection dues.[83]

In Safed the departure of Bonaparte's French troops (1799) unleashed a razzia on the Jewish quarter, with pillage, massacre, and a ransom of 50,000 piastres, raised to 75,000 piastres in 1810. In 1820 the notables were again imprisoned and a ransom demanded which increased the community's debt from 125,000 to 400,000 piastres. The same policy was applied in Tiberias in 1822, and was chronic up to 1852 (see appendix 1).[84]

As for the Jews of Jerusalem, James Buckingham provided an interesting note from 1816:

> Previous to the invasion of Syria by Buonaparte [1798], a law existed among the Turks that there should be no more than two thousand Jews in Jerusalem, on pain of death to those who exceeded that number. At that period, the Christians were all shut up in their convents, and the Jews in their quarter, and if Jerusalem had then been attacked by the French, it was intended by the Turks here to massacre all who were not Mohammedans without distinction of age or sex.[85]

In Nazareth and Bethlehem, Christians were in a majority, numbering about 1,200 in each town. In Jerusalem, Christians numbered from 3,000 to 3,500 in 1820, representing six different church denominations. The Churches were charged excessive ransoms to ensure the safety of pilgrims. During the Greco-Turkish war of liberation (1821–27), the Christian population of Jerusalem was forced to dress in black and to work on the fortifications of the city and they were punished by considerable ransoms. In 1824, as recorded in an Armenian chronicle:

> The governor of Damascus arrived in Jerusalem with a big force and through tortures forced the Greeks to pay 65,000 dahekan, the Latins 40,000, the Jews 100,000 [. . .] Armenians [. . .] 128,000. There was no money left neither to meet the needs of the [Armenian] Brotherhood nor to pay the mortgages. After the governor left the new mayor of Jerusalem started to torture some of the inhabitants and asked for heavy fines [. . .][86]

In Damascus in 1844, Namik Pasha ran short of money for his troops and resorted to extreme measures. Soldiers stopped Christians and Jews in the streets and entered their homes at night to force them to pay the *ferde* (income tax). "This soldiery committed the most deplorable violence against them and their families, and removed merchandise from shops as they pleased by sheer force."[87]

The eviction of *dhimmis* from all administrative office aggravated the impoverishment and decline of the communities. Muslim jurists based this exclusion on a number of koranic verses (3:27, 114; 5:56) and *hadiths* forbidding a *dhimmi* to exercise authority over a Muslim. The legal texts confirm this exclusion by citing all the humiliating dismissals of Christian officials under each caliph, going back as far as the first caliph Abu Bakr (632–34).[88] In fact, the survival of a Christian bureaucracy with *dhimmi* senior officials was actually the inevitable result of the Islamic conquests which reserved the military sector to warlike Muslim tribes, and assigned the administration of the vanquished Christian peoples to their coreligionists. Not only was the administrative skill of the Christians useful to the Muslim state, but their appointment to high positions also made it possible to bribe them and utilize them to crush uprisings led by their own coreligionists. In addition, Jewish and Christian *dhimmis* provided useful intermediaries as interpreters (*dragomans*) or ambassadors in negotiations with, or delicate missions to, the countries of the *dar al-harb*.

Despite the many administrative purges followed by forced conversions which Islamic jurists delight in listing, the continual flow of Christian slaves into every sector of activity, but particularly into positions close to the caliphs or sultans—as pages, eunuchs, soldiers, and officials—wove a network of affinity and protection with the *dhimmi* communities. And it was these neo-Muslims—the viziers and soldiers created by the Ottoman *devshirme*, for example—who were probably responsible for those calls for the tolerance and protection of the People of the Book, enshrined in the Koran, and who endeavored periodically to shield the *dhimmis* from the popular fanaticism fanned by the ulema, concerned as they were with adjusting practice to the orthodoxy of the texts.[89]

The Legal Domain

The legal position of the *dhimmi* constitutes the most important aspect of his condition because it determined all his rights in every area and his ability to have them recognized. The Muslim state accepted the jurisdiction of *dhimmi* religious courts insofar as it governed their civil and religious affairs.[90] The Roman and, to a lesser degree, the Byzantine state had already granted the Jews legal autonomy; the multireligious Muslim Empire extended this privilege to the vanquished peoples. However, Islamic law took precedence over *dhimmi* jurisdiction in litigation between Muslims and *dhimmis*. But, as the evidence of a *dhimmi* was inadmissible in Islamic courts, the *dhimmi* could not bear witness for or against a Muslim. All the jurisconsults recognize that only a free, adult Muslim can be a witness.[91] Judgments pronounced on the basis of the testimony of two witnesses who later proved to be infidels, slaves, or minors were nullified, but they were accepted if the witnesses repeated their statements when the cause of their disability was abolished, that is to say, respectively, by conversion to Islam, emancipation, or reaching adult age.[92] Moreover, according to the thirteenth-century jurist an-Nawawi, the recognized age for the majority of an infidel child was below that of a Muslim, apparently for fiscal reasons.[93]

This disability not only obliged *dhimmis* to buy Muslim witnesses and to bribe the kadis, but it removed any possibility for them to defend themselves against usurpations, accusations, theft, or abuse, and in particular the abduction of women and children. More than any other measure, this excessive vulnerability inflicted by the law branded fear and servility on the *dhimmi* mentality. It rigidified the partitioning of the communities, the *dhimmis* avoiding every pretext for conflict by limiting relations to a bare necessity. On the Muslim side, this conduct was in accordance with the koranic verses forbidding friendship and association with the People of the Book. This reservation was also imposed on foreigners as a Danish scholar traveling in the Orient warned in 1762:

> It will not be amiss to add one slight observation concerning the brokers of different nations. A stranger can not be too much on his guard against Mahometan brokers. [. . .] Through all the countries in the East, Mahometan merchants have the knavery to seek to irritate the Christians, when, after having duped them, they fear their resentment: And then, when any term of reproach is uttered by the strangers in the heat of passion, the rascally Mussulmans make a great noise, under pretence that their religion is abused, and threaten to complain to the magistrates. Several Europeans have been obliged to pay considerable sums by these arts of knaves who have previously cheated them.[94]

According to Islamic jurisdiction, the equality between the People of the Book made them subject to the talion among themselves only. A Jew could serve as guarantor (*aqilah*) and be responsible for a Christian, who could do the same for him, but not for a Muslim. Except for the Hanafi school, the jurists reject the talionic law between Muslims and *dhimmis*, the latter being inferior to the former. In effect, the validity of the talion requires: "That the guilty be not in a higher social position than the victim. That is why a Muslim could not be put to death for killing an infidel, who could even be a subject [*dhimmi*] of a Muslim prince."[95] The blood-crime could not be avenged if the Muslim's victim was a slave, a Jew, or a Christian.[96]

> The Muslim is not put to death for the murder of an infidel, but the infidel is for the murder of a Muslim. No talion between free man and slave, nor between Muslim and infidel. [. . .][97]

However, this opinion is disputed because, according to a tradition described by the jurist Yahya b. Adam (d. 818), the Prophet had ordered the execution of a Muslim who had killed a *dhimmi*.

In punishments involving monetary compensation, the blood of a Muslim has twice the value of a *dhimmi*'s blood.[98] In Shafi'i legislation:

> The Jew and the Christian are worth one-third of a Muslim, the pyrolate [Zoroastrian] and even the idolater having obtained a safe-conduct (*amân*), one fifteenth.[99]

Compared with the outlawed *harbi* whose life could be taken legitimately, the *dhimmi* as a protected tributary held a relatively privileged position.

In the mid-nineteenth century, when the emancipation of the *dhimmis* in the Ottoman Empire was decreed, none of the many reforms that had to be introduced was more systematically contested than the measure legalizing the admissibility of *dhimmi* evidence. This modification not only annulled a principle of faith establishing the superiority of Muslims over *dhimmis* in all domains, but it also eliminated the corporation of false witnesses and a source of illicit gain collected by the kadis.[100] To circumvent the refusal of the religious courts to take evidence from Jews and Christians, a proclamation by Sultan Abd al-Aziz transferred cases between Muslims and *dhimmis* from religious courts where, according to the *shari'a*, they had to be heard, to civil courts which received such evidence.[101] Commenting on this situation in the Balkans in 1876, Charles Brophy, the British vice-consul at Burgas—a port on the Black Sea, in Bulgaria—explained:

> [This] most important provision [the competence of civil courts to judge cases between Muslims and *dhimmis*] upon which hinges the acceptance or rejection of Christian evidence, is in the province either absolutely disregarded or resolutely defied; the Judges say openly "we are Sherah Memourlari, officers placed here to judge according to the Sheri [*shari'a*]; it is the only law we recognize, and it is the only law we shall administer". [ ]

No point in the whole of the Iradé will meet with such opposition as this substitution in certain cases of the civil for the sacred law, and I doubt whether the members of the Ulema will, in practice, ever thoroughly concede it, [for] they consider this innovation as a fundamental alteration in a system which according to their views is unalterable as long as Islamism exists, and as being a virtual negation of their religion.[102]

Traveling in Armenia, Robert Curzon mentions the refusal to hear Christian testimony in relation to that of a Muslim, and cites the case of an Armenian, tortured at Erzerum in 1843. "A woman's evidence is never taken, nor is that of a Christian or a foreigner held good in any case against a Mahomedan."[103]

Islamic law sentenced to death Muslims and *dhimmis* accused of criticism or blasphemy against the Islamic religion, the Koran, and the Prophet. According to the jurists, apostasy was recognizable by the following statements: first, that one did not believe in the existence of the Creator or his prophets; second, that Muhammad, or one of the other prophets, was an imposter; third, that one regarded as legal something strictly prohibited by the *ijma* (the consensus of the Muslim community); or fourth, forbade anything that was permissible by the *ijma;* fifth, that the regulations of the *ijma* were rejected; and lastly, that the veracity of Islam was doubted.[104] The accusation of blasphemy leveled against a *dhimmi,* whether true or false, often resulted in summary execution. It was primarily the increase in travel and information in the nineteenth century which makes it possible to assess the frequency of these situations and particularly the behavior patterns they induced. Traveling in North Africa at the beginning of the nineteenth century, Perceval Barton Lord noted:

> In Algiers, a Janissary, if so inclined, would stop and beat the first Jew he met in the street, without the latter daring to return, or even ward off the blows. His only resource was to run as fast as he could, until he had made his escape: complaint was worse than useless, for the cady always summoned the Janissary before him, and asked why he had beaten the Jew? The answer was, "because he has spoken ill of our holy religion"; upon which the Janissary was dismissed, and the Jew put to death. It is true the testimony of two Mussulmans was required to the fact of the Jew having abused their religion; but on such occasions witnesses were never wanting.[105]

Accusations of blasphemy provoked collective reprisals against Jews: in Tunis (1876), Hamadan (1876), Aleppo (1889), Suleymaniya (1895), Teheran (1897), and Mosul (1911).

The *dhimmi* was also forbidden to possess Muslim religious books, to discuss them with Muslims,[106] or to employ Muslim servants.[107] In 1880 in Entifa—a district of Marrakesh in Morocco—an elderly Jewish couple had engaged a poor Muslim woman to work for them. On the governor's orders, the husband, sixty-five-year-old Jacob Dahan, was nailed to the ground and beaten to death and his corpse was dragged through the streets by soldiers. The Jews were able to retrieve it for burial by paying a heavy ransom; the dead man's mule and livestock were confiscated.[108] Marriage or sexual relations between a *dhimmi* and a Muslim were punished by death,[109] as was conversion of a *dhimmi* Jew to Christianity, or a Christian to Judaism.[110]

Protection-Ransom Relationship

We will not examine here the complex processes whereby the *dhimmi* peasantry, still a demographic majority two or three centuries after the Islamic conquests, were eliminated from certain regions. It will be sufficient to illustrate—with the help of a few documents—the ambiguities of the protection-ransom relationship transposed into a religious context as it survived in a traditional society.

Some interesting evidence reveals the type of protection which enabled Jews to live in the Jabal Nafusa in Tripolitania:

> The Berbers, who are the owners of the land, do not show great hatred towards the Jews; instead, the Jews belittle themselves before the Berbers, who are constantly demanding homage, even though the Jews themselves are the pillars of the society, the craftsmen and merchants.
>
> Even before the conquest of the land by the Turks [1858], when the region was governed by neither ruler nor judge, the Jews lived in security, for every Jew had a Berber lord who championed his cause in any quarrel. When a wrong was done to a Jew and his lord let it pass in silence, this was considered to be a disgrace to the lord who had not protected his servant, the Jew. There were even times when the tribes went to battle in matters concerning a Jew.
>
> The Berber lord passed his Hebrew servant down to his children as an inheritance. If the Berber lord had many sons, each inherited a share in the servant. Each could also sell his share in the servant.[111]

This patron-client relationship in nineteenth-century Tripolitania, described by Mordechai Hakohen, a Libyan Jew born in 1856, differs from the usual type of servitude in that it is solely determined by religion. The prohibition on owning weapons condemns the *dhimmi* group to a vulnerability which makes Muslim protection essential. His vulnerability stems from the principle denying him the right to security of life and property, a right which must constantly be redeemed.

However, the Jew could redeem himself from his owner or owners and, on liberation, obtain a certificate testifying to his redemption. The Turks abolished this system and liberated the Jews. Even families that were not able to redeem themselves from slavery were emancipated, but in these cases the Berber lord could summon them and demand that they pay homage to him. The lord reciprocated by protecting them from attack by other Berbers.

According to another tradition, the Jews in the Jabal al-Gharbi—the Atlas region of Algeria today—had been brought in captivity from Jerusalem by an Arab king and sold into slavery to Muslims (Ishmaelites):

> [T]here is no Israelite family without an Ishmaelite master to whom the Israelite must make a token payment every year. The Ishmaelite may sell him to another, and this arrangement persisted until six or seven years ago, when the Ottoman rulers took the area from the Arabs.[112]

In the Mzab (southern Algeria), in Tafilalet and Atlas, before French colonization, the same bonds of slavery prohibited Jews from fleeing from their masters.[113] Throughout the nineteenth century, in some rural regions of the Maghreb—even into the twentieth century in Yemen—a Jew was forbidden on pain of death to leave his Muslim master to whom his body, family, and property belonged. In 1884, Charles de Foucauld observed the same situation in southern Morocco, and it was still applied to the Jews of Dades in the Grand Atlas in 1913.[114] "Protection," though in a far less radical form, also existed in nineteenth-century Bosnia, where: "Every proprietor [Muslim] was then supreme master of the peasants [Christian] located on his lands, and, in a rude way, afforded them protection."[115]

This ransom-protection system, which is the very basis of dhimmitude, governed relations between Christians and Kurds in Armenian Mesopotamia. In 1894, Paul Cambon, French ambassador at Constantinople, described the creation of Kurdish *Hamidiés* regiments as "the official organization for pillage at the expense of Armenian Christians." In these provinces the system of "persecutions and extortions" became intolerable "to populations who had become accustomed to their slavery." According to the ambassador, the Porte refused reforms and persisted "in maintaining a veritable regime of terror, arrests, assassinations, rape, etc. in Armenia."[116] At the same period, in Erzerum, French Consul Bergeron mentions the system of ransoming that existed in the Sassun region.[117] The context is also very similar to that of Serbian Christians in the Balkans subjected to their Albanian lords and to the Bosnian Muslims.

In August 1894—which marked the first stage of the mass slaughter of Armenians—all Christian villages in the Sassun region were burned down, the women raped, the inhabitants, regardless of age or sex, men, women, the old, and children, were put to the sword and their corpses thrown into mass graves. Under pressure from foreign powers, the Ottoman government ordered a commission of enquiry in which British, French, and Russian consular delegates in Erzerum participated. The Collective Report of this commission, dated 28 July 1895 from Mouch, included a section on Armenian-Kurdish relations. They were considered to be good within the protection-ransom context described above:

It should in fairness be added that, if relations between Kurds and Armenians appear satisfactory, it is because for a long time the latter, in order to obtain the help and protection of the Kurdish aghas in case of need, have been paying them an annual due in proportion to their resources, known by the name of *halif* and consisting of handing over to them a certain part of all that they harvest, heads of cattle, payment in kind, supplementing it with clothing, agricultural implements, etc. . . . When an Armenian peasant marries off his daughter, his agha levies as *halif* half the sum paid by the bridegroom to the future parents, according to the customs of the land.

Each village or each house is dependent on one or several aghas who regard these various levies as a property right to such an extent that they transfer them as an inheritance or by private sale.

If for whatever motive an Armenian refuses to pay, the agha compels him to do so by force, by stealing his livestock or causing him some injury; the aghas of the villages of Kavar and Talori were principally the Kurdish aghas of Sassun (Kharzan).[118]

In Yemen outside the central administration, Jews were protected by the sultan or by tribes until the mid-twentieth century. So lowly was their status under the law, that it was as shameful to kill one of them as it was to kill a Muslim woman.[119] If a Jew protected by a tribe was killed, this tribe retaliated by killing a Jew from the guilty tribe. The result was two Jews assassinated with no inconvenience to any Muslim. If a Muslim insulted or attacked a Jew, the Jew was not allowed to respond but could appeal to the protection of the sultan or the tribe to defend him. The matter could be submitted to a court—a court which refused to accept the Jew's testimony. It is easy to understand why the Yemenite Jew refrained from demanding justice. In these cases the dehumanization of the Jew transferred legal proceedings solely to the Muslim level, as if the Jews were reduced to objects whose disappearance or mutilation injured their Muslim owners.

These last examples taken from a study by Robert B. Serjeant, an eminent British orientalist, are intended to show how magnanimous was the protection granted to Yemenite Jews, especially in murder cases. His article—published in 1953, a few years after roughly 50,000 Jews had emigrated from Yemen to Israel—also contains the oft-repeated assertion that the status of *dhimmis* was better than that of Muslims. Serjeant quotes a Muslim author writing in Cairo in 1937 to demonstrate that Jews in Yemen enjoyed privileges denied to Muslims. Supporting this view, Serjeant goes further still:

My own impression is that from an economic point of view the Muslim peasant was often very much worse off than the Jewish craftsman in respect of tax-burdens.[120]

One should note here the placing of two different social classes (crafts-men and peasants, instead of Jewish craftsmen and Muslim craftsmen) at the same level, and the complete disparity in relation to the law of the two categories being compared—the Jew and the Muslim—who are assumed, nonetheless, to be equivalent. In fact, Muslims were the sole beneficiaries of state-financed religious, academic, and philanthropic benefits, whereas *dhimmi* communities had to be self-financed. And this does not take into account the complete dissymmetry between the rights of Muslims and those of *dhimmi* Jews. So integrated and so accepted is this dissymmetry that it is unconsciously excluded from comparative reasoning based on a spuri-ous equality.

As a whole, the toleration accorded the *dhimmi* populations took shape within a complex network of random violence and legal prohibitions which were at the very core of Islamic rule. It was created by war and doomed by its own militarist dynamic to be perpetuated in a body of legal and fiscal discriminatory measures when peace was restored. This development, con-sistent with the mentalities and religious concepts of the time, resulted from the processes whereby political and economic power was transferred from the vanquished indigenous populations to the conquering group. The specific principle of Islamic religious toleration, and the acquiescence of Christian religious leaders, prepared the way for these transformations which were precipitated by uncontrollable political circumstances. It is im-portant to reiterate once again that, for religious or social reasons or from financial motives, the Muslim state—whether Abbasid, Ottoman, or North African—frequently strove by the dispatch of troops to protect its *dhimmi* subjects from violence by the populace or rebel bands.

3

Religious and Social
Aspects of Dhimmitude

The guiding principles constituting the whole ideological structure of dhimmitude appear most emphatically in the fields of religion and human relations. These principles rest on three requirements: first, the compulsory degradation of the *dhimmi;* second, the differentiation between Muslims and infidels; and third, the separation of the latter—the last two requirements arise directly from the first.

To the believer, humiliating the *dhimmi* constitutes a good deed, an act of faith, and a religious duty, kept constantly alive in the *umma*'s consciousness by a series of ordinances meticulously governing, down to the smallest detail, the organization of degradation that is sacralized into an ethical code. Ibn an-Naqqash, a famous fourteenth-century Egyptian preacher and Shafi'i jurist, collected the ordinances of the early caliphs in his *fatwa*. In a letter to the governors of his empire, Umar II (717–20) ordered the dismissal of *dhimmi* officials because:

> [. . .] their removal is your duty, as is the destruction of their faith; bring them down to the place of shame and degradation that Allah has assigned them; and subsequently let each of you inform me what he will have done in his province.[1]

Ibn an-Naqqash recalls an ordinance of the caliph al-Amir bi-Ahkam Illah (1101–30):

> Now, the prior degradation of the infidels in this world before the afterlife—where it is their fate [to be degraded]—is considered an act of piety; and the imposition of their poll tax [*jizya*], "until they pay the *jizya* off-hand, being subdued" [Koran 9:29] is a divinely ordained obligation. As for the religious law, it enjoins the inclusion of all the infidels in the payment of the *jizya* with the exception, however, of those upon whom it cannot be imposed; and it is obligatory to follow in this respect the line laid down by Islamic tradition.
>
> In accordance with the above [obligations], the governors of the provinces in their administration must not exempt from the *jizya* a single *dhimmi,*

even if he be a distinguished member of his community; they must not, moreover, allow any of them to send the amount by a third party, even if he is one of the personalities or leaders of their community. The *dhimmi's* payment of his dues by a bill drawn on a Muslim, or by delegating a real believer to pay it in his name will not be tolerated. It must be exacted from him directly in order to vilify and humiliate him, so that Islam and its people may be exalted and the race of infidels brought low. The *jizya* will be imposed on all of them in full and without any exception.[2]

The Maghrebian mufti al-Wansharishi, who died in 1508, author of the *Kitab al-Mi'yar*, summed up this obligation in a *fatwa*: "God Almighty, the One, the All-Conquering, has created abasement to be inflicted on the accursed unbelievers, fetters and chains for them to drag from one place to the next as a demonstration of his power and of the superiority of Islam, and to honor his chosen Prophet."[3]

Islamic commandments relating to religion were not limited to the realm of degradation, quite typical of the general intolerance of the period. They were also written into the military legislation of *jihad*, the progress of battles and the conditions of surrender. These provisions, at once religious and military, governed the status of places of worship, thus perpetuating the triumphalism of the foreign invader and the humiliation of the vanquished native inhabitant in religious consciousness for more than a millennium.

Religion

The status of religious buildings was a major element in the controversies of the Middle Ages; it expressed conflicting religious interpretations, as well as politicoeconomic interests. This polemic opposed the supporters of a tolerance for the recognized religions, represented at the highest level of power, and their adversaries who favored their total eradication. It was this dynamic that would determine—in the course of time and over whole regions—the survival of churches and synagogues or their elimination, hence the destruction of their communities. In practice, the prohibition for believers to possess a place of worship meant the prohibition of their religion. Consequently, the status of these buildings reveals whether these religions were actually accepted, eliminated, or tolerated in semi-clandestinity.

In the course of the Arab conquest and during the following two or three centuries, chroniclers mention considerable destruction, compounded by the effects of violent earthquakes. In fact, from the eighth to the tenth century—much before the first Crusade—from Andalusia to Iraq, the magnificent basilicas and innumerable monasteries of Egypt, Syria, and Mesopotamia became little more than ruins. The immense domains in mortmain from which the Churches drew their wealth had been confiscated by the Muslim treasury. Ruined, humiliated, stripped of their property, the patriarchs were reduced at some periods to wandering throughout the land, going into hiding for fear of arrest or extortions often exacted by torture. In Egypt, under the patriarchate of Alexander II (705–30), monks were mutilated, taxed, and their religious orders banned.[4]

Judaism in the Orient, already weakened by the Church's intolerance, was forced out of some regions; in others, at the whim of fortune communities were able to regroup, and sometimes flourish, surviving around their constantly threatened synagogues. In the Ottoman Empire, however, Jews expelled from Spain (1492) and Portugal (1497) were welcomed by Sultan Bayazid II (1481–1512) and constituted dynamic communities in the empire. Other refugees found asylum in the Jewish communities of North Africa.

It would be impossible to list all the places of Jewish, and particularly Christian, worship which were Islamized and banned to their former owners. The cave of Machpela in Hebron is the most famous example: built by Herod the Great to house the tombs attributed to the Hebrew patriarchs and matriarchs, it was turned into a church at the time of the Crusades, was later converted into a mosque in 1266 by the Mamluk Sultan Baybars and, henceforth, banned to Jews and Christians. In 1862 the Prince of Wales was allowed to enter it by a special authorization granted by the Ottoman sultan, a sacrilege which necessitated the military occupation of the town. Ordinary Christians could not enter until the British Mandate in 1922, and the Jews only after Hebron came under Israeli administration in 1967. In Iraq, in former Nineveh opposite Mosul, the tomb attributed to the Prophet Jonah, once a place of Jewish, Christian, and Muslim pilgrimage, together with all the church buildings, was assigned to the Muslim *waqf* after the conversion of the Mongols to Islam. It was strictly banned to non-Muslims until World War I and the establishment of the British Mandate. The latest example was the tomb of the Hebrew Patriarch Joseph—within the boundaries of the town of Nablus, then under the protection of the Palestinian Authority —which was destroyed by a Palestinian mob soon after the outbreak of the second intifada in October 2000. It was immediately rebuilt as a mosque, its dome painted green. Since then, Palestinian groups have mounted unsuccessful attacks to take over the Tomb of the Hebrew Matriarch Rachel at the entrance to Bethlehem, which is under Israel's protection.

All Muslim jurists agree on the rules regarding churches and synagogues in the conquered countries. For Mawardi, writing in the eleventh century:

They [the *dhimmis*] are not allowed to erect new synagogues or churches in the territory of Islam and any built are to be demolished without compensation. They can restore ancient synagogues and churches that have fallen into ruin.[5]

Whether churches and synagogues survived depended on the circumstances in which the land had been conquered. In any town founded after the conquest, the construction of churches and synagogues was prohibited; in regions conquered by armed force, this prohibition was observed and the ancient buildings confiscated. In cases of submission by surrender, and only if a clause specified the preservation of these buildings, the indigenous *dhimmis* could retain them, while any modification was prohibited. The unanimous opinion was expressed by an-Nawawi in the thirteenth century:

> Infidels who are subjects of our Sovereign by virtue of surrender, must be forbidden to build churches or synagogues in a town we have founded, or whose inhabitants have embraced Islam of their own accord. As for places taken by attack, the infidels must refrain not only from building new churches and synagogues there, but also from using for their purposes such buildings which exist there. When, however, the country submitted by capitulation, the following cases must be distinguished:
>
> 1. If the capitulation treaty states that the land will be ours, but that the infidels will remain there by virtue of hereditary possession, and that they retain their churches or synagogues there, they will then be able to continue to use them; but if nothing has been decided on the subject of these buildings, they are forbidden to use them for their purpose.
> 2. If the capitulation treaty states that the infidels will remain owners of the land, they can not only continue to use their churches or synagogues, but also build new ones.[6]

Often, the populace or individuals denounced the slightest restoration carried out to the interior of the churches or synagogues and demanded their demolition. Under Caliph Ma'mun (813–33), the Muslims of Jerusalem complained that the dome of the Church of the Holy Sepulcher had been enlarged, making it higher than the Dome of the Rock. The patriarch Thomas was cast into prison, but escaped flagellation and saved his dome on payment of a heavy ransom.[7] Permission for minor restoration was bought at an exhorbitant price and gave rise to proceedings which were as interminable as they were detailed.[8] This provision and the motives behind it are set out in the *fatwa* by the eighteenth-century Maliki Sheikh al-Adawi:

> Now there is no doubt that one of the principal conditions of equity consists in banishing infidels from any distinction and any possibility of raising their status, and of reducing them to humiliation and abasement.
> The decisions made by our ulema state that they will not be permitted to

build new churches in Muslim countries, and that, if they build them, it is an obligation to demolish them. As for the reconstruction of those which have been destroyed, this is not possible in any manner; it would even be preferable not to allow these buildings to be repaired; and yet, is it not incredible: we have seen times when Muslim mosques fell into ruins, whereas infidels' churches were restored![9]

These destructions wiped out the *dhimmis'* culture and civilization. The remains of churches and synagogues scattered over North Africa, the Middle East, Armenia, and Mesopotamia reveal the extent of religious persecution in places where numerous *dhimmi* populations had once lived. The destruction of churches and synagogues is constantly mentioned from the time of the caliph Abd al-Malik (705–15) by the pseudo-Dionysius of Tell-Mahre, Michael the Syrian, and the chronicle of the Coptic patriarchs. The last Umayyad caliph, Marwan II (744–50), pillaged and destroyed many churches and monasteries in Egypt. Mahdi (775–85) and Harun al-Rashid (786–809) ordered the destruction of all the churches in the empire built after the Islamic conquest. Under the Fatimid caliph al-Hakim (996–1021), every church and synagogue in Egypt, Palestine, and Syria was demolished. The Church of the Holy Sepulcher was razed to its foundations, the linen and vessels plundered, and the wood of the sepulchral coffins stolen.[10] Al-Hakim subsequently permitted the destroyed buildings to be reconstructed.

Despite these prohibitions and demolitions, Christian *dhimmis* always built new churches, paying considerable sums of money to obtain permission. In 1662, the vizier Fazil Ahmed Köprülü Pasha (1661–76) was persuaded by a sufi that his indulgence toward Christians was causing plague, fires, and had halted Ottoman victories. He therefore ordered the churches to be demolished and the head carpenter and mason to be strangled, accusing them of having engaged the workers for these constructions.[11] In effect, the patriarchs in the *dar al-Islam* had to wage a fierce battle in order to preserve or build churches and monasteries. The Syriac chronicles allude to their incessant struggle to prevent demolition or confiscation. The prohibition on erecting new buildings heightened the bitterness of the quarrels between the different Churches when the Muslim authority transferred ownership from one of them to another.

The legal taxes paid by the *dhimmis* were augmented by ruinous extortions levied as "protection dues" for monasteries and synagogues by regional Bedouin chiefs, whose conflicts exposed *dhimmis* and pilgrims to constant insecurity and pillage. These "protection fees" proved more crushing in Palestine than elsewhere. Ransoms were demanded for the protection of holy places and fees for gaining access to them, praying there, and for changing residence, as well as a tax to prevent the desecration of cemeteries. Places of worship were subject to constant surveillance, as is shown by this extract taken from an Armenian chronicle dating from 1760:

> With different excuses the Moslems of Jerusalem asked for amounts of money, sometimes under the excuse that they [St. James Brotherhood, a monastic order] were building without permission, and sometimes that it should be re-examined [. . .] and when the Brotherhood was not subjected to their futile excuses they indicted them to the judges and the rulers, and caused them to pay fines. Although the clergy showed the official documents [. . .] but in vain, because not only they would not hear them, but scorned them for the reason that they had not renewed them by the new Sultan [. . .] Upon his arrival [the Governor of Damascus] to Jerusalem, he drained the blood of the clergy and dessicated their bones [. . .] Because even if the stones and the earth of the Holy Land turned into gold and silver, as in the days of Solomon, it would not be enough to satiate them.
> As for Governors, who made an annual tour through the towns, their aim was not to put things in order, but rather to molest the clergy [. . .][12]

In Jerusalem the Jews still had to give gratuities to the Turkish authorities throughout the nineteenth century in order to pray at the Western Wall, other sums to the Algerian Muslims living near the Wall, to the Silwan villagers to prevent the destruction of tombstones on the Mount of Olives, and to the Ta'amra Arabs of Bethlehem so that Rachel's tomb would not be destroyed. An additional sum was extorted by the Arab inhabitants of Bethlehem to permit Jews to visit this tomb. Another tax was levied to allow them to pray on Mount Zion. In 1863–64, the gratuity for access to the Western Wall had risen to 30,000 piastres, for the village of Silwan to 10,000, and for Bethlehem to 5,000; and this ransom system was practiced throughout the Holy Land. In addition, every Jewish traveler arriving at Jaffa was taxed and likewise had to pay in order to enter and leave Jerusalem. Moreover, non-Muslims, *dhimmis,* and travelers were subject to tolls on all the roads in Palestine, levied by Arab tribes for their own benefit.[13]

Worship

The rule ordaining contempt also applied to worship which had to be conducted in silence and humility. Wooden clappers, bells, crosses, icons, shofars, and banners were prohibited, as were all other visible or audible public manifestations. Some Muslim theologians tolerated processions by *dhimmis,* but solely in regions where they were in a majority.[14] Church bells were forbidden in the lands of Islam. According to a *hadith* recorded by Muslim, the eighth century compilator, the Prophet said: "The bell is the devil's pipe."

Dhimmis had to conduct burials of their dead in secret and without lamentations.[15] Even in 1889, the Jewish quarter of Baghdad was plundered and its cemetery confiscated because the funeral of a rabbi was considered ostentatious. The prejudices against the living continued after death, to be vented upon corpses doomed to hell, as maintained in Muslim tradition. According to some *hadiths*, not only did they have to expiate their own sins but also the sins of Muslims, who were thereby pardoned:

> When it will be the Day of Resurrection Allah would deliver to every Muslim a Jew or a Christian and say: "That is your rescue from Hell-Fire". (6665) "There would come people amongst the Muslims on the Day of Resurrection with as heavy sins as a mountain and Allah would forgive them and He would place in their stead the Jews and the Christians. (6668)[16]

Yet, the Koran also affirms: "No one amasses anything except upon himself, and no one bears the burden of another." (6:164)

The law commanded that Muslim graves be differentiated from those of *dhimmis*. Profanation and the leveling of the infidels' cemeteries was a general occurrence, a practice which continues till the present day in some countries. Until the beginning of the twentieth century, in Oujda and in the valley of western Tiaret in Morocco, Muslims defiled burial places in Jewish cemeteries and exhumed corpses to use in the ancestral magic rituals which Islam had not succeeded in eradicating. To avoid such desecrations, Jews refrained from placing tombstones on the graves of their dead.[17] On the other hand, firmans issued by the Ottoman sultan Murad III in April 1584, November 1585, and December 1587 forbade Muslims to plunder tombstones in the Jewish cemetery at the Golden Horn in Constantinople. These firmans enjoined them to cease their harassment and any attempt to drive out the Jews.[18] In March 1568, a firman by Selim II forbade pirates to plunder *dhimmis* on the island of Naxos or to take them as slaves.[19]

According to the Shafi'i rite, in cases when Muslim and *dhimmi* corpses are indistinguishably mixed all should be washed and prayers recited for them all, but with specific statements requesting that only Muslim souls should be granted peace.[20] Even the formulas for condolences differ depending on whether the deceased is a Muslim or a *dhimmi*.[21]

Conversion

Periods of forced conversion interrupted the protection-persecution rhythm which alternated throughout history within complex parameters and was governed by imponderable factors, combining individual personalities and political contingencies. As protection was guaranteed by the highest political authority—caliph or sultan—orders for conversion emanating from this source eliminated the possibility of any recourse. It would be tedious to cite the places and dates involved, because such orders were decreed under the Umayyads, Abbasids, Fatimids, and Mamluks—from Spain and the Maghreb to Yemen and Persia.[22] Even if they could be revoked by payment of heavy ransoms, they decimated whole communities and always caused permanent traumas.

In the Maghreb and Andalusia, the Berber Almohad persecutions (1130–1212) wreaked massive destruction on the Christian and Jewish populations. This destruction by sword, death, captivity, and conversion was described by the Jewish chronicler Abraham Ibn Daud and the poet Abraham Ibn Ezra.[23] Maimonides, doctor and philosopher, experienced it and had to flee Cordova with all his family in 1148, residing in Fez—disguised as a Muslim in 1160–65, before finding asylum in Fatimid Egypt.

Doubting the sincerity of the Jewish converts, Muslim "inquisitors" removed the children from such families and put them in the care of Muslim educators. The Jewish origin of several Judeo-Berber tribes in the Atlas mountains, and of Muslim families in Fez whose ancestors were forced to convert in 1165, 1275, 1465, and 1790–92 is known. The same is true of descendants of forced conversions in Libya in the period 1558–89. Jews were forced to convert to Islam in Tabriz in 1291 and 1338, and in Baghdad in 1333 and 1344. In Persia sporadic waves of forced conversions from the sixteenth to the beginning of the twentieth century decimated the Christian and particularly the Jewish communities. Conversion was encouraged by a law granting a converted heir preferential, if not exclusive, rights to an inheritance.

The removal and conversion of children from the *dhimmi* tributaries is a little-known aspect of forced conversion. Islamic law strictly prohibits children to be removed from tributaries in these circumstances, contrary to child-booty taken from infidels as a right of war in razzias, battles, and rebellions.

In practice, however, this prohibition, which protected *dhimmi* populations as a whole, was often flouted on a variety of pretexts. The most common cases involved children whose Jewish or Christian parents were overwhelmed by taxes they were unable to pay. Another practice, the *devshirme* system, has already been mentioned in connection with the Balkans. In addition, *dhimmi* sources from all quarters repeatedly mention the abduction of children of both sexes by nomads, soldiers, or individuals. This situation continued up to the twentieth century in the mountainous regions of Kurdistan and areas exposed to nomadic incursions.[24] In the Yemen, fatherless Jewish children of both sexes were taken from their mother or family, forcibly converted, and placed in state orphanages, where some of them underwent military training. The conversion of children to Islam was based on numerous *hadiths* asserting that every child was born a Muslim, based on Koran 30:29–30 (see ch. 2, n. 57). The removal of these children from their families thus "restored" children to the *umma*.

In Yemen, the law on forced conversion of fatherless Jewish children was retroactive. Even elderly men who had succeeded in escaping it in childhood were obliged to convert. The Orphans' Decree of 1922, strictly applied at the request of the Arab Palestinian delegation to the Hijaz in their Jedda declaration, remained in force until the Jews finally left Yemen in 1949–50. If the families involved or the leaders of the Jewish community attempted to save the children, they were tortured, imprisoned, and ransomed to make them reveal the children's hiding place. Children who refused to convert were threatened, punished, beaten, and chained in dark vaults.[25]

Degradation

Any analysis which pays even slight attention to the status of the *dhimmi* reveals that in certain respects it was inferior to that of the slave. Although the slave was deprived of his freedom he did not suffer the obligatory and constant degradation prescribed by religion. The contempt for the human being and his reduction to an inferior status—raised to a theological and political principle—constitutes a major aspect of the civilization of dhimmitude. It is the ignominy of nonbelieving which makes it legally permissible to take a *harbi*'s life and which legitimizes *jihad* and the *dhimmis'* disabilities.

Muslim legal texts attribute these rules to the first caliphs, but they were decreed progressively, depending on the political situations, which determined the dynamic of the Islamization of the conquered lands. Thus, it was during the first wave of Islamization—in Arab Islam which covered the whole Christian Near and Middle East—that these concepts developed and became uncompromisingly institutionalized. Here, a distinction must be made between the legal disabilities—generally borrowed from Byzantine legislation against Jews and schismatic Christians—and the principle of humiliation, taken as far as to deny the right to life for a *harbi* or a pagan. These two currents can overlap and complement each other but do not lose their separate identities. For example, a slave suffers from the curtailment of his rights; his body could be mutilated if he became a eunuch, but he was not compulsorily humiliated, and in Islamic civilization, as in Byzantine society, he could attain the highest offices. On the other hand, as the opprobrium imposed on the *dhimmi* represented a religious duty, it formed a basic element in his status as a protégé. This status would be abrogated if he attempted to free himself from it.[26]

One can even say that the corpus of his legal disabilities imprisoned the *dhimmi* in that state of ignominy and degradation which provided irrefutable proof of the triumph of Islam. Its superiority is inherent in the relationship between its strength and the humiliation forcibly imposed on others. This opinion, constantly stated in legal and religious texts, expresses a fundamental doctrinal element of government and foreign policy. When the reforms demanded by Europe in the nineteenth century attempted to abolish it, *dhimmi* populations were threatened.

The numerous sources consulted seem to confirm that measures to ensure humiliation were applied to Jewish and Christian *dhimmis* at all times over the whole *dar al-Islam*. Periods of relief were exceptional and temporary, resulting from ephemeral and circumstantial conjunctures. The many vituperations by kadis denouncing the freedoms that *dhimmis* enjoyed reflect a psychotic fixation rather than a true description of reality. Beyond any possible doubt, over the centuries, at the whim of circumstances, *dhimmis*—particularly Christian *dhimmis*—did infringe these regulations through the clemency of an individual sultan or thanks to a slave close to the central power. Others were able to free themselves from certain obligations by corruption or foreign protection, but these individual cases are in no way representative of the long-term situation of the *dhimmi* communities. Whatever the rulers' personal opinions, they were sometimes forced to save their thrones by yielding to the demands of a populace aroused by fanatical ringleaders.

Muslim theologians justify the humiliation of the *dhimmi* by koranic verses and *hadiths*, accusing the infidels of falsifying the Bible and of denying the superiority of the Koran by persisting in their error. However, this attitude contradicts some koranic verses which recognize pluralism and forbid religious constraint. It must therefore be attributed to political motives in a period of religiosity and intolerance. In Arab society where honor holds a preponderant role, the humiliation and mockery of the *dhimmi* reduce him to the lowest level of human life, and this humiliation did in fact generate many conversions among the educated classes. Community leaders were bound to oblige their *dhimmi* co-religionists to fulfill the required duties of self-abasement.[27]

No systematic study has listed or compared the variety of discriminatory practices developed in the many countries of the *dar al-Islam*, where difference did appear between Shi'ite and Sunni societies, these latter showing considerable variations among themselves. Some practices in Muslim guise perpetuate pre-Islamic customs, introduced by prejudiced converts, monks, prelates, and magistrates. All the legal disabilities and fiscal impositions already mentioned assuredly form part of this geographical panorama of the psychology of humiliation. The social practices which are grafted on to them can be divided into two categories: those common to the whole of the *dar al-Islam*, cited copiously in texts on the subject; and those confined to certain regions and resulting from specific local conditions. Four basic concepts have determined and molded these practices. First, the *dhimmi* has no rights other than those allowed him by the Islamic community; to enjoy them he must pay for them by humiliation; second, *dhimmis* collectively constitute the *fay* of the *umma*; third, the invalidity of *dhimmi* evidence; and last, the principle of separation between the faithful and the nonbelievers. The first translates a social context peculiar to Arabia into a theological form; the others, although presenting analogies with Byzantine anti-Jewish legislation, are justified according to jurists by koranic verses and *hadiths*.[28]

Common Elements

All the measures cited below are based on the principles of separation and differentiation.

Clothing

Differentiation in clothing was the subject of detailed regulations. Perhaps originally a safety measure adopted by an army of occupation which distrusted the indigenous population, this obligation was attributed to Umar Ibn al-Khattab "in order to distinguish them [non-Muslims] from Muslims at first glance."[29] Such an origin endowed the principle of differentiation with the normative and sacred character of a *hadith* and created a general rule which survived until the twentieth century in some regions. In Yemen, Jews were bound by it until 1950, the year they emigrated to Israel. Vestimentary regulations were laid down by the founders of the four juridical schools as early as the eighth century. They assigned to the *dhimmi* coarse cloth and specific colors for each religion and special belts (*zunnar*). Nor did the legislator fail to give precise details as to headgear: pointed caps (*qalansuwa*) or turbans, made of particular fabrics and color. Christians had to shave the front of their heads above their foreheads. According to an-Nawawi, the *dhimmi*

> [. . .] has to make himself distinguishable by a piece of yellow cloth and a belt over his clothing. If he enters a bath-house where there are Muslims, or if he undresses elsewhere in their presence, the infidel has to wear an iron or lead ring on his neck or else some other sign of servitude.[30]

Ordinances imposing these obligations were constantly decreed. In 849–50 the caliph al-Mutawakkil ordered that Christians and all *dhimmis* throughout his dominions be forced to cover their heads and shoulders with a yellow veil (*taylasan*) and wear a wide belt (*zunnar*). Their caps had to distinguish them from Muslims and their servants had to wear two wide visible pieces of a yellow tissue on their breasts and backs, being of a different color from their robe. Their turbans had to be yellow and their wives wrapped themselves in a yellow cloak (*izar*). *Dhimmis* had to use wooden saddles and stirrups and place two pommels on the rear saddle; their new places of worship were destroyed and a tenth of their dwellings seized and converted into either mosques or open spaces. In public baths they were forced to wear small bells, an order which remained in force for centuries. Demons' heads were nailed onto the doors of their houses. They were expelled from administrative posts and from positions which enabled them to exercise authority over Muslims. At the caliph's command, *dhimmi* graves were leveled to the ground, in order to differentiate them from Muslim graves. District chiefs were instructed to supervise the strict and complete execution of these orders and to punish any dissimulation and deviation by *dhimmis*. The distinctive signs had to be ostentatious for men and women, servants, and pack animals in order that they could be immediately identified.[31]

European pilgrims, struck by these vestimentary distinctions, provide abundant evidence of their implementation in the East, in the Maghreb, Iran, and in the Ottoman Empire. In some regions (Persia and Ifriqiyya) *dhimmis* were excluded from public baths; in others, such as Egypt, Palestine, and Syria, they had to wear small bells within.[32]

In Ifriqiyya the wearing of distinctive clothing was strictly supervised. In ninth-century Qairuan (Tunisia), the belt round the garments of Christians and Jews had to be conspicuous. Those who failed to wear the distinctive signs—belt or badge (*riqa*)—were whipped, imprisoned, and publicly humiliated. Al-Marrakushi, the thirteenth-century historian of the Almohads recorded:

> Toward the end of his reign [1198], Abu Yusuf [Abu Yusuf Ya'qub al-Mansur, 1184–99, Almohad ruler of Spain and North Africa] ordered the Jewish inhabitants of the Maghreb to make themselves conspicuous among the rest of the population by assuming a special attire consisting of dark blue garments, the sleeves of which were so wide as to reach to their feet and—instead of a turban—to hang over the ears a cap whose form was so ill-conceived as to be easily mistaken for a pack-saddle. This apparel became the costume of all the Jews of the Maghreb and remained obligatory until the end of the prince's reign and the beginning of that of his son Abu Abd Allah [Abu Muhammad Abd Allah al-Adil, the Just, 1224–27]. The latter made a concession only after appeals of all kinds had been made by the Jews, who had entreated all those whom they thought might be helpful to intercede on their behalf. Abu Abd Allah obliged them to wear yellow garments and turbans, the very costume they still wear in the present year 621 [1224]. Abu Yusuf's misgivings as to the sincerity of their conversion to Islam prompted him to take this measure and impose upon them a specific dress. "If I were sure," said he, "that they had really become Muslims, I would let them assimilate through marriage and other means; on the other hand, had I evidence that they had remained infidels I would have them massacred, reduce their

children to slavery and confiscate their belongings for the benefit of the believers." [pp.264–65]

In our lands safeguard [protection] is not granted either to Jews or Christians since the establishment of Masmudite[33] power, and no synagogue or
church exists in all the Muslim lands of the Maghreb. But the Jews in our
lands profess Islamism externally; they pray in mosques and teach the Koran
to their children, while complying with our religion and our law. Only Allah
knows what is hidden in their hearts and what their houses conceal.[34]

After noting that the Jews were plundered by the Moors every time a sultan died, the sixteenth-century writer Leon the African, formerly a Muslim,
described their attire:

None of them [the Jews] can wear shoes, they only have sandals made of
rushes. They wear black turbans on their heads. Those who wish to wear a
cap are obliged to sew a piece of red fabric on it.[35]

Despite marriages between the Seljuk sultans of Anatolia and Christian
princesses, these regulations seem to have been applied in their emirates.
Strangely enough, even the renowned Andalusian mystic Sheikh Muhyidin
Ibn Arabi, otherwise reputed for his tolerant attitude toward other faiths,
advised Sultan Kaykaus I (1211–20) to humiliate infidels by prohibiting the
use of bells and the building and restoration of churches and monasteries.
He reminded him of Umar's ordinances: the right of every Muslim to be
housed and fed for three nights in churches; the respectful behavior
toward Muslims required of infidels; the humility imposed on their wor-
ship, and the compulsory distinctive nature of their shoes, turbans, and
haircuts. They were forbidden to teach the Koran to their children, to use
Muslim names, and to own horses, fine saddles, and swords.[36] After the
Mongol prince Mahmud Ghazan (1295–1304) was converted to Islam, the
Mongol governor reinstated Umar's regulations in respect of Jews and
Christians in Anatolia. A fourteenth-century traveler in Babylon (near
Cairo) observed a multitude of Christians "who are called Centurins, or
Christians of the Belt, because they wear a wide belt and clothing which
distinguish them from others."[37]

Nor did the great Ottoman sultans fail to issue detailed orders on this
subject, specifying the texture of fabrics, style, and color. When, for example, the sultan Murad III (1574–95) received a letter from the kadi of Istanbul informing him that Jews and Christians had changed the style of their
clothing, turbans, and shoes, he wrote an order dated 5 August 1577 (20
Djemazi-ul-ewel, 985):

In the past this state of things was forbidden by an imperial *firman*. In no way
do I grant imperial consent to what the Jews and the community of *kiafirs*

[Christians] are wearing, such as has been explained, dress, turbans, and sandals [list of prohibited clothing follows]. You will take care that they return to dressing in accordance with the infidel model of former times; you will not let them wear Muslim dress nor allow them to assume a Muslim demeanor and you must prevent them from acting contrary to an imperial order. Those who do not see reason after this injunction and wear [forbidden] clothing contrary to my orders, will be publicly punished. Have the prime culprits arrested, imprison them, and keep me informed on the matter.[38]

On 27 April 1580, the same sultan sent another order forbidding *dhimmis* to wear turbans. Jews were required to wear red hats, Christians black, and both groups black shoes. Under Mahmud I (1730–54), headgear was manufactured for Muslims similar to the Jewish bonnet (*kaouk*). Consequently, on 3 April 1730 (15 Ramazan, 1141), the sultan wrote to the kadi of Istanbul:

Since it is difficult to establish a distinction from the point of view of clothing, it so happens that several Muslims, apart from the fact that they are instantly suspected [of being *dhimmis*], are also giving proof of wrongful belief, according to the dictum "Whoever makes friends of them [Jews and Christians] is one of them" [Koran 5:56], an occurrence which it is an important religious action to suppress.[39]

He ordered those in positions of responsibility to give

positive and strict orders and repeat them to their people so that henceforth they do not sew hats like those of the Jews, that is to say sewn with small stitches and with a base in the shape of a disc, and call for each to keep an eye on the other. In addition, let it be thoroughly understood by each of them that hereafter if word is heard that someone has sewn and sold a *kaouk* [hat] of this type, he will be arrested for not having obeyed the *sheri* [*shari'a*] and having acted against the imperial *firman* and will be hanged in front of his shop door. And you, who are the *shawush bashi* [head officer of the law], do not cease to watch over this matter in secret and unremittingly.[40]

Mustafa III (1757–74) renewed the same orders on 8 June 1758 (1 Chavval, 1170), reproduced here because they explain the significance attached to the differences in clothing:

While, according to religion and according to custom, Jewish and Christian *dhimmis* who live in Stanbul, center of the *khalifat* and its surroundings, had at all times to refrain from resembling Muslims in matters of clothing and in matters of external appearance, to preserve an attitude of humility in their demeanor and to observe the rules of politeness, yet for some time those named above have by the manners they affect not only exceeded the bounds of the *sheri* [*shari'a*] and of politeness, and, contrary to their obligations, worn [a list of prohibitions follows], and, without possessing *firmans*, ridden horses and traveled in boats with three pairs of oars, but there are also some among the Christians who, contrary to known custom, create and wear a type of *kalpak* [cap] made in a strange fashion from some half a pic of cloth, which deserves disapproval and disgust from the point of view of religion and custom. This fact having been established and prohibition of these attitudes being a religious necessity and a political duty, both the Jews and Christians being *rayas dhimmis* and since their attitude from the point of view of the *sheri* and of logic must be humility and abjection, [we instruct you to] issue a severe warning and hereafter prevent their dress from resembling that of Muslims and them from wearing [list of forbidden clothing follows]; nor traveling by horse or by a boat with three pairs of oars, without a *firman*.[41]

To transgress these regulations was considered so serious that in 1758 when the sultan was walking incognito in Constantinople and encountered a Jew wearing forbidden attire, he immediately ordered that he be beheaded for infringing them. The next day an Armenian guilty of the same crime suffered the same fate.[42] In 1827, two or three Jews from Constantinople converted to Protestantism; hoping to avoid reprisals from their coreligionists, they adopted European dress and hid among the Armenians. When they were recognized they were sentenced by a kadi to six months imprisonment, not for having changed their religion, but for their clothing. After the punishment had been carried out, a fresh sentence added a further three years imprisonment.[43]

On the other hand, discriminatory clothing and the ban on carrying arms did not exist in regions in European Turkey, Greece, Albania, and the towns and villages of the empire where Christians were in a majority. But in Turkish Bulgaria, according to the historian Iono Mitev, Muslim judges refused to accept testimony against Muslims given by Christians. Bulgarians were forbidden to carry arms or wear fine clothing; they could not mount a horse in the presence of Turks, build new churches or repair old ones without first obtaining an authorization; moreover Bulgarians also endured constant plundering and humiliations.[44] The last Ottoman firman concerning discriminatory clothing dates from 10 August 1837 and emanated from Sultan Mahmud II. Addressed to the chief rabbi of Istanbul, it charged him, in pursuance of his duties, with the obligation to enforce strict observance of these differentiations on his coreligionists; similar orders were conveyed to the Armenian, Greek, and Catholic patriarchs.[45]

The distinctive character of the tributaries' dress constituted a customary rule essential to their status, and it would be tedious to list all its variations. Many sources indicate that *dhimmis* were subject to these regulations until the nineteenth century. In 1875 the Jews of Tunisia were compelled to wear a blue or black burnous, yellow slippers, and a black cap. In the Mzab (southern Algeria) before French colonization, the Jews paid the *jizya* and lived in their own quarter, only leaving it dressed in black; they were forbidden to emigrate. The Jews of Morocco in Tafilalet and in the Atlas mountains were also subject to this disability.[46]

Several nineteenth-century travelers noticed that the Muslims of Jerusalem, Hebron, and Nablus were among the most fanatical. The Spanish traveler Domingo Badia y Leblich (Ali Bey) mentions the dark colors compulsory for Jews and Christians in Jerusalem. He notes that in Damascus neither Jews nor Christians could ride a horse or even a donkey; in Tripoli (Libya), Jews wore distinctive colors, as they did in Morocco, where they were forbidden to leave the *mellah* wearing shoes. When they encountered a Muslim notable in the street, they had to draw aside to the left, their bodies humbly bent over, on pain of being harshly beaten.[47] In Bukhara, as well as the usual restrictions concerning synagogues, the Anglican missionary Joseph Wolff noted (1832) that Jews were obliged to wear a discriminatory badge.[48] In Hamadan (1892 and 1902), the ayatollahs ordered Jews to wear a red circular patch as well as distinctive clothing. This obligation, also enforced in Shiraz and Teheran (1897), was opposed by the Shah. In 1910 Yomtob Semach, director of the new Alliance Israélite Universelle school in Yemen, was shocked by the discriminatory clothing which made Jews objects of ridicule.[49]

Just as *dhimmis* had to be distinguishable from Muslims, so their slaves were bound to bear witness to their masters' degradation by appropriate clothing.

Mounts

Dhimmis were forbidden to ride noble animals such as horses and camels. They were restricted to donkeys and, at certain periods, were only allowed to use these outside the town. Instead of saddles, only pack-saddles fitted with rough wooden stirrups were authorized:

> The infidel subject of our Sovereign cannot mount a horse, but is allowed a donkey or a mule, whatever their value; he must use an *ikaf* [pack-saddle] and wooden stirrups, because he is forbidden iron stirrups and saddle; on the road he must stand aside to allow a Muslim to pass; he should not be treated as an important personage or given the leading place at a gathering.[50]

Passing through Famagusta (Cyprus), Alexander Drummond, British consul at Aleppo (1751–58), described the discomfort of such a mount, not without a touch of humor:

> When I went to Famagusta, formerly Salamis, afterwards Constantia, at least the situations seem to agree, I rode upon a mule furnished with a ragged,

patched packsaddle, so bulky that I straggled like a beggar upon a woolpack; in lieu of a whip, I was provided with a sharp pointed stick about a foot long, with which I was directed to prick the lazy animal's shoulders when I wanted to quicken his pace; spurs would have been as useless as a whip, for my legs were so expanded, that I could not bring one heel within half a yard of the creature's side. All these circumstances rendered my seat so uneasy, that I was obliged to shift five hundred ways before I finished my journey; which, though no more than twenty-four miles, fatigued me as much as ever I was by riding above one hundred miles a day. As the Turks permit no Christian to ride into the town, I was obliged to dismount and walk along the bridge. This was no impolitic precaution with regard to me, who, by the splendor of my equipage, might have made a conquest of some peeping sultana.[51]

The same conditions reappear in all legal texts concerning the *dhimmis*. In about 1772, Sheikh al-Adawi stated in his *fatwa:*

In the opinion of several, even all ulema, it is in general not fitting that *dhimmis* be placed on an equal footing with ulema, emirs, and sherifs in respect of clothing and mounts. They can ride neither horses, mules, nor costly donkeys; they can not use expensive pack-saddles, and both princes and heads of state must not only forbid the use by them but are even obliged to punish and reduce them to a state of degradation and abasement.[. . .] they will not be permitted to raise their voices in the presence of Muslims, nor possess servants who follow them and, even less, clear a way for them in the street. They will not be allowed to wear clothes of fine fabrics; but they will on the contrary dress in rough and common garments; they will not be permitted to build their houses higher than those of Muslims; nor will they be allowed to decorate the outside of them. It is the duty of Muslim princes, to whom Allah has given authority, to prohibit all these things and to punish them and chastise them in case of disobedience.[52]

A famous eighteenth-century Egyptian jurist, Sheikh Damanhuri, director of the koranic University al-Azhar, summed up this point in 1739:

Neither Jew nor Christian should ride a horse, with or without saddle. They may ride asses with a packsaddle. They must not wear the *qaba* (full-sleeved garment), silk garments, turbans, but may wear quilted *qalansuwa* [conical bonnet] headgear. If they pass by a Muslim assembly, they must dismount, and they may ride only in an emergency such as sickness or leaving for the country, and their path is to be made narrow.[53]

Karsten Niebuhr, participating in a Danish scientific expedition, described this situation in 1761:

In Cairo no Christian or Jew may appear on horseback. They ride only asses, and must alight, upon meeting even the most inconsiderate Egyptian lord. Those lords appear always on horseback, with an insolent servant before them who, with a great staff in his hand, warns the riders on asses to shew the due marks of respect to his master, crying out *ensil* [*inzil*], get down. If the infidel fail to give instant obedience, he is beaten till he alight. A French merchant was drubbed on an occasion of this kind. Our physician, too, was insulted for being too tardy in alighting from his ass. For this reason, no European dares walk the streets without having a person to attend him who knows all those lords, and can give him notice when they approach. At first, when I went about in Cairo, I made my janissary go before, and my servant follow, both mounted on asses as well as myself. But, after having the mortification to see these two Mussulmans remain upon their beasts, while I was obliged to alight, I determined to walk on foot.

It is true, that in Egypt, these distinctions between the Mahometans and persons of other religions, are carried a greater length, than any where else through the East. Christians and Jews must alight even before the house of the Chief Cadi; before more than a score of other houses in which the magistrates distribute justice; before the gate of the janissaries; and before several mosques in high veneration for their sanctity; or by the quarter *El-Karafe*, in which are a great many tombs and houses of prayer; they are obliged to turn out of their way, to avoid these places, as even the ground on which they stand, is so sacred in the eyes of the people, that they will not suffer it to be profaned by the feet of infidels.[54]

And an English traveler, James Silk Buckingham, visiting Palestine in 1816 remarked:

The whole of our road from Nazareth to Sook-el-Khan had been more or less rugged and hilly, but on our departure from hence, we entered on a fertile plain. In our way across this, we met a party of Jews on asses, coming from Tiberias to the great public market, and conceiving me, from my Turkish dress and white turban, to be a Mohammedan, they all dismounted and passed by us on foot. These persecuted people are held in such opprobrium here, that it is forbidden to them to pass a mussulman mounted, while Christians are suffered to do so either on mules or asses, though to them it is also forbidden to ride on horseback without the express permission of the Pasha.[55]

The prohibition on riding horses remained in force for Jews until the beginning of the twentieth century in the countryside of Morocco, Libya, Iraq, and Persia, and in Yemen until their departure for Israel. Sometimes, if a *dhimmi* did not dismount from his ass fast enough, he would be thrown to the ground.[56]

The prohibition on *dhimmis* riding astride their mounts and the requirement to keep both legs on the same side was attributed to Umar Ibn Abd al-Aziz.[57] According to another tradition, it was Umar Ibn al-Khattab who included it in his orders relating to Christians in Syria. A decree by the imam Yahya promulgated in 1905 renewed this obligation for the Jews in Yemen, where it was implemented until 1950.

Behavior toward dhimmis

The hostility toward populations with different beliefs was not peculiar to Muslims; it also existed among all the peoples of dhimmitude. The barriers of hatred and mistrust preserved religious separatism more effectively than did the walls of any ghetto.

The obligation to tolerate the existence of *dhimmis* on the conquered lands and to come into everyday contact with them developed a reflection, a sort of behavior code, prescribing the conduct and language which the true believer should adopt toward *dhimmis* in the different circumstances of life. Here again three major principles emerge, governing the range of conduct: first, the prohibition on forming ties of friendship with Jews and Christians and adopting their opinions;[58] second, the prohibition on entering into discussions with them;[59] and last, the obligation to humiliate them.[60]

Consequently, for the believer to express his aversion to *dhimmis* publicly was a righteous act.

Moreover this situation [the appointment of *dhimmis* to employment] could not coexist with the opprobrium attached to them: for, to be invested with a position (*ouilaie*) is a mark of distinction which cannot be reconciled with the degradation reserved for infidels; and friendship (*ouelaie*) is a bond which cannot be combined with the absence of friendship and with the hatred which must be felt for them.[61]

Modes of greeting were formulated differently depending on whether they were addressed to a Muslim or a *dhimmi*. The manner of greetings was examined by famous jurists. For the renowned tenth-century Maghrebian Maliki jurist, al-Qayrawânî:

One should not be the first to say *salam* [blessing be upon you] to Jews or Christians; but when one has (inadvertently) said *salam* to a tributary, he should not be asked to consider it null and void. If a Jew or Christian greets you, you must reply "*alayka*" ["the same to you"] (nothing more). But you can also reply: "*alayka' s-silâm*," with *kasra* of the *sîn* [vocalized with an "i" and not an "a" to make it an insult], for it would then mean: "the stone," because, according to one opinion, this is permitted.[62]

Sheikh Damanhuri gave a ruling on the subject in the eighteenth century:

If you greeted one whom you considered a Muslim, only to learn he was a *dhimmi*, withdraw your word, pretending "he answered my salutations." If one of them salutes he is answered with "Same to you" only. If you correspond with one, you say: "Salutation to him who follows right guidance." But avoid congratulating, consoling, or visiting them, unless you expect the

person visited to convert to Islam. If you do expect so, visit him and proffer
Islam to him.[63]

According to the fourteenth-century Egyptian preacher ibn an-Naqqash:

> When a *dhimmi* sneezes, one should no longer say: "may Allah bless you!"
> but, "may Allah lead you to the right path!," or "may he improve your situa-
> tion."[64]

Condolences likewise varied with religion. According to the eighth-century jurist Abu Yusuf, a *dhimmi* must not come face to face with a Muslim
in the street but pass him to the left, the impure side; other jurists add the
obligation to make it difficult for him to proceed and to push him aside.
This practice is mentioned by European travelers to Palestine where Jews
and Christians were humiliated and insulted in the streets of Jerusalem,
Hebron, Tiberias, and Safed until the mid-nineteenth century.[65] In Palestine, Tripolitania, and Yemen, these demonstrations of hatred were frequently marked by abuse, sometimes accompanied by stone-
throwing—although the latter was not prescribed by law. The *dhimmi* had
to walk quickly and with lowered eyes. In countries where they were admitted to public baths, male and female *dhimmis* were forbidden to look upon
naked Muslims of their own sex.[66] Travelers mention these customs, which
survived in North Africa until the European colonization and in Yemen.

Dwelling places and traveling

The separation between Muslims and infidels represented a religious obligation based on many koranic verses and on *hadiths*. Al-Wansharishi (d.
1508) forbade Muslims to live among Christians because they would be
contaminated by the Christian presence, particularly if they had to sleep
and dwell in Christian houses.[67] As mentioned, Muslims were also forbidden to imitate the dress and gestures of Jews and Christians, to form ties of
friendship with them, or to enter into discussions with them.[68] The religious segregation was aimed at protecting the faith of the true believers.

The separation between individuals also operated at the level of the community by confining the different *dhimmi* groups to separate districts. Laws
concerning *dhimmi* houses obeyed the same principles as those governing
their appearance:

> Some jurists recommend, while others—and they are the majority—state
> that it is compulsory to forbid infidels to have houses higher than their Mus-
> lim neighbours, even to have them of the same height; however, this rule
> does not apply to infidels inhabiting a quarter apart.[69]

The houses of *dhimmis* had to be smaller than those of Muslims and of humble appearance, often painted in dark colors. In Constantinople and its surroundings Jewish houses were black, those of Armenians and Greeks brown or dark red. Certain districts and the proximity to venerated mosques were banned to *dhimmis*.[70]

Prohibitions on some changes of residence and access to certain cities or places have always existed. In 640 Umar Ibn al-Khattab, the second caliph, expelled Jews and Christians from Arabia in order to make the peninsula entirely Islamic; since then, Mecca and Medina were forbidden to all infidels. Texts mention the expulsion of Jews and Christians from Arabia.[71] Although Jews continued to live in Yemen they were only permitted to reside in strictly limited areas. Until well into the twentieth century they were forbidden to leave the country.[72] In the twelfth century, al-Idrisi (Edrisi) reported that the town of Aghmat-Waylan was inhabited exclusively by Jews. The Almoravid ruler Ali b. Yusuf (1106–42) forbade them to go to Marrakesh and to spend the night there on pain of losing their life and property; for those stranded there after sunset, "their life and their possessions were at the mercy of all."[73]

Visiting the Maghreb in 1870, the Chevalier de Hesse-Wartegg noted that in Tunis:[74]

Of all confessions not Mohammedan, the Catholics have alone obtained the right to live within the walls of the Moorish town; Jews and Protestants are obliged to have their temples and churches as well as their cemeteries outside. [p.178]

In Qairuan:

An infidel, whether Jew or Christian, is not allowed under any circumstances to enter this town, which is strongly walled in, and the fanaticism of the populace goes so far, that even the highest and most influential travellers can enter only in disguise, and furnished by an official order from the Bey to the Caid of the town. [p.237]

In Sfax:

The exclusiveness of Sfax is so great that an Arabian immigrant, whether he comes from Tunis or from the Oases, may not remain long in the town [. . .] Of course Christians are hated: not one lives in the town; they and the Jews— 2,000 in number—occupy a separate quarter on the sea-shore, which is lower than the town, and called Rabat. [p.270]

In 1876, Dr. Arthur Leared noted:

In the southern province of Sus the Jew is regarded as so indispensable to the prosperity of the country that he is not allowed to leave it. If he gets permission to go to Mogador to trade, it is only on condition that he leaves his wife and family, or some relation to whom he is known to be attached, as surety for his return.[75]

In 1890, another traveler, Dr. Robert Kerr, observed that at Salé in Morocco:[76]

> Several years ago the place was guarded, and no Christian or Jew was permitted to enter within the precincts of its sacred walls. The first who entered on scientific researches did so under an escort of soldiers; but now Christians not only freely walk about, but even enter and inspect the ruins of the sacred mosque. [p.51]
> Fez has two principal mosques, Maulie Edrees and the Karueen [. . .] Christians and Jews are not allowed to pass the streets in which its doors open. [p. 139]

Corvées

From the beginning of the Arab and Turkish conquests, *dhimmis* were subject to corvées for work in public services or on lands belonging to Muslim feudal lords.[77] In Egypt, in 852, various Coptic villages were raided to conscript galley slaves. In Bukhara and Samarqand, under the caliph Nasr al-Din Allah (1180–1225), *dhimmis* cleaned latrines and sewers and removed refuse and rubbish.[78] The requisitions involved in lodging and maintaining troops subjected the *dhimmis* to extortions and humiliation. The British consul in Jerusalem in the mid-nineteenth century, James Finn, still mentions these practices.[79] At the same period in Kurdistan, Jews, Nestorians, and Armenians were subject to tallage and corvées at the whim of the authorities.[80] Jews were also conscripted for public works in Tunisia: they had to carry out the mutilation of thieves required by koranic law, whereas Christians served as hangmen.[81] In Yemen, an edict of 1806 which remained in force until the Jews emigrated to Israel in 1950, obliged them to remove the carcasses of dead animals and clean the public latrines, even on the Sabbath. In Yemen and Morocco, Jews had to remove the brains from the decapitated heads of the sultan's enemies, salt them, and exhibit them on the walls of the town.[82] The Muslim population was also liable to corvées for public or military undertakings, but the most degrading tasks fell to *dhimmis*.

Regional Elements

The obligations described above and prescribed by the body of jurists at different periods formed the general constitutive elements of the *dhimmi* condition inscribed in the *shari'a,* and imposed with greater or lesser severity depending on the region and period concerned. They are to be found as much in the Balkans as in Anatolia, in Persia, in the Levant, Yemen, and the Maghreb. However, other features were added which remained localized. Thus, until the twentieth century in the Maghreb where Jews represented the only religious minority after the waning of Christianity, they were forbidden footwear in almost all the towns of Morocco except in their own quarter; this was also the case in the Algerian Sahara until 1912, and in Yemen till 1950.

In 1836–37, the Jews of Fez applied to Sultan Mulay Abd ar-Rahman for permission to build a *hammam* (public bath) in their quarter. The ulema had to be consulted for a decision on such an important matter. They drew up a dozen *fatwas* based on the scrupulous examination of legal literature since the beginning of Islam and the manner in which Morocco was designated: either as a Muslim land, a land which had surrendered, or a land conquered by force. Except for one scholar, whom his colleagues described as an ass, all agreed that the *hammam* should not be built. Their main reason for so doing was the need to maintain the Jews in a state of degradation and humiliation; but they also concluded that Jews should not be allowed to imitate the example of the illustrious men who endowed towns with *hammams;* that tributary subjects could not build anything after the Islamic conquest; and that constructing the *hammam* would make Jews the equals of Muslims. In 1898 the Jews of Fez again requested the right to have a *hammam* and again were refused for the same reasons.[83]

Travelers in Persia and Yemen at the beginning of the twentieth century noticed the low doors of *dhimmi* houses. In San'a (Yemen) the Jewish quarter had no garbage collection or lighting at night. In Bukhara a piece of cloth had to be hung over Jewish houses to distinguish them from those of Muslims. Prejudice was strongest among the shi'ite populations which considered *dhimmis* impure, forbidding them to go out in the rain and to handle foodstuffs, in order not to transmit their impurity. Shi'ites in Lebanon (Metawalies) abstained from drinks and any other food, such as bread and meat, that a Christian had touched. Any contact with Christians, even via intervening objects, was refused.[84]

Dhimmi Behavior

The law required from *dhimmis* a humble demeanor, eyes lowered, a hurried pace. They had to give way to Muslims in the street, remain standing in their presence and keep silent, only speaking to them when given permission. They were forbidden to defend themselves if attacked, or to raise a hand against a Muslim on pain of having it amputated. Any criticism of the Koran and Islamic law annuled the protection pact. In addition, the *dhimmi* was duty-bound to be grateful, since it was Islamic law that spared his life.

The whole corpus of these practices—and the description here is hardly exhaustive—formed an unchanging behavior pattern which was perpetuated from generation to generation for centuries. It was so deeply internalized that it escaped critical evaluation and invaded the realm of self-image, which was henceforth dominated by a conditioning in self-devaluation. The fact that the group was held responsible for the misdoings of one of its members bound the whole community in collective fear, stiffened by a millennium of cultural patterns. It locked the *dhimmi* into a world of degradation, conveyed by thousands of minute details of daily life. This situation, determined by a corpus of precise legislation and social behavior patterns based on prejudice and religious traditions, induced the same type of mentality in all *dhimmi* groups. It has four major characteristics: vulnerability, humiliation, gratitude, and alienation.

First, it must be stressed that the *dhimmi* mentality differs from the mentality of the Jew in Christendom, because Christianity's theology, history, and civilization is quite distinct from Islam's, whatever their reciprocal borrowings. Likewise, the *dhimmi*'s position is not analogous to the condition of the pariah in Hinduism, despite certain similarities in respect of impurity and the principle of separation.

The constitutive elements of this mentality can therefore only be apprehended in the basic texts defining this condition and its motivations, and in the reactions which they induced in its victims. It is in this psychological conditioning—distorted by silence, since the *dhimmi* is deprived of speech—that the mute dialogue between *umma* and *dhimmi* functioned.

The fundamental component of the *dhimmi* mentality is established from the moment he consents to submit to a system which removes his basic right to life. Whereas a *harbi*'s life and property are forfeited to a Muslim, in the case of a *dhimmi* his physical existence is the object of a monetary transaction valued on the basis of service to the *umma*.[85] However, all these regulations only appeared a century after the Muslim conquests, therefore, whatever may have been the Prophet's true intentions in respect of the vanquished—which is neither our subject nor within our competence to examine here—the jurisconsults' texts, drawn up one or two centuries after Muhammad's death, are very explicit and leave no room for doubt.

Two basic principles govern the *dhimmi* condition: protection and the perfection of the *umma*. The first determined the corpus of measures designed to make the *dhimmi* dependent on protection through his vulnerability; the second required his degradation in order for it to be proved.

The principle of protection follows from the right to kill the victim and appropriate his possessions, a practice inherent in primitive pre-Islamic

Bedouin society where the right to kill was modified by protection-clientel-ism, a principle which reappears in the *harbi* and *dhimmi* condition.[86] Consequently, extreme vulnerability is a basic characteristic of this status, the right to life not being legitimate per se but dependent on toleration granted by the *umma*. This vulnerability is achieved through prohibitions on testifying in Muslim courts, on bearing arms, and on possessing weapons. As, in addition, legitimate self-defense against a Muslim is regarded as aggression, the *dhimmi* is reduced to begging for peace and purchasing his innocence. This same vulnerability engenders the *dhimmi*'s gratitude to Islamic law which protects his life and his property and guarantees him limited rights on certain conditions.[87] In other words, the assimilation of the principle that the *dhimmi*'s existence is illegal enhances the value of Islamic tolerance which ensures that his life is spared.

Vulnerability and gratitude developed in the *dhimmi* the language of servility, flattery, and appreciation, a zone of mythical untruth, the only area where his testimony could be accepted. In this context, it is interesting to note that at a time of extreme Christian vulnerability and suffering, an Arab-Christian literature developed glorifying Arabism, Islamism, and a millennium of peaceful Muslim-Christian co-existence. This period witnessed the massacres of Christians in Kurdistan in 1843, in Syria and Lebanon between 1850 and 1860, then of the Armenians at the end of the nineteenth century, followed by their genocide between 1915 and 1918, the massacres of the Jacobites in 1920–25, and of the Assyrians in 1933–38, which culminated in their exodus from Iraq.

The second basic factor is rooted in the dogma of the perfection of the *umma*, a perfection linked to its sacred obligation to rule over the entire world. Any borrowing from another civilization is forbidden because perfection does not borrow from imperfection without damage to itself. The perfection of the *umma* implies the perfection of its history, its conquests, its government, and its laws; it also legitimizes the status of the *dhimmi* and the destruction of the evil cultures of the *dar al-harb*. However, the Bedouin conqueror's sense of superiority was rudely shaken when his conquests revealed the brilliant Persian and Mediterranean civilizations. This collision between the dogma of Arabo-Islamic superiority and concrete reality engendered the whole ritual of the debasement of the *dhimmi*. Arousing the conqueror's feelings of frustration and humiliation, this superiority complex compelled him to degrade the *dhimmi*—for example, by requiring Jews and Christians to dismount from their donkeys on encountering any Muslim, thereby attesting their deference to his superiority. Any manifestation of skill on the part of the *dhimmi* peoples constituted an arrogant challenge to this conviction of superiority, confirmed in practical terms by an institutionalized ritual of degradation. Unable to rise to the challenge, frus-

tration provoked murderous impulses to destroy the elements that contradicted this doctrine.

This attitude undoubtedly emanated from deep religious feelings. Criticism not only scandalized the believer's susceptibilities, but also cast doubt
on the legitimacy of privileges linked to his religion. The identification of
criticism with blasphemy safeguarded the inviolable conviction of perfection.

In a minority and under threat, the *umma*, implanted in the heart of the
most prestigious civilizations, worked out methods to defend and legitimize
itself. The assertion of its own superiority served as a compensatory valve in
the confrontation with the *dhimmi* peoples, heirs to great civilizations and
mastering their scientific and cultural dynamism. The law prohibited any
friendship and discussion with the *dhimmis*, as well as the smallest borrowing of ideas or conduct, the *umma* thus protecting itself by rigid prohibitions based on self-glorification. Triumphalism, superiority, the perfection
of the *umma*, and the wretchedness and abjection of the *dhimmi* blinded by
error, embodied the perfect order of dhimmitude in practice. Its contesta-
tion either by emancipation achieved through equality between Muslims
and *dhimmis*, or through the *dhimmis'* national liberation in their own country constituted a blasphemy and a bitter source of humiliation and rancor.
The same behavior patterns continued to exist even after the *umma*—with
its scholars and philosophers—had developed a brilliant civilization.

All these factors, which encompassed more than a millennium in some
regions—particularly Palestine, Syria, Egypt, the Maghreb, Yemen, Iraq,
and Persia—helped to create a particular type of sub-human society: that
of dhimmitude. Based on a principle which valued the right to life in monetary terms, respect for the individual was suppressed, henceforth justifying
the complex apparatus for the degradation which encompassed and accompanied him from cradle to grave. Language, culture, history—
evidence of the civilization of the *dhimmi* peoples—were proscribed,
effaced from memory, dismissed into nothingness. Not all these factors, it
is true, appeared with the same force and relentlessness everywhere. For
example, some practices were not introduced in the Ottoman Empire,
mostly governed by Islamized Christians—products of the *devshirme* system— and where the powerful Greek aristocracy linked to the patriarchate
still survived.

Actually, the insecurity and degradation of the *dhimmi* survived most per-
sistently in Arab societies, particularly those situated around the desert
oases. In this context, the fact that the protection of the People of the Book
was inscribed in the Prophet's commandments constituted the best safeguard, which caliphs and sultans attempted to observe throughout the up-
heavals of history. In a society where life is not considered intangible but
only respected within the socio-religious organization of a corpus of obliga-

tions and ransom, protection replaced the deficiency of the laws. In Morocco a large number of assassinations of Jews led the sultan in 1841 to announce that the Jews belonged to him; henceforth, whoever attacked them was attacking the sultan's property. Thus, it was not life which was pronounced inviolable and the supreme value, but the sultan's property. It is this context which clarifies the meaning of protection.

The behavior of *dhimmis* was frequently described by foreign observers.[88] Fear and humility formed its dominant characteristics. For Hommaire de Hell, the Christians of Turkey in the 1840s "have fallen into a state of degradation impossible to convey. When an archbishop appears before the pasha, he does so with a servile bearing which should only belong to a slave."[89] Another observer, Lord Broughton, describes the situation in 1809–10:[90]

> Those who have been in Turkey know that it is contrary to the nature of things for a man in the Greek habit [clothes of a *dhimmi*] to talk in any other than the most submissive cringing tone to a Turk; and on this account it is always preferable to engage a person accustomed to wear the dress of a Frank, a name that includes all those, of whatever nation, who are dressed in the small-clothes, the coat and the hat of civilized Europe. (1:19)
>
> A rayah [*dhimmi*], or subject, wearing with his robes the badge of slavery, dares not to utter the sentiments put into his mouth, and discharge the duties intrusted to him by a foreign minister. Even when he is backed by the presence of his ambassador, a decisive sentiment can scarcely, or only with a pale face and trembling limbs, be forced from his lips. (2:211)

In the 1870s, the Italian writer Edmondo De Amicis observed the humble and terrorized expressions of the Jews of Morocco with compassion. The British consul James Finn was moved to pity by the distress and panic of the Christians of Jerusalem and mentioned their frightened humility.[91] As late as January 1909, the British vice-consul in Mosul, H. E. Wilkie Young, noted that the attitude of the Muslims toward Christians and Jews,

> to whom [. . .] they are in a majority of ten to one, is that of a master towards slaves whom he treats with a certain lordly tolerance so long as they keep their place. Any sign of pretension to equality is promptly repressed. It is often noticed in the street that almost any Christian submissively makes way even for a Moslem child.[92]

Foreign contemporaries and *dhimmis* themselves keenly analyzed the characteristics developed by groups whose servility, fear, and humiliation formed the very conditions of their lives. In his book (1918) on the character of the "*raya*," the Serbian scholar, Jovan Cvijic, emphasizes the important role of mimicry as a means "to save themselves from harassment and ill treatment"—a protective mimetism that was specifically forbidden by Islamic law in order to maintain abusive behavior through differentiation. Cvijic considers that this moral mimicry accentuates submission to the Muslims because the *raya* "becomes increasingly accustomed to forming an inferior servile class whose duty it is to win the master's approval, to cringe before him and to please him." People "get used to hypocrisy and lowliness because this is necessary for them to live and to protect themselves from violence." Emphasizing that this mimicry leads to Islamization, the author notes on the subject of fear that "whole countries lived in terror often for months on end. There are regions where the Christian population has lived under the regime of fear from birth to death." Even after the liberation in 1912, he wrote, fear could still be read on the faces of Christians who had not yet fully realized their new condition.[93]

If these were the feelings of the Serb majority in the European provinces of the Ottoman Empire, one can imagine the distress of the small Jewish communities scattered among oases from Yemen to the Maghreb or of the tiny Armenian, Syriac, and Jewish groups engulfed in the Islamic expanse. To this fear can be attributed the exodus of Christians from the Levant which began after the large-scale massacres of 1860 in Lebanon and Damascus. The Arab nationalist movement in which Christians were prominent emerged at this period to combine political objectives with the trauma of fear and this tendency to mimicry. The concealment of the components of dhimmitude by the *dhimmis* results from their refusal to acknowledge them and led the victim to blame himself for his own misfortune. As a consequence of a total disintegration of his being, caused by the internalization of his degradation combined with omnipotent fear, the *dhimmi* mentality remains incapable of conceiving the values of man's dignity and freedom. These elements still persist in a contemporary trend among some Eastern Christians, the best apologists for systems which are destroying them.

Dhimmitude, because of differences in its parameters, has not produced a uniform psychological type. These brief comments only represent samples of a still unexplored domain, which calls for a comparative study to examine the religious, cultural, and behavioral aspects of each group in terms of local particularisms: a Greek's attitude to former glory differs from that of an Iraqi Nestorian, or a Copt, or a Jew from a town or a desert oasis, but all of whom are, nonetheless, *dhimmis*.

Dhimmitude and Inter-Church Rivalry

The Arab conquest which followed domination by Byzantium embraced a multitude of peoples from diverse ethnic groups, languages, and cultures. The Christianization of the ancient world, pursued since the conversion of

Constantine, represented not only the eradication of paganism but primarily an attempt for religious uniformization in the Eastern and Western Christian empires. The pagan world was collapsing and Christianity was emerging from the ruins. But in effecting its fusion with Christianity, paganism brought its beliefs, distortions, and constant sources of renewed schisms and conflicts. The institution of the Church, the formulation of worship and its liturgy, and the budding of a patristic literature, grew and developed amid a profusion of heresies and violent theological anathemas. Ethnic and cultural divisions blended into the temporal interests of the powerful Churches, heirs to the pagan priesthood's colossal wealth. The Church, linked with the imperial Byzantine power, attempted to combat these voices of dissent expressed in the Christological debate: Arianism (in North Africa and Spain), Nestorianism, and Monophysitism (in Mesopotamia, Egypt, Syria, Armenia). Throughout the Empire the struggle to unify the Christian faith gave rise to bloody religious revolts, the crucifixion of dissident monks, and murderous fanaticism supported by a repressive legislative apparatus, inspired by canon law.[94]

These conflicts between Church and State, and between the different Christian denominations, appeared at every level: at the levels of the priority of episcopal sees, the demarcation of dioceses, the autonomy of financial sources, and the appointment of bishops. At the level of dogma, the imperial authority intervened to impose the councils' doctrinal decisions on recalcitrant bishops. Lastly, a juridical conflict developed between the Byzantine state, heir to Roman jurisdiction with its respect for the different religions of its subjects, and the Church which tried to replace it with canon law in order to impose a rigid system of religious intolerance and exclusivism in all areas.

After the Arab conquest, Muslim caliphs and governors knew how to play on the inter-Christian dissension in order to impose Islam irrevocably on Christian countries. The Monophysite wish to be rid of the Chalcedonian Greeks had facilitated the Persian, and then the Arab, conquest of Egypt, Mesopotamia, and Syria; the conquest of Spain was organized by princes and dissident bishops (see pp. 115–16). The Arab advance into Armenia, then the Turkish conquest of Anatolia and the Balkans, were based on the same alliances and betrayals in high imperial and ecclesiastical circles. The alliance between the turban and the tiara constituted a major factor in the Islamic progression, the patriarch under Islam regaining the legislative and economic power which the Christian state had disputed. In fact, the rallying of the Eastern Churches to the Arab-Islamic government reflected the power struggles between the Christian state and the Churches. It was through this loophole that Islam, by gratifying the patriarchs' ambitions for economic and religious autonomy, was able to ensure their collaboration, amenability, and betrayal in the defeat of the Christian state.

However, the illusions were short-lived. Less than fifty years after the conquest, the wave of destructions of churches, amply recorded by Christian and Muslim chroniclers, swept over the whole *dar al-Islam*. Repression harshened under Harun al-Rashid (786–809), while his son, al-Ma'mun (813–33), dealt the death-blow to the Copts' revolts by massacres and deportations. This is the period—with a few remissions here and there—of that long hellish descent for the Churches, corroded by simony and the corruption established by the sale of ecclesiastical offices to the highest bidder—a system which ruined Christian communities and favored a trend toward Islamization.

As the inter-Christian divisions were an essential factor in stabilizing Islamic power, the authorities were quick to support and exploit them. The caliph was able to manage the large Christian populations, who constituted the majority of his subjects at the beginning of the conquests, by playing on the rivalries between Melchites, Monophysites, and Nestorians through the grant of a favor or the transfer of a church. The caliph entrusted to the patriarch the task of collecting the taxes extorted from his flock, leaving him only with a pittance. The chronicles record in detail these relationships based on money and violence and always involving torture, from the lowest social level to its summit. Equally, one should have few illusions about the appointment of high Christian officials, particularly to the Treasury. Integrated into this Islamic machinery for the destruction of Christendom, they could, by a gesture, temporarily slow it down, temper it, or exacerbate it, but could not abolish it.

The inter-Christian dissensions, embedded in history, were supplemented by internal schisms within the clergy, generated by the Islamic authorities' interference in the selection and appointment of patriarchs, choices which the synods often challenged. These conflicts, arising from the suffragans' personal ambitions, probably also reflected resistance within the clergy to the Islamic authority. Thus, this Muslim-Christian collaboration was established through the convergence of interests between the Islamic authority and a class of clergy and notables who administered their community in the service of the *umma*.[95] Appointed by the sultans, the patriarchs became their most obedient allies. The Bosnian Grand Vizier, Mehmed Sokolovic, a renegade, reestablished the patriarchate of Pec (1537) for two of his relatives, Macarius and Euthyme. This relationship, between the Islamic authority and the patriarchate in this Muslim-Christian fusion at the highest level, explains how dhimmitude for the people functioned, gained ground, and survived.

Christian Anti-Judaism and Dhimmitude

It was in the eastern Mediterranean Jewish diaspora—particularly Palestine, where Jews and Samaritans were the majority in the fourth century—

that the first Christian nucleii appeared and where, later, the Christian call for the destruction of Israel was formulated. This meant that the East, and particularly Palestine, was the theater for the unleashing of anti-Jewish passion. This is not the place to recount the whole history of antisemitism.[96] Two themes will suffice, the first because it determined the whole status of the *dhimmi* Churches, the second because it survives today in the anti-Zionism of the Arab Churches.

At the legal level, the Church's struggle against the Synagogue was expressed in the political, social, religious, and economic disabilities decreed by the first councils and introduced into canon law. Alternating pressure with threats against the emperor, some theologians imposed these laws within the jurisdiction of the Christian state. Promulgated in the codes of Theodosius II in 438 and Justinian in 534, they were applied throughout the Byzantine Empire. These codes, established after the break between the patriarchates (430 and 450), contained equally severe regulations against "heretics" and were therefore contested by the Eastern Churches. Nevertheless, disabilities for Jews decreed by earlier councils were written into canon law, the principal sources of which emanated from Eastern Christendom. These Collections of the Church Fathers' opinions were formulated into articles of law by the Councils or by individuals. The patristic literature is composed of various moral treatises, liturgical and legal compilations (the *Didachee*), and canonical rules (the *Didascalia*), written in Syria from the mid-second to the beginning of the fourth century. The apostolic *Constitutions*, also compiled in Syria at the beginning of the fifth century, constitutes the most important collection of canon law and liturgy, from which the *Constitutions* of the Egyptian Church were drawn (c. 450).

Anti-Judaism was not only expressed in religious literature, sermons, and conciliar laws but equally in the Syrian liturgy (for use in Jerusalem and Antioch). The dissemination of hostile prejudices provoked the destruction or confiscation of synagogues and the persecution of Jews, particularly in Palestine where the Church was confronted with the Jewish historical heritage which it sought to appropriate. The prohibition on residing in Jerusalem, which the Emperor Hadrian had inflicted on the Jews in 135 in order to suppress any renascent nationalism was later relaxed, but it was renewed by Constantine the Great two centuries later at the Church's request. Each year on the ninth of Av (August), the commemoration of the destruction of the Temple, the Jews had to purchase an authorization in order to be allowed to go to Jerusalem for their traditional lamentations. This exclusion of Jews from Jerusalem remained in force until the end of the fifth century and, at the demand of the Palestinian clergy, was reimposed by Heraclius in 620, accompanied by the expulsion of Jews from a three-mile radius of the city, and a ban on their entering within this limit.[97]

The de-Judaization of Jerusalem was a sacred principle of the Church, integrated into its policy of the systematic destruction of Palestinian Jewry.

After the Islamic conquest the legal status for Jews, formulated by the councils, became—by a process of transference—the status of all *dhimmis*, Christians and Jews. Transmitted to Islam through the conversion of Christian officials responsible for its implementation, it perpetuated, under Islamic rule, the war of the patriarchs and the conflict between Church and Synagogue. While these laws are for the most part duly classified and dated in conciliar canons or in Byzantine legal compilations, they reappear, however, in Islam in the form of *hadiths* attributed to the Prophet or to the first four caliphs, or in interpretations of the Koran. This process of Islamization took place quite rapidly since all the components of this status are already mentioned as early as the eighth century by the jurisconsults who founded the four schools of Muslim law.

Similarities can be observed in many areas. In the sphere of worship, at an indeterminate date, chants, and prayers in synagogues were forbidden if they were audible in neighboring churches. In that case, the synagogue was converted into a church, and the Jews were authorized to erect another building further away.[98] A similar measure decreeing silent worship was imposed on *dhimmis* by Islamic law; it determined the prohibition on bells and the construction of churches close to mosques. A Byzantine law of 415 forbade Jews to build new synagogues; in case of infraction the synagogue was converted into a church and the builders subject to fines. The same law prohibited the embellishment or restoration of synagogues unless they threatened to collapse, in which case restoration was authorized by a special permit.[99] Another law forbade synagogues being converted into churches, but once this infringement had been perpetrated it became irreversible;[100] the same law existed in Islam concerning places of *dhimmi* worship vis-à-vis mosques.

The Theodosian Code (438) and *Novellae*, and Justinian's Code (529) and *Novellae* (565), contained many laws excluding Jews from honorific offices, the army and, after 438, from all public office—the exercise of authority over a Christian being barred to them because: "those who are not orthodox Catholics must be deprived of honors so that their position be as lowly as their soul."[101] The same exclusion based on the same motives was adopted by Islamic jurisdiction.

Jews were forbidden to own Christian slaves and to criticize the Christian religion on pain of forfeiting their rights;[102] marriage to Christians of either sex was punished by death.[103] The inheritance of a Jewish convert to Christianity was privileged in relation to other heirs, but Jews could act as witnesses to wills.[104] The powers of Jewish courts were annulled if one party to a suit was a Christian.[105] In addition, Jews were subject to unequal penalties and special taxes. The Church Fathers also imposed religious separation

forbidding Christians to associate with Jews, to attend their religious ceremonies, or consult their doctors. In Spain in 613, a council prohibited Jews
who had been forcibly converted to revert to Judaism. All these laws and
measures, henceforth justified by *hadiths*, formed the Islamic legal framework imposed on Christians, who thus found themselves subjected to the
rules of degradation which their own councils had formulated for Jews.

However, under Islam, specific factors had worsened. Thus, *dhimmis* were
forbidden to own landed property as a result of their collective expropriation following on the Islamization of their land, whereas in the Byzantine
Empire Jews were only barred from possessing Church property. Similarly,
under Byzantine law Jews were exempt from corvées and a summons to appear in court on the Sabbath and religious festivals, whereas *dhimmis* were
specifically summoned to appear on their holy days. In the matter of testimony, evidence was accepted from a Jew if it were favorable to a Christian,
and Jews could act as witnesses, whereas a *dhimmi*'s evidence was unacceptable to Islamic courts in all cases involving a Muslim. Lastly, contrary to the
situation of the *dhimmi*, no regulations controlled dress, Christian books,
weapons, or the names of Jews; nor, under the Carolingians, the reversion
to Judaism of a Jewish convert to Christianity. In addition, the whole conceptual framework of *jihad* is nonexistent in Christianity so that the position of the Jews is not affected by the modalities of battles or territorial
conquests. The concepts of *fay*, the collective human tribute—the purchase
of life and protection as the supreme guarantees of life—are completely
alien to Christian dogma.

During the early European Middle Ages the situation of the Jews was constantly threatened by pressure from the clergy exerted on a royal power it
regarded as too liberal. Archbishop Agobard of Lyons (779–840), declared
that the councils' decisions, because they were presumed to express the
divine will, took precedence over royal jurisdiction. The intense legislative
activity within the Church of Rome from the time of Pope Gregory VII
(1073–85) led to compilations of canonical collections written in preceding centuries. The ancient anti-Jewish provisions, forgotten or lapsed, were
gradually reactivated by the popes. By the end of the Middle Ages the discriminatory and humiliating measures affecting the Jews were identical to
those imposed on the *dhimmis*. In particular, these included compulsory
segregation, exclusion from public and honorific office, and the prohibitions on holding positions conferring authority and on owning landed
property. The distinctive signs, headgear, and specific badges, imposed on
Jews and Muslims by the fourth Lateran Council in 1215, were directly inspired by the vestimentary regulation in Islamic lands; in Europe, at the
end of the Middle Ages Jews were required to wear the specific badge in a
prominent position. The reciprocal borrowings between Islam and Christendom were not solely legal; they also appeared in the theology, even sen-

tences from the Church Fathers, such as those of St. Augustine or St. Jerome, are to be found in the Koran.

The conditions which later allowed the development of a critical examination of the Churches' relationships with other religions, notably Judaism, did not appear in the *dar al-Islam*. There, no critical consideration of the texts and of the *dhimmis'* status has emerged that is comparable with the small—yet constant—trend within Christendom, which led to more conciliatory interpretations of this dogma. The *dhimmis* were emancipated because Europe demanded it and imposed it, not—Turkey excepted—by a process *sui generis* to Islamic society, like movements in the West which heralded secularization, equal rights, and abolished discrimination.

Under Islam, the position of the different Churches vis-à-vis the Synagogue scarcely altered. Firmly controlled by the Islamic authorities, notably the Ottomans, explosions of bloody inter-Christian fanaticism and Christian Judeophobia appeared less frequently as Islamic justice established parity between the Peoples of the Book. A few rare indications of cooperation between Jews and Christians, or of sympathy in a shared state of oppression can be found here and there in the sources. But these references only appear as exceptions, a silence which strengthens the impression of social segregation and mutual hostility. Although it cannot be concluded from this dearth of material that friendly relations between Jewish and Christian *dhimmis* did not exist, for history eliminates the banality of everyday life, only retaining the description of exceptional events.

The constantly renewed and often shared afflictions concurred to bring the communities closer. In 1264 in Cairo, Jews and Christians were led to the stake to be burned alive together. They redeemed their lives by paying considerable ransoms, although many died under torture.[106] It was in fact very rare for reprisals, revolts, and pillage to affect one religious community without affecting the other. The leaders of the Jews—Rabbanite and Karaite—and the Melchite and Jacobite communities were always summoned to appear together, especially by the Mamluk sultans, to be reproved, insulted, and reminded of their obligation to accept degrading practices on pain of death. A document signed in Cairo in 1454 by the representatives of the four communities notified them of the humiliations and restrictions of the *dhimma*. Apart from all the obligations already mentioned, it includes the prohibition on repairing churches and synagogues even if they were falling into ruin, the obligation to allow Muslims to enter them at any hour of the day or night, of shaving the front of their heads, of not possessing any weapon, of praying quietly, of burying their dead in silence, and of never striking or swearing at a Muslim.[107]

The disunity of the Churches and a Judeo-Christian discord, however, formed a constant plank of Islamic policy. In the Ottoman Empire the authorities utilized Jews to carry out its basest acts against Christians, profiting doubly from the humiliation of the Christians and from their rekindled vindictiveness toward the Jews. Apart from these political manipulations, there were also the harmful effects arising from patriarchs selected by caliphs and sultans for their bigotry and submissiveness to the designs of the Islamic authorities. Despite religious separation based on exclusivism and elitism that had been raised to the level of state policy, the jurisdictional discrimination in Christianity concerning Jews—and in Islam regarding Jews and Christians—one would like to believe that any fraternization, when it occurred, indicated broader emotions of generosity than those created by a shared conditioning for mutual execration.

From the long process of agony which the Christian world endured under Islamization, one accusation emerges fairly frequently: the incrimination of Jews for the misfortunes of Christians. Such an attitude was, in the first place, dogmatic—rooted as it was in the tradition of the demonization of the Jews. Strongly embedded in the Eastern Churches, it petrified the depiction of Jews as the embodiment of Evil. The dispersion of Israel and its degradation, retribution, and divine punishment, proved the Church's election. Henceforth, reduced to the identical position it had created for the Jews in order to supplant them, the Church had to exculpate itself by projecting Evil on to the Jews.[108] This demonization provided a theological and eschatological explanation for the misfortunes of the Christians, now absolved, and thus served as an outlet for anger and frustration. In fact, anti-Jewish doctrine was formulated by the Councils before the coming of Islam, but political contingencies obviously exacerbated it. Without minimizing the doctrinal apparatus of Christian Judeophobia, it is still difficult to separate the Western Christian anti-Jewish persecutions of the Middle Ages from the political context of the Muslim-Christian confrontations. Attacked on its own lands, retreating ceaselessly under the pitiless blows of *jihad*-wars, Christendom adopted two attitudes toward the Jews: self-exculpation and deflected aggression. As has already been seen, the Emperor Heraclius, at the instigation of the Palestinian clergy, blamed Jews for the destruction which the Persians, Nestorians, and Monophysites had inflicted on the Melchites (614–28). This was the signal for barbaric killings throughout the empire. The demonization of the Jews represented a strongly rooted tradition in the mentality of the Eastern clergy.[109]

While the accusations of treachery leveled against Jews ("a Jew," "the Jews") are noteworthy for their collective anonymity, on the other hand, Christians who collaborated with Muslim armies—princes, bishops, governors, tribes, or mercenaries—are known historical persons, designated by name and office. During the Arab invasion of the seventh century, Tagrit (Iraq) was betrayed by the Monophysite Archbishop Marutha, Hira (Iraq) by its Nestorian bishop, and Egypt ceded by the Melchite Governor-Bishop

Cyrus. Michael the Syrian mentions collaboration by the Coptic patriarch Benjamin; Damascus was surrendered by its Melchite governor, Mansur b. Sarjun, who received from the Arabs the administration of the provinces. One of the leaders of Hims (Syria), Abu Ju'ayd, is also recorded as a traitor to the Byzantines and as having been active in the capture of Jerusalem, which was handed over without a battle by the patriarch Sophronius. The invasion of Spain was organized by Prince Julian and by Bishop Oppas.

The Christian Arab tribes—Monophysite and Nestorian—who provided the Muslims with information or assisted them in the seventh century are well known. Fully documented, likewise, are the defections by Armenian mercenaries, the accession of Christian collaborators to the highest offices under the caliphate, the goodwill toward the Islamic authority on the part of the Nestorian, Monophysite, and Melchite patriarchs.[110] The history of Islam's advance over Christian lands might be read as a conflict between the patriarchs in which their religious, political, and economic rivalries, and their confrontations with the imperial Christian power played their part. Even if caliphs and sultans occasionally called on the services of Jewish financiers, doctors, and counsellors, their numbers were insignificant compared with the numbers of Christians, *dhimmis* or converts, functioning in the entourage of the Islamic authority. It was this collaboration at the highest level which really determined the course of history for the mass of Christian populations. The marginal position of "a Jew" or "Jews" within Christendom could never have transformed the Christian empire to such an extent. Peddled around Europe, these accusations from the Orient caused repeated persecution and expulsion of Jews on the orders of the Christian kings. The treachery of Christian governors and clergy in the Levant, North Africa, and Spain was transferred to the Jews collectively.

When the road to Syria was opened up to Muhammad through his many contacts with eastern bishops, Heraclius responded to reports that a circumcized people was seizing his empire by ordering the forced conversion of the Jews. At the emperor's request, Dagobert, king of the Franks, ordered that they be banished or baptized.[111] Who else but the Palestinian Church could incarnate *Verus Israel*, the 'true Israel'?—a fundamental theme in anti-Jewish polemic. And while the Christian empire was collapsing, the Patriarch of Jerusalem Sophronius urged the caliph Umar Ibn al-Khattab to maintain the exclusion of the Jews from the Holy City. Despite the mortal blows that Islam was dealing to Christendom, it was again the Patriarch of Jerusalem who, in 932–39, asked the Eastern and Western Roman emperors to decree the banishment or conversion of the Jews, causing new persecution in the Byzantine Empire and in Europe.[112] And when, in 1009, the caliph al-Hakim ordered the destruction of all churches and synagogues and the suppression of the *dhimmi* religions, reprisals were unleashed against the Jews in Europe, whom the Eastern clergy accused of instigating the persecution that al-Hakim had decreed and of which they themselves were the victims.[113] It is true that a few Jewish officials emerge from the thousand years of history but they were often just as tyrannical as the others, and such situations arose from specific circumstances and remain exceptions. Deprived of all political or legislative power, these Christian or Jewish individuals were only the executants of the system which utilized them.

In the eleventh century, besides the advance of the Almoravids in Spain, the increased power of the Seljukid Turks in Mesopotamia, Syria, Palestine, and particularly Armenia which they put to fire and sword, was among the major causes of the first Crusade in 1096. Depending on the political circumstances, Greek Orthodox, Monophysite, and Nestorian bishops collaborated with the Muslim troops against the Crusaders. Yet the accusation that the Jews had committed treason in support of the Muslims caused a wave of reprisals against them in the West. For a millennium the Christian world, brought face to face with *jihad*, suffered the ravages of war, the burning of towns, and the slaughter or enslavement of populations. Terrorized refugees fled to Christian lands spreading fear of the invaders and horror-stricken accounts of barbarous destruction. The suffering of wars and defeats were augmented by the widespread humiliation and debasement of the Cross beneath the Crescent. Christian princes, powerless to stop the Islamic advance, transferred their frustration upon the Jews in their realms, although the Jewish populations had suffered as much as others in the Orient. The persecution of Jews in the West cannot be dissociated from the political context of the Muslim-Christian wars. In 1063, however, Pope Alexander II condemned the identification of Jews with Muslims. War was permissible, he wrote, against the latter who were attacking Christians everywhere, but not against the Jews who were loyal subjects.[114]

The identification of the Jews with Christendom's Muslim persecutors was expressed in medieval religious iconography, especially Crucifixions, in which Jews were sometimes depicted as Turkish soldiers with physical features borrowed from that Asiatic-Arab world which was marching toward the West from Bukhara and Baghdad, and through Spain, its *jihad* armies flanked with kadis.[115] The contact that the West then experienced with the exacerbated Judeophobia of Eastern Christianity in the context of *jihad* was a factor in the deterioration of the Jewish condition in Europe. Other borrowings from Islam included a custom established in Toulouse (France) at the beginning of the eleventh century. Every year at Easter the Jewish community was represented by one of its members who was displayed on the parvis of the cathedral where a Christian slapped his face, a reminder of the *jizya* ritual.[116]

The indictment of the Jews for the misfortunes of Christians exculpated the *dhimmi* Christendoms, by transfering their impotent aggressiveness to the scapegoat. Nostalgia for past glory and the humiliation of sharing a common status with the Jews stirred up permanent Judeophobia which exploded in renewed ritual murder accusations and in acts of aggression against Jewish *dhimmis*, particularly by the Greeks. It must be understood, however, that Christian Judeophobia was set in the wider conflictual context of religious intolerance which contributed so much to the Islamic advance. But whereas schismatic Christian *dhimmis* benefited from the protection of Byzantine, Latin, and later Russian Christian sovereigns, the Jews' vulnerability made them privileged objects for revenge deflected from its real target. And in the same way that a distinctive badge humiliated the Church under the Crescent, it humiliated the Synagogue under the Cross. The flight of Christian populations from Armenia, Anatolia, Greece, Serbia, and Bulgaria was matched by the expulsion from Christian towns of Jews, themselves wandering victims of *jihad*, tossed between temporary protection, ransoming, persecution, and massacre.

This Christian syndrome of displaced aggressiveness, which took the form of Christian-transferred violence in the *dar al-Islam*, has traveled through history and still appears today. It can be seen, for instance, in the numerous ritual murder accusations that Christian *dhimmis* brought against Jews. These accusations proliferated in the nineteenth century, a period when uprisings by Orthodox Christians and Western military supremacy exacerbated Muslim anti-Christian fanaticism. Greek Orthodox *dhimmis* felt particularly vulnerable in this context of war and lived in a state of terror. Extracts from the report of the French consular agent in Damascus, Jean-Baptiste Beaudin, reflects the atmosphere in 1833, a year after Muhammad Ali took control of the region from the Ottoman sultan:

> The only real cause of their [the Muslims of Damascus] discontent has its source in the fanaticism and hatred which they have for everyone who does not profess their religion. Being accustomed in Damascus to treat Christians, Jews, and even Europeans with the greatest contempt and the first in particular as lowly slaves, whereas today Christians, like Jews, can ride on horseback, as everywhere else in Syria, without being beaten and abused by the people [. . .] But if, unfortunately, there was a reaction, the first signal for revolt would be a massacre of Christians and the pillage of their properties.
>
> At present Europeans can come and go in Damascus, retaining their own costumes.[117]

In 1835, Beaudin explained the situation:

> Deeply-rooted fanaticism does not easily tolerate the equality which Muhammad Ali seeks to establish between all religions. Those here accustomed to regard Christians and Jews as lowly slaves find it hard to see themselves their equals; the continual arrival of European travelers is also very difficult for the Damascans, particularly when they see them on horseback wandering

through the bazaars, it is then that one hears professions of faith, the *La Illa,* and *La Alla,* and especially muttered abuse.[118]

At this period, a revolt broke out in Galilee and Samaria (1831–34) when Egyptian troops under Ibrahim Pasha tried to break the power of the regional Bedouin chiefs and impose reforms. Rabbi Isaac b. Salomon Farhi (d. 1853) described in his biography how this affected the Jews of Safed and Hebron in Palestine.

> They [the *fellahin*] entered the town [Safed] on the day after the festival of Pentecost in the year 5594 [1834] and vented their anger pitilessly on the Jews. They were even robbed of their clothes and the men, women, and children were abandoned without garments. For our sins, several Jews were killed and their wives raped. Even after having completely stripped them, they were in no way left in peace, because other Arabs arrived who showered them with blows in order to make them reveal hiding places containing their objects of value. Consequently, the Jews abandoned their houses and fled to the fields. There, like the wild animals of nature, the men, women, and children lived as naked as on the day they were born, covered with shame but without the slightest garment on their bodies unless it were rags. Thus they remained in this distress for twenty-four days on end.
>
> In the month of Av 5594 [August 1834] the army of Ibrahim Pasha burst into Hebron, holy city of the Patriarchs, in order to fight the Turks of the town who had rebelled. [Ibrahim] authorized his soldiers to plunder the town as much as they wished for three days.
>
> For our sins, they broke out with fury and vented their anger on the Jewish quarter which they pillaged with terrifying cruelty. A certain rabbi, renowned for his saintliness, piety, and learning despite his youth was beaten up when he left his home. They also found an aged sage there, the cantor of Hebron, named Rabbi Issakhar Hasun. He was confined to bed with a serious illness. They broke into his house and decapitated him while he was stretched out on his couch. In addition they slaughtered European Jews and publicly raped their wives. Then they turned toward the synagogue where they snatched the Torah scrolls from the Holy Ark, trampled on them, and tore them in pieces. Then they stripped the men, women and children and left them naked. Although all this only lasted for some twenty hours, the disaster was greater than that of Safed.[119]

In 1843, a year after the French consulate was opened in Jerusalem, the consul witnessed an ancestral practice established by the Eastern Churches toward Jews:

> The protection that the French consul is called upon to exercise in respect of the Jew of Algeria, residing in, or passing through, Jerusalem has given me the opportunity for a serious and successful attack on certain customs <u>stamped</u> with <u>cruelty</u> and <u>barbarity</u> among the population of that town. [underlined in the original]

A police ordinance forbids the Israelites to cross the parvis of the Church of the Holy Sepulcher. Up to this day, the unfortunate Jews who inadvertently venture to cross this place were assailed by a crowd of fanatical Christians or Muslims. These madmen crush their victims with blows, wound them with weapons, several times even, and have gone so far as to <u>slaughter</u> them without mercy. This atrocity was committed under the administration of Ibrahim Pasha, in the presence of the Muslim authority, who remained cold and indifferent to these assassinations. This horrible outrage went completely unpunished.

Some three weeks ago, a French Jewish protégé, M. Messaoud, recently arrived in Jerusalem and unaware of the prohibition imposed on his coreligionists, crossed in front of the Holy Sepulcher. Recognized by the Greeks as belonging to the Israelite religion, he was crushed with blows from an iron bar by these miserable wretches and came to lodge a complaint at the consulate, covered with wounds and with a bloody head. I did not hesitate; I immediately asked the Pasha for the instantaneous arrest and punishment of the culprits. I obtained it, but this enforcement created great and lively emotion in the city.

The superiors of the various monasteries came to entreat me to have the offenders released, for the honor of the religion, they said. In their hatred and scorn for the Jews, they alleged in the most serious way in the world, that it was an ancient custom for Turks and Christians, in such a case to <u>kill Jews with impunity</u>, that this custom being established from time immemorial had the force of law. I was inexorable and told them that the <u>law of God was even older</u>, and that it forbade the killing of one's fellows. They had no answer to this argument.[120] [passages underlined in the original]

The remainder of the letter reports that the Pasha himself had the offenders punished because a Muslim court would have acquitted them, and that the heads of monasteries were "urgently requesting" the assailants' release. Three years later the British consul had to intervene on behalf of a foreign Jew who was almost killed in the same circumstances.[121]

A letter from Consul Outrey in Damascus to the French ambassador at Constantinople (31 March 1858) describes the Muslim frustration after the Crimean War, when the European powers sided with Turkey against Russia and then obliged the Ottoman sultan to abolish the legal discrimination against the *dhimmis*.

Monsieur l'Ambassadeur,

Yesterday evening I received the dispatch dated the 15th of this month in which Your Excellency was pleased to inform me of the wish expressed by my colleague from England to have foreign flags hung on the various consulates established in Damascus.

I fear that Mr. Brand, in requesting this innovation very shortly after his arrival here, has not taken sufficient account of the general spirit which exists among the Muslims of our town in respect of Europeans. One cannot close one's eyes to the fact that since the last war the old fanaticism which cloaked all Christians in the same feeling of mistrust has changed into a repressed hatred, all the more profound for being powerless. The Muslims do not forgive us for the obvious superiority which we have over them, even less for the privileges which the Powers have granted the Christians and the influence of Europe which they instinctively resent, the product of a moral malaise which a practised eye can perceive in almost every class of the population. It is vexing to have to add that these malevolent attitudes are not only sustained by the ulema, which is very natural, but also and primarily, by the army officers who generally show very little reserve in their language . . .[122]

In 1860—after two decades of anti-Christian violence in Palestine, Lebanon, and Syria—some 12,000 Christian men, women, and children were slaughtered by Muslims and Druses in atrocious circumstances in Lebanon, and about 10,000 more in Damascus. Although the rampaging Muslims had acted within sight of all, including the foreign consuls, Christian survivors falsely accused Jews of participating in these massacres and called for vengeance. Only the forceful action of their coreligionists in Europe—led by Sir Moses Montefiore and Adolphe Crémieux—saved the Jews of Damascus from bloodthirsty Christian retribution.[123]

Tension between Christians and Jews in the Ottoman Empire was widespread. Hence, when a Jew, who was an Algerian subject, was imprisoned in Aleppo in 1889 charged with blasphemy, the French consul refused to intervene. He pretexted the situation in Crete where the continual reprisals of the Turks against rebellious Christians had provoked attacks there by the Christians on Jews. It was in Palestine, however, that the most wretched aspects of Jewish life were experienced, under the combined blows of Christian and Muslim fanaticism. This situation was noted by all foreign pilgrims and also by the European consuls in Jerusalem after 1839, when the Turks allowed consulates to open in the city. Although Christians were henceforth forbidden to kill Jews with impunity in front of the Holy Sepulcher, the prohibition on approaching it remained in force. As late as August 1908 priests, particularly the Greek Orthodox, violently attacked Jews whom they judged to be violating this ban.

During the Greek war of independence (1821–32) thousands of Jews were slaughtered by Greeks, in revenge for all the humiliations and murders inflicted on them by the Turks.[124] Greek anti-Judaism, which had been reflected in periodically renewed laws, aggression, murders, and religious calumnies now had free play. Naturally, in such a context of terror there was no lack of ritual murder accusations; denunciations were commonplace also among antagonistic Christians and the clergy, and even at the highest level of the Greek Church hierarchy and its notables. In this cycle of uprisings and reprisals, the Porte—more than ever prone to divide in order to rule—often stoked the hatred between the various religious groups and sustained their conflicts.

These anti-Jewish outbursts also appeared soon after the independence of Bulgaria and Romania. They express the humiliation of the Christians and their revolt, not only against their Muslim oppressors, but also against having been associated in their humiliation with the Jews—a people whom they scorned and oppressed. Mob violence against the Jews or their expulsion—as had been the case during the Spanish Inquisition—would thus restore to Christians, freed from dhimmitude, their dignity, supremacy, and their ancient right to persecute the Jews. Such feelings paved the way for the Nazi extermination of the Jews in the Balkans during the Shoah—with the exception of Bulgaria—bringing a millennium of Jewish history there to an end.

4

Modernity: A Time of Hope and a Time of Ashes

After a millennium of confrontation between Islam and Christendom, the nineteenth century culminated in multiple challenges. Science and political and cultural revolutions destroyed the old order everywhere, abolishing slavery and the humiliation of the infidel. Even more important were the military challenges of the despised *dar al-harb* with its technological superiority. Introduced by the colonial armies, secularism replaced the *shari'a* with new legal systems which suppressed the sectarianism and religious segregation of dhimmitude. Opposed to the *dhimmi's* abasement, the West propounded the equality of human rights; to the concept of Islamic toleration, it put forward the principle of respect for life; to the subjection of the *dhimmi*, it proposed emancipation and freedom.

Three simultaneous movements rocked Islamic societies in the nineteenth century: colonization, national revolts by the subjected *raya* populations in Europe overlapping with the interplay of European rivalries, and emancipation imposed by the West. Hundreds of thousands died in the struggles waged by the Serbian, Greek, Romanian, and Bulgarian peoples to achieve independence, while from 1839 to1876 the European Powers strove to oblige the Ottoman sultan to abrogate the *dhimma* and to recognize, albeit in theory only, equality between Muslims and *dhimmis*. Elsewhere—in Africa and Asia—the advance of the European colonial armies destroyed the Islamic order, proving the supremacy of the *dar al-harb*. Thus, modernity and the secularization of traditional Muslim societies freed the *dhimmis* from a millennium of degradation.

From the time that Sultan Abd al-Majid promulgated the emancipation edict (*Hatt-i Humayun*) of 18 February 1856, European consuls in the Ottoman Empire strove to enforce compliance with two major principles: the right for Christians and Jews to give evidence in Islamic courts when a Muslim was a party, and respect for the life and property of non-Muslims. Acceptance of these principles symbolized the abandonment of the concepts of Muslim superiority over infidels, of *jihad*, of *harbi* and *dhimmi* — intended to be replaced by the principle of equal rights. In both cases their

123

efforts failed. In the European Ottoman provinces, particularly in Bosnia and Herzegovina until Muslim rule ended (1878), the kadis rejected evidence from Christian Serbs and denied them rights to possess land, to build new churches, repair old ones, or install church bells.

The Bosnian beys refused all the reforms improving the lot of Christians. With endemic Serb uprisings threatening European peace, the Powers intervened with the sultan. The *iradé* of 2 October 1875, followed by an imperial firman (30 November–12 December 1875), confirmed the rights of Christians to own land and to build churches and schools. The legal and fiscal systems were improved; the obligation for testamentary wills by *dhimmis* to conform to the *shari'a* was annulled, as were corvées, compulsory requisitions, and extortions (*jerimeh*). However, Bosnian Muslim obstruction prevented any progress and none of these reforms was ever enforced.

Elsewhere, it was colonization which altered traditional social patterns. The principle of equality stirred up periodic massacres of *dhimmis* as Europe's control on the *dar al-Islam* tightened. Indeed, such an upheaval could only provoke violent opposition. The flight of Muslim populations from regions liberated by Christians in the Balkans, or conquered by colonial wars—as well as the Russian advance in the Caucasus, and the British conquest of India—hardened fanaticism and increased bitterness and humiliation for Muslims ruled by foreign infidel powers. Consequently, despite ostensible improvements, the reforms promised by the Porte were hardly ever implemented. The wars and struggles in which the *dhimmis* were the prize represented a conflict of civilization where they were both the beneficiaries and the victims. The difficulties of applying the reforms (*Tanzimat*) lay in the fact that the modernization of all sectors of the Ottoman Empire introduced a European conceptual apparatus into the *dar al-Islam* at a period of political and military confrontation. Consequently, the *umma* saw the *dhimmis'* emancipation and the equality of rights that abolished the koranic order of supremacy over infidels as the ideological tool to humble Islam. Secularism, modernization, and equality of rights were considered as an anti-Islamic onslaught.

In European Turkey, bloody strife spread during decades. In the Asian and African Ottoman provinces—with the exception of Egypt, under a British Protectorate from 1882—the emancipation of the *dhimmis* appeared as a violation of the divine law ordaining the submission of infidels and their degradation. The killing and sufferings of Muslims fleeing the Balkans, humiliated by the victories of their erstwhile subjected *dhimmis*, increased the fears and vulnerability of Eastern Christians, particularly the Greek Melchites. In the provinces of Damascus, Sidon, and Acre—corresponding to the Syrian, Lebanese, and Palestinian regions—foreign interference aggravated local conflicts. Furthermore, violence and insecurity were exacerbated by the arrival in these regions of considerable numbers of Muslim refugees: Algerians fleeing French colonization in the 1830s, led by the Emir Abd al-Qadir, now resided in Damascus and Jerusalem; Muslims driven out of the Caucasian region by Russians after their defeat in 1878; as well as Bosnians and Albanian Muslims camped in and near Haifa, Acre, Caesarea, Jerusalem, Amman, and elsewhere. The emancipation of the *dhimmis*, achieved in a context of rivalries, political instability, and religious hatred provoked massacres of Christians in Lebanon and Damascus (1860). European military intervention restored order and forced recognition of the administrative autonomy of the Ottoman province of Lebanon (Organic Regulation of 9 June 1861).

In Asia, the Russian advance into the Caucasus in the 1830s had already caused bloody reactions against many Jewish communities in Persia, which were plundered and decimated in Tabriz, Ardabil, Zanjan, and in other areas of Azerbaijan. In some towns, such as Mashhad (1839), they were obliged to convert to Islam or face death.

A brief survey will illustrate the traditional condition of dhimmitude in Persia at this period. In 1866, the head of the Hamadan Jewish community was imprisoned, put in chains, and threatened with death. The same year in Balforuch (a province of Hamadan), the disappearance of a young Muslim provoked the forced Islamization of Jews: eighteen were killed and two burned alive. In Hamadan in 1875, a fanatic mullah preached the slaughter of the Jews; one of them, accused of blasphemy, was burned alive by the mob. In Teheran on 16 May 1877, the Jewish quarter was invaded and its inhabitants attacked, while a mullah published a *fatwa* forcing Jews to wear a distinctive badge.

In Isfahan in 1889 a ritual murder accusation unleashed several days of anti-Jewish violence and threats of extermination. On 10 August 1889 in the same town, Muslims accused Jewish pilgrims of throwing stones, of attacking a kadi, and of profaning a mosque with brandy. The mob immediately broke the hands and legs of some hundred pilgrims and injured all the others. Isfahan Jews were attacked in the streets the next day and had to hide in their homes; two who ventured out were killed. Their corpses were dragged through the streets and dumped in the Jewish quarter when night fell. On the morrow, some women were raped and the kadi signed a petition for the Jews to be exterminated. The shah's son, Prince Zil-Sultan, hastened to protect the victims but the brutality continued. Two months later, on 5 October, a Muslim who had struck a Jew then accused him of the same offense; Jews were immediately beaten up and their quarter plundered. Only the arrival of Prince Zil-Sultan prevented a general massacre. This report also mentions efforts by "Christian priests," Mirza Norollah in particular, to help the Jews, thereby saving a large number and constantly assisting them. Another report a month later (7 November) related the circumstances of riots which involved a Jewish holy place in Sangan, a village near Isfahan.

In winter 1892–93 the Hamadan Shi'ite clergy subjected the Jews to humiliating regulations, including the wearing of a distinctive badge, while noncompliance was punished by death or forced conversion; thirty notables—with knives at their throats — were forced to convert. For more than forty days Jews were besieged in their homes, pursued, and beaten to death if they left them, while Jews and Zoroastrians were massacred in Yezd and Shiraz. In 1897 the mullahs of Hamadan put posters in the mosques calling for the killing of the Jews. The following year, in Lar, a mullah forbade Muslims to deal with Jews and sell them any foodstuffs; already in dire financial straits, the Jewish community was called on to repay a debt within a given period or convert collectively to Islam. On 18 January 1900, in Teheran, a crowd gathered outside the mosque after an inflammatory sermon, and then plundered the Jewish quarter, attacking its inhabitants and wounding many; in 1907 in Shiraz and the region of Fars, the army had to intervene to save the Jews; in 1909 in Durab (in the region of Shiraz), the Jewish quarter and the synagogue were plundered, Torah scrolls burned, houses ransacked, and seventeen Jews obliged to convert, while the remainder fled. The same scenario occurred in Kirmanshah where a child was killed and all the houses of Jews plundered.[1]

The increase of violence and murders against Jews by fanaticized mobs prompted the representatives of the European powers to express their worries to the Persian government. However, in spite of the shah's efforts to control the situation, atrocities continued.

On 19 May 1910 Nissani Machallah, a Jewish teacher at the school of the Alliance Israélite Universelle (AIU) in Shiraz, was brutally murdered in the street by a fanatic young sayyid for asking him why he was beating two elderly Jews with an iron chain. The murderer was released three months later since no Jewish witness dared identify him for fear of being assassinated. In October the local police chief, Ibrahim Monchi Zadeh, posted on every mosque door and public buildings the following declaration:

> Considering that the principal aim of the police administration is to assure the general security and tranquillity;
> Considering that, besides this, the Jews have been from all times, and still are, under the safeguard and protection of Islam;
> We inform all the Jews that they should feel themselves to be safe and protected by the police. If someone should molest them, mistreat them, or commit a crime against them, they should inform the police so that the culprit will be arrested and punished, in conformity with the Constitution, and the "Shari'a" laws.
> The police has always been very assiduous in providing tranquillity for the Jews and they can, with all confidence and hope, go about their occupations.[2]

On 30 October another false ritual murder accusation provided the pretext for plundering the Jewish quarter of Shiraz, initiated by the soldiers of the military governor of the town, Nasr ed-Dowlet. Mr.Nataf, director of the AIU in Shiraz, reported how:

In the space of a few hours, in less time than is needed to describe it, 6,000 men, women, children and the elderly were stripped of everything they possessed. [. . .] In short, the outcome of yesterday's events is as follows: 12 people dead and about 50 more or less seriously injured, whilst the five to six thousand people comprising the Shiraz community now possess nothing in the world but the few tatters which they were wearing when their quarter was invaded.[3]

These accounts illustrate the protection that the Shah and his officials accorded the victims by sending orders to governors forbidding violence, dispatching troops, and imposing severe punishments on the perpetrators. Also relevant is the solidarity that existed between *dhimmis*. Lastly, in all these tragic situations, European diplomatic missions, when they existed, supplied humanitarian aid and political support by exerting pressure on the authorities. The same situations recurred when repeated massacres of Jews took place in Morocco at this period, despite the sultan's efforts to avert them and impose penalties against the perpetrators. They express the conflict between the modern values of respect for life and human dignity and the condition of dhimmitude.

This confrontation opposed the political authority, concerned with temporal contingencies, and the religious authority, pillar of a tradition guaranteeing its privileges. Over and beyond the economic and political conflicts a great movement was emerging, transforming thought, ethics, and multireligious relationships, and in which Europeans and modernist Muslims participated side by side, a dynamic born at the very heart of dhimmitude—a terrain par excellence for the rediscovery of the human being beneath the degradation of the *dhimmi*. Since this conflict involved the fundamental notions of the relationship with other religions, it consequently required a reappraisal of the dominant group's self-image. The processes whereby the *dhimmis* were emancipated thus gave rise to bloody reactions against infidels who were claiming equality with Muslims.

In the Ottoman Empire the irredentism of the various emanations of Christian nationalism—Greek, Serbian, Montenegrian, and Bulgarian—sustained a continuous cycle of wars and massacres.[4] In the context of dhimmitude, one can note the constant application of the political and military principles of *jihad* in accordance with the texts of Muslim jurisconsults and evidence supplied by chroniclers. The case of Armenia in the 1890s allows a comparison of military practice with the religious duties of *jihad*, because it produced a considerable documentation, in voluminous

reports by consuls and joint commissions of inquiry appointed by the Great
Powers and the sultan.

It is important to remember that the Muslim population refused to implement the reforms abolishing the inferiority and vulnerability of Jews and
Christians, on the pretext that this principle of equality was contrary to the
shari'a. In 1894 the Armenians in Sassun rebelled against the protection-
ransom system described above and were massacred. The European Powers, who had signed the Treaty of Berlin with Turkey (13 July 1878), then
required Sultan Abd al-Hamid II to follow a plan of reform in accordance
with clause 61 of the Treaty.[5]

Actually, in the provinces of Mesopotamia which had a very large Christian population, these Ottoman reforms under the provisions of the Treaty
of Berlin not only comprised the government's obligations to its subjects
but also its pledges to the Powers who had signed the treaty. This renewed
plan to implement reforms in the Armenian provinces was presented on
11 May 1895 to the sultan who signed it on 17 October. According to Meyrier, French vice-consul at Diyarbakir, the uprising began on 22 October
1895 when the sultan's consent to the reforms was known. This point is also
emphasized in the report that Rev. Père Celestino Da Desto, the Vatican's
representative and head of the Capuchin order in Malatia, sent to Carlier,
French vice-consul at Sivas, on 28 November 1895. The report begins:

> The news that certain [Armenian] provinces were going to receive reforms
> had aroused great discontent among the Muslims. Their provocative attitude
> was giving Christians cause for concern.[6]

After the 1894–96 massacres in the provinces of Mesopotamia, the chief
dragoman (interpreter) at the British embassy, Gerald H. Fitzmaurice, explained the rules of *shari'a* law:

> [The perpetrators] are guided in their general action by the prescriptions of
> the Sheri Law. That law prescribes that if the "rayah" [*dhimmi*] Christian
> attempts, by having recourse to foreign powers, to overstep the limits of priv-
> ileges allowed to them by their Mussulman masters, and free themselves
> from their bondage, their lives and property are to be forfeited, and are at
> the mercy of the Mussulmans. To the Turkish mind the Armenians had tried
> to overstep those limits by appealing to foreign powers, especially England.
> They, therefore, considered it their religious duty and a righteous thing to
> destroy and seize the lives and property of the Armenians [. . .][7]

At Urfa in October 1895, again in the last days of December, and then
on 16 and 17 January 1896, the mob and the army massacred more than
ten thousand Armenians, while women and children were sold in public
squares. Those who had taken refuge in the Armenian cathedral were

hacked down, or ritually slaughtered, after the recitation of sacred verses by clerics. Everything—human beings and Bibles—was sprinkled with petrol and set alight, while five mullahs gave praise to Allah. For several days the streets of the town were cluttered with piles of corpses. Finally, the Jews received orders to bury the bodies; they carried out this macabre corvée for a week, forced to drag the corpses with cords to the prepared public ditches. The role of gravediggers, assigned them by the Porte, gave rise to virulent banter in European antisemitic circles.[8]

This episode is interesting because it indicates the Porte's manipulation of religious antagonisms. Similar tactics were employed during the Greek war of independence (1821–32), accompanied by murderous rage against the Jewish *dhimmis* by the Greeks. It was easy then for the Porte to be seen by Europeans as a moral rampart against such Christian barbarity, all the more so as the Greeks took their revenge on the Jews for the humiliations and murders that the Turks were inflicting on them.

The 1894–96 massacre of Armenians in central Anatolia claimed as many as 250,000 victims and led to a large number of conversions to Islam.[9] Converted couples were obliged to divorce and remarry, each with a new Muslim spouse. If they reverted to Christianity, they were killed.[10] In Constantinople, the British ambassador, Sir Philip Currie, informed his French colleague, Paul Cambon, that he had mentioned the wave of forced conversions to the sultan on 15 January. The sultan expressed astonishment and on 25 January his first secretary showed a telegram to the ambassador, signed by the

> [. . .] Protestant, Catholic and Gregorian Armenian leaders from Biredjik, stating that the Armenians of that town having lived in complete security and happiness under the just regime of the sultan, without their lives and possessions having been in danger, were desirous of embracing the religion of Muhammad. The dispatch added that this wish was spontaneous, no one having suggested this proposal to them.[11]

The same report from Currie gives the results of the inquiry conducted by Fitz-Maurice, British vice-consul in Smyrna, made with the sultan's assent. This inquiry revealed that the population of Biredjik numbered 240 households on the day of the massacre:

> After 150 Christians had been massacred, the survivors, numbering 1,500 Gregorians, Protestants and Catholics, converted to Islam in front of the bleeding corpses of their parents and under pressure from the crowd. Not a single Christian remains in Biredjik.

This example illustrates the contradictory versions of the same facts and the sources of information available to historians when they wish to deny or confirm the practice of forced conversions in the history of dhimmitude. The evaluation of documents from *dhimmi* sources falls within the same context of historical criticism. From Diyarbakir, French Vice-Consul Meyrier observed in 1895 the submission on the part of the Armenian clergy and notables to pressure from the new Turkish governor, Aniz Pasha, a notorious fanatic. Aniz forced them to send a letter to the sultan extolling his virtues. Three weeks later the entire Christian population was killed.[12]

In July 1908 the Young Turks' coup d'état restored the 1876 constitution, whose liberal principles guaranteeing individual liberty and equal rights and duties contradicted those of the *shari'a*. In Constantinople, and especially in the Arab provinces of the empire, traditionalist forces demanded that the *shari'a* be restored and the constitution and equal rights abolished. In Baghdad, it was rumored that, as Jews had become equals to Muslims, they could now defend themselves if attacked. For several hours on 14 October 1908 a crowd of rioters attacked every Jew who passed, "in order to recall them to a respectful attitude."[13] In Mosul, Christians were openly abused in the street. The Muslim Union movement, strongly entrenched in Damascus, Homs, Hama, Aleppo, Beirut, and Sidon terrorized Christians and demanded that the *shari'a* be restored. Furthermore, Bulgarian independence, Austria's annexation of Bosnia-Herzegovina in 1878, and the return of Crete to Greece in 1908 exacerbated anti-Western feelings and antagonism toward non-Muslims.

In these circumstances the twentieth century opened with a mass slaughter of Armenians in Sassun (1904). In April 1909 about 25,000 Armenian men, women, and children were butchered and burned alive in Adana, while the warships of Britain, France, Italy, Austria, Germany, Russia, and the United States were anchored in the nearby port city of Mersin, "paralyzed by confusion and uncertainty."[14]

The general insecurity and terror exacerbated conflicts among the *dhimmis* themselves. The expansion of the educational system in both Christian and Jewish communities had created parallel modernization and reform movements. From the end of the nineteenth century religious hostility was supplemented by economic competition between *dhimmis* and their political polarization in the doctrines of Arab nationalism and Zionism.

Political and Theological Rivalry in Europe
and the 1840 Damascus Blood Libel

It was during the nineteenth century that the formulation of European designs on Palestine were conceived, making of the Jewish people not only a surety and a hostage but, in the next century, the victim of a genocidal war. These political designs hinged on the Great Powers' geostrategic, colo-

nial, and economic rivalries in regard to the Ottoman Empire. Their conflicts were embittered by divergent millennial Christian theological and
eschatalogical implications related to the Holy Land and to the Jewish
people.

Political Conflicts

Ever since Bonaparte's expedition to Egypt (1798–99), France planned
to establish a great Arab empire in the Levant under its governance. It,
therefore, set about strengthening the power of Muhammad Ali, an Albanian officer from the Ottoman army, nominated pasha of Egypt. At the
request of Sultan Mahmud II (1803–39), Muhammad Ali sent the Egyptian
army to subdue a Greek revolt. In 1823 the re-attachment of Crete to the
pashalik of Egypt created a base from which to attack the Greeks. Egyptian
troops led by Ibrahim Pasha, the adopted son of Muhammad Ali, proceeded to devastate the island completely: villages were burned down, plantations uprooted, populations driven out or led away as slaves, and vast
numbers of Greek slaves were deported to Egypt. This policy was pursued
in the Morea where Ibrahim organized systematic devastation, with massive
Islamization of Greek children. He sent sacks of heads and ears to the sultan in Constantinople and cargoes of Greek slaves to Egypt.[15]

In 1829 France envisaged—under its patronage—the reunification of
the three regencies of Tripoli, Tunis, and Algiers with Egypt, and encouraged its protégé, Muhammad Ali, to conquer Syria, Palestine, and Mesopotamia. In 1832 Ibrahim Pasha succeeded in breaking the power of the local
chiefs and in placing Syria, Lebanon, and Palestine under the government
of the pasha of Egypt. France, protector of Catholic interests, was allowed
to develop a network of Catholic institutions there. This was the beginning
of a grand French Arab policy intended to ensure the preeminence of
France in the Mediterranean, and of the papacy's long-term interests. Literature was published extolling the splendid virtues of the Arabs and the in-
calculable benefits anticipated from close collaboration with them.[16]
Notwithstanding a more liberal attitude toward *dhimmis*, the fiscal extortions and the cruelty of Ibrahim Pasha in Syria led the Druse and the Maronite populations to revolt. The British government was quick to support
the insurgents by sending British advisers, money, and weapons. In fact,
the expansion of French ambitions in the Arab-Ottoman provinces, linked
to the Latin Church's increased influence, posed a threat to British strategic interests.

Theological Conflicts

The disintegration of the Ottoman Empire unleashed in Palestine a political and religious competition between the three major streams of Chris-

tianity: Catholicism, Orthodoxy, and Protestantism. All three expanded missionary activities among *dhimmis,* both Christians and Jews. With political and financial support from European governments, they promoted Christian colonization in Jerusalem and the Holy Land after 1836, and increased the organization of pilgrimages, the building and restoration of churches and monasteries, and the purchase of land. Sheltered by French diplomatic protection, the papacy enlarged its establishment in the East via Uniatism, thanks to considerable subsidies given to local Uniate churches. The linkage of Eastern Churches to Rome caused the sultan to issue a firman in 1834 forbidding movement from one Christian communion to another. Contributions to the holy places flowed into Palestine from the whole Catholic world. However, the Uniate movement, which transferred the orthodox *dhimmis* from the protection of Russia to that of Rome and France, worried Imperial Russia, causing her to strengthen the religious and political presence of Orthodoxy in Jerusalem.

This re-Christianization policy in the Holy Land by two rival Christian factions clashed with certain Protestant concepts which favored the restoration of the Jews to their ancient heritage, a prelude to conversion to Christianity in a millenarian vision. Thus, three contradictory visions divided Christendom: the Russian Orthodox which acted through the Orthodox *dhimmis;* the Latin, pretexting Arabism, which was infiltrating through Catholic Ottoman subjects in order to extend the influence of France and the Holy See; and the third, the Protestant millenarian movement which used the Jews to gain a footing in the Holy Land.

From the seventeenth century the Christian millenarian movement in England and elsewhere had been publishing studies advocating the return of the Jews to their homeland.[17] In the late 1830s, at the prompting of Lord Shaftesbury—stepfather-in-law to Viscount Palmerston—this faction fought for the granting of British consular protection to Jews in Palestine in order to protect them from Muslim and Christian fanaticism. On 31 January 1839, Palmerston, then British foreign secretary, had instructed Britain's first vice-consul in Jerusalem, "to afford Protection to the Jews generally." To the young Queen Victoria, he even quoted the prophet Jeremiah: "Judah shall be saved and Israel live in peace at home." (23:6).[18]

In a letter to Lord Palmerston, dated 25 May 1839, Vice-Consul William Tanner Young described the situation of the Jews in Palestine:

> The Pasha [Ibrahim Pasha] has shown much more consideration for the Jews than His people have. I have heard several acknowledge that they enjoy more peace and tranquillity under this Government, than ever they have enjoyed here before. Still, the Jew in Jerusalem is not estimated in value, much above a dog—and scarcely a day passes that I do not hear of some act of Tyranny and oppression against a Jew—chiefly by the soldiers, who enter

their Houses and borrow whatever they require without asking any permission—sometimes they return the article, but more frequently not. In two instances, I have succeeded in obtaining justice for Jews against Turks—But it is quite a new thing in the eyes of these people to claim justice for a Jew—and I have good reason to think that my endeavours to protect the Jews, have been—and may be for some little time to come, detrimental to my influence with other classes—Christians as well as Turks—If a Jew my Lord, were to attempt to pass the door of the Church of the Holy Sepulchre, it would in all probability cost him his life—this is not very Christian like, considering Christ Himself was a Jew—And were a Jew here, to fly for safety, he would seek it sooner in a Mussulman's house than in that of a Christian.[19]

After mentioning a new Proclamation decreed in Jerusalem, "forbidding the Jews from praying in their own Houses,"[20] vice-consul Young added:

So soon as the Plague is reported to be in the City, the Jews at once become the object of cupidity to every employé in the quarantine service, who, with the Native practitioners in medicine, rob and oppress them to the last degree. From one individual alone, of the better class, they succeeded lately in obtaining 4,000 piastres, equal to £40 Sterling in bribes—His son was sick with the fever—they declared it to be Plague—set a guard on his house, deprived him of all means of obtaining medical assistance—the patient died, and then, on his refusing to satisfy their demands—they threatened to burn everything in his House. This My Lord is not a solitary instance.
What the Jew has to endure, at all hands, is not to be told.
Like the miserable dog without an owner he is kicked by one because he crosses his path, and cuffed by another because he cries out—to seek redress he is afraid, lest it bring worse upon him; he thinks it better to endure than to live in the expectation of his complaint being revenged upon him. Brought up from infancy to look upon his civil disabilities everywhere as a mark of degradation, his heart becomes the cradle of fear and suspicion—he finds he is trusted by none—and therefore he lives himself without confidence in any.

By granting protection to the Jews, Britain enlarged its zone of influence and placed Jews on an equal footing with Christians. In addition, this policy introduced a Protestant presence into the Holy Land where the exclusive religious protectorate of Catholic France was dominant.

The authorization from the Ottoman sultan for a British vice-consulate in Jerusalem was the first such concession. Its responsibility extended to the whole of Palestine, a country whose borders did not even exist on a map at that period and whose provinces were each attached to various administrative centers. Consequently, the British government resorted to biblical history as a basis to define Palestinian territory. Not only was Great Britain the only country to boast a consulate in Jerusalem at that time—France opened its consulate in 1843—but it also sought to obtain permission from the sultan to build a large church for the reformed religion, a construction that was forbidden by Islamic law.

These encroachments by Anglicanism and Prussian Protestantism in the Holy Land disturbed royalist France, which had benefited, particularly since the seventeenth century, from an exclusive right over the Holy Places (firman of 1620, confirmed in 1740). Besides, Catholic France supported the papacy which, via Uniatism, was gathering the *raya* churches into the bosom of the Holy See, and simultaneously strengthened French influence in the Ottoman Empire. Thus, Rome's religious interests closely overlapped with the economic and political expansion of France. Britain's penetration of Palestine, which competed with France's patronage, was challenged by the French government and by ultramontane circles. For the latter, the "Protestant danger" was added to the "Jewish danger" as Britain made no secret of its intentions to protect the Jews and to encourage the rebirth of their ancient homeland. Above all, the return of the Jews to the Holy Land threatened the Christian teaching of the deicidal Jewish people, fallen from grace, expiating the crucifixion of Jesus by their abasement, their exile, and their humiliation in Jerusalem.

To combat Protestant and proto-Zionist British penetration, France used its Muslim ally, Muhammad Ali, as the instrument of its Arab policy and supported his claims on Syria and Palestine (1831–40). The establishment of several Latin missionary institutions in the Levant, connected with French protection, gathered indigenous Catholic and Uniate Christians under French patronage and favored its political and religious hold over the region. Between London and Paris a confrontation began for the control of Syria and the Holy Land. Over and beyond Anglo-French strategic and economic rivalries, two fundamentally opposing theological concepts clashed: the Catholic concept of the Jews as a deicidal people; and the Protestant millenarian vision of a reborn Israel.

Meanwhile, the cruelty of Egyptian oppression roused the populations to revolt. In Crete, the Egyptian governors established a regime of pitiless terror, menacing both Christians and Turks with collective massacre.[21] In Syria, the whole Lebanese mountain rose up against Ibrahim and even the Maronites, age-old allies of France, threatened to join Britain which had promised to restore the Kingdom of Israel in Palestine and to create a Christian state in Lebanon. France found its position seriously jeopardized and the French consular agent felt that, in the war between the pasha of Egypt and the sultan, "much innocent blood would be shed, particularly by Syrian and Damascan fanaticism which would take advantage of this circumstance to destroy the Christian, and especially the European, name."[22]

It was in this context—in which the political and religious interests of the Great Powers in the Levant, particularly in Palestine, intermingled—that the disappearance of Father Thomas, a Capuchin monk from Sardinia under French protection, and his servant, Ibrahim Amara, occurred. In February 1840, Count de Ratti-Menton, the French consul, and Sherif Pasha, the Egyptian governor of the town, accused the Damascus Jewish community of ritual murder without any proof. The French consul immediately had some Jewish notables arrested, and instituted a search of their houses and the whole quarter. Sometimes in his presence, and for several weeks, the accused underwent torture—including genital torture—mutilation and burnings, accompanied by extortions, floggings, and the imprisonment of men, women, and sixty-three children torn away from their families. Two adults died under torture and one converted to Islam to save his life. Crowds of Christians and Muslims, stirred up by high ranking ecclesiastics in the hierarchies of their communities, called for the massacre of all the Jews of Damascus and the plunder of their possessions.

The "Damascus Affair" broke out during negotiations by the Quadruple Alliance (England, Prussia, Russia, Austria), conducted by Britain, to expel Muhammad Ali from Syria and Palestine.[23] During the ministry of Prime Minister Louis Adolphe Thiers (February–October 1840), France had been excluded from the Alliance; it found itself totally isolated and reduced to carrying on a war against the European Powers alone if it persisted in supporting the pasha against Turkey. Its prestige was tarnished and "perfidious Albion" had destroyed the dream of a Franco-Arab empire extending from Algiers to Alexandretta (Turkey). The Egyptian pasha was called on to return Crete to the sultan as well as the Syrian provinces, where even the Maronites were deserting France. In addition, Austria and the Protestant countries were criticizing the French consul's barbarous conduct in Damascus. Some Catholic theologians, but primarily the Protestants, refused to accept the accusations of ritual murder and the torture inflicted on the Jewish martyrs. Even distant America was moved by the affair. On 14 August 1840 Secretary of State John Forsyth wrote to U.S. Consul John Gliddon in Alexandria:

Sir:—In common with all civilized nations, the people of the United States have learned with horror, the atrocious crimes imputed to the Jews of Damascus, and the cruelties of which they have been the victims. The President fully participates in the public feeling, and he cannot refrain from expressing equal surprise and pain, that in this advanced age, such unnatural practices should be ascribed to any portion of the religious world, and such barbarous measures be resorted to, in order to compel the confession of imputed guilt; the offenses of which these unfortunate people are charged, resemble too much those which, in less enlightened times, were made the pretexts of fanatical persecution or mercenary extortion, to permit a doubt that they are equally unfounded.

The President has witnessed, with the most lively satisfaction, the effort of several of the Christian Governments of Europe, to suppress or mitigate these horrors, and he has learned with no common gratification, their partial success.[24]

In France the Thiers government consistently supported its consul's action, and the ultramontane and governmental press exploited the affair by a campaign to defame Judaism. Throughout Europe books, press comments, and articles recounted with sadistic details the alleged ritual murders committed by Jews on Christians. Consul Ratti-Menton assumed the stature of a national hero entrusted with a sacred mission: to reveal to the horrified Christian and Muslim worlds the satanic machinations of the Jews and their hatred of Christians. Standing alone in the face of the concealed and corrupting forces of "international Jewry," he defended heroically the prestige and glory of France and Catholicism.

This vilification of the Jews by the French government took place in a context of a European policy in which the emancipation of the Jews was being strongly challenged; in addition, it related to precise objectives in France's Arab policy. The struggle against Britain closely linked the ambitions of Muhammad Ali and those of France, and via that coup, orchestrated by the Egyptian governor and the French consul, France proclaimed its right of patronage over Christians in the Ottoman Empire. The French consul's attack on the Jews aimed to restore the tarnished French influence on the international scene and in the Levant. The criminalization of Jewry not only threatened the recent emancipation of the Jews in some European countries, but above all it rallied to France all the Western Christian factions which objected to their emancipation.

In addition, the smear campaign discredited the British policy of protecting the Jews in the Orient and its plan to restore them to the Holy Land, which would thereby be lost to France. It was also aimed at proving that the Jews were unworthy of the emancipation granted to *raya*s in the Ottoman Empire by the edict of Gulhane promulgated on 3 November 1839. Greek Orthodox and Catholic Christian circles had opposed the abolition of the Jews' legal disabilities, considering that only Christians should qualify for European protection and equality with Muslims.

In the absence of corpses, even murder could not be proved, and when a Jewish delegation representing the French and British communities—led by Adolphe Crémieux and Sir Moses Montefiore—demanded that the case be reopened in order to carry out the judicial enquiry on the basis of penal deontology and not of torture, France refused to allow the documents to be examined. The Jewish victims had been tortured to force them to confess to this crime so that a political dossier could be used against Jewish emancipation. In a context of Anglo-French and Catholic-Protestant rivalries, it would also discredit the proto-Zionist Protestant movement. This rivalry continued throughout the nineteenth century in the Orient, particularly in Palestine.

On 5 June 1840, an article was published in *Sud,* a Marseilles newspaper. It exposed the Jews' alleged "implacable hatred" against the nations, but especially against Christians, victims of their barbarous ritual murders, their usury, their perfidy and their rapacity. In spite of Jewish demoniac machinations, profusely expounded by the author, the Holy See had always dealt kindly with this nation, the enemy of mankind. The Jews—the article claimed—were only waiting for the moment to subjugate and assassinate Christians. Since their emancipation, Jews were accused of acquiring immense wealth by extorting money from Muslims and Christians. In Asia and Europe, they had displayed a crazed insolence with their bogus prophesies of a future restoration in their homeland:

> The current insolence of the Jews, both in Europe and Asia, the alleged prophesies that they put into circulation, their constant efforts to recreate themselves into a national body, their immense wealth, all this has attracted little attention from our so-called politicians, solely occupied in winning or retaining ministerial appointments. But this influence, these false prophesies, even these efforts have for some years been noticed by all honest men, by all true Christians.

The author then concluded by stating:

> Whatever will be the end result of this horrible affair [the disappearance of Father Thomas and his servant], it demonstrated this truth, that between followers of the Thalmud [*sic*] and the Christians, no peace whatsoever is possible, and that the deicide people is the irreconcilable enemy of Christians and Muslims.

The *Sud* article was reprinted in the section "Faits Divers" (Miscellaneous facts) of a two-volume book published in Paris by Achille Laurent, *Relations Historiques des Affaires de Syrie depuis 1840 jusqu'en 1842.*[25] It reproduced the complete procedure conducted by the French consul with the justification of all his allegations against the Jews of Damascus, and of Judaism. The book also included a description and a historical survey of the alleged ritual murders performed by the Jews on their Christian victims. One notices throughout, and in the letters and newspaper articles republished in the "Faits Divers" pages, a permanent current aimed at associating Muslims and Turks in the anti-Jewish accusations and hatred expressed by the French consular authorities and the local Churches. Before and after its publication in 1846, wide publicity was given in the French government-influenced and clerical press to these alleged Jewish ritual crimes.

French and Vatican Arab Policy: The Anti-Jewish Fulcrum

The great Arab uprising against the Ottoman sultan which France had sought in the 1830s did not occur for want of a concept which would unify ethnically diverse and mutually hostile populations. The missionaries who had flocked to the Levant helped to fill this gap. From the 1840s they set about teaching and modernizing the Arabic language, the centralizing pole of a future Arab nation which would detach the Arabic-speaking provinces from the Ottoman Empire. Thus, the concept of an Arab nation was born in the French Catholic missions of the Levant. After the massacres of Christians in Syria between 1840 and 1860, the Christians clung to Arabism in order to surmount the religious conflicts and strengthen a policy of rapprochement with the Muslims.

The Damascus Affair marks the start of a French opposition to what can be called proto-Zionism. It combines the colonial interests of French imperialism in the Arab provinces with the exploitation of an anti-Jewish theology. The French protectorate over the Catholic *rayas* directed them to Arabization, and used them as agents of its anti-Zionist Arab policy. Simultaneously, the Judeophobic campaign frequently renewed blood libel accusations in Europe, in Russia, and in the Ottoman Empire where Christian *rayas* endeavored to associate with Muslims. This was the beginning of the polarization of the Eastern Christian communities, Arabized by Catholic missions, in the anti-Jewish and anti-Zionist campaign, and the appearance of a theme that was to have a great future: a struggle that would unite Christians and Muslims against the "Jewish enemy."

In April 1847, the British consul in Beirut, Colonel Hugh Rose, informed Lord Palmerston that a Christian child in Dayr al-Qamar (Lebanon) having disappeared, the Christians immediately accused the Jews. The French consul-general, Bourée, secretly advised the Turkish governor in Damascus, Kiamil Pasha

> to refer the matter to the Grand Vizier as one of peculiar importance. Mr. Bourée assumed the fact that the Jewish religious ordinances do prescribe the use of Christian blood in their Paschal rites.[26]

The local Christians had asked the authorities to arrest all the Jews of Dayr al-Qamar, and nine were imprisoned. On instructions, however, Kiamil Pasha forbade the Christians in Beirut to insult or offend the Jews and he proceeded to examine the matter with justice. Consul Rose's letter continues:

> As there was no evidence against the Jews, except the vulgar belief that they used Christian blood in their Paschal rites, and must therefore have killed the child, Kiamil Pasha ordered the Jews in prison at Deir el-Kamar to be set at liberty and brought to Beyrout, after the holidays, to answer any charge which might be brought against them. The Christians have declined to prosecute the Jews before a legal tribunal.

But the matter did not stop there. A month later, in collaboration with the French consul, the Christians of Dayr al-Qamar declared that "they had now found a Druze who had actually seen a Jew throw the body of the Christian child on the road." Rose informed Henry Wellesley, British minister plenipotentiary in Constantinople, that Bourée

> interfered three times to predispose the mind of the Turkish authority against them [the Jews], even going so far as to say that he felt convinced from what he had learnt at Deir el-Kamar that the Jews had murdered the child.

Referring to Viscount Palmerston's circular of 21 April 1841 concerning the protection of the Jews from oppression, Consul Rose tried to ensure a fair trial of the Jews by the Turkish tribunal. His efforts succeeded and he concluded his letter:

> The Jews were tried; the Druze evidence appears to have been imaginary for he never appeared; the prosecutor grounded his accusation principally on the allegation that the Jews use Christian blood for religious purposes.
> The Mehkame [tribunal] acquitted the Jews, firstly because there was no evidence whatever to prove that they had committed the murder, and secondly because the accusation that the Jews use blood in their religious ceremonies was disproved by the Firman received in Syria in 1841 which states that strict search had been made into the Jewish writings and that no trace of such a practice is there to be found.[27]

The same year, Joseph Simoni, the British consul in Damascus, informed Wellesley in Constantinople of an incident in Baalbek, following the incitement of Beaudin, the then acting French consul. Christians had "industriously circulated reports" of two other blood libels against the Jews—one concerning a Christian boy, the other a Muslim woman.[28]

In the wake of these events, similar accusations were renewed almost every year in the Ottoman Empire. Their instigators who caused the imprisonment, torture, and death of innocent people and the pillage of communities were never prosecuted as criminals. Ratti-Menton who was at the origin of this libelous campaign had the support of his government; he became a senior diplomat, receiving the decoration of Officer of the Légion d'Honneur in 1861, just before his retirement. Accusations and legal proceedings were aimed at establishing a political and judicial criminal record which was kept alive in the collective Christian consciousness by repetition. Emancipation may have abolished the walls of the ghetto, but they were thus replaced by gratuitous incitement to general hatred, incriminating the Jews collectively as a people, as well as their religion.

For the instruction of the faithful, a funerary plaque was placed in the chapel of the Latin Convent of the Capuchins in Damascus to perpetuate the memory of Father Thomas. The brief inscription in Italian, and the more explicit one in Arabic, accused "the Jews" of his murder. In December 1840, Sir Moses Montefiore went to Rome to request the pope to have this calumny removed from the church. He first met Mr. Aubin, acting agent for the British government, who reported to him the words of Signor Capucini, the Holy See's Under Secretary of State

> that all the people about the pope were persuaded that the Jews had murdered Father Tommaso, and even *if all the witnesses in the world were brought before the pope to prove the contrary*, neither he nor his people would be convinced, and he could do nothing more. [italics in the original][29]

His efforts to see the pope having proved unsuccessful, Sir Moses did meet Cardinal Riverola, the protector of the Capuchins, who told him that he could not order the removal of the stone because the Convent of the Capuchins in Damascus "was under the protection of the French authority, who had caused it to be erected."[30] Montefiore, however, had obtained the firman from the Ottoman sultan (6 November 1840) which refuted the practice of ritual murder in Judaism. After the retreat from Syria of the Egyptian army, the sultan ordered Sherif Pasha to liberate the Jewish prisoners in Damascus. According to letters received by Sir Moses, the Jews were freed

> to the great joy, not only of the Jews of Damascus, but also of all the Musulmans of that city. The unfortunate men were accompanied by bands of music, and thousands of persons, Jews and Moslems. They first went to Synagogue to return thanks for their delivery, and then to their respective dwellings. All the distinguished Mussulman merchants paid them visits of congratulations, expressing their firm belief in their innocence. The Christians maintained silence, denoting thereby their dissatisfaction at the justice of the Pasha [Sherif Pasha]. The blood of the four unhappy men who have died under torture has not been sufficient to satisfy these people.[31]

After the Dayr al-Qamar event—and other Christian blood libel accusations against the Jews in several places, including Jerusalem in 1847—the Jews of Rome wrote to Montefiore in May 1850 during the pontificate of Pope Pius IX:

> We are now more oppressed than ever; no Christian is allowed to be in a Jew's house, either as servant or companion. The pope will receive neither an address nor a deputation from the Jews.[32]

Although Prime Minister Thiers and Consul Ratti-Menton occasionally expressed doubts about the guilt of the tortured and imprisoned Jews in Damascus, they were both convinced that it was necessary to inform public opinion about the criminal nature of the Jewish religion, as was explained in the *Sud* article of 5 June 1840:

> We are very far from wishing to deduce from these precedents that the Jews, prosecuted at this moment in Damascus, are necessarily the assassins of Father Thomas; but it is important to enlighten public opinion about facts which are generally little known and which demonstrate that the attack of which the venerable monk was a victim, was not the first of the same genre, whereby the Jews, through a false and fanatical interpretation of their laws, have brought dishonor on themselves in [pursuance of] their secret rites, whatever the rabbis, great or small, and the advocate Crémieux can say.[33]

In the sphere of its foreign policy, France was pursuing the colonization of Algeria, while claiming in the Orient to be the protector of the Eastern Christians and the Muslims against a "Jewish peril," which it had invented for political purposes. This policy, endorsed by the papacy, sustained its prestige and Catholic control over the Christian Holy Places. The campaign to demonize the Jews, disseminated via church channels, undermined Protestant encroachments and particularly the British project to allow Jews to return to their homeland. In addition, Eastern Christians and their Churches were mobilized in this anti-Jewish struggle. The consequences of such a policy were described seventy years later by Henry Harris Jessup—a prominent personality in the American Presbyterian Church in Beirut. Having lived for fifty-three years in the Middle East, he described in 1911 the attitude of the local Churches to the Jews:

> They are hated intensely by all the sects, but more especially by the Greeks and Latins. In the gradations of Oriental cursing, it is tolerably reasonable to call a man a donkey, somewhat severe to call him a dog, contemptuous to call him a swine, but withering to the last degree to call him a Jew.
> The animosity of the nominal Christian sects against the Jews is most relentless and unreasoning. They believe that the Jews kill Christian children every year at the Passover and mingle their blood with the Passover bread. Almost every year in the spring, this senseless charge is brought against the Jews . . . the Jews of Beirut and Damascus are obliged to pay heavy blackmail every year to the Greek and Latin "lewd fellows of the baser sort" who threaten to raise a mob against them for killing Christian children . . . and not only do they regard them as children of hell but would rejoice to send them there if they could.[34] [inverted commas in the text]

The Protocols of the Learned Elders of Zion

Thus the return of the Jews to Palestine, contemporary with an immigration of Levantine Christian refugees, unleashed antisemitic passions in Europe. At the end of the century, French religious and extreme-right parties called for the abolition of the republican laws, the segregation of the Jews in ghettos—as had been done by Pope Pius IX in Rome—and the restoration of their traditional discriminatory status, in order to remove their means of political and economic action. Closely associated with the European antisemitic movements, the Eastern Churches—particularly the Palestinian Churches—integrated European antisemitism into the machinery of hatred and linked it to Arab-Muslim anti-Zionism. After the First Zionist Congress in Basle (1897), a two-stage Christian-Muslim strategy was developed: the fabrication of *The Protocols of the Learned Elders of Zion,* and its incorporation into Arab nationalism. Only this latter aspect will be examined here.

The Protocols were forged in Paris between 1897 and 1898 by plagiarizing a diatribe against Napoleon III, written by Maurice Joly in 1864. It is known that the original manuscript was written in French, but the clumsiness of the style indicates a foreign hand. The 1905 version of *The Protocols* in Russian differed from the previous book, published in 1901 by Nilus, a conspiratorial Russian monk; this new book claimed to reproduce the "minutes" of the first Zionist Congress. Despite a dig at the Protestants, it entreats the Christian world and its governments to overcome their divisions in order to unite against Judaism and Zionism. Actually, the most systematic propaganda in the 1880s and 1890s about the Jewish conspiracy emanated from the Jesuits as a reaction to Zionism.[35] In his masterly study on the origins and history of *The Protocols'* international diffusion, Norman Cohn describes the worldwide ecclesiastical networks that played a decisive role in their wide dissemination.[36] Moreover, France saw Zionism as a threat to the exclusive protectorate that it had exercised for centuries over Christendom's Holy Places in Palestine. After the emergence of Zionism, the linguistic concept of an Arab nation turned into a political militancy in favor of Arab nationalism—as an anti-Jewish, Muslim-Christian movement, strongly supported by the clergy.

The Protocols, a Christian work of anti-Zionist political theology, was symbiotically connected by Arab Christians with the concept of an Arab nation, an ideology uniting Christendom and Islamdom. This symbiosis is revealed in a book by Negib Azoury, *Le Réveil de la Nation Arabe* (*The Awakening of the Arab Nation*), published in Paris in January 1905. A Latin Catholic close to the Jesuits, Azoury was born in Lebanon in 1873, studied in Paris in the mid-1890s, and lived there toward the end of 1904 till 1908, frequently returning to Cairo. From 1898 to 1904 he was an assistant to the Turkish governor of Jerusalem, Kiazim Bey.[37]

For Azoury, France and Rome represented two basic political poles of an Arab nation which extended over the whole Levant, except for Egypt. This Arab nation not only gathered Arab Christians and Muslims together in Palestine, but it also represented all the branches of Christianity. Hence,

Arabism embodied the nucleus of the Muslim-Christian symbiosis, bringing together the whole of Christendom and Islamdom against Israel. For Azoury, the pillars of this symbiosis would be the papacy, as a unifying force of Christianity in its entirety through the Uniate movement; and the Caliphate on the Muslim side. Both institutions, of irreproachable morality, would coordinate their activity in perfect harmony, under the political aegis and military protection and collaboration of France.

According to Azoury, the Ottoman sultan was unworthy to be caliph, and the caliphate should revert to an Arab prince who would exercise it in Arabia, a sort of replica of the Vatican. The caliph, a Muslim counterpart of the pope, would only exercise spiritual authority over all Muslims. Christians and Muslims, united in an Arab nation under French protectorate, would seal the alliance of Islam and Christianity in their common battle against Zionism. In his preface, he quotes at length his own manifesto, circulated to officials and notables in the Levant. He points out that the Arab movement "comes just at the moment when Israel is so close to succeeding, in order to destroy its [Israel's] plans for universal domination."[38] "With the aim of facilitating understanding of the *Jewish Peril,*" the author decided to examine "only the detailed geography of Palestine which constitutes a complete miniature of the future Arab empire."[39]

Azoury further explains that his present book "will allow the reader to realize the unique idea that we are recommending in our two books." He is referring to *Le Réveil de la Nation Arabe* and a forthcoming book, *Le Péril Juif Universel (The Universal Jewish Peril)*, both united in the same concept. The link between traditional Christian anti-Judaism and the Christian involvement in anti-Zionism and Arabism is thereby acknowledged. Azoury declares that he has exposed the universal nature of the Jewish peril from a new and entirely unknown point of view.[40]

Then, in the conclusion to a supplementary foreword, Azoury explains:

> In writing our two books, *Le Réveil de la Nation Arabe* and *Le Péril Juif Universel,* we have risen above all religious prejudice [regarding the differences between the Eastern Christian Churches], and set aside our own feelings and convictions. We have only envisaged the question from a political point of view, as we have studied it for six years in a post which we have recently relinquished, against the wishes even of the sultan, in order to undertake a sacrosanct work of patriotism, justice, and humanity. Throughout this entire period, we have been intimately linked with our compatriots and in constant contact with the Jews, whom we have observed in the very country which is the most active theatre of their silent and pernicious efforts.[41]

In his call for a Muslim-Christian unity under the dual spiritual authority of the pope and the caliph, in an Arab nation under French protectorate, Azoury develops the themes of *The Protocols*. He might have had direct links

or access to the forgers who fabricated them, all the more so as he repeatedly states—with his clumsy turn of phrase—that he is the author of the
forthcoming book, Le Péril Juif Universel.[42] Israeli historian Eliezer Be'eri
mentions that Azoury's book was published with assistance from the French
government or Catholic church support.[43]

Azoury had an important French contact in Paris, the director of the Imprimerie Nationale. In January 1906, back in Cairo—probably with French
government aid—he wrote to his French patron in Paris offering to organize an uprising in Syria in favor of France for 100,000 francs.[44]

In 1906, Farid Georges Kassab, a pro-Zionist, anti-clerical, Greek Orthodox Christian from Lebanon, published in Paris a virulent attack on
Azoury's book, in which he condemned papal policy which aimed at making the new Arab Empire into a branch of the Roman curia.

> What is extremely interesting and likely is that the Roman Curia, loyal to
> its principles and traditions, and with its shaven-headed groups is working to
> bring about the emergence of a Muslim kingdom. Solely to this end, and in
> an amicable way, it [the curia] will continue to recruit bands of sympathetic
> monks in Europe, send them to the East in order to help its establishment
> [the Muslim kingdom] and to prepare the hearts of Christians, instilling in
> them [Arab] national feeling and bring them closer to Muslims from whom
> they have been estranged.
>
> Because, and no one can doubt it, the Roman curia and its bands, such as
> the excellent and very reverend Jesuits, are actively and sincerely working to
> re-establish unity and love between [these] two indigenous peoples—
> formerly closely united, of the same race, of almost the same spirit, having
> the same language, the same history, the same government.[45]

In 1909, the Beirut Arab review, al-Machriq, printed Muhammad's alleged protection edict, contained in the ancient Chronique de Séert. This
apocryphal text informs Muslims of their duty to protect and love all the
Christians in the world, a religious obligation arising from the assistance
that Christians had given the Muslims in propagating Islam and in the
struggle against its enemies, particularly the Jews. This document stresses
the devotion of Christians to the Islamic cause,

> their steadfastness in observing the pact that they entered into after their
> interview with me [Muhammad] and to which I have agreed: because the
> bishops and monks showed unshakable loyalty in their attachment to my
> cause, the devotedness of their promises, confirming the propagation of my
> mission and by supporting my doctrine.[46]

The publication of this Judeophobic text in an erudite journal in 1909,
clearly inspired by local religious circles, was symptomatic of the combination of fear and aggressive deviancy which made up the context of dhimmi-

tude. At such a cruel period of Muslim-Christian strife, when entire Christian villages were being eradicated in Cilicia by fire and sword, the Syrian Churches attempted to protect themselves by deflecting the *jihad* onto the Jews—a modern stratagem which will be discussed later. This local element was compounded by antisemitic policies in Europe. After the First Zionist Congress in Basle in 1897—Negib Azoury attended the Seventh Zionist Congress in July 1905[47]—opposition to the restoration of a Jewish state in its Palestinian homeland was organized at a theological, strategic, and political level. In its thousand-year struggle against the Jews, the Church aimed to revive and exploit Islamic Judeophobia. On its road to independence, Israel had to confront the Church—both in the East and the West—that had driven it out of Jerusalem, condemning it to exile and degradation; at the same time, in its ancestral homeland, it would have to fight against the laws of *jihad* which imposed on Jews—and also on Christians—the humiliation of dhimmitude.

5

The Mandate Period (1921–1956)

After World War I the victorious Powers—France, Great Britain, Italy, and the United States of America—held the geostrategic keys to the Middle East. The disputed lands with their scarred borders were then still smoldering from the collapse of empires. Meeting at the newly created League of Nations in Geneva, the Allied Powers, masters of History, were then approached by the representatives of ancient peoples coming to testify to the ethnic pluralism in the Orient and to demand justice. Somewhat naively, they argued that war, extermination, and pillage should not alienate their rights.

President Woodrow Wilson's speech to the U.S. Congress on 8 January 1918, setting out the fundamental peace conditions, had confirmed their hopes. The twelfth point, referring to the Ottoman Empire, specified:

The Turkish portions of the present Ottoman Empire should be assured a secure sovereignty, but the other nationalities which are now under Turkish rule should be assured an undoubted security of life and an absolutely unmolested opportunity of autonomous development [. . .]

In his conclusion, Wilson emphasized that the entire peace program had a principle:

An evident principle runs through the whole program I have outlined. It is the principle of justice to all peoples and nationalities, and their right to live on equal terms of liberty and safety with one another, whether they be strong or weak. Unless this principle be made its foundation no part of the structure of international justice can stand.[1]

In fact, although the Entente Powers clearly accepted the ethnoreligious pluralism of the East, its recognition in terms of political geography and strategy presented virtually insurmountable difficulties.

Against this concept of states integrated into multireligious and cultural regional coexistence emerged the monolithic plan for a gigantic Arab Nation, free from all foreign interference and encompassing Arabia, Mesopotamia, Syria, Lebanon, and Palestine under the government of a supposedly enlightened caliph, in effect, Husayn, Sharif of Mecca.[2] Such a return to the seventh century situation would reconstitute the Islamic government of the Umayyad Empire, imposing dhimmitude as prescribed by the *shari'a* for Jews and Christians, who had only recently been emancipated with difficulty and through constant pressure and intervention by the Powers. This would not only negate the Wilsonian principle but would relegitimize Arab-Muslim imperialism over these peoples who had been its victims for centuries.

In support of his ambitious plan, Sharif Husayn referred to the tolerance shown to Christians by Umar Ibn al-Khattab, the second caliph to whom Muslim jurists specifically attribute the humiliating *dhimmi* status. In a letter to Sir Henry McMahon,[3] the Sharif of Mecca declared that "Christian brothers" would enjoy the same civil rights as Muslims, insofar as these rights accorded with the general interests of the whole Arab Nation. This reservation covered the restrictions Islamic laws imposed on non-Muslims. In the sharif's own country, Arabia, these laws prohibited his "Christian Arab brothers" from any expression of their religious worship and banned any Christian presence in Mecca and Medina.

France, whose zone of influence in Lebanon, Syria, and Cilicia (on the Turkish frontier) was included in the caliphate's plan, denounced the Sharif of Mecca's aspirations as an imperialist pan-Islamic policy, contrary to the concept of secular nationalism. Moreover, a decade earlier the same sharif had ordered the flogging at Mecca and Ta'if of some individuals found guilty of talking of freedom and the Turkish constitution after it was reestablished in Istanbul as a result of the Young Turk coup d'état of 1908.[4] In addition, whatever their differences, all religious minorities were agreed on one point: the need for European mandates to protect them. It was, in fact, in the Syrian desert of Dayr al-Zur that Kurdish and Arab tribes had completed the Turks' dirty work of eliminating the Armenians, and their aggression toward other minorities had with difficulty been controlled by promises of the caliphate's restoration.

Christian Nationalisms

Armenian

In the aftermath of a war in which France lost nearly two million men and Great Britain more than a million; when a third of the Lebanese population had perished in a famine imposed by the Turks (1914–17); and while Christian survivors of massacres and deportations were straggling along the roads in the Levant, a desire for freedom gave new hope to the remnants of peoples who had survived the desolation. The Armenians—after the genocidal horrors they had suffered and their support for the Allied armies—could hope that their national rights would be recognized. In January 1918, British Prime Minister David Lloyd George, French Premier Georges Clemenceau, and President Woodrow Wilson acknowledged Armenia's right to national existence. But the treaty of Brest-Litovsk between Turkey and Bolshevik Russia (3 March 1918) once again abandoned the territories of Transcaucasia, populated by Armenians, to the Turks. The Bolsheviks' volte-face and the Georgians' defection facilitated Turkish reconquest. As the Allies refrained from sending help, Turkish troops, with Azerbaijani forces, seized Baku (September 1918). For three days bandits and soldiers, aided by the Muslim population, indulged in pillage, extortion, rape, and torture of the Armenian population, some twenty thousand of whom were slaughtered.[5]

At the Paris Peace Conference (January 1919) the Armenian delegates, Avetis Aharonian and Boghos Nubar Pasha, pleaded their case eloquently. But while the Allies were drawing the frontiers of a mythical Armenia in the still-born treaty of Sèvres (10 August 1920), Mustafa Kemal (Ataturk), a military genius and an astute politician, gathered the dispersed Turkish army and put an end to any dreams of Armenian, Assyrian, and Kurdish independence by his devastating military campaigns. Embittered by Russia's defection, the Armenians demanded, in vain, an Armenian state in Cilicia under French or American mandate. The Allies, who had utilized them in their campaigns, now thought only of strengthening Kemalist Turkey against the Bolshevik threat, and to gain the goodwill of their colonized Muslim peoples from North Africa to India.[6]

Nestorian and Chaldean Assyrians

The murderous fury that had fallen on the Armenians did not spare other Christian communities. In the villages around Mosul, where both Armenians and Assyrians lived, massacres had caused the exodus of around 50,000 Assyrian-Chaldeans.[7] Almost as many men, women, and old people were tortured and killed, their churches burned down, and their precious religious texts that had been preserved for centuries disappeared in the destruction. Like the Armenians, they desperately tried to reach the British lines, fleeing Turkey. Several thousand more died of exhaustion and starvation in camps near Baghdad.

On 7 November 1918, the Anglo-French Declaration recognized the principle of an autonomous government for the Assyrians, and the following year the Assyrian delegation asked at the Peace Conference for a state stretching from Diyarbakir to Iraq, whereas others envisaged a territory in Upper Mesopotamia under British mandate. Appearing before the American King-Crane Commission in August 1919, the Chaldean patriarch demanded that Assyrian-Chaldeans and Jacobites be granted a state under European protection in their ancestral homeland, Mesopotamia and the Jazira (Iraq). But in August 1921, Britain—still dreaming of restoring the "Golden Age" of the Abbasid Caliphate throughout the whole Near East— entrusted the throne of Iraq to the Emir Faisal, third son of the Sharif of Mecca.[8]

In the course of discussions at the Lausanne Conference (December 1922) on the delimitation of the Turko-Iraqi frontier, the British delegate, Lord Curzon, remarked that the Nestorian Assyrians, driven out and decimated by the Turks, would fight to the death against the return of control "to a people who to them were the symbol of oppression." The Turkish delegate, Ismet Pasha, replied that the Nestorians had acted treacherously "towards their Muslim compatriots, *with whom they had been living side by side in complete tranquillity for centuries*" (italics, B.Y.).[9] At the Constantinople Conference (May 1924), the Turkish government rejected frontier adjustments in favor of the Assyrians. Citing the equal rights of all without distinction of race or religion, it stated that the interests of the Muslim majority should not be sacrificed to those of Christians because its national aspirations took precedence over all other considerations. The delegate added that the Nestorians "would still find in Turkish territory the tranquillity and prosperity which *they enjoyed there for centuries*" (italics, B.Y.).[10] It is noteworthy that the British delegate's reply contained the Nestorians' radically contrary opinion of their past, as well as these comments:

> In spite of their isolated position in the heart of a country under Turkish rule, the small Assyrian people, in the very early days of the Great War, determined to espouse the cause of the Allies and to seize the opportunity to break away from the rule of those whom their past history has led them to regard as their persistent oppressors. They endured great sufferings as the result of this decision. They were driven from their own country and died in thousands in their flight to Iraq.[11]

In the conclusion of its report on the frontier between Turkey and Iraq, the Commission recommended the protection of minorities and stated:

> We think, however, that the arrangements made for the benefit of minorities might remain a dead letter if no effective supervision were exercised locally.[12]

Syrian-Lebanese

During this decade (1915–25), while a million and a half to two million Christians—Armenians and Assyrians—were being exterminated and tortured or fled in terrified hordes along the roads from Mesopotamia and Syria, the Christians of the Levant remained as divided as ever.

The Lebanese Christians were indisputably the best endowed of all the non-Muslim peoples of the empire. Possessing an autonomous territory since 1861, they could boast the best schools in the East and formed the most free and developed community in the region. But despite these advantages, religious and feudal sectarianism deeply divided Lebanese society, while constant Christian emigration to the United States, Latin America, and Africa jeopardized the long-term political stability of Lebanon.

Already, at the First Arab Conference (Paris, 18–23 June 1913),[13] the arguments for Arab nationalism had hardly met with the unanimous approval of the Lebanese and Syrian Christians who formed half the delegation. At the 1919 Peace Conference, the Lebanese delegation, through the Maronite patriarch, Elias Pierre Hayek, asserted its total independence from Syria and claimed a specific historical and cultural national character, despite sharing a common language with the Arab world.[14] The Maronites in particular fiercely defended an autonomous Lebanese identity and demanded the return of territories—Beirut, Tripoli, and the Beqa'a—which had been assigned to them in 1860, and whose confiscation by Turkey had left Lebanon in a nonviable state.

Meanwhile, another Christian current, which was supported by Greek Orthodox, Uniates, and Protestants, and which divided the Maronites, rejected the idea of a Lebanese Christian and Jewish independence. Fighting for an Arab nation, which would be a secular version of the caliphate and would encompass Syria, Lebanon, and Palestine, and later even Iraq, this movement attracted clergy and laymen. Supported by the American King-Crane Commission (June 1919), it advocated the creation of a large secular, democratic, and multi-cultural Syria where complete religious freedom and minority rights would be guaranteed. According to the Commission, circumstances were propitious to attempt a "trial" of ethno-religious pluralism in an Arab state governed by King Faisal. Stating that a separation of religions and peoples would prove disastrous, the Commission recommended including Lebanon in an Arab state as a considerable Christian presence would counterbalance a "reactionary Muslim" policy. In the Commission's view, rather than confining their interests to the narrow bounds of a Christian Lebanon, the Lebanese should merge into a Syrian-Lebanese state, thereby participating in the needs and problems of the Muslim majority, and sharing its existence in order to understand "the other half."[15] An opinion probably strongly influenced by American missionaries, given the document's naively moralizing tone and its faith in the anticipated perfection of Faisal's future Arab government.

The divergences in Christian discourse corresponded to the religious sectarianism and political clientelism of the Christian minorities toward the protecting states. These differences, however, disappeared in one unanimous demand: the protection of a European or an American mandate. Thus, regardless of the contradiction, all the Christian leaders acknowledged the need for protection against the same Arab-Muslim populations with whom they were pretending to fraternize in the cause of Arab nationalism.

As for the Muslims of Syria, they specifically demanded a return to the caliphate. The notables and Bedouin chiefs supported Faisal's claims to the caliphate. His promise to free them from all foreign interference provided hope for a return to the *shari'a* and the old order, which had made of Syria and Palestine the most fanatical regions of the Levant for centuries.

Threatened by the caliphate's pan-Islamism and the return of dhimmitude, Eastern Christians were of two minds: some desired autonomy, others integration within the Muslim majority through a secular Arab nationalism. Even though the King-Crane report was generally regarded as propaganda at the time[16]—it called for an American mandate for Anatolia, Armenia, and the whole Levant—the report also included the basic ideas which were to constitute the credo of political movements until the present day. First, one finds in it the Manichean contrast between bad Turks and good Arabs. The Turks are attributed with all the vices of a fanatical oriental theocracy. The Arabs, on the other hand, are credited with a gloriously tolerant past. Hence, the magic formula of "Arab nationalism" was a guarantee that impartial justice and democratic institutions would be at the service of every citizen of the future multireligious Arab nation. According to the authors' report, this model of social perfection would be worth the sacrifice of Armenian, Lebanese, Jewish, or any other territorial independence. This proposal, supported by the American missionaries of the Syrian Protestant College at Beirut (later the American University), became the foundation of the total Arabization of Arabic-speaking Christians and of their struggle against any autonomist movement. The conclusion of the King-Crane report highlights, in order to disprove it, the contrary opinion held by some Christians:

> Certain Christians, on the other hand, affirmed that the sentiment of Syrian [Arab] Nationalism is new and feeble, and that the expressions of it made before the Commission gave a false impression. They claimed that the Christians who adhere to this view do so as making a desperate effort to live on good terms with the Moslem majority, and that the Moslems much prefer a pan-Arabic or Pan-Islamic scheme, and would quickly abandon Syrian nationalism if they saw a chance for the success of either of these ideas. (p. xxvi)

Jewish Nationalism: Zionism

Jews collectively avoided involvement in Muslim-Christian problems, unlike the majority of Christian Arabs who joined the fight against Zionism. Transmitted by the Arab Churches, by European pilgrims and through numerous contacts with France and Russia, Western antisemitism in its modern forms spread in the Levant through the channel of indigenous Christians.[17] Christian immigrants to Palestine, even though survivors of the massacres in Syria, Lebanon, and Iraq perpetrated by Muslims, supported the Jerusalem Churches—traditionally the most Judeophobic—and later became the most zealous servants of Islamic causes.

But other Christian currents expressed different views. In spring 1913, for example, some Christian members of the Decentralization Party and the Reform Committee in Beirut adopted a favorable attitude toward Jewish immigration into Palestine. Indeed, politicians—even Muslims, Arabs, and Turks—envisaged the possibility of some compromise with the Zionists at that period. However, the aims of these compromises were different for each group. In fact, if some Muslims accepted limited Jewish immigration, they saw it solely as part of the program to strengthen the *dar al-Islam* by the accretion of capital and technology.[18] Local Christians, on the other hand, were concerned about the emigration of their own people and about Ottoman policy aimed at settling in Syria tens of thousands of Muslims driven out of Macedonia by the Balkan wars (1912–13). These Christians viewed the autonomy of another minority—the Jews—as a stabilizing element in the region.[19]

From the outbreak of hostilities in 1914, the Turkish authorities had expelled more than eleven thousand Jews of Russian origin from Palestine. Housed by the British authorities in camps in Alexandria and Cairo, most of the able-bodied males enlisted in the British army where they formed a "Zion" army corps under the command of Joseph Trumpeldor. This situation jeopardized the security of their coreligionists in the Turkish provinces where any secessionism, whether ethnic or religious, was crushed with the utmost cruelty. As the British troops approached Jerusalem in March 1917, the Turkish governor of Syria-Palestine, Jemal Pasha, ordered the immediate deportation of three hundred Jerusalem Jews, threatening them with the same fate as the Armenians. In Jaffa several Jews were killed and about 8,000 cruelly expelled following an order of evacuation dated 28 March 1917, while the whole Jewish quarter was destroyed and pillaged by Bedouin hordes.[20] But Germany, afraid of being compromised by her Turkish ally, interceded on several occasions with Istanbul on behalf of the Jews, emphasizing the use that Allied propaganda would make of these excesses in the United States.[21] In Syria and Iraq large numbers of Jews and Christians had to enroll in the Ottoman armies or pay a ransom for exemption, sometimes even under torture. Those who refused were hanged, while hundreds of mobilized Jews never returned from the front.[22]

By the Balfour Declaration of 2 November 1917 the British government acknowledged that it viewed "with favour the establishment in Palestine of a national home for the Jewish people and will use their best endeavours to facilitate the achievement of this object [. . .]". The following year, the Muslim-Christian Association (MCA) was formed in Jaffa with the tacit approval of the British Military Administration in Palestine and developed branches in the country's principal towns.[23] Controlled by the Military Administration, the MCA formed the anti-Zionist political platform for Palestinian Muslims and Christians and constituted the political tool created by the British administration, directed toward the annulment of the Balfour Declaration. The ambivalence of British policy seems to have been a gesture in response to Islamic agitation, which was sustained by Mustapha Kemal's call to all Muslims to conduct a *jihad* against the Allies. In a letter of 19 December 1920 to Sir Herbert Samuel, the British High Commissioner, Musa Kazem al-Husayni, president of Arab (Muslim-Christian) Palestinian Congress—former governor of Jaffa during the last years of the Ottoman Empire—called for the restoration of the *shari'a*.[24] In another letter dated 12 February 1921 he informed the Secretary of State for the Colonies, Winston Churchill, that the Muslims and Christians of Palestine were asking, in the name of the Muslim and Christian world, for the abrogation of the Balfour Declaration.[25] On 28 March 1921 a delegation from the Haifa Congress, which included a large proportion of Christians, sent Churchill a memorandum which set out the arguments of *The Protocols of the Learned Elders of Zion*.[26] Arab nationalism and *The Protocols* became indissociable themes of the same Christian policy aimed at nullifying any Jewish rights to Palestine, under the Arab—and later the Palestinian—political label. A Jerusalem memorandum of 9 July 1921 to the High Commissioner from the executive committee of the Fourth Arab Palestinian Congress conjures up the idyll of a harmonious past coexistence of all elements of the population.[27]

Here it is important to examine the anti-Jewish arguments uniting Christians and Muslims, because they have determined important political developments of the twentieth century up to the present day. In a letter of 23 March 1919 the Jerusalem section of the MCA stated:

> One of the most important rules of the country is preventing the Jew from permanently settling in Palestine, but they are allowed to stay for a short period after which they are required to return from whence they came.[28]

The Muslim-Christian alliance against the Jews was based on the following principles as they were set out:

- The obligation to demand and to maintain the exile and dispersion of the Jewish people.
- That Palestine belonged solely to Christians and Muslims; they alone should control it and the Jews had no place in it.
- The Jews had no religious relics, nor connections with Palestine, and consequently had no historic right there.
- The Arabs were living in Palestine before the Jews.
- The MCA rejected the use of Hebrew as an official language and only recognized Arabic; it opposed the designation of towns and provinces by their biblical names.
- The MCA listed the diabolical characteristics of the Jewish people mentioned in *The Protocols of the Learned Elders of Zion* in order to demonstrate the peril of a Jewish state.
- The Arabs were the creators of science and of civilization whereas the Jews were destroyers and the agents of Evil.[29]

For a century, Christian and Muslim spokesmen constantly, and in unison, hammered out these affirmations; they amalgamated the Christian principles of supersession and deicide with the theological principles of *jihad*. After World War I, Ronald Storrs noted that "Arabism does not exist [. . .] Arab merits, defects, rights, and grievances are essentially local in character, even when reinforced by the Vatican and by the relics of Pan-Islam."[30] The British military and civil administration also strengthened the Muslim-Christian Arab camp: "Zionism had at least united (for the first time in history) Arab Moslems and Christians, who now opposed a single front to the Mandatory" (parenthesis in the original).[31] The statutes of the MCA were drawn up on 20 May 1920 under Britain's aegis, represented by Chief of Staff Colonel B. H. Waters Taylor. From the start, the Association received financial aid and support from the Mandate authority.[32] The British administration in Palestine was to become so antisemitic that in 1937 (speaking before the Peel Royal Commission) Colonel Wedgwood described the

> crypto-Fascist officials, whose objections to Parliament had taken the place of objections to the Jews; there is no change [possible] except by a complete reform of the Administration in Palestine.[33]

In Europe, where antisemitic violence was openly expressed at the beginning of the century, the possibility of Jewish sovereignty in Palestine aroused radical opposition from lay and ecclesiastical circles. The anti-Zionist struggle, shared by Christians and Muslims in Palestine, helped to strengthen their only common ground because, while the Muslims supported Islamic Pan-Arabism,[34] the Christians for their part desperately demanded the protection of a British or American mandate, depending on the political clientelisms of each community.[35] In addition, the Italian occupation of Libya (1911–12), the Balkan wars (1912–13), and the arrival of Muslim refugees from Europe, had exacerbated anti-Christian feeling. The shouts of "Palestine is our land and the Jews are our dogs," which accompanied Judeophobic demonstrations,[36] evoked Christian memories of those times when the word "Christian" was used rather than "Jew." The defeats that Christian armies had inflicted on Turkey and on the Muslim world for more than a century, and counter calls to *jihad*, combined with Islamic propaganda, provoked expressions of hostility toward Christians in Palestine. The sense of insecurity was particularly apparent among the Melchites, linked by their religious hierarchy to Greece, a country which dreamed of driving the Turks out of the Dardanelles and restoring in Constantinople the glories of Byzantium.

After Faisal was evicted from Syria by the French in July 1920, Syrian nationalists claimed that the Balfour Declaration and the French mandate over Syria and Lebanon broke promises that London had given the Sharif of Mecca. Although these accusations were belied by the Sykes-Picot and Husayn-MacMahon correspondence, the Foreign Office disseminated and utilized them in pursuance of its Islamophile policy, led by historian Arnold Toynbee, director of studies from 1925 to 1955 at Chatham House, the Royal Institute of International Affairs.[37] By challenging the legitimacy of Zionism, this propaganda aimed at disarming the hostility of Muslims in the British Empire. It also created guilt feelings in Arabophile British circles.[38]

World War I sealed the fate of Ottomanism, that is to say the utopia of a peaceful multireligious and multicultural coexistence in a country where the Islamic majority held political power. By attributing this defeat to Turkish fanaticism, Great Britain was able to resurrect the same utopia in the guise of Arab nationalism. The geostrategic interests of the mandatory states led to a conciliatory policy toward the Muslim populations. European colonial administrations, fearing the hatred of their colonized Muslim subjects, stifled the autonomist inclinations of the ethnoreligious minorities, based on national rights and concern for security. Whatever may have been Anglo-French rivalries in their Arab policy, Christians were invited to merge into the Islamic majority in order to become ferments of modernization and Westernization, guinea pigs for the new Arab formula of a Muslim-Christian symbiosis which was to fill the ideological void created by the collapse of Ottomanism. Arab nationalism, symbol of peaceful religious pluralism, was transmuted into an exclusive mystical dogma, an instrument for the destruction of all other cultures and any idea of independence.

However, the League of Nations had refuted the hegemonic claims of an Arab caliphate stretching from Armenia to Egypt and had recognized the ethnic and cultural pluralism of these regions, as well as the rights of non-Arab and non-Muslim indigenous peoples. Henceforth, the principle of self-determination developed at two conflicting levels: the level of the *umma;* and of the indigenous ethnoreligious minorities which it had colonized. Thus, the Muslims required that Europe recognize this principle—which was moreover a European concept—where they themselves were concerned, but refused to acknowledge it in respect of the peoples they had subjected, expropriated, and exploited. Only the Zionist project survived all obstacles. In fact, it provided the Muslim-Christian entente with a Judeophobic cement and an empathy in their anti-Zionist discourse at a period of total insecurity for the Christians.

At the San Remo Conference (April 1920) the League of Nations included the achievement of the Jewish homeland among the goals of the mandate assigned to Great Britain. The preamble to the mandate, which recognized the Jewish people's historical link with Palestine, henceforth grounded their right to a national home in international law. After the Lausanne Peace Treaty (24 July 1923), a legal and political framework formed by the mandates was set in place. The Zionists pursued the road to a territorial independence. The Christians in the Arab regions—except for the Copts and a Maronite faction—fought for Arab nationalism which became, in the name of Muslim-Christian symbiosis, the basis for the struggle against Zionism and against the colonial powers. The dice for the future were cast. Europe had set up two opposite dynamics: one leading to a sovereign Jewish state, the other to its destruction from a Muslim-Christian entente which it had created.

The Inter-War Period

The two decades of the inter-war period saw radical transformations in the Middle East. The Arab provinces of the Ottoman Empire were delimited by arbitrary frontiers to please the mandatory states, whereby new countries were created and constitutions promulgated: in Iraq (1924), Lebanon (1926), and Syria (1930), which confirmed the religious freedom and equality of their citizens.

The autonomist claims of Kurds, Armenians, and Assyrians were stifled by the emergence of two vast Arab entities: Syria and Iraq, under French and British mandate respectively. Having placed Faisal on the throne of Iraq after his flight from Damascus, Britain attempted to disarm nationalist opposition by attaching to Iraq the rich oil region of Mosul, claimed by Turkey (1925–26). The mandatory administration then equipped Iraq—one of the most backward provinces of the Ottoman Empire—with a national army, a government, a constitution (1924), and a parliament (1925).

The French withdrawal from Cilicia (Ankara Agreement of 1920) provoked the emigration of Armenians, Syriacs, Jacobite, and Uniates. In 1921–22 they abandoned their ancient villages in the Adana and Urfa region and fled behind the Anglo-French lines. A year later (1923) an exchange of populations took place: 1,300,000 Greeks left Anatolia against 400,000 Turks from Thrace. In 1925, some 150,000 Armenian refugees from the genocide were able to rejoin their coreligionists in Baghdad, Cairo, and other cities in the Middle East. Assisted by local communities and the mandatory governments, they rapidly achieved economic autonomy and even obtained important social positions.

Palestine, designated by the League of Nations Mandate as the Jewish national homeland, was stripped of three-quarters of its delimited area in September 1922. This new region now formed the Arab Palestinian Emirate of Transjordania under British mandate headed by the Emir Abdallah, the third son of the Sharif of Mecca. Jews were forbidden to reside there, whereas Christian refugees found security.

In June 1922, Winston Churchill published a White Paper defining British policy on Palestine. It specified that the Jewish people were there, "as of right and not on sufferance."[39]

The establishment of the mandates aroused intense political opposition in traditionalist and nationalist Arab-Muslim circles. Since the nineteenth century, European powers had not only supported, willy-nilly, the independence of the European Christian peoples subjected by the Turks, but they had imposed an autonomous regime on Lebanon (1860), invaded Egypt (1882), and North Africa between 1830 and 1912, as well as the Indian Sultanate. Now they were directly governing the Middle East, the very heart of Islam.

During 1924–25, the frontiers of the new Arab states placed under European mandate were stabilized, while the Christian populations of Anatolia and Mesopotamia—deported, seeking refuge, or fleeing war zones—continued to leave their homes for countries under European control or the United States. In 1925, the Muslim Kurds rose in revolt against the "atheist government of Ankara" and demanded autonomy, the restoration of religious laws and the sultanate.[40] The Turks crushed this revolt and took advantage of it to disarm the Assyrian-Chaldeans and Jacobite Christians who suffered plunder, rape, and assassinations before being deported.[41]

At the special request of the Foreign Office, the Anglo-Iraqi treaty (1930), which provided for a British withdrawal, included no guarantee for the Assyrians. It considered that any separatist measure would damage Assyrian integration into the new state which, being Arab, could be expected to be democratic and tolerant. Scarcely convinced of this truism, the Assyrians requested that they be granted an autonomous territory and be concentrated in one region. The Colonial Secretary opposed it, objecting that the triviality of the religious quarrels did not justify a system of guarantees, which might hinder the integration of the Assyrians, and consequently do them a disservice. In addition, publicizing their fears could only strengthen religious animosity against them.[42] As a result of this attitude, the Assyrian situation became untenable: having supported the Allies during the war and supplied the British with auxiliary troops (levies) to crush the Kurdish and Shi'ite rebellions, they now saw themselves sacrificed to London's Arabophile policy.

Britain withdrew from Iraq in 1932, leaving total power to King Faisal. That summer, the Iraqis, with tacit British support, brutally crushed an uprising by the former levies. The following year (March 1933), the Assyrian patriarch, Mar Eshai Shimun, was invited to Baghdad where he was imprisoned on a charge of having asked the Permanent Mandate Commission for a system of autonomy. Saved by British intervention, he was taken to Cyprus. Five months later, on the orders of Prime Minister Rashid Ali al-Kaylani, Iraqi forces, commanded by General Bakr Sidki, mowed down six hundred Assyrian men, women, and children at Simel, near Mosul. Bedouins and Kurds then joined in the slaughter, in which sixty-five Nestorian villages in northern Iraq were plundered and burned down, priests were tortured, and Christians were forced to renounce their religion, while others in Dohuk were deported, and about a hundred were shot.

In 1934, the Assyrians again called for an autonomous area under European mandate in their homeland. The scheme failed, impaired by the colonial authorities' policy of Arab appeasement. The patriarchs of the Jacobite and Chaldean (Nestorian) Uniate churches (united with Rome) took a totally different line. Advised by the Vatican, they proclaimed their loyalty to the new Iraqi state and total confidence in the goodwill of their Muslim compatriots.

The massacres of the Armenians and Assyrians had terrorized all the non-Muslim communities of the Middle East. They had seen the Armenians and Assyrians betrayed and abandoned to slaughter, even though they had trusted the European states and joined the European war against the Turks in the hope of obtaining an area of freedom in their ancestral homeland. Without an army or any military experience, conditioned by centuries of servitude, seduced by fallacious promises, they had thrown themselves into the war, giving unstinting aid to the Allies.[43] Henceforth victims of self-interested bargaining and intrigues by the Great Powers, decimated and outlawed, they were the very incarnation of the demise of hope. At the time when the provisional Constitution of Iraq was being drafted, the Assyrian–Chaldean hierarchy even refused a specifically Christian representation to the Chamber of Deputies, alleging that the Christians had total confidence in their Muslim compatriots. It accused the Europeans of utilizing "Christian rights" in order to divide Christians and Muslims. One of their newspapers recalled the fate of the Assyrians and Armenians "who put their trust in the Christian powers of Europe and were practically exterminated in consequence."[44]

These events provoked a new exodus of about ten thousand Nestorians and quickened the flow of Christian emigration to Europe and the United States, to Syria and Lebanon under French mandate, or to Transjordania and Palestine under British mandate. Syria benefited economically from this Christian flow of refugees; the French authorities settled at Homs, Damascus, and Aleppo a hundred thousand Armenians, Assyrians, Jacobites, and Uniates who had fled Anatolia and Iraq. In August 1937, another massacre of Christians at Amuda, in the Jazira under Syrian administration, gave further impetus to the Christian autonomist movement. Anticipating the withdrawal of the French mandate in 1939, this movement, led by Cardinal Ignatius Tappuni, stressed the dangers incurred by Christians in northeastern Syria and elsewhere and called for measures which would guarantee the security of all communities. The transfer of the sanjak of Alexandretta to Turkey in 1939 caused the further flight of thousands of Armenians to Syria.[45]

Traumatized by these events, the Syrian Christians committed themselves totally to the doctrine of Arab nationalism. The most intransigent exponents of a Muslim-Christian brotherhood, they dedicated themselves to extolling at both a political and a literary level the greatness and tolerance of Islamic civilization. Enthusiastic supporters of a great secular and democratic Arab nation, they fought against the existence of autonomous states based on the cultural, historical, and linguistic pluralism of the East; a pluralism which had justified the independence of Lebanon and the Armenian, Assyrian, Kurdish, and Jewish nationalist movements. Rejecting religious sectarianism, the Christian Arab nationalists proceeded to de-Christianize and deculturize their community. This development which favored Marxist militantism, or Islamization in subsequent decades, caused divisions inside these communities between the religious hierarchies and the forces of secularization.[46] In particular, it raised a problem of political identification between traditional religious loyalty and pan-Arab political, even pan-Islamic, militantism.

In Palestine, mutual mistrust and hostility between Muslims and Christians continued to exist despite the colonial administration's efforts to unify their positions. The Turkish victories over the Greeks in 1924, the conflicts in Mesopotamia and Syria, and the Islamic masses' hatred of Western Christian rule had poisoned Muslim-Christian relations. Moreover, recurrent anti-Jewish violence since 1920 culminated in the uprisings of August 1929, when Arab bands plundered villages and districts, killing 133 Jews, and injuring 339 more in Jerusalem, Hebron, Safed, and elsewhere. The uprising followed a Jewish request for authorization to place a few benches and a screen in the two meters narrow passage in front of the Western Wall of the Temple Mount in Jerusalem, where for thirteen centuries Jews had paid the Muslim authorities for the right to pray at their holiest shrine, often to the sound of jeers. After spending some months debating the crucial problem of the right of a few elderly Jewish men to sit down when praying, the British administration settled for the status-quo in favor of the Muslims who carried on a violent campaign ranging from huge demonstrations to multiple petitions "to safeguard their religious rights."[47] The severity of the pogroms prompted the British to react with a few executions and fines from which Christians were exempted as they had barely participated in the riots. This situation exacerbated the animosity of the Muslims who criticized the Christians for their passivity. The murder of a Christian journalist, Jamil al-Bahri, by a Muslim the following summer divided the two communities still further. Sporadic attacks on Christians by bands of Muslims occurred in many Palestinian towns, and in Lod a church was desecrated.[48] Some Christian notables presented petitions to the administration denying any connection with the MCA and the Muslims.[49] In the years that followed, the tragedy of the Assyrians in Mesopotamia and the worsening of religious tensions worried the Christians in Palestine, prompting them to draw closer to the Muslims. In a confidential letter to the Colonial Secretary on 15 August 1931, the British High Commissioner, Sir John Chancellor, explained:

> Christian Arab leaders, moreover, have admitted to me that in establishing close political relations with the Moslems the Christians have not been uninfluenced by fears of the treatment they might suffer at the hands of the Moslem majority in certain eventualities.[50]

In December 1934 the Muslim Supreme Council (MSC) pronounced a *fatwa* forbidding the sale of Palestinian land on the grounds that it belonged to Allah. Strong pressure was applied to persuade Christians to participate in this campaign, with Islamic overtones. Only one responded: a Greek Orthodox, Ilyas Qanawati, who publicized a statement warning that "whoever sold or acted as a broker in selling even the smallest part of [. . .] the motherland to the Jews [. . .] would be considered as one who had betrayed Christianity and might expect the Church's curse and excommunication."[51] During the Arab revolt (1936–39), which involved very few Christians, bands of villagers and Bedouins sowed terror by extortions and pillage. If the Christian villagers refused to supply them with men, weapons, and provisions, their vines were uprooted and their women raped. The rebels forced the Christian population to observe the weekly day of rest on Friday instead of Sunday and to replace the tarboosh by the kaffiyeh for men, whereas women were forced to wear the veil. Often orders to boycott

Jews also included Christians. At the end of 1936, when Lebanese Christians obtained recognition of Lebanon's autonomy which their Muslim compatriots disputed, the anti-Christian campaign in Palestine intensified. Muslims marched through the Christian village of Bir Zayt near Ramallah chanting: "We are going to kill the Christians."[52]

Under the British administration, Palestinian Christians, privileged by their education, obtained positions of responsibility, which increased Muslim animosity.[53] This social ascent also caused Christian opposition to Jewish immigration, a source of economic competition but also a dynamic of development.

The situation was different in Egypt, where for a period of some generations an aristocracy close to the Palace and a Muslim intellectual elite did their utmost to foster modernization of the country and a change in attitudes. Whereas in Syria Arab tribes who formed the majority of the population outside the towns retained a sense of Arab-Islamic unity, in Egypt an autonomist policy distinct from pan-Arabism had been growing since the time of Muhammad Ali. Nevertheless, the Islamic University of al-Azhar in Cairo remained a pan-Islamic and xenophobic center fighting for restoration of the *shari'a*. Lord Cromer, the British governor (1883–1907), and his successor, Sir Eldon Gorst (1907–11) thought they could allay this hostility by a policy of marginalizing the Copts.[54] Since the reign of the Khedive Ismail (1863–79), the Copts, together with the Jews, had been associated with the vast politicocultural movement led by Muslim liberal intellectuals. On this basis, Muslims, Copts, and Jews joined together in the Wafdist movement, fought for Egypt's independence and the emergence of modern political and legal institutions.

Founded in 1919 and led by Sa'ad Zaglul, the Wafd succeeded in forcing Britain to accept the independence of Egypt in 1922. Many outstanding Copts militated in this party and when Zaglul died in 1927, a Copt, Makram Ebeid Pasha (1888–1961), took over the leadership. In 1923, the Egyptian constitution recognized certain guarantees for non-Muslims and the equality of all religions in accordance with established custom.[55] Within the Wafd, Coptic personalities such as Wissa Wassef, Makram Ebeid Pasha, and Salama Mussa fought for a secular state, separation of religious and political power, equality of rights, and a total British withdrawal. This struggle attracted a large number of Jews that included Léon Castro, Joseph Cattaoui, and Zakki Orebi.

At this period, Jews and Christians, helped by the postwar situation, economic development, and above all political liberalism, gained distinction in the press and the industrial sector. After independence, however, the Egyptian government encouraged discrimination against the employment of Jews.[56] The nationality law of 27 February 1929 required that Jews—and only Jews—should provide proof of uninterrupted residence in the country since 1849, which was often impossible to supply; less than ten percent succeeded. The Jews, former Ottoman subjects, now became a stateless population of "local subjects," discriminated against on the job market. Moreover, King Fuad's claims to the caliphate was reiterated by his son Faruq (1936–52). The creation of the pan-Islamist confraternity of the Muslim Brothers in 1928 fueled a re-Islamization of the political apparatus and an intensification of koranic teaching in schools. At that time the rector of al-Azhar, Mustapha al-Maraghi, in order to discredit the popular Wafd party, accused the Copts of controlling it and launched a press and radio campaign against them. In February 1938, al-Maraghi proclaimed on the radio that for Muslims to befriend Copts was to go against Allah's law; he also declared that Egyptian social, political, and legal institutions had to be based on religion.[57]

Ambiguous Security

The establishment of mandates which transformed Arab-speaking provinces into Europe's semi-colonies gave rise to immense frustration. The Muslim masses and the traditionalists had hoped that the return of the caliphate would restore the *shari'a* and, consequently, annul the freedoms that had been granted to non-Muslims under pressure from the West. However, not only did the *dar al-Islam* continue to diminish, but the humiliation of occupation by infidels now affected mainly the Arabs. Victorious Europe, with its numerous technicians, imposed new legislation everywhere and improved public safety and administration. The communications network, the public education, and the health sectors were expanded, gradually breaking down traditional social structures. The departure from the Arab provinces of the Turkish administrative cadres left a void which in Iraq and Syria was often filled by Christians and Jews, educated at local European schools. Modernization allowed members of the religious minorities to gain distinction in the civil administration, banking, industry, journalism, and cultural life. Churches, monasteries, and synagogues were built or restored, publicly confirming the existence of the erstwhile humiliated tolerated religions. The Syrian Jazira—a depopulated region, traversed by bands of nomads until World War I—was transformed into rich agricultural land by the afflux of Christian refugees from Turkey. However, the improvement in living conditions and the proclamation of a Lebanese republic in 1926 did not interrupt Christian migration to the towns, to Europe, and to the Americas.

In reality, even if the era of dhimmitude had apparently ended under the guardianship of the colonial regimes, traditional political positions continued to exist and the orientations of the *umma* remained irreconcilable with that of the minorities. Despite different tactics, the minorities were seeking a region where they could enjoy security and freedom. Assyrians, Maronites, and Jews envisaged it in the form of autonomy, whereas the Greek Orthodox and Protestants looked to secularism to obtain it by a change in the political institutions of Muslim societies.[58] Two conflicting principles confronted one another: territorial sovereignty, or dilution within the Islamic environment to restrain its intolerant factions.

The contradictory tendencies among Christians did not only express the differences between the protecting states but, more precisely, Christian vulnerability in a period characterized by massive population movements which threw tens of thousands of Christians on the roads, fleeing to zones under European protection. Terrified by the barbarity of the reprisals punishing autonomist rebellions, those refugees who had abandoned home and country were particularly responsive to Arab nationalism, the only hope of integration into their Islamic environment. In fact, so traumatizing was the experience of massacres and deportations of the past decades that each Christian community voiced views reflecting its own need for security in its specific environment.

For example, at the Paris peace conference in January 1919 the Jacobite bishop of Syria and future patriarch Ignatius Afram I Barsum defended the rights of Arabs rather than those of his community to the great delight of the Arab delegation.[59] The repercussions within the Palestinian Greek Orthodox communities of the conflicts between Athens and Istanbul have already been noted. Although the Melkite communities' desire at the beginning of the century to Arabize totally the religious hierarchy was based on linguistic factors, it still revealed their sense of vulnerability at the time of the Greek-Turkish wars, a vulnerability compensated by a rhetoric glorifying Islam coupled with a virulent denigration of Christianity and Europe professed by their most nationalist intellectuals.[60] Observers noted in 1926 that "the dearest thought of every young local Orthodox Christian [Melkite] is that he is an Arab, and his most cherished aspirations are those of Arab nationalism, which he shares with his Moslem fellow countrymen."[61] Some ten years later another witness noted that the Jews in Palestine were unanimously for Zionism, whereas on the Arab-Christian side, solidarity transcended the old divisions between Muslims and Christians.[62] The hysterical and paranoid Arabophilia of Khalil al-Sakakini, a Greek Orthodox Palestinian, like so many of his coreligionists, expresses the acute sense of his own vulnerability. Above all, it offered a community—only recently barely tolerated—the opportunity to assimilate into the majority at a price of constantly adopting anti-Jewish policies, coupled with defamation of the West and, sometimes, even of one's own religion.[63]

In short, the three options open to Christians—autonomy (Assyrians),

secular nationalism (Syrians), a call for European mandates (Lebanese)—
were all totally rejected by Islamic circles who specifically demanded the
reestablishment of the caliphate, the end of all foreign interference including the principle of secularism, and a return to the *shari'a*. Moreover, to
Muslims, the protection of the European mandates, demanded by the
Christians, symbolized a humiliating domination by infidels.

The colonial administrations readily favored the interests of the Muslim
population in an effort to gain their support. At a political level, an ambigu-
ous relationship combining interdependence and hostility was set up between colonizers and Christian minorities. Arnold Toynbee's turnaround
has already been mentioned (see note 37). The denial of the Armenian
genocide, their indictment for the massacres of which they were the victims, the abandonment of the Assyrians, and the delegitimization of Zionism by invoking fictitious pledges to the Arabs, were symptomatic of the
disrepute henceforth sullying the ethno-religious communities' aspirations
to freedom.[64]

After World War I, Arab-speaking Christians, conscious of their vulnerability, totally supported the nationalist and anti-Zionist policy of their Muslim compatriots. But the dice were loaded, for the struggle of Muslims
against colonialism, channeled into pan-Arabism or pan-Islamism, were
rooted in a historic theological bedrock of wars against Christendom. The
frustration and humiliation caused by Christendom's superiority and its
victories rebounded on the Christian *dhimmis* whom Europe had emancipated.

Thus, the period 1920–40 offers contrasting aspects. Under the colonial
regimes, Christians and Jews enjoyed complete freedom at an economic
level and were present in the highest strata of the political organs in Egypt,
Iraq, and—for Christians only—in Syria. Nonetheless, their position remained tenuous and dependent on the colonial administration. This combination of political and economic progress by the ethnoreligious
minorities, on the one hand, and foreign occupation on the other, further
compromised them and concealed the real precariousness of their position. This vulnerability increased during the 1930s when the polarization
of forces which led to World War II locked them into the geostrategic and
economic interests of the Great Powers.

Taunted with their attachment to the *dar al-harb*, non-Muslims were
blamed even more for their rapid ascension on the social ladder, an easy
adaptation to modernity, and their inventive ability which made them the
leaders of economic and industrial development and catapulted them into
positions of prestige and authority. To the traditionalist Muslim populations, the total reversal of the Islamic social order brought about by the
colonial administrations constituted the supreme humiliation. At the political level, the struggle to restore non-Islamic sovereignty over land con-

quered by *jihad,* whether this undertaking was independentist (Lebanese or Zionist) or secular militantism opposed to the *shari'a,* represented the same ideological commitment of the two People of the Book. It was the same effort to break the theological alternative between *jihad* or the *dhimma,* and to enforce recognition of equal rights. The first option involved armed confrontation; the second choice imposed the compromises of dhimmitude. Although the goals were similar, the current of Arab nationalism, integrated into the anticolonial struggle, appeared to be the trend of the future.

Muslim-Christian Anti-Zionism

The principle of a national homeland in Palestine for the Jews, an indigenous population reduced in the Holy Land to the lowest level of dhimmitude by Muslims, and to theological contempt by the Churches, appeared blasphemous to the Muslim and Christian Arab world. The Vatican pursued the policy initiated by the Church Fathers in the fourth and fifth centuries. The Church had based its supersession theology on the eventual disintegration of Palestinian Jewry, the banishment of Jews from Jerusalem and their relegation to a degraded status. Henceforth, the defense of Islam now became the Vatican's weapon to prevent the restoration of the Jewish state.

The Christian teaching on the Jewish people—a fallen deicidal people—is directly relevant to our subject because it links theological anti-Judaism to the political delegitimization of the State of Israel. In his analysis of *The Protocols of the Elders of Zion,* the French sociologist Pierre-André Taguieff explains the ecclesiastical origins of the shift from anti-Judaism to anti-Zionism, as expressed by the Jesuits since 1898.[65]. Because Zionism represented an unacceptable challenge to the Church's doctrine, the Vatican fought it unremittingly.

In a letter from Jerusalem, dated 25 January 1919, Cardinal Francis Bourne, Roman Catholic Archbishop of Westminster, regarded Zionism as a movement which was "quite contrary to Christian sensitivity and tradition." Jews could live in Palestine, "but that they should *ever again* dominate and rule the country would be an outrage to Christianity and its Divine Founder" (italics added).[66] In the course of discussions at the League of Nations in Geneva, on the provisions of the Palestine Mandate, Lord Balfour wrote to Sir Maurice Hankey, Secretary to the Cabinet, on the objections raised by the Vatican. He explained that

the Vatican would seem to have redoubled its efforts to stir up opposition to the draft mandate for Palestine as it stands at present. At all events the extent of the campaign undertaken by the Vatican can scarcely have been realised in London. It is no exaggeration to say that the reluctance of the French, Polish, Spanish, Italian and Brazilian representatives on the Council to discuss now the Palestine mandate [. . .] has been due to the representations which have been made to their Governments by the Papal representatives.[67]

In summer 1922, Ronald Storrs, then Civil Governor of Jerusalem, undertook a journey to Rome at his own expense to reassure Pope Pius XI who "had evidently been receiving alarmist reports as to the 'preponderating influence of the Jews.' "[68]

On 17 April 1937, Cardinal Eugenio Pacelli, Secretary of State and future Pope Pius XII, declared on the occasion of his visit to the seven basilicas of Rome:

Bow your head, my Christian brethren, before these sacred altars, and remember that a crucified God intended to make us the Chosen People, and that He, destroying the only Temple which the ancient deicide people had been granted [*distruggendo l'unico tempio concesso all'antico popolo deicido*], revealed the infinity of his compassion by taking delight in being with us and among us.[69]

Even after World War II, *L'Osservatore Romano* (14 May 1948) commented on the restoration of the State of Israel:

Modern Zionism is not the true heir of biblical Israel, it is a secular state, and for this reason the Holy Land and its sacred places belong to Christendom, the true Israel.[70]

In July 1949, *La Documentation Catholique*, the official bulletin of the French Catholic Church, following the publication of the encyclical *In Redemptoris Nostri*, declared:

[W]e have now, after careful investigations, arrived at least at part of the truth, and we can only agree with a statement frequently heard that Zionism is Nazism in a new guise.[71]

This was a period when—through Catholic channels in Europe—Nazi criminals were still seeking refuge in Arab lands, in Latin America, and in other countries.[72]

The Christian response to Zionism developed in two areas, at the level of theological doctrine and the political aspect involving European interests in Muslim countries. After the Balfour Declaration (1917), and especially the League of Nations' recognition of the Jewish national home in Palestine, anti-Jewish propaganda linked to slanderous and racist indoctrination spread throughout Europe, bolstered by overwhelming political, religious, and economic forces. In spite of Jewish and strong Christian opposition during this period, those movements strengthened the networks of the anti-Jewish International in the West, the United States, Latin America, the Arab countries, and especially in Syria and Palestine. Anti-Jewish political polarization, defined in a racist perspective by Hitler in his *Mein Kampf* (*My Struggle*) (1925), would lead inevitably to the Shoah, the consequence of an intentional policy of plundering, eradicating, and exterminating the Jews in a "final solution."

The political domain of European anti-Zionism then encompassed a considerable number of factors. For the Vatican, and certain currents in the reformed Churches, anti-Zionism played a crucial role in its rapprochement with Islam. It allowed the hostility of the Muslim world to be focused on Zionism. It still provided the Churches and the Vatican with a role as privileged allies to Muslims by the dissemination of antisemitic Arab propaganda in Europe.

At the level of states, the anti-Zionist policy corresponded to the interests of Europe in the Muslim world. In this respect, it scarcely differed from that adopted for the Eastern Question concerning the Christian peoples in the Ottoman Empire. But, whereas for Christians the Churches and public opinion attempted to restrain the state's political cynicism, anti-Zionism on the other hand—with a few exceptions—aroused a general consensus. In addition, the Armenian genocide which Europe could have opposed more firmly, and the sacrifice of Armenia on the altar of a European-Islamic entente created pent-up frustrations which were released by the demonization of the Jews.

The sacrifice of Christians to Muslim antagonism is discreetly alluded to by Jerusalem Governor Ronald Storrs:

> The supposed indignation of "His Majesty's sixty million loyal Indian subjects", who appeared alternatively under the journalese disguise of "Moslem Susceptibilities", delayed many reforms in the Near and Middle East, kept several million Orthodox Christians as "Rayahs" under Ottoman domination, and helped to paralyse intervention in the torture and massacre of countless innocent Armenians.[73]

After World War I, the mechanisms in the functionality of anti-Zionism in Euro-Arab policies and in a Muslim-Christian symbiosis, were established: first, the diversion onto the Jews of the hostility of the Muslim peoples, colonized and humiliated by Europe; second, the Euro-Arab alliance and cooperation against Zionism, notably in the program to exterminate the Jews in World War II; third, the Muslim-Christian rapprochement.

The Mandatory powers and particularly local Christian communities, themselves threatened by the wave of Islamic Arabism, directed all nationalist frustrations into the struggle against Zionism, even defining its political arguments.[74] Most virulent were the Palestinian Churches, heirs to an old Judeophobic tradition. The conspiratorial theories of *The Protocols of the Elders of Zion,* and accusations of ritual crimes—frequent among the Greek Orthodox communities—were brought together in Nazi antisemitism.

The American millionaire Charles Crane, one of the cosignatories of the 1919 King-Crane Commission's report, who became the patron of George Antonius, a Lebanese Greek Orthodox, was an enthusiastic admirer of Hitler and Nazism. Antonius had been one of three members of the abortive "Ligue de la Patrie Arabe," founded by Negib Azoury at the turn of the century, which was based on the antisemitic "Ligue de la Patrie Française" (the third member was Eugène Jung). At meetings with Arab leaders organized by Antonius in the 1930s, Crane mingled theological and political anti-Judaism to convince them of the maleficence of the Jews and Zionism.[75] These concoctions reached Muslims through Christian channels and formed the basis of the Muslim-Christian alliance cemented in anti-Zionism, while in the country itself the Arab revolt against Palestinian Jews (1936–39) bred an inflammatory instability which led the British government at that crucial period to limit Jewish—and only Jewish—immigration into Palestine by the White Paper of 1939.

However, the interests of the colonial powers and of the Arab-speaking Christian minorities did not always coincide and were often contradictory. For the many members of Arab Christian communities, the anti-Zionist battle provided a breathing space and enhanced their position as agents for transmitting Christian antisemitism throughout the Islamic world. It supplied them with an anchorage in an Islamic environment where religious identification was detrimental to Christians, generally associated with European colonizers or with the Greeks, who were considered as the traditional enemies of Islam. Moreover, Christian support strengthened the Muslims position with the Western governments. Although some Muslim notables understood the strategic advantages of the Christian alliance, yet prejudice remained deep-rooted among the people and in religious circles. In the 1930s, the insecurity felt by Christians induced self-hatred, a rejection of Christianity and a tendency toward Islamization.

Other Christian factions, particularly the Maronites, nevertheless dissociated themselves from anti-Zionism. The Maronite Patriarch of Antioch, Antun [Antoine-Pierre] Arida (1932–54), condemned the persecution of the Jews in Europe and welcomed cooperation with Zionists. He considered the Zionist ideal as a model for Lebanon and advocated a small Christian state, a land of refuge for the persecuted. While the Arab press, both Muslim and Christian, extolled Nazi ideology, Mgr. Arida rejected it and wished to cooperate with the Zionists, praising their work of reconstruction in Palestine.[76] In Beirut in 1945, a pamphlet in Arabic, French, and English, entitled: "S.O.S. Lebanon: A Homeland for the Christians of the Near East" was widely circulated. Prepared by the historian Fuad Afram Bustany's group and the Maronite Archbishop of Beirut, Ignace Mubarak, who assumed responsibility, it rejected the term "Arab" as erroneous when applied to all the Christians in the Orient. After recalling the miserable *dhimmi* status of the past, it affirmed that Arabism equals Islamism (see appendix 3). The pamphlet's cover and title page included a pertinent quotation from Mgr. Arida himself.[77] The Vatican responded to this "provocation" by elevating the Syriac patriarch, Ignatius Tappuni, to the rank of cardinal. Newly arrived in Beirut, Tappuni stood at the head of 3,500 worshippers; he was appointed senior Catholic prelate to the Lebanon.[78] Vatican policy obliged the pro-Zionist Patriarch of Antioch to resign in 1954, and attempted to turn away pro-Israeli postulants, contrary to the community's wishes.[79]

From the beginning of the thirties, Nazi propaganda spread successfully in Arab countries where its antisemitic themes aroused enthusiasm and general support. Calls to murder Jews created a climate of hate. From the 1920s, free antisemitic brochures were widely distributed, as well as Arabic translations of *Mein Kampf* and *The Protocols of the Elders of Zion.*[80] The first Arabic translation of *The Protocols* from the French edition appeared in the review, *Raqib Shayun* (15 January 1926), published by the Roman Catholic community of Jerusalem.[81] This propaganda, repeated by the Arab press and radio, was contested by the Egyptian Jewish community, but its legal actions were obstructed by the government.[82]

Arab anti-Zionist agitation was at its most virulent in the French Arab colonies and in territories under French mandate. In North Africa the anti-Jewish movement spread from one town to the next, erupting into pogroms in Rabat, Casablanca, Oran, Mostaganem, and Sus; in Constantine, twenty-five Jews were killed in 1934, including six women whose throats were cut and three small children, while dozens were gravely injured. In 1936 the ulema of Algeria, obeying instructions from the Grand Mufti of Jerusalem, Haj Amin al-Husayni, ordered a general boycott of Jews.

In Syria under French mandate, the nationalist parties called for total independence. The return to Turkey of the district of Alexandretta, coveted by the Syrians, heightened French-Syrian tensions. In these difficult circumstances,—and as a diversion—a Syrian government-backed Committee for the Defense of Palestine organized a Congress at Bloudan (near Damascus) from 8–10 September 1937. The five hundred delegates from neighboring Arab countries included a considerable number of Christian intellectuals, members of the upper clergy and a journalist representing the Nazi press agency.

A former prime minister of Iraq, Naji as-Suweidi Pasha, was nominated as president of the Congress and informed the participants what should be their ultimate goal:

> Besides it was not enough to appeal to moral principles. [. . .] It is our duty to exterminate and finish off this parasite [Palestinian Jewry] currently established in a part of the Arab body, otherwise it will threaten us with extermination.

One of the vice-presidents of the Congress was Amir Shakib Arslan, a Syrian Druze, who represented the Syrian-Palestinian Congress to the League of Nations in Geneva. Editor of the periodical *La Nation Arabe* from 1930, later financed by the Nazis, Shakib Arslan proposed that an appeal be made for the defense of Palestine to Christian religious leaders, as well as to Muslim dignitaries worldwide.

The Mufti of Jerusalem was forbidden to participate by the British authorities but sent a message of support. The intervention of the Greek Orthodox Bishop of Damascus, Mgr. Ignatos Hereké, representing the Patriarch, called for a Muslim-Christian union against Zionism, as did many other speakers. Bishop Hereké also pleaded for a Muslim-Christian entente:

> Let us imitate the Jews, let us unite. The Crusaders of the Middle Ages had pretended that they were guaranteeing the security of the Holy Places [. . .] Since then, the Arabs are the noblest keepers of the holiness of these places, beginning with Umar Ibn al-Khattab who conquered them, until Salah al-Din ibn Ayyub [Saladin] who pushed back the aggresssors.

Among the many working commissions, one dealing with propaganda planned the dissemination of books and tracts in the Islamic, Arab, and Western worlds. It also decided on the dispatch of delegations and the development of anti-Zionist opinion, by brochures and lectures to be given in schools, mosques, and churches.[83]

Anti-Zionist agitation continued to erupt in the ensuing years in the territories under the French mandate and in the Syrian-Lebanese press. In British India, Nehru and the Muslim deputies showed their hostility to Zionism; in Brazil, Lebanese-Syrian emigrés created a propaganda office. Italy intensified its antisemitic and anti-Zionist broadcasts in Arabic from a radio station in Bari. European secret agents supplied Palestinian terrorists with arms. International anti-Zionism before World War II became a vast movement of pro-Arab solidarity, structured and disseminated by intellectuals, politicians, and networks of mosques and churches.

Until 1939, Nazi ideology was propagated on billboards, by information bulletins in the Arab press, through personal contact, by the financing of travel to Germany and of scholarships to study there.[84] In Palestine, on the

Prophet's birthday in May 1937, Italian and German flags were flown side by side with portraits of Hitler and Mussolini.[85] This militancy combined antisemitism and the Arab struggle against colonialism.

After 1939, weapons and money from Germany poured into Arab nationalist circles, in particular to the Palestinian Arabs. Hitlerian propaganda, expounded on no fewer than five weekly radio programs to Arab countries, was particularly active in Syria where the Palestinian Arab High Command operated. Spread by Arab intellectuals, this propaganda intensified after the visit by Nazi officers in 1937. Contacts also became closer between top-level Germans and Muslim religious leaders, including the most distinguished among them, such as the Mufti of Jerusalem.[86]

Many paramilitary organizations on the fascist model were created in Arab countries between 1937 and 1939. In Egypt the list included the Blue Shirts (Wafd), Green Shirts, Territorial Army (royalist), and the religious militias of the Muslim Brothers. All these youth organizations kept an atmosphere of revolt alive in the Arab capitals. In August 1939, the Egyptian cabinet of the Germanophile Prime Minister Ali Maher included several pro-Nazi and Muslim Brotherhood ministers.

Anti-Judaism created identical situations throughout the Arab world: economic discrimination, sporadic assassinations, the burning of synagogues, bombings, and attempted murders. In Iraq, dozens of Jewish civil servants in the ministries of Finance and Transport were dismissed in 1934. The following year a decree limited the admission of Jews to state secondary and high schools. Emigration to Palestine was prohibited and the teaching of Hebrew forbidden, except when reading the Bible, and then without a translation or any interpretation. Inflammatory sermons in mosques and massive demonstrations punctuated by shouts of "Death to the Jews" encouraged violence. Jews were stabbed in the streets or in their shops in Aden (1933), Baghdad (September 1936), Basra (1936), and Damascus (1938). Bombs thrown into synagogues claimed several victims in Baghdad (September 1936), Beirut (24 July and 7 August 1938), Cairo, Mansurah, Mahalla, and Asyut (July 1939). The Nazi victories intensified this campaign; fired with enthusiasm, mobs announced a great massacre of the Jews.[87]

During 1941, contacts at the highest level were maintained between the Nazis, Arab nationalists, and Egyptian and Iraqi officers. In April, Rashid Ali al-Kaylani, allied to the Axis forces, seized power in Iraq. The presence in Baghdad of the Mufti of Jerusalem, an enthusiastic ally of Hitler, spurred a campaign of provocations, arrests, and anti-Jewish violence. Despite Rashid Ali's flight on 29 May at the approach of the British forces, Iraqi soldiers, police and members of youth groups seized Jewish pedestrians, bound them hand and foot, and threw them under the wheels of tramcars; others were stabbed. Murder, pillage, rape, and the burning of Jewish shops and houses continued for two days during which 170 to 180 Jews were killed and several hundred injured.[88]

On 28 November 1941, the Mufti of Jerusalem, accompanied by Joachim von Ribbentrop, the German minister of Foreign Affairs, met Hitler in Berlin to discuss the Arab-Nazi alliance and the methods to exterminate the Jews. At the end of December, al-Kaylani—strengthened by the support of the Arab nationalists—submitted a plan to the Germans for a treaty between Germany, Iraq, Syria, Lebanon, Transjordan, and the Palestinian Arabs.

The pro-Nazi revolt in Iraq aroused immense enthusiasm in Egypt. For young army officers like Anwar Sadat, impatient to throw off British guardianship: "It was the first sign of the liberation of the Arab world, and we [the officers] followed the course of the revolt with admiration."[89] Distrusting the Egyptian army, the British authorities forced it to evacuate the Mersa Matruh region (November 1941). When the Afrika Korps arrived in El-Alamein in 1942, crowds shouted "Rommel! Rommel!" in the streets of Cairo.[90]

With Europe in the north occupied by the Axis, and the pro-Nazi hysteria of the Arab peoples in the southern and eastern Mediterranean, Oriental Jewry was virtually trapped. The Vichy government ruled over the French Arab colonies in North Africa, Lebanon, and Syria, while fascist Italy controlled Tripolitania, and Rommel stood at the gates of Alexandria. In the East, Arab nationalists in Baghdad had already shown their intentions by fomenting a massacre of Jews in 1941, which British troops, camped outside the city, had failed to prevent. During this same period, Jewish youths in Baghdad, Cairo, and elsewhere formed self-defense groups. Brave they certainly were, but their resources were derisory in such a context.

6

From the Jewish Exodus to
the Christian Exodus

After World War II the Arab nationalist movements intensified their fight against the Jewish national liberation movement. The main justification for this struggle was drawn from the legal and historic foundations of dhimmitude, mandatory for Jews no less than for Christians, as the crushing of the Armenians and Assyrians in previous decades had demonstrated. Anti-Zionist terrorism was merely the modern version of *jihad*.

Conscious of this danger and aware that the mandates would soon end, Arabic-speaking Christians committed themselves totally to anti-Zionist Arab nationalism, a policy which was moreover encouraged by Britain, France, and the Vatican. The amalgam of fear and traditional anti-Judaism formed a corrosive ideological terrain which structured, inspired, and guided certain aspects of the anti-Zionist policy expressed by the Christian wing of Arab nationalism.

Since the 1930s, close contacts based on ideological affinities had united Muslim nationalist leaders with the Nazis. Consequently, many Nazis found asylum after the war in Egypt and Syria where they held important posts under Arabized names. Cairo, seat of the Arab League, created in 1945 with British Foreign Office influence, became a political cauldron. Pan-Arabists and Islamists, led by the Muslim Brotherhood, stirred up political violence, strikes, and riots against the discredited regime of King Faruq and the British occupation. Invited by the king, who backed the Islamists, the Mufti of Jerusalem, Haj Amin al-Husayni—fearful of being tried as a war criminal at Nuremberg—found refuge in Egypt from May 1946, before moving to Beirut in 1962. During the war the Allied forces were able to control the situation and impose security, but the withdrawal of their armies and the nationalist and xenophobic violence which accompanied the Arab countries' struggles for independence contributed to a deterioration in the situation of all the Jewish communities throughout the Middle East. The Arab press in general launched an anti-Jewish campaign and some newspapers, particularly *Misr al-Fatat* (Egypt), published extracts from *The Protocols of the Elders of Zion*.[1]

173

In Damascus, rioters plundered the Jewish quarter in January 1944 and again in May 1945. The following month Jacques Franco, assistant director of the Alliance Israélite Universelle school of Damascus, was murdered. On 18 November—the Muslim holiday of Qurban Bairam—a rowdy mob led by students attacked the Great Synagogue in Aleppo, beating some elderly men and burning prayerbooks in the street.

In Egypt, the anniversary of the Balfour Declaration brought anti-Jewish agitation in Cairo, Alexandria, Mansurah, Tanta, and Port Said, leaving some ten dead and 350 wounded (2 and 3 November 1945). Initiated by the Green Shirts of the "Young Egypt" (*Misr al-Fatat*) organization, led by Ahmad Husayn, thousands of demonstrators burst into the streets, shouting "Death to the Jews!" In Alexandria demonstrators went on a rampage, burning the Jewish quarter where they stabbed and raped many, and destroyed three synagogues and the Jewish hospital. In Cairo, rioters plundered and set fire to a synagogue and communal premises. Old-age homes, schools, and hospitals were completely ransacked. Twenty-seven Torah scrolls were desecrated and burned in the streets. During the weeks preceding the pogroms, the aged, nearly blind, Chief Rabbi Haim Nahum reported receiving threatening letters. In the press, secular and religious leaders exhorted him to condemn Zionism and denounce the Balfour Declaration.[2]

The fever reached Libya where more pogroms took place from 4 to 7 November 1945 in Tripoli and the surrounding area: Zanzur, Zawiya, Cussabat, and Zitlin. At least 130 Jews were killed, 450 seriously injured, and others forced to convert to Islam, while about two thousand were driven from their homes; shops were destroyed, nine synagogues attacked, and twenty-five Torah scrolls and more than two thousand prayerbooks desecrated. According to an official report by the president of the Tripoli Jewish community, Zachino Habib:

> In order to carry out the slaughter, the attackers used various weapons: knives, daggers, sticks, clubs, iron bars, revolvers, and even hand-grenades. Generally, the victim was first struck on the head with a solid, blunt instrument and, after being knocked down, was finished off with a knife, dagger, or, in some cases, by having his throat cut.
>
> In Zanzur and Amrus [Suk al-Juma'] in particular, after having killed or injured their victims, the attackers poured benzine or petroleum over them and set them on fire, and ultimately those killed were so charred as to be unrecognizable. Grenades were used especially at Amrus against the synagogue as well as the houses. On some of the bodies signs of unimaginable cruelty could be discerned.[3]

According to observers, rioters of all ages pillaged and slaughtered to cries of "*Jihad fil-kuffar*" (*jihad* against the unbelievers); the women encouraged them with shouts of joy, while wealthy Muslim notables stood by as passive onlookers.[4] The memorandum of the Jewish community stated:

> The Arabs attacked Jews in obedience to mysterious orders. Their outburst of bestial violence has no plausible motive. For fifty hours they hunted men down, attacked houses and shops, killed men, women, old and young, horribly tortured and dismembered Jews isolated in the interior [of the country]—all of this with the proven complicity of the local Arab police and the most absolute inertia on the part of the administration and armed forces of the occupying power [British Military Administration] responsible for protecting order.[5]

It is noteworthy that such criminal acts against the Jewish civilian population were perpetrated after World War II in Arab countries under French control (Syria and North Africa) or British rule (Aden, Egypt, Libya, Palestine).

In the ensuing years, the anti-Jewish campaign in the Arab world intensified, with Jewish quarters attacked and synagogues and houses burned down (Damascus, 1947). Bombs were thrown at schools and synagogues in Beirut (May 1946), Alexandria (January 1947), and Libya (June 1948). In Aleppo in December 1947, the populace killed an indeterminate number of Jews and set fire to seven synagogues—including the most ancient one— and broke into 60 shops and 150 houses. Jews were arbitrarily arrested and tortured, and emigration to Palestine was prohibited on pain of death.[6] In British-controlled Aden, mobs attacked the Jewish quarter on 2 and 3 December 1947, burned down schools and thirty houses, plundered 114 shops, killed 82 Jews and injured 76, according to the official count. In the Sheikh Othman refugee camp for Yemenite Jews, houses, schools, businesses, and synagogues were set alight and plundered.[7]

As early as 19 January 1948, the World Jewish Congress (WJC) had submitted a detailed memorandum to the United Nations that included the text of a law drafted by the political committee of the Arab League. In view of the pogroms that had already occurred, and the statements made at the General Assembly by Arab spokesmen that, should the UN Resolution 181 (Palestine Partition) of 29 November 1947 be implemented, Arab governments would not be able to guarantee the safety of the Jewish communities, the WJC expressed its worst fears that "the very survival of the Jewish communities in certain Arab and Moslem countries is in serious danger unless preventive action is taken without delay."[8]

On 18 January 1948, in a long documented article, the WJC announced that its president, Dr. Stephen Wise, had called on U.S. Secretary of State George Marshall to intervene. Its opening paragraph stated:

> Between 800,000 and a million Jews in the Middle East and Africa, exclusive of Palestine, are in "the greatest danger of destruction" at the hands of Mos-

lems being incited to holy war over the partition of Palestine. [inverted commas in the original]

This article, with its final subheading: "Crime of Arabs is Genocide" appeared less than three years after the end of World War II, and almost a year before the United Nations General Assembly adopted the Convention on the Prevention and Punishment of Genocide and the Universal Declaration of Human Rights (9 and 10 December 1948). The article warned:

Acts of violence already perpetrated, together with those contemplated, being clearly aimed at the total destruction of the Jews, constitute genocide which, under the resolutions of the General Assembly, is a crime under international law.[9]

The day after Israel's declaration of independence (15 May 1948) the armies of five Arab countries, assisted by Arab Palestinians, invaded the new state. Fiery sermons in Arab capitals, calls to carnage amplified by loud speakers in the streets, and broadcast by radio produced a climate of collective hysteria. The humiliation of the defeats and the traumatizing exodus of the Palestinian Arabs from the battle zones exacerbated tensions. Jews in Arab countries were indiscriminately stabbed in the streets, and bombs were thrown at their homes, shops, and synagogues. In the Cairo Jewish quarter on 6, 20, 28 June and 17–20 July, 1 August, and 22 September 1948, more than 60 Jews were killed and 400 wounded. Attacks took place in Beirut on 3 and 9 January, 24 May, and in July 1948; and in Baghdad on 27 April 1948. In Damascus in February 1948, bombs were placed in the Jewish quarter, and on 5 August 1949 scores of Jews were killed and wounded when a bomb was thrown into a synagogue.[10] On 7 June 1948, at Oujda in French Morocco, on the border with Algeria, rioters stabbed five Jews and injured thirty, plundering stalls and houses;[11] the same evening, in nearby Djerada, thirty-nine Jews were killed and thirty more seriously injured, out of a Jewish community of about a hundred; on 12 June, in Tripoli (Libya), under British rule, Arab bands again plundered the Jewish quarter, killing a hundred and twenty and injuring and mutilating several hundred more men, women—including the elderly—and children.[12]

At the governmental level these pogroms carried out by mobs were accompanied by a policy of terror, anonymous threats, dismissals, and economic harassment with sequestration and confiscation of property. In Egypt, Iraq, and Syria Jewish students and teachers were expelled from the universities and civil servants dismissed, mail censored, and houses subjected to searches and investigations. Arbitrary arrests were made at night, while the immediate eviction of Jews from public places, police surveillance, prohibition on travel, and extortion of funds expressed a sadistic revenge against defenseless communities. Young Jews defied the prohibition and braved the dangers of emigrating to Palestine; if arrested, they were imprisoned and tortured, even executed after Zionism was declared a capital crime.[13]

In March 1950, the Iraqi government promulgated a law authorizing Jews to leave Iraq on condition that they abandoned all their possessions and left with a maximum of £50 per adult and £20 per child. The *fatwa* by Sheikh Muhammad al-Kharisi forbidding the purchase of their property forced them to abandon it. From June 1950 to June 1951, more than 110,000 Jews emigrated to Israel, an additional 13,000 or so had fled clandestinely via Iran in the preceding years. In 1952, no more than 6,000 Jews remained in Iraq from a community numbering 140,000 in 1949, which had originated after the Assyrian and Babylonian Exiles of the eighth to the sixth centuries B.C.E.

After the Arab-Israel armistice of March 1949, discriminatory measures against Jews in Arab lands decreased, but Israel's victory and the humiliation of the defeats strengthened xenophobia. Political violence and criminal outrages increased, although the ideology and political anti-Zionist discourse differed from the revolutionary agitation carried on by communist and nationalist groups. The numerous Nazi war criminals who had found asylum in Egypt and Syria orchestrated a campaign of anti-Jewish defamation.[14] Arab and Islamic nationalist circles flaunted admiration for Hitler and his regime, denying the genocide of the Jews and the extermination camps. This commonplace attitude was voiced in tones of derision in Egypt as early as the 1950s, well before it was converted into a negationist theory in France.

In the following decades, the wars of 1956, 1967, and 1973 revived political tensions. Police measures hardened and the arrest of large numbers of Jews in Syria, Egypt, and Iraq took place in 1956, and again in 1967, with torture, expulsions, dismissals, and hangings (in Iraq, January and August 1969).[15] Bloody riots also broke out in Tunisia, Algeria, and Aden.

Only Lebanon pursued a different policy, all the more remarkable in its environment of hysterical hatred. In 1947 and 1948, and in 1967, Christian police forces protected the Jewish quarter of Beirut, Jewish refugees from Syria and Iraq were welcomed, and no discriminatory measures were decreed in spite of the arrival of Arab Palestinian refugees.[16]

Indeed, the pro-Zionist trend of Mgr. Arida continued during the 1940s under the leadership of the Maronite Bishop of Beirut, Mgr. Ignace Mubarak. This Christian nationalist movement, which had wide popular support, especially in Mount Lebanon, called for a Christian Lebanese homeland for Eastern Christianity, alongside a Jewish Palestine. On 30 May 1946 a Maronite-Zionist treaty was signed between the Maronite Church and the Jewish Agency. However, under pressures from both France and the Vatican, this Christian trend calling for a free Lebanon was marginalized and defeated, even though Mgr. Mubarak maintained this position in his courageous letter of 5 August 1947 to the chairman of the UNSCOP Committee of Enquiry on the Palestinian Question.[17]

It would be superfluous here to describe in detail the wave of violence which swept through the whole Near East and Maghreb. Xenophobia revived the old traditions of the *dhimma*, camouflaged by terms such as Arab nationalism and socialism. The Arab *dhimma* replaced the Islamic *dhimma*. The Arab-Israeli conflict released a latent hatred, formerly held in check by the Western colonial administration. Sporadic, like a recurrent fever, it worsened in the 1950s and the 1960s awakening the tradition among the populace to plunder and kill the *dhimmis* with impunity. Some governments—in Tunisia and Morocco—strove to control popular fanaticism, but in Libya, Syria, Egypt, and Iraq it was the authorities who tolerated, even encouraged, the violence against innocent civilians by mobs inflamed with widespread calls to murder. The Arab nationalists who released these collective passions spoke the same language of hatred and contempt as in past centuries.

At the World Islamic Congress meeting in Amman, Jordan, on 22 September 1967, it was resolved:

> *Jews in Arab Countries:* The Congress is certain that the Jewish communities living in Islamic countries do not appreciate the Muslims' good treatment and protection over the centuries. The Congress declares that the Jews residing in Arab countries who contact the Zionist circles or the State of Israel do not deserve the protection and care which Islam provides for the free non-Muslim subjects living in Islamic countries. Muslim Islamic [*sic*] Governments should treat them as aggressive combatants. Similarly, the Islamic peoples, individually and collectively, should boycott them and treat them as deadly enemies.[18]

Thus, Jewish communities, which had survived for thousands of years, disappeared from Arab-Muslim lands within a generation. Their crime was to have had links with those who had rebelled against the *dhimma* and had liberated a part of their ancient land.[19]

These events, however, were integrated into a wide context of guerrilla warfare against British and French colonization. European rule represented the *dar al-harb*'s humiliating control—responsible for the limitation of the *shari'a*—and the unlawful emancipation of Jews and Christians, who now benefited from equal rights with Muslims. The revolutionary climate was also a product of deep-seated social, economic, and political changes, often accompanied in the Orient by coups d'état, purges, and executions. The economic recession following the war and the rural exodus worsened the misery of an illiterate sub-proletariat, victim of poverty, unemployment, and political demagogues.

"After Saturday Comes Sunday"

In the conceptual and political context of *jihad*, Zionism represented for the Jews the only means of freeing themselves from the *dhimma*. Among Christian Arab nationalists, the same desire for emancipation took the form of the struggle—not without its dangers—to secularize Islamic society. Consequently, the Islamists' battle, coupled with anti-Zionism, was also directed against Christians too. In Egypt, on 27 March 1947, the Coptic church of Zagazig was burned down during a religious service by members of the Muslim Brotherhood. The burning of other churches in Alexandria and Upper Egypt at that time was accompanied by anti-Christian demonstrations punctuated by slogans such as:

Today it is Zionism's turn, tomorrow it will be Christianity's; today is Saturday, tomorrow will be Sunday.[20]

In Egypt, the Muslim Brotherhood demanded the restoration of the *shari'a* and the Islamization of the state, while in Lebanon the centrifugal forces of Pan-Islamism fought for Lebanon's integration into Syria, and for an ending of Christian political power. The Emir Abdallah of Transjordan, brother of King Faisal of Iraq, wrote in 1947 that Arab nationalism had to restore the government of the Koran and the *shari'a*, which had been replaced by European law under the Turks.[21] For Nuri al-Sa'id, prime minister of Iraq, Arab nationalism, linked to Islam, represented "an aspiration to restore the great and tolerant civilization of the early Caliphate."[22]

The uprooting of the Jews amid hysteria, pillage, and murder heightened the Judeophobia of the Christian Arab nationalists, in particular Greek Orthodox members. The anguished world of dhimmitude allowed neither solidarity nor compassion.[23] For the Jews, the history of dhimmitude was drawing to a close. Their hasty or clandestine departure and the abandonment of the vestiges of a millennial community existence—fully understood by Christians—was only one of the tragic episodes in their shared destiny, among those cataclysms which for a century had driven hundreds of thousands of Christians along the roads to exile.

At an economic level, Christian industrialists and merchants rejoiced at the eviction of rivals and the ruin of the whole Jewish commercial sector through nationalization, state confiscations, or pillage. At the political level, the anti-Jewish measures were integrated into a revolutionary context combining socialism and a progressive Islamization of the state-controlled institutions, particularly in Egypt under Nasser, which was soon to become a model for the Arab world. Consequently, Christian attitudes were expressed as a dialogue between two contradictory, yet complementary, Christian voices—a pro-Arab hysterical exhilaration, contrasted by a silent anxiousness—while an exodus of Christians, parallel to the exodus of the Jews, could be observed as early as the 1950s.

The Christian Struggle Against Dhimmitude

Egypt

Although Copts, Jews, and Muslims had joined forces to accelerate the secularization and modernization of Egypt, the Islamization of the state entailed different consequences for each religious community. For the Copts—thought to represent about ten percent of the population—a return to the condition under the *shari'a* which the Islamists had been demanding for more than a century, meant the restoration of dhimmitude with the marginalizing and humiliation of the Christian population— justified by the principle of the inferiority of non-Muslim religions. Hence, the Copts' opposition to the *shari'a* exposed them, together with liberal Muslims, to the vindictive rage of Islamist circles.

Nasser's accession to power in 1952 furthered the Islamization of national life. The abolition of the ecclesiastical courts in 1955 (Law 462) placed the Copts under the jurisdiction of national courts, presided over by Muslim judges (kadis), from which Christian judges were excluded. In cases where there was a conflict of laws, the Muslim judges applied Islamic law, under the terms of successive Egyptian constitutions (1923, 1930, 1956), which stipulated that Islam was the state religion. Under Sadat (1970–81), the 1971 constitution specified that "the principles of Islamic law are a principal source of legislation" (art. 2). This provision was qualified on 30 April 1980 when parliament adopted an amendment stating that the *shari'a* was *the* principal source of legislation. From 1971, the *shari'a* became the criterion for the constitutionality of laws, the basis for their promulgation or rejection.

The Ottoman firman of 18 February 1856, requiring the sultan's approval for the restoration, enlargement or building of new churches—no longer applied under British rule—was reinstituted by a ministerial decree in 1934. Thereafter, any church building, alteration of places of worship or interior restoration—even of a toilet—depended on obtaining a royal, later a presidential, permit which was seldom granted.

The Copts reacted by expanding the teaching of their civilization and language. In the political sphere the Association of the Coptic Nation[24] called for a secular and Egyptian constitution, freedom of religion, and equal rights. Assisted by the Muslim liberal current, the Copts protested strongly against the Islamic grip on all state institutions and thereby on the life of the nation. Their opposition to the clause making Islam the state religion was demonstrated as early as 1952 by a large number of articles in the press, in publications, memoranda, and petitions to the government. This resistance exposed them to the hatred of the Islamists, and when, in the 1970s, Sadat favored the latter in order to stifle the communists, anti-Copt violence erupted, during which churches were burned and Christians were lynched, robbed, abused, murdered, and raped.[25] In 1981, bloody riots and the burning of three churches in Zawya al-Hamra (a suburb of Cairo) caused thirty-five deaths, of which twenty-five were Copts. In addition, the civil war in Lebanon which the populace regarded as a religious conflict fanned tension. These events took place during Sadat's difficult peace negotiations with Israel. Vilified by the Islamic world, the PLO, and the international Left, excluded from the Arab League and the Organization of the Islamic Conference (1979), criticized by France which was opposed to an Egyptian-Israel peace treaty, Sadat also felt trapped by the Islamists' provocations. He worried that his tarnished public image risked weakening the Western support needed to rescue his country from the economic and other disasters of Nasser's rule. The attacks on Copts by Islamists, and the opposition of international pro-Palestinian lobbies—especially in France—to a peace treaty with Israel aimed at stifling his policy of reconciliation and modernization.[26]

On several occasions—in 1971, in December 1976, and during 1977—the civil and religious bodies representing the Copts sent petitions to the government, exposing the fanaticism, the violation of their rights and liberties, and the religious persecution which they were sustaining. In the United States and Canada, the Coptic diaspora set to work to denounce publicly the violations of human rights suffered by their coreligionists. The Copts, who proudly preserve the memory of their origin and history, understood that the re-Islamization of political life would condemn them to exclusion.

The Copts' struggle against this revived dhimmitude provoked violent reprisals led by the Islamists.[27] The plunder and destruction of Coptic houses and shops; the burning down and vandalism of churches, districts, and villages; threats and physical aggression against an unarmed civilian population; even collective killings have, tragically, filled the Coptic chronicles and columns in the international press since the 1970s. Numerous Muslims from among the people, the intellectuals, and political personalities strongly condemned this criminal activity. Some of them were assassinated—such as the writer Farag Foda (8 June 1992), defender of both secularism and the Copts. Others, who advocated a reinterpretation of their religious texts—allowing the ethics of the Koran to be related to modernity and a peaceful coexistence with other nations—persist in their struggle despite the dangers. However, the mixture and cumulative effects of poverty and illiteracy, coupled with tyranny and corruption, has maintained an explosive social background breeding fanatical demagogy.

Lebanon

It is difficult to embrace in all its dimensions the desperate and tragic war fought by the Lebanese Christians against the various Islamic, Syrian, and Palestinian forces, backed—at the international level—by a disparate alliance of the Arab League, the communists, and Third World forces, all sustained by European theological anti-Zionism. The struggle of the Lebanese Christians, like that of the Copts in Egypt, took place against a background of a millennial resistance, fought henceforth at a national level, and not as a religious community. In addition, the Lebanese war nurtured a dramatic and desperate internecine war, uniting feudal clientelism (Arabism, communism, Nasserism), and economical, political, and religious conflicts.[28] Indeed, corruption, blindness, the short-term policy of venality, and compromise all concurred in this descent into hell, when even the most honest and the most lucid were rocked by the contradictions and ambiguities of a binational Muslim-Christian state.

Lebanon rested on two pillars: hope of Muslim-Christian coexistence born in spite of the trauma of the 1860 massacres, and sustained by the Vatican and French colonial policies; and a fragile intercommunity equilibrium where Christian preeminence guaranteed the freedom of non-Muslims. With the insight of a statesman, Charles Malik, then Lebanese Minister for Foreign Affairs, posed the fundamental questions of Muslim-Christian coexistence in a speech, published in an article (1952) entitled "The Near East: The Search for Truth."[29] Truth, he declares, lies in the duty to know the Bedouin mentality, the mob's dominion over the leaders, and the pre-eminence of rhetoric over thought. He raised the essential question: whether compromise and modifications were possible in Islam, allowing a genuine awakening to "others." He lucidly pointed to the fascination of the Arabs with their past history, their desire to restore it in its integrality, and to the disturbing expansion of age-old fanaticism on the morrow of attaining independence.

Opposed to the political concept of the state, a missionary religious stream of thought appeared among some Lebanese Christians. Its most extreme terms were expressed by Abbé Youakim Moubarac (not to be confused with the pro-Zionist Bishop Ignace Mubarak), who favored an ever-growing missionary action to the whole Third World, at the service of Islamic aims while rejecting the nationalist formula of the state. As he put it:

> The problem boils down to this: are the Catholics going to make Lebanon a bastion or a radiant center in the heart of the Arab world.[30]

This trend refused the "regrouping of Eastern Christians within the frontiers of a small Lebanon" as an attitude of fear concealing a repressed desire for opposition, aggression, withdrawal, distrust.[31] "The small Lebanon curled up upon itself"[32] was unworthy of its mission and the bastion had to be changed into a wide-open center.[33]

This evangelizing conception of Lebanon envisaged Muslim-Christian coexistence in political utopias constructed on the basis of charity, love, and service. At the time when the Islamization process of the Middle East was accelerating, Abbé Moubarac was proclaiming his conviction that the separation between spiritual and temporal in Islam was imminent.[34] Citing the example of Pakistan,[35] he rejected the option of secularization, and three years before the Lebanese civil war engulfed the country, suggested a Muslim-Christian council to govern Lebanon.[36] He claimed that the teaching of Christianity by a Muslim, and of Islam by a Christian, at a Lebanese university would ensure perfect social fusion.[37] In fact, the conception of Lebanon which Moubarac advocated recreated the framework of dhimmitude, where relative religious freedom and civil autonomy were united under the political domination of Islam. This inter-Christian struggle between clergy and laymen encouraged the Islamophile churchmen—Catholics, Uniates, and Orthodox—to fight alongside the Palestinians in Lebanon in order to destroy the political and national structures of Christian power. This confused situation resulted from the unification of two separate domains: the religious and eschatological domain, and the imperatives of Christian political survival. Moubarac interpreted the end of Christian political power as a religious liberation which would restore to the Church the vocation that Islam had assigned to it: a service of charity and love toward Muslims. This policy was in perfect line with Vatican politics since the nineteenth century. But, at a political and secular level, Christianity in Lebanon, possessing political power, represented the challenge of Christian freedom at a parity with Islam, and radiating a hope for all the Middle East Christians. However, this freedom depended on the conciliation within the same nation of the aspirations of pan-Islamic domination, supported by Lebanese Muslims and the whole Arab hinterland, and the multicultural and egalitarian secularism of the Westernized Christians.

According to Christian politicians, the plan to Islamize Lebanon had already been more or less openly admitted since 1958, just over a decade after independence. Then, the Nasserian left-wing movements and the Islamic forces fighting for Lebanon's union with Syria and Egypt (United Arab Republic) provoked a Lebanese civil war.[38] Only American intervention, requested by President Camille Chamoun, saved the country's independence. Chamoun later explained the situation:

> Indeed, Islam, whose dogma cannot tolerate any authority parallel or superior to its own, accepted Lebanon only if [Islam] dominated it.[39]

In 1975, Hussein al-Kouatly, one of the leaders of Dar al-Fatwa—a Lebanese Sunni institution disseminating *fatwas* (legal opinions)—published a declaration, specifying:

> The position of Lebanon is very clear on one point: it is that the true Muslim cannot assume a neutral attitude towards the state [. . .] Either the head of state is a Muslim and the law [is] Muslim law, then he will be in agreement with the state and will support it; or the head of state is a non-Muslim and the law [is] non-Muslim, then he will reject the state, oppose it and work to destroy it, peacefully or violently, overtly or secretly [. . .] This position is logical because Islam is a complete system and an all-embracing attitude.[40]

The Cairo Agreement (3 November 1969) imposed by Egypt, Syria, and the Lebanese Muslims legalized the PLO's military operations in Lebanon on the pretext that terrorist raids into Israeli territory were justified. Sponsored by the Arab-Muslim and communist world, the PLO, henceforth, became a more powerful organization for subversion and terrorism worldwide.[41] Hostage to the PLO's anti-Zionist *jihad*, multicultural Lebanon—in regard to Islamic law, a state as illegal as the Jewish state—abandoned by the Arab League and the West, reverted to the traditional resistance of the Christian mountain-dwellers. For Chamoun, the causes, nature, and objectives of the war against Lebanon waged by the Palestinians and the Muslim forces, which erupted in 1975, hardly differed from those of the 1958 conflict: that is, Lebanon's Islamization.[42]

In fact, the Lebanese-Palestinian conflict brought together all the constituents of dhimmitude. On the Muslim side, the Lebanese population remained faithful to its Syrian and pan-Arab allegiance, giving unconditional support to the Palestinians, thereby undermining the Lebanese state.[43] But in the Christian camp, the customary dissension between leaders, their corruptibility and their clientelism, were increased by Syrian provocations and by the deliberate PLO tactics of creating internecine Christian strife. Some groups of Armenians, whose allegiance was to the Soviet Union, joined PLO terrorist camps, while others belatedly supported the Lebanese Forces which embraced various Christian parties. Whereas Suleiman Frangieh (President, 1970–76) willingly played the Syrian game,[44] the communists, the majority of whom were Greek Orthodox, backed Arafat and the "Islamo-progressist" camp, while the Palestinian Christians unanimously lined up behind the PLO.

For Abbé Moubarac, the concept of Lebanon as the defender of Christianity was a delusion, a hypocrisy, and a policy unworthy of the Gospel.[45] He saw the Cairo Agreements as an invitation and summons from destiny "to commit Lebanon to the struggle and to sets its mark on the future of the whole sphere to which it belongs." Only such a commitment was worthy of its history and destiny; and if it could not honor that obligation, it deserved the destruction that would be its fate![46] This grandiose commitment was the service to the Palestinian cause and the eradication of Israel. "Freed from both fear and egoism," by the pressure of events: "The moment has come for Lebanon, allegedly Christian, to discover a youthful vigor and an evangelical revival by its immersion into the depth of this [Arab] mass." Lebanon should reject

> the capitalist and pleasure-seeking West, which sullies its shores and pollutes the air of its summits, the moment has come to convert all the vital energy of the Christian communities and no longer put their institutions solely at the service of Christians but also, even primarily, at the service of non-Christians. [. . .] a pressing invitation is given to the Church of God which is in Lebanon to achieve this wish for the benefit of the mass of non-Christians, who, just like the poor of Jesus Christ, are placed under the rod of the Zionist occupation and of the local [Christian Lebanese] potentate in the pay of the foreign power.[47]

In January 1976, at Damur south of Beirut, where the bodies of 582 Christian women, children, and the elderly lay, butchered and trampled by the Palestinians, the walls of desecrated churches bore the words in Arabic: "Today Damur, tomorrow Palestine."[48]

One element specific to the context of dhimmitude should be noted: the Lebanese Christians were betrayed by the very people whom they had welcomed and whose cause they had untiringly defended. They suffered abductions, destruction, and massacres during the war years by PLO bands, armed to the hilt by Arab countries and the Soviet Union. Iran, Iraq, Syria, Egypt, Libya, and Algeria participated in this carnage by their hostile policy or by sending funds, military equipment, mercenaries, or troops.[49]

While the PLO was arming on a massive scale, Abbé Moubarac, with his anti-Israeli obsession, was recommending

> the formation of the mass of Lebanese people into the sort of non-violent resistance, which should make it equivalent to a radioactive cell in the Middle East, disintegrating the process of violence and removing the Zionist system's raison d'être [. . .].[50]

This is not the place to recapitulate the events of the Lebanese war which have been analyzed in numerous books. For Abbé Moubarac, the destruction of Christian temporal power restored to the Church its real vocation of love for Islam, cementing a Muslim-Christian ecumenism which would liberate Jerusalem by returning the Israelis to the status of *dhimmis* initiated by the Church. But for Christian politicians, the Lebanese conflict meant something quite different. Camille Chamoun describes the condition of the *dhimmi*,[51] the fate of the Armenians,[52] and the impossible coexistence of Muslims and Christians, separated by an unbridgeable gulf, by different "concepts of a religious, cultural, political and social nature, above all, different allegiances."[53] However, it was President-elect Bashir Gemayel whose words and deeds bear witness to the conflict between dhimmitude and freedom, and expose the lie of a peaceful Muslim-Christian past coexistence and the fallacious Palestinian-Christian alliance as a fatal source of compromise and the surrender of principles.[54]

Within the context of dhimmitude, it was through the action of a *dhimmi* that the dream of a free Lebanon disintegrated: the assassination of Bashir Gemayel on 14 September 1982 by a Christian in the pay of Syria. European politicians, aligned in support of Arab policy and consequently hostile to Bashir Gemayel's candidature,[55] stifled a cowardly sigh of relief at his untimely assassination. In this way, the possibility of a Lebanese-Israeli peace treaty disappeared. Envisaged by a Christian president, it would have jeopardized Europe's commercial relations with the Arab world. The "Palestinian affair" had become

> the first and greatest Arab cause: the one that conditioned the evolution of their [the Arabs'] relations with the outside world, great and small powers.[56]

The isolation of the Lebanese Christians[57] resulted from European economic interests and was justified by a campaign of hostile disinformation.[58] The destruction of Lebanon confirmed the balance of the traditional forces of dhimmitude: the political gains of *jihad* against the financial advantages granted to European governments.

From the *Millet* to Citizenship

To conclude this rapid overview of some thirty years, certain behavioral patterns can be observed which are common to all *dhimmi* groups although they are modified by variations in demographic and political situations. The basic, immediately striking, characteristic is the absence of any coordination or alliance between the groups. Friendly or sympathetic contact is confined to personal relationships, whereas religious sectarianism, economic rivalry, and mutual antipathy ensure that each community remains segregated. This conservative self-security attitude also led to isolationism, a source of weakness. This is the mentality of the *millets*, juxtaposed religious entities separated by a hostility which perpetuates submission, and maintains an active participation and instrumentalization in mutual self-destruction. European colonization broke this Islamic order only superficially because those who fraternized under the colonial regime were solely Jewish and Christian schoolchildren, and pupils from the Muslim elite, attending secular and religious European educational institutions. But these generations were later scattered to the winds of exodus.

Connected with this sociological fragmentation coexists a lack of an over-all and shared vision of the dimension of dhimmitude. A few Lebanese personalities followed a different path: the Maronite Patriarch of Antioch, Antun Arida; the Maronite Archbishop of Beirut, Ignace Mubarak; and the jurist Antoine Fattal were among the most articulate. Several factors, some of which have already been mentioned, explain this myopia, primarily motivated by the rivalry of political clientelisms and by a historical amnesia, adopted as an axiom of survival.

At the economic level the over-riding prevalence of commerce and trade can be observed among the minorities, the principal agents of the modernization of the Arab-Muslim countries. In this field too, the accumulation of wealth perpetuated a tradition in which money governed the redeeming of life and communal rights. The visible, often ostentatious, enrichment of non-Muslims under colonization broke the Islamic order while maintaining the economic rivalry and mercantile spirit, all the more preponderant as most Jewish and Christian students emigrated to Europe to complete their studies and remained there. This brain drain accelerated with the stifling of culture resulting from the development of fanaticism after independence was achieved.

General amnesia remains the basic characteristic shared in varying degrees by all groups except the Copts. The history of dhimmitude—which could never be written or even mentioned in Islamic circles—is still totally neglected except by a few rare, daring scholars. Under colonization, this amnesia was manifested in a general mistrust of Muslims. Ancestral *dhimmi* fear survived in the form of vague terrors, driving Jews and Christians to shut themselves up in their homes at the slightest alarm. Among Christians, this anguish was counterbalanced by philo-Arabism.

The same attitude also appears among the Jews, due to their greater vulnerability in the Islamic environment, notably through the atomization of small rural communities in the Maghreb. Uprooting, destructions, the exodus to the towns in the contemporary period heightened deculturization resulting from isolation and oppression, although Jewish scholars from Morocco, Tunisia, and Egypt have left valuable testimonies. The myth of the "golden age" in Andalusia and in the Ottoman Empire, recycled by European Jewish scholars since the nineteenth century, was propagated in a historical vacuum filled by the perverted dogma of "tolerance"—a term which betrayed its ambiguity when these same laws, in their European form, were judged oppressive.

Educated at the schools of the Alliance Israélite Universelle, the Jewish elites in the Maghreb learned the history of Western Judaism. After World War II, traumatized by the Nazi genocide, perpetrated amid the general indifference of the Christian world, the Jewish intellectuals of the Maghreb sublimated their condition under Islam. This trend is particularly conspicuous among Israelis of Moroccan origin. Muslim Judeophobia was at that time exclusively attributed to the Machiavellism of the European colonizers who had set the communities against each other the better to dominate them. This thesis, also propagated in the East from the 1920s, had driven young Jews and Christians, smitten with an egalitarian ideal, to enroll in communist parties and movements of national independence. As for Jews from more modest backgrounds, their amnesia—a veritable abyss in history—was masked by religious practices which took the place of collective memory. Thus, the trauma of the Shoah, and the desire for peace between Israel and the Arab world, gave credence to the dogma of tolerance.

Some historians have contrasted the political passivity of Jews from the Middle East in the twentieth century with Christian activism there. But after World War I, the Judeophobia in political life, polarized by Arab nationalists and the anti-Zionist struggles, barred Jewish participation. Political liberalism, an epiphenomenon of colonization, barely extended over two to four decades, depending on the country. In addition, the genocide of the Armenians and the massacres of the Assyrians prompted the Jews to observe the greatest caution vis-à-vis Zionism. From the 1930s the development of Arab pro-Nazism and the intensification of Judeophobia in the Orient led them to prepare their self-defense. The absence of stability and security made political involvement impracticable in the following decade, which saw the massacre of Jews in Baghdad in June 1941, and numerous anti-Jewish riots and pogroms throughout the 1940s, culminating in the subsequent massive exodus of whole communities. In fact, Israel's destruction became—as with Nazi ideology—a central theme of Arab nationalism, many of whose ideologues were prominent Arab Christians, both Syrians and Palestinians.

Among Christians, historical memory and awareness of a separate identity from that of the *umma* was particularly apparent among the Armenians, Copts, and Maronites, giving rise to varied behavioral patterns. The Armenians—an ancient people who had always preserved their language, history and culture—concentrated their resentment on the Turks, although the Kurds, the Syrians, and the Iraqi Arab populations, as well as the Bedouins had participated in the genocide and the enslavement and conversion of Armenian women and children. Traumatized by the past, dispersed over the Arab-Islamic terrain, the Armenian refugees in Lebanon, loyal to the Armenian Soviet Republic, were instrumentalized by the Soviet-dominated left-wing terrorist movement. In the decade 1970–80, these ASALA militants were trained in the Palestinian terrorist camps in Lebanon, Syria, and Iraq, while other Armenians fought in the Dashnak movement which was allied to Maronite forces.[59] To the best of our knowledge, there seems to have been no indication that the Armenians were conscious of dhimmitude as a common destiny determined by Islamic laws for all Christian communities. This unawareness led them to join, and to collaborate with, the "*Palestino-Islamo-Progressistes*"—as they were labeled in the political French jargon. Participation by some Armenian groups in the activities of the PLO was scarcely helpful to Lebanese resistance. Having regained territorial independence, the Armenians limited their struggle to force Turkey to acknowledge responsibility for the genocide they had suffered.

Faced with the danger of the Islamization of their country, the political awareness of the Copts was a totally different matter. A population rooted in its homeland, the Copts always took pride in their ancient pharaonic origins and preserved the unhappy memory—similar to the memory of European Jewry—of past humiliations and sufferings. Some writings evince an acute awareness of their resistance to an inflexible Muslim desire to eliminate them. The wrists of Coptic children display a tattooed cross, an ostentatious claim of indestructible identity. Unlike the Jews, the structures of dhimmitude were familiar to them. Thus in 1910 the Coptic writer Kyriakos Mikhail commented in the following terms on the assassination of the Coptic Prime Minister Butrus Ghali by a Muslim:

> Boutrous [Ghali] Pasha belonged to a people under tribute, and a conscientious Mohammedan is bound to look upon assassination as a light punishment for the tributary Christian who dares to assume semi-independent government rule over a Mohammedan population.[60]

Ronald Storrs, who was in Cairo during this period as an official of the Colonial Administration, mentions that, although the Sheikh of al-Azhar proclaimed over the grave that "few Moslems have done for their country the good this Christian did," the public temperature rose to boiling point. Wardani, the assassin, became a national hero, acclaimed by bands of students patrolling the streets singing, "Wardani! Wardani! That slew the Nazarene."[61]

In 1936 Father Marcos Sergios sent a report to the patriarch of Alexandria and to the Coptic community council, in which he listed existing discriminations which were tempting the Copts to convert to Islam. Emphasizing their very critical situation, he wrote:

> The situation will become more and more difficult from one year to the next. Coptic Christianity has survived till today by coping with the persecution of past centuries and it will have to confront and cope with a dark future.[62]

Unlike the Syrian and Lebanese Christian Arabists who declared themselves more Arab than the Arabs, the Copts never considered themselves

Arabs. Similar to other Christians, but without ever renouncing their identity, they attempted to secularize Egyptian nationalism, struggling against the Islamization of society. In the exacerbated Arabization of the Nasserian period, they protested at the discrimination they suffered. Whereas the Christian Syrian and Lebanese Arabists evaded the whole problem of dhimmitude in Arab nationalism, the Coptic representatives unambiguously denounced the return of practices which were still very present in their memory. In his indictment of discriminatory measures against the Copts in 1953, Ibrahim Fehmi Hilal, president of the Association of the Coptic Nation, wrote:

> Preceding generations have up to now suffered injustice with patience and discretion. Today the awakening has become evident; the spirit, open; reason, alert; and feelings quite different from what they were.[63]

Confronted with the pan-Arabism wave, the Copts resumed the teaching of their language, history, and civilization. Abroad, the diaspora mobilized and campaigned to support the struggle of the Copts in Egypt by publicly denouncing the oppression they were suffering, thereby demonstrating loyalty to the past, courage in the struggle, and solidarity.

In the Memorandum of the Community Council of the Bishopric of Asyut, relating the anti-Copt events of 7 to 22 August 1977, the signatories deplored the passivity of the Christian leaders. Claiming that the right to complain was a basic human right, they denounced the government's plan which aimed to present the victim as the criminal.

Another Memorandum on the Current Events of October 1977, signed "The Coptic People," criticized the docility of the clergy and the representatives of the Copts in the face of the aggressive acts suffered by their coreligionists. As in the preceding memorandum, the protesters denounced the attitude of those who condemned the disclosure of facts and found it "strange that the oppressed raised their voices against the oppressor" even preventing the victim's complaints. The document mentions "oppressions" exerted in order to impose silence, practiced by a clergy resigned to suffer injustice and agreeing to yield certain Christian rights in return for mutual understanding and harmony with the Muslim majority. This horse-trading in rights, carried on by the notables—the document suggested—betrayed the community's interests because these compromises underlined the clergy's practical inability to resolve political problems.

These mechanisms of dhimmitude—the docility of the notables who imposed silence on their community when threatened, and the clergy's inability to assume a political role—were thus perfectly discerned and denounced by Copts. But this policy was probably the price for the protection of innocent lives. However that may be, the memoranda sent to the government by the patriarch Shenuda III in the 1970s and his vehement protests—supported by other Coptic representatives—pledged to ensure the security of his flock and respect for Christianity. It bore witness to a courage and dignity which contrasted with the silence and servility of the Syrian Arab Churches.

In the Syrian-Lebanese group, which also included the Palestinians, perceptions of dhimmitude differed according to Maronite, Greek Orthodox, or Uniate affiliation and political clientelism. Although Muslim-Christian brotherly collaboration in Arabism and Judeophobia had concealed all reference to dhimmitude, Maronite personalities analyzed the seeds of religious conflict. In fact, the clarity of analysis and courage of their political vision set it apart from the servility of the anti-Zionist, Christian, pan-Arab current and brought it closer to the Coptic attitude. Some Lebanese Christians denounced past persecutions and humiliations and discerned a pan-Islamism in Arabism which stimulated them to claim an autonomous Christian homeland in Lebanon. This current forcefully asserted Judeo-Christian solidarity in dhimmitude and the identity of the claims of the two Peoples of the Book in the historical cradle of their civilization. Defended by the Patriarch Antun Arida and Archbishop Ignace Mubarak, this trend was thwarted by the Vatican, the Arabists, and a European pro-Muslim policy. These opinions always remained in a minority.

Through Arab nationalism, the Syrians and Lebanese Christians were sometimes able to make a brilliant contribution to the contemporary history of the Arab countries in the realm of politics, culture, and journalism. It was they who thrust on to Islamic society the concepts of cultural and religious pluralism, of peaceful Muslim-Christian coexistence, and the golden age of the first caliphs. However, Charles Malik, Camille Chamoun, and other Christian personalities were hardly unaware of the difficulties and ambiguities of Muslim-Christian coexistence; and it was a Lebanese, Antoine Fattal, who first perceived the general legal and historical aspect of the *dhimmi* status, usually evaded in the theory of tolerance and the golden age. Consequently, the problem of dhimmitude—although the word had not yet been coined—remained a major concern for Lebanese Christendom in its political aspect: the suppression of Christian freedom.

During the Lebanese war, when the Palestinians—entrusted by the European leftists with the plan for a multicultural and democratic secular state—exploded this myth in blood and horror, the Lebanese Christians recovered the sense of their history. Without transition, the youth of the "dolce vita" rediscovered the bellicose virtues of their ancestors. The political discourse of the Lebanese nationalists at the beginning of the century, and the denunciation of the oppression of Christianity inherent in Islam, supported the ideological battle. Lebanese resistance, like that of the Copts, rejected the bartering in compromises which curtailed rights.

"Compromise and protection are well known to us, and like twins they originate from the same stock," Bashir Gemayel declared.[64] Recalling religious intolerance the day of his assassination, he announced the reconstruction of churches destroyed by the Palestinians and commented: "But had we been in Syria or Egypt, we would not even have had the right to restore the smallest church, which risked falling into ruins."[65] Hence, the essential condition for survival required the knowledge of *dhimmi* history, the exposure of the lie, and the need for truth:

> But what has happened to us, has happened because we did not have respect for truth, because truth very often frightened us; in Lebanon, we were not used to speaking the truth: very often the truth frightened us because we were afraid [. . .] And when we awakened, we realized that we only had a superficial knowledge of our own cause, that we did not have the slightest idea of the basic foundations of our identity and our raisons d'être. Everything was only a gloss, everything was nothing but falsification, everything was only a lie.[66]

Bashir Gemayel explained this existential meaning of the Resistance in another address he delivered a few hours before he was assassinated. To make Lebanon a country

> where we will be able to live with our heads held high, without anyone coming up and saying to us: "to the left," "walk on the left-hand side," as we were told in the time of the Turks, because we were Christians; without someone forcing us to wear some distinctive sign on our body and our clothing to mark us out as Christians; without us being citizens living in the "dhimmitude" of others. Henceforth, we refuse to live in anyone's "dhimmitude"! We no longer wish to be under the protection of anyone![67]

In contrast with these demands for freedom and dignity, the Syrian and Palestinian Christians—the majority of them Melchites or Protestants—were conspicuous for their Islamophile militantism. It was in anti-Zionism that the Palestinian Christians in particular, strongly supported by European anti-Zionist movements—communist, clerical or Islamophile—sealed their alliance with the Muslims and their participation in Arab political life. Mainly emigrants from Lebanon and Syria, giving their allegiance to a Third-World leftist ideology, they fought at every level of the PLO and in the Palestinian terrorist organizations. As early as 1923, an Orthodox Christian from Tulkarem, Khalil Isa Al-Sabbâgh, led a large-scale raid on the Jewish village of Hadera.[68] Slavishly serving Islamic aims, Syrian and Palestinian Christians propagated the Arab theses of Western guilt and evilness. Their ideologists, such as the pro-Nazi Antun Sa'adé, or the cofounder of the Ba'ath party, Michel Aflak, who later converted to Islam, advocated the theology of "Palestinianism" and undermined the Christian struggle against dhimmitude. Terrorist leaders and supporters: George Habash, Nayif Hawatma, Wadi Haddad, Abu Nidal, Kamal Nasser, Father Sakkab, the Syrian Greek Catholic Archbishop Hilarion Capucci—the most prominent from many others—helped to divide and weaken Eastern Christianity at a period that was crucial for its survival.[69]

This trend also included the missionary movement favoring the *millet* structure which granted power to the Church in the Islamic system. Abbé Moubarac supported this regime of community coexistence which, in his view, would open up to missiology the vast field of the Third World. Such a grandiose task would have been nullified by a small Christian nationalist Lebanon, turned in upon itself, on the model of Israel. Such a Lebanon would betray the vocation of charity which Islam conferred on the Church, and would cause it to evade the obligation of restoring to the Jews— through the destruction of Zionism—the place that Islam assigned to them, by bringing Judaism back to its essential nature: to "hope against all hope."[70] At a time when all the structures of Christian existence in the East were decomposing, Abbé Moubarac classified the different meanings of Arabness. It was incumbent on the Muslims, he said, "to learn for themselves what they need from the Christians in order to form the community of believers that the Koran desired," a rather sibylline sentence implying dhimmitude. As for the Christians, they had to promote that egalitarian community, "independently of any numerical calculation," with a view to fulfilling the major injunctions of the political future "of the countries of the Revelation." The contradiction between the koranic system and multireligious equality escaped Moubarac, unless he envisaged the possibility of a Muslim-Christian egalitarian coexistence solely in the fulfillment of "the major injunction." This consisted in "perfecting the Muslim-Christian entente" by the "*de-Zionization of Palestine*" ("*désionisation de la Palestine*"— italics in the original) with which Judaism must cooperate.[71] The success of this battle, aimed at Israel's total eradication, involved the destruction of a closed, exclusivist Lebanon and the elimination of a Maronitism and a pro-Zionist Chamounism.[72]

Faris al-Khuri, the Christian prime minister of Syria in 1954, stigmatized the Arab politicians who envisaged a possibility of peace with Israel.

> Whether they return the refugees or not, peace must not be concluded with Israel in any form. I do not believe that the Arabs would approve such a peace so long as the Jews remain settled in that spot—the heart of the Arab state—threatening all those around them and spreading corruption and evil . . . How could we find it possible to make peace with them while they remain there?[73]

Did this type of statement express a Christian desire to use Muslim strength to eliminate a Jewish national sovereignty which the Church condemned, or did it reflect the insecurity of a minority trying to direct hostility onto a third party? It is true that Syria under the presidency of Colonel Adib Shishakli (1953–54) was in the grip of a wave of Arabization which threatened religious and ethnic minorities with extinction, even ordering that names be Arabized on pain of withdrawal of Syrian citizenship. In Egypt, Christian men Arabized their names overnight. The promulgation of coercive measures in the political and religious spheres to benefit Islamic preponderance caused a fresh wave of Christian emigration to Lebanon and Europe. By and large this policy was integrated into a context of anti-Christian incidents in Egypt, in Syria (1949), even in Israel, where Muslims had attacked Christians in a church of Nazareth, leaving one dead and four injured (1950), and in Amman against Armenian scouts (1953). However isolated these incidents were, nonetheless they revealed, after the independence of Arab states, the persistence of a behavior that Christian factions had sanctioned a few years before against Jews, behavior which Pierre Rondot defined in 1956 as: "ancestral habits," "a certain spirit of vexation inherited from the past," "violent outbursts, suddenly issuing from the masses under the influence of ancient instincts and feelings which evolution has not yet eliminated."[74] Despite the movement of Muslim-Christian brotherhood (World Fellowship of Muslims and Christians), founded at Bhamdoun (Lebanon) on 22–27 April 1954, the situation of the Christians was deteriorating.

One might wonder if Arabic-speaking Christians had any option, or if anti-Jewish virulence constituted their only guarantee of survival in the Islamic environment. All this notwithstanding, the opinions of the Islamophile ecclesiastical faction remove any ambiguity. Israel is inconceivable, writes Moubarac, "for the conscience of the Arab world, Christian as much as Muslim,"[75] and "the occupation of Jerusalem is for us, as for Islam, an intolerable challenge: it will be brought to an end by every means."[76] Even if the Arab states would sign a peace treaty with the State of Israel, he himself would refuse to accept it on grounds of faith and through loyalty to the memory of Louis Massignon.[77] As he expressed it:

> But we know and testify that Islam's vocation is to bring about the triumph of a certain number of divine laws over the temporal city by confronting Jews and Christians, thereby provoking them in a certain number of privileged places to something other than the crusade.[78]

For Abbé Moubarac, Israel represents a sacrilege since it had broken the vocation assigned it by Islam; and it would be through the mediation of the Islamic vocation for Jerusalem that—through a Muslim-Christian union—the destruction of Zionism and the return of the Jews to exile among the nations, or to dhimmitude, would be fulfilled.

7

Jihad and *Dhimma:* Modern Formulations

The Themes

The previous chapters have expounded the permanent presence throughout history of pan-Islamic movements centered on *jihad,* and on the restoration of a caliphate in the twentieth century, which would unite religious and political power. These movements were both stimulated and consolidated by the impact of Westernization which eroded the dogma of Islam's superiority. In addition, the abolition by the colonial administration of the *shari'a*'s discrimination vis-à-vis non-Muslims heightened the resentment of the Muslim population. The social ascent of erstwhile *dhimmi* communities humiliated the clerical classes and the petite bourgeoisie, who saw their privileges disappear under colonization. They reacted by seeking refuge in a past of mythical perfection, basking in the glory of the dazzling conquests of former times. Nostalgia for lost domination was from the start expressed in political terms, as in India against British power, and then in a general Muslim refusal in 1947 to be integrated into a modern secular state of the Indian Union. This secessionism gave birth to two independent Muslim states on the Indian sub-continent: West Pakistan, and East Pakistan (later Bangladesh).

Except for a Westernized minority, *jihad* constituted the driving force and the ideological foundation for the claims on European states and the decolonization wars against them. Muslim intellectuals have been surprised at the Western interpretation of these movements as new developments, when they are actually integrated into the historical and sociological fabric of the Muslim peoples. Khurshid Ahmad emphasizes the historical continuity of Islamic movements in the *dar al-Islam* and their deliberate omission by Western observers of the Islamic scene.[1]

In fact, what makes these movements original is not the statement of a millennial politicoreligious ideology, endlessly expounded in legal and theological writings, but their actualization through ideologies and modern state structures, their worldwide diffusion, and their transposition into international policy. These ideologies were developed, not in an obscurantist or traditional milieu but by intellectuals, graduates of American and

European universities. However, it is important to distinguish between the previous Muslim nationalist anti-colonial struggles and the Islamist movements. Moreover, the Islamist movements are hardly representative of all opinion in the Muslim world. In fact, both at international forums and in every strata of the population, these movements are to various degrees disputed and contested in North Africa and the Middle East, particularly in Turkey, but also in Pakistan and through the Iranian and Sudanese opposition groups. As a result, non-Islamist Muslims themselves have suffered attacks and assassination attempts. However, as the various political forces in the Muslim world are not the subject of this study, these few guidelines merely indicate the areas of interaction between ethnoreligious minorities.[2] Here, only those measures in the Islamists' program which concern these minorities will be mentioned, as they are relevant to dhimmitude.

The Islamist Conception of the Universe and the Origin of Islam

The ideological justifications for the Islamist political systems were first formulated by Muslims in British India, particularly, by the respected Islamic scholars Muhammad Iqbal (1876–1938), and Abu l-Ala Mawdudi (1903–81).

The Koran states that Islam is Allah's religion:

> Verily the religion in Allah's sight is Islam; and those to whom the Book has been given did not differ until after the knowledge [of revealed religion] had come to them, out of jealously among themselves; if anyone disbelieves in the signs of Allah, Allah is quick to reckon. (3:17)

As Allah created the world it follows that the whole world is Islamic, as explained by Mawdudi:[3]

> As the entire creation obeys the law of God, the whole universe, therefore, literally follows the religion of Islam—for Islam signifies nothing but obedience and submission of [sic] Allah, the Lord of the Universe. The sun, the moon, the earth, and all other heavenly bodies are thus "Muslim." So is the case with air, water, and heat, stones, trees, and animals. Everything in the universe is "Muslim" for it obeys God by submission to His laws. (p.10) [inverted commas in the original]

Even a non-Muslim, whose body is subject to the laws of nature, is Muslim:

> His very tongue which, on account of his ignorance advocates the denial of God or professes multiple deities, is in its very nature a "Muslim." His head which he wantonly bows to others besides Allah is a *born Muslim*. His heart wherein, through his lack of true knowledge, he cherishes love and rever-

ence for others, is "Muslim" by intuition. These are all obedient to the Divine Law, and their functions and movements are governed by the injunctions of that law alone. (p.10) [italics in the original]

Although all mankind is born Muslim, the individual can choose:

Here he has been given the freedom of choice—and it is the way a person exercises this freedom which divides mankind into two groups; believers and non-believers. (p.11)

Since Adam, Islam was the religion of all the prophets:

God's true Prophets were raised in all countries: in every land and people. They all possessed one and the same religion—the religion of Islam. (p.37)

The concept of a dualist mankind divided between believers and unbelievers constitutes a fundamental ideological and political basis, as Mawdudi explains:[4]

Kufr literally means "to cover" or "to conceal." The man who denies God is called *Kafir* (concealer) because he conceals *by his disbelief* what is inherent in his nature and embalmed in his own soul—for, indeed, his nature is instinctively imbued with "Islam." His whole body, every sinew and every fibre, functions in obedience to that instinct. Each and every particle of existence—living or lifeless—functions in accordance with "Islam" and is fulfilling the duty that has been assigned to it. (p.12)

But one who disobeys God and resorts to *Kufr* is the person who perpetrates the greatest injustice, for he uses all these powers of body and mind to rebel against the course of nature and becomes an unwilling instrument in the drama of disobedience. He forces his head to bow down before deities other than God and cherishes in his heart the love, reverence, and fear of other powers in utter disregard to the instinctive urge of these organs. (p.13)

He [the *Kafir*] will, without the least compunction, shed blood, violate other men's rights, be cruel to them, and create disorder and destruction in the world. His perverted thoughts and ambitions, his blurred vision and disturbed scale of values, and his evil-spelling activities would make life bitter for him and for all around him. Such a man would destroy the calm and poise of life on earth. And in the life hereafter he would be held guilty for the crimes he committed upon his nature, his powers, and resources. Every organ of his body—his very brain, eyes, nose, hands, and feet—will complain against the injustice and cruelty he had done unto them. Every tissue of his being will decry him before God Who, as the very fountain of justice, will award him for the fullest punishment he deserves. This is the inglorious consequence of *Kufr*. It leads to the blind alleys of utter failure, here and hereafter. (p.15)

Where there is no Islam there is *Kufr*. Its form and nature may be different, but in any way it would be *Kufr* and nothing but *Kufr*. (p.25) [all italics in the original]

Islamist ideology advocates the restoration of a state which would apply all the injunctions of the Koran and the *sunna,* on the model of the politicosocial organization created at Medina by Muhammad and the first four caliphs (632–61). Acccording to the ideologist of the Sudanese regime, Hasan al-Turabi, the universal characteristics of the Islamic state

> [. . .] derive from the teachings of the Quran as embodied in the political practice of the Prophet Muhammad and constitute an eternal model that Muslims are bound to adopt as a perfect standard for all time.[5]

Mawdudi explains the ideological foundation of this state by the doctrine of *tawhid,* the unity of Allah and of the koranic revelation. This unity places on Muslims the religious obligation to accomplish the Divine will on earth. The will of Allah revealed to Muhammad in the Koran and the *sunna* was intended for mankind. As the sole keeper of the True Revelation, the Islamic community is distinguished from other peoples by two characteristics: the election (Koran, 3:106) and the perfection attached to the laws of Allah, implemented in the *shari'a:*

> The *shari'ah* stipulates the law of God and provides guidance for the regulation of life in the best interests of man[6]

These two characteristics—the *umma*'s election and perfection, linked to the koranic revelation and the *shari'a*—justify its role as Allah's vicegerent on earth.[7] Power which is not consonant with the *shari'a*—that is, Allah's will—is considered illegitimate and usurped, because only Islamic—that is, Allah's—law must prevail. This concept bestows legitimacy of authority and power at an international level exclusively on the *umma.* It confirms the supremacy of its authority over all other peoples by its divine election. The same principle legitimizes *jihad.*[8]

The primacy of the Islamic *umma* was reaffirmed in the Cairo Declaration on Human Rights in Islam (CDHRI), adopted in Cairo on 5 August 1990, whose first two preambulary paragraphs declare:

> The Member States of the Organization of the Islamic Conference,
> *Reaffirming* the civilizing and historical role of the Islamic Ummah which God made the best nation that has given mankind a universal and well-balanced civilization in which harmony is established between this life and the hereafter and knowledge is combined with faith; and the role that this Ummah should play to guide a humanity confused by competing trends and ideologies and to provide solutions to the chronic problems of this materialistic civilization.
> *Wishing* to contribute to the efforts of mankind to assert human rights, to protect man from exploitation and persecution, and to affirm his freedom and right to a dignified life in accordance with the Islamic Shari'ah.[9]

For its domestic policy, the Islamic state must be established by the total eradication of all non-Islamic thought, influence, and institution, that is to say, by eliminating the slightest external influence introduced by colonization or by concepts borrowed from other cultures. This return to an orthodoxy which pre-dates the intrusion of the West prolongs the decolonization struggle for moral and institutional purification. This is the classic concept of the rejection of infidel and inferior civilizations from which Islam, by virtue of its superiority and perfection, could not borrow anything without sullying itself.[10]

Mawdudi recalls that "the Holy Prophet (peace be upon him) has positively and forcefully forbidden the Muslims to assume the culture and mode of life of non-Muslims."[11] This rejection of the world outside the *umma* forms the basis of a whole vocabulary of demonization which relates to the traditional demonology of the *dar al-harb,* victimizing the Arab Christians, Jews, and other minority groups. Khurshid Ahmad places responsibility for the resurgence of the Islamic movement and its political program on the colonial government whose Western-type secular society constitutes a blasphemy in an Islamic state where the *shari'a* must be recognized as the source of all jurisdiction.[12]

The promulgation of laws in accordance with the Koran and the *shari'a* requires the political domain to be limited exclusively to parties professing Islamic ideology and whose candidates know koranic law. Consequently, only Muslims should possess the right to vote.[13]

After the establishment of the *shari'a*, the next stage will consist of eliminating the territorial divisions (national boundaries), introduced by colonization that are a source of weakness to the *umma.* This Islamic reunification will create an enormous demographic, political, economic, and military power. Psychologically conditioned by the sacred spirit of *jihad,* the *umma* will then be able to pursue its historic mission: world conquest in order to impose the *shari'a* worldwide. In a national radio broadcast soon after he came to power in 1979, the Ayatollah Khomeini described Israel as "the enemy of humanity throughout the world." He also declared: "The governments of the world should know that Islam cannot be defeated. Islam will be victorious in all countries of the world, and Islam and the teachings of the Koran will prevail all over the world."[14]

For the leading Egyptian Islamist thinker Sayed Qutb, *jihad* is continual and must be waged until Judgement Day.[15]

This conception of foreign policy is integrated into the classic concept of a world divided into the Good, the *dar al-Islam*, and the Evil, the *dar al-harb,* confronting one another in an obligatory and eternal *jihad.* The legitimacy of any non-Islamic political or legal authority is totally rejected. This rejection exempts Muslims from any duty to obey laws which are not in accordance with the *shari'a* and encourages subversive movements.[16] Immigrant communities, in particular, are duty-bound to create their own autonomous Islamic states in order to liberate from disbelief the territory in which they have settled. Any impediment to Islamic expansion, such as a challenge to the autonomy of these communities, or restrictions on the development of a network of mosques and koranic centers, is regarded as war against Allah, justifying *jihad* on the part of the *umma*. In the realm of international relations, the principle of the primacy of Islamic over all other law is reaffirmed, annulling any agreement not in accordance with the *shari'a*.

The Islamists' political message on this subject can be summarized as follows:

1. The perfection of the *shari'a* follows from Allah's perfection; to cast doubts on one is tantamount to casting doubts on the other. The *shari'a* is an expression of Allah's will through the medium of Muhammad and as such is eternal, immutable, and perfect.[17]
2. The perfection of the *shari'a* is reflected on the *umma,* an Islamic community which, through its laws and actions, is an incarnation of this perfection.
3. The *dhimma* is incorporated into the *shari'a* and possesses its attributes of perfection. The dogma formed by these three postulates is not open to discussion.
4. In the realm of international policy, the *umma*'s perfection earns it a vicegerent's role on earth to govern mankind.
5. This role as mankind's guide carries with it the obligation to pursue *jihad* in order to impose the *shari'a* worldwide.
     The success of *jihad* consists of three essential steps:
   a) The restoration of the *shari'a* in all Muslim countries;
   b) The re-Islamization of new generations by the elimination of all concepts borrowed from foreigners;
   c) The unification of the military and human potential of the *umma*.

Resistance to this policy determines two types of battle zone: 1) Regional conflicts to re-Islamize countries which had once belonged to the Islamic area, the *dar al-Islam*: Lebanon, Israel, Bosnia, Kosovo, Kashmir, and other regions; 2) Conflicts to impose the *shari'a* in Muslim countries.

Repressed History

The concealment of *jihad* and dhimmitude in the West, and particularly in the Communist bloc, has helped to freeze, without resolving, ethnoreligious conflicts. Yet only an impartial examination of Islamic imperialism might clear the way for a reconciliation with those peoples who were its victims. This step is indispensable for a non-Islamic national entity to be recognized as legitimate, the only way to annul the justification for *jihad*. This field of reflection has not yet been tackled. The suppression of history—or worse its distortion—has reopened the venomous return of the past, while in former Yugoslavia the repression of history unleashed a barbaric war.

To anyone with some knowledge of the centuries-old history of Serbian resistance to Ottoman domination, it was obvious that the return of any form of Islamic power in Bosnia-Herzegovina would be rejected by Orthodox Serbs. The five centuries of "harmonious and peaceful coexistence" under Islamic rule, cited by Bosnian President Alija Izetbegovic, belong to the theological dogma of the perfection of the *shari'a* and the *dhimma*.[18] For the Orthodox Serbs, however, this same period is considered one of massacre, pillage, slavery, deportation, and the exile of Christian populations. In their eyes it was a regime which found its justification in the usurpation of their land and denial of their rights; hence it represented the exact opposite of a peaceful, multicultural coexistence based on a system of social and political justice. Thus, two conceptions of history clashed, having never before been confronted. On the one hand, there is the version of the *dhimmi* victims; on the other, that of the conquerors, through *jihad*.

In their wars of emancipation—and, later, of liberation—the Orthodox Serbs found that their bitterest adversaries were their Muslim compatriots, attached to their religious privileges and their domination over the humiliated Christians.[19] During World War II Axis forces invaded Yugoslavia and sponsored the creation of a Nazi Croat state (Ustashi) with which many Bosnian Muslims cooperated. At the prompting of the Mufti of Jerusalem, Haj Amin al-Husayni, they formed military corps, including the 13th (Hanjar) Waffen SS Division, some of which were trained in France. Early in the war, these Muslim Slavs actively participated in the policies of the Ustashi Croats and Nazis in the genocide of hundreds of thousands of Orthodox Serbs, Jews, and gypsies. Even their German allies were shocked by the bestial atrocities committed then in Yugoslavia.[20]

The Nazis encouraged secessionist claims by Muslims, some of whose leaders cited the traditional peaceful coexistence under Islam to denounce later these atrocities which they imputed to the Croats—although Muslim participation in the massacres was notorious.[21] In fact, these allegations aimed at exploiting the inter-Christian conflicts between Catholic Croats and Orthodox Serbs which had facilitated Islam's expansion for a millennium.

Under the authoritarian Communist rule of Tito—a Croat—the Muslim religion benefited from being recognized as Muslim nationality. It was the only group defined by religious criteria, whereas others were characterized by their ethnic differences. The deliberate policy of allowing the Islamization of the Orthodox Serbian homeland (Kosovo and Bosnia-Herzegovina) to continue also earned Tito the economic and political support of the Islamic world and perpetuated inter-Christian schisms. The communist dogma of human brotherhood once again froze the conflicts without resolving them. In 1991, before the conflict erupted, the English edition of Alija Izetbegovic's Islamic Declaration (1970) was published in Sarajevo. It specifically stated: "There can be neither peace nor coexistence between the Islamic faith and non-Islamic social and political institutions." And his conclusion affirmed:

> The Islamic movement must, and can, take over power as soon as it is morally and numerically so strong that it can not only destroy the existing non-Islamic power, but also build up a new Islamic one.[22]

Underneath the camouflage of "the multicultural Islamic state" and the "five hundred years of peaceful coexistence," Bosnian Serbs recognized the *shari'a* system which had decimated them. Hence, the cruelty of the fighting in Bosnia reflected the historical confrontation which, instead of being settled by dialogue, erupted in hatred. Its barbarity expresses the revenge of repressed history, a parody of the distorted myth of idyllic coexistence. Izetbegovic described the Canadian UN commander, Major-General Lewis W. MacKenzie, as "an ignorant man" for his statement in New York that

> "both sides" in the war were filled with hatred. According to Izetbegovic, this could only have been said by someone who knew nothing of Sarajevo's Muslims and their "500-year tradition of tolerance". (inverted commas in the original)[23]

Izetbegovic's reference to an "Ottoman paradise" scandalized Serbs, Greeks, and Armenians. Innocent individuals regardless of religion have become victims of a past which, because it was buried in silence, vengefully returns, accompanied by appalling acts of violence. Those responsible are the politicians who, to safeguard their own interests, tried to impose the myth of tolerance on their victims.

Today, diverse conflicts are tearing Muslim countries apart. Islamist movements develop on different fronts and at a variety of levels. Strategies of territorial reconquest of the *dar al-harb* are being developed in Kashmir, Indonesia, the Philippines, on different Balkan fronts, in the Caucasus, in Israel, Lebanon, Sudan, Nigeria, and elsewhere.

In the West, the Islamists are fighting for in-depth re-Islamization of millions of Muslim immigrants contaminated by the civilization of *kufr*. Their efforts to convert Christians are having considerable success particularly in pro-Palestinian and anti-Jewish Christian circles. The Islamic doctrine regards the whole Earth as Allah's patrimony entrusted to the *umma*. Thus, from an Islamic viewpoint, the right to immigrate and settle in foreign countries is theologically justified. Muslims cite the example of Christians in Islamic lands in order to demand the establishment of the *shari'a* in a Western legal area. Yet the very limited rights of Christian minorities under Islam only apply in their countries of origin conquered by *jihad* and not in Arabia, the cradle of Islam. The rights of indigenous non-Muslim minorities in their own country and the rights of millions of Muslim immigrants in Europe and the Americas do not follow the same parameters. The huge Muslim immigration to Europe differs on two main points from the *indigenous ethnic dhimmi* communities, to which it is often compared:

1. Muslim immigration to the Western world is recent and alien;
2. This immigration should be comparable to a hypothetical Western immigration in modern times into Muslim countries, including Arabia, on the same demographic scale.

Other bloody confrontations are ravaging a number of Muslim countries in the form of inter-Muslim, politicoreligious wars, as in Algeria, Egypt, Pakistan, Afghanistan, and in other regions. Hostages of this violence, the non-Muslim minorities have to choose between a suitcase, a coffin, or dhimmitude. In recent years, the Islamist concept of *jihad* against the infidel has filtered through to the general public, despite much obfuscation in the Western press. From Indonesia to the Philippines, from Afghanistan to Sudan, from Egypt to Algeria, from Gaza to New York, London, and Paris, calls to *jihad* repeat the same themes, integrated into the same ideological structure. Such homogeneity cannot be improvised, nor is it the result of circumstantial external factors. On the contrary, it is integrated into a permanent historical trend, based on legal, ideological, and cultural foundations. But it would be unfair to omit the manipulation by outside agents of the compulsory nature of *jihad*. Thus, even if *jihad* is an Islamic concept, it also provided the screen for a "Christian" war. This was the Vatican's anti-Israel policy alongside the Palestinian Christians, and the Western Arabist trend; the struggle of the French anti-Zionist and anti-American policies in their conquest of Arab markets; the ideological war of the Soviet Union against Israel and the United States; the latter's war against the Soviet takeover in Afghanistan.

The adoption of *jihad* as a tool in geostrategic and economic rivalries and theological hatred will be discussed later. It suits the masked adversaries to advance their pawns, concealed beneath other banners, as, for example, the anti-Zionist policies of Europe and the ex-Soviet Union—because the war against Israel also has European ramifications. In the context of the adoption of *jihad* by external parties, *jihad* becomes—as so often in history—a Muslim-Christian, and not an exclusively Islamic war. It is sad that the Muslim peoples, today the principal victims of these ideologies of war, should willingly be encouraged to espouse this role.

The various strategies of *jihad* in all its complexities on a world scale cannot be analyzed in this study, but modern *jihad* will be examined in two different contexts: the cases of Sudan and Israel. The situation in Sudan has the advantage of a substantial documentation, provided by human rights defenders and the UN's Special Rapporteur on Sudan from 1993–98. In addition, the Islamist government in Khartoum asserted that it was acting in accordance with Islamic law. Its strategy can easily be compared with the original texts and the history of *jihad*, that is to say, of the Islamic institutional and legal organization for war. As for the Israeli-Arab war, we consider it a typical context of dhimmitude because it also involves—although hidden—a Judeo-Christian conflict.

Jihad in Southern Sudan

In Sudan, the same ethnic and religious conflicts, polarized by the restoration of the *shari'a*, set the Arabized and Islamized North against the African, Christian, and animist South, the traditional source of slaves for the North. Since independence (1 January 1956) the dual process of the Arabization and Islamization of the South provoked a civil war claiming hundreds of thousands of victims. The Agreement of Addis Ababa (1972) recognized the regional autonomy of the South and guaranteed its complete cultural and religious freedom. But the restoration of the *shari'a* (1983) by President Muhammad Ja'far Numeiri, applicable even to the Christians in the North, rekindled the civil war. A coup d'état occurred during negotiations on suspension of the *shari'a* (1989), bringing to power General Omar al-Bashir and the Islamist party, the National Islamic Front (NIF) headed by Hasan al-Turabi. Since then, the Islamic regime has pursued a policy of ethnic and religious cleansing and extermination in the South. Massacres, repression, deportation of populations, and famine intensified considerably following the Gulf War (1991). Soon after, the Sudanese government obtained massive supplies of arms from Iran, another fundamentalist regime. Rony Brauman, the then Chairman of the International Council of Doctors Without Borders (Médecins Sans Frontières) spoke of a "genuine process of extermination."[24] Reports mention "a deliberate—one could say, planned—policy of ethnic and religious cleansing and extermination."[25] Within the framework of its *jihad*, the junta in power also sent heavily armed militias to the Nuba mountains south of El-Obeid, hitherto spared from war. On 16 February 1993, Father Hubert Barbier, who had worked in Africa for twenty-three years, nine of them in Sudan, provided evidence to the United Nations Commission on Human Rights in Geneva:

> The Nuba, of African origin, had been massacred by the thousands, their wives often raped and carried off into slavery together with their children. The area liberated as a result of ethnic-religious cleansing had been occupied by Islamised African tribes from the north. Repression was increasing throughout the south at the present time.[26]
>
> More than 150,000 Nuba families have been forcibly removed from their traditional homeland and relocated elsewhere in the northern Arab desert of that region. Their traditional home and fertile agricultural lands have been repopulated with ethnic Arab tribes. More than 20,000 Nuba children have been sold into slavery with the fullest knowledge and connivance of the regime.[27]

In the neighborhood of Khartoum, where civilian populations—mainly from the South—had massed, the NIF regime planned a policy of massive deportations. From November 1991 more than half a million people were deported and confined in camps in a desert zone, with no food and water. The distribution of food and medical aid was controlled by the Islamists and subject to the blackmail of conversion to Islam.

The Report covering 1993 on the situation of human rights in Sudan was presented to the Commission on Human Rights in February 1994 by the UN Special Rapporteur (UNSR), Dr. Gaspar Biro.[28] He stressed the abduction of women and children deported for slavery and forced labor in the Bahr al-Ghazal, Southern Kordofan, and the Nuba mountains. These actions, perpetrated on a massive scale by the Popular Defence Forces (PDF), the Mujahedin, and the army escorts of trains from Babanusa to Wau were accompanied by pillage, looting of cattle, killings, and rape. (§ 62–65) In reference to religious violations, the report cites forced conversions in various parts of the country, particularly in the deportation camps, the persecution of priests, and the destruction of churches (§ 76–80), the declaration of *jihad* on non-Muslims, particularly Christians (§ 78), the death penalty for apostasy (§ 79–80), discrimination against women (§ 102–106), and the reintroduction of corporal punishment (§ 59). On 12 February following the publication of this report, Sudanese president Omar al-Bashir stated in Khartoum that Dr. Biro was "an enemy of Islam and of the Islamic laws" for publishing what the president called a "blasphemous" report. On 17 February 1994, Sudan's delegation circulated a warning at the Commission on Human Rights entitled, "Attack on Islam"; it also submitted an official letter accusing the Special Rapporteur of making a "vicious attack on the religion of Islam."[29]

The confusion between the political and religious domains emerges very clearly here. Thus, any criticism on policies and human rights violations can be called blasphemy.

In his 1996 Report covering the year 1995, the UNSR wrote that since the resumption of the civil war in southern Sudan in 1983, it has recently been estimated that about two million Africans have lost their lives. In the Nuba mountains, a large number of civilians, including women and children, Christians as well as Muslims, have been killed in deliberate and indiscriminate attacks, or summarily executed (§ 8). In the war in South Sudan, war prisoners are the exception (§ 9). Mosques "were reportedly desecrated, looted and burnt down, allegedly because of the officially expressed claim that the central Government 'knows better Islam' than the indigenous Nubans." (§ 41)[30]

After raids on Nuba villages outside the framework of armed clashes with rebels or after their defeat, the report mentions indiscriminate killings of civilians, regularly accompanied by the burning of houses, churches, mosques, and looting, including the theft of cattle. Mass deportation of civilians—"at least 30,000 civilians from camps around Kadugli during the summer of 1992"—and the abduction of women and children for the purpose of enslavement, were also routine practice. Widespread abuse of women, including the rape of young girls by soldiers and members of the PDF, was regularly reported. (§ 96)

> Reports continue to be received of enforced Islamization in the government-controlled area in the conflict zones and among displaced southerners in northern Sudan. Food and relief, including medicines and clothes, are among the means used to force people to convert to the Islamic religion. The displaced persons who reject Islam are refused shelter and relief. (§ 42)
>
> Alarming reports were received of cases in southern Sudan where those who refused to convert and to send their children to a *khalwa* [koranic school], were killed. During his recent mission, the Special Rapporteur received testimonies, including an eye-witness account, of the summary execution of 12 civilians, men, women and children, at Lobonok on 3 May 1995, at noon. At the end of April 1995, following fighting which reportedly had lasted almost three months, government troops entered Lobonok. The local population was forced to convert to Islam, children were dressed in white jellaba and given Arabic names. Although some adults did convert to receive food, the group mentioned above was executed because they refused to convert and to send their children to the *khalwa*. (§ 43)

Abduction, slavery, and forced Islamization of children—as described here—are similar to those mentioned in the historical records relating to *jihad*, in different regions and in past centuries. In the conclusions to his 1996 Report, Dr. Biro noted:

> [T]he Special Rapporteur continues to receive reports of the practice of arbitrarily rounding up children from the streets of the major towns of

northern Sudan, including the capital city, and of sending them to special camps where: (a) they are subjected to cruel and inhuman treatment; (b) they are ideologically indoctrinated; (c) non-Muslims are forcibly converted to Islam and have their identity changed by being given Arabic names; and (d) in some cases, they are trained by the military in order to be sent to southern Sudan to fight the war. (§ 49)

Women and children continue to be among the most vulnerable groups targeted deliberately by agents acting for and in the name of the Government of the Sudan. In this respect, the following must be taken into consideration:

a) The passivity of the Government of the Sudan regarding the cases of slavery, servitude, slave trade, including the abduction of women and children, traffic in and sale of children, forced labour and similar institutions and practices brought to its attention;

b) The complete disregard by the Government of the Sudan of the calls upon it by the Commission on Human Rights in its resolution 1995/77 to put to an end these practices, and its failure to hold the perpetrators responsible in conformity with the relevant provisions of the Sudanese Criminal Act of 1991;

c) The lack of measures to ensure that members of racial, ethnic and religious minorities, especially children and women, are protected from violations, atrocities, and abuses of this type. (§ 88)

A *fatwa* issued in April [22] 1992 and publicly supported at the highest government level explicitly sets forth the status of all those who oppose the GOS [Government of Sudan]:

"The rebels in south Kordofan and southern Sudan started their rebellion against the State and declared war against the Muslims. Their main aims are: killing the Muslims, desecrating mosques, burning and defiling the Koran and raping Muslim women. In so doing, they are encouraged by the enemies of Islam and Muslims: these foes are the Zionists, the Christians and the arrogant people who provide them with provisions and arms. Therefore, an insurgent who was previously a Muslim is now an apostate; and a non-Muslim is a non-believer standing as a bulwark against the spread of Islam, and Islam has granted the freedom of killing both of them." (§ 97) [this *fatwa* was already mentioned in the UNSR's 1994 Report covering the year 1993: E/CN.4/48/1994, § 78.]

Jihad against Israel

By anti-Zionism we mean the strategy aimed at eliminating the State of Israel. This strategy employs a variety of techniques: local and international terrorism; the delegitimization of the state through a defamatory campaign in the media and the appropriation of Israel's history by a supersessionist maneuver. Anti-Zionism is made up of two strands: the Islamic and the Christian. The latter is not easily identifiable because it is camouflaged in the Islamic movement which it nourishes, guides, and enriches by the addition of traditional Christian and Nazi anti-Judaism.

The Muslim Strand

Islamic anti-Zionism has its roots in the politicoreligious concept of *jihad,* which opposes any non-Islamic political authority anywhere. Peace is only granted to the People of the Book (Jews and Christians) who submit to dhimmitude. The war against Israel is a war against *dhimmis* who have revolted; its aim is to restore the supremacy of Islamic law. Yet Muslim countries, such as Iran under the shah, and Turkey, which had repudiated these outdated concepts and embraced modernity, maintained good relations with Israel. Ottoman Turkey had recognized the autonomy and independence of its former European-Christian provinces since the nineteenth century. It had integrated into its empire—that included Armenia, Lebanon, and Palestine—the millions of Muslim refugees driven out of the Caucasian regions, and of the new Greek and Slav Christian states which were liberated from dhimmitude.

Islamic anti-Zionism rejects all the national characteristics—language, Jewish history, and civilization of Israel—and only recognizes religious rights for *dhimmis.* This ambiguity between war and tolerance has misled a number of analysts who are not conversant with the context of dhimmitude within a *jihad* mentality.

Countless studies of the Arab-Israeli conflict have been published. Here we will refrain from describing it yet again in all its complexity; instead, we will follow the plan of this study and limit ourselves to defining its ideological and historical structural elements within the concepts of *jihad* and *dhimma.*

In January 1998, Sheikh Yusef al-Qaradawi, spiritual leader of the Muslim Brotherhood Movement, confirmed the basic principles commanding the *umma*'s relations with the People of the Book, whom:

> according to the view of Islamic law [are divided into] three types: *Ahl Al-D[h]'imma,* namely non-Muslims under the protection of Islam; *Ahl Al-'Ahd,* namely, non-Muslims in temporary contract with Islam; and *Ahl Al-Harb,* namely non-Muslims in state of war with Islam. Each type has rules that are unique to it.[31]

The *jihad* against Israel is expressed by a dogma (ideology) and by its strategy, comprising military, terrorist, and economic operations (boycott), through propaganda (demonization) and corruption (winning over hearts and minds).

The Muslim-Christian Strand

An Islamized Christianity, as has been described, represents a historical trend which has been active since the beginnings of Islam. It is a fundamental force in the whole history of the Islamic conquests and their hold over the conquered Christian peoples. This trend, in which all the inter-Christian and Judeo-Christian religious rivalries overlap, appeared in the political and military collusion of the Christian hierarchies, or was expressed in the syncretistic form of Sufism at the time when numerous monks were converted to Islam. Few analysts have studied this Muslim-Christian trend which spread from the Orient to Europe. Here, it will be examined only in its modern anti-Zionist form forged in the Holy Land by religious missionaries and which polarized European theological and political rivalries.

After the Arab conquest of Palestine the Christians lost their dominant position and the privileges which had allowed them legally to confiscate and destroy synagogues and to persecute Palestinian Jewry. As in the rest of the *dar al-Islam,* the Jews and Christians of Palestine were expropriated by the laws of *jihad* and suffered the scourges of Arab conquest and colonization by tribes which had emigrated from north and south Arabia. The division of Palestine into provinces, each administratively attached to various Syrian centers, destroyed its character as a geographically defined national unit. It became a land open to migration by nomads dependent on their flocks' transhumance, while only a few agglomerations, with prestigious biblical names, assured the *dhimmis* a dearly purchased and precarious security.

The Arab conquerors imposed the same discriminatory measures on the Christians that the Church had inflicted on the Jews. Nevertheless, the powerful protection of Christian monarchs contrived to procure them privileges which gave them superiority over the Jews. After the Crusades, Christianity in Palestine was primarily represented by foreign monastic orders which ensured the custody of its holy places.

In the mid-nineteenth century, the European powers, which were embarking on the purchase of large urban and rural domains, favored the Christianization of the Holy Land. The earlier waves of Syrian-Lebanese Greek Orthodox, Uniate, and Catholic refugees were swollen after World War I by Christian survivors of massacres in Anatolia, Iraq, and Syria: Armenians, Syriacs, and Nestorians. As a result, a substantial heterogeneity characterized the Christian population of the Holy Land, unlike the other ethno-religious *dhimmi* groups elsewhere in the Middle East: Copts, Armenians, Maronites, Greeks. This historical context explains the diversity of the Christians in Palestine.

Judeophobia

It is not generally known that Syro-Palestinian Christianity nurtured the most virulent Judeophobic sources, whose poisonous manifestations shocked both consuls and travelers up to the end of the nineteenth century. Anti-Jewish hatred was unleashed in Syria-Palestine by frequent accusations of alleged ritual crimes and the murder of Jews. The diverse religious orders and the crowds of Christian pilgrims, particularly at Easter, exacerbated latent mass fanaticism. This Christian aggressiveness was motivated by the doctrine which proved the election of the New Alliance, and the caducity of the Old Alliance, through the degradation of the Jews in their own land. The de-Judaization of Palestine and the persecution of Jews in their homeland were therefore represented as pious deeds. This doctrinal element is precisely what gave the Christian community in Palestine its historical character of extreme and fanatical Judeophobia.

The adoption of Arabic by the *dhimmis* in Syria and Palestine was imposed under the administrative reform of the Caliph Abd al-Malik (685–705), and the prohibition of a non-Arabic language in government offices. This transformation increased with the domination of these regions by Muslim Bedouin dynasties whose tribes had emigrated from Arabia and the Syrian deserts. Arabization of the Near-East was accompanied by great destruction and the persecution of *dhimmis*, especially Christians—particularly in Jerusalem—in retaliation for attempts at the Byzantine reconquest in Syria.

The Greek Orthodox rite was dominant in the cities, whereas Jacobites were widespread in rural regions. After the Crusades, Christianity—already much weakened by earlier centuries of oppression—was restricted from the fourteenth century to a minimal presence in the Holy Land, limited to Christianity's sacred sites. Only the "protection" from Christian states, negotiated with the Islamic authority, could maintain a presence which was tolerated by the Muslim populations solely on payment of multiple charges. This symbolic guardianship, perpetuated over the centuries in the ruins and humiliations of dhimmitude—an identical condition to that which Eastern Christians had previously imposed on Jews—was constantly jeopardized by the multifarious dissensions within Christendom.

From the seventeenth century, the economic privileges linked to French protection encouraged Uniatism (with the Vatican) and the emigration of Christians from Syria to the Palestinian coastal towns of Acre, Jaffa, and Gaza.[32] In 1841, after Muhammad Ali had withdrawn from the Ottoman Syro-Palestinian provinces, the European powers had envisaged the internationalization of Jerusalem and Bethlehem, considered as Christian holy cities. Jerusalem became the center of religious rivalries between the Anglo-Prussian archbishopric founded in January 1842 to develop Protestant influence through conversions, and the Catholic patriarchate established there in July 1847, to promote Catholic interests through Uniatism.

Anti-Zionism

As has been seen, Christian immigration into Palestine in the nineteenth century, contemporary with Jewish immigration, was integrated into a policy of European religious rivalries and of the Christianization of the country. France, the papacy, Austria-Hungary, later Germany, and Russia and Greece for the Orthodox, sustained this movement with political and financial means far superior to that available to the Jews. In this context of politicoreligious imperialism, Zionism was perceived as a danger which could not be defeated by military operations since the Jews were civilian populations scattered over numerous countries. The combat against Zionism utilized other tactics: defamation and incitement to hatred. As Zionism gained ground in twentieth-century Palestine, this campaign reached a crescendo that would lead to a policy, culminating in the near total extermination of European Jewry.

Primarily spread through church networks, the anti-Jewish strategy extended to all Europe and the Ottoman Empire, utilizing political, racist, and religious resources. In Palestine itself—a land of the utmost interest to the Christian world—the Western nations could only intervene through their Christian protégés. But the latter consisted solely of minority groups, divided among themselves and lacking any political power. Only their alliance with the Muslims could overcome Zionism. Islam thus became the savior of Catholicism and Orthodoxy against the "Jewish threat." The de-Judaization of Palestine that had been pursued for more than a millennium was now challenged by a continuous, unstoppable Jewish immigration. Endowed with the historical sacred mission of maintaining Israel in exile, the Syrian and Palestinian Christians denounced Jewish immigrants and land purchases to the Turkish authorities and conducted a virulent, anti-Jewish press campaign among Muslims. It should be noted that the de-Judaization of Palestine required a collection of discriminatory political measures applying exclusively to Jews—and only to them—in their homeland. However, European Zionists—Christians and Jews alike—had sufficient influence and financial means to circumvent this policy. The exacerbation of antisemitism at the turn of the century, as Zionism became established in Palestine, can be followed in the French ultramontane and European antisemitic press. Other national factors were, of course, involved but the reintroduction of a special status for Jews, and the confiscation of their wealth as demanded in Europe by the antisemites and the Catholic clergy, aimed also at neutralizing Zionism. Through their family connections all over the Levant, Palestinian Christians, the clergy in particular, relayed to the Muslim world the baggage of European anti-Jewish hatred of which they were the lungs and voice. It was within the Palestinian Christian ranks that the Arab-Fascist and Nazi movements developed in the Orient, finally collaborating with the Axis forces and backing the pillage and extermination of European Jewry, conceived as the "final solution" for the Jews—and for Zionism as well.

Manipulation and Dhimmitude

The religious heterogeneity of Christians in the Holy Land and the deprivations of their refugee populations constituted a favorable terrain for manipulation and intrigue by foreign imperialist powers. Arab nationalism, by bringing Christians and Muslims together in the same anti-Jewish battle, restricted the fragmentation of the Churches and the consequent centrifugal drift. However, Eastern Christians did not unanimously accept this policy. Many challenged the Arabization policy imposed on them by their clergy, and the Western colonial powers eager to protect their own religious and political interests and to combat Zionism. In Palestine, Christian proponents of Arabism were recruited from among the clergy, civil servants, intellectuals, primarily linked to the Roman Curia and France, and from among Western Arabists.

The evolution of the Christians' political trends in Palestine falls into two phases: the Arab phase from 1922 to 1967, followed by the Palestinian phase. The first corresponds to Christian involvement exclusively in Arabism and the rejection of regional national identities, including a "Palestinian" identity which the Jews had accepted in mandated Palestine until 1948. The following Palestinian phase after 1967 consists of a search for identity, formed in opposition to Israel but modeled on Jewish identity. This imitation comes from a Christian source, since Christians, not Muslims, knew the Bible well. Through Christian mediation, biblical history, appropriated from the Israelis, was transferred to the Palestinians. Whatever the apparent specific features of the two phases—Arab-Palestinians being part of the Arab-Muslim culture and history—both claimed official recognition of historical precedence and legitimacy over Israel, and its elimination. It is therefore possible to discern three different strands which converge in anti-Zionism:

(1) The Arab-Islamic strand which hinges on the ideology of *jihad* and places the Israelis in the ranks of infidel countries, destined to disappear. This strand is as much anti-Christian as it is anti-Jewish.

(2) The Arab-Christian strand in which the traditional anti-Jewish currents of the Orient and Europe coalesce and are masked by the Arab—later Palestinian—cause. The Christian element surfaces in

the construction of a political rhetoric designed to seduce Western opinion by resorting to various levels of European antisemitism concealed under ideological leftist or humanitarian slogans. Its more sophisticated Christological themes are easily identifiable as is its policy of supersession which transfers Israel's historical patrimony to Arab Palestinians. It has been seen that the concept of an "Arab Nation" was of French manufacture, produced by religious institutions in the Levant. The battle for "Arab Palestine" was nothing more than the Christian subterfuge for the Islamic *jihad* against Israel; the aims are identical, only the rhetoric is different.

(3) The European antisemitic strand, which feeds, guides, and supports the preceding strand both financially and politically. The Vatican's involvement in the Palestinian cause and its links with the PLO are known.[33] Charles de Gaulle's doubts about Israel's legitimacy, voiced at a press conference on 27 November 1967, facilitated French ideological and political support for the undermining of Israel's security.[34] These last two aspects—and particularly the similarity between the PLO's charter (1968), to which a considerable number of PLO Christians contributed, and the Islamic Constitution of Hamas (1988)—will be examined below.

From Third-Worldism to Islamism

A number of observers have noted the Islamization process of Third-Worldist revolutionary concepts, the result of alliances and amalgamations between leftwingers, communists, and Islamist revolutionary movements.[35] In 1982, a well-informed Iranian journalist, Amir Taheri, indicated that Geidar-Ali Ali-Zadeh, alias Aliyev—appointed deputy prime minister by Yuri Andropov, and since 1995 president of Azerbaijan—was in charge of relations with communist parties in Muslim countries. Born into a traditional Shi'ite family from Azerbaijan, "Mr. Aliyev was known in Middle Eastern Marxist circles as the chief advocate of 'a revolutionary alliance between fundamentalist Islam and Soviet socialism'."[36] According to Aliyev, "the fundamentalists must be used to mobilize the masses in the name of religion in a holy war against 'Western Imperialism'."[37] This policy was adopted by the communist parties until the collapse of the Soviet regime in 1991.

Many of the leading thinkers of the Islamist movements were graduates of prestigious Western universities: Sayed Qutb spent some years in the United States (1948–51); the Iranian ideologist Ali Shariati was a student of Professor Jacques Berque in Paris;[38] Turabi studied in London and at the Sorbonne. Faced with the dramatic economic and social problems of Islamic societies, these Westernized intellectuals translated European political concepts into an Islamic frame. Humiliations and frustrations were channeled into an anti-West mold, whereas the glorification of Islamic superiority filled the gap between narcissistic nostalgia and intolerable realities. Six weeks after Iraq's invasion of Kuwait on 2 August 1990, and as preparation for the Gulf War began, Jacques Berque, conscious of this psychological factor, declared:

> [The Arabs] weigh heavily on the flanks of Europe, even in its very heart, with the immigrants [sic]. The humiliation of the Arab world is a luxury which we can not afford.[39]

In many respects Islamism seems to be modeled on pan-Arabism, in the pan-Islamic version of the majority of Muslim circles, and not in its primarily literary expression as developed by Christians. In fact, the Islamist program of world subversion—applied also to Muslim states, which do not adopt the *shari'a* and are linked to the West—is modeled on pan-Arabism. Reassessed in a religious concept, the target is the whole world, the *dar al-harb,* and not solely Israel.

This argument appears as the other side of the coin in a 1973 article by Berque which sets out the anti-Zionist dogma and the Arab geopolitical tactics needed for the State of Israel's demise. Born in 1910, brought up in the antisemitic atmosphere of the French colony of Algeria, it is not surprising that Berque should see Israel through the prism of the conspiracy myth. Sharing with the Arab world a Judeophobic paranoia, he developed every anti-Zionist argument, which the Islamists later adopted to demonize the West. The demonization of Israel, which he adapts indiscriminately to suit the Arab or the Islamist cause, displaced the Palestinian struggle from the realm of history to the sphere of metaphysics—the enemy representing the ontological evil, as in the Nazi fashion. Thus, the author explains that the Palestinian affair is the only conflict in the whole of world history to be tragic in the Aristotelian sense for "the essential is there, because the Eye ['*Regard'*] is watching" [sic].[40] Thus, the destruction of peoples and cultures by Islam's conquests through *jihad,* the Armenian genocide, not to mention deportation, slavery, apartheid, the Shoah are all eclipsed because, on a miniscule territory, a small nation has been able to restore its independence in a part of its ancestral homeland. The demonological, Nazi-type interpretation of the history of Israel, which the erstwhile incumbent of the Chair of Social History of Contemporary Islam, and eminent professor at the Collège de France, shared with the Arab world, is applied by the Islamists to the whole of the *dar al-harb.*

Preoccupied with Arab tactics for destroying Israel, Jacques Berque formulated a world strategy which would set "true internationalism" against "cosmopolitan Zionism."[41]

> In such a situation, it is no longer classical warfare that solicits attention, but guerrilla combat, assassination attempts, moral resilience, the explosion of the collective psychism: actions which the chronicle of the past quarter of a century have shown to be the peoples' adequate response to injustice.[42]

These calls to murder worldwide helped to justify the international terrorist campaign in the 1970s against the Jews. The French government bestowed the highest honors on Jacques Berque in his lifetime (d. 1995).

During the wars of decolonization, the traditional religious substrata were molded into a Western political language, often forged by Arab Christian communists and Third World trends. Today, the Islamists' prime aim consists of purifying the *dar al-Islam* of concepts imported from the *dar al-harb* and propagated by transgressing *dhimmis,* eager to escape from Islamic law. Nationalism, the separation of religion and politics, secularism, equality of the sexes and religions, symbolize the diabolical tactics imposed by a Western conspiracy to destroy Islam.

This camouflaging of the ideology of *jihad* through a Western type Third-Worldist phraseology was particularly evident in the PLO's speeches, most probably because of leftist and Marxist Christians' involvement in anti-Zionism. In a 1969 article, Berque had already formulated the thesis of the international significance of combating Israel.[43] However deliberately vague stylistically, he describes Israeli "excess" as "inexpiable",[44] and articulates the plan and the tactics of an anti-Zionist movement which would involve all the peoples of the Earth.[45] In this perspective, as with Vichy-Nazi propaganda, Israel becomes the enemy of mankind.

This thesis will be examined here in two texts which supplement and complement each other: the Charter of the PLO (1968) and the Constitution of *Hamas* (1988).[46] Despite the conflict between the PLO and *Hamas,* the homology of these texts vis-à-vis Israel seems to point to a power struggle rather than an ideological conflict. In article 25 of its Constitution of August 18, 1988, *Hamas* proclaims its respect for and sympathy with the Palestinian nationalist movements—nationalism, for *Hamas,* arising out of religious faith (art. 12). This support is assured them so long as these movements "do not owe their loyalty to the East or the West" (art. 26).

> Under the influence of the circumstances which surrounded the founding of the PLO, and the ideological invasion which has swept the Arab world since the rout of the Crusades [Western colonialists], and which has been reinforced by orientalism and the Christian mission[aries], the PLO has adopted the idea of a secular state, and so we think of it. Secular thought is

diametrically opposed to religious thought [. . .] The Islamic nature of Palestine is part of our religion [. . .]

Until that happens [i.e. the PLO adopts Islam as the guideline for life], the position of the *Hamas* towards the PLO is one of a son towards his father, a brother towards his brother, and a relative towards his relative [. . .]. (art. 27)

The common aim of the two movements—the destruction of the State of Israel—is based on the same assumption: that Israel's independence is illegal.[47] *Hamas* refers to the Islamic law whereby lands conquered by *jihad* constitute "an Islamic *waqf* throughout the generations and until the Day of Resurrection." This prescription, based on the decisions of the second caliph Umar ibn al-Khattab and the opinion of Ali, the fourth caliph—at the time of the conquest of Iraq in 635–42—is equally valid for all lands Islamized by *jihad* (*Hamas,* art. 11). This would include, *inter alia:* Spain, Portugal, Sicily, Greece, all the Balkans, Armenia, India, and so on. This conception is integrated into an ideology in which the *dar al-harb* is delegitimized globally.[48]

In the PLO's charter, an Arab state will replace the State of Israel; for *Hamas,* this state will be Islamic, yet both versions are idyllically described (PLO Charter, art. 16; *Hamas* Constitution, art. 6 and 31). *Hamas* expanded these ideas in classic terms:

[It] strives to raise the banner of Allah over every inch of Palestine. Only under the shadow of Islam could the members of all religions coexist in safety and security for their lives, properties and rights. In the absence of Islam, conflict arises, oppression reigns, corruption is rampant and struggles and wars prevail. (art. 6)

[*Hamas*] is committed to the tolerance inherent in Islam as regards attitudes toward other religions [. . .] Under the shadow of Islam it is possible for the members of the three religions: Islam, Christianity and Judaism, to coexist in safety and security. Safety and security can only prevail under the shadow of Islam, and recent and ancient history is the best witness to that effect. The members of other religions must desist from struggling against Islam over sovereignty in this region. For if they were to gain the upper hand, fighting, torture and uprooting would follow; they would be fed up with each other, to say nothing of members of other religions. The past and the present are full of evidence to that effect [. . .]

Islam accords his rights to everyone who has rights and averts aggression against the rights of others. (art. 31)

This, therefore, is a call for the idyllic state of dhimmitude for the Jews—and for anti-Zionist Christians. This future of peace and prosperity in the Islamic state which would supplant Israel was favorably described by Ismail R. al-Faruqi, a Palestinian professor of Islamic Studies at Temple University, Philadelphia.[49]

According to the author, in this new state—where Jews would no longer be Israelis—the Muslim leader will be able to repeat the message which the Turkish conqueror of Constantinople in 1453 sent to the Greek patriarch who, for his collaboration, was rewarded with Islam's protection. This is hardly a convincing conclusion in view of the almost total disappearance of the Greek population of Anatolia in the twentieth century, and the doubts today of even the Patriarchate of Constantinople's survival.

But the denial of national characteristics is not limited to Israel alone; it is rooted in a conception of mankind, which should be compulsorily subjected to the *shari'a*. Nationalism has no legitimacy whatsoever and, as *Hamas* says, "When Islam appears, all the forces of unbelief unite to confront it, because the community of unbelief is one" (art. 22)—that is, the *dar al-harb,* the region of war.

In the same way as the PLO claimed the whole of Palestine as Arab land (Charter, arts. 2, 21, 28), *Hamas,* which rejects all secular nationalism, acknowledges no legitimacy other than Islamic (arts. 11, 21, 13, etc.). And in the same way as Arab Palestine constitutes an inseparable part of the Arab homeland (Charter, art. 1), so Islamic Palestine is integrated into the Islamic *umma* (*Hamas,* art. 2). The means for eliminating the State of Israel are *jihad* (Charter, art. 9; Constitution, 13, 3, etc.).[50] The PLO cites the solidarity of the Arab world (Charter, art. 1, 10, 15), *Hamas* stresses Muslim solidarity (Constitution, art. 7, 15)—a solidarity justified at an ideological, strategical and operational level (Charter, 13, 14, 15; Constitution, 14, 25, 27, 29 to 33). This military strategy refers to the concept of concentric circles expanding to embrace all the peoples of the earth,[51] a concept which becomes worldwide *jihad* in the *Hamas* version because the community of unbelief (*kufr*) is one. The Charter (art. 8, 12, 27), like the *Hamas* Constitution (art. 25, 27), endorses the internal contradictions of the Arab or Islamic anti-Zionist forces as tactical necessities destined to disappear.

Jihad is also waged at an ideological level in order to modify teaching and purge it of

> all vestiges of the ideological invasion which has been brought about by orientalists and missionaries. That invasion had begun overtaking this area [following] the defeat of the Crusader armies by Salah ad-Din al-Ayyubi [Saladin]. (*Hamas* Constitution, art. 15)

This ideological invasion by the Crusaders—Christendom—violated Muslim ideals and heritage and paved the way for imperialism. (art. 15) All the Islamist movements insist on *jihad* against the "ideological invasion" as a necessary intellectual cleansing operation, an indispensable condition for the establishment of the Islamic state. In Islamist symbolic language, the Tartars represent the communists (Russians), and the Crusaders represent Western Christians. (art. 35)

Particular importance is attached to Arab education (Charter, art. 7) and, for *Hamas*, Islamic education (Constitution, arts. 15, 29, 30). The demonization of the enemy is expressed in the Charter by Third-Worldist, Marxist phraseology (arts. 22, 23), and in the *Hamas* Constitution in Islamic language, which replaces imperialism with the international conspiracy fomented against Islam by the Crusades and the Tartars, whose Machiavellian creation is Israel. The forces of money and sabotage of the Jewish enemy come from: "Freemasons, Rotary Clubs, Lions Clubs, B'nai B'rith and the like," which are the sources of imperialism and corruption, responsible for the French Revolution (1789), both World Wars, as well as the creation of the League of Nations and the United Nations; and for the destruction of the caliphate, and world revolutions: "Their plan is embodied in *The Protocols of the Elders of Zion*" (arts. 22, 28, 32). In the same way as the PLO regarded itself as the nucleus of the Arab revolution and demanded as a legitimate right the pursuit of guerrilla warfare on Israel's borderlands, so *Hamas* claimed this same right in all Islamic countries (art.28). It is true that the PLO modified its position in November 1988 at Algiers. The collapse of communism and Arafat's support for Saddam Hussein at the time of the invasion of Kuwait (August 1990) had helped to weaken the PLO considerably. It forfeited support from the fabulous financial resources of the Gulf states which had enabled it to assert itself at a political and international level, and in the media. This situation and the election of the Rabin-Peres government in Israel (June 1992) brought a spectacular Israel-Palestinian rapprochement by August 1993.

The disintegration of the Soviet Union and international pressures on Israel for concessions opened the way for an Israel-Palestinian treaty of mutual recognition that was signed in Washington on 13 September 1993, a prerequisite for the establishment of peace between Israel and the Arab states. On 14 December 1998, in Gaza, the Palestinian National Congress—in the presence of President Clinton, and on live television—publicly amended the articles concerning Israel's illegitimacy in the PLO's 1968 Charter.

But for all modern Islamists, the aim of *jihad* will always remain the expansion of Islam—by war or by persuasion—over the entire world, and the establishment worldwide of the *shari'a*, the law of Allah. The concept of *dar al-harb* embraces all non-Muslim countries; they constitute the empire of Evil and ignorance, the *jahiliyya*—the Arabic word used for the "paganism" that preceded Islam. It is the religious duty of Muslims to replace it with the empire of Good and of True Faith, which is Islam.

Hamas transposed the ideology and tactics of *jihad*—as expressed in terms of Arab nationalism by Christian Arabs in the Third-Worldist jargon of the sixties—into an Islamic language with its historical categories. All this notwithstanding, some Christian Arab theologians called for the regen-

eration of the Arab soul by the destruction of the State of Israel, such as
Georges Khodr, Metropolitan of Byblos and Mt. Lebanon, in 1970.

> The grace of this new birth [of the Arab soul] is only acquired through a
> restored Palestine.[52]

The illegitimacy of Israel is incorporated into the illegitimacy of the West
as a whole, the stages in Israel's destruction by Islamists, analyzed by Jacques Berque as a process of unification and universalization, are applied
globally: unity of the Islamic world; demonization of the West; division of
roles between subversive, destabilizing terrorist movements and the legal
facade of the state.

This interdependence between the West and Israel is hardly the result of
circumstantial events, for it is integrated into the very origin of Islamic
dogma. In no way is it the demonology of Israel which is reflected onto
the West but rather the reverse, with the whole emotional charge of the
uninterrupted conflict between Christian and Muslim states. The exploitation of anti-Zionist paranoia by European governments and the automatic
majority at the United Nations fostered the rejection of the 1979 peace
treaty between Israel and Egypt for ten years, and the legitimization of Palestinian terrorism which later boomeranged on the West, the former Soviet
Union, and also the Muslim world. This did not correspond only to geostrategic and economic interests, but also revealed a policy of self-protection
consisting of diverting aggression onto a third party (displaced aggressiv-
ity), a traditional policy of the Arabic Christian communities in the East,
now transposed to the level of European states.

The Anti-Zionist, Missionary, and Third-Worldist Movement

In the same way as the destruction of the Lebanese Christian bastion
would unleash the advance of the Church in the Third World, so—for this
movement—the Western fortress had to be opened to a Muslim immigration in order to bring about the fusion of the two shores of the Mediterranean. The mixing of populations and the abolition of frontiers opened the
missiological field, conceived as the area for the Church's charitable duties
in the service of Islam.

At the theological level, the Muslim-Christian fusion required a search
for common ground. In the tradition of Louis Massignon, this pursuit consisted of "de-Bible-izing" the Bible, by favoring an interpretation in the
light of a koranic reading. The meeting and the journey common to the
Christian and the Muslim required a certain "conversion to Islam" (dia-
logic attitude), "an Hijran exodic itinerary."[53] These are the necessary pre-

conditions for a return to Islamic Abrahamism, which was thereafter conceived as being at the origin of Judaism and Christianity, and consequently reversed the order of relations between the three religions.[54] The Islamic reading of the Bible suppresses the Judeo-Christian affiliation in order to attach the Gospels to the Koran, in particular through the adoption of the koranic interpretation of Jesus Christ's genealogy.[55] This exegesis led Youakim Moubarac in the early 1970s to proclaim in his confused and emphatic style, that:

> The Islamic vocation of Jerusalem is thus an ecumenical urgency incumbent on Christianity . . .[56]

In other words, the Christian denial of Israel's right in Jerusalem calls on Christianity to buttress Islam's duty to force Judaism back to dhimmitude. Likewise, the Christians themselves are made dependent on the Islamic order.[57] Moubarac also proposes the Islamic formula for Christians.

At a political level this activism was based on the exemplary Lebanese model, whose principal aim is to assert a Muslim-Christian brotherhood against Zionism.[58]

> Lebanon is the eldest son of the peaceful cohabitation of Islam and Christianity.
> It is in Lebanon, therefore, that the whole complex of Muslim-Christian relationships must be encountered and experienced, not only for that country but also for the rest of the world. It is in Lebanon that this must be conceived and institutionalized. It is in Lebanon that the formulas of interfaith and international life must be turned into reality, in so far as the evolution of the present world still depends on those two major factors of its past evolution which are Islam and Christianity.[59]

In 1967, the Lebanese and Yugoslavian models of a Muslim-Christian peaceful coexistence were put forward as a justification for the demise of the State of Israel. This Christian vocation in the service of Islam gave the Arab Christian clergy a political role which was of prime importance to the Arab governments. Their apostolic mission in the West included spreading Islamic propaganda through Western religious channels; encouraging and giving practical or moral support to anti-Israeli terrorism (using the theme of Palestinian despair); demonizing Israel; vindicating Islam and, above all, concealing the Islamization and religious purification of Arab societies with all its discriminatory and humiliating restrictions in respect of Christians.

In the West, this trend militated for a European and a Church "Muslim policy". The abolition of frontiers and of "chauvinist" nationalisms would allow the merging of both shores of the Mediterranean. The missiological field thus opened wide would encourage mass Muslim emigration into Europe and the emergence of a Muslim-European bloc hostile to Israel, as well as a counterweight to the influence of the United States. At a theological level, and in a salvific perspective, past Islamic conquests of Christian countries were vindicated, thus justifying the modern Islamic advance into Europe. As Abbé Moubarac explained:

I, as a Christian and a priest, I believe and I testify that Muslims are as much at home and rightfully so in St. Sophia [in Istanbul] as in Aqsa [in Jerusalem], and as they must one day be at home again in the mosque of Cordova, whose Christian additions—transforming it into a church—are an insult to pure beauty.[60]

The criminalization of Zionism in the West, which the Eastern Arab Churches made a basic and essential condition of the Muslim-Christian rapprochement,[61] conferred on the elimination of the Jewish state a priority over defending the rights of their own communities. This procedure explains the silence that hid the deterioration in the condition of Christians, whose Church leaders had the responsibility to protect, but who today are blamed by many community members for their myopia.

Islamic biblical exegesis and anti-Zionism developed the self-hatred syndrome, familiar to Christendoms in the East. Reading the Bible, particularly certain psalms, became painful. For Moubarac

it is not just the psalms; there are even whole books of the Bible that have become difficult for me, because they are infinitely painful to read [. . .][62]

The psalms become "the most intolerable shock" to bear. The "spiritual perversion of the exegesis" needs to be counterbalanced:

I turn to the Koran as a sort of Old Testament which serves as an antidote to the first. In a sense, the Koran becomes my desert Psalter.[63]

The Judeophobia at the very heart of the Church—generating hatred of its theological roots—as well as Islamophilia, are illustrated in this description of Louis Massignon by his faithful disciple Youakim Moubarac:

It is not accurate to say that Massignon loved Ishmael and Israel with the same love. I would say rather that this Christian tried to heal the uncircumcized heart of Israel in his Abrahamic heart, while loving Muslims passionately. The Muslims—that is, all the non-Jews, all the non-Christians, everyone who does not have a share in the promise and its privileges—[are] all those excluded, humiliated and abused, within the Jewish people, as within the Muslim people, and everywhere. Massignon has passionately defended the

koranic protest against the arrogant exclusiveness of the Jews and the crimi-
nally oppressive egoism of those who call themselves Christian.[64]

The amalgamation between Muslims, the poor and the "excluded" appears at a theological level:

> The position of Islam honors the monotheism of Abraham and the messia-
> nity of Jesus, both of which abolished Jewish and Christian "privileges."[65]

As is well known, the theme of "exclusion" became a major argument in
Third-Worldist ideology. But one wonders how theologians are able to ignore the universal blessings for mankind expounded in the Bible, and the
exclusion from salvation decreed by a considerable number of koranic
verses in regard to Jews, Christians, and other non-Muslim peoples, condemned to eternal torture in hell. Likewise, it only needs a glance at the
map to realize that it is precisely the vast territory conquered by Islam that
turned Christians and Jews into excluded and humiliated peoples, whose
much-vaunted "privileges" in their former homelands belong to the imaginary.

Third-Worldist missionary work, based on the rejection of Judeo-Christianity—identified with capitalist exploitation and a system of theological
exclusion—expanded, through the clergy, the movement of Islamization
in Europe by conversion to Islam and Muslim immigration, particularly
from the 1970s till today.

8

The Return of Dhimmitude

Arabization was the vector of Islamization, just as Arab nationalism was the vehicle of *jihad*. The homology of the two processes not only forms a basic principle of faith for the Arab *umma*—as noted by Hasan al-Banna, founder of the Muslim Brotherhood Movement in 1928—but their interdependence was always emphasized by Arab Christian politicians and ideologists.

Motivations for Islamization were numerous; they include the legitimate desire of a society to recover its roots and its own values. However, the re-Islamization movements are not solely cultural or pietist, but also political. And, insofar as the rejection of non-Islamic—particularly Jewish or Christian—norms is inscribed in several verses of the Koran, this re-Islamization engenders the radical elimination of any foreign legal, social or ideological element.[1]

The same problem occurred in the nineteenth century when it came to carrying out the reforms and modernization of the Ottoman Empire, hence Ubicini's repeated advice:[2]

> that the [Ottoman] government for its part, insofar as it will want to introduce new reforms, take care to present them as an application of the principles of the Koran and not as borrowings from Europe; after that one will see all opposition cease [. . .] (1:142)
> that the Porte, for its part, take care to present the new reforms as a direct emanation from the Koran in order to make them acceptable to the people [. . .] (2:422)

Abbé Moubarac felt that "secularism should not be presented by its advocates as a Western invention [. . .]," but rather as a "resumption" of a tradition rooted in the East. In order for secularism to have some chance of success there, he advised Christians to accept Muslim law, not only as a source of law but as the primary source of law. On this condition, he wrote, Islam would accept secularism, and the Christian communities would recover their specific rights[3]—which means dhimmitude, a system always praised by the Church, as it could thereby retain full control over its congregations.

This illustrates the inescapable necessity of Islamizing modern Western ideas if they are to be introduced into the Arab East. This attitude of doctrinal rejection is linked to the demonization of the *dar al-harb*, born of the problematic relationship to non-Muslim entities—that is, the Crusading West, Israel, and other regions. It unleashes a process of ideological vilification disseminated by religious, educational, and political networks that are integrated into the movement of re-Islamization.[4]

On the political scene, the adoption of the *shari'a* as the ethical and legal criterion reactivates the practices, customs, and laws which had permeated Islamic civilization for more than a millennium, remaining throughout as ideal reference models. This return to past jurisdiction allows a comparison between the laws and the social and political consequences of their application today, with similar situations reported in ancient chronicles. And this is even more feasible as the present status of non-Muslims in a modern Islamist state is now the subject of considerable discussion. It is set out by Muslim politicians in vague and conciliatory terms which still present some contradictions with current practices.[5]

In the early 1990s the current situation of the Christians in the predominantly Islamic countries has emerged from being a taboo subject, and was mentioned in a few publications which appeared in the United States and Europe, often in unofficial information leaflets for internal use. It has also been debated occasionally in various international forums, and sometimes evoked in reports to United Nations bodies. The following documentation is mainly from these UN human rights sources.

Countries Applying the *Shari'a*

Saudi Arabia

The *shari'a* is strictly applied in Saudi Arabia and the practice of Islam is compulsory. The Christian population numbers between half a million to a million immigrant workers. Churches, the import of Bibles, prayerbooks, and the celebration of their religion are strictly forbidden. The religious police severely punish any infraction by the destruction of unauthorized chapels, altars, missals, and any religious cult object. Officiants are hunted down, imprisoned, kept in solitary confinement and, at best, expelled.

Apart from a few American diplomats—and soldiers during the Gulf War—no Jew is tolerated on Saudi territory. Judeophobia is integrated into educational programs and into the politicoreligious doctrines of the kingdom.[6] The impurity and defilement attributed to non-Muslims prohibits their presence in Mecca or Medina. This conviction is shared by the whole Muslim world. All the koranic punishments are applied.[7] All this notwithstanding, Saudi Arabia received the necessary "regional" backing to be nominated as one of the fifty-three member States of the UN Commission on Human Rights, from 2001.

Iran

Christians (mainly Armenians), Jews, Zoroastrians, and Baha'is form the indigenous non-Muslim population of Iran. The restoration of the *shari'a* by the Ayatollah Khomeini led to the expulsion of the majority of foreign priests and pastors and the closure of all their religious schools in 1980. The Islamic government reimposed punishment by mutilation, stoning for adultery, execution for apostasy or blasphemy, the rejection of testimony in an Islamic court by a non-Muslim when a Muslim is involved, and discrimination in employment. Prohibitions affect the building of churches and synagogues and the import of Christian and Jewish books and journals which are subject to strict control. The Islamization of non-Muslims takes place via the lex talionis which discriminates against the non-Muslim, and in the army, which is structured by the ideology of *jihad*. The state controls the compulsory religious education of non-Muslim schoolchildren. School teaching—geography, history, literature—is imbued with anti-Christian and anti-Jewish material, and totally Islamized. Non-Muslims, globally designated as *kafir* (unbelievers), are denigrated in the media, mosques, and schools.

The following facts are extracted from the Report for 1992 on the Situation of Human Rights in the Islamic Republic of Iran by Mr. Reynaldo Galindo Pohl, the UNSR.[8] It mentions cases of imprisonment and torture of Muslims who converted to Christianity, and of Armenian and Assyrian pastors (§ 244–50), the dissolution of the Iranian Bible Society in 1990, the closure of Christian libraries, the confiscation of all Christian books, and in 1991 of 20,000 copies of the New Testament in Farsi (§ 250). A few extracts illustrate this situation:

251. It has been reported that all Christian activities are checked by the Ministry of Culture and Islamic Guidance, which is responsible for religious minorities in the Islamic Republic of Iran. Christians must receive permission to print their church newsletters and are not allowed to build new church buildings. They are only allowed to renovate old church buildings provided they do not add any new construction.
252. It has been reported that Armenian and Assyrian Christians are not allowed to pray or read their sacred books out loud at home or in churches, lest Muslims hear their prayers; they are not allowed to print their religious books or sell them in public places and markets and they are not allowed to congregate in the streets during their religious festivals. Armenian and Assyrian Christians are not permitted to broadcast or display their ceremonial re-

ligious rituals on radio or television or to publish any picture of their religious ceremonies in newspapers and magazines and they are not allowed to install the cross on their churches or houses. Obtaining wine for communion services is severely punished and Christian schools must now teach the Islamic understanding of Jesus as 'one of 120,000 prophets'.[9]

By the terms of the Constitution of the Islamic Republic of Iran, and in official documents, Baha'is are regarded as belonging to a "misguided dissident sect" and, hence, do not benefit from any protection, not even that granted *dhimmis*, according to the definitions provided in this report:

227. Neither Baha'i marriages nor divorces are legally recognized in the Islamic Republic of Iran. Baha'is continue to be deprived of inheritance rights. For the past 12 years, the Baha'i community has been denied the right of assembly and the right to elect and maintain its administrative institutions. These institutions constitute the core of religious community life, considering that there is no clergy in the Baha'i faith. Without administrative institutions the very existence of the Baha'is as a viable religious community is said to be seriously endangered. As individuals, Baha'is are officially considered "unprotected infidels" and, therefore, their civil rights and liberties are often ignored. The non-recognition of their religion manifests itself in various ways, including the denial of the basic right to express their religious beliefs freely.

309. As regards followers of the Baha'i faith, there have been numerous confirmed and documented cases of harassment, arbitrary detention, confiscation of property, expulsion from the home and discrimination in general. As has been pointed out in the part of this report relating to developments [in Isfahan, Teheran, and Yazd], 1992 has seen two Baha'is sentenced to death because of their religious faith; at least one member of this community has been executed during the year. [. . .]

310 (c). As regards their legal and social position, the following guidelines are hereby adopted [by the Iranian government]: (i) they shall be permitted to lead a modest life similar to that of the population in general; (ii) to the extent that this does not constitute encouragement for them to persist in their status as Baha'is, they shall be allowed the normal means to live like all other Iranian citizens, such as ration books, passports, death certificates and work permits; (iii) employment shall be refused to persons identifying themselves as Baha'is; (iv) they shall also be denied positions of influence, for example, in the education sector.

Relevant to this subject are further extracts from Mr. Galindo Pohl's Report for the year 1994 to the UN Commission on Human Rights:[10]

52. The Baha'is in Mash[h]ad are reportedly facing major hurdles in carrying on their professional and commercial activities. Throughout the country, many Baha'is dismissed from the public sector on account of their religious beliefs are still unemployed and receive no financial assistance, grant or pension. It has even been reported that some Baha'is dismissed

from the public sector were required to return the salaries and pensions they had received when they were working. Baha'i farmers are still denied access to farm cooperatives, which often provide the only opportunity to obtain credits, seed, fertilizers and pesticides.

53. It has been alleged that marriage, divorce and the right to inherit among the Baha'is continue to be unrecognized in law. Major difficulties, mentioned in information received previously, remain in obtaining passports and exit visas. It is asserted that young Baha'is continue to be denied access to higher education and, for the Baha'i community as a whole, the right to meet freely, to elect their representatives and to maintain their administrative institutions. The cemeteries, holy places, historical sites and administrative centres of the Baha'i community remain confiscated or have been destroyed. It is said that the Baha'is must bury their dead on waste land specified by the Government and that they are not entitled to identify the graves of their loved ones.

105. Property of Baha'is resident at Ilkhchi and Saryan has been confiscated. Pressure on the Baha'i community has been particularly severe in the city of Mashhad. Cemeteries, historic sites, administrative centres and property confiscated in 1979 have not been returned to the community.

Concerning the situation of Christians, this same Report indicates:

102. The Bible Society of Iran and the Garden of Evangelism society remain closed. The closure of the Christian church at Gorgan has also been reported. The Christian churches at Mash[h]ad, Sari, Ahwaz, Kerman and Kermanshah have been closed. The church at Orumiyeh is open but only one religious service is permitted each week. Christian religious services are permitted in the Armenian and Syrian languages but not in Farsi. Christian church leaders have signed written promises not to permit Muslim believers to attend their religious services. [. . .] Reports have also been received of alleged acts of aggression, persecution and threats against other Protestant ministers and Christian converts at Kermanshah [details were given of two cases].

42. In its November 7, 1994 issue, [the newspaper] *Kayhan* reported that the Government of Tehran had banned the manufacture and sale of clothing, footwear and accessories with unsuitable patterns or letters from the Latin alphabet on them. The decision is reported to be based on the need to preserve the country's culture and national and religious traditions and to guarantee proper respect for the national literature and language.

In his conclusion, the Special Representative recommends, *inter alia:*

110 (h). There must be an end to the harassment and discrimination to which members of the Baha'i community are subjected because of their religious convictions, mainly in matters of marriage, divorce, succession, issue of passports and exit visas, rights of ownership and free possession of their places of worship, cemeteries, historic sites and administrative centres. Careful attention should also be given to the legal situation of Baha'is who are in

prison, particularly those who have been sentenced to death or accused of apostasy.

110 (i). There must also be an end to acts of surveillance, hostility and discrimination against Protestants, particularly converts from Islam; permission should be given for the re-opening of churches, chapels, libraries, bookshops and other Christian premises that have been closed down and for the construction of new premises; and the right to hold services in Farsi without being kept under surveillance by agents of the security forces should be guaranteed.

In his Report to the UN Commission on Human Rights for the year 1995 the new UNSR, Mr. Maurice Copithorne, stated that the Islamic Penal Code of the Islamic Republic of Iran may apply the death penalty and other punishments for offenses deserving Islamic punishment, like apostasy and sexual relations by a non-Muslim with a Muslim woman.[11]

Mr. Copithorne's Report for the year 1997 noted public executions, the use of stonings in large cities, lashes, and amputations for offenses. It also mentions discrimination and persecution against Baha'is, "including extra-judicial executions, arbitrary detentions, refusal of entry to universities, confiscation of property and dismissal from employment," and religious persecution.[12]

His Report covering the year 1998 gives details of the laws on the status of minorities which contain numerous discriminatory provisions against non-Muslims.[13] In Annex 4, he gives examples from the Islamic Criminal Code, in which the law provides punishment if the victim of a murder is a Muslim, but if the victim is a non-Muslim, the law is silent and therefore no punishment needs to be enforced (art. 207). A non-Muslim man is condemned to death for sexual relations with a Muslim man or woman, while a Muslim is subjected to a hundred lashes. Some provisions in the Islamic Civil Code (arts. 121, 297, 300, 881) and in the Constitution (163) enforce discriminations against non-Muslims in the domain of inheritance, judiciary profession, and blood money. In his Report for the year 1999, the Special Representative confirmed that the situation of the Baha'is remains serious. He also drew attention in Annex 2 to manifold irregularities in the arrest of thirteen Iranian Jews accused of spying for Israel.[14]

Mr. Maurice Glélé-Ahanhanzo, the UNSR on Contemporary Forms of Racism, Racial Discrimination, Xenophobia and Related Intolerance, has a section (H) on the Islamic Republic of Iran in his Report for the year 1999 in which he described the constant police surveillance of the Jewish community by the Iranian authorities, and their discriminatory policy in regard to Jewish schools and the employment and travel of Jews.[15]

Sudan

As already described in the previous chapter, the application of the shari'a in 1983 reignited a rebellion by the Christian and animist South, heightening a latent revolutionary situation. The restoration of the *shari'a* imposed the already mentioned provisions of Islamic law: mutilation, corporal punishment, the death penalty for apostasy and blasphemy, a hundred strokes of the whip for adultery, and, depending on the case, crucifixion of the corpses of the tortured. In the field of education, study of Islam is compulsory and admission to university includes an examination on Islamic science. The teaching of Arabic, the official state language— although English is more common in southern Sudan—is based largely on the utilization of Islamic texts. Permission to build new churches is refused. In many places, Christian prayer meetings, regarded as open churches, are forbidden. Foreign priests and nuns are expelled, repressed, or admitted with difficulty, while ecclesiastical personnel, even Sudanese, are subject to continual harassment: closure of prayer centers, expulsions, attacks on churches, arbitrary arrests, confiscation of schools, and a ban on changing residence.

Pressure to convert to Islam is applied by blackmail in regard to humanitarian food aid intended for the millions of internally displaced and starving populations, by intimidation and threats directed at prisoners, invalids, nurses and students. Christianity is decried in the media, schools, and religious sermons.[16] This situation has not changed since Sudan was declared an Islamic state in 1989.

Pakistan

Although Pakistan is outside the scope of this study, it is worth mentioning some legal measures which illustrate a certain uniformity of Islamic jurisdiction in Muslim countries although their cultures are different. Pakistan, which obtained its independence in 1947, rejected Mohammad Ali Jinnah's principle of a secular state and became a Muslim state in 1956. During the presidency of General Zia ul-Haq (1977–88), a Federal Shariat Court (FSC) was instituted to exercise jurisdiction in cases involving Islamic laws. It had to examine any law or provision of law, and validate it only if it was in accordance with koranic jurisdiction. In 1984, the president introduced the Hudood (Punishment) Ordinances which "define crimes against Islam" and edict their punishment according to Islamic laws.[17]

The laws concerning blasphemy are found in section 295–B and 295–C of the Pakistan Penal Code, the latter prescribing death. In 1997, a Christian village in the Punjab, Shantinagar, was set ablaze by a mob protesting an alleged blasphemous offense.

In January 1999, a joint written statement was submitted to the Commission on Human Rights by Franciscans International, the Commission of the Churches on International Affairs of the World Council of Churches, and the World Alliance of Reformed Churches.[18] The following excerpts are taken from this statement:

> The Blasphemy Laws in their present form have become a source of victimization and persecution of minorities in the country. Minorities suffer all manner of humiliations through false accusations made under these laws. In the present climate of hate, intolerance and violence in Pakistan, the Blasphemy Laws have become a major tool in the hands of extremist elements to settle personal scores against members of religious minorities, particularly Christians. [. . .] Since the mandatory death sentence was introduced as a result of Amendment Act No. 3 (1986) to Section 295–C, many innocent people have lost their lives, including some accused persons who had not been brought to trial. [. . .]
>
> In the present context, lawyers who appear in court on behalf of accused persons in blasphemy cases are the targets of intimidation and threats. [. . .] In view of continuing threats and intimidation, it has become increasingly difficult to engage the services of lawyers to defend cases registered under the Blasphemy Laws. (§ 7–8)

On 6 May 1998, John Joseph, the Catholic Bishop of Faisalabad and Chairman of the Human Rights Commission established by the Catholic Bishops' Conference of Pakistan, publicly committed suicide in front of the law court in Sahiwal which, a few days before, had pronounced a death sentence on yet another young Christian from Punjab, falsely accused of blasphemy. His desperate act aimed at calling world attention to Pakistan's blasphemy law which has claimed many innocent lives.

In 1979, an amendment to Pakistan's electoral laws changed the previous system of joint electorate to a system of separate electorates. The above-mentioned joint written statement explains how:

> The amendment was introduced at the request of the religious-political parties that subscribe to the view that non-Muslims in Pakistan are "Zimmis" [dhimmis] or second-class citizens. During the past two decades, successive Governments in Pakistan have followed discriminatory policies that have prevented non-Muslims from holding key positions in the civil service and in the higher judiciary. [. . .]
>
> This policy of discrimination among voters on grounds of religion has cut off the non-Muslim citizen of Pakistan from the mainstream of national political life. Further, it has denied them the right to participate directly in the national decision-making processes as well as in the framing of national economic, social and cultural policies. (§ 4–5)

Soon after the coup d'état and the fall of Prime Minister Nawar Sharif in December 1999, the new head of state, General Pervez Musharraf, explained the guiding principles of a new human rights policy, "entrenched in the values of human dignity, justice and equality, enshrined in Islam."[19]

He promised to suppress the abuses of the Blasphemy Laws and to improve the status of women, and specifically condemned the "honor killings" of women.

However, less than a month later—under threats and pressure from Islamic clerics and twenty rightist religious parties—General Musharraf withdrew his plan to prevent abuses of the Blasphemy Law. Musharraf told reporters: "As it was the unanimous demand of the Ulema, Mashaikh (religious scholars) and of the people, I have decided to do away with the procedural change." He said that the government would consult religious scholars on Islamic issues.[20] The religious parties had threatened a nationwide strike if Musharraf went ahead with the plan for reform. Christians and other non-Muslim minority communities have often called for repeal of the blasphemy law.

Countries Adapting the *Shari'a*

Egypt

The Egyptian Islamist trend, although challenged from the nineteenth century and repudiated by official Islam linked to the government, demands the strict restoration of the *shari'a.* Today, extremist currents advocate the elimination of Muslim opponents, Westernized intellectuals and politicians, likened to the "hypocrites" of the Prophet's day.

As in other countries previously referred to, dhimmitude can be observed on two levels: laws and customs. In the legal sphere, some Islamic laws, obsolete during British rule, have been restored. Hence, the building of new churches or the renovation of old ones and their annexes—even a temporary tent in the courtyard or the modernization of toilets—were prohibited. These constraints were designed to humiliate a tolerated religion. Already before Sadat's assassination in 1981, and then under President Hosni Mubarak, the restrictions were extended to all Coptic institutions: church halls, hospitals, bishops' residences, and so on. In the region of Asyut (Dariut), Sohag and Alexandria, a number of churches which had been repaired without permission were destroyed or pillaged. Except at Christmas and Easter, only Islamic programs are televised.

In Cairo, the state confiscated fifteen historic churches and transferred the ownership of lands in mortmain (*waqf*), held by the Church, to the Minister of Islamic Affairs (1968), thereby curtailing community social benefits to the poor. Regarding religious matters, the memorandum issued by the Coptic patriarchate (17 December 1976) mentions "bloody attacks on several occasions when they [the Copts] want to build a church." Coptic history from the first to the seventh century was removed from textbooks and educational programs. In August 1976, and the following year, external religious manifestations, such as decorations, illuminations, and processions provoked hostile demonstrations against Copts. Stones especially prepared for the purpose had been thrown at a cathedral, two evangelical churches, and Christian shops and houses. On those lands left to the patriarchate, a building presumed to be a church was demolished in 1973 and a mosque was built there in 1976. References can be found to other attempts, abortive or successful, to build mosques on confiscated land belonging to the patriarchate, or on Christian property.[21]

Court decisions in favor of Christians and against Muslims are not carried out. The police and postal service neglect complaints by Copts. In some places in Upper Egypt, "protection" dues—the old *jizya*—are added to other extortions and to the prohibition of publicly celebrating Christian religious festivals, marriages or funerals. Recently the law again imposed prescriptions on apostasy, conversion from Islam and the marriage of a Muslim woman with a Christian man.[22] Similarly, various discriminatory measures prevent Copts from attaining positions of responsibility or posts, which would give them authority over a Muslim. Thus, high rank in the army, administration, universities, magistrature, police, banks, and industrial and commercial companies are closed to them.

In the field of education, primary schools refuse to appoint Copts as Arabic teachers after the fifth year. Even in the private education sector, the teaching of the Arabic language and literature is exclusively reserved for Muslim teachers. Diplomas from Coptic religious institutions have less academic credit than those granted by Muslim institutions. Compulsory educational textbooks inculcate the superiority of Islam over the other religions which presumably will be eliminated in time. This situation designates Christian pupils as infidels in the eyes of their schoolmates and even their teachers.

Regarding prejudices and customs, the previously mentioned memorandum of the St. Synod to the Egyptian government (February 1977) stressed the campaign of defamation—both in the media and the press—against Christianity, its dogma, and its clergy. The media disseminated abuse in respect of Christians, who are called infidels, exhortations to a *jihad* against them, and sarcastic comments ridiculing Christianity. Priests are sometimes chased by children and adolescents throwing stones and rubbish, while Muslim bystanders do nothing to stop them. Insults in respect of Christians and Christianity are a general phenomenon for young and old, in the streets, schools, workplace and public transport. Attempts at Islamization via school, pressure, corruption, blackmail, and above all contempt and discrimination at every level of social life represent—to quote the Coptic lawyer Ibrahim Fehmi Hilal—a "passive war of extermination" of the Copts who "are dying from the slow doses of poison seeping into their body."

Reports from Copts note their under-representation in parliamentary bodies and also cases of the forced Islamization of young Christians. Henceforth, churches must be protected against projectiles by walls and guards, while insecurity and discrimination are accelerating a Coptic emigration movement.[23]

The sporadic attacks against Copts which started in the 1970s intensified in the 1980s and 1990s. Since 1992, the Islamists' war against the Copts has taken the form of stone-throwing, stabbings, shooting, bombs, and arson. This hate campaign provoked reprobation and indignation in non-Islamist Egyptian circles and stirred the government of president Mubarak, himself threatened by the Islamist terror, to promulgate measures ensuring the protection of the Copts. Nonetheless, the deterioration in the economic and social situation, the corruption of the regime, and the attacks perpetrated by the Islamists are increasing insecurity and religious racism. Bloody assassination attempts on "infidel" tourists such as the massacres on 18 September 1997 in Cairo and at Luxor on 17 November 1997, necessitated severe protection measures, humiliating for the government. These circumstances are somewhat reminiscent of earlier times when bodyguards ensured the safety of travelers from the *dar al-harb*.

To satisfy pressure from Islamists, innocent Copts are severely condemned for the religious clashes and even for attacks on tourists (see pp. 246–47). When the government puts pressure on the Islamists, large numbers of Christians are also arrested in an effort to appease public opinion by what appears to be an even-handed policy but which actually does not distinguish between guilty and innocent. Many imams teach that Christians and Jews are infidels, creating an atmosphere of hatred, contempt and intolerance. According to the Rev. Keith Roderick, who gave testimony at a U.S. Congressional hearing in 1998:

> The Egyptian government has allowed the Copts to be used as human safety valves in an attempt to deflect the Islamists' anger against the Mubarak regime.[24]

In the 1990s, attacks on Copts increased in Lower and Upper Egypt, in Al-Zawiyah Al–Hamra, Ain Shams, Imbaba, Sanabu, Asyut, Aswan, Minya, and other cities and suburbs of Cairo and Alexandria.[25] Monks were killed in monasteries and priests stabbed in the street. Mass killings occurred in churches (1994, in Assiut; and 1995, 1996, 1997, in Abu Qurqas, Minya Province); bullets and explosives targeted churches. In the countryside, money extortions from Copts (as *jizya*) were followed by torture and execution for those who refused to comply. After the murder on 4 August 1998 of two young Copts by a Muslim in Al-Kosheh village (Upper Egypt), police rounded up more than twelve hundred Coptic villagers and abused and terrorized whole families. Men were tortured, women and children were threatened and maltreated in an attempt to extort confessions from them, in order to "prove" that the Copts had perpetrated the murders. On 31 December 1999, Muslims from Al-Kosheh and the surrounding villages gathered and went on a rampage against Christians, looting, burning, and killing during three days with the collaboration of some local police. Calls to *jihad* against Christians in the name of Allah poured from the minaret and the populace. Twenty-one Copts were killed, some brutally mutilated. The local police were accused of negligence and connivance.

Egyptian intellectuals, journalists, liberals, and Egyptian human rights organizations accused the government of disseminating a culture of intolerance and rejection of the non-Muslims, especially through the education system and the media. Journalists reported religious instigation against other religions launched by Muslim preachers in the mosques of Cairo and its suburbs. They denounced the official media, owned and run by the government, which presented programs that slandered Christian beliefs and provoked anti-Christian hatred. According to these sources, those who are directly or indirectly accountable for the mass killings of Copts and for the destruction of their properties—including police and high-ranking executive authorities and politicians—were not brought to justice.

Members of the Coptic minority were terrorized by the public climate and the official policies under which they were living; they feared public or official retaliation if they publicly denounced either the legal system or their persecution. The Church leadership in Cairo warned of a government policy of "covering-up, by counterbalancing or by turning the victims as criminals!"[26]

Iraq

Although Iraq boasts of having a secular government, the UN Special Rapporteur on the situation of human rights in Iraq wrote in his report for the year 1994:

Decree No.59 of 4 June 1994 prescribes: amputation of the right hand at the wrist for a first offence of theft over 5,000 Iraqi dinars (well under US$10 at the present real rate of exchange); amputation of the left foot at the ankle for a second offence; and death for a third offence. Decree No.109 of 18 August 1994 prescribes the 'tattooing' or 'branding' (it appears to be a branding in practice) with an 'X' between the eyebrows of all persons having suffered legally prescribed amputations. Decree No.115 of 25 August 1994 prescribes the cutting off of the auricle of one ear of each person evading military service, deserting military service, or sheltering any evader or deserter of military service.[27]

Palestinian Administration

Palestine as a territorial entity defined by geographical frontiers was only legally constituted after World War I in the context of the mandate granted to Great Britain by the League of Nations, in order to establish the Jewish national homeland. Henceforth, it was "Palestinian Jews" who identified themselves with "Palestine," whereas from the 1920s Christians and Muslims challenged a separate Palestinian identity in the name of a Greater Syria, or of Arab nationalism. It was only after 1967 that they all claimed a Palestinian identity within an Islamic framework, integrated into the Arab nation. However, it is important to emphasize that the diverse Christian groups in the Holy Land adopted varying attitudes toward Israel, ranging from open sympathy to total identification with PLO terrorism and the most extreme theological anti-Jewish prejudices.

Despite the fact that Palestinian Christians militated in the PLO and supported anti-Israeli terrorism, their situation has incessantly deteriorated. In fact, discrimination against non-Muslims had been apparent since the end of the British mandate in Transjordan, which covered 77 percent of the original 1921 League of Nations Mandate of Palestine. This was the case also in parts of Western Palestine (Judea and Samaria) between 1948 and 1967 which had been incorporated into the Kingdom of Jordan in 1949 henceforth, called—by the British Foreign Office and the Jordanian authorities—"the *West Bank* of the Hashemite Kingdom of Jordan." All Palestinian Jews were henceforth expelled, their houses and possessions transferred to Muslims, all their synagogues destroyed, and their cemeteries desecrated. In the Jewish cemetery on the Mount of Olives in Jerusalem, 38,000 tombstones were destroyed or re-employed in military forts and latrines. Access for Jews to their holy places in Jerusalem and throughout Jordan was barred. A Jordanian law on citizenship stipulated that any person could become a citizen providing he was not Jewish.[28]

From 1953, the Jordanian administration undertook to Islamize the Christian quarter of the Old City of Jerusalem by laws forbidding Christians to buy land and houses and by establishing strict control over their social and educational institutions.[29] It ordered the compulsory closure of schools on Muslim holidays and authorized mosques to be built near churches, thus preventing any possibility of enlargement.

Under Israeli administration (from 1967), numerous churches and ecclesiastical properties in Jerusalem were restored with financial assistance from the government or the Municipality. The renovated monuments included the Augusta Victoria hospital on the Mount of Olives and the Syrian Catholic church on the Nablus Road. Similarly, the Syriac Orthodox community received a million dollars toward work to strengthen St. Mark's Church. Considerable economic aid was also provided for the Maronite community. However a large number of Christian institutions chose to refuse this gesture from the State of Israel.[30]

Restorations, renovations, or constructions of churches and Christian community centers with the financial participation of the Jewish state in the Old City of Jerusalem, in Bethlehem, and in Galilee were probably interpreted as a provocation at a time when the restoration of the *shari'a* in Muslim countries effectively prohibited the expansion of the Christian religion, while Judea-Samaria (the West Bank) was "under occupation" by Israel.

Under Jordanian administration, Christian schools had to fight to retain their European curricula. During the Israeli administration, which refrained from interfering in their educational programs, the same schools adopted the Jordanian curriculum in 1973. It is true that since the 1960s, the majority of those who benefited from the communal organizations of the Greek-Orthodox Palestinians were Muslims. Identifying with the anti-Israeli struggle of the Palestinian Arabs, these organizations refrained from establishing contacts with Israel.

Although abusive slogans profaning Christian cemeteries had appeared earlier, the situation of Christians in the Muslim environment began to deteriorate from the 1970s and has worsened considerably since the first *intifada* started (December 1987). This insecurity, stirred up by the Islamists, led the Palestinian *dhimmi* Churches to proclaim their solidarity with the *intifada*. At Easter 1988, their representatives cancelled festivities and paid a visit to the Palestinian mufti, Sa'd al-Din al-Alami. On 30 March 1988 the Latin Patriarch Michel Sabbah accused Israel—confronted with Arab-Palestinian terrorism—of imposing security measures which literally inflicted "the sufferings of the passion of Jesus on the Arab Christians."[31]

In Bethlehem, Christmas and Easter celebrations were often marred by threats and intimidation, as Islamists considered them a violation of the *intifada*. Christian businesses were set alight if an order to strike was disobeyed. The burning down of a religious school in Bethlehem (21 December 1990) was followed by attacks by masked Palestinians on a Carmelite monastery[32] and on a Christian school (12 March 1991). The profanation of a Greek Orthodox cemetery, where crosses were destroyed and bodies exhumed and mutilated, led the Arab Palestinian clergy to appease their Muslim environment by pressuring the international community to impose sanctions against Israel.

On 30 March 1991 the municipality of Bethlehem circulated a Declaration, which stated:

In view of the constant criminal attacks on the religious institutions, private and public properties including the violation of tombs and the desecration of the relics of the dead in the city of Bethlehem, the representatives of the

institutions and societies and a crowd of citizens hastened to the Municipal
Hall of Bethlehem to discuss the late events and to take the necessary measures to confront these vicious attacks and eradicate the premeditated acts
of damage such as burglaries of religious and educational institutions, and
commercial stores, car thefts and car burning, drug trafficking, and the defaming of honorable and upright people.[33]

Profanation of churches, attacks on nuns, the assassination of Arab Palestinian Christians and foreign pilgrims, as well as the violation of graves and
anti-Christian graffiti continued alongside the burning down of Christian
centers and restaurants by *Hamas* in Ramallah (16 March 1992), and terrorist operations by masked Palestinians. This campaign of intimidation and
threats formed an Islamic policy which aimed at accelerating the departure
of Christians from Cisjordan[34]; it also constituted leverage for pressuring
the international community to act against Israel.

Despite the Christian leaders' passivity in the face of *Hamas*, anti-Christian terror worsened in the territories intended to become an exclusive secular Muslim-Christian Palestinian state cleansed of Jews. However, the
graffiti as well as violence against Christian institutions did not diminish
despite the anti-Israel campaign pursued by the Eastern Churches and
propagated by Western theological channels. In 1991, for example, out of
245 Palestinians killed by other Palestinians for collaboration with Israel or
vendettas, more than half of them were Christians. In Hebron, the Russian
Orthodox church had to be protected by a high wall, immediately covered
with Islamist graffiti, and in Bethlehem barbed wire encircled the Baptist
church. This deterioration in the social climate developed within the
power struggle between the Palestinian ex-communist faction, mostly
Christian, and the *Hamas* Islamists.

In other Muslim countries, discrimination against Christians occurs to a
varying extent, reproducing traditional behavior patterns, but being also
marked by the impact of the Gulf War, conflicts in the former Yugoslavia,
and internal power struggles. This study does not examine other Muslim-
Christian conflicts—in East Timor, in the Moluccan Islands and other regions of Indonesia, in the Philippines and elsewhere—although one can
often discern there the same pattern, determined by the *jihad* ideology, its
tactics, and its strategy.

Causes of the Christian Exodus

The re-Islamization of the Arab countries, which started at the time of
their independence, engendered a process of legal discrimination against
non-Muslim minorities. The struggles for independence, from the nineteenth century, had recycled into anti-imperialism the traditional rejection

of the Christian *dar al-harb*. Arab Christians—prisoners of this mechanism and of their policy of secularization—were duped by Arab nationalism which in reality was reconstructing the Arab Muslim *umma*.

After World War I the refusal of the Western Powers to create autonomous and protected Christian zones provoked a Christian emigration that had begun as early as the nineteenth century. This exodus gathered pace with the independence of the Arab countries, political instability, the succession of military dictatorships, and repeated coups d'état. The chronic conflict between the secular Christian minorities and the Muslim majorities became acrimonious at the time when the new states formulated their constitutional norms and jurisprudence. The swift propagation of Khomeinism on receptive ground accelerated the wave of Islamization demanded by an ever-growing base. Europe's deliberate blindness to the destruction of Lebanese Christianity—"more Arab than the Arabs"—and secularism's defeat created the incentive for Eastern Christians to emigrate en masse.[35]

In the 1990s the dissolution of Arab communist parties, deprived of Soviet subsidies, discredited the Christians who formed their principal adherents, mainly of Greek Orthodox origin. Confronted with the return of the religious faction whom they had always fought, they were now triply threatened: as communists, Christians, and secularists. In addition, the words "secular" and "assimilationist" (in sympathy with the West), tended to become accusations, even worse than "Zionist." Consequently, while ex-communist Muslims were rejoining the ranks of the Islamists, the Christians were significantly intensifying their emigration. Besides, many conflicts in the last decade—in Afghanistan, Sudan, Iraq, Bosnia, Kosovo, Chechnya, and East Timor—are being interpreted by Islamists in the context of the traditional *jihad* against Christianity. Hence, it is no longer possible to restrict, solely to Israel, the identification of the "Evil" which is now overflowing into the Christian, Hindu, and other regions of the *dar al-harb*. Some Islamist factions denounced Christian Palestinians, even those associated with PLO terrorism, as traitors and accomplices of a new crusade by the West. Their accusers cite tradition to deny them, as Christians, the right to speak on behalf of Muslims. The Euro-Arab anti-Zionist alliance—forged as a formidable economic, political, and military media pressure group against Israel—is today boomeranging on its instigators, accused of conspiring against Islam. Henceforth, a tidal wave of hatred, which they themselves had helped to orchestrate, amplified by the Islamist current, now targets them directly.

A disastrous internal situation compounds these political factors. The galloping demography of Muslim countries breeds poverty and illiteracy; it paralyzes development and generates a violence which is recycled by the Islamic religious classes, fundamentally hostile to non-Muslims. Political instability and unemployment worsen interfaith tensions. The Eastern Christians react to this situation with a diversity which expresses the variations in dhimmitude, ranging from total alienation to awareness of their fundamental human rights and liberty.

The Tactics Adopted

The Tactics of Dhimmitude

Silence

The general silence about this situation, which has been endemic for several decades, may at first lead one to believe that the persecution of non-Muslims in Islamic countries, like dhimmitude itself, is an expressly taboo subject. This prohibition emanates from the Churches themselves, particularly the Eastern *dhimmi* Churches. Hence, the refusal to testify concerning their own situation is perpetuated, especially if this evidence implies criticism of an Arab-Muslim government, or the *shari'a*.

Nonetheless, three sorts of message are expressed in this vacuum: the silence of the terrorized victim, the silence enforced by the government which oppresses him, and the deliberate deafness of the international community—a factor which will be discussed later.

Testimony Prohibited

The failure to provide testimony emanates from two sources: the Churches in the Islamic lands and the respective governments of these countries. The first enforce silence through fear of reprisals against inoffensive and unarmed Christian populations. This is the very basis for the silence of *dhimmis*, duty-bound by their own Churches to remain silent. Consequently, Christians in Muslim countries observe the greatest discretion. The traditional fear reflex created by the accusation of collusion with the *dar al-harb* aggravates their situation. Were it not for the struggle by the Christian diaspora communities—particularly the Copts—their real situation would scarcely be known to the outside world.

In April 1980, during President Sadat's visit to Washington, Copts demonstrated against the assassinations and discrimination targeting their co-religionists in Egypt. This expression of freedom scandalized Sadat. In his speech in Cairo on 14 May 1980 he criticized the Copts for expressing their grievances publicly and slandering Islam by charging it with discriminating against non-Muslims. He warned the Copts not to mobilize a Christian front, probably meaning the pressure of Western public opinion. Sadat justified the legitimacy of the *shari'a* in Egypt, a country where both the state and its president were Muslim. He twice stated that Islam constituted the best guarantee of security for the Copts in Egypt, thus implicitly confirming their dhimmitude, since Islam and not their inherent human rights guaranteed their security.

The same dogmatic attitude is apparent in Sudan. In his address to Pope John Paul II in Khartoum (10 February 1993), Sudanese President Omar al-Bashir denied any religious persecution and forced conversion to Islam in Sudan, affirming as proof that Islam condemned intolerance and enjoined Muslims to adopt an attitude of veneration and not just of benevolence toward non-Muslims.

Imprisoned in its clear conscience, based on the rejection of evidence from non-Muslims, the *umma* has always refused to reconsider the history of *jihad* and the foundations of dhimmitude. Hence, today as in the past, the *dhimmi*'s complaints clash with the perfection of Islamic law, which reduces the plaintiff to silence.

The Indictment of Scapegoats

The most vicious expression of psychological terrorism consists of driving the victim to justify publicly his oppressor. Unlike the Copts, who— together with a fringe of liberal Muslims—struggled from the early twentieth century against extremist behavior patterns and the discriminations of the *shari'a*, the Arab Palestinian Churches diverted incrimination onto scapegoats. Islamic fundamentalism and the Christian exodus were ascribed to Israel, and to the West, guilty of having failed to eliminate the Jewish state, as if *jihad* and *shari'a* were not Islamic concepts which required identical conditions of submission from the People of the Book, both Jews and Christians.

These ideas, current in the West, are not only perverted, but they are totally ineffectual in solving the problem, whose roots are thereby masked. In fact, Koran, *sunna,* and *shari'a* form a distinct whole, evolving through the interdependence of their elements, and from which—according to doctrine—all foreign contributions must be rejected. And it is within this religious, legal, and political system which is being reconstituted—after a brief disappearance imposed by colonization—that the age-old tactics of *jihad* and dhimmitude are being reformulated.

In regard to Muslims, this traditional position was expressed at the trial (July 1994) of the assassins of Dr. Farag Foda, the secularist Egyptian writer, international consultant on agricultural development programs, and defender of the Copts. Sheikh Muhammad al-Ghazali, a foremost theologian and official of Al Azhar, testified in favor of the Islamist killer, stating:

A secularist represents a danger to society and the nation that must be eliminated. It is the duty of the government to kill him.[36]

For the mainstream religious hierarchy to which al-Ghazali belonged, the separation of religion and state constitutes apostasy; and an apostate should be put to death. A month earlier al-Ghazali had declared:

Whoever declares publicly that he demands the non-application of the *shari'a* is an apostate and has to be killed. Whoever kills such a person commits *ifti'at* against the government. Islam knows no punishment for *ifti'at* .[37]

Like many other Egyptian intellectuals, Egyptian Nobel laureate for literature Naguib Mahfouz was threatened with death by Islamists at that time and had to be placed under police protection after being stabbed. Islamic clerics regularly distributed hundreds of cassettes urging Muslims to avoid Christians. On one cassette, Sheikh Umar Abd al-Kafi stated that Muslims must not shake hands with Christians, nor offer them good wishes on their festive occasions, nor accompany them on walks.[38]

Having freely chosen anti-Zionism from the end of the nineteenth century as an indefectible Muslim-Christian alliance, the Palestinian *dhimmi* Churches have experienced a veritable descent into hell. The participation or support of some high-ranking churchmen in terrorist activities was strengthened by their moral endorsement of the *intifada.* But earlier "*intifadas*" since 1953 in Egypt had transformed the Copts into a target for stone-throwing in certain areas. In other Muslim countries—such as Algeria, Sudan, Nigeria, East Timor, and the Moluccas in Indonesia—more "*intifadas*" have led to church burning, the profanation of cemeteries, the murder of Christians, and a campaign inciting them to leave their country.

Since 1967, the Palestinian *dhimmi* Churches have adopted a policy which aimed at forming a united front against Israel by identifying totally with the Arab Palestinian cause. They also strove to associate the whole Christian world in solidarity with the Palestinians and to promote an anti-Israel campaign in the West. This policy reshaped Negib Azoury's turn-of-the-century anti-Judaic themes and revived his strategy. Arab nationalism, which had earlier been a cement to unify all the Eastern Christian communities with Islam against Israel, was replaced by Arab Palestinianism. It is not surprising that this old dream was represented by the Jerusalem *Justice and Peace Commission*, a Catholic body established in 1971, that emphasized in its pamphlets the common cause of Christians and Muslims against Israel in the Holy Land. The "Jewish Peril" of pre-Shoah Europe was reincarnated for post-Shoah Europe in the State of Israel, with its corollary, the sacralization of a salvific Arab Palestinian cause. This policy intensified with the terrorist and anti-Christian pressure of the *intifada.* The clergy's reaction was predictable: unconditional support for the *intifada* and unilateral condemnation of Israel.

In Judea and Samaria (Cisjordan) the outbreak of the *intifada* in December 1987 unleashed a wave of violence, assassinations, strikes, and abusive anti-Christian slogans which caused economic disaster and heightened the emigration of Christians.

In Israeli villages, the Christians—generally ex-communists—felt threatened by the increased power of the Islamists. A statement in 1986 attributed to Kamal Khatib, Islamist chief of Cana, a village in Galilee, near Nazareth, expressed the wish to establish an Islamic state in Palestine and treated George Habash and Archbishop Hilarion Capucci as new Crusaders in the Islamic sense of the term.[39] Posters appeared in the village proclaiming the Islamic state of Palestine symbolized by a Koran and crossed swords. In Acre, Samir Asai, an Islamist leader, explained his refusal to collaborate with communists by the koranic ban on associating with infidels.[40] In November 1987, a Palestinian Islamist monthly *Al-Sirat,* described Christians in the PLO as Crusaders.[41] This situation led the patriarchs and archbishops of Jerusalem to sign a declaration of support for the Palestinians (Week of Prayers, 24 and 31 January 1988) and to call on Churches worldwide to side with the Palestinians. Such an attitude immediately drew a strong response from the International Christian Embassy in Jerusalem (Proclamation, 14 April 1988), as well as from other theologians and clergy.[42] Their declaration stated that true reconciliation could only be achieved if Christians took the lead by confessing that for two millennia they had failed to practice justice. Refusing the partisan politization of the Palestinian Churches, they

> pray for a [Christian] unity that is not based on the common denominator of either hatred of Jews or replacement theology, but for the only Christian unity that is faithful to Scriptural requirement, that of being grafted into the cultivated olive tree, Israel.

Once again, on 27 April 1989, the "Heads of the Christian Communities in Jerusalem" appealed to the international community to denounce Israel, omitting all mention of the acts of terrorism which necessitated security measures in order to maintain public order. In November 1989 the Middle East Council of Churches (MECC) organized an international conference in Geneva to launch a movement, "Christians for Peace in the Holy Land." The MECC's Secretary-General Gabriel Habib proposed that a month-long campaign be launched internationally among Churches to emphasize the rights of the Palestinians, presented as martyrs, with the Israelis as brutal oppressors. A great deal of publicity was given to a declaration by the leaders of Christian communities in Jerusalem calling on churches

worldwide to pray and take action from Palm Sunday to Pentecost on behalf of the Palestinians, and for peace in the Middle East. In the eyes of
many Western theologians, however, the unilateral nature, the accusations
and the implications of these declarations resembled a new form of anti-
Israeli propaganda "under cover of prayer." Such methods brought cen-
sure from many Christian religious and secular circles who circulated a
prayer emphasizing that thanks were due to the Jewish people who had
received and transmitted the message of the Bible, a message that had
reached the most remote nations.[43] At this period, Christians had to refrain
from celebrating their religious holidays for fear of Muslim neighbors who
considered any signs of celebration as a violation of the *intifada*.

During and after the Gulf War the explosion of hostile feelings toward
the West exposed all Christians in Muslim countries to the greatest danger.
Consequently, the Arab *dhimmi* Churches again proclaimed their allegiance to the *intifada* and strove to pacify the Islamic environment by intensifying an international campaign against Israel through the MECC. On 2
April 1990, and again on 28 May 1990 at the opening session of an emergency Arab League Conference held in Baghdad—two months before he
invaded Kuwait—Saddam Hussein threatened to incinerate half of Israel.
Just prior to this Conference, Diodoros, the Greek Orthodox Patriarch of
Palestine and Jordan, thanked Saddam Hussein in eloquent terms for his
noble anti-Israel declaration concerning the lease of the hospice of St. John
in Jerusalem, sold by an Armenian to an Orthodox Jewish group:

> Allah sent Saddam Hussein as the commander to realize a victory for Iraq
> and the liberation of Palestine, and if God wills, the liberation of Palestine
> will come through Saddam Hussein. The war against Israel is not on behalf
> of one convent or one building but for the homeland, and it will continue
> until the liberation of the entire homeland. This subject has proven the
> unity of the Palestinian people, Christians and Muslims.[44]

In fact, the Christians' fear of their Islamic environment—and not of the
Israeli "occupation"—was so great that Bishop Naim Nassar of the Lutheran evangelical church of Jordan called for international protection.[45]
However, in January 1991, Iraqi Scud missiles fell on Israel as thousands
of Palestinians cheered on their terraces in the Jerusalem area while Arab
populations from North Africa to Iraq applauded and rejoiced. In June
1993, Christian Aid, a British charitable organization that had campaigned
ceaselessly against Israel, launched a "special action" for the Arab Palestinian cause, giving it wide publicity in the columns of the London *Church
Times*. The seminar (18 June) for the "Christians of the Holy Land" under
the auspices of the World Islamic Trust, Christian Aid, and MECC repeated
the customary accusations.[46] In 1994, after the Oslo Agreements between

Israel and the PLO, Christian Aid published a "prayer calendar" showing how to pray for the Arab Palestinians on *every* day of the year.

All this notwithstanding, the *Wall Street Journal* (1 July 1994) reported that Muslims would not sell land in Palestine to Christians and that Christian facilities and clubs had been attacked by Muslim extremists. Christian graves, crosses, and statues had been desecrated; Christians had suffered physical abuse, beatings, and Molotov cocktail attacks. In 1994, Christians were stabbed by a gang of fifty Muslim youths who ransacked a pool hall frequented by Christian youths near the Church of the Holy Sepulcher. Chanting anti-Christian slogans, the rioters broke chairs, tables, and other objects. In April 1997, Israeli Christians complained of the blasphemous abuse of the cross by Muslims. This somber situation contributes to the steep decline in the Christian population in all the regions controlled by the Palestinian Authority. In those areas, Christian cemeteries were being vandalized and destroyed, and churches burgled. The telephone lines of monasteries were cut and convents attacked. Fear of retaliation prevented people from speaking. Controlling the Church leaders, the Palestinian Authority pressurized them to act as advocates against Israel.[47]

Their compliance having been ensured by anti-Christian terrorism, the Palestinian Arab Churches served as channels to spread anti-Zionist racism on an international scale via the worldwide network of Western Churches. In fact, they see the Israelis as a superceded people with neither historical, political, nor religious rights in its own country. This attitude reveals the traditional two-thousand-year-old thesis of the Eastern Churches which conforms to the theology of supersession, the Church replacing Israel as *Verus Israel*, the true Israel.

As in the Middle Ages, when the Crusaders marched to the Holy Land and massacred the Jews in Europe because Muslims in the East were exterminating Christians, so these Churches, threatened by Islamism today, intensified anti-Zionism in the West in order to influence public opinion and encourage a policy of sanctions against Israel.

Muslims who persecute Palestinian Christians are not held responsible for their actions, but the harm they cause is transferred to Israel's account for the purpose of demonizing and reiterating international sanctions against it. This situation is very typical of the dhimmitude relationship.

The Tactics of Freedom

The Copts

Whereas the Arab Palestinian Christians, as a community, represent an extreme case of alienation through dhimmitude, the Copts on the contrary, though in a far more dangerous minority situation, chose to react courageously. In a memorandum to the Egyptian government, dated February 1977, the Holy Synod clearly described the religious conflict based on Christian opposition to Islamic penal norms and other provisions of koranic law. Rejection of the *shari'a,* it stated, involved the implicit non-acceptance of the Islamic religion as offering divine legislation to regulate social and political relationships between individuals. This rejection placed the Christians of Egypt in a particularly delicate position because the Muslims among whom they lived interpreted it as a calumny against Islam. Islamic religion and *shari'a* constituted a single entity; any criticism of *shari'a,* that is to say of the political and social jurisdiction governing modern Muslim societies, became a blasphemy.[48]

As early as 1953, Ibrahim Fehmi Hilal, had shown his concern about the re-establishment of the *shari'a,* comparing the Christians' position to that of slaves. If Islam was the state religion, he reasoned, then the state taught that the Muslims were on the right path and the Copts misled. He pointed out that koranic law determined the punishments for crime and theft solely on evidence from Muslims, and noted that "*aggression against non-Muslims is permitted with the protection of the law*" (italics in the original). He not only denounced the government, but also the representative bodies of the Copts and their religious leaders who, at international religious congresses, denied that Copts were being persecuted. A sense of patriotic duty drove them to claim that Egypt did not experience fanaticism, and to praise the peaceful coexistence of Christians and Muslims, thereby describing an idyllic image which did not correspond to reality. For Fehmi Hilal, those discriminatory measures were aimed at eliminating the Christians and constituted a unilateral civil war against them:

A peaceful war of extermination, which aims to kill one member after another of the body of Christians, so that the suffering be not severe and the cries not heard. Unfortunately, all this takes place behind the scenes, covered by the most moving humanitarian scenario, all decorated with olive branches, the sign of peace; by the ceremonial embrace between Crescent and Cross, the sign of love between Christians and Muslims; by slogans glittering with fraternity, national unity, racial non-discrimination, equality, respect for religions and beliefs, and the era of freedom.[49]

Consistently, despite the danger and their isolation, the Copts demanded that their rights be respected. Those in the diaspora, who had emigrated to the United States, Canada, and Australia strove—through a campaign of publications and activism—to inform public opinion and governments about the violation of the human rights of Copts in their ancestral homeland. They denounced the restoration of the *jizya* by Islamic groups in Upper Egypt and the many assassinations of Christians who refused to be thus held hostage to ransom.

On 12 March 1998 Nagi Kheir, spokesman of the American Coptic Association, submitted a written statement on the persecution of Christians in Egypt to the U.S. Secretary of State's Advisory Committee on Religious Freedom Abroad. He stressed that in addition to harassment and persecution by the government, Christians were vulnerable to violent attacks by Muslim extremist groups. These groups, with the collaboration of the Egyptian security forces, abducted and raped Christian women and girls, forcing them to convert to Islam. Violence against Christians included attacks on churches, their private properties, homes, and businesses. Conversions of Christians were encouraged by offers of material reward, such as money, jobs, and apartments. It was made easy for Copts to run up debts by the offer of loans which, if not paid, incurred sanctions that were abolished by conversion to Islam. Coptic history, language, and culture were neglected in schools and universities, if not forbidden domains.

Kheir mentioned the case of a Coptic physician, Dr. Neseem Abdel-Malek, formerly the director of the El-Kanka mental hospital in Cairo, whose sentence to hard labor for life by an Egyptian military court was confirmed on 1 January 1998. He was charged with accepting a bribe for releasing an Islamist patient, Saber Farahat Abul-Ulla, who then, with his brother Muhammad, killed nine German tourists and their Egyptian driver outside the Cairo Museum on 18 September 1997. The charge was based on the sole testimony of the same extremist Muslim who was previously involved in several attacks on Copts and the killing of four foreign tourists in 1993 outside the Cairo Semiramis hotel. On that occasion he was certified as mentally ill and interned. At his second trial in November 1997 Saber Farahat declared to the military court that it was lawful for him to take the money and blood of Christians according to the teachings of the Prophet of Islam to which he referred: "I have been ordered to fight the people till they say there is no God but Allah and Mohammed is his messenger." Just before his execution six months later, Saber stated "that the people he killed were infidels and that he would have killed more if he had had the chance."[50] Despite the killer's previous internment for insanity, the court refused Dr. Abdel-Malek's denial of the bribery charge, even though he was absent from the hospital on the weekend when Saber was given a pass by his Muslim colleague, who was then on duty.

In its Report to the Commission on Human Rights, dated 17 December 1999, the UN Working Group on Arbitrary Detention noted "that the trial against Dr Neseem Abdel-Malek suffered from serious deficiencies. Thus, although a civilian, he was tried by a military court." The charge, "by a certified insane killer who had previously stated that his acts were part of his crusade [*jihad*] for God and that he would target 'infidels', was totally insufficient evidence to convict a Coptic hospital doctor to 25 years of prison." The Working Group concluded that Dr. Abdel-Malek was not accorded a fair trial, as "the violation [of his human rights] is of such gravity as to confer an arbitrary character to his continued detention."[51] Although no appeal is allowed after an Egyptian military tribunal's decision, his sentence was reduced in January 2000 from twenty-five to ten years, perhaps as a result of this UN "Opinion," pressures from nongovernmental organizations (NGOs), and the earlier appeal to President Mubarak by U.S. Congressman Frank Wolf on his visit to Cairo in July 1998.

Nagi Kheir also mentioned the case of Father Augustinus, a Coptic priest of Al-Shahedein church in Marsa-Matrouh in Lower Egypt. He was charged in 1997 by the Egyptian authorities for constructing an arch over the front door of his church and painting an internal room without prior presidential permission. The case was referred to the criminal and not the civil court on the basis of Law 7, 1996. Father Augustinus was finally summoned on 19 April 1997—a great humiliation as it was Easter Sunday. However, the charges against him were finally dropped.[52]

The spokesman of the American Coptic Association also stressed that the efforts of the Copts to seek support from the international community were motivated by their moral obligation to reach out to those who suffer. He also insisted on the international community's duty to speak up, thereby ending those persecutions and humiliations.

On 9 September 1998 René Wadlow and David Littman, representatives of the Association for World Education (AWE) in Geneva, who had initiated the appeal to the UN Working Group on Arbitrary Detention (UNWGAD) concerning the Abdel-Malek case, received a faxed letter from Rev. Gabriel Abdel-Messih, a Coptic priest of the Angel Mikhail church in Al-Kosheh village, describing the atrocities recently committed there. It concluded: "We call upon the human rights organizations to save the Christians of Kosheh, who are being subjected to torture by the Egyptian Security Forces without any justification or legal ground." An update (18 September) from Bishop Wisa followed.[53]

On 6 and 13 April 2000, Littman intervened at the UN Commission on Human Rights regarding the 1998 atrocities in Al-Kosheh and the further massacres of twenty-one Copts between 31 December 1999 and 4 January 2000; he also referred to the case of Dr. Abdel-Malek, citing the opinion of the UNWGAD.[54]

The Lebanese Christians

As Bashir Gemayel explained, the causes of the Lebanese war (1975–91) were clearly denounced by Christian leaders. They were: Arab-Islamic irredentism, the annexationist aims of Damascus, and the desire to:

Kill the greatest number [of Christians], make others leave [. . .], in the same spirit and by the same technique, in such a way as to depopulate the coveted regions in order to change the demographic and cultural texture of the country.[55]

Speaking on 26 August 1980 to an important French delegation led by Marie-Madeleine Fourcade, President of the Comité d'Action de la Résistance française, Gemayel declared:

> Spearhead of the Arab cause, as they [the Palestinians] claim, must we understand that this cause also aims at destroying the Christians of Lebanon? "The Tel Aviv road goes through Junieh," the Palestinian leaders proclaim since the start of this war. For a long time one wondered why the conquest of Palestine has to take place via the conquest of Kesruan. Kadhafi has just answered that question: because a Christian, just like a Jew, a Druse, or an Alawite is not a full citizen and cannot exercise political rights in any of the countries which were once conquered by Islam.[56]

Three months earlier Gemayel stated that Arab unionism had created irredentist currents in the country and, by means of Palestinian aggression, these current have carried the state along. Because: "The Palestinians have established the international power center of subversion and of terrorism [here] from where they scour the whole world."[57]

The Sudanese Christians and Animists

Since 1983 the Sudanese Christians in the South felt threatened by the re-establishment of the *shari'a* and defended themselves by armed force. Like the Copts and Lebanese, they denounced the real causes of the *jihad* war that has killed an estimated two million persons, causing the internal displacement of some four million southerners, and hundreds of thousands of refugees into neighboring countries. In a letter of 20 August 1992 to the Secretary-General of the United Nations, Boutros Boutros Ghali, a meeting of the Peace Forum in Nairobi condemned the destruction of the African languages and cultures by forced Arabization and genocide by Islamization, with the abduction and conversion of children and slavery. These facts were confirmed in the Report (for the year 1996) to the Commission on Human Rights by the UNSR for Sudan, Dr. Gaspar Biro, in which he stressed that the situation vis-à-vis political and civil rights and fundamental freedoms had not improved. He mentions arbitrary arrests on a massive scale, detention without due process, torture and degrading treatment, camps for children, forced Islamization of Christians and animists, and abductions of refugees from southern Sudan (mainly children from refugee camps). In both his reports for 1995 and 1996, he concluded

> that the abduction of persons, mainly women and children, belonging to racial, ethnic and religious minorities from southern Sudan, the Nuba

Mountains and the Ingassema Hills areas, their subjection to the slave trade, including traffic in and sale of children and women, slavery, servitude, forced labour and similar practices are taking place with the knowledge of the Government of the Sudan.[58]

There was no real change in Khartoum's policy in subsequent years. Harassment of believers and church personnel by government agents, including the interruption of prayers and religious processions had increased.

From 1995 till April 2001, Christian Solidarity International (CSI), a Zurich-based humanitarian, nongovernmental organization (NGO), was able to free 47,720 African slaves in Sudan. In the United States, the American Anti-Slavery Group led by its president, Charles Jacobs, engaged in a campaign to heighten public awareness of this "crime against humanity."

On 15 November 2000, the Committee on Conscience of the United States Holocaust Memorial Museum issued a genocide alert for Sudan with an exhibit called "Genocide Warning: Sudan." Lomole Simeon Mwonga, Chancellor of the Episcopalian Diocese of Khartoum, warned that

entire communities are being erased and the international community is being quiet. If the international community does not move in, those people will be erased and it will be too late.

On 20 November, Reuters described a meeting between four freed women and U.S. Assistant Secretary of State for African Affairs Dr. Susan Rice—on a rare visit by a senior U.S. offiicial to South Sudan—who told journalists in the southern town of Rumbek:

Part of why I am here is to show the world that despite what the government in Khartoum says, despite what some of our partners in the European Union may want to pretend . . . slavery exists, it has to be acknowledged and it has to be addressed.

Finally, in an address delivered on 6 December 2000 commemorating Human Rights Day (10 December), U.S. President Bill Clinton condemned the scourge of slavery in Sudan and praised

the students, religious communities, and human rights activists who have done so much to publicize the atrocities of Sudan.

The Pakistani Christians

In Pakistan, voices are raised publicly denouncing religious discrimination and the systematic expulsion of members of non-Muslim minorities from positions of responsibility. The blasphemy laws are particularly dangerous since they are exploited by malicious individuals making false accusations. In 1998 a Pakistani Catholic priest, Father Anjou P. T. Soares, considered that international pressure on Pakistan was more than ever necessary to prevent the worst. In his opinion, the law on blasphemy, for which Bishop John Joseph "has given his life by committing suicide as a sign of protest," obliged Christians to censor themselves constantly.[59] Father Soares gave an accurate description of the traditional *dhimmi* attitude:

> Now it is fear which prevails. When they realise that I am a Christian, people would love to know my opinion. I keep quiet. I now avoid talking religion even with childhood friends. At any moment I can be accused of blasphemy.

He explained that it "has become increasingly difficult in every area of life for minority groups such as Christians to lead a normal existence. In Pakistan, you [the Christians] are faced with pressure and hostile attitudes the whole time."

Consequently, there was no shortage of detailed reports on the real causes of the Muslim-Christian problems, either in ecclesiastical circles or European chancelleries. Thus, Eastern Christians launched two totally conflicting messages, specifically for the international community: one was Arabophile and anti-Zionist; the other was an appeal for help. We shall examine which appeal the West chose to receive and transmit and what were the reasons for that choice.

The Consensus of Silence

The prohibition on testifying does not only set up an inner prison of silence but also a wall which blocks complaints that are even denied a hearing. As the Copts recognized, the person attacked was accused of complaining. In November 1979 a Coptic delegation contacted the Egyptian National Council of Churches to obtain international support. The Council refused even to receive the delegation.[60] The tireless struggle of the Copts in the diaspora met with indifference and threats.[61]

The Sudanese bishops for their part realized that the international media reporting events in the Persian Gulf, former Yugoslavia, and Somalia, as well as the oppression of the Shi'ites and Kurds in Iraq, almost systematically ignored the horrible genocide being perpetrated in Sudan. Priests who denounced the abuses frequently suffered threats and intimidation. In June 1994, a small CSI team visited Sudan to assess the need for humanitarian aid and medical supplies. Their brief report on that visit to the churches and the international community includes the following message from Mgr. Macram Gassis, the Roman Catholic Bishop of El–Obeid in Sudan.

This visit has given us a deeper knowledge of the immensity of the suffering of the people. My message to leaders in USA, Canada, Europe is: Too many years, months, days were spent on discussions—on ways and means to rescue the dying and afflicted people of Southern Sudan and the Nuba Mountains. There is no more time left at our disposal in order to save them. The silence of the leaders in Europe, USA and Canada and their procrastination— tomorrow and tomorrow—is definitely giving a helping hand to the Government of Sudan to eliminate its people through genocide and ethnic cleansing. The indifference and silence of Christian leaders is condoning the inhuman acts being perpetrated by the regime and their silence is killing our people.

In January 1995 the Bishop reiterated his call to another visiting delegation from CSI. Speaking of the Sudanese Christians, he said:

They tell us that they feel forgotten by the world; that even the Church seems to forget them. [. . .] We want to tell our brothers and sisters abroad that we are suffering a genocide in our country, especially in the Nuba Mountains. Slavery is a reality—now, men and women are taken and sold as slaves. [. . .] This is a holy war—a *jihad*, with hatred in those who attack us. Listen to their words . . . they say they are going to kill us "infidels." [. . .] Dear brothers and sisters, be our voice. We are hungry, persecuted, naked, with no schools. But we are dignified. We have maintained our dignity and we live full of hope that the day of liberation will come.

At the World Council of Churches' Eighth Assembly in Harare, Zimbabwe (December 1998), the Bishop of Torit (Sudan), the Rev. Paride Taban, asked the churches to intercede with the international community to stop the slaughter in southern Sudan. Recalling Western help to the Kurds, Bosnians, and Kosovars, he said that the Sudanese people were asking: "Are we not worthy human people to be protected from the Sudanese air force?" He added: "They told me to speak out here, to be their voice." He promised to try, "to be their voice and bring their message and cry to the world. Can anyone help me, delegates of this great fellowship of Christians from all over the world?"

The Lebanese for their part considered themselves victims of the disinformation propaganda in wartime which replaced silence. Bashir Gemayel explained it in 1979:

White then seems to be black and everything becomes obscure. Thus one has even gone so far as to refuse us the right not to let ourselves be slaughtered [. . .]. I am thinking of all those grand journalists, writers, prelates and politicians who have insulted and slandered us, dragged us in the mud with their good faith. The Lebanese resistance irritates them, disturbs their routine of clear consciences.[62]

The reasons for this distortion of the truth did not escape Bashir Gemayel:

Because we [Lebanese Christians] have mocked the world for forty years, the world has mocked us. Because we have deceived the world for forty years, the world in turn has deceived us.[63]

It was thus a consensus of silence, as much self-imposed through fear of reprisals, as from the deafnesss of the outside world. Faced with this passivity, Gemayel explained its causes in his 22 March 1979 article in *Le Monde:*

This capitulation by the West—what Solzenitsyn calls the decline of courage—is attributed by some to a syndrome, a component of Europe's atavistic antisemitism which culminated in the massacre of six million Jews. From this, it seems, comes that guilt feeling of the Western Christian, which drives him always to self-culpability for sins, even imaginary ones. Also, as someone wrote recently, "*when the ancient Lebanese Church was threatened with annihilation, a good part of Western Catholic opinion, particularly French, sided with the* 'Islamo-progressists' *against the* 'Christian-conservatives', *to the amazement of the Israelis.*" Aware, it seems, of the persistence of its demons, and afraid of its power to hurt, *homo occidentalis* today is mutilating himself.[64] [italics in the original]

France and the Holy See were totally opposed to an Israel-Maronite rapprochement which risked undermining the policy of a Muslim-Christian symbiosis and Israel's isolation. The Vatican felt that supporting the Palestinian cause was a prime objective, even more important than defending Christian rights. As the Palestinian Christians never represented more than a negligible proportion of the population, the Vatican's policy was motivated by the obsessive centrality given, since the nineteenth century, to the Church's battle against Zionism.

In the above-mentioned speech to the French delegation on 26 August 1980, Bashir Gemayel mentioned the free zone in south Lebanon and declared:

All the rest [of Lebanon] is bent under the yoke of a new power out of the darkness, the Palestinian power. The power of money being of prime importance, it pumps out oil in order to buy consciences, fuel subversion and spread terror. Hence its dominion over both sides: it holds the Arab countries, which it ransoms, at its mercy, intimidates the nations of Europe and America, supports cruel dictators in Third World countries, employing blackmail, lies, and arrogance everywhere which is always rewarded, alas, in the world of politics [. . .] Although a power from the darkness, it assumes the guise of a resistance movement in order to beg for charity from the free world, whereas here it acts as an aggressor against the Lebanese people, who had freely opened wide their doors to the Palestinian refugees. For almost six years they have kept this country plunged into an infernal violence: bombardment of urban agglomerations, destruction of businesses and institutions, drastic destruction of some towns and villages, massacres, pillage, sequestration of people and vicious terrorism by exploding booby-trapped cars in places where they can claim the most victims. This is a recapitulation of the doings of those people on whose behalf the chancelleries of the civilized world are striving throughout the year, and for whose favors the old nations of Europe are competing.[65]

This was the personal tragic experience of a Lebanese Christian, freely elected as president in 1982, and then assassinated. It was interpreted differently by the Palestinian poet, Mahmud Darwish, a member of the PLO, who lived in Beirut from 1972 to 1982:

In Beirut the Palestinians found an unprecedented political platform. There, the Palestinian cause experienced a boom at the military, political and informational level. [. . .] Beirut is dear to the heart of every fighter because it was there that our free and independent political personality was forged. It was there that we gained an international dimension. I would add that the Arab world's powerlessness to reproduce in its own lands the values which flourished in Beirut has made that city the prey of the Israelis. Their purpose was not only to expel us but to empty Beirut of its contents, of its plans for democracy, of the right to be different, of freedom [. . .] Therefore, Israel unleashed a war, the results of which were guaranteed.[66]

During the visit by Pope John Paul II to a Syrian-controlled Lebanon in May 1997, Pierre Najm, a spokeman for local Catholic youth organizations made a moving plea at the shrine to Our Lady of Harissa, north of Beirut:

We ask you, you who came here to give us hope, to give hope, to dare to say out loud that which we are afraid to say, and which we have lost the habit of expressing. Be our courage, and call things by their real names.[67]

The causes of the consensus of silence fall into three interdependent groups: first, economic interests; second, anti-Zionism; and last, the myth of Muslim-Christian idyllic coexistence, or the Andalusian myth which is linked to the first two.

From the 1970s the policy of the European governments, particularly France, was determined by their arms sales to Arab countries and by their oil and energy policy. In this optic, France became the occult protector of Palestinian rights, establishing close relations with the PLO, even opposing

Sadat's visit to Jerusalem in November 1977 and the Israel-Egypt peace process.[68]

In order to harness Arab oil wealth securely to Europe, the ideologists of the Euro-Arab movement conceived a blueprint for the future Euro-Arab entente around a Mediterranean matrix of socioeconomic ecumenism. Arab immigration was intended to play a preponderant role in this plan with its historic contribution: the tolerance of the caliphate and the multireligious coexistence of medieval Islam in Europe. This golden age of dhimmitude formed the model for the social and political projects for Europe in the twenty-first century where European Arabists dreamed of recreating a utopian Islamic Andalusia.[69] This plan for the future, conceived mainly in French laboratories of Islamology, was rooted in the dogma of an idyllic past of peaceful coexistence that had only been destroyed by the Crusades, by Christian fanaticism, and, in the modern period, by Zionism. Strongly defended by European ideologists, this dogma seemed irrefutable, since it was embedded in their economic and geostrategic state interests. Similar to the communist paradise, it was an object of faith and not of proof. Since Israel had destroyed this Muslim-Christian symbiosis, the necessary condition for its restoration required the demise of the Jewish state, the source of the evil, and its eventual replacement by a multireligious Palestine of earlier times which would revive the Christian paradise of dhimmitude. In 1969 Jacques Berque was already criticizing Lebanon for its failure to contribute to what he called "the cause"—that is to say, the Muslim-Christian alliance against Israel. He described as "scandalous confrontations" the Christians' rebellion against the sacrifices that the anti-Zionist policy required of them. Moreover, as Israel's destruction was justified by the Palestinian program of multiracial "coexistence," it was imperative that Lebanon demonstrate its excellence, even if this dialogue "was a fake."[70]

In the conclusion of his book on the Eastern Christians (1979), Robert Brenton Betts developed the same idea:

> For Israel itself, a successful Christian-Muslim experiment makes Lebanon the most dangerous of all enemies to Zionist survival, for it is a living example of the kind of society the Palestinians have lately advocated in place of the narrowly nationalistic and ethnically based state that is Israel today.[71]

The very same idea was put forward by many others, including Mgr. George Khodr, Metropolitan of Byblos and Mt. Lebanon:

> Any renunciation of Arabness in the last resort can only be of service to the Zionist thesis, according to which no political harmony is possible in the Middle East between the religious communities . . .[72]

Echoes are clearly discernable here from the criticisms expressed in the 1922 King-Crane Commission's Report regarding the Lebanese Christian nationalists. However, this comment reveals above all the subconscious attribution to Israel of the motives of its enemies. Indeed, it is the wish to eradicate Israel that has cemented the Muslim-Christian entente, whereas Zionism is in no way correlated with the type of relationships between Christians and Muslims. The justification for the State of Israel lies in the principle of freedom and of the sovereign right of peoples—including Jews—in their own country. This principle has allowed the linguistic and cultural renaissance of Israeli society, comparable moreover to the renaissance of the Balkan states from the nineteenth century. The excellence of Muslim-Christian coexistence in Lebanon no more undermines the legitimacy of Israel than it besmirches the legitimacy of the states set up in the former Ottoman Empire or of any other state in the world. Exhibiting the Lebanese showcase, be it beautiful or ugly, no more makes it a correlate of Israel's legitimacy than that of France, Greece, or the United States. The incoherence of this reasoning lies in an imaginary and totally false causality between terms which are barely placed in an interdependent relationship. In fact, Zionism does not result from persecutions of Christians committed by Muslims, whereas this is precisely the case with the restoration of Christian states in the Hispanic and Balkan regions. The Muslim-Christian symbiosis (in Lebanon and in Palestine) should, consequently, serve as a justification for the disappearance of Christian countries, if it is acknowledged that Islamic tolerance constitutes the sole determining criterion of any national sovereignty in lands once a part of the *dar al-Islam*.

Despite its obvious absurdity, this proposition—often repeated by Christians—in fact, merely represents a weak argument by the Christian *dhimmi*, a sort of plea in order to appease the oppressor by means of anti-Zionism. The integration of Christians into the *umma* is not claimed on the basis of legal legitimacy but as a weapon against Israel. In an improvised speech at a banquet given by the President of Syria to the leaders of the Muslim and Christian communities in 1957, the Syrian Patriarch Sayegh declared that propagandists against Israel should

> proclaim the existence within the Arab world of Christian communities enjoying the same rights and the same duties as the Muslims [. . .][73]

This theme has been constantly hammered since then throughout the Middle East. Too fearful to denounce the oppression of Christians in the Muslim world, the *dhimmi* clergies resorted to this subterfuge by pretending that Muslim respect for Christian rights constituted the best weapon against Israel. This obstinate attitude of hate reinforced the West's silence, concealing the persecutions of the Christians in the Muslim world. Thus, Abbé Youakim Moubarac described Lebanon,

> that country, the weakest and most deprived confronting Israel, is its most implacable adversary. I will rather say that the very existence of a multi-racial and multireligious Lebanon is the most serious offense to the Jewish state [. . .].[74]

This type of reasoning—at a time when the Palestino-Islamists were pre-paring to destroy Lebanon—illustrates the perverted mentality of the *dhimmi*, who refuses to denounce his real oppressor and substitutes an-other. This propaganda imposed the taboos of disinformation; it did a dis-service to the whole community of Eastern Christians if, as the historian Robert Brenton Betts wrote, their future is irrevocably linked to the destiny of the Lebanese Christian communities.[75]

In September 1989, Gabriel Habib, Secretary General of the Middle East Council of Churches, expressed the same worry:

> If the position of Christians in Lebanon is shaken, it will confirm the second-class status for the fourteen million other Christians in the Arab world and there will be little hope for them to get equal treatment.[76]

The anti-Israel Euro-Arab current aimed at serving Christian interests by accusing Israel, but the indissociability of Jew and Christian and their simi-larity in Islamic conception sparked a dynamic for the destruction of East-ern Christianity. The refrain of a Muslim-Christian peaceful coexistence stifled the voices of the Copts and Lebanese Christians. Since *jihad* had been effaced from history, the genocide and enslavement of Christians and animists in southern Sudan became a non-event. And when the Lebanese martyrdom revealed—through blood and flames—the true face of secular and multicultural Palestine, defamation of the Christian victims safe-guarded the ideology.

Pierre Rondot, a French Middle East specialist, is quoted as saying in 1981: "The Christians of Lebanon have committed an unpardonable sin by appealing to Israel! They would do better to disappear with honor."[77] In other words, contact with Israel contaminates. The Catholic Church, in particular, discouraged the plan for a Christian secessionist enclave and condemned the Maronites' rapprochement with Israel; it warned them that an entente with the Jewish state would put fifteen million Christians in the Arab world in danger.[78]

The fear of reprisals against Christians in the whole Middle East helped to conceal the real aspects of the Lebanese conflict and caused an escala-tion in the demonization of the Jewish State on a world scale, thus encour-aging Palestinian anti-Jewish terrorism in Europe. The international anti-

Zionist campaign of the 1970s developed in the context of the extreme in-security of the Eastern Christian populations and has unmasked their ter-ror within the Islamic environment.[79] Mgr. Youssef Moussayer, the Syrian Catholic Archbishop of Damascus, courageously declared in 1980: "We are the Muslims' number one enemies. They resort to fine words to appease us, but they seek to exterminate us."[80] In Europe, anti-Zionist propaganda primarily served to protect Eastern Christians from Palestinian assassina-tion attempts and as a lubricating agent in the economic field.

Disarray: Reality Conflicting with Ideology

In this chapter four policies toward dhimmitude have been noted: first, negationism on the part of *dhimmis,* conditioned by a regime of silence and fear; second, the attitude of Christians who denounce and fight it; third, the silence of European states, based on their economic and geostrategic interests; and, last, the denunciation of Israel by both the pro-Palestinian clerical current and the Euro-Arab alliance as the main cause of Islamist terrorism, which even encompassed the persecution of Christians commit-ted by Muslims. In an April 1996 article in *Le Monde,* just before his official visit to Lebanon and Egypt, President Jacques Chirac—expressing the opin-ion of the European Union—was quoted as stating that "the slowness of the peace process and the Palestinian people's frustration" were the cause of Islamic terrorism.[81] This opinion is shared by Muslim intellectuals, immi-grants in Europe, who explain most Muslim-Christian conflicts by alleged European support for Israel—a support which, according to them, de-stroyed the former golden age of dhimmitude. This current attributes to Israel a centrality similar to that which Nazi ideology conferred on "Israel" and "World Jewry." These not so uncommon opinions—expressed also by many European politicians—are not just defamatory, but are either cynical or illustrative of sheer ignorance. For Islamist terrorism, which has devel-oped on all continents, is grounded in Islamic policies emanating from their doctrines which justify them and which pre-date—by a thousand years and more—the creation of the State of Israel in 1948.

Faced with the perennity of Israel, the massive exodus of Christians, the intensification of *jihad,* and Islamic radicalism, various solutions were sug-gested. Some of the clergy invite their flocks to remain in Muslim countries in order to win the crown of martyrdom, but the latter often reacted to this appeal by a mass exodus. Gemayel had already made the point: "The Vati-can should also understand that the Christians of Lebanon are not experi-mental material for the Muslim-Christian dialogue."[82]

Another policy, practiced currently, consisted of intensifying the delegi-timization of Israel through the controlled media in the hope of thereby guaranteeing the survival of Eastern Christians. In order to lead the international community to align with the Palestinian cause, the *dhimmi* Churches in Jerusalem ascribed to Israel the persecutions inflicted on the Christians by the first *intifada* (1987–93). This tactic, however, was condemned and combated by Christian clergy and laymen in Israel and the West. Perhaps the most radical submission to Islamist demands was found in the Arab Anglican Church, which preached the "de-Zionization of the Bible," by eliminating the words "Zion" and "Israel" from psalms and biblical texts used in the liturgy. This process had already been undertaken by Nazi Churches in the 1930s. Some theological trends stigmatize theologians who give biblical readings from the Bible (!) and even recommend a koranic interpretation.

"De-Zionization" of the Bible having proved an impossible undertaking, some of the Arab Palestinian clergy are currently campaigning to induce the Church to forego the Old Testament and all spiritual links with Judaism, retaining only the Gospels. This attitude of self-mutilation, as a result of schizophrenic hatred of the very essence of one's own Christian spirituality, represents the final stage of dhimmitude before conversion to Islam. However, even this denial of the self, an extreme consequence of Arab-Christian anti-Judaism, will not be enough to improve the situation of Christians, who are persecuted because they are Christians, trinitarians, and—according to Muslims—falsifiers of the true Gospels. Only their adhesion to the Koran would change the condition of the Christian *dhimmis* and not their hatred of Israel, since the oppression and humiliation they endure are prescribed for Christians, per se, unrelated to the existence of Israel. Thus in 1978, Abu Iyad, Arafat's right-hand man, described the Lebanese Christian fighters as "Lebanese Crusaders," their leaders "displaying the cross on their breast," their soldiers "always sporting the cross."[83]

The same trend, inspired by the Syrian Melchite Bishop Neophytos Edelby, recommended in the 1970s that the Eastern Christians abandon "their minority psychosis," plunge totally into the Islamic world in which they live, and serve it with love and humility.[84] The theme of serving the Muslim with love and goodwill as a form of tribute for the Christian presence in Islamic lands is widespread. Yet, the hope that Christian goodwill and charity will be recognized seems utopian, since by their very essence, Jews and Christians— at a religious level—represent Evil for the Islamists, whatever they do. Besides, this attitude is unrealistic since Christians refuse to become *dhimmis* again as is proved by their exodus. More so, it is immoral by its denial of human equality, for it requires saintliness from one category of the population which is forced, in order to survive, to serve another religious group that considers itself to be superior. The contrast should be noted between this invitation to love, and the incitement, often by the same clergy, to hate or reject the Israelis.

Faced with such a dramatic situation at the human level and with the destruction of the diverse Christian cultures in their historic birthplace, the Western Churches are fighting strenuously for the assimilation, matched with full political rights, of millions of Muslim who have emigrated to Europe in the last thirty years within the framework of a future European-Muslim civilization. This claim made by clergymen on behalf of recent immigrants is motivated, not only on the grounds of the imperatives of human rights, but in the hope—often proclaimed—of obtaining equivalent rights in Muslim countries for indigenous Christian communities, which preceded the Islamic conquest. However, this reasoning is based on the principle of reciprocity between equals, a principle denied in countries applying or influenced by the *shari'a*, which rejects the equality between Muslims and non-Muslims. Furthermore, the idea of tolerance is nowadays replacing the principle of rights, as implied in speeches by Muslim jurists and responsible politicians. Fehmi Hilal had already expressed it clearly in his 1953 analysis addressed to Egypt's Constitution Commission:

> Difficulties, obstacles and iniquitous laws have been instituted for the purpose of limiting the Copts' freedom to build their churches. [. . .] And when they [Muslims holding responsible positions] find themselves forced to grant us permission to build a church, they think this constitutes an act of generosity toward us.[85]

Another policy, primarily developed by the Christian members of the PLO, the Syrian-Lebanese, and the proponents of the Muslim-Christian dialogue, consists of generally assigning to the West a moral attitude of self-guilt vis-à-vis Islam—of contrition and repentance for the Crusades, colonialism, and having "created" the State of Israel. In this way, the West's remorse and humiliation—and not their rights—would be surety for the survival of Eastern Christian communities. These policies, peculiar to some of the pro-Palestinian, Islamized Churches, and anti-Zionist circles compose, *inter alia*, the networks for the spread of a humble *dhimmi* mentality in the West.

It is obvious that all these policies of submission, humiliation, and an inferior's love for a superior—in order to justify an existence dedicated to his service—as well as support for traditional European antisemitism, are perfectly integrated into the context of dhimmitude which they help to sustain. It is hardly surprising that they emanate from the *dhimmi* Churches themselves, which have pursued this policy for more than thirteen centuries, thus helping to reduce the majority Christian populations to the status of a remnant minority. Today, the *dhimmi* Churches strive conscientiously

to impose these same policies on the West, thus leading all their populations toward a radiant future of dhimmitude. Stripped of all power in Muslim countries, their dignity greatly reduced by a conception which
sanctions the Christian presence solely on the basis of the service constantly
rendered to the *umma*, these Christians fulfill the objectives of Islamic policy to perfection by weaving the fabric of dhimmitude into Western societies.

The situation was lucidly analyzed in a Memorandum of October 1977 entitled "Egypt and the Copts," which commented on the Coptic hierarchy:

> 1. Some disclaim and criticize the disclosure of the truth for itself. Even
> more, they even find it strange that the oppressed victim raises his voice
> against the oppressor. Instead of telling the person who hits not to hit, we
> see them telling the person who has been hit not to complain. Notwithstand-
> ing all that, they do him no justice. [. . .]
> 2. If one seeks to justify the positions of the religious leaders by referring
> to their capacity as men of religion, this does not alter the fact that these
> positions are no less political positions, which leave no possibility of excuse
> to someone who understands nothing of the ruses of politics. But, because
> of their capacity as men of religion, they have nothing to do with politics.
> Why therefore do they dabble in things of which they have no knowledge? Is
> politics not a science exactly in the same way as medicine, architecture or law?
> *If the person who has not studied medicine starts to care for the sick, the latter are
> inevitably condemned to death.*[86] [italics in the original]

It could not have been better expressed. The consensus of silence imposed by the *dhimmi* Churches ensures moral impunity for persecution
which is accelerating the Christians' departure. This silence is also in keeping with the Arabophile policy of Europe and lends credence to the axiom
of a "peaceful coexistence" within Islam.[87] Lebanon—whatever the realities—was obliged to demonstrate in blood, suffering, and agony the perfection of this coexistence which projected the future Palestinian paradise, to
be built on Israel's demise. Guilty of having blasphemed the doctrine, the
Lebanese Christians were abused and abandoned like the Armenians, Assyrians, Copts, Sudanese, and others in Asia.[88]

European, particularly French, economic interests in the Arab world required a laxist and integrationist policy toward the flow of millions of Muslim immigrants into Europe. The theme of Andalusia provided arguments
to check the anti-immigration movements, which could have poisoned
Euro-Arab economic exchanges and obstructed the emergence of a future
Euro-Arab entity politically opposed to the United States. Hostility toward
America and Israel was not only fed by the communist and leftist trends,
but also by the heritage of the French Vichy regime of pro-Nazi collaborators, which had survived in the postwar decades, and had permeated the

French administration up to the highest ranks. It is in this international context of "affairisme," including arms sales, that European governments —preaching the universality of human rights values—yielded to Palestinian international terrorism in the 1970s, while concealing the discriminatory measures weighing upon the Eastern Christian populations in the Middle East.

In 1982 the WCC, the Vatican, and the Anglican Church accused Coptic groups abroad who denounced discrimination of being paid by Israel—as if the *shari'a* laws were an Israeli invention.[89] Analyzing the failures by Christian religious bodies to condemn this oppression, historian Herbert Schlossberg interviewed Marston Speight of the American National Council of Churches (NCC) in August 1989. Schlossberg summarized the answer he received:[90]

> [Marston Speight] was at a loss to suggest any source of information on the Muslim persecution of Christians, so rare had such events been. He knew of no current cases. When there is trouble, he says, it is usually because of economic and political factors. He claims to believe that Muslims have a better record on human rights than Christians do in modern times as well as in the past. (p.194)

Schlossberg mentions a telephone interview two days earlier with Charles Kimball, another Islamic specialist at the NCC, who

> views the problems of Christians living in Islamic lands as not very different from those of anyone living where another religion is dominant. The problem for him is that Christians in the West have a negative predisposition toward Muslims and do not consider what Christians do to Muslims. He is concerned that stereotypes about Muslims are being perpetuated and points out that in places like Syria and Iraq Christians are not persecuted; rulers even parade their Christians. (p.194)

However, if there is no persecution, the proof of a beneficent Muslim rule toward Christians is unnecessary.

According to an *Associated Press* dispatch of 24 November 1999—only six weeks before the second massacre at Al-Kosheh—the Archbishop of Canterbury rejected suggestions that Egypt's Christians were persecuted, saying that he saw no evidence of bias toward the religious minority: "I haven't encountered any hostilities toward Christians in Egypt." He affirmed that perceptions in the West of Egypt's Coptic Christian minority being persecuted were probably because "the further away you are from a situation, the greater the possibility of distortion."

Archbishop George Carey was on a one-day visit to Egypt as head of the Church of England. He had come to promote Christian-Muslim dialogue. He met with the Grand Sheikh of Al-Azhar, Muhammad Sayed Tantawi, and Coptic Pope Shenuda. The same report mentions that: "The Egyptian government is sensitive to charges that it discriminates against Coptic Christians."

This conflict between ethics, politics, and economic interests is particularly dramatic in the case of Sudan. In May 2000 Amnesty International accused the Khartoum government troops of driving

> people out of their homes by committing gross human rights violations; male villagers were killed in mass executions; women and children were nailed to trees with iron spikes.

Attacking Amnesty for its "moral bankruptcy" the Sudanese embassy in London replied that

> The Sudan government holds a bi-weekly regular dialogue with the European Union , where no one has ever brought or discussed information or reports similar to those circulated by Amnesty on Sudan.[91]

A Ray of Hope?

In such a context, the results obtained by Christians who denounced dhimmitude and slavery in Sudan are all the more noteworthy. On 26 June 1992, the Assyrian National Congress, the American Coptic Associations, and the World Lebanese Organization held a leadership meeting in Washington, D.C., to examine national, ethnic, cultural, and fundamental human rights in their home countries. At the conclusion of their meeting, the parties announced the formation of a coordination committee to be called the Mashrek Committee, headed by Sargon Dadesho, chairman of the Assyrian National Congress, Shawky F. Karas, president of the American Coptic Associations, and Walid Phares, member of the executive committee of the World Lebanese Organization. In 1994 a Coalition for the Defense of Human Rights in Islamic Countries was created; it called for an International Day of Prayer and Remembrance for the Church in Iran (20 November 1994). A Coalition for the Defense of Human Rights under Islamization was also formed at that time in Washington, focusing on the situation of religious minorities in the Islamic world.

On 23 January 1996, Freedom House's Puebla Program sponsored a consultation on the "Global Persecution of Christians" with more than a hundred leaders of key Christian organizations and churches. Following this meeting, the National Association of Evangelicals (NAE) issued a Statement of Conscience. After a description of the actual persecutions, the Statement published "Facts, Principles and a Call to Action." This text is noteworthy in several respects. It contains, in the good Christian tradition, a confession of the errors committed: "We confess our own culpability in

failing to do all within our power to alleviate the suffering of those persecuted for their religious beliefs." This Call to Action constitutes a historical
event and a genuine revolution compared with the earlier attitude of silent
indifference. Among the most important steps here recommended are:
first, public acknowledgment of current widespread and mounting anti-
Christian persecution, and its public condemnation; second, the elimination of any "option of silence" regarding persecutions from the annual reports of the U.S. State Department's Human Rights Bureau; third, the
appointment of a special presidential adviser on religious freedom; and
last, to apply economic pressure by a significant reduction in foreign aid to
countries guilty of persecuting Christians. Other important steps stressed
political leverage to press for the reform of American foreign policy. In
August 1996, Freedom House published *In the Lion's Den: A Primer on
Mounting Christian Persecution around the World and how American Christians
can respond.* The opinions of various Christians on the Church, the media,
and the politically correct silence on the persecution of Christians were
cited.

This sudden awakening was followed by a campaign of information for
the American public, combined with political pressure at the State level.
By a bill on 24 September 1996 the U.S. Senate unequivocally condemned
religious persecution and encouraged the president to take organizational
steps to strengthen American policies aimed at combating religious persecution. On 29 September 1996 the World Evangelical Fellowship organized
an International Day of Prayer for the Persecuted Church, observed by
thousands of evangelical churches throughout the United States. It proclaimed the last Sunday in September of every year thereafter as an international day of prayer on behalf of persecuted Christians, while the first
Sunday in November was dedicated to Christians suffering for their faith in
Muslim countries. In 1997, Paul Marshall (with Lela Gilbert) published a
compilation on the persecution of Christians worldwide and why they were
being ignored—with an evocative title, *Their Blood Cries Out.*[92]

Following more massacres of Copts in early 1997, testimonies were presented in April to New York's City Council in preparation for the forthcoming legislation to impose economic pressure on countries guilty of
persecuting Christians. In May 1997 the Freedom from Religious Persecution Act was introduced by Congressman Frank Wolf of Virginia and Senator Arlen Specter of Pennsylvania, after the U.S. Senate Foreign Relations
Subcommittee on Near Eastern and South Asian Affairs chaired by Senator
Sam Brownback of Kansas held a public hearing on religious persecution
in the Middle East.[93] On 8 July 1997 the representatives of four thousand
churches gathered in New York City to pray for martyrs and persecuted
Copts. Books were also published on this topic, as well as Muslim and Western reactions to this public campaign against religious persecution. The

1997 bill was replaced by another bill (H.R. 2431) and signed by President Clinton on 27 October 1998. In December 1998 a new U.S. Commission on International Religious Persecution was established by the 105th Congress to monitor religious abuses and ensure an appropriate response from the U.S. government. Its first chairman was Elliott Abrams, former assistant secretary of state for International Organization Affairs, for Human Rights and Humanitarian Affairs, and for Inter-American Affairs during the Reagan administration (1981–88).

On 28 June 2000, leaders of Mideast Christian Organizations in the United States formed a national conference, named MECHRIC (Middle East Christian Conference). The announcement was made at a meeting convened at the U.S. Capitol by Freedom House's Center for Religious Freedom and U.S. Senator Sam Brownback. Professor Walid Phares, elected as MECHRIC's coordinator, declared:

> The plight of Middle East Christians is grossly overlooked in U.S. foreign policy and under-represented in the American political debate. This conference aims to reverse these parameters. Today we made history. From now on, there will be a voice representing the voiceless communities of the Middle East in America. Middle East Christians will have a house to express their freedom. And more importantly, the American people and international public opinion will be able to see another dimension of the region. For many decades, the birthplace of the three monotheist religions witnessed the development of only two political and spiritual cultures. Today the third culture of the region will take its natural place under the sun. From now on, with the formation of MECHRIC, Middle East Christians in America will assume their historic responsibilities towards their mother communities to ensure them a better future.

Finally, on the *jihad* front in southern Sudan, the government's use of slavery was officially denounced by the U.S. State Department and publicly by President Clinton in December 2000. This success resulted from the tireless efforts of CSI to free the slaves, and to bring this "crime against humanity," via the media, to the attention of the world and the "international community." In the conclusion to his wide-ranging article on past and present slavery in Sudan, John Eibner—leader of CSI's anti-slavery program—observed:

> The sad truth must be acknowledged: Sudanese slaves and other victims of the National Islamic Front's genocidal jihad count for little in a world preoccupied with other matters. Millions of lives have been lost and disrupted while the world has largely turned a blind eye toward gross violations of human rights in Sudan. [The Dinkas] can count on my colleagues and me, as well as a growing number of abolitionists for support until the last slave is free.[94]

On the threshold of the twentieth century, Eastern Christians could have hoped for an auspicious future. Instead, from massacres to exoduses, from Western rejections to abandonment and defamation, today they are fleeing from Arab-Muslim regions where the *shari'a* prevails.

As the century drew to a close, Islam returned to Islamism, the *dar al-harb* to the *jihad* threat, and the Christians to dhimmitude. However, in their fight for survival, the latter lacked neither courage nor intelligence. Every formula was tried: liberal parliamentary government; secular nationalism; anti-Western militancy; socialism; Marxism; Judeophobia; and even terrorism—all in vain. Only one policy was strictly taboo as it terrified Western powers: the denunciation of Arab-Muslim imperialism and the agonizing centuries of dhimmitude. Thus, *jihad* and dhimmitude—as types of relationship between the *umma* and the People of the Bible—borne along by the Islamist tide, now threaten the entire world's future stability.

From the break-up of fake ideologies, buried history emerged. Beneath the trap of "the harmonious multicultural coexistence," based on the *shari'a*, dhimmitude expanded. Euro-Arabism engendered its foundation myth: "the Andalusian Golden Age," while anti-Zionism concealed Christian suffering which, had it been revealed, might have broken the isolation deliberately imposed on Israel by European political and economic interests and by Christianity's theological anti-Judaism. Created to destroy Israel, "Palestinianism" is destroying Eastern Christianity instead.

9

Expansion of Inter-*Dhimmi* Conflicts in the Modern Period

After decolonization, Arab Christian communities were determined to integrate into their Islamic environment by adopting the policies of Arab states. Suspected of allegiance to the West, their only option was anti-Westernism coupled with an excessive Judeophobia, two components essential for survival in a conflictual context.

The prolongation of inter-*dhimmi* conflicts manifested itself mainly at three levels: the political level of the inter-Arab forum; the religious level in the theology of Palestinianism; and, on the international level, in the propagation worldwide of anti-Zionism by neo-Nazi, communist, Third-Worldist, and theological channels. We have evoked earlier the Christian Arabs' instrumentality in spreading anti-Zionism and will attempt here to assess these elements in a more general framework.

The Political Domain: Christian Dhimmitude and Anti-Zionism

As has been frequently mentioned, Christian Judeophobia in former Christian countries, and subsequently Islamized, represents a permanent historical trend. It is identical in its theological conception to traditional European antisemitism in both its religious and political manifestations. However, it did not express the totality of Eastern Christian opinions.

At the beginning of this century, exchanges between European capitals and their Arab colonies propagated European antisemitism via Arab Christians, and their clergy. Yet to attribute the origin of Islamic anti-Judaism to European antisemitism is unjustified and has no basis except in the obfuscation of dhimmitude from history. It is important to distinguish in the Levant the different fields of anti-Judaism. The European trend was fed by theological sources and economic, political, and social factors, while in the Eastern Christian sphere the same elements are to be found but transposed to the Eastern Churches' version, and in the specific context of a Christianity persecuted by Islam. Finally, the specific Islamic field was based on the

Koran, *hadiths,* and the *shari'a* where Christianophobia and Judeophobia intermingle. The interactions of these trends in the modern period scarcely obscure their specific characters.

In fact, the context of dhimmitude is certainly the most important of all the different sources that converge in Arab Christian anti-Zionism. This is the only domain that will be examined here, the others already forming the subject of relevant specialized studies, particularly William Nicholls's outstanding book, *Christian Antisemitism, A History of Hate.*[1] It should also be specified that the Judeophobia of Christian *dhimmis* represents only one of many inter-*dhimmi* conflicts. The reciprocal antagonisms of the various Eastern Churches have been hardened by a century of massacres in the *dar al-Islam* against one or another community. The Christian national movements striving for independence and emancipation brought terror and death over an area stretching from the Balkans to Damascus and Mesopotamia, only stopping at the gates of Egypt under British rule. The Jewish national movement was the pretext of a campaign of terror and pillage in the Middle East, North Africa, and Yemen against Jewish communities. The *dhimmis'* survival depended on the willingness of the colonial powers to intervene. However, as has been shown, the latter dissuaded the Christian autonomists in their Arab colonies, encouraging them to join the struggle for Arab nationalism, which had their support in the Levant against Zionism. This political option had its roots in the axiom that the true Islam— "Arab Islam"—in reality incarnated a tolerant and democratic political ideal. Hence the importance, as has already been stressed, in conceptualizing the myth of Islam's Andalusian "Golden Age." European politicians became convinced of their ability to transpose this myth in modern times, simply because they had invented it for the past. In fact, it was nothing more than a political slogan which permitted Western countries to manipulate political forces on the Middle East chessboard.

This allegiance to Arabism, fed by the trauma of ordeals, sentenced the Arab Christian communities to a long course of fragmentation and depersonalization, since cultural Arabization implied the abandonment of their Syriac culture. The repression of *dhimmi* history fostered the glorification of Arab-Islamic conquests and civilization, notwithstanding the identification of Arabism with Islam. Fixed in the dogma and symbolized by the early expulsion of Arab Jews and Christians from the Hijaz, Arabism henceforth became incompatible with secularism. This fact was echoed in a January 1995 message to the international community and to the world's Churches from Catholic Bishop Paride Taban of Torit in Sudan, when he declared: "The Arab language has been imposed on the Africans against their will as a vehicle of Islamization and of creating an Islamic State."[2] This opinion was shared by the overwhelming majority of the southern Sudanese and expressed on many occasions in the 1990s.

Except for the independentist Christian Lebanese fringe, the Arab-speaking Christians of the Middle East passionately joined in the anti-Zionist struggle in reaction to their own insecurity and their desire to integrate into the *umma*. Among those who, in the 1930s, gained distinction as theoreticians of anti-Zionism and channels of Nazi hatred were Alfred Roch, a Catholic connected with the French embassy in Jerusalem and vice-president of the pro-Nazi Palestinian movement founded by the Grand Mufti of Jerusalem, Haj Amin al-Husayni; Yaqub Faraj, member of the Arab High Committee, presided over by the same mufti; as well as Georges Antonius and Isa al-Isa. Terrorists were even recruited from among the Anglican clergy (Rev. Ilyas al-Khuri, member of a terrorist commando group in 1969 and—after his expulsion to Jordan by Israel—of the PLO's Executive Committee); from the Catholic clergy (Father Ibrahim Ayyad, suspected of having collaborated in the assassination of King Abdallah of Jordania); and from the Greek Catholic clergy, Archbishop of Jerusalem Hilarion Capucci, who collaborated in PLO terrorist actions. Capucci, a Syrian from Aleppo, was caught transporting explosives into Israel in his official car. At his trial in 1974 he upbraided:

> The vile conquerors who came from the darkness to desecrate the holy city of Jerusalem, cradle of two religions, Christianity and Islam. Only Jesus Christ, who weeps in Heaven over the fate of Jerusalem has the right to judge me.[3]

For Abbé Moubarac, Israel's liberation of Jerusalem was a rape and even a ritual crime.[4] This theological faction strove to strengthen Islamic prejudice against Jews and to reinforce them by Christian racist stereotypes.

In the leftist parties, Christian anti-Zionists were not less prominent. Michel Aflaq, a Greek Orthodox Syrian, one of the founders of the Ba'ath party, targeted Israel as the primary enemy. Aflaq had studied in France during World War II, residing there for long periods. As with Judaism in the Nazi ideology, Israel's eradication acquired a centrality in the party's policy and its rhetoric of hate. The Political Manifesto of the Tenth National Conference of the Socialist Arab Ba'ath Party (1–10 March 1970) urged the Party to bring international public opinion to understand that Zionism is a danger that threatened the destiny of mankind. Constantine Zurayk, a leading Lebanese intellectual, had earlier accused Zionism of threatening the very existence of the Arabs. Represented at the highest level in the whole range of Arab anti-Zionist movements, Syrian and Palestinian Christians unsparingly supported Palestinian terrorist movements. This Muslim-Christian symbiosis extended into the collusion of Palestinian organizations with European neo-Nazi and terrorist groups. Only the Lebanese autonomist faction, courageously anchored in its tradition of liberty—

disavowed by the Vatican and France—could defend the independence of the other People of the Book because, by so doing, it was defending its own independence.

The theme of Muslim-Christian brotherly association symbolized by Lebanon, in contrast with the isolation of Israel, appeared in Europe after the 1967 Six-Day War at every level of international policy, and in the economic boycott of the Jewish state imposed by the Arab League.[5] It was also expressed in scholarly books. Fernand Braudel, a former member of the extreme right-wing movement of the 1930s, the "Camelots du Roy," chose as a subtitle to a chapter of his study on *The Mediterranean*, "One civilization against the rest: the destiny of the Jews."[6] The whole book deals with the bloody sixteenth-century inter-European wars and their confrontations with the Ottoman *jihad*, involving countries and populations on three continents bordering the Mediterranean. But the author's tone is light-hearted and he reassures us: "All the conflicts discussed so far have been confined to a dialogue between two civilizations." However, in the case of the Jews, every civilization was implicated.[7] The Jews learned "cunning and obstinacy" from the Talmud.[8] According to him, they were an Asiatic people foreign to Europe, being vigilant and aggressive; the Talmud had made them much more intolerant than the Christians at the beginning of the sixteenth century, in the opinion of an author cited by Braudel, but which he then generously balances as "probably an exaggeration." Perhaps Braudel had in mind the Inquisition . . . He then goes on to examine "The ubiquity of Jewish communities" (a subtitle),[9] which enabled the Jews to settle in France in the guise of Christians. After having justified the expulsion of the Jews from Spain, he comments:

> The one thing of which we can be certain is that the destiny of Israel, its strength, its survival and its misfortunes are all the consequence of its remaining irreducible, refusing to be diluted, that is of being a civilization faithful to itself. Every civilization is its own heaven and hell.[10]

In regard to Muslim-Christian cooperation, Pierre Rondot wrote in 1953 that, "behind the national idea, Islamic sentiment forms the most powerful factor to bring into play against the Zionist invaders."[11]

In Israel, it was the Arab Palestinian Churches which were the most irreducible opponents of Christian integration into Israeli society, promoting a totally opposite attitude to Christian efforts of assimilation in Muslim countries. Was this a response to the precariousness of Christian existence in an Islamic environment? The Christian and Jewish populations of the Holy Land had suffered the perverse humiliations of dhimmitude more than elsewhere. Numerically very weak in the mid-nineteenth century, the Palestinian Christian population—as has already been mentioned—was swelled by refugees fleeing massacres in Lebanon, Syria, Anatolia, Mesopotamia, and Armenia in the nineteenth and twentieth centuries. The extermination of the Armenians, perpetrated in the very heart of the Syrian-Iraqi Arab populations, had branded the Christian soul with terror. In 1949, about 35 percent of the Christian population—roughly 40,000—had remained inside the frontiers of the State of Israel; today—half a century later—their number is about 110,000 in Israel, which does not include those now under the Palestinian Authority (less than 35,000) and in Jerusalem (less than 10,000).

Here, it is worth recalling that the same violence which prompted Arab Christian ideologues to seek Israel's demise contributed to their own communities' self-destruction. Fighting against the rights of the Jews, they thereby fought against their own rights. Relentlessly opposed to Israel, it was the Christian in themselves they wished to kill. Thus, Khalil Sakakini—the first secretary of the Palestinian Arab Congress in the 1920s—mentions in his journal the arrival in 1914 of a delegation of Greek Orthodox clergy and laymen initiating a proposal to create a party to protect Christian interests. Sakakini refused point blank, citing the preeminence of Arab over Christian interests.[12] Michel Aflaq, who became a Muslim in later life, invited Christians to discover the Islam within themselves, as the most incorruptible and precious essence of their Arabness.[13] In an essay dated 1940, he wrote:

> There is no fear of conflict between nationalism (Arab) and religion because like religion, it [nationalism] flows from the heart and seed of the will of God; they move forward arm in arm, supporting one another, particularly when religion represents the genius of nationality and is in harmony with its nature.[14]

The sanctification of Arab nationalism after World War I by Arab Christian factions, whose paranoic ravings present many affinities with contemporary fascist and Nazi rapturous exultation, demonstrates the ecstasy of a minority's mystic communion with a majority which only tolerates it via a system of exclusion. The morbid devotion and hysterical fanaticism of the nationalist discourse of Arab Christians display the minority syndrome created by a violent and insecure political situation. Its negative aspects—including anti-Jewish paroxysms, going so far as to justify antisemitic crimes—proceed from Christianity's struggle for survival in an Islamic environment. However, they are also and primarily an expression of the old anti-Zionist Christian trend underlying Arab nationalism, regarded as the weapon that would eliminate Israel.

These political options also derived from the directives of the King-Crane Commission's report, abandoned by the U.S. State Department, for which it was accused of being "spineless" by its promoters. The introduction to this text published in 1922 stresses two basic points:[15]

It pronounces the doom of Zionism. It portrays an incredible co-operation between Moslems and Christians, in pursuit of the goal of "self-determination." (2, col. 2)

Citing the danger of pan-Islamism, the report brushes it aside with evasive arguments:

The fundamental question in this connection, and, indeed, in several other great immediate problems, is the basal attitude of the Christians toward the Moslem world: Shall this be friendly or hostile? (26, col. 3)

As for the establishment of secular nationalism in "Greater Syria" under Faisal's rule, this would be achieved if the mandatory administration (preferably American) governed the Syrian peoples "frankly and loyally."

As if goodness and loyalty—even if they were recognized and repaid with gratitude—were elements in determining policy! This confusion between ethics and politics on the part of the Commission upset the balance of Muslim-Christian relations.[16] The Christians' duty to love Islam (without demanding reciprocity), expressed by Aflaq and so many others, drew the Arab Christian communities into a self-destructive spiral of compromise through its over-enthusiastic zeal—while eliciting no gratitude from the Islamic world. Moreover, this behavior pattern perpetuates the conduct of the *dhimmi* whose existence is only tolerated for the service he owes the *umma*, a service for which he must expect no thanks but which he gives gratefully since it spares his life.

All in all, the long-term consequences of anti-Zionist Western policies penalized Eastern Christians more than Jews. Weak, divided, wooed by opposing political and economic interests, they were incapable of defending themselves against the destructive forces emanating from their deadly alliance. Given the local and international political context, one might ask if there were any other option open to the Arab-speaking Christian communities than to be the channel for spreading European antisemitism in the East. From the 1960s the trend was reversed: anti-Zionist Arab clergy, particularly Palestinian, were the best propagandists of Judeophobia in the West as well as zealous servants of Islamic political interests in Europe. For thirty years they played a determining role in the wave of Islamization which reached the West, spurred along and buoyed up by the course of events, and by the corruptive power of petrodollars. For both, the Arab-Israel conflict constituted a passionate, obsessive element of Muslim-Christian entente. After decolonization, this dynamic brought Europe important advantages in the political, economic, and strategic domains in exchange for an anti-Zionist policy. It permitted a revengeful and xenophobic bitterness of Muslim peoples—colonized by Europe—to be transferred, released, and focused on Israel; it also constituted a protection "ransom" for Eastern Christians against international Arab terrorism and Christianophobia.

The Theological Domain: Redemptive
Palestine versus Israel's Iniquity

From 1963, the Vatican's decision to revise the Church's position on the role of the Jews in the crucifixion of Jesus infuriated many of the Muslim intelligentsia, although Islam does not accept the Gospels' account of the crucifixion (Koran 4:156–58). In fact, it was the Judeo-Christian rapprochement and the rehabilitation of the Jewish people that really angered the Muslim world. Consequently, exposed to very strong pressure from the Arab League, the Uniate Eastern Churches (Jacobite, Nestorian, and Greek) fought by every means against the policy of reconciliation with Judaism adopted by Pope John XXIII. They opposed the declarations of the Second Vatican Council (October 1962–65) which rejected the charge of "deicide" against the Jewish people in the *Nostra Aetate* declaration, and they succeeded in replacing it with a watered-down version. They exploited several arguments: the text had to satisfy the Muslims;[17] a balance was required to avoid offending them and harming Christians living in Arab lands; finally, the Arabophile Catholic factions demanded the establishment of a parity between Jews and Muslims.[18]

On the political plane, "the persecutions that such a declaration risk unleashing against Christendom in the Arab world" were cited, emphasizing that the Council and all Catholics would suffer from such an "error."[19] In order to satisfy "the furthermost ecumenical extension" (the Muslim world), the *dhimmi* Arab clergy considered that the passage which annulled the collective accusation of deicide against the Jews was untimely and demanded its removal.[20] Muslim protests "against the disculpation of the Jewish people" were made—according to the *dhimmi* bishops, advocates of the Muslim cause—in "a perfectly authentic pursuit" of the Koran, a demand "for the honor of God and of both Christ and the Virgin."[21] The Jews were summoned to do honor to the Virgin, "thus satisfying the combined claims of Islam and Christianity."[22]

Abbé Moubarac stressed that:

On the evidence of a great contemporary Muslim author, Good Friday is the culminating point of iniquity in the world. All the crimes and all the injustices which are committed throughout historical time were materialized and "carried out" on that day in the person of Christ'. [inverted commas in the text][23]

The Jewish people were "the principal agent of an entire sinful mankind," Moubarac continues, and "blame cannot be placed on this mankind for a deed for which its prime author is absolved." Thus, Islamic and Christian anti-Judaism mutually strengthened each other in order to torpedo the Judeo-Christian rapprochement. Therefore, wrote Moubarac in a veiled threat to the Council: "there is essentially, and there will always be, a third participant [in the Judeo-Christian dialogue]: the Muslim world."[24] Such arguments enhanced Islam with the arbiter's role of the two thousand years of Judeo-Christian relations, as if the Vatican should examine them through an Islamic prism. This self-imposed dependence on Islam had immense symbolic value, since it enabled the avoidance of a Christian doctrinal reform vis-à-vis Judaism, thereby hindering Judeo-Christian reconciliation.

On the texts concerning relations between Church and Synagogue, Moubarac accepts the acknowledgment of persecutions committed by Christians against Jews but, returning to his idea of compassion in opprobrium, he considers that the Christian must "place himself in the same attitude toward the people of Israel as Jesus crucified [toward the Jews]."[25] As it was impossible to strike out the conciliar text, Moubarac suggested several improvements [*sic*] and amendments. He approved the prohibition on speaking of a "condemned nation" or "deicide," which allowed the exegetists and theologians to

gradually educate Christian consciousness to a spirituality of compassion and communion with sinful Israel, "that witness" and "vicarial cause" of the sin of all mankind [. . .] and, in any case, in order to avoid the belief that a Judeo-Christian reconciliation can come about independently of Islam and, *a fortiori*, against it, the paragraph on the Jews should be followed by a passage which links it to the preceding paragraph on the Muslims. [. . .] (inverted commas in the text)[26]

Thus, the Vatican Council submitted to Islamic pressure in a field of historical and theological exegesis concerning exclusively Jews and Christians, where Islam had no place. This inaugurated a process which made the Vatican's relation to Jews a hostage of Muslim states, through threats of reprisals against the Eastern Christian communities. Although Islamic pressure via the Arab *dhimmi* clergy had succeeded in removing a paragraph specifically annulling the accusation of deicide against the Jews, the Vatican and its representatives in Arab countries, nonetheless, had to redeem themselves by anti-Israeli statements. In Jerusalem, then under Jordanian rule, and in Aleppo—both traditional centers of anti-Jewish hatred—crowds of

Christians demonstrated in the streets and hissed the Council, while the Greek Orthodox and Jacobite *dhimmi* patriarchs outdid each other in anti-Jewish declarations.[27]

Islamic interference in an exclusively Christian ethical and exegetical domain concerning the origins of Christianity and the development of its thought and its history sowed divisions in the very heart of the different Churches. It opposed one school of theologians in the West against other Western and Arab anti-Jewish Catholics. The first was working for the moral purification of Christianity through a critical self-examination, while the other united all the dynamics of antisemitism and dhimmitude, stiffened and structured by powerful Islamic pressures.

Although Moubarac speaks bitterly of his many enemies, without naming them, and of the obstructions to his publications, it seems that his ideas presided over the international anti-Israel campaign propagated by Third-Worldist religious trends. Thus, after Vatican II, Muslim circles constantly returned to the deicide theme. In 1978, only six months after Sadat's visit to Jerusalem, Anis Mansur, editor of the Egyptian magazine *October*, wrote in an introduction to an article by a Copt (Zaki Shanuda al-Muhami):

> The Jews doubted him [Jesus], tormented him, passed judgment on him, and crucified him. He cursed them until the Day of Judgment. But the Jews began to deceive the Christians all over the world, until in the end they were successful in washing the blood of Jesus from their hands. This happened in the Vatican Council of ten years ago.

The article ends with this conclusion:

> So did Jesus continue in the Via Dolorosa in order to redeem humanity. But were the Jews able to destroy him? Not at all! For the Jews failed in this. And no matter how they have persisted until today in denying their failure, they did fail. Jesus will continue to proclaim peace forever. This is the peace the Jews loathe; just as it happened before that they detested what Jesus proclaimed.[28]

The Palestinian poet Mahmud Darwish, although a proclaimed communist, found the material for his anti-Israel inspiration in the Bible. As an Arab and a Palestinian Muslim, he appropriates the history of the Jewish people and adapts it. Identifying Arab Palestine with Christ crucified by Israel, he tries to unite Christendom and Islam in the same hatred of Israelis, dispossessed of their history, their prophets (all Islamized), and their legitimacy in favor of an Islamic Palestine where the Cross is used to construct the *minbar* (from where the *khutbah*, or sermon, is delivered in the mosque), an allusion to Islam's retrieval of Christianity and its Islamization.[29]

The same process of reactivating hatred was adopted by the Arab press during the Gulf crisis, particularly in Syria. The Damascus government daily, *Tishrin (October)*, published an article in February 1991 on the theme, "Muslims and Christians: same fight against Israel," which stated:

How does it happen that today one acquits those who crucified Christ and do not cease to kill and crucify his disciples, and to sully his sacred values?[30]

It was after the *Nostra Aetate* declaration that the Christological themes of Palestinianism developed, based on the traditional Judeophobic schemas of the crucifixion, and introduced via the Arab Churches and the Euro-Arab current. The militancy of many Christians, including some priests within the PLO's ranks led to a stricter system of anti-terrorist surveillance in Israel. This crime prevention policy transformed the assassins into Christian martyrs in the cause of a new theology of Palestinianism, modernizing medieval Christian Judeophobic legends. The Arab Palestinian Churches transfigured the Arab Palestinian terrorist into a Christ-like image. In the long tradition of Syrian-Palestinian Christianity, the assassinations of Jews was thus hallowed. In a lecture in Paris on 2 June 1970 Mgr. Georges Khodr, Metropolitan of Byblos and Mt. Lebanon, following Abbé Youakim Moubarac, stressed:

You know what place Christian symbols occupy in contemporary Arab poetry, particularly that of the Palestinian resistance. It is not for me to tell the Muslims what force the evangelical ferment would contribute to the Arab cause.[31]

And he went further in his conclusion: "On June 5, 1967 I chose Arabness because on that day I saw that Jesus of Nazareth had become a Palestinian refugee."[32] The recycling of Christian religious symbols in the Arab-Muslim war on Israel was carried out at the instigation of Arab clergymen. Thirty years later, in 1997, at Har Homa, a stony hillside in the Judean desert overlooking Jerusalem, three Arabs had themselves bound to crosses to protest the building of houses on land owned by a Jew. This housing project sparked intense protests in Europe, and especially in the Arab countries where houses of Jews, property, and entire quarters had been confiscated and plundered—and in Palestine, including Jerusalem—at different periods for more than a millennium, and right up to the last decades of the twentieth century. The only protest about this sacrilegious utilization of the Cross that is known to the author came from two Christians living in Jerusalem, Patrick and Nicola Goodenough, who wrote to the *Jerusalem Post* to express their indignation against

the continued and blasphemous abuse of the symbols of our faith by the followers of another. [. . .] Not only did it denigrate our Lord, it was also an unsubtle attempt to resurrect, in the minds of viewers worldwide, the libel of deicide which prompted centuries of Jewish suffering.[33]

As the campaign of incitement to hatred through Christian religious symbols seemed to have been accepted by the highest ecclesiastical authorities it aroused no official protest, although it demeaned Christianity.

On 11 December 2000—two weeks before the Christmas Jubilee—a New Palestinian daily, *Intifada*, displayed on one-half of its front page a provocative caricature, showing a crucified young woman called "Palestine"—with blood flowing from her pierced hands and feet. A long spear transfixes her body to the cross, its protruding point embossed with a star of David, and an American flag at the shaft end. Blood spurts from her martyred body down upon a trio of huddled, caricatured Jews, who are looking up, grimacing at the crucified woman meant to represent Jesus/Palestine. Three days later, on 14 December, another spiritual message appeared in *Intifada*, alongside a battered cross, this time without the crucifixion scene, but with a prayer to "My Lord the Betrayed" "betrayed by the contemptible treasonable kiss," and ending: "O Son of The Virgin, they cannot overcome you twice . . ." (*PMW*).

To my knowledge, no Church body reacted before or after Christmas to this defamation of Christianity and hate-propaganda against Jews and Judaism in Jerusalem at the close of the Jubilee Year 2000. However, in Geneva, an ecumenical letter of protest dated 17 December ("Détournement de Symbole Religieux: parodie de prière et de crucifixion en Palestine . . ."/ "Abuse of a Religious Symbol: a parody of a prayer, and crucifixion in Palestine") was sent by Abbé Alain-René Arbez and the Rev. Bernard Buunk to the Association for World Education (AWE) requesting it to lodge a formal complaint with the appropriate bodies at the United Nations. This was done by the AWE on 21 December in an urgent appeal—enclosing their letter and the caricatures—to the UN Special Rapporteurs on Religious Intolerance and on Racism (Mr. Abdelfattah Amor and Mr. Maurice Glélé-Ahanhanzo), asking them to act under the Commission on Human Rights Resolution 1999/82 and 2000/84: "Defamation of Religions."

The Muslim-Christian appropriation of the Shoah aggravated this theological trend. Hence, Bishop Khodr could say: "The Jews of Auschwitz, Dachau, the boys and girls of Palestine, they were the Church [. . .]."[34] And again: "Their mass exodus [of the Palestinians] would be a historical and cultural genocide in all cases."[35]

In short, as Moubarac had defined it, this Christian compassion for the Jews—the "vicarial cause" of the sin of mankind—had to be accompanied by an unremitting war against Israel, whose restoration refuted the theology of hate. An indissociable relationship linked the demonization of the Jews with Christian compassion toward them. Such a perverse reasoning turned a heretofore racist ethic into a charitable undertaking. The identification of Israel with Evil assigned the symbol of Good to Palestine, moral regenerator of mankind but, above all, it provided the factor that cemented the joint Muslim-Christian pursuit to destroy Evil. In addition, Israel—"vicarial cause" of human iniquity—liberated the European conscience from the culpability of antisemitism and the Shoah, allowing a justification for a new Crusade against Israel. Thus, in this combination of pity for the demonized Jews, and of politicide for Israel, was planned the whole anti-Israeli campaign. It was developed by the Arabophile and pro-Palestinian Churches since Vatican II, making Israel—to quote Jacques Berque—"the inexpiable evil." This position explains the stigmatization of Israel's defensive actions and the silence surrounding the attacks which provoked them; since these attacks were perpetrated against the devil, they lost all noxiousness and, as Israel is the incarnation of evil, it is impossible to commit evil by striving to abolish it. Thus, as Moubarac explained, Vatican II in the end turned to the detriment of the Jews.[36]

The Arab states, having maintained and exacerbated Christian Judeophobia through historical falsification, pressure, and threats, also strove with the *dhimmi* Churches to prevent the Vatican from recognizing Israel.[37] From the Protestant side, official statements by the World Council of Churches (WCC) on the Jewish people were published in Geneva in 1988. Paul van Buren, professor of systematic theology at the University of Heidelberg, commented on contemporary theological issues regarding the State of Israel:

> Nothing in the church's tradition has prepared it for dealing with the State of Israel. Indeed, tradition has assumed as a matter of theological principle that a Jewish state was an impossibility: the Jews, we have taught, having rejected their Messiah and so their own inheritance, are condemned to wander the face of the earth in exile, until they turn to Christ or are confronted by him upon his return in glory. It is therefore not surprising that the churches have had difficulty in accounting for this new phenomenon, and that no consensus has yet arisen concerning the State of Israel. Furthermore, the absence of any analysis of the relationship between the Jewish people and the Land in all major documents of the WCC may be due to understandable apprehensions: fear of awakening eschatological fervour; aversion to the sacralization of any territory or institution; concern for the predicament of the Palestinians or of Christians in Arab or Islamic lands.[38]

Examining the Churches' policy on Jews and Israel, Professor Emeritus (of Religious Studies of the University of British Columbia, Vancouver) William Nicholls wrote:

> Perhaps we should not feel surprise, in view of this history of hate, at the total failure of these churches and their leaders to have any empathy with

Jews and their causes and their extreme readiness to sympathize with their sworn enemies.[39]

By winning over the clergy, the Arab League spread anti-Zionism at both local and international levels. This success occurred against a background of terrorism and assassinations, threatening Christian Arabs. Muslim blackmail of Christians proved advantageous: the more Christians were killed in the Middle East, the more the West pronounced Israel responsible. The murder of Christians during the first *intifada* stirred up anti-Zionist sentiments worldwide, and caused the European Community to impose retaliatory economic and political sanctions against the Jewish State.

The exoneration of Muslim policy for anti-Christian persecutions in order to transfer blame on Israel accounts for the conspiracy of silence about Christian suffering in Muslim lands, for which Israel was made responsible. The whole anti-Zionist campaign emanating from clerical bodies concealed the humiliations and discriminatory measures which their Islamic environment was inflicting on Christians in the same period. Jacques Ellul, the French sociologist and Protestant theologian who constantly fought against Christian Judeophobia, referred to this "concealment"— this policy of "silence"—in regard to Islamic expansion and dhimmitude. In what was to be his last analysis written soon after the Gulf War of 1991, he insisted on this point:

> I would say *carefully concealing*—so widespread is the agreement on this silence that it can only be the results of a tacit agreement based on implicit presupposition. [italics in the original][40]

Silence in respect of the oppressing Muslim states and virulent accusations at an international level against Israel constituted a policy of psychological release and compensation, set in a context of a millennium of Christian dhimmitude, reflected back on to the Synagogue by the Church. In addition, the Eastern Churches attributed the problems of the Muslim-Christian rapprochement to the pro-Zionist Western Churches.[41]

Many Christian theologians strongly opposed these anti-Zionist trends, such as the American Reinhold Niebuhr, editor from 1941–66 of the journal, *Christianity and Crisis*. After the Six-Day War, the editorial changed "with, as the inevitable outcome, total acceptance of the Arab case . . . Reinhold Niebuhr would have no part in this betrayal."[42]

Focusing libellous propaganda on Israel at the international level formed the shield protecting Christians from Muslim fanaticism. Thus, during the civil war in Lebanon when Christian resistance to PLO terrorism had put various Christian communities in danger, a hysterical anti-Israeli campaign was unleashed in the West and by the Communist world.

Incitement to hatred and propaganda attributed to Israel the destruction of Lebanon, perpetrated by the PLO and its allies. At the international level, the policy of protecting Christians and Western interests by defaming Israel dominated Vatican and European diplomacy in the Middle East. It reappeared during the Gulf crisis from August 1990 when the Vatican, supported by France, strove to establish a "linkage" between Israel and Iraq's invasion and destruction of Kuwait.[43] This strategy was based on fear of Muslim anti-Christian reprisals, provoked by the coalition of the West against Saddam Hussein, despite the participation of Muslim and Arab states, and Israel's neutrality. The Eastern patriarchs condemned the Gulf War as "an international plot directed against Christians in the Middle East" to force them to emigrate.[44]

Like a true *dhimmi*, the new Latin Patriarch of Jerusalem Bishop Michel Sabbah (nominated on 12 December 1987) stated that the danger did not originate from Islamic fundamentalism but from Israel and the United States.[45] France was drawn into the coalition despite itself. After a round of excuses and promises to the Arab countries, French pro-Arab politicians denounced Israel as the source of anti-Western Arab-Muslim feeling.

During the Gulf War (January–February 1991), Israel agreed to assume the role of a *dhimmi* state by foregoing its self-defense against Iraqi Scuds. And it did so amid the silence of the Western nations, champions of human rights. Despite this, at the conclusion of a synod convened by the Pope on 4–5 March 1991, after the war, a spokesman for the Holy See stated that the United Nations was resorting to double standards and was favoring Israel. The Patriarch of Jerusalem declared that "the sole secure frontier for the Jewish State is justice, reconciliation and forgiveness."[46] The idea that the State of Israel represents an injustice, which implies that its nonexistence incarnates justice, is frequently voiced by Christians—both clergy and secular—on behalf of the Palestinian cause. On 21 July 2000 the Geneva newspaper *Le Temps* published an interview with Tarek Mitri, a Lebanese Greek Orthodox sociologist, responsible for interreligious relations at the World Council of Churches in Geneva. For him, any arrangement between Israel and the Palestinians over Jerusalem required an essential condition:

> First, the recognition that an injustice has been done to the Palestinians as a result of the creation of the State of Israel. And it should now be corrected. The modalities to accomplish this are a detail.

In his thorough research on the ideology that led to the Holocaust and its genocidal methods, Daniel Goldhagen states that the conception of Jews in medieval Christendom "was one which held the Jews to violate the moral order of the world." It becomes difficult for antisemites "to see the Jews'

actions, even their existence, other than as desecration and defilement."
As he put it:

> The fundamental nature of antisemitism of this kind is different from the
> great variety of antisemitisms that are not colored in this way. They are more
> tenacious, arouse more passion, usually provoke and support a wider variety
> of more serious and inflammatory charges against the Jews, and inhere
> within them a greater potential for violent and deadly anti-Jewish action.
> Conceptions of Jews that hold them to be destructive of the moral order, that
> demonize them, can be and have been based on different understandings of
> the source of the Jews' perniciousness, clearly including both religious and
> racial understandings of Jews. The former was the case in medieval Chris-
> tendom, the latter in Germany during its Nazi period.[47]

The interpretation of Israel as an injustice and not as historical redress
for a crime committed against the Jewish people—robbed of its identity,
history, and human rights—transformed the rehumanization of the victim
into a conceded favor, with the implication that this favor is temporary. It
is a favor that Israel, the victim of this crime, must seek through pardon
which implies that its independence—always according to the traditional
Church criteria—is an error which justifies its continued condemnation.

The Vatican's anti-Israeli and anti-West stance during the Gulf War
aroused sharp criticism. In an article entitled "Vaticant, the Pope's war record," the Catholic author, Furio Colombo, noted that the Pope only protested after the nineteenth Iraqi Scud had fallen on Israel, although about
double that number had been discharged. He commented that it was the
first time since 1947 that a pope had mentioned the State of Israel by name,
an omission which obfuscated its existence.

> In his thinking on the Middle East, the pope has long had his own "new
> world order" in mind. The relationship between the Catholic Church and
> Islam clearly takes precedence for the Vatican over the relationship between
> the Catholic Church and Judaism. And even over the one between the Cath-
> olic Church and the Western world.[48]

As has been shown, Arab nationalism was initially a tool of French imperialism in the Ottoman provinces against British interests. From the mid-
nineteenth century it served the anti-Zionist campaign led by France and
the papacy via the activism of Arab Christians. After the failure of Arab nationalism to eliminate Israel, the Uniate, Orthodox, and Latin Catholic
Churches in the Holy Land strove from the 1970s to construct an Arab-
Palestinian identity hostile to Israel and shared by Christians and Muslims.
In 1970, the Catholic Justice and Peace Commission was established in Jerusalem under the supervision of the apostolic delegate of the Vatican; in
1983, it issued a pamphlet entitled "Moslems and Christians on the Road

Together," emphasizing cultural and historical unity as well as their common Palestinian cause. It affirmed that Palestinian Christians should consider that their Arabism and their relations with Islam were an integral part of their Christian personality, their vocation, and their mission.[49] Catholic-sponsored centers, as well as publications, stressed Arab Christian and Muslim unity in their struggle against Israel. This political involvement of the Arab Palestinian Churches against Israel was backed by the European Community and gained media coverage. In 1983, al-Liqa, a Catholic Center for studying the Muslim and Catholic heritage in the Holy Land, was established. The Center has been strongly politicized since 1987 and was used for spreading anti-Israeli propaganda through international Catholic channels and the media.

It is particularly instructive to examine the anti-Zionist Christian argument in its new Palestinian garb, as described in two books by Anglican clergymen. The language used here—contrary to the virulence of the preceding period—is stuffed with expressions of compassion, justice, and peace toward an evil Israel. The argument is polarized by two conflicting centers: the Church, symbol of truth and of a suffering justice; and Israel, usurper and oppressor of the innocent. Between these two poles circulate the compassion of Justice, symbolized by the Church—toward Sin, personified by Israel. This Marcionite conception dominates Canon Naim Stifan Ateek's book, *Justice and Only Justice. A Palestinian Theology of Liberation.*[50]

Throughout its chapters, the author sets out the infallibility of the Church's justice, which expresses the divine will through its religious body. The author's absolute conviction that he knows the justice of God impregnates his thought and lends his judgments on Israel a trenchant certainty unaffected by doubts. The Israel that Ateek weighs on his scales is the Israel of the deicide people, a usurper, devoid of any rights in its homeland—just as the Arab Palestinian Christian leaders stated in 1923 when they presented Winston Churchill with a copy of *The Protocols of the Elders of Zion.* Ateek's numerous biblical references do not concern the ancestors of the Jews, but of the Church and Christianized pagan peoples, pre-existing in biblical Israel, the sole heirs of Israel's heritage. He reluctantly admits that Israel does not persecute the Churches, but he immediately corrects himself, declaring that the Church was attacked as part of a national Palestinian entity, a fiction belied by the extreme fragmentation of the Christian communities in the Holy Land. In fact, the Bishopric of Palestine never constituted an ethnic autocephalous Church, unlike the Coptic, Greek, Armenian, Assyrian, Serbian, and other Churches elsewhere in the world.

As its name indicates, the Arab Palestinian Church is not related to Israel. It is the Christian *Verus Israel,* preexisting in biblical Israel, of which it alone assumes the heritage—the Jews being stripped of all rights, even their name and identity. This Church is not neutral since it utilizes all its international ramifications to delegitimize the Jewish state. In order to attain "Justice and Peace," Ateek recommends that this Church follow a strategy that he calls a dual imperative: prophetic and political. The prophetic imperative requires the Arab Palestinian Church to analyze and interpret political events theologically.[51] Thus, he calls for the de-Zionization of the Bible and the de-mythologization of the State of Israel.[52] But a few pages further on he forbids the Israelis and their Christian friends from exercising this same right in interpreting the Bible as, in his opinion, the only valid interpretation is that of the Palestinian Christians based on *their* justice. Ateek explains that this theological imperative of interpretation comprises the underlying substance of the Church's strategy and is based on a theological understanding of Justice and Peace. However, this theological understanding of Justice and Peace is rooted in the denial of the rights of Jews in their own land, a conviction which impregnates all Ateek's thought and reasoning. The second element of this dual imperative consists of a strategy which the author modestly presents as a great discovery. He proposes to unify all the Palestinian Churches with those from the East and West, to act together: "Working for peace makes the Church focus on a common Christian concern." The unity of the Church would provide greater involvement and centrality. The Church should create a "Center for Peace" and should look to the United Nations as the best forum for establishing the criteria for justice.[53] In particular, this Center should reach out to the West with the aim of de-Zionizing the Bible and proving Israel's usurpation.

One only need replace the magic words "Justice and Peace" by "the international Jewish peril" and Azoury's old tactics resurface, advocating the unification of all the Eastern and Western Churches under the authority of the Vatican in order to eliminate Israel. The alliance between world Christendom and Islam in Arab nationalism is thus replaced by Palestinianism. Canon Ateek may have dug up this plan to internationalize hatred of Israel in some old box of documents from the Latin convents in Jerusalem. Since 1905, rivers of blood have flowed from this serpent of hatred which enveloped the world. It contributed to the genocide of the Jews that was sealed by the Nazi-Palestinian handshake between the Grand Mufti of Jerusalem and Hitler on 28 November 1941, and by the silence of the Churches during World War II. This unification of the Churches for which the Latin Patriarch Michel Sabbah—supported by the Anglican and Lutheran bishops—obsessively worked, produced a campaign of anti-Israeli vilification in the Western media during the 1980s. Ateek considers himself "an observer of history", but his ignorance in matters relating to antisemitism and the Shoah is appalling. Likewise, the criteria of justice that he attributes to the United Nations are highly objectionable since the General Assembly's automatic majority adopted resolution 3379 equating Zionism with a form of racism on 10 November 1975, the thirty-seventh anniversary commemorating the 1938 Nazi Kristallnacht. This lapsus casts a grim shadow on his flowing style that abounds in love, peace, justice, and forgiveness.

Canon Ateek's argument is impregnated with false symmetries and the principle of supersession. Thus, the historical sameness that he invents between Israelis and Arab Palestinians voids fourteen centuries of Christian antisemitism, which has no equivalence in the European-Arab relationship. Likewise, it wipes out more than thirteen centuries of dhimmitude imposed on the Jews by the invaders from Arabia. This historical situation places the two terms—Arabs and Jews in the Holy Land—in an asymmetrical, and not an equal relationship, because it was the Jews who were expropriated, exploited, dehumanized, and decimated *after* the Arab invasion. Similarly, he places the Shoah—a policy of total extermination of the Jews—on a parity with the flight of Arab Palestinians who were defeated in the course of a war, which they waged in conjunction with neighboring Arab armies to crush the Jews and Israel's rebirth. Ateek's statement shows abysmal ignorance on the part of a Christian; in fact, it reveals the *concealment* of a stratagem aimed at shifting onto Israel the Christian guilt toward it, by a gratuitous accusation of "genocide" against Palestinians. Inspired by this false symmetry which enlightens us on his conception of justice, Ateek would like to see Yad Vashem display Palestinian history as a counterbalance. He seems unaware that it has been represented there for some time by the photographs of the Palestinian Grand Mufti Haj Amin al-Husayni celebrating with Hitler in Berlin, saluting the Nazi Arab legion which—with other Muslim soldiers—became an S.S. unit for Germany, and his declaration on Radio Berlin (1 March 1944):

> Kill the Jews wherever you find them. This pleases God, history, and religion. This saves your honour. God is with you.[54]

Ateek admits that the Palestinians have always denied the Holocaust; he recommends that they acknowledge it now, but accompanied by a Palestinian symmetry. Because they too have had their genocide: both Christians and Muslims, brotherly victims of Israeli "Nazis." Although the Israelis have no rights, Ateek nevertheless advises the Palestinians to accept Israel, but solely on the basis of the Holocaust:

> The Palestinians, as hosts, have to come to accept giving the Jews the best part of Palestine [i.e. in the remaining part of Western Palestine], not because they had any right to it, not because of the Balfour Declaration, and not even because of antisemitism, but because of the Holocaust.[55]

Antisemitism being hatred of Jews, how is it logically possible to separate this hatred from the process of their total extermination in the Shoah? If not hatred, then perhaps it is the compassion, peace, and justice of Christianity which led to their genocide?

> The Palestinians can, therefore, look the Jews in the eye and say that the only justification that they can accept today for the presence of Israel is the Holocaust. And with a new, magnanimous attitude they should say to the Jews, we will accept you and share the land with you.[56]

This attitude is typical of dhimmitude: Israel is magnanimously tolerated, but its rights are denied. This concept is in accordance with the principle of supersession, which appropriates the Jewish people's rights by transferring their history to the Church, whose origin is placed before the birth of Jesus. Thus, modern Israel has no right to assume the heritage of a four-thousand-year-old history, including, *inter alia,* a long period of dhimmitude in Arabized Palestine; it is a usurping nonexistent entity, proclaiming an identity which is not its own by right.

The author is anxious to inform us—in case we have not already understood—that he has succeeded through love and forgiveness in overcoming the hatred that, since childhood, he vowed toward Jews.[57] It is a pointless confession since his thought patterns are set in the perverted mold defined by Abbé Moubarac, which masks hatred by compassion.

Naim Stifan Ateek's book was greeted with a chorus of praise by pro-Palestinian Christian circles when it was published in 1989. Some elements of their moralizing and political arguments should be mentioned here: the banalization of the false symmetries, which cancel Israel's history and rights; likewise, the statement that only the Holocaust legitimizes Israel's existence enables the author to deny the historic rights and identity of the Jewish people. *In fact, the reverse is true: Zionism preceded the Holocaust, and the Shoah was the war to exterminate all Jews in order to eradicate Zionism, which explains the collusive silence throughout most of Europe to allow the crime to be perpetrated.*

The book by Kenneth Cragg, *The Arab Christian,* takes the reader into the same opaque world where the words justice, peace, love, and, above all, compassion flourish on nearly every page, masking inadmissible sentiments.[58] But Anglican Bishop Cragg has a far more ambitious aim than Canon Ateek's superficial book, and his convoluted style runs through every register of hatred camouflaged as compassion.[59]

In order to endow the Arab Palestinians with a historical legitimacy as ancient as Israel's, Cragg identifies the Arabs with the Philistines. With a magic stroke of his pen he abolishes those numerous Arab chronicles which glorify the vicissitudes of the Arab-Muslim conquests and the deportation of the peasantry. He overlooks the continuous migration of tribes from Arabia over the centuries, with whom, until recent times, the Muslims of Palestine proudly identified themselves. All these chronicles which may be found in major libraries worldwide that conscientiously list the Bedouin ancestries and the names and alliances of their tribes, are now implicitly denied and replaced by an imaginary relationship to an obscure population, known to posterity through its conflicts with the Israelites. No link exists between the Philistines—polytheist immigrants from the Aegean islands, speaking a non-Semitic language—and Semites from the Arabian peninsula who were Islamized in the seventh century. No historical continuity, nor a religious, ethnic, and cultural identity connects these two groups. Cragg is conscious, however, of the poor reputation of the Philistines, and by a feat of legerdemain reverses the roles, in contempt of elementary historical deontology, thereby discrediting biblical Israel in order to rehabilitate the Philistines as the ancestors of the modern Arab Palestinians.

One is dumbfounded at the efforts and passion that the former assistant Anglican Bishop of Jerusalem (from 1970–73; and in an "honorary" capacity from 1973–85) expends on a game which he himself invented, rigged with distorting mirrors. Conversely, these anti-Jewish tactics are more detrimental to Christianity by the glorification of a pagan culture dominated by sanguinary gods. Acknowledging finally the misfortunes of the Christian *dhimmis,* Cragg accuses Europe of having provoked the Islamic reprisals against the Christians by resisting the Muslim invaders. Instead of fighting them, European Christians should have learned from Eastern Christian Churches, whose conduct seems to Cragg "an index to truth"[60] and a model of how to submit to, and live with, Islam. This submission comprises "a wisdom of sufferance," a wisdom analyzed by historians in terms of continual collusion and collaboration with Muslim leaders on the part of the Christian religious and political hierarchy for their personal interests. Europe, having defended itself first against the Arab, and then the Turkish, invaders is twice guilty in respect of the Eastern Christians, and guilty vis-à-vis the Muslims. By constantly reexamining European guilt for the Crusades, Bishop Cragg minimizes the causes: the destruction of churches in the Holy Land, the assassinations, abductions, and forced conversions of pilgrims, and the *jihad* ravages in Armenia. In 1998, this assumption of guilt for the Crusades even moved groups of repentant Christians to travel through the Middle East—former Christian lands—to ask Muslim forgiveness.

Cragg strives to create a sense of European guilt toward Muslims and the Eastern Christians (Copts, Armenians, Syriacs, Greeks, all of whom he wrongly calls Arabs), on the lines of Christian thinking on antisemitism and the Shoah. He seems to be unaware that these groups were not always fragmented and impotent minorities, but had once formed national majorities, some with their own armies. Their destruction is primarily the result of the corruption of their religious leaders, as well as of conflicts between the different Christian factions. No symmetry exists between these situations, however tragic they were, and the doctrine of deicide with all its legal, political, and exterminatory consequences for the Jewish minorities in the Christian East and in Europe. Likewise, the author is not afraid of ridicule when he places on an equal footing the history of *jihad* on three continents with the history of European imperialism, and the recent Jewish settlements of Gush Emunim . . . in Judea. As he deftly puts it:

> Indeed, the history of Jihad, of Crusade, of the Gush Emunim in every faith . . .[61]

In other words, the intention is to place Islamic and Christian imperialisms worldwide, over more than a millennium on the same level as an Israeli political movement expressed solely in Judea, a province known by that geographical name from biblical times till the end of the British Mandate. In the same vein, Latin Patriarch Michel Sabbah suggested that, "just as Western Christians had had to repent for the treatment of Jews, so Jews would have to repent for their treatment of Palestinians."[62] In this way, sixteen centuries of persecution culminating in the Shoah are equated in a false symmetry with the Jewish victims' liberation from both Christian antisemitism and Muslim dhimmitude.

Returning to classic antisemitism but in the form enhanced by the theological language of compassion, Bishop Cragg reflects on the Arab Ba'ath party's thinking, and its Christian sponsors, declaring, *inter alia*:

> Was 'Aflaq invoking a mystical concept of eternal peoplehood and sacred mission, as if to counter Jewish election with an Arab vocation, or to translate the Christian dimension of "people of God" into Bergsonian ideals of an Arab *élan vital*?[63]

Arab nationalism, as a political and ideological tactic to oppose Zionism was clearly set out in the King-Crane Commission's report and in innumerable declarations and writings by nationalist Arabs, both Christian and Muslim. According to a Lebanese, Joseph Aboujaoude:

> The concept of an "Arab Nation" was used officially for the first time in June 1913 at the sessions of the Arab Congress held in Paris. The emphasis in the works of the congress is placed on the rights of Arabs inside the [Ottoman] Empire and on the wish of the Turks to impose their language and their traditions, while preserving Arab-Ottoman relationships. There is never any allusion to frontiers or to territorial delimitation. Which allows one to conclude that until that time the concept of an Arab Nation was not far removed from the concept of an Islamic Nation.[64]

As the religious and legal persecution of *dhimmi* Christians could no longer be concealed, Cragg resigns himself to examining it. His analysis of Muslim-Christian relations reveals the whole fabric of the Christian anti-semitism which is subjacent. This fabric is much less evident in Ateek than in Cragg, who treats it in a more sophisticated manner by conjuring up a demonizing Christology of Israel. Therein can be seen the continuity in some European and Arab Christian theological trends, transcending history, of a focusing of Evil on one human group: the Jews—and now on Israel. This fabric of hate is particularly apparent in the Israel-Palestine-Lebanon—that is to say, in the Judeo-Muslim-Christian—relationship. As has been shown, Muslim-Christian relationships in Lebanon did not represent a reality by themselves but were exploited as a weapon against Israel. This anti-Israeli argument induced its authors to attribute to the Jewish state the diabolic intention to destroy the Muslim-Christian idyll. The proclamation of such a symbiosis is intended to highlight a Christianity which displays a fraternal, trusting, and welcoming relationship with Islam. The purpose was to create an effect of contrast with an isolated Israel, with its "Jewish implacability"—"Palestinianism is grimly held within that built-in suspicion of or distrust in the rest of humanity so characteristic of Jewish anxiety."[65] These contrasting images abound in a whole corpus of ecclesiastical and secular European-*dhimmi* literature. It is because it destroyed this politico-media fallacy that the Lebanese Christian resistance was condemned. And as Lebanon was ravaged by the PLO—that privileged ally of Euro-Arabism—those men who had invented these fallacies, not being in a position to denounce their allies, accused Israel of their own intentions.

Cragg stigmatizes the Lebanese Christian resistance; he considers its alliance with Israel as the height of treason against Christian values and mankind. "[T]he malevolence of Israel is mainly responsible for the failure of the Lebanese experiment for a Muslim-Christian symbiosis."[66] Hence, he states: "In all the given factors of the Arab scene, the tragedy of Lebanon is the neighborhood of Israel."[67] But how then to explain the genocidal *jihad* war against the Christians and animists in Sudan, and the Muslim-Christian conflicts in Egypt, Algeria, Nigeria, Pakistan, the Philippines, Indonesia, the Balkans, the Caucasian region, and elsewhere in the world?

To attribute to Israel the destruction of Lebanon perpetrated by the Muslim-Palestinian *jihad* reveals two tendencies: first, the impossibility for this faction of denouncing Muslim responsibility for the destruction of Christian political power; and, consequently, the obligation to transfer the blame to Israel by the depraved conditioning of dhimmitude, and in accordance with the theological principle of the incarnation of evil. Second, this argument reveals, apart from its foolishness, the theological, political, and media-controlled strategy of the anti-Zionist war. In his chapter on Lebanon, the author ill-humoredly harries the Maronites, accused of being responsible for the Lebanese disaster: "The tragedy of Lebanon is the tragedy of the Maronites writ large."[68] This is hardly a flattering image, especially as he considers Maronites to be similar to the Israelis. On the other hand, he admires the Greek Orthodox, who knew how to adapt the requirements of dhimmitude by collaborating with the destruction of Christian political power in order to contribute, "by a common dedication," to the supreme goal of Arabness demanded by Islam, an aim which he discreetly omits to mention. Like Abbé Moubarac.

Ateek only mentions the Holocaust superficially. For Cragg it forms an obsession, but in the context of the false parity which places the Arab Palestinians in a history modeled on Israel's. From his pen flow analogies between Nazis and Israelis, Menahem Begin and

> the bunkers of Berlin in 1945 and the grim end of Hitler in a clear anticipation of a parallel "final solution" for Lebanon by the eviction of the Palestinians. The element of grim triumphalism in the Israeli psyche was unmistakable. Reckoning in Lebanon would be vicarious vengeance for the Holocaust.[69]

These and many others arguments, developed by European and Arab Christian theologians, are part of a fixed theological system in which the Jews and Israel symbolize the essence of Evil, an eternal evil which is the enemy of Goodness and Justice, identified with Palestine. Facing the satanic principle incarnated by the Zionist state stands the Palestinian people, crucified on the Cross, wearing the crown of thorns, an incarnation of an Arab Palestinian Jesus, in which Islam and Christianity mystically unite in oneness.

In his conclusion Cragg wonders how to create, and to express, a "Palestinian liberation theology." He acknowledges the irrelevance of Hebrew scriptures in this context, and finds inspiration in the New Testament, and in his conviction "that there is redemption *within* suffering." He then proposes Dostoevsky's idea in *The Possessed* of " 'a God-bearing people', whose responsibility to evil lay in the will to transmute it into good." He recalls the Muslim, as well as the Christian urge in poetry,

> to identify with suffering, to be on behalf of the people in the voicing of despair, so that evil is not silenced, dismissed, disregarded—which is the way of untruth—but held, pilloried, taken for the evil it is. To that extent it is being borne, carried in the heart, and essentially known. In that sense it is right to liken oppressors to Judas Iscariot and to identify the crown of thorns. Poetry is thus the acceptance of evil, the vocal realization that it has been suffered. [. . .]But this is not liberation. [. . .] But is there an acceptance that can go further, an acceptance that, while letting the wrong be the wrong it is and poignantly saying so, nevertheless outlives it in the will to suffer, and suffer toward an end beyond it and because of it?

Such was and is the principle of Jesus's cross. It is not a political solution, draws no maps on territories, negotiates no treaties. But it liberates from the evil imprisoning the future and releases hope from the bondage of the past. After more than a century of political Zionism on the move, after four decades of exile or distraint, it is clear that Arab Palestinians are a martyr people, with Poles, Armenians, and many others.[70]

Not only are Jews detested because of the suffering that Christian anti-semites have inflicted on them for two millennia, but Christian associates and friends of Israel even more so. As mentioned, he is particularly vindictive in respect of the Maronites and their Lebanese-Christian allies, a people martyred by the Palestinians. The more he demonstrates the diabolic character of Israel, the more his style overflows with compassion. This display of compassion, justice, and peace is all the more nauseating in that it disguises the vice of hatred as a virtue. For Bishop Cragg, the future restoration of Palestine on the demise of Israel would restore perfection and purity to the world, a policy not so different to that of the Nazis, which had already led to the greatest slaughter houses of history.

Since the mission of the Palestinian Arabs is to suffer in order to expose Evil, one can understand the pathological obsession of the *dhimmi* Arab Churches and their contacts in Europe to proclaim and tirelessly pillory the demonic essence of Israel. Research into the genocide of the Jews reactively fostered the transfer of this Jewish martyrology to the Palestinians. The more horrible the Shoah was, the more its victims are blamed, and the more indispensable becomes the Palestinian mediation which permits the transfer of the executioner's guilt to his victim. As a result, this Palestine, crucified by Israel, represents a morbid and essential necessity which gathers together the passions of all the European and Arab, neo-Nazi, and anti-Jewish trends, as well as the schizophrenic perversions of dhimmitude.

This inversion of roles, travestizing the Jews as Nazis for having successfully resisted the combined Arab genocidal assaults from the 1930s, was first developed by British historian Arnold Toynbee during the 1950s.[71] In his conclusion to a subsequent book on Palestine, Kenneth Cragg provides more personal insights, such as:

Christians were used to Zachariah's Song: "Blessed be the Lord God of Israel" alongside their bitter exile at the hand of the (to them less than 'blessed') Lord of Ben Gurion, Begin, Shamir and Rabin. The same song made double reference to "the hands of our enemies" and "them that hate us", i.e. the new Philistines.[72]

As already mentioned, this anti-Zionism is scarcely representative of the whole body of opinion of Eastern Christians, most of whom react as hostages struck dumb with fear. Habib Malik, son of Lebanon's former foreign minister, Charles Malik, analyzed the problem in a 1998 article:

> Last, the Middle East Council of Churches appears on the verge of broadening its hitherto exclusive fixation on the Arab-Israeli conflict and the Palestinian problem to include such vital issues on its agenda of priorities as the welfare of native non-Muslim minority communities (mainly the Christians), the state of human rights and fundamental freedoms in the region, women's issues, and Christian unity. [parentheses in the original][73]

This exclusive fixation on the Palestinians, nourished by a paranoid Judeophobia is in fact the determining cause of the careful *concealment* and, henceforth, an apparently irreversible aggravation of Christian dhimmitude in Islamic lands. In a subsequent incisive article on the Palestinian Christians, Malik concludes that their mentality is symptomatic of the perverse effects of dhimmitude, based on an absolute ignorance of history and its replacement by a mythical Muslim-Christian symbiosis:

> By and large, Palestinian Christians have looked to Palestinian nationalism for a meeting ground with their Palestinian Muslim counterparts. This point of intersection has all too often been mythologized by intellectuals and clergymen who never tire of insisting that harmony has always prevailed between Muslims and Christians in Palestine.[74]

According to Malik, to believe that the solution of the Palestinian conflict will abolish all anti-Christian persecution in the region—as Palestinian Christians pretend—reveals all the fear and ignorance of the *dhimmi*. Here it should be added that the Christian *dhimmi* discourse merely echoes the theories of its oppressors. Proponents of Islamic interests, the Palestinian Christians bear a heavy historical responsibility for having imposed an exclusive anti-Zionist focus on the Christian world at a decisive period in the survival of Eastern—and above all, of Lebanese—Christianity, a focus which allows the whole history of dhimmitude and its modern aggravations to be camouflaged. In many respects, this Arab Palestinian Christianity is directly responsible for the West's indifferent and collusive silence on the contemporary dhimmitude of Eastern Christians. Commenting on the simplistic ignorance of these Palestinian *dhimmis*, Malik writes in the same article:

> Once again, removing Israel from the equation and satisfying the Palestinians beyond their wildest dreams would not eliminate the violence against non-Muslims inherent in political Islam. Second, this interpretation is not shared by the vast majority of the region's Christians, whether *dhimmi* or free.

For Malik, the alienation of the *dhimmi,* so deeply internalized by the Palestinian Christian, is doubled by a Marcionite tendency.

Palestinian Christians further differ from other Christian communities in the region in their acute discomfort with the Jewish Bible.

He noticed that they cannot bear to recite certain psalms or to read the biblical stories, and commented:

In the spirit of Marcion, some Palestinian Christians in their liturgies have excised or doctored specific references to the Old Testament and to the People of Israel.

Calling them contemporary Marcionists, Malik concludes:

This misdirected and unnecessary alienation of Palestinian Christians from the Old Testament ought not to be encouraged. [. . .] Whichever way one looks at it (except as an expression of the prevailing *dhimmi* motif), Palestinian Christianity is unrepresentative of the wider Christian communities scattered throughout the Middle East. [parentheses in the original]

The Muslim-Christian front against Israel gave rise to various comments in the Israeli press. The *Jerusalem Post* published a long editorial in 1992, entitled "The Churches' anti-Israel Crusade," which emphasized the attempts by the *dhimmi* Palestinian Churches to follow the PLO in an attempt to "de-Judaize Jesus" and "Palestinize" him and the Apostles. It referred to their silence in respect of the Palestinians' anti-Christian persecution and terrorism.[75] In 1998, Muslim attacks on Christians at Nazareth concerning a piece of land in front of the Basilica of the Annunciation caused Latin Patriarch Michel Sabbah to accuse Israel of these disturbances. The papal nuncio added his criticism to these accusations. An article by Deborah Sonntag in the *International Herald Tribune* of 24 November 1999 (from the *New York Times*) had a title on its first page: "Israel Sows Divisions on Mosque," which continued on page 10 with another title: "VATICAN: Israel is Fomenting Discord Between Christians and Muslims, Church Says." A year earlier, the director of the Christian Communities department in the Religious Affairs Ministry, Uri Mor, rejected—as he had done in 1992—any attempt by Bishop Sabbah, or the leader of any other Christian community, to blame Israel for Muslim attacks on Christians.[76] What makes these Christian accusations so ridiculous is that they were motivated by exclusively Muslim demands: the construction near the basilica of a mosque, topped by a high minaret, on the tomb of Shihab ad-Din, a hero of the *jihad* against the Crusaders.

The Patriarch's accusations were all the more inappropriate as the Latin

Patriarchate of Palestine had often been at the root of anti-Jewish hatred in the Christian and Muslim worlds. In an interview given on the subject of this mosque to *Al-Ahram Hebdo* (Cairo) in December 1999, Sabbah declared: "the problem is not the construction of a mosque, rather it is to spread discord [. . .] We must, above all, maintain the Muslim-Christian force."

The Judeo-Christian conflicts have been examined here in the context of dhimmitude, that is to say, in relation to an Islamized Christianity. As Muhammad Hussein Fadlallah—the spiritual leader of the Lebanese Hizbollah movement—declared in 1995:

> Even the Christians living in the Arab world unconsciously think with an Islamic mentality; although they do not have an Islamic affiliation, they take in Islamic civilization as they do the air they breathe like the fragrance of a rose.[77]

The inter-Christian conflicts emanating from the same context of dhimmitude have been mentioned briefly. In his book, *Between Damascus and Jerusalem: Lebanon and Middle East Peace,* Professor Malik differentiates between the Christian factions which resist Islamization and the "[p]ure 'resignationists' or assimilationists."[78] According to the author, this latter group includes "various strands of ideological Arabists and those who promote the idea of a Greater Syria." The assimilationist trend

> comes closer to a form of quasi-*dhimmi* status. Interestingly, the position of one Christian group is very often motivated more by a desire to set itself apart from another Christian tendency than to resist or accommodate the Muslims.[79]

Any study of Christian dhimmitude should consider the diverse and contradictory trends which corroded and tore apart the *dhimmi* Christian communities—within a context of anti-Judaism, inter-Christian conflicts, and European-Muslim relations.

The Internationalization of Hate

One could ask whether the dynamics of dhimmitude examined above are still apparent at an international level today and, if so, what form they take. In fact, from the beginning of its geographical expansion political Islam was always actively present in Judeo-Christian and inter-European conflicts, and the contests between different Christian Churches such as the struggle of Monophysites against Diophysites. In the modern period, it has been shown that from 1830–40, the French ultramontane parties and the papacy conceived their policy of Arabizing the Levantine Christian groups as an instrument of French and Catholic influence in the Near East. The Damascus Blood Libel of 1840 initiated a French policy of incriminating Jewry in order to suppress Jewish emancipation, neutralize the interests of Anglo-Prussian Protestantism in the Holy Land, and crush proto-Zionism.

This French and Catholic policy, banding Muslims and Christians against "Jewish rapacity," reached a peak of violence in the last decades of the nineteenth century in French Algeria. In 1882 Abbé Chabauty launched the slogan: "The Jew, that's the enemy," taken up by Abbé Martinez in 1890, and by Abbé Hippolyte Gayraud in 1896, who declared: "I consider it axiomatic, theologically, historically and canonically, that the Jew is the enemy."[80] It became a leitmotif. On the pretext that the Jews were exploiting the Arabs, the French colonists called for the repeal of the Crémieux decree of 1870, which had granted French citizenship to all the Jews of Algeria. The French antisemitic party demanded a return to the laws of dhimmitude for the Jews, similar to their former status in Christendom. The anti-Jewish campaign burst into riots, pillages, and massacres in Mostaganem, Oran, and Algiers (1896–97). Geneviève Dermanjian notes that: "The antisemite thus presents himself as the Muslim's friend and educator, his natural protector against the rapacious Israelite."[81]

> The stamp of the anti-Jewish league showed a [French] colonist and an Arab placing their feet on the back of a prostrate Jew. It is noteworthy on this score that antisemites, who take upon themselves the duty of protecting "the Arab against the Jew," and who counted for a long time on his antisemitism, are determined to associate him [the Arab] with Europeans in anti-Jewish engravings.[82] [inverted commas in the original]

This same structure can be applied to Palestine, where—from the beginning of the twentieth century—the Arab Christians, the Vatican, and European antisemitic parties proclaimed themselves the protectors of Palestine against Israel. As early as 1880, the French Catholic newspaper *La Croix* published a text by Abbé Dutartre waving the threat of a Jewish peril in the form of a powerful State of Israel where the Jews would rebuild their capital.[83] Anglo-French strategic rivalries in the Middle East fueled the war of Catholic slander against Jews and Protestants. It has also been noted that in the international context European states gave up protecting the rights, security, and even the survival of Christian *dhimmis* at the beginning of the century, fearing the reprisals of the millions of Muslims in their vast colonies. Hence, Arab or Turkish Islam played a considerable part in European policy in every period.

However, mention should be made in the modern period of the political convergence regarding the extermination of the Jews between the European Nazi and fascist parties on the one hand, and the Arab nationalists—particularly the Syrian, Egyptian, Iraqi, and Palestinian fascists—on the other. Muslims collaborated through pro-Nazi movements in Nazi and anti-semitic propaganda; and Arab journals financed by Hitler's regime were published in Latin America and Spain. Arab soldiers in Palestinian units were integrated into the Axis forces (*Deutsch-Arabische Lehrabteilung*) and a Nazi Arab legion.[84] This alliance is corroborated by the fact that Muslims in Europe and Asia were the only religious group to be spared by the Nazi extermination machine. After the war, collaboration continued through the emigration of Nazi criminals to several Arab countries, where massacres and pillage of Jews occurred (see chapter 6, above), and through Arab-Nazi historical revisionism.[85] Today, the Islamists' support for extreme right-wing anti-Jewish movements, and for neo-Nazis and their propaganda strengthens the forces working toward the destructuration of Europe by corrupting the very foundations of its civilization.

In the 1960s France's pro-Arab policy utilized anti-American and anti-Israeli propaganda to promote its economic and strategic interests in Muslim countries. Also in the 1970s pressure from Islamic states succeeded in restricting Judeo-Christian reconciliation. More recently, Muslim irredentism in the Balkans—linked to a worldwide Islamism, wittingly supported by Western Europe and the United States—made the difficult reconciliation between the three great streams of Christianity even more problematic. Thus, the internationalization of regional conflicts led to the reemergence of those great politico-religious axes—Orthodox, Catholic, Protestant—which for centuries had crossed Europe and the Islamic world. These conflictual lines persisted into the nineteenth and twentieth centuries despite short-term circumstantial variations. Today, these same axes serve as ideological and structural channels for the expansion of dhimmitude to the West in a fractured Christianity.

The 1967 Six-Day War revealed to the Arab countries the importance of Western public opinion. This was perceived by them to be massively and spontaneously pro-Israeli. In September 1968 the fourth Conference of the Academy of Islamic Research, held at the University of al-Azhar in Cairo, examined all the doctrinal and historical aspects of *jihad*. In addition to armed struggle, it also emphasized the importance of *jihad* by the written and spoken word, that is, propaganda. The proceedings of the Conference were published in Arabic and in English.[86]

The second International Conference in Support of the Arab Peoples was held in Cairo on 25–26 January 1969. It assembled delegates from seventy-four countries and fifteen international organizations, representing a wide spectrum of politicians, public opinion makers, and intellectuals, among whom were British historian Arnold Toynbee and French Arabist

Jacques Berque. The chief object of the conference was to emphasize the hostility to Zionism, and the solidarity with the Arab population of Palestine. In its appeal, the conference stressed

> that all information media should be mobilized to enlighten world public opinion, kept in ignorance and confusion by deceitful propaganda on the part of Israel and its supporters.
>
> It is an incumbent moral and political duty of all participants to this conference to reveal the truth and spread it through the press, the radio, television, demonstrations, visits of delegations, and the organization of seminars and conferences in the West and through all continents.

The Conference issued twenty-three resolutions on mobilization, among them the following practical measures:

(1) Special committees are to be established to coordinate activities on this issue. Such activities are to be directed in the way most suitable to the individual conditions of each country. Special committees can be created or maintained on particular issues.

(7) To appeal to all international and national organizations and committees to organize public demonstrations, exhibitions, publications, films, etc., dealing with the background, causes, current events, Israeli atrocities, refugees, Palestinian resistance, etc., according to the possibilities in each country.

(9) Special emphasis to be placed on the mobilization of public opinion in countries where governments are taking a negative stand or helping Israeli aggression.

(15) The conference decided to form special parliamentary groups, where they did not exist, and to use the parliamentary platform for promoting support of the Arab people and the Palestinian resistance.

(19) It also decided to organize two seminars on the Middle East issue, one in Western Europe and one in the United States.

(22) Representatives would organize, on return from the conference, special meetings and publications, and utilize the press, radio and television media to popularize the conference's decisions in the most appropriate way for each individual country.

Among the 54 members of the Sponsoring Committee, 46 were from Europe: 32 from Western Europe (France, Italy, England, Belgium, Cyprus), 11 from the communist countries (Yugoslavia, Poland, East Germany, Hungary), 2 from Chile, and 1 from the United States.

Twenty-four years after the extermination of European Jewry, anti-Zionism—like antisemitism—consisted of an ideology divided into topics, which were intended for worldwide diffusion through a media network, operating at all social levels. This policy aimed to transform the balance of forces in international opinion, transferring the capital of sympathy which the Israelis enjoyed until then to the Palestinians. Thus, the triangular relationships of dhimmitude—Muslims, Christians, Jews—emerged from the traditional inter-communal level to take on international proportions.

The Arab states—backed mainly, but not exclusively by Saudi Arabia—contributed vast sums to universities, centers for Islamic studies, international communications agencies, and private and governmental organizations in order to win over world opinion.[87] This propaganda, an effective war machine, was labeled: "the re-establishment of even-handed judgement."

Today, the laws of the ideology market are well known, as are the ways in which their global dissemination function. The anti-Zionism market returned to the anti-Jewish themes of the 1890–1945 period, substituting the word "Zionist" for "Jew." As Jacques Ellul had explained in his book on propaganda (1962), the myth "slips simply into the pre-existing mold and therein creates new beliefs."[88] In this way, the themes of Euro-Arab anti-Zionist propaganda were grafted on to a reflex reaction, previously conditioned by antisemitism. "Propaganda merely uses the existent material. It does not create it."[89]

Just as the Judeo-Christian rapprochement was contested on the theological and political plane, the principle of a Judeo-Christian civilization in Europe had to be eliminated by producing and constantly propagating Judeophobia. Hamadi Essid, head of the Arab League Mission at Paris, and its permanent delegate to UNESCO, told a meeting in 1970: "For some time there has been a catch-phrase: 'Judeo-Christian values.' This slogan is directed against the Arabs" [sic].[90] The Arabs reject the term "Judeo-Christian civilization" and replace it with "Abrahamic civilization," because as Abraham was a Muslim according to the Koran, it follows that Western civilization not only *includes* the Islamic dimension, but *is* Islamic in its essence.[91]

At the end of the 1960s, national groups of "Solidarity with the Palestinian Resistance and the Arab peoples" were formed throughout Europe and especially at the United Nations. Delegates of these European committees and left-wing Catholics groups such as *Témoignage Chrétien* took part in all the anti-Israel manifestations. The first World Conference of "Christians for Palestine" was held in Beirut on 7–9 May 1970. Its organizers rejoiced at the ecumenical nature of this conference, which was attended by more than 300 Christians: Catholics, Greek Orthodox, Anglicans, and other Protestants, coming from some thirty countries. It was said to have made a considerable impact on the Christian populations of the West. For the Arab League, this conference was of major interest for the Arab peoples. As for the Christians in the Middle East, they were "anxious to bring to their brothers in the West and in Eastern Europe, a testimony not only of their solidarity, but also of their identity with the Arab peoples of the region where they form an integral part."[92] Notwithstanding this fraternity, clashes had occurred in April 1969 between the Lebanese army and the PLO in the south and in the Bekaa Valley.

Thus, the same politico-religious fulcrum of European Judeophobia against Israel re-emerged after World War II, engulfing *dhimmi* Christianity in its machinery. This was the beginning of the great offensive in the West, with the *dhimmi* Churches and Arab-Christian intellectuals as soldiers and propagandists for Islamic causes. The many "prestigious and influential" personalities present at the 1970 conference included the popular Abbé Pierre, whose anti-Jewish remarks and support for the negationist philosopher Roger Garaudy—a convert to Islam—would scandalize the French episcopate and public opinion nearly three decades later. Also present was Georges Montaron, director of *Témoignage Chrétien*, who was "the soul of that meeting in Beirut and who, last year in Cairo, had played a vital role within the French delegation at the world congress in support of the Palestinian people."[93] The conference was inaugurated by the Christian president of Lebanon, Charles Hélou. According to the Geneva bulletin of the League of Arab States—widely circulated at the United Nations and elsewhere—one of its aims consisted in informing Christians throughout the world about the Palestinians. A few years later the PLO was instrumental in destroying Lebanon, while Bashir Gemayel denounced the great imposture imposed on his country; he then appealed in vain for help to European politicians and the Western Churches, who were ideologically allied to its enemies.

At a lecture he gave in Cairo at the Dar es-Salam Center on 22 November 1970 entitled "The Arab World and Western Opinion," Montaron cited three fundamental reasons for the European ignorance of the Arab world: the scarcity of information exchanges; the great humility of the Christian Arabs and their lack of assertiveness; lastly, the occult Zionist propaganda. Referring to the successes of European Jews, Montaron stated: "If you succeeded in making from authentic Oriental Arabs, authentic Frenchmen or Englishmen—what influence you would wield!"[94] European pro-Palestinian lobbies often expressed the wish to build up a Euro-Arab population that would fight for Arab causes against Zionism. This policy motivated the solidarity movement of churches, intellectuals, and politicians in favor of massive Muslim immigration to Western countries from the 1970s. Their lobbies attributed to Zionist propaganda the natural sympathy that millions of Europeans felt for Israel, that is to say, false and misleading information destined to be unmasked by a Palestine solidarity movement.

On an official visit to Lebanon in summer 1971, Jean de Lipkowski,

French secretary of state for foreign affairs, told a press conference that a separate partial settlement in the Middle East was unacceptable. He pointed out that in the previous year France—although still isolated and taxed with partiality toward the Arab world by the European Community— had now succeeded in imposing its views.

The 1967 war had dashed the age-old Christian refusal of Jewish residence, or sovereignty over Jerusalem. This sparked off a Euro-Arab solidarity movement which gave a global dimension to the anti-Israeli campaign. These international committees for solidarity with the Palestinian people included eminent politicians, intellectuals, and clergymen. The days of anti-Jewish hatred seemed to be returning with international Palestinian terrorism. Once again Jewish synagogues, schools, and cultural centers in Europe became targets for criminal attacks, requiring security measures for their protection, reinforced by armed guards as in wartime. The same thing happened in October 2000 soon after the second *intifada* was fueled by Arafat's decision, prepared three months earlier.

From 1969, numerous and converging maneuvers within international organizations had tended to isolate Israel, bringing condemnation and ostracism from the international community. The Arab League—with the backing of the Soviet bloc, Third World countries, and the European Community on France's initiative—used these mechanisms for their propaganda war of defamation, through the World Trade Organization, the World Health Organization, the Commission on Human Rights, UNESCO, particularly in 1974–75 when the PLO was granted observer status in these and other United Nations bodies.

In an article published in *Le Monde* on 22 July 1975 the president of the Paris-based International League against Racism and Antisemitism (LICRA), Jean-Pierre Bloch, stated that "racism and antisemitism have become the instruments of the politics of those states which launched these maneuvers." He concluded:

> It is scandalous to allow the language of liberalism and democracy to be misused for the profit of a policy that aims at ostracizing Israel from the community of nations. Indeed, the only way of discrediting Israel—following the old tradition of antisemitism—was to make the world believe that the existence of the Jewish State was incompatible with civilization [he was referring to the UNESCO resolution], incompatible with health, incompatible with women's liberation, incompatible with human rights, and so on and so on.
>
> Such is the power of words over the minds of men that, today, Israel and its allies see themselves counted among the enemies of mankind.
>
> Jean Cassou [a well-known French writer] was perfectly right when he said that anti-Zionism is a wonderful invention: from now on it enables everyone to be antisemitic in total serenity and without embarrassment.

On 10 November 1975 the General Assembly of the United Nations adopted resolution 3379, which "determines that Zionism is a form of racism and racial discrimination," a formula initiated by a Syrian Christian, Fa'iz A. Sayigh (1922–80), the son of a Syrian Presbyterian pastor. Sayigh was a former member of the fascist Syrian Social Nationalist Party (SSNP) created by Antun Sa'ada, a Greek Orthodox Syrian. The party collaborated with the Axis in the 1940s and attracted many Palestinians and Lebanese who became major figures in politics and worldwide terrorism.[95] Under cover of a program to eliminate racism, UN resolution 3379 sanctioned the vilification of Israel, thereby initiating a strategy which combined the justification of terrorism against Israel with virtuous condemnation of racism and antisemitism.[96]

This campaign increased after the direct peace negotiations between Egypt and Israel began in November 1977. In a lecture given to the diplomatic press association in Paris on 6 December 1979, Shedli Klibi, Secretary-General of the League of Arab States, deplored the recent Israel-Egypt peace agreement and announced[97]

> the opening of an Arab information campaign in the widest sense. The Tunis summit has made very precise recommendations so that a concerted campaign be mounted aimed at all friendly countries, and particularly toward Europe. We attribute a particular importance to Western Europe because we believe that Europe can and must play a key role, first for itself, and to influence international, and especially American, opinion.
>
> Thus, we think that the campaign that will be directed to Western Europe will be crucial.

Klibi referred to UN General Assembly resolution 3236, adopted by the automatic majority on 22 November 1974 after Arafat addressed that body as the PLO's chairman. For the first time, a UN resolution referred to the Palestinian people, rather than to "refugees." To the question of a journalist: how the UN Security Council's resolution 242, which only referred to "refugees," could be modified, Klibi replied:

> That is where your role as Europeans can be effective. To start with, the concept of "refugees" should be replaced by that of "Palestinian people." And the consequences of this theoretical modification should also be realized so that this people would be placed in a position to have its state. That is where Europe can play a specific role, a dynamic role, a driving role [. . .] I would like France to play a role in this direction, and to be, within the European Community, a sort of motive force—that France should take the role as leader, and that the whole European Community would play a role in this direction.

The Israel-Egyptian peace treaty—signed in March 1979—relaunched the Arab League's struggle against Israel using every means, particularly, political. "That is why I have said," Klibi explained,

> that information is going to assume an especial, primary, importance in this strategy. Information directed toward all the international communities, and above all directed toward Europe and America.

To a journalist who expressed a favorable opinion on the peace treaty, Klibi replied: "If you think that the principal belligerents are Egypt and Israel, you are mistaken. The principal belligerents are the Arabs on one hand, and Israel, on the other."

Thus, the Arab League's covert propaganda campaign was directed toward the West with a certain European complicity, and against a background of Palestinian international terrorism and hostage-taking in Lebanon. Euro-Arab militancy was not only apparent in state policy and in the widespread anti-Israeli media coverage, but in the close association and collaboration at the highest level of politicians, intellectuals, journalists, and the clergy. The speeches and publications of the time show that the PLO's ideology, strategy, propaganda, and phraseology were conceived, formulated, and imposed by Europeans on a reluctant Western public opinion.

As described earlier, the *dhimmi* clergy who espoused the Arab cause and who found justification for the destruction of Israel were affiliated to European Churches that had been established belatedly in the Middle East during the nineteenth century, through the colonial protection of European states. Thus, the Churches which best reconciled dhimmitude and Judeophobia were the Arab Catholics, the Uniate, Anglican, and Lutheran Churches, all connected with Europe. It is no surprise, therefore, that these channels devised and diffused the propaganda that aimed at identifying the Israelis as Nazis. For instance, in 1969, Father Khuri declared in Amman that the Israeli attitude vis-à-vis the Arabs (the word "Arabs," not "Palestinians", was still current then) reminded him of Nazism and its policy of mass extermination of the Jews.[98] As has been shown, this trend amplified and, after an anti-Israel declaration at Easter in April 1989 by the *dhimmi* Palestinian Churches, Anglican Bishop Samir Kafity reportedly told his Israeli critics: "You condemned us for keeping silent during the Holocaust. We are raising our voices now in order to prevent more acts of murder."[99] However, these same Palestinian Churches had never publicly condemned the Palestinian Arab collaboration with the Axis powers, and—as Lukasz Hirszowicz wrote—the Mufti of Jerusalem's "ominous role in the extermination of European Jewry," although documentary proof of this was presented at the Nuremberg trials when he was indicted as a war criminal.[100] Even before World War II, Haj Amin al-Husayni—the most intransigent anti-Jewish Arab leader, responsible for the murder of Palestinian Jews since 1921—was subsidized by Italy and later by Nazi Germany.[101] In his investigation related to the mufti, who occupied a supreme place in the Axis Arab policy, S.S. Obergruppenführer Erwin Etter gave his opinion that

> the Arab population is indissolubly connected with the Jewish question. The Jews are the Arabs' deadly enemies just as they are the deadly enemies of Germany. Whoever in [Nazi] Germany occupies himself with Arab problems must be a convinced and uncompromising enemy of the Jews.[102]

At a period when American historians were, for the first time, uncovering the history of the extermination of European Jewry and revealing the political and religious implications, a virulent campaign was launched in Europe to present the Israelis as Nazi criminals. This destructive policy, which focused on Israel, boomeranged on the Christian *dhimmis* with irreversible consequences because it constituted a smokescreen concealing their oppression. It is a remarkable fact that it was during this period, when the PLO was active in the destruction of Lebanon, that from Europe emanated hate-filled invective against Israel, whose prime minister from 1977 was Menahem Begin, a Holocaust survivor. At a press conference—after Israel's Air Force had destroyed Iraq's French-built nuclear reactor "Osirak" on 7 June 1981—he declared: "There won't be another Holocaust in History. Never again, never again."[103]

Thus, the wave of incitement to hatred and eventual politicide, which swept across Europe with varying degrees of intensity, resulted from the breakdown of taboos surrounding the genocide of European Jewry. Following in the footsteps of Simon Wiesenthal, historians and the traumatized victims of the Shoah began to break the silence and to gather up the debris of their history. Public opinion had been partially informed by a few books and films about the extermination camps. In 1961 the Eichmann trial for the first time projected the genocide of European Jewry on to the international scene. Religious historian William Nicholls noted that: "Christians did not begin to confront the Holocaust as a theological and ethical challenge to themselves until the sixties." He concluded that, in the light of the history of antisemitism, "the picture of the Jewish people in the minds of Christians outside as well as inside Germany predisposed them to indifference to, or even unconscious connivance with, the Nazi onslaught upon Jews."[104] In the 1960s, books on the Shoah were published by Jewish and Christian historians. "The 1960s may well have been the high point of corporate Christian sensitivity to 'the Jewish question' in its transformed post-Holocaust form."[105]

It was within this context, when the extermination of European Jewry by the Nazis and their accomplices was being revealed that a campaign to portray Israel as a Nazi state, to identify the Arab Palestinians with the Jewish victims, and historical negationism as an "anti-Zionist tactic" was planned.[106] This demonizing propaganda which inversed roles constituted the response to the disclosure of history, a revenge concocted with the public or covert encouragement of many politicians, intellectuals, and Christian clergymen. In other words, it was the disclosure of the Shoah's connivances which provoked, as a counterpart, the violent and immediate transformation of traditional Judeophobia into heinous anti-Zionism. Hence, from the late 1960s, the years of international terrorism for the Palestinian cause renewed the war against Israel. This militancy led to the establishment of Euro-Arab networks in the West within an international solidarity of crime with which several governments connived. It was this context which implanted the syndromes of dhimmitude in Europe and accelerated the disintegration of the *dhimmi* Eastern Christian communities, an evolution which was masked by the Euro-Arab propaganda war against Israel.

Anti-Zionist dogma was diffused worldwide by radio, television, the press, and United Nations' educational publications, particularly those equating Zionism with racism. Along the lines of Shedli Klibi's program already mentioned, France became the motor of this Arab League strategy. Henceforth, as historian Robert Wistrich described it:

> Above all, the French televisual media created a climate of disinformation and unprecedented hostility towards Israel with its ceaseless use of emotionally charged Holocaustal terminology, which undoubtedly intensified latent antisemitic sentiment that had never altogether disappeared in France. The French Communist Party, through its manifold channels of influence, added its own Soviet-inspired legends of fascism and Zionism as inseparable 'Siamese twins'; to this motley chorus one would have to add the left-wing Catholics of *Témoignage Chrétien*, a section of the French Socialist Party, the various Franco-Arab and Franco-Palestinian associations and the myriad promoters of anti-American Third World ideologies in France.[107]

This determination was integrated into Europe's strategic and economic interests and, in particular, into the policy of those socialist-communist governments involved in creating a Euro-Arab bloc opposed to the United States and Israel—a policy which aroused considerable opposition to the Gulf War of 1990–91, especially in France.[108] Not to be outdone, Arabist Jacques Berque, a fanatical admirer of the Arab world and of Saddam Hussein—the "secularist" tyrant—included among the virtues of his regime that Iraq had become "a redoubtable potential adversary for Israel."[109]

It was during the Gulf War that Syria endeavored to revive the blood libel accusation, first instigated in 1840 by the French Consul against the Jews of

Damascus. At the UN Commission on Human Rights, in a right of reply on 8 February 1991 to a statement by David Littman (the then representative of the World Union for Progressive Judaism), Syrian representative Nabila Chaalan tried to propagate a book, *The Matzah of Zion* (1983). Holding it in her hand, she launched into a diatribe against Zionism and "its barbaric practices." She announced to the plenum meeting of the Commission that:

> Those who read the book and learn about the reasons for Father Toma's murder would clearly understand the reality of Zionist racism. [. . .] We should like to urge all members of the Commission to read this very important work that demonstrates unequivocally the historical reality of Zionist racism.

The book had a preface written by Syria's Defense Minister, General Mustafa Tlass, and Littman had quoted from Tlass's preface:

> The Jew can kill you and take your blood in order to make his Zionist bread. I hope that I have done my duty in presenting the practices of the enemy of our historic nation. Allah aid this project.

Tlass's words were similar to those used in 1840 by French Consul Ratti-Menton, who had boasted that it was his duty to unmask Judaism's practices for Christians and Muslims alike.

Already in August 1986 *The Matzah of Zion* had been brought to the attention of the U.S. State Department and the foreign ministries of major Western countries by the Simon Wiesenthal Center. It was also denounced then in Paris at a time when General Tlass was about to receive a French University doctorate for his thesis on Soviet Marshal Georgi Zukhov. Trying again for a doctorate in 1999—this time with a thesis on "Greater Syria"—the 1986 "*affaire*" caught up with Tlass. As Professor Yves Lacoste, his academic supervisor, then explained in a letter to the LICRA dated 24 September—published with his consent—the idea to facilitate Tlass's wish to obtain a doctorate in 1986 had originated within the entourage of President Mitterand. It was to thank the Syrian Minister for his help in freeing the French hostages in Beirut during the 1980s. According to Lacoste, for ten years the French foreign ministry services in Damascus urged that the doctorate procedure continue.

Syria's blood libel revival at the United Nations elicited protests from only 28 out of 118 governments present, and 14 out of 120 NGOs. According to David Littman, "all efforts over the next weeks to convince the delegation of the World Council of Churches to react failed. This was also the case with the Holy See's delegation."[110]

The recrudescence of Judeophobia in Europe also aroused strong opposition from Christian lay and religious circles. It was mainly expressed by historical research and theological studies for re-Judaizing Christian sources. However, this important work had only a limited impact on public opinion, as the delegitimization of Israel was integrated into Europe's political and economic strategy. Consequently, it enjoyed the support of the senior ranks of the political parties, the religious hierarchies, and a constant media campaign. This strategy was based on the dissociation of Judaism as a religion from its national historical features. The rehabilitation of the first was counterbalanced by the delegitimization of the second. If applied to the French nation, this conception would mean the acceptance of their religion in France but not of their French national rights. The case would be the same for all nations. In fact, this concept conforms to the Muslim political view of the *umma,* which recognized the religious rights of non-Muslims within the *dhimma* "protection," but not their national and sovereign rights.

In Europe, the denial of Israel's national rights in its ancestral homeland was accompanied by ever-increasing emphasis on the "inalienable rights of the Palestinian people" and a future Palestine with its capital in Jerusalem, which was acknowledged even before its existence as a sovereign state had been recognized. Total disequilibrium characterized this state of permanent Palestinian militancy and the process of rapprochement with Judaism, limited solely to the religious level and cautiously restricted to modest publications in order not to irritate the many Muslim countries united in the powerful Organization of the Islamic Conference—today numbering fifty-six states.

This disequilibrium created by state and United Nations-inspired anti-Zionism limited the impact of important achievements by a whole Christian intelligentsia engaged in fighting world antisemitism and anti-Zionism. Condemned by their own religious hierarchy, boycotted by politicians and much of the media, reduced to silence and often threatened by Arab terrorism, these Christian intellectuals preserved the moral health of public opinion, assiduously manipulated by the many currents of anti-Zionism, which henceforth constituted an occult, central element in European policy.

10

The Politics of Dhimmitude in Europe

In this chapter we shall summarize themes that are specific to dhimmitude and consequently apply equally to Jews and Christians, to Israel, and to the West in general. This thematic emerges from the actual configuration of dhimmitude, where the homology of Jew and Christian implements the transference, interpenetration, and identification of the two entities: Israel and the Christian West. This fusion is rooted in the structure and the rationalization of the Islamic conceptions related to the People of the Book. Their negative projection upon Israel is a striking illustration of the permanence of the various facets built into the *dhimmi* condition and its stereotypes.

However, it is important to point out the difference between, for instance, a modernized and secularized Turkey and an Islamist Arabism whose anti-Zionist *jihad*—as well as its policy toward its Christian minorities, and the aggravation of an anti-West Islamist feeling—are evidence of the fixity of a religious and historical tradition. There are several reasons for these differences, but the most important concern the role of the Arabs as the creators of the initial conceptions of dhimmitude, which they then transmitted to the peoples whom they later Islamized. In addition, harsh European criticism of the Ottoman regime in the nineteenth century constrained the Turkish elites to embark on reforms in every sphere.

The situation in respect of the Arab peoples was the reverse. Europe's Arabophile policy, with its servile praise of Arab tolerance and civilization, blocked any process of Arab self-criticism. The reforms which the Ottomans—and then European colonization—imposed on the Arab Islamic societies created insurmountable frustrations, fostered by a mythical vision of Arab glory and the absence of any critical opinion of the past. The blockages were strengthened over the last fifty years by the encouragement of a *jihad* against Israel and its endorsement by currents of Euro-Arab anti-Zionism. This trend replaced the history of dhimmitude with the foundation myths of Palestinianism that were linked to a century of silence on the persecution of Christian minorities throughout the Arab world. This negationism eliminated any possibility of self-criticism by the Arab intelligentsia.

An attempt will be made here to examine the most typical Islamic components of dhimmitude, as well as the European policies of collaboration and support which strengthened them in the Arabized countries and in Western Europe.

The Islamic Components of Dhimmitude

The Perfection of Jihad

What gives to *jihad* its just and sacred character is the noxiousness and illegitimacy of the *dar al-harb*. Considered to be of a divine nature, *jihad* brings peace and happiness to the conquered, subjected peoples. For Hasan al-Banna, founder of the Muslim Brotherhood, the Islamic conquest did not involve victorious conquerors and vanquished enemies but simply friendly and affectionate brethren.[1] The application of the traditional rules of *jihad* were observed in recent years in various conflicts, particularly in Israel, Sudan, Algeria, Afghanistan, Kashmir, Indonesia, and the former Soviet republics in the Caucasus (particularly Chechnya) and Central Asia, a prey to Islamist unrest.

As *jihad* does not give rise to overt criticism, Muslim scholars attribute the origin of Muslim-Christian conflicts to the Machiavellianism of the Crusades. Consequently, the incessant Islamic wars from the seventh century—throughout the Christian Orient and beyond—from Armenia to Spain and on the Mediterranean coasts, are rarely mentioned, let alone criticized. Likewise, the modernist Arabist thinking attributes the origin of the conflicts between Islam and the West to the period of colonialism from the nineteenth century, and to Zionism in the twentieth century.

The Perfection of the Shari'a

All currents in modern Islamism praise the Islamic juridical provisions of the *shari'a* concerning the *dhimmi*. For Sayed Qutb, the oppression they may have suffered—a just retribution for the depravity of the party of Satan whom they personify—actually confirms the perfection of the *shari'a*.[2] For Hasan al-Turabi, the Islamic state "is subject to the higher norms of the *shariah* that represent the will of God."[3] According to the Palestinian Ismail R. al-Faruqi, professor in the department of Islamic Studies at Temple University:

> an Islamic state whose constitution is the Quran, whose law is the *shariah*, and whose constituency is only partly non-Muslim [. . .] Such an Islamic state is the heaven for world Jewry, as well as the protector and defender of

prophecy and its people against all outside attack. [. . .] Such lasting peace cannot be assured to the Jews anywhere except by Islam and under its political dominion.[4]

As history has proved, so he maintains:

Except for the briefest intervals in which Muslims have suffered even more than Jews or Christians at the hand of a corrupt ruler, the history of Islam's tolerance and coexistence with Judaism and Christianity is pure white. Throughout the fourteen centuries of its existence, its record is without blemish.[5]

According to Hamas, only Islamic law permits the three Abrahamic religions to coexist in peace, security, and justice (art. 6 and 31). At an "Inter-Cultural Conference" held in Teheran in May 1999, Sheikh Yusuf Salamah, Under-Secretary of Religious Endowment (*Awqaf*), representing the Palestinian Authority, praised the seventh-century *dhimmi* status "as the proper paradigm for relations between Muslims and Christians today."[6]

To my knowledge, no critical historical work on the theory of *dar al-harb, jihad,* and the *dhimma* has yet been published by Arab historians, even those teaching in European and American universities. This attitude is also common among Muslims in Asia. Concerning the teaching of Islam in France, the Grand Mufti of Marseilles, Soheib Bencheikh al-Hocine, wrote: "How can one teach in France a theology which emanates from a division of the world into a 'territory of Islam' and a 'territory of war', as all the Islamic juridical schools state?"[7] In his book (published in 1962) on the theory and sources of Islamic law for non-Muslims, Md. Alauddin al-Azhari, a Pakistani scholar from Dacca, stated: "It should be noted here that the theory of *Dar al-Islam* and *Dar al-Harb* no longer operates in our modern world, because most of the Muslim countries have not enforced the Shari'a law." Examining Islamic law on *jihad,* the author concluded: "*Jihad* is compulsory as ordered in the Qur'an and as enjoined in the Traditions."[8]

A few days after the invasion of Kuwait in August 1990, the then Mufti of Jerusalem, Sheikh Sa'ad a-Din al-Alami, appealed to Saddam Hussein:

From the Blessed Aqsa Mosque, the third holiest place to Islam, and on behalf of the Islamic world and Islamic Law, we are calling upon you to remove the impurity of the Americans and their underlings from the Hijazi land, to purify those Muslim Holy Lands from the desecration of the American troops and their aides, and to salvage the Holy Cities of Mecca and Medina . . . Allah will help you against your enemy and the enemies of Islam.[9]

In Cisjordan, the Muslim Supreme Council called on all Muslims to rise up against the multinational coalition created to liberate Kuwait: "Tell the Americans that Islamic lands are out-of-bounds for non-Muslims."[10]

The Iranian revolution and the collapse of communism destroyed the screens meticulously constructed to conceal reality. For the Palestinian Muslim Brotherhood there is a

> great culture clash in progress between the Islamic nation with its historical tradition, its faith and exemplary civilisation, and the West with its crusading spirit. [. . .] This was a struggle between the divine and the satanic forces.[11]

The attribution of stereotypes to Jews and Christians appeared from the beginnings of Islam.[12] The political and religious conflicts and the fanaticism of the period had integrated these negative assessments into an ideological and institutional theological structure which emerges from contemporary writings by Islamists. Since Ayatollah Khomeini's establishment of the Islamic Republic of Iran in 1979, numerous publications have familiarized the Western public with the religious foundations of the Islamist movement.

The fundamentalist press mirrors the traditional attitude of scorn and derision which the *umma* adopted toward the infidel nations:

> Real peace will come when Jerusalem and Palestine are liberated from the hands of those mean descendants of monkeys and pigs [. . .] The Islamic uprising in occupied Palestine will become a full-fledged war, because when the war breaks out, it will purify Muslims from all their elements of weakness and dishonour as they face the scum of the earth, those nameless people [. . .] This is a generation that knows [. . .] that its security, future and civilisation are hanging upon the liberation of Jerusalem from those disgusting people, and of Palestine from the descendants of monkeys, pigs and pagans.[13]

These unflattering terms are applied to Jews, Christians, communists, Baha'is and other non-Muslims. In December 1998 Zain Abu Bakr Mehdar, a 28-year-old Yemeni, led an extremist Islamic group that abducted sixteen Western tourists on a desert road near Aden. Four of them were killed. At his trial, Mehdar told the court that the tourists were "grandchildren of pigs and monkeys." "God sent them to us, so we took them," he said. "If I live, I will kill some more."[14]

The Islamic Supersessionism

As has been mentioned, Muslim theologians refuted the Western chronological interpretation of history which located the appearance of Islam in the seventh century, posterior, therefore, to Judaism and Christianity. Mawdudi associates the origin of Islam with the origins of mankind: "The day Adam and Eve were sent down to live on earth, Allah told them that they were His servants and He was their Master and Creator." He told them and mankind that he would reward them if he was pleased, but would punish them if they would not heed his commands:

> This was the simple beginning of Islam. Adam and Eve invited their children to follow the Islamic way of life. They and their children and their later generations followed the teachings of Islam as propounded by Prophet Adam (peace be upon him) for quite a long period.[15] [parentheses in the original]

Allah sent prophets to sinful mankind:

> In short, they were asked to perform a mission—to make people righteous and true Muslims. These noble people entrusted with this great mission were called Prophets or Messengers of Allah. Allah sent these Prophets to different nations and countries. All of them were honest, truthful, and people of noble character. All of them preached the same religion—Islam. To mention a few names—Noah, Abraham, Moses, Jesus [. . .] The people who followed the Prophets became Muslims. [. . .] Having forgotten the teachings of Islam, later generations of Muslims themselves gradually sank into disbelief. Whenever such a situation arose, God sent a Prophet or Messenger to revive Islam. (p. 4–5)

In another book Mawdudi expands the same theses, and then specifies:

> Although the religion taught by Jesus Christ (peace be upon him) was none but *Islam*, his followers reduced it into a hotch-potch called Christianity [. . .][16] [italics in the original]

A contemporary Iranian shi'ite scholar in Islamic jurisprudence, Abbasali Amid Zanjani, has devoted a book to the examination in modern terms of the Islamic principles of jurisprudence, according to what he calls the Law of the Tribute Agreement—which is, in fact, the *jizya*, resulting from the *dhimma* pact of protection.[17] Zanjani explains the Islamic position:

> Islam recognises the religion of Moses, Christ and Zoroaster as three holy heavenly creeds announced to the human society by the above prophets on behalf of the Creator of the universe. But it believes that none of the said creeds possessed an eternal aspect, and they had successively been abolished until with the universal call of Islam, Christianity, too, which in its own time was in its ideological evolutionary stage, was abrogated. (p. 90)

In a note, the author clarifies his theory:

> The religions which are now followed by the Zoroastrians (fire worshippers), the Jews and the Christians are nothing but a handful of legends fabricated by the fancies of a number of the pseudo-men of religion. Their original

heavenly book had been distorted and their real beliefs and precepts have for long left them. (p. 91) [parentheses in the original]

The Islamization of the Bible has had considerable cultural and political consequences. Essentially, the appropriation of Judaism's religious inheritance is harming the Christians, since it is also their inheritance. But, above all, the Islamization of the Bible erases all the richness of the Judeo-Christian, historical, and archaeological scholarship of biblical criticism and exegesis. Religious negationism also cancels the historicity of the civilizations which enriched human knowledge before Islam appeared in the seventh century. This historical negationism, inherent in the Islamic doctrine which gives Islam temporal precedence over Judaism and Christianity, disturbs the religious identification of the Christian *dhimmis* and of the European and Arab Christian current, which deliberately ignores it. In June 1999 the Arab Palestinian press published an ongoing controversy between Sheikh Kamal Khatib, vice-chairman of the Islamic Movement of Israel, and the Catholic Archbishop of the Galilee, Butrus al-Muallam. The Archbishop had rejected the seventh-century *dhimmi* status for Palestinian Christians in a debate, stressing that Christian roots in the Holy Land preceded Islam. Sheikh Khatib answered angrily:

> What do you mean when you say you were here before the appearance of Islam? It means that Islam is a foreign phenomenon here . . . You should know that for us Islam is not only the religion of the Prophet Muhammad, but also the religion of Moses, Jesus and Abraham.[18]

Here it can be noted, not without some irony, that for nearly 2000 years Christians have used this same supersessionist argument against the Jews—still repeated nowadays—to dispute their historical and national rights to their ancestral homeland. This historical negationism applies to all the pre-Islamic civilizations: Coptic, Syriac, Assyrian, Phoenician, and so on; studying them is ascribed to demonic motives on the part of the West and of Orientalists, as agents of colonialism and its conspiracies. The latter, in particular, are accused of wanting to poison and weaken Islam through the study of the languages and civilizations of the countries conquered by *jihad*.[19]

In his scholarly examination of the Orientalists, J.D.J. Waardenburg also covers the more recent encounters, with a comprehensive bibliography up to 1988. In 1992 a whole dossier was devoted to the subject by *PISAI* (Rome). In "The Question of Orientalism" (1982), Bernard Lewis analyzed the much propagated popularized account (1978) by Edward Said, an Egyptian-born American scholar of literature, close to the PLO until the Oslo Accords when he resigned; he posed as a Palestinian refugee until the fabled account of his early life was revealed.

In a 1973 text, Tunisian academic Abd al-Latif al-Shuwayrif, writing in the journal of the Tunis Faculty of Theology, refers to the destructive poisons of Orientalism. The Orientalists have sown duplicity and depravity concealed "under the name of research programs, freedom of thought, and aspirations to development and revival." Few Orientalists have "surpassed the inherited bitterness of the Crusades."[20] In fact, the subversive and dominant conspirator is the West as a whole. The rejection of Western "ideological pollution" forms a central theme of Islamism. The struggle aims at the restoration of the *shari'a* by the elimination of the pseudo-Islamic governments and any law that does not conform to the *shari'a*. Writing in 1991, Abd al-Azim Mahmud al-Dib, responsible for the law section at the *Shari'a* faculty of Qatar university, explained that the purpose of the Orientalists' interest in the Pharaonic, Babylonian, Assyrian, and other civilizations is to cause a schism among Muslims and curtail the history of Islam and of the Muslims.[21]

Here, it is appropriate to recall the different conception of time in Judeo-Christian societies, and in Islam where Adam and Eve are regarded as Muslims. In a note to Mawdudi's book, cited earlier, its editor, Khurshid Ahmad, wrote:

> There is a common misconception, mostly among the Western writers, that Islam owes its origin to the Prophet Muhammad (peace be upon him) and some of the writers even go to the extent of calling him "the founder of Islam." This is a travesty of truth. Islam has been the religion of all the Prophets of God and all of them have brought the same message from Him. Prophets have not been the founders of Islam; they have only been the messengers of it. Islam consists of the Divine Revelation conveyed to mankind by the truthful Prophets.[22]

Khomeini never tired of denouncing the conspiracy by Orientalists in the pay of imperialism. Here again, historical negationism is not limited solely to Israel, but encompasses the whole of non-Arab and non-Muslim history and peoples. Today in Egypt, not even the pyramids, the avenues of sphinxes, and the obelisks escape the Islamists' condemnation.[23] A. L. Tibawi devoted a study to the maltreatment of Islam as a religion and as a civilization:

> Briefly diagnosed, the origin of this great distortion is the persistence in studying Islam and the Arabs through the application of Western European categories by Christians and Jews who cannot free themselves of their inherited prejudices.[24]

European Policies of Dhimmitude

The propagation of dhimmitude in the West is a function of its submission to the Islamic policy of de-Judaizing Christianity, a drive which proceeds from Israel's centrality to the international relations of the Islamist states and the Arab countries. In this context, the Eastern Christian communities become hostages to the anti-Israeli policies that Islamic states require from the West. Like Nazism, the anti-Zionist Islamic policy exploits Christian antisemitism in Europe and strives to de-Judaize Christianity by the denial of its Jewish origins and support for Marcionism. The Jewish people is thereby stripped of its identity by the denial of a historical continuity with biblical Israel. These tactics undermine and weaken the core of the Judeo-Christian West, and particularly of Christianity in its symbiotic and fundamental relationship with Judaism.

This section will examine those European currents that are spreading and accrediting in Europe the demonization theories specific to the *dar al-harb*, the esteem for and promotion of *jihad* and *shari'a*, and of their corollary: negationism. This movement develops a set of flagellatory attitudes aimed at incriminating the West. We will call this tendency the European-*dhimmi* current because—although it consists of a majority of European intellectuals, politicians, and clergy—its concepts are common to those of dhimmitude. Forming part of traditional Christian Judeophobia, the European-*dhimmi* movement develops an anti-European brand of anti-Christianity combined with its anti-Zionism. Its reasoning follows from the rejection of the history of the Shoah, which is only accepted via its backlash on Israel by way of its "equivalent": the Palestinian *nakba* (disaster) of 1948.

The advocates of this current show little originality and are content to repeat servilely the usual inculpatory anti-Western Islamic recriminations, thereby accrediting and justifying them. In order to impose negationist Islamic criteria of history, they employ maximum media coverage to channel and spread their campaign against Orientalists and Western historians. It is noteworthy that this trend encourages the West to conform to one of the basic rules of dhimmitude which expressly forbids Christians and Jews to criticize Islamic history and doctrine. Although some Orientalists did show religious prejudices at the beginning of the century, these opinions were much less hostile than those expressed by Muslims—then and now—in respect of non-Muslims, and particularly of their specific religions.[25]

The European-Dhimmi Current: The Inculpation of Israel and the West

For the Islamist movement, the delegitimization of Israel is embedded in the universal theological context of the *dar al-harb*, whereas the parallel European delegitimization crusade cites the Arab-Israel wars and a commitment to the "Palestinian refugees." Yet all Islamic territories were conquered by *jihad*-wars which provoked refugees, slavery, and massacres on three continents. In addition, all the Christian *dhimmi* peoples who gained their freedom waged far crueler wars than did Israel, accompanied by exchanges of populations and the expulsion of millions of Muslims. The refusal to accept an independent Israel endows the laws of *jihad* with a definitive legitimacy. As *jihad* barely differentiate between nations but applies indiscriminately to all non-Muslims, the latter are, *ipso facto,* in the same category as the Israelis. Thus, the theological concept of the *dar al-harb*—what is by divine will Islamic territory illegally controlled by infidels—unites all non-Muslim countries in the same theological illegitimacy.

The statement that Israel represents an injustice constituted a central theme in the pro-Palestinian policy emanating from circles in the Vatican, the World Council of Churches, and in European countries. Israel's declaration of independence (1948) meant the end of the exile imposed on the Jews by the Christian doctrine of the deicide and the abrogation of the institutionalized laws of *jihad* for Jews and Christians.

Israel's rebirth followed a war of total extermination waged against the Jews of Europe.[26] The nascent Jewish state was then attacked by five Arab states, backed by the Arabs of Palestine. This politicidal war was accompanied by pogroms in Arab countries, pillage, and the exodus of Jewish communities, followed by the subsequent wars (1956, 1967, 1973, and constant Arab guerilla attacks). Despite all this, it is Israel's survival that is called an "injustice." Thus Arab Palestine, born of *jihad,* is considered a legitimate entity; but a reborn Israel, liberated from dhimmitude, is considered an injustice. This same principle which proclaims the laws of *jihad* to be just and definitive, thereby undermines the legitimacy of the West itself.

The Islamist rejection of Israel is based on the *dhimmi* status—a theological obligation for both Jew and Christian. Likewise, any delegitimization of Israel by Western political currents reinforces the delegitimization of the West. If Israel ought not to exist *de jure,* the same reasoning must apply to Europe, America, and any other place in the world; if the Jew must be a *dhimmi,* the Christian too. Thus, the history and ideology of dhimmitude has tied the destinies of Jews and Christians into an indissoluble bond.

Christian Eulogy of Jihad and Dhimma

The Islamic conception of a *jihad* spreading peacefully without bloodshed is repeated and taught in Western universities. This interpretation feeds an ideal vision of Islamic society and nourishes the nostalgic desire for its future restoration in Europe. Anglican Bishop Kenneth Cragg, who had a determinant influence on the formulation of "Palestinianism" thinking in many Church circles and beyond, attributes the origin and the responsibility for the Muslim-Christian conflicts to the initial resistance that Europe offered to the Islamic conquests and to the Crusades—not to the concepts of *jihad* and *dar al-harb.* Georges Corm—Lebanese Minister of Finance from 1997 to 2000—maintained an eloquent silence on the Muslim-

Christian conflicts, even during the civil war in Lebanon, the destruction of which he attributed solely to the Israelis in his book published in 1991. Under the heading "Religious Minorities," he devotes only eighteen lines to Christian minorities, whereas nearly twenty-eight are reserved for the Jews.[27] In fact, the author is a perfect representative of left-wing Arab Christians who burned their Christianity in the flames of Arabism, a screen for its own destruction. Wandering from mirage to mirage in his Arab passions, he casts a blind eye on the millennial ruins of Eastern Christendom.

John L. Esposito, a former professor of Middle East Studies at the College of the Holy Cross, is currently Professor of Religion and International Affairs at Georgetown University and Director of the Center for Muslim-Christian Understanding: History and International Affairs at the Edmund A. Walsh School of Foreign Service. As he wrote in the preface (1988) to his book, *Islam. The Straight Path*, he endeavored to "enable readers to understand and appreciate what Muslims believe and practice."[28]. Passing over in silence the centuries of anti-Christian *jihad*, he considers that:

> Five centuries [seventh to eleventh] of peaceful coexistence elapsed before political events and an imperial-papal power play led to centuries-long series of so-called holy wars that pitted Christendom against Islam and left an enduring legacy of misunderstanding and distrust.

Hence, he totally ignores the concepts of *jihad* and *dar al-harb* mentioned in innumerable *hadiths*. In his subsequent study, *The Islamic Threat. Myth or Reality?* (1992), Esposito devotes a page to "Non-Muslims in the Islamic State," which has a ten-line quotation extolling the pacifism of the Arab conquest.[29] The text describes the benefits of the Islamic conquest which had originated in Arabia and was pursued for a millennium: in Mesopotamia, Syria, Egypt, North Africa, Spain, southern Europe (Italy and Sicily); and in the East: Armenia, Anatolia, and Greece, not to mention Asia. This single page also includes a description of the status of non-Muslims— meaning the populations of all these conquered lands—and ends with a description of the Crusades (three pages). Esposito uses another quotation to stress that the Islamic conquests destroyed very little.

> Up till 1000 the West was a poor, backward and illiterate region [. . .] while for four centuries, Islam enjoyed an internal peace and security, untroubled save for domestic wars, and thus was able to build up a brilliant and impressive urban culture.[30]

Yet in reality, and not in an imaginary version of history, Islam's military advance continued without interruption in Spain and against the Byzantine Empire, in the Mediterranean basin, in Mesopotamia, in Armenia, and in Asia. Then, the author describes the arrival of the Ottomans (two pages) and the unleashing of Western fanaticism against them, although "many in the Balkans saw the Ottomans as liberators."[31]

Esposito lists, but does not discuss, the origins and causes cited by Muslim politicians today to justify their aversion to the West. These causes are: the Crusades, the Inquisition, colonialism, imperialism, missionaries, Orientalists, the abolition of the caliphate (in fact, abolished by a secular Turk, Kemal Ataturk), the destruction of the Ottoman Empire, nationalism, and secularism. However, in 1983, Esposito himself edited a volume, *Voices of Resurgent Islam*, with articles by Islamist scholars, some of whom expound the legal and historical koranic sources for the hostility toward the People of the Book. According to them, these sources date back to early Islamic times, hence they pre-date the Crusades, the modern State of Israel, and "the centuries" of European colonialism that englobed Arab countries for a maximum period in Algeria of a hundred and thirty years—all in all, an insignificant period compared with the centuries of Islamic imperialism on three continents. Despite the Islamists' texts, published under his editorship, Esposito maintains that it was only in the nineteenth century (which contradicts his use of the term, "the centuries") that the "European Christian colonizers were now rejected as infidels, the enemies of Islam."[32] He does not acknowledge the whole context of *jihad,* nor the meaning of the *amân,* the clause that temporarily suspends the right of any Muslim whomsoever to shed the blood of a *harbi,*[33] a provision which was at the origin of the Ottoman *Capitulations* treaties with European states from the sixteenth century.

The much-used arguments of Western culpability and the victimization of Muslim populations is generously developed in explaining Muslim hostility to the West. Hence, the West is accused of having created Israel, an offshoot of European neo-colonialism:

Nothing symbolized the reality of Western neocolonialism more than the creation and expansion of the State of Israel—a Western state established in the midst of the Arab world—protected and sustained by massive American aid.[34]

The thematic structure of this type of Western apologetic literature—certainly not exhaustive—is summarized below:

—historical negationism consisting of suppressing or sketching, in a page or a paragraph, one thousand years of *jihad* which is presented as a peaceful conquest, generally welcomed by the vanquished populations;

—the omission of Christian and, in particular, Muslim sources describing the methods of conquests: pillage, enslavement, deportation, massacres, and so on;

—the mythical historical version of "centuries" of "peaceful coexistence," masking the processes which transformed majorities into minorities, constantly at risk of extinction;

—an obligatory self-incrimination for the Crusades, the Inquisition, imperialism, colonialism, Israel, and other intrusions into the *dar al-Islam*;

—servile criticism of the rational tools of historical knowledge, created by earlier European Orientalists and historians.

These arguments form the basis of Western unilateral and masochistic self-incrimination, a traditional *dhimmi* behavior.

Historical Negationism and the Andalusian Myth

One of the themes developed in the West in lectures and writings was the Andalusian myth of "peaceful coexistence" and the "golden age." This theme propagated the Islamic version of the perfection of the *shari'a*, engendering the same mechanisms of historical amnesia in Europe as in the Eastern Christian communities.

The theme of Islamic tolerance is rooted in the nineteenth-century European policy of the balance of power adopted in order to contain the pan-Slav Russian upsurge, pan-Hellenism, and Austrian expansionism. A political and ideological weapon, it justified the defense of the territorial integrity of the multinational Ottoman Empire in the context of its modernization and the emancipation of its non-Muslim subjects.[35] France adopted an Arab version of this theme to serve its colonial ambitions in the Ottoman Arab territories. After World War I, "Ottoman tolerance" was metamorphosed into "peaceful coexistence under the first Arab caliphs," that is to say, under the *shari'a*, a not very different jurisdiction to that of the Afghan Talibans today. This theme formed the cornerstone of Muslim-Christian Arab nationalism in Palestine and an ideological weapon against claims to independence by Israel and other *dhimmi* peoples.

Obviously, this myth of peaceful coexistence strengthens Islamic doctrine. It confirms the perfection of the *shari'a*, even in one of its most severe manifestations, the Malikite rite, applied in the Maghreb and in Spain. In fact, the slightest criticism of the *dhimmi* status is rejected, as it undermines the doctrine of the perfection of Islamic law and government. Consequently, the praise of the tolerance and justice of Islamic government, accompanied by gratitude, constituted an integral part of the obligations required of the *dhimmi* and was specified in the *dhimma* treaties.

Today, the themes of happy and peaceful coexistence under Islamic law are hawked around the West via Jewish and Christian *dhimmi* networks. Those taken over by the Turks vaunt Ottomanism; others, sponsored by the Arab League, glorify the Muslim-Christian religious symbiosis in the Arab empire. This theme, modernized in the 1960s by the anti-Zionist European movement, justified the elimination of Israel and its replacement by a "secular and democratic Arab Palestine, the multicultural Arab Palestinian State." It polarized the anti-Israel conflict, the glorification of international terrorism, integrated into the anti-Jewish *jihad,* which was translated into the "Palestinian just cause," fertile soil for the blossoming of historical negationism. Three main trends sprang from this source: 1) the Marcionite Christian current which integrated the Nazi themes of the de-Judaization of the Church; 2) the inculpation of the West and its self-incrimination; 3) the Islamization of Christianity.

The Founding Myths of Palestinianism

Palestine as a political project of the 1960s was constructed by the PLO's Christian and Muslim strategists, assisted by European advisers. The combined Euro-Arab militancy for Palestine conceived the ideological and political context of negationism and of historical amnesia. In his statement to the General Assembly of the United Nations on 13 November 1974,[36] Yasser Arafat, chairman of the PLO, nostalgically recalled in lyrical terms the Palestinian Golden Age before 1881—aided by his many Christian advisers:

> Every segment of the population enjoyed the religious tolerance characteristic of our civilization. Palestine was then a verdant land, inhabited mainly by an Arab people in the course of building its life and dynamically enriching its indigenous culture. (§ 31–32)
> [. . .] The world must know that Palestine was the cradle of the most ancient cultures and civilization. Its Arab people were engaged in farming and building, spreading culture throughout the land for thousands of years, setting an example in the practice of [religious tolerance and] freedom of worship, acting as faithful guardians of the holy places of all religions. (§ 40)

In contrast to this idyllic description, Negib Azoury, founding father of the Muslim-Christian war against "the universal Jewish peril," recalled the neglected and abandoned condition of Palestine in 1904, and compared it with the verdant, overpopulated land of the Bible.[37] As an official of the Jerusalem municipality, he traveled across

> all that glorious region [the Jordan valley] from north to south without encountering a single inhabited village, or half a hectare [an acre] of ploughed land, or even a single meter of irrigation: all is desert; the fertilizing waters of the Jordan, sad and silent, flow uselessly toward the Dead Sea; this is the

picture which best expresses the desolation which the Turkish government maintains in the countries still under its rule. (p. 18)

As for the Tiberias region:

Today completely uncultivated [. . .] apart from the town of Tiberias, totally populated by Jews, there is not a single hamlet on those glorious shores; and four or five wretched boats, for the use of tourists, have replaced the fleets of yore. The whole of the Jordan valley is the personal property of the Sultan, who does not want to exploit it, or to rent it, still less to sell it. (p. 19)

In the Esdraelon valley he barely found twenty-five villages in an abandoned countryside: "that is why only a tenth part of this fertile plain [of Sharon] is cultivated." (p. 20) After describing the lamentable state of abandonment and depopulation of Palestine, Azoury commiserates with its "wretched" inhabitants "who vegetate in poverty, living in filthy huts, almost never changing their clothes and eating only one miserable meal a day" (p. 23).

As other reliable sources confirm, all land in Palestine belonged to the Ottoman sultan, in accordance with the terms of the Islamic conquest. Palestine, which never was an "Arab land," divided into plots registered to Arab landowners, constituted war booty, like all the conquered territories of the *dar al-harb* from Spain to the Indies. Cradle of the two religions of the People of the Book, who only survived there in the most extreme humiliation, "Arab Palestine" represents Islam's triumph over these two religions. During the nineteenth century, European warships frequently cruised the open seas off the Palestinian coasts to prevent a general massacre of Christians.[38]

Numerous sources describe the oppression of Christians, and particularly of Jews, in Palestine. Over the centuries the land was devastated and pillaged as a result of constant internecine feuds of roving, invading occupiers: Arab and Turkoman tribes, Moors from Spain, and—from the late eighteenth century—many Muslims fleeing from the Caucasus, Algeria, and the Balkans.

During his travels in the Levant in 1698, Canon Antoine Morison, from Bar-le-Duc in France, noted that the ancient Land of the Bible could not be conceived from the actual desolated state of "Judea in particular, or Palestine in general." He observed that the Jews in Jerusalem are "there in misery and under the most cruel and shameful slavery," and although a large community, they lived under regular extortions. He observed that descendants of Moors who had been expelled from Spain were numerous in Palestine.[39]

Similar descriptions were given by travelers at different times, but it is only from the mid-nineteenth century with the improvement of security that truly scientific explorations began with the travels in 1838 of an American, Edward Robinson, and his three-volume work of 1841.[40]

This was the first of a series of geographical, historical, and archaeological surveys in Jerusalem and throughout the Holy Land from 1865 to 1914 for the Palestine Exploration Fund by Britons like Charles Wilson, Charles Warren, Claude Condor, Horatio Herbert Kitchener, Leonard Woolley, T.E. Lawrence, and others; and Frenchmen such as Charles de Vogüe, Charles Clermont-Ganneau, and Victor Guérin. The latter's seven-volume study of 1868, following his explorations in 1863, contains this appreciation:

> With the Bible and history books in his hand, he who attempts to rediscover in a land formerly so fertile and densely populated—now scarcely cultivated and inhabited—the traces of towns which have disappeared, finds, assuredly, ruins everywhere: but these ruins are often very unclear, having been for ages turned topsy-turvy, bristling with undergrowth, and not easily accessible. A considerable number of them have even been almost entirely erased from the earth, and only names have survived of several once famous cities, which have been as if annihilated.[41]

Guérin describes at random the utter desolation of the towns and villages of Judea, Samaria, and Galilee (the titles of his three sections); the ruined churches where animals were herded, and the fanaticism of the Moors. Latin Christians were the least numerous of the scattered Christian population. Thus, from a population of 600 persons in Bayt Sahur near Bethlehem, 60 were Muslims, 50 Catholics, and 490 schismatic Christians. The Christian village of Bir Zeit had about 1,800 inhabitants, of whom only 140 were Latin Catholics, the others being Greek Orthodox and Muslims.

The Muslim-Christian Supersessionist Trend

At a press conference at the United Nations in Geneva on 2 September 1983 Yasser Arafat declared:

> We were under Roman imperialism. We sent a Palestinian fisherman, called St. Peter to Rome; he not only occupied Rome, but also won the hearts of the people. We know how to resist imperialism and occupation.[42]

With a conniving smile, Arafat ended the press conference with these startling words: "Jesus Christ was the first Palestinian fedayeen who carried his sword along the road on which today the Palestinians carry their cross." This travesty—in comparing Jesus with a Muslim fedayeen, literally a fighter against Christians for the triumph of Islam—provoked no public reaction then from the audience of over a hundred journalists, and no protest later from delegates of the official Churches in Geneva, members of the World Council of Churches, nor from the Holy See. This justifies the presumption of Muslim-Christian collusion, which had also been apparent in Geneva a dozen years earlier when a poster depicting Jesus nailed to a Star of David with the word "Palestine" was confiscated by the Genevan police. Syrian Greek Catholic Archbishop Hilarion Capucci—when caught smuggling arms—had already stated that "Jesus Christ was the first feda-yeen. I am just following his example."[43] The politicization of Jesus—the incarnation of God for Christians—to serve the Palestinian cause in the war against Israel, was thus initiated and disseminated to the public by the high-est levels of the Levantine Catholic hierarchy.

Among the many themes developed by the theology of Palestinian Mar-cionism—opposed by many Western Christian theologians—the de-Juda-ization of the Bible by its "Palestinization," or the strategy of supersession, plays a leading role. Stripped of its history and of its identity, the State of Israel is no more than an imposter which has usurped a name, a history, and a portion of land. Such an interpretation that disguises Zionism as im-perialism vis-à-vis Zion, and the Jews in Judea and Samaria as colonists, re-veals a Christian source because its biblical Jewish events transferred to the Palestinians do not appear in the Koran. For example, David's sling is ab-sent from the Koran but, through Christian mediation, it becomes a super-sessionist image favored by the Western media.

The substitution of an Arab Palestinian identity to a biblical Jewish con-text aims to transfer the Jewish historical heritage to Palestinian Islam. Moreover, the appropriation of Judeo-Christian culture is a fundamental element of Islamic doctrine since the many prophets of the Bible, and Jesus himself, are mentioned in the Koran and revered solely as Muslims, who—it is claimed—taught Islam before Muhammad. Thus the Jewish and Christian religions, dispossessed of their historical foundations, are re-duced to mere fictions.

The *dhimmi* Churches developed an Arabized interpretation of the Gos-pels, combining traditional anti-Judaism with the psychological condition-ing of dhimmitude. Jesus, his mother Mary, and the Apostles, thus identified with Palestinian Arabs, lost their Jewish historical and cultural dimension. This Islamization of the Jewish sources of Christianity, dissem-inated through European *dhimmi* church networks, popularized the Is-lamic version of the Arab origins of Christianity. It increased the disintegration of Christian identity, grafting on to the *dhimmi*'s cultural am-nesia the falsification of the Christian faith's foundations.

Some Western clergymen have propagated the Arabization of Jesus and the Apostles in accordance with Islamic interpretations, in iconography, and in teaching. Thus, when Father Christian Delorme, defender of the Arabs in France, condemned right-wing extremist Jean-Marie Le Pen, he explained: "But he [Le Pen] forgets that Jesus was an Arab Jew from Palestine."[44]

The Arabization of Jesus in "Palestine"—which, in his lifetime and one hundred years later was still called Judea, as all ancient authors and the Gospels attest—also implies the Arabization of his ancestry, which Christian doctrine traces back to King David. By such logic, this clergy confirms the Islamic theory that Jesus and the Hebrew patriarchs and prophets were all Muslims, the terms "Arab" and "Muslim" being synonymous.

Driven to make an ultimate denial in order to survive in an Islamic milieu, some Churches—particularly Protestant—since 1948 have erased the words "Israel" and "Zion" from their liturgy. They even proposed the omission of Old Testament readings from Church services, that is to say the spiritual sources of the teaching of Jesus and his Apostles.[45] In 1988, the Anglican synod of New Zealand, under pressure from the Anglican bishop of Jerusalem, went a step further and removed the words "Zion" and "Israel" from the Anglican psalter. Also part of the same current are Abbé Moubarac's efforts to prove, on the basis of a verse of the Koran, that Mary was not "racially" Jewish. These *dhimmi* and Islamic alterations and interpolations in Christian doctrine and worship strengthened the divisions in the very bosom of the Churches. They provided those Churches with a Marcionite or Islamic-Christian syncretic tendency in Europe, as well as in the United States, and elsewhere.

The Incrimination of the West and Its Manipulation

Whereas in the 1960s Christian theologians in Europe were engaged in a long and painful process of self-criticism and moral purification through the examination of antisemitism, the Arab Churches at that time were initiating a Muslim-Christian dialogue. It was intended to reassure the Muslim world and to introduce it as a mediator and counter-balance to the Jewish-Christian rapprochement. It is noteworthy that this Muslim-Christian dialogue had started in the 1930s, at the height of the Church's period of increased antisemitism.

Commenting on the encyclical *Nostra Aetate* (1965), William Nicholls wrote:

Above all, the document never mentions the need for Christian repentance, nor does it ask forgiveness from the Jews, though elsewhere the documents of the council do ask forgiveness for the Church from Protestants, Eastern Orthodox, and Muslims. This is perhaps the greatest weakness of the statement. Perhaps it would not have passed the council if it had. But the absence of mention of repentance has allowed many Catholic apologists to speak of the achievement of the council on the question of the Jews in triumphalist terms, as a sign of great progress, rather than as the first beginning of reparation of an infinite deficit.[46]

On 12 March 1970, at a demonstration of solidarity with the Palestinians in Brussels, Bernard Schreiner, general representative of the "Christian Witness" groups and former president of the National Union of Students of France, declared that the Church's favorable attitude toward Israel was conditioned by its remorse.[47] In fact, the Vatican had always supported the Palestinian cause against the State of Israel, which it had refused to recognize. In addition, at that time, no Church or state, except Germany, had officially shown "remorse" toward Israel or the Jews, victims of the Shoah.

At this period, Christian theologians were voicing modifications to Christian doctrine on the Jews in extremely measured and circumspect terms. The Arab states, by exploiting their *dhimmi* Church leaders, and using blackmail and threats directed at Eastern Christian communities, did their utmost to impede this timid rapprochement accompanied by economic and political pressure. Publications by Western historians and intellectuals on the sources and history of Christian antisemitism created a parallel Arabophile Western literature which duplicated Jewish history, but in an Islamic victimized version. The analysis of Christian antisemitism, undertaken in a very precise and well-documented context—theology, jurisdiction, history—was transferred into the totally different context of Muslim-Christian relations. In contrast, the latter is structured by a millennium of Islamic conquests and the subjection of numerous Christian lands and peoples. As a Jewish expansion on Christian territories similar to Muslim imperialist history does not exist, this history was omitted altogether in order to maintain a parity—even a false parity—between Judaism and Islam. Similarly, the whole Muslim anti-Christian theological, juridical, and historical system of dhimmitude, having no equivalent in Judaism, was erased.

The argument of remorse to explain to Muslims the spontaneous popular Christian sympathy with Israel was used with considerable success by the Arab League. During the International Conference on the Palestine Question on 29 August 1984 in Geneva, the secretary-general of the Arab League. Shedli Klibi, declared:

> Zionism has turned the persecution of the Jews into a bargaining matter with European states and peoples. It has implanted a guilt complex in these states and peoples and in order to wipe out the West's responsibility for the crimes committed in the West against the Jews, Zionism requires the Western conscience to wipe out the crimes perpetrated by the Zionists against the Arabs, as well as those they are counting on perpetrating to complete the achievement of their expansionist and aggressive ambitions in the region.[48]

This remorse, according to Klibi, prevented Westerners from dealing severely with Israel. The idea that Israel was born and lived off the guilt of the Western states motivated the whole campaign to inculpate the West vis-à-vis the Muslims, and particularly the Palestinians. The European-*dhimmi* movement exploited this theme on two fronts: 1) the denial of the Shoah, regarded as anti-Palestinian political blackmail; 2) the symmetrical incrimination of Europe vis-à-vis the Palestinians and Muslims by the takeover of Jewish history.

Consequently, a Muslim-Christian line of reasoning developed, inculpating Christianity to counterbalance the "Judeo-Christian dialogue," as if there was the slightest resemblance between the history of the Jews in Christendom and the history of the Islamic *jihad* which had imposed dhimmitude on conquered Christian and Jewish populations on three continents. The denunciation of the Crusades, of imperialism, and a century or more of colonialism, like the accusation that Europe had collaborated in the creation of Israel, tended to imply that Europe owed a moral debt to the Arab Palestinians and the Muslim world that was equivalent to two millennia of Christian antisemitism and a policy to exterminate the entire Jewish people.

Laymen and clergy rallied to this argumentation. Despite its moralizing tone, it served as a perverted counterbalance to Judeo-Christian history through a symmetrical attribution of guilt on Christians in respect of Muslims. European taboos and the policies of blocking information for fifty years on the extermination of the Jews during World War II and the pillage of their property contributed indirectly to the Arab war against Israel. Only the scholarly work on this subject by Jewish and Christian historians, mainly in America and Canada obliged politicians to recall this past. It was Christian public opinion which demanded that Western politicians acknowledge past crimes and repudiate antisemitism.

By accusing the Jews of using the Shoah as blackmail, the desire for purification on the part of Christianity was belittled, as was the reconciliation with its religious origins through atonement. In fact, in this way only the Arabs and the Palestinians benefited from the Shoah, because the European governments counterbalanced acknowledgment of the genocide of the Jews and Judaism by an anti-Israel and pro-Palestinian policy.

In 1983, when the sixth assembly of the World Council of Churches met in Vancouver, William Nicholls noticed that its statement included a new theme, stressing that Christians in the West should recognize

> that their guilt over the fate of the Jews in their countries may have influenced their views of the conflict in the Middle East and has often led to uncritical support of the policies of the state of Israel, thereby ignoring the plight of the Palestinian people and their rights.[49]

This policy brought forth propaganda which skillfully amalgamated the Palestinian Arabs with the persecuted Jews of Europe on the one hand, and the Israelis with the Nazis, on the other. The transfer of European guilt to the Israelis cast the Palestinians as victims on two counts: victims of Europe which, according to the Arab version, created Israel; and victims of Israeli "Nazism." In addition, the Euro-Arab lobbies exploited the history of anti-semitism to castigate Western public opinion, reticent to mass Muslim immigration from a dozen Muslim states, which, hardly tolerated their own remnant Christian *dhimmis*. Thus Jewish history, documented by numerous Jewish and Christian scholars, served anti-Zionist and pro-Arab European policies, but the same Jewish history was described as Jewish blackmail in respect of Israel. This opinion, expressed at both the political and the religious level, defended the "right" of an Arab Palestine, but condemned the "injustice" of Israel's existence.

In 1997 the trial of Maurice Papon, chief of police in Lyons under the French Vichy government during World War II, broke a taboo after half a century regarding France's anti-Jewish policy and its responsibility in the deportation of Jews, including children. The trial brought an explosion of anti-Zionism, fanned to the maximum by the Euro-Muslim lobbies. Activists in the Jewish community were accused of being "manipulators," and taxed with wanting to "inculpate public opinion in European countries." Paul Cousseran, a distinguished civil servant, active in the French Resistance, even stressed in the Paris newspaper *Le Figaro*:

> In my opinion it [the Papon trial] is a question of conditioning this public opinion, and the governing classes, so that they feel obliged to defend the State of Israel unconditionally, *"even when it commits very great stupidities."*[50] [italics and inverted commas in the original]

Thus, anti-Zionism would seem to require that French war criminals like Papon should not be judged as their trials could benefit Israel. Jewish history and juridical and historical deontology once again became the hostages of French-Arab interests and their pro-Palestinian policy.

In its unilateral aspect, the inculpation of the West by pro-Arab lobbies accorded with the tradition of demonizing the *dar al-harb*. Supported at the highest political and religious level in Europe, propagated by academics and writers, this unilateral accusation established an anti-Zionist and anti-Western culture fed by a twofold negationism: of the Shoah, and of *jihad*.

The whole campaign to accuse the West seems to be fashioned on the model of the Judeo-Christian dialogue. Actually, one can discern the same process already mentioned of substituting history and identity, which makes it possible to replace the Jews by Muslims. But Muslim-Christian relations, determined by *jihad* and dhimmitude in former Christian lands, can never be integrated into a scale of equivalence with Judeo-Christian relations.

Condemnation of only one example of barbarity (Europe's) introduces discrimination against the evaded sufferings of other populations, thereby annulling the principle of equality. Ostensibly claiming to be moral, this process becomes immoral, suspect, and eminently selective because it is diminishing and tendentious, and therefore falsifying and politically oriented. For Muslim-Christian violence does not take place between unequal entities, but between states and armies, animated by the same motives; hence, it should be established in a context of reciprocities regarding the "duty of memory"—for the Crusades, as well as for *jihad*. It is the perverse principle of false symmetries between Jews and Muslims in relation to Christians that conceals the history of *jihad* and of dhimmitude—for they have no parallels in Jewish history.

Some clergymen and European politicians utilized the Shoah to inculpate public opinion, hostile to the immigration of millions of Muslims into Europe during the last three decades. This tactic, which aggravates antisemitism, simply transformed Jewish history into a Trojan horse for increased immigration. It is noteworthy that the numerous Muslim populations in Nazi-occupied countries—France, the Balkans, the Caucasus—were never assigned a special status, nor did they suffer deportation and extermination in Europe, but there was a discriminatory status for Jews and there was an extermination of Jews. Hence, the extermination of the Jews—perpetrated with the approbation and connivance of the Palestinian leadership in Berlin during the war—was not a problem of immigration but a premeditated strategy against Zionism, endorsed by those in the religious hierarchies, who considered Zionism contrary to Christian teaching which condemned the deicide people to exile and to wandering.

In the 1970s, the confusion in Europe between anti-Judaism and anti-Arab xenophobia caused by massive immigration, led to the inclusion of recent Arab immigration into the two millennia-old Jewish history in Christendom. Playing on the guilt of the Christian West toward the Jews, certain antiracist movements—which included Jews among them—likened the condition of the economic migrant to that of the European Jew during World War II. Other than a few political refugees—among whom were well-known Islamists—the Muslim immigrants to Europe are voluntary economic emigrants who were not persecuted in their native lands. In addition, the problems connected with Muslim—or any other immigration—are not comparable with the problematics of two millennia of Christian antisemitism. Jewish history serves as a camouflage for unpopular policies which exploited the inculpation of public opinion concerning the extermination of the Jews during the war. The linking of xenophobia—from which North African and Turkish immigrants suffer—to the extermination of European Jewry, not only concealed the history of two thousand years of anti-Judaism, it also reduced the Shoah to a modern problem posed by xenophobia and immigration. By appropriating and transferring European guilt to another context, it constitutes a cynical and dangerous process, because it does not resolve the real problem. Moreover, it brings no solution to the immigrants' specific problems in their relationship with their environment. It is not surprising that the revisionist, negationist, and racist theses are widely disseminated by these anti-Zionist immigrant circles which, at another level, exploit the Shoah.[51] For example, on 5 February 1994, Muslim organizations from several French towns demonstrated in Grenoble on the question of whether Muslim girls should be authorized to cover their hair with a scarf at school. According to the Paris newspaper, *Le Monde*, of 8 February 1994 (p. 15):

> Most of the demonstrators sported armbands representing the crescent of Islam in yellow on a black ground, matched with this slogan: "When is it our turn?" an explicit allusion to the yellow star imposed on Jews under the Nazi occupation.

This comparison reduced the Shoah to a problem concerning the wearing of head scarves at a secular state-school. In addition, France's policy toward North African immigration cannot be compared in any way to the policy of the Nazis and their French Vichy collaborators toward the Jews. It is noteworthy that discriminatory signs on clothing were invented in early Arab-Islamic jurisdiction and imposed on Jews and Christians by Muslims up to the nineteenth century, when Europe required their abolition in the Ottoman Empire. They were taken over from Islam by Christendom for Jews and Muslims in 1215 by the Church's Fourth Lateran Council.

One can see that the theories that heap blame on the West are often diffused by the same anti-Zionist propaganda networks; in other words, the same indivisible entity of the People of the Book is the object of the same unilateral hostile campaign.

The Eastern Christians' incrimination of the West is part of a historical tradition of self-protection similar, moreover, to their present anti-Zionism. Theirs is a policy of integrating into the *umma*, a policy which does not, however, lessen their vulnerability. This is the case with the Iraqi Christians, closely linked to and compromised by Saddam Hussein's regime and exposed to the risk of reprisals after his fall from power. Heirs to *dhimmi* Christian viziers in the service of the caliphs, *dhimmi* patriarchs and intellectuals today constitute powerful pressure groups, advancing Islamic interests in the West. Imprisoned in the traps of history and hostage to the blackmail upon their communities, they form the conveyor belts of dhimmitude in the West. However, this policy is increasingly challenged and repudiated in the Arab Christian diasporas, now aware of the counter-truths appearing in the statements that the *dhimmi* propagandists circulate abroad. Consequently, these contradictions are creating a real schism between the *dhimmi* clergy and intellectuals, and their Christian compatriots who have immigrated to the West.[52]

The Islamization of Western Culture

Among the topics already listed, we should note the tendency to overestimate Western civilization's debt to the civilization of medieval Islam, despite historical and archaeological evidence. This interpretation of history resulted from resolutions and recommendations issued in September 1968 at the end of the second session of the fourth conference of the Academy of Islamic Research at Al-Azhar University in Cairo.

> The conference recommends the publication of a detailed book in diverse tongues, to be circulated on a large scale pointing out the viewpoint of Islamic civilization regarding the Rights of Man and drawing a comparison between it and that of Western Civilization.
> The conference recommends the preparation of a historical and scientific study explaining the impact of Muslim civilization and teachings on the movements of political, social and religious reform in the West, since the age of European Renaissance.[53]

Consequently, a spate of works written in the past twenty years by distinguished Western Arabists has magnified this Islamic contribution to European civilization. Like the other currents, it manifested a desire to compensate the declarations of Vatican II, the "*Orientations*" of the French episcopate (1973) and of the Vatican (1975), on the theological, spiritual, and cultural relationship between Judaism and Christianity.

In September 1991, the Parliamentary Assembly of the Council of Europe held an Assembly debate on the contribution of Islamic civilization to European culture. It was recalled that this was simply a follow-up to the previous Resolution 885 (1987) on the Jewish contribution to European culture. Following the colloquy held by the Committee on Culture and Education in Paris, the Assembly issued recommendations on the contribution of Islamic civilization to European culture. The Muslim and European scholars who participated stressed the superiority of Islamic civilization and the humanism of the "golden age," compared with Europe's obscurantism. This affirmation is noteworthy as the *shari'a* was the only Islamic law practiced during this "golden age." In his Explanatory Memorandum, the Spanish socialist rapporteur, Luis Maria de Puig, stated that

> both the reports and our discussion re-affirmed the Islamic civilisation's enormous influence on West European culture. It is an established fact

that—in a wide variety of philosophy, science, art, architecture, town-plan-
ning, medicine, language, everyday life and lastly, culture—we cannot explain the history of Europe without taking into account all that is of Islamic
origin.[54]

The rapporteur deplored the conflicts caused by the Crusades, the Inquisition, European imperialism and colonialism, and the paternalism and
ambiguity on the Israeli-Palestinian problem (p. 15). In his paper, Omar
Khalifa al-Hamdi, secretary-general of the National Council for Arab Culture, wrote that it was

> necessary to lay bare the reasons that have prompted the concealment of the
> Arab role in the building of contemporary civilisation. The real reasons why
> the Arabs have been subjected over the centuries to calumnies, aggression
> and attempts to obscure their identity must be identified.
>   The importance of such a revision of historical concepts and outlook will
> escape none of the participants in this colloquy, for the contacts between the
> Muslims and Europe have in the past engendered events of the gravest kind,
> such as the Crusades, European colonialism, the foundation of the State of
> Israel and, lastly, the Gulf War. (pp. 170–71)

Members of the conference emphasized "the debt that Europeans owed
to the cultural heritage of Islam." Hence, the Parliamentary Assembly of
the Council of Europe adopted numerous recommendations concerning
the development of Arabic and Islamic studies in different fields, such as
education, media, and culture. For their part, the Muslim representatives
asked for the opening of European universities to Muslim students and the
transfer of Western technology to their countries, considered by them as
logical political demands since European culture had an Arab-Muslim
origin.

Seven years later, speaking at the Ismaili Center in London on 8 October
1998, British Foreign Secretary Robin Cook stated:

> It is the most wonderful reminder in the very heart of London that the roots
> of our culture are not just Greek or Roman in origin, but Islamic as well.
> Islamic art, science and philosophy have helped to shape who we are and
> how we think.

After stressing "the debt our culture owes to Islam," he added: "Islam
laid the intellectual foundations for large portions of Western civilisation."[55] Such assertions are obviously motivated by electoral and economic
interests, but they may also be viewed as political tactics to facilitate the
integration of millions of Muslim immigrants into a European culture with
Islamic roots. Since Islamic doctrine forbids Muslims to accept the influence of infidel cultures and requires the acknowledgment of Islamic pres-

tige, European ministers are not loath to proclaim the Islamic origin of, or contribution to, Western science, the arts, and even its civilization.

This problem already arose at the beginning of the nineteenth century when the modernization of the Ottoman Empire was in process, but was temporarily overlooked by colonization which imposed Western concepts on Muslim populations in Asia and Africa. Today, at the dawn of the twenty-first century, the conflict of civilization is reemerging again on European soil in the context of an Islamic immigration. For Zanjani—expressing the normative Islamist position—Islamic law forbids cultural dependence and any cultural accord which subordinates Muslim culture to that of foreigners (non-Muslims). As he put it: "Islam strongly rejects such a friendship and forbids the Muslims from engaging in such a treason" (p. 254). He quotes numerous koranic verses forbidding friendship with non-Muslims,

for the preservation of the Muslim's independence, personality, prestige, leadership, devotion, unity and solidarity in order to prevent some weak and flexible Muslims from turning to self-surrender, self-losing, reliance and acceptance of the leadership of non-Muslim groups [. . .] (p. 258)
"Whoever loves a people he is of them. A man is (counted) with those whom he loves."
The type of friendship which is forbidden in the said *ayah* [Koran, 5:56] is of the last kind, namely affection which produces spiritual attraction, depriving one of one's [word missing in text] and moral impression, and leadership. Obviously such a friendship by the Muslims would involve the loss of independence and leadership in favour of others, transformation of the Islamic morals and ways, and inclination towards those of the non-Muslims, and ultimate perversion. (p. 262)

Zanjani justifies the struggle against these polluted ideas, foreign to the *shari'a*, by quoting the koranic verse 4:140b: "And Allah will never give the disbelievers a way against the believers" (p. 295), and also the *hadith*: "Islam surmounts, not surmounted."

The same Muslim London magazine *Q-News* which reproduced the British Foreign Secretary's speech carried two headlines: "Rushdie will never be safe, say British Muslims," and: "An overwhelming majority of British Muslims continue to regard the blaspheming author as a legitimate target" (p. 10).

In an article in *The Guardian* (27 August 1999), Faisal Bodi, the news editor of *Q-News*, deplored the British Labor government's threat to expel a Pakistani cleric who had called for *jihad*, commenting that:

In the global village, Britain is not immune to the flames of the Kashmir conflict.[. . .] Over the years the Muslim community has invested heavily in [the] Labour [Party], boosting its rank and file membership, mainly in the hope that it can force the issue on Kashmir, where so many of them have their roots. With Labour in power, Muslims are looking for a return on their investment.

On 20 December 1999, the Shari'ah Court of the United Kingdom issued a *fatwa* (Case No. Xmas/M/42) prohibiting any Muslim from participating in Christmas or Christian New Year celebrations taking place in the Millennium Dome. Sheikh Omar Bakri Muhammad, the Principal Judge of the Court, gave several reasons for this. For example, it was forbidden for Muslims

> to imitate the non-Muslims (i.e. Kuffar) in their religious or ritual celebrations such as celebrating Christmas or the Christian calendar. There are many sayings of the Messenger Muhammad (saw) forbidding the Muslims to copy the Mushrikeen (polytheists) and Jews and Christians. There are also narrations ordering Muslims to be different from the Mushrikeen, the Jews and Christians, in relation to following anything which is part of their religion.[56] [parenthesis explanations in the original]

Symptoms of Dhimmitude in the West

It was in the early 1970s, with the outbreak of Arab Palestinian terrorism worldwide, that dhimmitude erupted on European soil through violence and death deliberately inflicted on one category of person: the Jews, who were singled out as in the Nazi period by their religion. Security precautions and instructions posted on synagogues and Jewish community buildings implied that being Jewish and practicing the Jewish religion in Europe might again incur the risk of death, and that the freedom of religion and freedom of thought had been restricted.

Among the various terrorist movements which appeared in the 1960s, a distinction should be made between terrorism inspired by anarchist and revolutionary European thought, and the terrorism linked to *jihad*—an element in a global strategy. Even if the trail left by the various terrorist networks indicate a collaboration in tactics and assassination attempts, their ideologies remain different. Hence, the propagation of dhimmitude in the West emanates from a strategy of terrorism belonging to the *jihad* civilization, whoever the mercenaries may be.

The alliance and compromises of some European governments with the PLO, especially France and Italy, in the 1970s led to shady deals with several Arab Palestinian terrorist groups. To neutralize this terrorism on European soil required defamatory propaganda against Zionism and Israel, whose demonization was integrated into Europe's economic and security requirements. This anti-Israel strategy renewed traditional antisemitism in Europe and elsewhere. Such compromises, and the emigration within two or three decades of several million foreign Muslim nationals, principally from Africa and Asia, imported the seeds of the conflicts stemming from dhimmitude. Increased insecurity required armed guards at synagogues and Jewish cultural centers throughout Europe, an obligation still in the year 2001 on all religious holidays and other occasions.[57] The threat of terrorism restricted various circles from expressing solidarity with Israel. In addition, the economic boycott and intellectual terrorism reproduced in Europe the instability and marginalization inherent in the *dhimmi* condition.

As the situation of the Jews foreshadows the situation of the Christians, and as the destinies of the People of the Book were always parallel and overlapping, the study of one thus reflects the other like a mirror image. Hence, the terrorist threat in the ensuing years inevitably involved Eastern Christians who were hostile to the PLO, as well as European civilians.

Consequently, because of the ideological structures of dhimmitude, Jewish insecurity was transposed to the Christian diasporas, who also became victims of *jihad* strategies: Copts, Assyrians, and Lebanese who had found refuge in the West. The same campaign of threats and intimidation was waged against individuals daring to criticize their countries of origin or Islamic discrimination and persecution. Varying forms of intellectual terrorism were practiced with even greater severity against European Muslims whose opinions were often judged blasphemous.

The policies of dhimmitude are clearly seen in Europe in the decades-long taboo of condemning the persecution of Christians and the violation of human rights in Muslim countries, and by the decade-long silence on the subject of the slavery and genocide in southern Sudan carried out by Northern Arab government forces against black African Christians and animists. This abstentionist policy by Europe, while claiming to defend human rights, obeys a fundamental law of dhimmitude: *dhimmi* minorities are forbidden on pain of death to appeal for help to outsiders, or to propagate ideas considered hostile to Islam. *Dhimmis* who request help from Christian countries are deprived of all the rights and privileges they had obtained through the *dhimma* tribute agreement and "of the right of immunity of life and property."[58] This silence, in order to protect the Christian communities of Islam, is a symptom of the West's implicit submission to the laws of the *shari'a*. During his visit to Egypt in January 2000, Pope John Paul II implicitly submitted to these regulations when he refrained from mentioning the recent massacres of the Copts perpetrated at al-Kosheh in Upper Egypt between 31 December 1999 and 4 January 2000. This situation forced the religious leaders of the Copts to withdraw into an isolation conducive to their own destruction, a system which prohibits victims from testifying against their tormentors.

The two principal causes of European dhimmitude emanate from historical negationism and the Muslim world's unilateral inculpation of the West, the first process leading to the second. To deny the black pages of European history is, of course, absurd; they are well known and are condemned by Western historians. What is reprehensible about the Islamic practice of incriminating Christian Europe concerns its mimicry of another history— the history of Judeo-Christian relations. But this history is special for two reasons: first, Israel occupies an exceptional place in Christianity since it was the source from which it sprang; and second, the Christian struggle against Israel was not directed at a sovereign nation but at a theological entity, and at a religious community and people characterized by the concepts of supersession and deicide. These two factors are totally foreign to the Church's relationship with Islam and other religions. On the contrary, Muslim-Christian relations are structured within an Islamic theology which, with regard to the People of the Book, associates the principle of supersession with a policy of conquest (*jihad*) and domination (dhimmitude). It is in this context which has been totally erased that these relationships must be examined. Consequently, this inculpation-victimization relationship proves to be a trick with distorting mirrors whereby Islam replaces Judaism.

Of course, no encouragement is too great for inter-religious dialogue which respects the freedom and dignity of both parties. For example, the condemnation of European anti-Muslim stereotypes should have been balanced by an equally vigorous condemnation of the Islamic stereotypes of the People of the Book, whose humiliation, particularly in the Holy Land, was institutionalized up to the nineteenth century to a degree rarely attained elsewhere. Not only was this step not taken but it was also blocked by anti-Zionism and historical aphasia, fabricating an idyllic past.

Zanjani devotes several pages of his book to the koranic rules permitting Muslims to hold discussions with the People of the Book. And the rules to which the Christians should submit in order to maintain a dialogue only admit of approval and not to any criticism of Islam from the People of the Book (*dhimmi* behavior patterns). Citing the evidence of history, Zanjani thinks that Muslims should favor exchanges with Christian priests, the clergy and theologians, since they have always encouraged the propagation and supremacy of Islam.[59] And, in fact, during decades of dialogue which preceded Vatican Council II and Judeo-Christian dialogue, the official Churches did maintain a compliant silence on the persecution of Christians in Islamic countries and developed an anti-Jewish and anti-Zionist cultural system of references. One can scarcely suspect the Christian participants of naivete in the Muslim-Christian dialogue; all are knowledgeable theologians, Islamic scholars, and Arabists. History will judge their silence concerning the destruction of Eastern—particularly Lebanese— Christianity by Syria and the Palestinians; their responsibility for the diffusion of dhimmitude in Europe; their passive obedience to political pressures ; and, above all, their obsessive desire to see the demise of Israel, willy-nilly.

Nonetheless, it seems that this Christian passivity, which reproduced in Europe the respectful and conciliatory *dhimmi* attitude, is being challenged in some Christian circles. For example, at a colloquium on the situation of religious minorities which the Group for Muslim-Christian Friendship held in Paris on 6–7 December 1997, certain interventions—such as that by Father Maurice Borrmans of the Pontifical Institute of Arab Studies (PISAI), among others—referred to the difficulties of Christians in Muslim lands; Father Hubert Barbier quoted Monseigneur Gabriel Zubeir Wako, the Archbishop of Khartoum:

> The identity of non-Muslim Sudanese is virtually unrecognized. The *shari'a* treats them as handicapped, people who lack something. A non-Muslim is not normal.[60]

The conclusion of the article by Alain Chevalérias analyzing the two days of discussions leaves one perplexed:

> However, one cannot help praising the courage of its organizers who, for the first time at this type of gathering, dared to depart from a flattering mono-logue for Muslims, but too often remote from reality.

Did it require so much courage to state the truth in France at the end of 1997? Which authorities required its replacement for such a long time by "a flattering monologue for Muslims"? Remarks by a well-known Lebanese priest, Michel Hayek, in a lecture on 6 March 1967 in Paris are relevant in this context:

> Let us break a taboo and a political prohibition by clearly confessing what we suffer in the flesh and the Christian consciousness, namely that Islam has been the most appalling scourge that has ever befallen the Church, as a re-sult of which Christian sensibility has remained traumatized until the present day.[61]

One day historians should elucidate the source—and the aims—of this "taboo," and the "political prohibition" surrounding it.

Consequences of the Dogma of Victimization

The duplication of Jewish history in an Islamic version emanates from anti-Zionist European political and theological circles. It aims, first, to in-culpate the West in regard to the Arabs in order to justify pro-Palestinian propaganda and policy; and second, to condition a reluctant Western public opinion to a deliberate and massive Muslim immigration policy in Europe. This strategy has numerous consequences. At a historical level, the doctrine of victimization has effectively placed a taboo on the whole history of *jihad*, the slave system, and dhimmitude. Pressure from the Arab League and the Eastern Churches has imposed a policy of preserving a false balance between Judeo-Christian relations and Muslim-Christian relations. This situation has blocked discussion of the characterizations of the People of the Book in Islam at a theological, juridical, and historical level, and, therefore, it hindered any possibility of an egalitarian relationship between Muslims and non-Muslims. Such conduct reproduces the traditional *dhimmi* behavior patterns, the more so that in the West this system is considered as a perfect model of multiculturalism which can be reimposed in the twenty-first century.

At a political level, the dogma of victimization, product of the mythological history of "the harmonious millennial multiculturalism" exemplified by the "Andalusia" myth, concealed the realities: the emergence of radical religious trends and the disappearance of the Eastern Christian communities. This situation established complex dissymmetrical relations between East and West. The self-incrimination of the erstwhile colonial powers was matched by the moral irreproachability felt by an Islam spread over the remnants of the conquered Christian and Jewish populations. However, this history is perfectly well known. Pierre Rondot, who cannot be suspected of Judeophilia, recalls the history of the ten centuries when Christians were forced to live "in fear and humiliation." For him, as a sign of election, they were "humiliated, insulted, reviled," and he concludes:

> One should not say too much about their long and often painful and unequal association with Islam in the sphere of public life: just enough to inform oneself and not to irritate.[62]

The contribution of Arab Christian militancy to the Islamic cause was predominant in Europe and the Americas. For the *dhimmi* Churches, which had remained loyal to the theology of supersession, the demise of the Jewish state by the Palestinian arbiters of justice constituted a powerful motive to identify with the Muslim world. The symbiosis of anti-Zionism and Christological anti-Jewish themes is expressed at the highest level of the Christian hierarchy when Israelis are excluded from their national and historical heritage, which is transferred to a Muslim-Christian Arab Palestine. This reasoning propagated in Europe the conception of the Palestinian as arbiter of a salvific justice for the world, and the savior of Christendom by the defeat of Evil, personified by Israel (i.e., the theology of Palestinianism). In this way occurred the conjunction of the theology of supersession and the theology of Palestinianism—a policy condemned and refuted by numerous Christian circles, both lay and theological.

Vehicle of Arab policy, the mercenaries of Eastern Christianity, themselves emanating from the long tradition of dhimmitude, substituted the Palestinian problem for the problem of the Christian *dhimmis,* whose survival was subordinated to Israel's demise. By focusing international attention on Israel, they thereby imposed a fatal silence on the oppression of the Christian *dhimmis;* on the destruction of Lebanese Christianity by the Palestinians, and the Syrianization and Islamization of Lebanon as described by Habib Malik; and on the genocide of the Christians in southern Sudan and in East Timor. The theology of Palestinianism and corruption masked the permanent deterioration in the living conditions of the Christians in Islamic lands, similar to the process which already in the past had brought about the disappearance of the Jews in the Islamic world, according to the well-known and confirmed Arab adage: "after Saturday comes Sunday." Thus, the exodus which had eliminated the ancient Jewish communities was being reenacted for the Christian communities. The major error was to have attributed to Israel the origin and cause of the Muslim-Christian problems in order to conceal the theological, political, sociological, and historical structures of Christian dhimmitude from which they emanate.

The spokesmen for Palestinianism—members of the clergy, bishops, priests, and pastors—introduced into the Palestinian system of symbols a Christological conception, rooted in the theology of the deicidal people. Under pressure and threats from the Arab states, the *dhimmi* Eastern Churches constituted an important element in delaying Judeo-Christian rapprochement and simultaneously facilitated the implantation of Islam in Europe, while introducing a form of dhimmitude relationship there, the only one that they knew well, and which gave them a semblance of importance. Thus, they militated for the retention of the deicidal designation attached to the Jews and spread a specific Judeophobic brand of anti-Zionism among the Western Churches, presenting it as a guarantee of their own survival in Muslim lands. Indeed, other opinions did exist in Lebanese Christian circles, but the local and international political context and, above all, widespread terrorism did not permit their free expression.

Although opposed in the West by Christian religious and lay currents, Arabophile activism, supported by the powerful Muslim lobbies, as well as the communists, and strongly backed by European politicians from both the Left and Right parties, swept through Europe from the 1960s, particularly after the Six-Day War. The theology of Palestinianism, created by the Eastern Churches, integrated into the policy of Europe's "Arab interests," required the establishment in the West of a sizable anti-Zionist production industry with all its Judeophobic derivatives.

Euro-American Rivalries and Islam

In the 1990s Muslim countries became more assertive on the international scene, at a time when Muslim immigration to the West greatly increased. Cultural and religious differences were expressed in sharper contrasts. Wars with religious incentives flared up worldwide between Muslims and Christians. Such developments, whose symptoms had been masked by the cold war, prompted scholars to seek the historical background to modern conflicts. In 1996, Samuel P. Huntington published *The Clash of Civilizations*,[63] a comprehensive work of research on geostrategy, linking history with modern trends, in which he asserted that: "Intense antagonisms and violent conflicts are pervasive between local Muslims and non-Muslim peoples" (p. 255). He analyzed what he called "The Islamic Resurgence" and the re-Islamization of Muslim countries (pp.109–20), and also described the situation in Bosnia (pp. 267–71). In Asia, he remarked:

> Muslim assertiveness stems in considerable measure from social mobilization and population growth. [. . .] Population growth in Muslim countries, and particularly the expansion of the fifteen-to-twenty-four-year-old age cohort, provides recruits for fundamentalism, terrorism, insurgency, and migration. Economic growth strengthens Asian governments; demographic growth threatens Muslim governments and non-Muslim societies. (p. 103)

Huntington stressed that regional conflicts are aggravated by a Muslim diaspora involvement and *jihadist* camps. In the 1970–80 period, Lebanon, Algeria, and the former Yugoslavia sheltered camps which trained terrorists from all over the world for the *jihad* against Israel. These *jihadist* camps later served as a model for camps in Afghanistan, Bosnia, Chechnya, the Philippines, and Kashmir.[64]

A recent well-documented book in French by Alexandre Del Valle examines Islamic international strategy. According to the author, Islamic immigration to Europe, the re-Islamization of Bosnia and Kosovo, and the destabilization of the Balkans have shifted the "front lines" of conflicts within Europe itself, as he explains:

> The frontier between the Islamic world and Europe, which formerly went through the Rabat-Algiers-Tunis-Alexandria line to the south of the Mediterranean, henceforth crosses the great European capitals.[65]

This situation is the obvious result of the policy initiated by General de Gaulle in the 1960s. The plan for a vast Euro-Arab geostrategic Mediterranean block by the mixture and interpenetration of populations from both shores (multiculturalism), has already been mentioned. Some French politicians envisaged this block as the basis for a strategic and economic alliance in which France would play the role of the protector of Islam and the Palestinians against America and Israel. It was hoped that a pro-French Islam would facilitate the retention of former colonies within the French orbit and spread the influence of French culture—the so-called *Francophonie*—associated with the benefits of an enormous market, reaching to Islamic Africa.

This project for a Euro-Arab unification was not new. On 25 October 1941, Hitler told the Italian minister Count Ciano that in the battle against America he envisaged "the common interests of a unified Europe within an economic zone completed by the African colonies."[66] It should be noted that France's Arab policy is constantly expressed in anti-Zionist overtones, throwing doubt on the permanency and legitimacy of Israel, allegedly set up by Jewish colonists on Arab Palestinian lands. The image of the "eternal Jew," of "a restless wanderer who has no home and who cannot find peace" is reinforced by anti-Zionist support.[67]

In the international context, the Muslim policy of conquest has always astutely profited from the religious, economic, and strategic rivalries of the West. Without going back as far as the alliance of Francis I with the Ottomans against the Emperor Charles V (1525), France was the first to play the Arab card against England in the nineteenth and twentieth centuries. Bonaparte in Egypt declared himself a Muslim protector of Islam against the Turks. Under the Restoration (1818–30), France dreamed of an Arab empire, a dream pursued by Napoleon III who wanted to create an Arab kingdom. Historian Alain Boyer recalls that: "France with its colonial empire declared itself a Muslim power, the protector of Islam, but with a paternalistic attitude."[68]

France continued to pursue its colonial Muslim dream—both protective and paternalistic—after decolonization. Thus, after 1962, France supported the most radical ideologies—Nasserism, the Ba'ath party in Syria and Iraq, the PLO, and the Front de Libération Nationale (Algeria)—which claimed to be secular but whose only secularity lay in the Christian defense of Islamic interests. For Arab Islam was never secular, neither pro-French nor pro-Western. France bowed to the directives of the Arab League, with the boycott of Israel; it opposed the Egyptian-Israeli peace treaty in 1979 and conferred a status of respectability on the PLO.

On the subject of terrorism, Jacques Frémeaux noted that: "The French were very much spared the terrorism which attacks the nationals, the interests, or the supporters of Israel." After citing a few cases of terrorism, he asks: "Is this relatively privileged situation the fruit of a more or less tacit entente with movements capable of organizing terrorist acts?"[69] How should this privileged situation in which terrorism only targeted Jews be understood? Frémeaux explains it as follows:

One must obviously also take into account France's Arab friendships with
the PLO in particular, but also with the collection of states which support
the most radical Palestinian movements.

France even had the privilege in 1978 of facilitating the emergence of
the first twentieth-century Islamic state: Iran, after the fall of the Shah, an
ally of America and Israel. After the European Parliament had received Arafat (September 1988), the French, Italian, Greek, and Spanish governments were said to be seeking "an allusion to a necessary division of
Palestine based on the 1947 UN Partition plan."[70] That is to say, the dis-
membering of Israel on the nonrealistic boundaries accepted by the Jewish
leadership then, but refused by all the Arab governments including the
Arab Palestinians. These anti-Israeli policies went hand in hand with massive business dealings, arms sales, and military technology involving colossal profits. Those operations concealed the emigration to Europe of
millions of Muslims, welcomed and protected by the Churches and diverse
organizations, financed by states which were still unwilling to restore booty
taken from the victims of the Shoah, and acknowledging the states' respon-
sibilities. Hence, there is no need to resort to theories of "Judeo-Masonic"
or "Judeo-Protestant" conspiracies against the papacy or the Greek Orthodox Church, hatched in America, to explain the irreversible process of Europe's Islamization. This policy was desired, planned, executed, and
proclaimed by its own, democratically elected leaders, and its spiritual
guides.

Today, the United States and Europe compete for the favor of the Muslim world by once again abandoning the victimized peoples to its mercies.
It is a long time since Europe has neglected the Christians of Muslim lands
and adopted an eliminationist anti-Zionism. The Gulf War against Saddam
Hussein on the question of oil interests (1991) was redeemed by the destruction of Yugoslavia and the creation of new centers of Islamist influence in the heart of the Balkans, planned to be integrated into the
European Union.[71] In this Euro-American competition, once again the
small nations are sacrificed. Numerous authors have noted that in Central
Europe the re-Islamization of Bosnia and Kosovo—to be followed by Macedonia—and the anti-Serb *jihad* were polarizing the economic and military
aid of the Muslim countries on a worldwide scale. This extraordinary militantism was encouraged, administered, and directed by the European powers and the United States. A media campaign of generalized demonization
of the Serbs aimed at neutralizing all opposition to NATO's anti-Serb war,
was waged with terrifying cynicism. The war to annihilate Serbia was intended to punish the crimes of Milosevic and his regime, but the media
campaigns endeavored to calm the anti-Westernism in the Muslim world,
and of Muslim immigrants in Europe. It also helped to gain forgiveness

for the war in Iraq by a strong pro-Muslim counterbalancing policy in the Balkans.[72]

It can be noted that NATO's war against the Serbs repeated, though on a far larger scale, the Euro-Palestinian tactics: control of the media world-wide; uniformization of information; collective demonization of the Serbs, and not solely of Milosevic's criminal regime; and banalization of the Shoah by pillaging Jewish and Serbian history. For years already, Europe had established the essential points of its anti-Israeli propaganda: disguising the Arab Palestinians—whose World War II leadership had been allied to the Nazis—as victims of the "Israeli Nazis." Moreover, as we have shown, this process emanated from the Greek Orthodox, Catholic, and Protestant clergy. This same referential framework of stereotypes, amalgams, and mirror-accusations was applied against the Serbs in the Balkan wars. Since it lacked any truth and rationality, it can be repeated against any group.[73]

Numerous French authors have tried to blame America for the emergence of Islamism, which they contrast with the secular Arab nationalism that France promoted. But this opinion is born of a policy seeking a scapegoat, for Arab nationalism has never been secular. As Henri Boulad, an Egyptian Jesuit, and a specialist in Islam, states in an article: "L'Islamisme, c'est l'islam" ("Islamism is Islam"):

This statement is perfectly consistent with history and geography, with the Koran and the sunna, with the life of Muhammad and the evolution of Islam, with what Islam says about itself. I reject the position of people—Muslims or Christians—who bury their heads in the sand like ostriches, beat about the bush, refuse to view the situation objectively, or take their wishes for realities, on behalf of dialogue and tolerance.[74]

The situation which is developing in Europe today is conducive to xenophobia and violence against blacks and immigrants, while European Jews are being targeted by Muslim immigrants. The present dangerous and chaotic situation is the result of the incredible irresponsibility of European leaders during the past three decades.

This period is characterized—in the specific sphere which concerns us here—by a schizophrenic policy which combined a Christian reconciliation with a rootless Jewish people, associated to an eliminationist policy in regard to the State of Israel. "Palestine" reactivates the process of substitution destined to destroy Israel. These mechanisms transfer Europe's culpability and the silence of the various Churches upon an alleged Nazified Israel, accused of perpetrating a similar Holocaust on their Palestinian victims. This usurped Jewish history was expressed on 29 November 2000 at the United Nations in Geneva by the Palestinian ambassador and permanent observer, Nabil Ramlawi, at the annual Day of Solidarity with the Palestinian People. Before a large assembly of UN officials and ambassadors, Ramlawi strayed from his circulated text to describe the Jews, and the Israelis of today:

> Their crimes can reach anybody anywhere in the world. Even Europe itself. Europe knows that very well. And America knows that also very well. There is not a single person in the world who does not know that. A group of criminal gangs from the various areas of the world came to Palestine to set up a State, a State that commits crimes from 1948 until now, perpetually before the eyes of the world. The civilized world hides behind closed eyes and a silent tongue [. . .] as though the West's guilt complex concerning the past could only engender another complex, another complex which will be borne by the Palestinian people [with the West] as a prominent feature of their historic struggle and for which, if necessary, they will arbitrarily blame others in the future.[75]

It is this cauldron of seething hatred that has engulfed thirteen centuries of a history, recorded in thousands of books, concerning the dhimmitude of Jews in their own land: the massacres and deportations, the destruction of Jewish towns and villages, the expropriations and pillage of their patrimony, the extortions, humiliations, and misery. Moreover, the condemnation to nonexistence of this Jewish history in its own land, in Israel (Palestine), has condemned to the same nonexistence the same Christian history.[76]

11

Conclusion

Historical Assessment: Political Prejudices and Interests

In his two-volume study of the Ottoman reforms, Edouard Engelhardt, French minister plenipotentiary, examined the condition of Christians in the European and Mediterranean regions governed by the *shari'a*.[1] He noted the koranic laws punishing blasphemy and apostasy, the refusal to accept Christian testimony in Islamic courts, the interdiction on infidels owning land, and their exclusion from different magistratures and teaching. He stated that pan-Islamism, which appeared in the 1870s

> nourished among [the Muslim masses] the hatred of the foreigner: It had the nature of a protest against institutions borrowed from Christian states [. . .] it was the negation of the principle of secularization without which reform could not succeed. (2:116–17)

Engelhardt noted the frightened submission of the Christians confronted with the tracking down of infidels by the Muslim reactionary movement which was opposed to their emancipation, and referred to the collection of taxes by the farmers-general

> [which was] arbitrary, iniquitous and oppressive. Probably in the course of time, the *raya* was no longer exposed to the shameful slap on the face by which the tax collector asserted his authority; but he has been despoiled with impunity. (2:137)

He concluded his first volume, published in 1882, by noting that the same problems which existed before the Crimean war (1853–56) existed twenty-five years later.

> Muslim society has not yet broken with the prejudices which make the conquered peoples subordinate [. . .] the raya remains inferior to the Osmanlis; in fact he is not rehabilitated; the two classes persist in their age-old hostility; the fanaticism of the early days has not relented. (1:111)

341

Even the thriving liberal Muslim class rejected "civil and political equality, that is to say, the assimilation of the conquered with the conquerors." (2:171) Those who represented that class were

> would-be pupils of Western schools, of a dubious nature, indifferent, corrupt, who, with rare exceptions, had gained nothing from their contact with civilization except an unintelligent scepticism and the feeling of their relative inferiority, matched with all the hatred that European superiority inspired in them. [. . .] There were in fact a few Christians at the lower levels of the hierarchy, as if to bear witness to the fact that equality was not an empty word; but these latter were for the most part unworthy of that origin for which they were seeking to gain forgiveness, veritable renegades without a public apostasy, shamelessly betraying the interests of their faith, pitilessly pressuring their coreligionists, and, by their own doing, bringing contempt on the authority to which other[s] brought hate. (1:254–55)

Engelhardt's pertinent work analyzed the condition of Christians in the Ottoman Empire in the period from 1826 to the early 1880s, but much of it could have been written today. The author noted that *dhimmi* clergy and financiers collaborated in the oppression of their own communities, a situation which still exists. Engelhardt points out that the reforms imposed by Europe aimed to rescue the Christians from their abasement and to erase all abusive terms referring to them from official documents. He describes the conflicts in the Balkans and the Christian grievances in Bosnia and Herzegovina. Christians demanded an end to their fiscal exploitation by Muslim landowners and the billeting of soldiers in their homes; they asked for respect toward their religion, permission to build schools and churches, to use bells, to own land, and the right to testify in courts. In 1878, during the Albanian disturbance, he noted that

> for the Mohammedan Albanians, like the renegade begs [beys] of Bosnia, it was primarily a question of maintaining their religious, political and social preponderance, and to escape from a Christian power. (2:248)

Historians, diplomats, and travelers, particularly in the nineteenth century, have left a large number of comments about the condition of the *dhimmis* whom they observed. As the great majority of these travelers could not have known the Muslim legal texts, the fact that their first-hand descriptions—of behavior in the street, for example (walking on the left side, dismounting when passing a distinguished Muslim), greetings, clothing, and so on—accord with the rules, proves that these rules were customarily applied. The travelers, and particularly the European consuls, generally felt some degree of compassion for these *dhimmi* populations, attributing their servile behavior to the oppression they suffered—although other opinions were voiced. But in general, up to the 1950s and the 1960s, it was still possible to read true descriptions of the *dhimmi* condition written by people who had observed it at close quarters.

World War I overturned the traditional world of dhimmitude and marked the start of a period of discontinuity. The Islamic-*dhimmi* war within the world conflagration enabled Turkey to eliminate ethno-Christian irredentisms by the genocide of the Armenians and the expulsion of the Greeks from Anatolia in an exchange of populations. In the Arab provinces, colonization replaced the *shari'a* with European legislation. The loss of former privileges, particularly the privilege of humiliating the *dhimmi*, nourished the persistent bitterness and hostility toward Europe. Modernization was built in a historical context, concealing but not destroying its ideological foundations.

The inter-war period, when the Shoah was incubating in Europe, is also relevant to the present subject. In fact anti-Zionism was the motive force which assembled, connected, and polarized the European antisemitic movements in the Syrian-Palestinian Christian communities, the United States, and the powerful transmission points in the Vatican with the Muslim world. Gradually, its ideology was built into Arab nationalism which welded the Muslim-Christian alliance in the common battle against the Jews. Such was the polluted ground on which the necrosis of the Christian memory developed, with its offshoot, the Christian trend to glorify Arab Islamism. This policy, challenged by some Eastern Christians, was—willy-nilly — imposed on them, from outside. It is noteworthy that important works by historians recalling certain aspects of the *dhimmi* condition were still being published at this period. In his study of Egypt published in 1930 Muhammad Sabry referred to historic events which, barely thirty years later, discreet censorship in academia would have overlooked or suppressed. He described how

> [Muhammad Ali] abolished all the humiliations afflicting the Christians who did not have the right to mount a horse or wear certain colors in the presence of their "superiors," the Muslims. [. . .] The Capitulations or privileges granted to Europeans by the Ottoman sultans were specifically justified by the state of insecurity and fanaticism in which the Empire found itself at this period.[2] [inverted commas in the original]

Describing Egypt's conquest of the Sudan (1820–22), Sabry sees no reason to conceal the massacres of the victims whose severed ears were sent in bagfuls to Cairo. The campaign aimed to collect gold to finance Muhammad Ali's wars and take 40,000 slaves. From Sennar, Muhammad Ali's son, Ismail, "launched his troops in all directions in pursuit of slaves, made continual razzias on the population in order to send to Aswan the Negroes [Nubians] destined to form the kernel of the new army." Ismail's extortions and cruelty put the populations to flight. The murder of the Egyptian general was avenged by the massacre of 30,000 Africans in the Sennar region.[3]

In the context of the Egyptian conquests of Mesopotamia, Syria, and Palestine, Sabry includes many descriptions of the anarchy prevailing there, the system of ransoming, and the plundering and humiliations practiced in Palestine, particularly in respect of non-Muslims. He reproduces the letter from British Consul-General Charles August Murray, which praises Muhammad Ali's reforms and recalls the long years when no Christian could walk in Aleppo or Damascus or any town under the Sultan's direct control, "secure from insult and abuse."[4]

In the same year in which Sabry published his book (1930), Arthur Stanley Tritton published *The Caliphs and their Non-Muslim Subjects. A Critical Study of the Covenant of Umar,* a pioneering work on this subject. In 1958, Antoine Fattal's fundamental research, *Le Statut Légal des Non-Musulmans en Pays d'Islam,* appeared in Beirut. Like Tritton's work, it expressed the opposite viewpoint of the Arabophile and negationist current, already largely represented. In this basic study, the author—a Lebanese Christian jurist—examined every aspect of the legal condition of the non-Muslims according to *shari'a* stipulations until the Ottoman era. But the general trend after World War II followed European economic interests vis-à-vis the Arab world and the West's desire for conciliation with the Arab-Muslim peoples in the context of the cold war and the communist threat. At the dawn of the nuclear age, the pressing need to go beyond history to attain a universal peace became an imperative. Moreover, the Muslim-Christian ideological struggle against Zionism broadened into historical negationism and the delegitimization of Israel. Henceforth, this policy continued the prewar antisemitic movement, but at another level. The theme of an ideal multireligious tolerance in the *dar al-Islam* would serve in future geostrategic, political, and anti-Jewish objectives.

Commenting on the status of the Jewish communities in Yemen in the late 1940s, Professor Robert Serjeant explained[5]:

Judging by Arabic sources, the Jews of South Arabia were not hardly treated by Muslim rulers, who in general seem to have dealt with them in fairly strict accordance with the provisions of the shari'ah relating to the protected faiths. (p. 118)

And again:

Individual Jews or communities were not, of course, always safe from occasional acts of fanaticism and, like the Muslim peasant, they must doubtless have been subject at times to unconstitutional exactions. (p. 119)

Three pages later, the author mentions the forced conversion of Jews in the town of Habban, which he visited during six days in December 1947, and the removal from his Jewish mother of a boy whose father had converted to Islam. Commenting on the dispatch of the little boy to another town to study the Koran, the author writes: "Even in the lawless and turbulent Wahidi Sultanate of that time there was quite clearly a certain regard for legal nicety where the *Dhimmi* was concerned. [...]"[6] The author seems to regard the forced conversion of a Jewish child and its removal from its mother in terms of "legal nicety."

A few sentences further on the author mentions the massacre and plunder of Jews in Aden on 30 November 1947 and the choice given to them: they "either accepted Islam or emigrated, the latter alternative being entirely voluntary, I believe."[7] This is a confused formula, for how can the alternative of apostasy or emigration express a choice which is not forced on the victim?

For William Montgomery Watt, the eminent theologian—Emeritus Professor in Arabic and Islamic Studies at the University of Edinburgh—the effective protection of "minorities" was a point of honor for the Arab tribes:

In the light of this fact it is not surprising that Islamic states have on the whole had an excellent record in respect of the treatment of non-Muslim minorities—it was a matter of honour for them to treat them well! In the case of the "protected minorities" under the early caliphs the idea of protection had a central place.[8]

It is surprising to find the large Christian majorities at the period of the first caliphs already described as "minorities." In a brief description of the *dhimma*, the author continues:

The Christians retained their churches and the Jews their synagogues. The later theory was that they had no permission to build new ones, but this rule, like many of the other petty rules about *dhimmis*, was probably not always observed. Rather exceptionally the cathedral of St. John the Baptist in Damascus was shared by Muslims and Christians until the reign of al-Walid I (705–715) when on some pretext the whole was transformed into a mosque.

On the whole the *dhimmis* had a tolerable life, though in some regions there was a deterioration after about the thirteenth century.[9]

The author acknowledges "some minor disabilities" and attributes the prohibition on serving in the army to town dwellers' repugnance to fighting, but also to the fact that *dhimmis* felt no obligation to participate in the defense of the country since they paid for their protection. Watt also considers that "the position of the *dhimmis* was moderately satisfactory," but they remained a kind of "second class citizen."[10] Mentioning in the book's epilogue "the disappearance—or perhaps one should say fossilization—of most of the Christian culture of the region," he adds: "There was nothing dramatic about what happened; it was a gentle death, a phasing out."[11]

This conciliatory spirit encouraged Professor Montgomery Watt twenty years earlier (1956) to take issue with certain historians who described what he calls "the alleged harshness of the sentence" on the Jews of Medina in 628 as "savage and inhuman."[12] But according to Muslim jurists, the fate of the Banu Qurayza had also determined the fate of Christians who faced the choice between Islam or *jihad* on three continents. The author's opinion shows very little compassion for all these victims. Even though he quite rightly attempts to put these data into context, there is no need to abandon one's own ethical criteria by blaming the victims. In this vein, the author regards the Arabian Jews' feeling of exclusivist election as a theological obstacle. However, as the Jews maintained good relations with their pagan environment and strengthened their connections by marriage, it would seem that elitist exclusivism was more characteristic of Christianity and of Islam which condemned "infidels" to eternal hell-fire—a concept totally alien to Judaism. In fact, Muhammad reproached the Jews for their friendly relations with the pagan Arabs.

As for the accusations leveled at the Jews of Medina, which the author adopts uncritically, there are four possible objections. First, in order to establish and prove the veracity of a claim, historical discipline requires the comparison of different sources. But as only very biased Muslim sources allege Jewish guilt, the accusations which motivated the execution of from 600 to 900 men, the enslavement of their women and children, and the plundering of their possessions are far from established according to the norms of Western historiography. Second, the author complacently repeats as correct the demonological characteristics attributed to Jews to explain their refusal to convert, although probably very few of these simple peasants would have concerned themselves with the Prophet's still incomplete teaching. Third, the author states that the Medina Jews "had opposed the Prophet with all their might," but accounts clearly show that they were under constant attack. Nowhere is there mention of Jewish warriors assailing Muslims; on the contrary, the picture is of dispossessed or murdered Jewish peasants. The *hadiths* describe Jews going out to the fields, spade on shoulder even at the time of Muhammad's attack on Khaybar. On the subject of their theological "aggressiveness," which the distinguished professor—himself an eminent Christian theologian—holds against the Jews, one should note that there is no proof of this assertion, merely that the Jews remained faithful to their own Scriptures, as recorded in the Bible. Moreover, Christians who did not convert and who refused to submit to Islam acted no differently and suffered exactly the same fate as the Medina Jews.

The author shares this "theological aggressiveness" since he himself did not convert to Islam. Christian and Jewish "theological aggressiveness" is based on their refusal of a koranic interpretation of their Holy Scriptures. The Koran gives different versions of biblical episodes and people. Thus, Abraham, Moses, Jesus, and others are alleged to be "Muslims."

On another register, a book by Princeton Professor Mark Cohen falls into this negationist category of replacing dhimmitude with a model of Muslim-Jewish peaceful coexistence. In his *Under Cross and Crescent* (1994), the author utilizes Christian anti-Judaism the better to emphasize Islamic benevolent tolerance and to denounce, unflaggingly, what he refers to as "the neo-lachrymose conception of Jewish-Arab History". In order to prove his thesis, Cohen explains: "For comparative purposes, I have found it fruitful to focus on the Latin West and mainly on the *northern* lands" (italics in the original). With candor, he explains: "The contrasts in the North are simply more vivid and less encumbered than in the South [of Europe], hence the reciprocal light cast on Jewish-gentile relations in Islam shines more brightly."[13] Here, it is therefore a question of the effect of contrast which determines general judgments, a specious argument because they are based on selected parameters and unfounded hypotheses which would be disproved in other areas, such as Arabia, the Sahara desert regions, and Palestine.[14]

Cohen's selective method is clearly apparent in his geographical divisions. Christian regions where Jewish life flourished are ignored because the less drastic condition of the Jews does not lend itself to the desired contrast. Thereupon, the author explains the better condition of the Jews in Provence (southern France) by proximity to the Islamic model. Similarly, in his search for contrasts he totally forgets the Jewish condition in the Arabian peninsula, the heart of Islam. He also ignores Palestine where indigenous Jews suffered expropriation, the evil of Bedouin Arab tribalism, permanent ransoming, destruction of synagogues, all designed to eliminate them from their historical homeland; likewise, he refrains from analyzing the Muslim East under the Mongols in Iraq, Persia, and Afghanistan. Rather, over and above the differences, one can detect some analogies and mutual borrowings between the Christian and Muslim civilizations on territories and among peoples who passed from one to the other, through war or conversion. In particular, the principles emerge of fallen peoples, excluded from divine love and therefore demonized; and of the supersessionist theory in regard, respectively, to the two prior religions.

Christianity, born of a Jewish nucleus, was structured by the Church *against* Judaism which became the theological enemy, having forfeited the Promise transferred by divine grace to the Church, the new "Israel." Islam for its part, born into Arab paganism, also developed a politicojuridical system *against* its predecessors, the People of the Book: Jews and Christians.

Against the Judeo-Christian civilization, it built the foundations of an Islamic empire conquered from the civilization it was supplanting and where, in the beginning, Muslims were always a foreign, conquering minority. In the conception of *jihad*, the theological enemy is no longer the Jew but all the peoples, the world of the infidel—the *dar al-harb*, which resists the Islamic advance.

Islamic anti-Judaism is certainly a Christian by-product, and the negative features of Jews in the Koran are those attributed to them through Christian theology and exegesis. However, this malicious baggage was reinterpreted and assimilated in the light of Muhammad's experiences and in the sociocultural context of Arabia. By sticking exclusively to the European context, Mark Cohen drains Islam of all its specific aspects which do not have equivalents in Christianity. For example, he neglects the fact that the condition of Jews in Islam is not solely part of a theological, but also of a political concept. The *dhimmis* are the Muslims' *fay* or booty, and "protection" is determined by the concept of *jihad* which opens up four possibilities: conversion, tribute, enslavement, or death. The condition of the Jews was therefore set within a different political context from that of Europe. Here we must also note the absence of the concept of personal rights, which makes the principle of protection indispensable to life. This aspect is manifest in the condition of the Jews in the Arabian peninsula, the Sahara regions, and in North Africa—regions which Professor Cohen does not even bother to mention. Preferring to show that Christianity had stronger motivation to persecute the Jews, he has not proved that Jews were actually less oppressed under Islam. The two propositions are not necessarily linked, hence the lack of an anti-Armenian theology did not prevent the genocide of the Armenians by the Turks. Cohen fails to explain why Oriental Jews, who constituted the majority of world Jewry before the Islamic conquest, had already dramatically shrunk by the eleventh century in Palestine, Mesopotamia, Egypt, and North Africa. Byzantine Christian law forbade Jews to live in Jerusalem, but they were very numerous in many Palestinian provinces—remaining the majority in some places. In fact, it was the system of dhimmitude that destroyed Palestinian Jewry, as it did the other *dhimmi* ethnic groups.

In terms of comparative history, it is important to emphasize that dhimmitude constitutes a global condition, not solely of Jews but common to Jews and Christians alike. It exploits the rehabilitation of one community against the other, and vice versa. In addition, any comparison with Europe up to the twelfth century must take cognizance of the disparity between the Eastern communities, survivors of the once-flourishing Mediterranean Jewish world, and the smaller communities in the West. Judaism—formerly widely represented in Arabia, Persia (especially Mesopotamia), Egypt, Syria, Palestine, and North Africa—was, by the twelfth century, reduced in some places to bare nuclei of communities, even if indigenous traditions of scholarship succeeded in maintaining an outstanding tradition. This decline matched the decline of those Christendoms which had become minorities in the *umma*. In the world of Islam, stretching from Spain to India, the scattered Jewish communities were harmless, but this did not prevent the Muslim religious authorities from employing similar mechanisms of demonization and oppression.

The Church Fathers called the Jews the enemies of God, but John of Nikious was nonetheless scandalized when the Muslim invaders, in their turn, designated Christians similarly as the enemies of God: an expression very common in the Koran to describe Jews, Christians, and other non-Muslims. St. Jerome declared that the man who wanted to remain faithful to his Lord and master could not at the same time be friends with the person who was His enemy. The same thought, expressed in several *sura* of the Koran and by the Muslim jurists, entailed identical segregationist measures, promulgated in Christendom and in Islamdom.

All the anti-Jewish legislation, conceived in a specific theological context by the Church Fathers passed into Islam, but in the enlarged context of *jihad*, mingling military conquest with theology. Remaining in force throughout the Islamic Empire, this legislation was neglected in Europe until the twelfth century when it reappeared alongside work compiling canon law. One might ask: by what artificial means did Professor Cohen wax indignant at these laws in Europe, but considers them benign in Islam, thus implying a human difference vis-à-vis victims of identical laws. In 1215, the Fourth Lateran Council forced Jews and Saracens (Muslims in Spain) to be distinguished by dress from Christians (canon 68). For Cohen, this law "promulgated for the first time a prescription that is perhaps the most infamous piece of ecclesiastical Jewry law during the Middle Ages" (p.38). Yet this law was clearly borrowed from Islam, which had imposed vestimentary differentiation on Jews and Christians six hundred years earlier from the end of the seventh century. Islamic laws governed the appearance of non-Muslims from head to toe, their headgear, disparate shoes, shoelaces, the style and color of their clothing, the little bells they had to wear in bathhouses and in the street, the rules concerning mounts, saddles, stirrups, houses, the segregation in separate districts with closed doors. Maybe the author does not consider all these rules—already numerous and detailed well before 1215—as ignominious, but as symptoms of a benign Muslim-Jewish symbiosis? It is this dehumanizing gaze brought to bear on the *dhimmi* which adorns dhimmitude with such attractive qualities.

Around the thirteenth century, a large number of humiliating and discriminatory rules decreed by the popes in respect of the Jews were identical to those imposed on the *dhimmis* as early as the eighth to ninth centuries.[15] These restrictions, generally of Christian origin, concerned their exclusion from public and honorific office, the prohibition on holding positions conferring authority, on owning land, and on mixed marriage; and the obligation to wear distinguishing signs visibly. Cohen restricts himself to the "Pact of Umar," a very limited text which makes no mention of the variety of the means of oppression and humiliation in respect of the *dhimmi*, such as walking on the left of Muslims, being disarmed, the prohibition on *dhimmis* defending themselves or answering insults, the abduction of children, the ignominious corvées, the rejection of their testimony in an Islamic court, and so on. He mentions as proof of their good integration the fact that Jews had their transactions signed by Muslim judges, but the reason for this is probably the exact opposite. According to the eleventh-century jurist Mawardi, the Muslim judge does not accept the decisions of a *dhimmi* judge, hence Jews were obliged to have recourse to the kadi to prevent the annulment of a document, which a contestant might bring before an Islamic court. One could argue that Mawardi's opinion is disputed by other jurists, but this does not invalidate it.

Style also plays its part. The description of the history of the Jews in Christendom employs a somber vocabulary with lengthy comments on the sufferings of the victims. There is nothing comparable on Jewish life under Islam considered to have unfolded in the delights of dhimmitude. The author regrets that European Jews lacked the privilege of the *jizya*—the blood ransom—because he argues that it guaranteed the *dhimmi*'s rights. But the whole history of dhimmitude demonstrates that the *jizya* has not prevented extortions, pillage, deportations, murders, and massacres. Under Christendom, the separation of political and spiritual powers—inherited from Judaism—limited the *odium theologicum* and made it possible in the last two centuries to restrain religious fanaticism. In Islam, the two powers are combined so that the ruler's military might serves religious ends. Not surprisingly, it is this system, combining politics, jurisdiction, and theology that Mark Cohen so admires.

Cohen's method is the product of a Manichean and simplistic vision of history which, sliced into segments of time and space, provides a contrast between Christendom and Islam especially for contemporary political and academic correctness. It is not our aim to minimize Christian anti-Judaism—in fact, frequently denounced in these pages—but to reject the principle of falsifying comparisons which actually forms part of the manipulation of dhimmitude today. This manipulation consisted of sustaining the conflicts between the different Churches, between the Eastern and Western Churches, and Judeo-Christian discord, by concealing the whole historical area of dhimmitude. It has already been shown that imputing to the Jews the massacres of Christians perpetrated by Muslims provoked Christian reprisals against Jews in different regions of Europe—which, in turn, led the Jews to make common cause with the Muslims against Christians in the Levant. These manifestations of anti-*dhimmi* violence and hatred, which were manipulated to the advantage of the third party, form the very substance of dhimmitude.

Today, the history of Christian anti-Judaism and criticism of European colonialism are being discovered by Muslim politicians in order to glorify Islamic goodness and tolerance, and to claim moral superiority over Europe. Jewish history in this context thus becomes a tool to attack the West, usurped by Muslim and pro-Muslim factions who conceal the history of *jihad.* Professor Cohen's method is similar to that of Eastern Christians who exploit anti-Judaism as a tactic to bring about a rapprochement with the Arab world. Thus, animosity between Jews and Christians constitutes the best apology for a military-theocratic system which has systematically oppressed the adherents of both religions.

The fact that Jews and Christians shared exactly the same *dhimmi* condition means that both populations must be judged on exactly the same criteria. Discriminatory or dehumanizing measures cannot be justified selectively to accord with Christianophobia or Judeophobia, even if such measures were in keeping with the mentalities and mores of the time. It is precisely by examining this condition in the different communities, whatever their reciprocal antagonisms, which will allow one to rise above prejudice, however deeply concealed, in order to discover the universal essence of the human being.

The Muslim-Christian conciliation movement salvaged the Judeophobic arguments which the two religious traditions held in common. It exploited Jewish-Muslim polemics and set out to prove that Islam granted a privileged status to Christianity as compared with Judaism. This attitude was rooted in a Christian *dhimmi* tradition which always maintained that the Christian was superior to the Jewish *dhimmi;* consequently, the leveling of their condition in shared degradation constituted an additional humiliation. Above all, the conciliation movement aimed to establish a relationship of esteem and mutual confidence between Muslims and Christians which would guarantee peace as well as security for the Eastern Churches. The best means of achieving this undertaking appeared to be the secularization of Islamic societies and unconditional support for the anti-Zionist struggle, this support being conceived as the Christian "service" to the *umma.* Perhaps, in the blood-stained dawn of the twentieth century there was no other way. Nonetheless, many Christians were opposed to Arab nationalism. In fact, by associating local Christians with the rejection of the Christian West, this doctrine increased the Christian *dhimmis'* schizophrenia. In addition, the replacement of history with the myth of a carefree past coexistence developed aphasia in populations cut off from their history and torn between atavistic terror and a pious lie. Lastly, the principle whereby the *dhimmis'* existence was justified by services rendered to Islam—the very foundation of the concept of toleration as opposed to the concept of natural rights—was recycled in anti-Zionist Christian militancy, particularly through clerical and Judeophobic channels in the West.

Historical negationism, which concealed the notions of *dar al-harb*, *dhimma*, and *dhimmi*—traditionally connected with Christians—made it possible for the demonization of the Jews to be reformulated and to reappear in the demonization of Judaism and Israel, considered responsible for all the misfortunes of Eastern Christendom.

Since the early 1990s a few books have mentioned the dhimmitude of Jews and Christians in Islamic lands. Jean-Pierre Valognes's important study in French (1994), already cited, displays different levels of analysis including an encyclopedic documentation on every Eastern Christian community. But however valuable his research, it represents a monumental history of *dhimmi* Christianity and not a study of dhimmitude itself, which must necessarily integrate the Jewish dimension.

Apart from his contribution to history, Valognes has shown rare courage in this era of disinformation by divulging the inviolable secret buried in the mutilated Christian memory and also in the archives of the Quai d'Orsay, the French foreign ministry, that chronicle the persecution of the Christians in Islamic lands. Nevertheless it is regrettable that he has avoided the even more tragic fate of *dhimmi* Jewry—particularly in its Palestinian homeland—who suffered a genuine physical and cultural genocide.

Several of my various publications in French, English, and Hebrew on *dhimmis* and dhimmitude have elicited scores of reviews since 1980. Most contain constructive comments or challenging objections. Two of them labeled my work "neo-lachrymose," but labels simply hide a paucity of argument. V. Poggi, a Jesuit priest, discusses an interesting and widely accepted idea: that it is best to vaunt Islam's tolerance in order to encourage it, rather than to denounce persecutions which would risk aggravating Islamic fanatical tendencies. However this attitude, which has been the norm for decades, was firmly opposed by Father Richard John Neuhaus—a Catholic priest and editor-in-chief of *First Things*, a New York monthly journal of religion and public life—in two powerful articles to which we shall refer later.[16] Other arguments explain away the anti-Christian persecutions entirely by contextualization. Jews are barely mentioned. This opinion ignores the basic theological and legal texts determining the status of conquered non-Muslim peoples. Islam-*dhimmi* relationships are interpreted in terms of a context of conjunctural causes, chance circumstances emanating from external sources such as the Crusades or colonization. This kind of interpretation was formulated by a Church specialist questioned by Herbert Schlossberg (see p. 261). Apart from obvious errors, such an explanation conceives the Muslim world as a static mass, devoid of any autonomous dynamic, whose only policies are reactions to stimuli from Europe, whereas the exact opposite corresponds to the historical reality.

In the course of history, dhimmitude has played a leading role in the political, economic, and religious spheres. Till today it is evident in a multitude of areas and its current dynamics have been discussed in the three previous chapters.

The Policy of European States toward *Dhimmis*

The nineteenth and twentieth centuries were turning-points in *dhimmi* history. There is a clear similarity between the independence movements of the Christians and Jews of the Ottoman Empire, despite the different contexts. The two groups struggled in their historic homeland to move from their status as a religious community to a status of national sovereignty. The similarity is also apparent in the justifications and policies of the forces that oppressed them. As far as the European powers are concerned, there is a visible concordance in the geostrategic and economic structural schemas they adopted toward the *dhimmis*, whether Christian or Jewish.

In the last two centuries, the European powers have followed the same policies toward the various Christian ethnic groups in the Ottoman Empire, alternating between help and obstruction, depending on the interplay of their own interests. In the second half of the nineteenth century two major developments influenced the European powers' policy toward the *dhimmis*: the extent of their economic and strategic interests in the Ottoman Empire; and Muslim opinion in Europe's old and new colonies in Asia and Africa. Consequently, European policy was one of appeasement toward Muslims who—from India to Algeria—were revolted by the abolition of the *shari'a*, colonization, and the emancipation of the infidels.[17]

The strategic interests of the European powers favored the maintenance of dhimmitude, propitious to manipulation and interference, rather than ethno-Christian independence. Thus, in the 1820s when pro-Hellenic public opinion hampered the Powers' policy, they resorted to censorship and to propaganda denigrating the Greeks, similar to the current anti-Israeli propaganda. Nineteenth-century philo-Ottoman literature invoked the negative characteristics of the Balkan *raya* people in order to challenge their right to independence.

In the 1840s France totally rejected the Maronite independentist movement, preferring a policy of diluting the Christians within the Islamic population rather than promoting their sovereignty. At the end of the nineteenth century a "conspiracy of silence" in France, Germany, and Britain attempted to conceal the 1894–96 massacres of the Armenians, or to incriminate them for their own sufferings.

On the morrow of World War I the ethnoreligious communities of the Arab provinces of the defunct Ottoman Empire opted for two different policies: territorial sovereignty or dilution in the Islamic environment. This last option accorded with the interests of Europe which regarded the Christians as ferments of secularization and modernization in Muslim societies, and as agents of its influence. It, therefore, sacrificed the Christian autonomies to the pro-Muslim policies in its own colonies. The Christian communities submitted to this policy, often under duress, and actively supported pan-Arabism and Arab nationalism, whereas the Jewish project for national sovereignty was to culminate in the creation of the State of Israel.

Europe had invested the Christian Arabs with a historic mission: to modernize Islam by the relativization of its basic concepts of domination, the only evolution which would have allowed a relationship to the non-Muslim on a basis of equality. Far from understanding that this role also related to the Jews and that it involved combined action, the Christian Arab nationalists, manipulated by European ambitions toward Palestine, exploited Islamic anti-Judaism as an agent for their own security and integration into the Muslim environment. In addition, the continuation of the Arab-Israeli conflict offered a respite and an opportunity to increase the importance of Western interests in Arab countries, and conversely to disseminate pro-Islamic propaganda in the West.

Twentieth-century French and Vatican policy toward Zionism scarcely differed from the goals of the 1840s, when France's "Arab and Muslim" colonial policy coveted the Mediterranean basin. As with the Christians, the national independence movement of the Jews was subject to the fluctuations of European interests. It was Muslim "opinion" in the colonies which had determined the dual policies of cover-up and nonintervention during massacres of Christians and even a genocide of Armenians. At a Cabinet meeting on 27 January 1939 which discussed Britain's subsequent harsh anti-Jewish policy, Colonial Secretary Malcolm MacDonald stated—three months before the White Paper, limiting Jewish immigration—that: "He was satisfied that we could not afford to forfeit the confidence and friendship of a large part of the Moslem world."[18]

The anti-*dhimmi* structure in which Christian nationalisms were directly involved also applied to Zionism, but on an infinitely more tragic scale as it incorporated a theological war which led to the extermination of European Jewry. The campaign of incitement to hatred, which had grown immeasurably since the 1840s, assumed an unparalleled and international dimension in April 1920, just before and after the League of Nations' recognition of a British Mandate for Palestine, and Prime Minister Lloyd George's determination to create a Jewish National Home.[19]

As the Evian Conference in July 1938 was to demonstrate so vividly, no state was prepared to receive Jews on their territory, nor in their vast under-populated colonies. It was said that Jewish immigration into those colonies with strong Muslim majorities would aggravate the tensions between the colonial administration and the Muslims. The West's policies of obstruction and indifference to their rescue, condemned the Jews to a planned Nazi program of extermination.[20] In a 20 July Cabinet Committee on Refugees after the Evian Conference, British Home Secretary Sir Samuel Hoare

> warned his colleagues that while he was anxious to do his best, there was a good deal of feeling growing up in this country—a feeling which was reflected in Parliament—against the admission of Jews to British territory.[21]

It is clear from the well-documented description provided by Sir Martin Gilbert that the Jews were sacrificed to an Arab appeasement policy. Moreover, the "universal Jewish peril" syndrome limited physical and financial concerted help being granted to the trapped and hunted Jewish populations of Europe.

Britain's position before the war was best summed up at a meeting of the Cabinet's Palestine Committee on 20 April 1939—just before the White Paper was finalized. Gilbert explains how

> Neville Chamberlain declared, with all the authority of his Premiership, that it was of "immense importance" from the point of view of strategy, "to have the Moslem world with us," and he added: "If we must offend one side, let us offend the Jews rather than the Arabs."[22]

The two interrelated European concepts: "Idyllic Muslim tolerance" and the "Universal Jewish Peril," laid down a policy in this field that spanned the whole twentieth century. It was to lead to the extermination of most of European Jewry, the abandonment of the Christian and Jewish *dhimmis*, and ultimately to the development of European dhimmitude in the last decades of the century.

During World War II the allied governments and most religious hierarchies often censored or minimized information on the genocide of the Jews, a genocide which was clearly intended to solve the problem of Zionism which no European government wanted—that is, a Jewish state with Jerusalem as its capital. This refusal to recognize the Shoah continued even after the war. The Euro-Arab anti-Zionist alliances were renewed and strengthened after the war by the reinstatement of the political, administrative, and religious antisemitic elites of the prewar period. Anti-Zionism naturally replaced anti-Judaism. After the Eichmann trial (1961), and as facts about the Shoah were revealed, political and religious antisemitism was recycled in support of Arab nationalism and Palestinism. In the 1960s, through the media and a pro-Arab policy, an anti-Zionist culture developed in Europe nourished by an assertive and distasteful contempt for Israel. Historians will have to clarify what part European antisemitism played in the banalization of anti-Zionism, as distinct from the enormous pressures and threats emanating from the Arab League.

Even more severe negationism was imposed on the history of Christian dhimmitude and on the current situation of Christians in Muslim countries. The few Christian organizations which struggled to break the silence—whether Coptic, Lebanese, Armenian, Syriac, or Sudanese—had meager or no financial resources, and other more active NGOs were often intimidated.

A recent case concerning the Zurich-based nongovernmental organization CSI illustrates this point. Since the mid-1990s it had constantly alerted the UN Commission on Human Rights (UNCHR) and world public opinion to the slavery and genocide perpetrated by the Khartoum government's *jihad*-war against black African Christians and animists in southern Sudan. Using a procedural pretext, as a result of SPLM leader Colonel John Garang's statement under CSI's auspices at the UNCHR (23 March 1999), the Government of Sudan filed a complaint with the UN Committee on NGOs. It requested that CSI be stripped of its consultative status at the United Nations. In a crude show trial "without due process"—the term used by U.S. delegate Seth Winnick—twelve of the Committee's nineteen members recommended to accept Sudan's harsh sentence (17 June 1999). However, due to a blatantly flawed procedure, the UN Economic and Social Council (ECOSOC) voted to return the case to the Committee on NGOs, which on 7 September confirmed its previous "recommandation" for CSI's exclusion. All twelve states—of the nineteen members—that voted against CSI have deplorable records in flouting human rights norms in their own countries (Algeria, China, Cuba, Ethiopia, India, Lebanon, Pakistan, Russia, Senegal, Sudan, Tunisia, Turkey). Finally, at a special ECOSOC meeting held in New York on 26 October 1999, twenty-four out of its fifty-four member states voted in favor of the exclusion of CSI from the UN, fourteen against, while fifteen abstained, and one member was absent. The mixed bag of additional "yes" voters included: Indonesia, Morocco, Oman, Saudi Arabia, Syria, and Japan. Fourteen Western, and like-minded states, voted "against" (Belgium, Bulgaria, Canada, Czech Republic, Denmark, Germany, Iceland, Latvia, Lesotho, New Zealand, Norway, Poland, United Kingdom, and the United States). By deliberately choosing to "abstain"—alongside ten countries from Central Africa and South America, and two others—France, Italy, and Spain caused a dramatic split within the European Union and in the Western democratic camp on a major issue: slavery in the Sudan. The Holy See was conspicuous by its silence alongside the World Council of Churches, and other NGOs.

Only two weeks before this ECOSOC vote, Sudan's procedural argument was contradicted in the publication of an Arab League statement used by Sudan's Minister of External Relations, Dr. Mustafa Osman Ismail:

> The Ministerial Council of the Arab League in its last meeting has reviewed the misleading and hostile campaigns being waged by some organizations such as Christian Solidarity International (CSI) against Sudan. By disseminating false information about the slave trade in the Sudan, CSI is instigating hatred among the Sudanese: Christians and Muslims, as well as painting a bad image of Islam. The Council has unanimously agreed that the reports are there to tarnish the image of Sudan, destabilize it, and preach hatred and should therefore be faced. A copy of this decision was sent to the Chairman of the Security Council.[23]

Speaking in response to ECOSOC's exclusion vote of 26 October 1999, CSI International President Rev. Hans-J. Stückelberger condemned this manipulation of UN institutions by dictatorial regimes:

> We deplore the power that repressive regimes have acquired to subvert the rule of law within the UN system. It does the UN no credit to support the efforts of a regime that is committing a clear plan of crimes against humanity, including the enslavement of its own people, and to punish an NGO for exposing those crimes to the world. We renew our appeal to UN Secretary-General Kofi Annan, and to the UN High Commissioner for Human Rights, Mrs. Mary Robinson, to condemn the Government of Sudan's well-documented role in the enslavement of black African women and children, and to work energetically toward the punishment of the perpetrators of these cruel deeds by an international war tribunal.[24]

According to John Eibner—the pioneer of CSI's antislavery program—Europe's readiness to appease the Arab world on the issue of Sudanese slavery was crucial to the success of the Government of Sudan's efforts to strip CSI of its consultative status at the UN.

This anti-*dhimmi* political convergence on the part of European and Muslim governments inevitably eroded the survival of Christianity in Muslim countries. Such a political consensus obeyed complex imperatives spread in numerous sectors. The political motives unfurled in geostrategy and a global economy. The neutralization of Islamic terrorism by a laxist policy of concessions and subventions ensured the protection—in Muslim countries—of Western interests, and of foreign non-Muslims in a context of international economic rivalries.

At a religious level, the Churches are concerned with preserving the Christian heritage in the Islamized lands of its origins. While combining Christianity's "service" to Islam with anti-Judaism and anti-Zionism propaganda, they continue to obfuscate Muslim anti-Christianity by a self-imposed silence. In Europe, this "service" consists of welcoming Muslim immigrants, likened by widespread propaganda to the Jewish victims of the Holocaust, which several Arab Muslim countries still belittle or refuse to recognize at all.

Dhimmitude and Christian "Service" to the *Umma*

The idea of Christianity's "service" to Islam has always existed in the Eastern Christian communities. It influenced the erstwhile welcome that the Eastern clergy accorded Arab armies as well as their collaboration with the caliphs. This service to the *umma* is moreover inherent in dhimmitude, since Jews and Christians are only tolerated in terms of their economic or political profitability to the *umma*. As the Lebanese tragedy showed, they can expect neither gratitude nor friendship from this service, which merely buys them the right to live in their own country once Islamized. In addition, the "service" to the *umma* which European *dhimmi* movements proclaim—whether it be a political or financial commitment—constitutes the very condition of dhimmitude. Abbasali Zanjani examines at length the role of the minorities, especially the clergy, in promoting Islamic interests.

> Undoubtedly, the role of the minorities [*dhimmis* tolerated through the tribute agreement] may be considerable in promoting the true goals of the Islamic cooperation and good understanding through these activities. That is the way adopted by Islam in its relations with the minorities to which it attaches great value.
>
> In view of the above explanations, it becomes clear that the minorities play a significant part in social activities. They cooperate with the Muslims in cultural, hygienic, medical fields, in aiding the needy and indigent, in fighting poverty and social problems, or even acting independently in such fruitful tasks.

Zanjani specifies the framework of the activities allowed to minorities. They can engage

> in any other task which may promote the social, moral and economic amelioration of the united Islamic society, and any activity which is not contrary to the interests of Islam and to the articles of the tribute [*jizya*] agreements and other existing treaties.[25]

In view of the advance of Islamization in the West today, it can be reckoned that the Christian *dhimmi* communities have carried out diligently the role entrusted to them.

The idea of "service" is distinct from charity because the former involves political coercion if it is compulsory. It derives from an individual choice which could not be imposed as an imperative condition of survival on a whole community whose existence would then be limited to the service of Islamic expansionist policies. In this context, the disappearance of the Christians from the East is explicable as is the animosity of many toward their Islamophile *dhimmi* clergy. They reproach them for neglecting the service owed to the Christian community, while providing a voluntary service to the *umma*. Particularly repellent to them is the designation of the humbled and the excluded—common terms for an Islamized Christian theology—to qualify the Muslim world, when they themselves, in fact, are humiliated and excluded.

The policies of the Islamized Churches have aroused some criticism since 1996 in France. A book, *Vivre avec l'Islam? (Live with Islam?)*, is a collection of opinions from numerous religious and lay Christians on Islam and its relationship with non-Muslims.[26] For the first time—and this is its originality—the source of the conflicts are set out; some texts even discretely repudiate the policy of the Islamized Churches in France, an exception to the national consensus. Another innovation appears in a masterly analysis in this same book by a Lebanese, Jean Sleiman ("Violence et Sacré dans le Coran"/"Violence and Holiness in the Koran").

In his book, *Trois Tentations dans l'Eglise (Three Temptations in the Church)*, the French scholar, professor of social sciences, and Membre de l'Institut, Alain Besançon, examined the Islamic temptation within the Church. He noted that past efforts by illustrious theologians to seek a rapprochement with Islam had led to a deformation of the meaning of Christianity by distancing it from Judaism.[27] In Besançon's opinion, the sympathy for the Arab world at the beginning of the century was connected with the apogee of the French colonial empire in Africa, in an imperial and missionary perspective—in other words, with the institutional support of State and Church. He observed with regret that Vatican II had opened the floodgates to "a mass literature" of Islamophile propaganda poured out by priests, rather than to a structured reflection requiring equality in the dialogue with Islam. This Islamized Christianity, cut off from its biblical roots and placed in a position of false symmetry in respect of Judaism and Islam, easily develops into Marcionism. Besançon states that the rapprochement with Islam

> aims to place the Muslims in a relationship which would be the relationship of the Christians to the Jews [. . .] But the result of this effort is to wrench the Christians from their biblical roots, push them down their gnosticizing or Marcionite slope, and weakens them in relation to Islam which pays them nothing in return. They become enemies of the Jews without becoming friends of the Muslims. (p. 220)

For Besançon, it was "this mutual and unnatural hatred" between Jews and Christians which led to a "reactional" sympathy for Islam.

A recent example of this is the fabrication by some Christian circles of the Palestinians as a substitute for the persecuted Jew, which aims to erase certain errors committed during the Nazi period and only succeeds in repeating them. (p. 221, n.1)

This mutual hatred between Jews and Christians mentioned by Besançon—it might also be extended to include the mutual hatred between Churches, from which Islam benefits—has a name in the strategy of *jihad*: it is the Divine Law of Mutual Repulsion. This alleged law was discussed at length after the Six-Day War in 1967 by Sheikh Nadim al-Jisr, a Lebanese member of the Academy of Islamic Research, comparing it with the Anglo-French conflict against Russia during the Crimean War aimed at preserving the integrity of the Ottoman Empire.[28]

The sheikh also mentioned another law which according to him was contained in two verses of the Koran (42:39 and 2:216): the law of Response to Challenge, "as a merit of the true believer, and as a blessing." For clarification, al-Jisr gave the example of Greece during World War I, when

western Anatolia could be ceded to Greece, in conformity with an alleged historical claim, no echo of which has ever been heard for three thousand years; a case that is quite identical with the farcical tragi-comedy played nowadays by Israel, with the aid of the same Allies, against the Arabs. (p. 120)

Had this attack against Anatolia been launched by France, Britain, or the United States of America, there would have been no disgrace to the Turkish people to bear patiently the aggression for some time. But if the attack came from the small Greek State, which had been until recent times, one of the dependencies of the Ottoman Empire, the might of which had previously aroused terror in Europe, then, this would be the Challenge that led to the desperate battle of Sakaria, (on the 14th of August to the 7th of September 1921), in which the Turks had so utterly routed their enemies that they did not wipe their swords stained with Greek blood, save in the seashore of Smyrna. (p. 121)

In conclusion to his commentaries on "the struggle amongst nations"; and "on the effects produced by the law of Challenge referred to in the Quran as of great value"; and "by the law of Mutual Repulse, termed by God the Almighty, a sign of the Grace and Favour (He has conferred upon mankind)"; Sheikh al-Jisr announced, concerning the future battle against Israel:

It lies hidden behind the favourable circumstances, to be adjusted by Divine Destiny for the operation of the law of Mutual Repulse, accuring [*sic*] on a day that will not be so far away. (p.122)

A few years later civil war broke out among the Lebanese Christian communities. Probably for him, the Divine Law of Mutual Repulse brought the

Syrian army into Lebanon at the demand of one Christian faction fighting other Christians.

Arab Nationalism and the Minority Syndrome

In the period between the two World Wars Christian discourse propagating Arab nationalism carried Christianity's "service" for Islamic causes into the twentieth century. Far from working for the abolition of dhimmitude, Arab nationalism justified and glorified Arab Islamic domination over the indigenous Christian peoples whom it had subjected. With the basic aim of destroying the Jewish national liberation movement, it failed to liberate the Christians and to alter Islam's relationships with the People of the Book. This choice trapped the Arab Christian communities, locking them into a spiral of compromise and self-denials which reduced their human status to mere calculations of the services they could render to the Arab-Islamic causes.

Arab nationalism enhanced the choice of dhimmitude by certain Christian theological currents which rejected the principle of territoriality in favor of merging into the *umma*.[29] This was conducive to the interpenetration of the theological and political domains, characteristic of the Eastern clergy, who cumulated all the powers over their community in their collaboration with the Muslim state erected on the ruins of Christian states.

In the modern period, the militancy of the *dhimmi* Churches to "free" themselves from a Christian political structure in Lebanon helped to remove the legal conventions guaranteeing the liberties of Lebanese Christians. In addition, the centrifugal forces of the Christians' economic clientelisms in the Arab world increased the political inability to discern and define the indispensable tools for defending rights and liberties in Lebanon. Anti-Zionism compensated this deficiency, providing a shield for the Christian communities, hostages of terrorist blackmail in their own country. In this context, the anti-Israeli and anti-West clamor on the part of certain Christian circles expressed the language of the hostage's identification with his oppressor—what I have called the *dhimmi* syndrome.

Arab nationalism was based on the axiom of peaceful, multireligious coexistence. After the decolonization of the Arab countries, political instability and Islamization—in Iran and in Turkey, as well—accelerated the exodus of the Jewish and Christian communities from these countries, voiding the multireligious project of its substance, a theme that was soon to be stressed in Europe.

The minority syndromes in Islamic and Christian majority societies respectively—resulting from the processes of integration or rejection of minority groups—present similarities but also differences, because Judeo-

Christian relations are not identical with Muslim-*dhimmi* relations at a legal and historical level. This syndrome formulates the interiorization by a minority of the stereotypes projected on to it by a hostile majority with which it is seeking to assimilate. It was expressed differently with *dhimmi* Jews than with *dhimmi* Christians for two main reasons. First, *dhimmi* Jewry disappeared after the decolonization of North Africa and the Middle East; but, above all, unlike the Christians of the Levant, the *dhimmi* Jews were not subject to the profound deculturation and historical amnesia resulting from Arabization. This process, which consisted of substituting a fictitious identity for their own, aimed to make the Christians more acceptable to the Islamic majority. Besides, the European states utilized them as agents to spread their influence. Through Arabized Christians, European or Russian policies could radicalize and provide an ideological framework for the Muslim-Christian confrontation with Zionism. As Alain Boyer, a French specialist on contemporary religious history, wrote:

> It is France's cultural activity which, inspired by the principle of nationalities and of the nation-state, favored the birth of the Arab national movement, particularly among the Lebanese Christians, at the very end of the nineteenth century, in opposition to Turkish oppression; it was the nationalist phenomenon (unity of the Arab world) in the place of the religious aspect (Muslim unity which could have united the Turks with the Muslim Arabs).[30] [parentheses in the text]

However, not all Christian *dhimmis* were affected in the same way by the minority pathology and its exploitation by the rival interests of the Powers. The Coptic, Armenian, Syriac, and Maronite ethnoreligious communities were able to preserve the balance of their identity, rooted in their historical memory. The most affected were the Arabized Christians: Uniates won over to Catholicism and to French patronage; Syrian-Palestinian Christians, and Armenians—all recent emigrés or refugees in countries under European mandate—whose identity was built around anti-Zionism. To these must be added the Greek Orthodox, hiding within Arabism at the time of the nineteenth-century Greek-Turkish wars which continued until World War I.

These groups were breeding grounds for identity-amnesia, the interiorization of self-hatred, so often described apropos the Christian janissary, the unwavering soldier of Islamic causes. The extreme anti-Jewish feeling on the part of a Christianity enslaved by Islam, a pawn of European antisemitic patronage and of its imperialist and economic interests, has constituted a millennial historical trend. This painful reality is still exacerbating the bitter hatred of Israel felt by Christian Palestinians—all the more so since most of the laws of dhimmitude had been created originally by the Church against Judaism, including Palestinian Jewry.

Service to Islamic causes in the West imposed total historical amnesia on

Arab Christians. Some of them even became the most virulent critics of the West which had emancipated them from a millennial system of debasement.

The submissive and cautious attitude imposed by the *dhimmi* clergy and by Europeans weakened the Eastern Christians. Condemned to silence, they mutely suffered persecutions and humiliations. The people who should have protected them—their religious leaders, and intellectuals—passionately defended the interests of their oppressors. Not surprisingly. For a century they had served them on every anti-European, anti-American, and anti-Zionist front. Victims of their own elites and of Western policy, the Eastern Christians continued to flee from Muslim countries, having servilely and agonizingly fulfilled the *dhimmi* destiny of service to the *umma*.

Today, this question is tormenting the Eastern Christian diaspora in the West, who are endeavoring to save their historical memory from annihilation. In the United States, the Maronite grassroots organizations reject those whom they call "Arabist" politicians—Christians who are the tools of Arab lobbies. According to their spokesmen, the American Maronite Union (AMU)—a national chapter of the World Maronite Union—was created to promote the Maronite identity. Thanks to the Arabist lobby, it has been largely marginalized and demonized over the past decades by the dominant media, academic circles, and the American foreign policy establishment.

Lebanese organizations within the AMU blame the Arabists for the anti-Lebanese Christian stereotypes adopted by the Western press during the Lebanese war. They think that these Arabist forces not only oppressed the Maronites in Lebanon, but also extended their activities into the United States by a propaganda campaign launched by a multitude of Arab-influenced, Arab-controlled, Arab-financed lobbies. According to the AMU, Arabists infiltrated their community associations, took over their clubs and institutions, and claimed to represent the American Maronites vis-à-vis the U.S. government. The AMU accuses Arabist power of defeating every project developed by the Maronites of Lebanon, subverting their claims, and demonizing their community in the eyes of the press and academia. It claims that the most dramatic chapter in the Arabist onslaught was the role played by Arabists of Maronite descent who, they say, caused the most harm to their community, particularly James Zogby, the director of the Arab American Institute.

According to Tom Harb, an AMU member, in his letter (30 June 2000) to Dr. Ed. Soma, chairman of the National Apostolate of the Maronites (NAM) at its 37th Annual Convention:

Since 1975, the Maronites of Lebanon were submitted to two campaigns aiming at undermining their history, identity, demographic presence and fundamental rights. In our mother country, the Maronites were submitted to massacres (Beit Mellat, Chekka, Damur, Aishiye, Shuf, Aley, Iqlim, East Saida), to 15 years of harsh bombardments in East Beirut and Zahle, and to the ethnic cleansing of more than 600,000 people. About 100,000 Maronites were killed in the multiple wars waged against our villages and cities. In 1990, a Syrian invasion ended the last free enclave w[h]ere the Maronites and other Lebanese Christians withstood several assaults for many years. During the 1990s, the Maronites and other Lebanese Christians were submitted to persecution. Their leaders exiled, murdered, and jailed, their Church and Patriarch put under pressure, and their youth savagely repressed. This on-slaught was and still is led by a vast coalition of Arab-Islamist forces including the Syrian occupation, the Islamist Fundamentalists and the radical Palestin-ians. This Arabist coalition was responsible for the defeat, decline and the oppression of the Lebanese Christians, and particularly of the Maronites in Lebanon. Politically, the Arabists rejected the Maronites legitimate claims in several occasions.[31]

On 14 June 2000, Colonel Charbel Barakat, from the South Lebanon Civilian Committees and Lebanese Christian Refugees in Israel, gave testi-mony before the U.S. Senate Foreign Relations Committee's subcommittee on Near Eastern and South Asian Affairs. This historic document high-lights the real background to the south Lebanon tragedy as well as its his-torical roots. Colonel Barakat stressed: "*Worse than the physical tragedy was the assassination of the truth*" (italics, B.Y.). He then described the resistance (from 1976) of the south Lebanese villagers against the PLO and pro-Syr-ian assaults. In 1978, the Christian enclaves were able to link up with each other as a result of the withdrawal of the PLO and allied forces following Israel's Litani operation. From 1979, the South Lebanon enclave fought against pro-Syrian Islamist militias, and Hizbollah. Colonel Barakat ob-served that most Western governments and the United Nations sided with the oppressive pro-Syrian regime in Beirut. In contrast with Bosnia, Ko-sovo, and the Palestinians, the South Lebanese Army (SLA) had never been allowed to achieve political representation, and the various world bodies refused to grant it that opportunity,he added. Hence, with the Is-raeli unilateral withdrawal (23 May 2000), the population of the enclave was at the mercy of the Hizbollah and the pro-Syrian regime in Beirut. It was an abandonment by the international community. However: "*Not only were they abandoned by the international community, but they have no official cause recognized as such*" (italics, B.Y.), Barakat remarked. After describing the op-pression of the south Lebanese population by the Hizbollah, Charbel Bara-kat concluded his testimony:

In view of the above facts, we cannot but conclude that the South Lebanon community, which was isolated because of a civil war and denied its political rights by the current pro-Syrian regime in Beirut, was punished for defending itself and for believing in popular and cultural peace across the border [with Israel] for the last quarter of a century. [. . .]

This community was never heard, its aspiration never legitimized and its security and freedom never guaranteed. The international community did not listen to its fears prior to the Israeli withdrawal, and did not recognize its tragedy after it unfolded.

Moreover, the native SLA was demonized as "collaborators" and "mercenaries" while Hizbollah was upgraded and rewarded. [. . .]

In sum we, the native population of South Lebanon, were not liberated but forced to leave. Those who stayed behind are not free but under oppression. And worse, our cause as refugees and oppressed is not even recognized by the international community.[32]

This shameful policy of the international community illustrates perfectly the strategy of dhimmitude which brought about the destruction of Christian communities by Christians themselves. The Lebanese Christian resistance was doubly punished by the Christian West: 1) because its revolt bore witness to its freedom and the justice of its cause; 2) because it was allied to Israel. Like those Christians who saved Jews at the time of the Shoah and were criticized, shunned, or punished by their governments for so doing.

For a century—in relation to Islam—European antisemitic and anti-Zionist policies had striven to maintain the hatred and separation between Jews and Christians. Thus, most "Arabists" rejected the normal interpretation of the koranic verse forbidding Muslims to have relationships with Jews and Christians on the grounds that they were friends with each other. They claimed that this verse meant that the Christians were friends with fellow Christians, and the Jews with their fellow Jews—and not that Jews and Christians were friends with one another.

However, Muslims often refuted such explanations. In a Friday sermon on 13 October 2000, in the Zayed bin Sultan Aal Nahyan mosque in Gaza, broadcast live on the official Palestinian Authority (PA) television, Dr. Ahmad Abu Halabiya, member of the PA-appointed "Fatwa Council" and former acting Rector of the Islamic University in Gaza, explained:[33]

[. . .] Allah the almighty has called upon us not to ally with the Jews or the Christians, not to like them, not to become their partners, not to support them, and not to sign agreements with them. And he who does that is one of them, as Allah said: "O you who believe, do not take the Jews and the Christians as allies, for they are allies of one another. Who from among you takes them as allies will indeed be one of them. [. . .]"

[. . .] The Jews are the allies of the Christians, and the Christians are the allies of the Jews, despite the enmity that exists between them.

Have no mercy on the Jews, no matter where they are, in any country. Fight them wherever you are. Wherever you meet them, kill them. Wherever you are, kill those Jews and those Americans who are like them.

Thus, the strategy of dhimmitude strove not only to destroy Christians by manipulating one group against another, but also, as has already been seen, to sabotage any Judeo-Christian rapprochement. It was for this rapprochement that the Christians of south Lebanon were punished so harshly. For European anti-Zionists, Christian Arabism's ultimate goal was the destruction of Israel. This is why any Eastern Christian alliance with Israel was viewed as a betrayal, and the traitors deserved the utmost contempt and hatred. This is also why European politicians, as a general rule, never recognized the Christian Lebanese cause, nor any *dhimmi* cause.

The abandonment of the Christian *dhimmis* by the Western powers, and the silence of the Churches about the persecutions they endured—although states and Churches were perfectly informed on the subject—are reminiscent of similar attitudes during the genocide of both the Armenians and the Jews. So serious is this moral indifference that it now threatens the very survival of the West.

Old Teachings in New Bottles

The anti-Zionist policy which developed in Europe from the end of the 1960s came from two sources: governments and Churches. These two sources coalesce but their aims and characteristics are different. Governments protect their states' strategic and economic interests in the Muslim world by a consensus of silence on conflicts, persecutions, and the massacres of Christians by Muslims, for which they frequently blame Israel, as being the source of all troubles.

On 12 February 2001, the newly elected Greek Catholic Melkite Patriarch of Antioch, Gregory III, celebrated mass in the Basilica of St. Peter's in the Vatican with Pope John Paul II, accompanied by a group of 700 Melkite pilgrims from the five continents. The patriarch declared that, for him, the pope represented "a precious support for the Palestinian cause."

> One cannot allow a particular people [Israel] to derange the peace and the equilibrium of such a large number of Arab countries, spreading wars and hatred, ruining them economically, and thus putting the Christian presence in danger.

The patriarch insisted that the Catholic Melkites were "Arab and Christian." They formed "the Church of the Arabs" and even "the Church of Islam, partner of Islam and bearer of the Church of Christ to this world." He added that the Melkite Church—born in 1724 and united with Rome—was the greatest catalyst in the Near East, the greatest protagonist of the Arab cause, and above all the Palestinian cause.

In his study of eliminationist antisemitism, Goldhagen notes:

> The language and accusations of racist antisemitism leave no doubt that the
> Jew was the source of, and was more or less identified with, everything awry
> in society.[34]

States practice a materialistic and nonhumanitarian policy except when
humanitarianism is politically profitable. Anti-Zionism, institutionalized in
political discourse and in the media, aimed to condition public opinion
and neutralize its opposition by disinformation or omission. Anti-Zionism,
like antisemitism, had already acquired a solid and wide institutional and
political support. Referring to eliminationist antisemitism, Goldhagen explains that, by the eve of World War I,

> a discourse—namely a discussion structured by a stable framework with
> widely accepted reference points, images, and explicit elaborations—had for
> over thirty years been in place with regard to the Jews. (p. 80)

The same analysis could be applied to anti-Zionism. This frame of reference with regard to Israel was "Zionism equals racism"—and Israel equals
injustice, nazism, colonization, occupied lands, and so on. In connection
with the banalization of genocide, Goldhagen mentioned:

> The toll of these decades of verbal, literary, institutionally organized, and
> political antisemitism was wearing down even those who, true to Enlighten-
> ment principles, had resisted the demonization of the Jews. (p. 81)

In his book, *L'Antisémitisme de Plume 1940–1944*, Taguieff examined the
political, literary, and media sources of state antisemitism, and anti-Jewish
racism in France at that period:

> The propagandist state favored the constitution, diffusion and inculcation
> of standardized themes of a mass political culture [. . .] of anti-Jewish inspira-
> tion.[35]

The same structure was applied in Europe to anti-Zionism in order to
mobilize and condition a popular public opinion which originally had
been favorable to Israel and hesitant about the alignment of a policy—at
first French-inspired, then European—on the Arab theses which two decades later were replacing the Nazi theses of the 1930s.

Anti-Zionism as an ideology represents an eliminationist policy. It expresses all the characteristics of Nazi genocidal antisemitism in which the
Jews manifested—according to Goldhagen—"a central cultural symbol, the
symbol of all that was awry in the world" (p. 67). No other conflict had

acquired such obsessional cosmological centrality. Anti-Zionists—like anti-semites before them, and now—wanted to believe that the demise of Israel as a state would again inaugurate a Muslim-Christian golden age. As Gold-hagen expressed it:

> Nazi common sense—that the Jews must disappear forever were the millennium to come—was at the root of the genocidal impulse. (p. 163)

This genocidal impulse took the form of the obfuscation of the human, cultural, and historical reality of Israel, of its continuity in history, and of its legitimacy. The suppression of the word "Israel"—and Jerusalem as its capital—already implied a social and political death.

For more than a century, these theses have been disseminated throughout the world to form an accumulation of documentation against Israel. No cause has been so much proclaimed and debated at the United Nations, in European, and Islamic countries on every continent before and after the Shoah than the delegitimization of Israel. European antisemitism moved almost uninterruptedly from pre-war anti-Judaism and antisemitism to anti-Zionism, supported covertly or openly by a certain European left, or right wing political parties, as well as religious hierarchies. One can discern here different interests at work, depending on the theological, political, strategic, or economic context.

First, theological anti-Zionism, which represents a majority current in the Church, pursues a long-term eliminationist policy. Its absolute priority, as the Latin Patriarch of Jerusalem Michel Sabbah explained, consisted of maintaining a Muslim-Christian force, irrespective of the price to be paid in Christian victims. Once again, anti-Zionism is diffused in the same way as was the traditional antisemitism spread by the Churches in the nineteenth and twentieth centuries: by sermons, circulars, directives. This same mechanism is put at the service of a virulent anti-Zionism and of pro-Palestinianism, although it is indiscernable whether the initiative comes from the Churches or from those states which ask their religious hierarchies to condition their communities to an anti-Zionist policy. This antisemitic/anti-Zionist propaganda, distributed in the West by the representative centers of the Churches, is remote-controlled and fashioned by the Palestinian Arab Churches in Jerusalem, *dhimmi* Churches, bound to Islamic policy by terror and centuries of dhimmitude.

During the beginning of the second *intifada*—from October into 2001—priests and pastors sent e-mail messages from Jerusalem inciting hatred of Israel. One such text was sent on 2 October 2000 by Father Stephane Joulain, a French Coordinator of the Jerusalem-based Catholic Office of Justice and Peace and of the Integrality of Creation (JPIC). It came from the Office of the White Fathers and was intended for widespread distribution as its heading indicates, printed in bold characters and underlined: "For Publication." Fr. Joulain accused Ariel Sharon of responsibility for the massacres of Sabra and Chatilla, committed, as is well known, by Christian militias, whose civilian populations had suffered far greater massacres at the hands of the Palestinians, led by Arafat in Lebanon, all of which had rarely been mentioned. Joulain accused Israel of being entirely responsible for the murderous Palestinian *tanzim* attacks on the Jewish neighborhood of Gilo (Jerusalem), in accordance with the demonological theological vision of Israel. As with all antisemites—and like the Nazis who projected the cause of their pathological hatred onto the Jews—he claimed that Israel itself had created the violence and the hatred. The "Justice and Peace" organization called on the international community "to take the sanctions necessary to isolate it [Israel]," in other words, to reinstate the former status for the Jews maintained by the Church over the centuries. Father Joulain's conclusion was unambiguous:

> In the twenty-first century the international community cannot tolerate the presence in its ranks of a country which is still in military occupation of land belonging to another people and which utilizes such violence. If one tolerates compromises of fundamental human rights, all mankind will suffer.[36]

Thus the international community was called upon—by a Catholic White Father in Jerusalem, connected to a Catholic organization—to expel Israel from the community of nations, a reminder of the prohibition on the right of the Jews to exist, making them the "universal peril" threatening mankind. In an "NB," after providing full details on his organization, Fr. Joulain acknowledges that his text does not represent the official position of the Churches in the Holy Land, but only the coordinating office of the JPIC in Jerusalem.

On 21 February 2001, an article appeared in the Palestinian Authority's daily *Al-Ayyam* in which the chairman of the Palestinian National Council, Salim Az-Za'anun, warned that the PLO was preparing to contest Israel's membership in the United Nations. (*PMW*)

Goldhagen's work on eliminationist antisemitism as a latent ideology of extermination could equally be applied to anti-Zionism. Anti-Zionism and Palestinianism developed as monstrous appendages of the Shoah, by way of a stratagem of substitution and the outlet of repressed hatred, which transferred the history of the Holocaust to the Palestinian Arabs. This calculation is all the more cynical in that leaders of the Palestinian Arabs at that time—both Muslim and Christian—were the most fervent admirers and allies of Hitler, whose genocidal strategy they had adopted.

Palestinianism, as set out by numerous Christian clergymen, draws on the two essential elements of theological anti-Judaism: 1) supersession: the

Muslim and Christian Arab "Palestinian people" replacing Israel; 2) the demonization of the Jewish people for seizing a country which is not theirs. This theology of substitution has three aspects: theological; historical; and political.

The theological argument challenges Israel's identity and three millennia of history in its homeland, including its martyrdom during thirteen centuries of dhimmitude under Islam. This represents a return to the cycle of existential negationism in which Israel is *not* Israel, but the usurper of an identity, of a history, and of a land, all of which are not its own. This Christian current claims that Jesus and the Jews of Judea in the first century were Palestinian Arabs. No longer is it the Church—too weak compared with Islam—which supplants Israel, but Arabism or "Palestinianism," the matrix of Muslim-Christianity (see below, p. 388).

The Muslim supersessionist current claims that the whole biblical history of Israel and Christianity is Islamic history, that all the Prophets, Kings of Israel and Judea, and Jesus were Muslims. That the People of the Book should dare to challenge this statement is intolerable arrogance for an Islamic theologian. Jews and Christians are thus deprived of their Holy Scriptures and of their salvific value. The biblical geography of Israel, in which villages and towns with Hebrew names indicate Jewish agglomerations, likewise constitutes the Muslim heritage. Although few Palestinian towns are mentioned in Arab writings until well after the Muslim colonization of the country, the history of Israel is considered Muslim history, in the same way as the whole history of mankind is considered Muslim history.

As a prelude to the probable emergence of a Palestinian state, the myths of Palestinianism are being conceived in Europe. This involves creating a national Muslim-Christian history which would stretch back to the eighth century Arabization of the Palestinian Christians, celebrated as the dawn of Muslim-Christian nationalism. In fact, this Arabization was imposed on the *dhimmis* by Caliph Abd al-Malik (685–705) who ordered the Arabization of the whole administration of the Byzantine and Sassanid territories occupied by the conquering Arabs. All *dhimmis,* and not only the Christians of Palestine, were forced to accept this Arabization, although they were forbidden to use the Arabic alphabet, considered too sacred for infidels. Whatever efforts are used to reinvent history, all the documents bear witness to the dhimmitude of Christians and Jews in a Palestine colonized by Arabs. The anachronistic projection of a Palestinian Muslim-Christian nationalism onto the eighth century, whereas the invaders originated from a multitude of tribes from Arabia, is irrational. National sentiment did not even exist among these Bedouin tribes; how could it exist between them and the Christians whom they had despoiled?

"Palestinianism" deliberately masked the ideological elements of the processes which destroyed the Christian and Jewish communities in the

Muslim countries and caused their exodus. It developed the networks of dhimmitude in the West which propagated Arab victimization themes and Western guilt toward them. This tendency revived the Christian *dhimmis'* language of servile conciliation.

Such a policy, as has been seen, which obeyed the demands and directives of the Arab League, was denounced and challenged by numerous writers. If anti-Zionism today is a subculture of defamation widespread in Western Europe since the 1960s, it is because it has benefited from the unofficial approval of the highest political and religious authorities.

The Armenian Genocide and the Shoah

The Armenian genocide, perpetrated in the Anatolian and Arab provinces of the Turkish Empire (1915–17), and the genocide of European Jewry some twenty-five years later, have been the subject of much discussion by specialists. Without entering into the core of these debates, it is still possible to observe certain similarities—but also great differences—in several aspects of these two monstrous crimes.

The Armenian genocide is a tragic extension of a long history of dhimmitude, marked in the course of conquests and invasions by deportations, enslavement, and massacres. These events, to which the chroniclers sometimes devote a few words, are followed by periods of silence, marking the places where the former peoples once lived.

The Armenians' fate belongs to the cycles of an institutionalized war of conquest. Its laws decreed in the eighth century by theologian-jurists—and still not revoked—prescribe the punishment of enemy combatants by repressive measures which modern international law has defined and decreed as "genocide." These measures are: the slaughter of all pubescent males, deportation, and enslavement of women and children. If the population submits, they are spared genocide, as inscribed in the *jihad*-war, and are protected; if they rebel, the genocidal law is restored. The repetitive recurrence of these theological and political events forms the historic background of dhimmitude.

The Jewish position in relation to traditional Christianity—officially abolished after Vatican II—also occupies a central place of a religious and political nature: the de-Judaization of Jerusalem and the condemnation of the Jews to wander among the nations.

It should be stressed that even if the *dhimmi* status of the Armenians and the condition of the Jews in the Christian communities overlap in the area of politics and religion, these areas do not represent identical situations. First, politics and religion are kept separate in Christian societies, a separation that Islam forbids. Although generally theoretical, this separation allowed some political independence from the Church and from canon law. This opening, which grew with modernity, enabled Christians to abolish the discriminatory status that applied to Jews, to impose their emancipation, and even to encourage Zionism. The genocide of European Jews was not an inevitability. It was not predetermined in Judeo-Christian relations, even if the eliminationist current was expressed in widespread antisemitic circles from the end of the nineteenth century, and by the pogromist policies in Russia and in the Balkans. As numerous Christian theologians have noted, the genocide of the Jews—a phase in Israel's elimination—represents the most serious flaw in Christian thought and ethics.

This diversity in Christian policies toward the Jews which existed throughout the centuries did not develop in Islam. Muslim involvement in the emancipation of the *dhimmis* is nonexistent in the whole history of dhimmitude. In fact, the Armenian genocide was programmed into the context of *jihad* and only a foreign intervention could have prevented it. There were certainly individual acts of heroism by Muslims on behalf of Armenians, but solely out of compassion and on individual initiatives. Apart from these differences in the respective groups of persecutors, there are two basic elements that are characteristic of the Holocaust, but absent from the Armenian genocide: 1) genetic racism; 2) a policy aiming at the total extermination of a human group.

However, bonds do exist linking these two human catastrophes, separated by a generation. The situation of Zionist Jews in Ottoman Palestine was similar to the position of the Armenians throughout the empire. This shared danger gave birth to a genre of Zionist literature in the early twentieth century which identified with the Armenians' tragedy and displayed deep empathy for their indescribable suffering. It is undeniable that Zionism had placed the Jews of the Ottoman Empire in an identical potential situation to that initiated by the Christian nationalisms in their Islamized lands. The reforms demanded by the Armenians in their provinces were not dissimilar to those claimed by the Jews in Palestine. As far as the Turks and the Arabs were concerned, the Armenian struggle—like that of Palestinian Jewry—aimed to revive their mother tongue, recover their religious freedom, civil autonomy, security, and the right to study their national and historical heritage, which had been confiscated by Islamic occupation and colonization, whether Turkish or Arab.

In his book, *The Banality of Indifference*, Yair Auron, an Israeli scholar, has published an important study on the attitudes of the different Jewish political movements toward the Armenians from the early twentieth century.[37] Perpetrated in the heart of the Arab provinces, the massacres of the Armenians constituted a traumatizing potential threat for all Christians, and Jews—particularly the Zionists—in the Turkish empire. The government of the Young Turks made no secret of its intention to inflict upon the Jews in

Palestine the same fate as they had reserved for the Armenians. Consequently, this shared context of national emancipation encouraged the identification of certain Zionist circles with the Armenian martyrdom.

From other aspects, however, the situation of the Jews was totally different from that of the Armenians. The Jews of the Turkish Empire were a small percentage of the world Jewish population and, for centuries, the Turkish authorities had protected them from the religious fanaticism—often including murder—of Christian *rayas,* particularly Roman Catholic and Greek Orthodox Syrian-Palestinians. The majority of the European Jewish population at the turn of the century lived in a fundamentally hostile culture—manifested by blood libel accusations, pogroms, and defamation, institutionalized by Church teaching and doctrine, combined with political propaganda. Thus, unlike the Armenians, a Christian people, the Jews were threatened by multiple dangers deriving, not only from Zionism in Palestine, but equally and in no small measure from antisemitism in the Christian world.

Moreover, it was in Christianized Europe that the Holocaust had been planned, announced, and executed. The genocidal crimes committed by Muslims against the rebel Christian populations were reproduced by the Germans—allied with the Turks during World War I—against the Jews during World War II. The Nazi were supported—either actively, or through a self-imposed silence, or the refusal to save the victims—by a Europe which had recently betrayed the Armenians and the Eastern Christians of the Levant. Reports of the extermination of the Armenians which Palestinian Jews—mainly Aaron Aaronsohn of the pro-British Nili group—sent to the allies and, above all, the activity of the American ambassador Henry Morgenthau, himself a Jew, strongly influenced American and British opinion. American Jewry's activism had contributed to America's entry into the war and consequently to Germany's defeat. These two factors increased Hitler's paranoid anti-Jewish fixation—being a soldier of a routed German army, which had decamped from the Levant and its Armenian charnel-houses.

The extermination of the Armenians was perpetrated in Anatolia, Iraq, and Syria. Arab officers in the Turkish army had also been directly involved and the local Arab populations of these provinces benefited by way of booty and slaves. As Aaron Aaronsohn wrote at the time in his report "Pro-Armenia":

> It might be asked: what part of the population or of the organized public services was carrying out those wholesale destructions of Armenian life and property. The reply is that no class of the Mohammedan population, rich or poor, high or low, young or old, men or women kept away from murdering and robbing, which of course does not mean to say that every individual Mohammedan is to be blamed without exceptions. A few noteworthy exceptions

were reported, cases of individual help tendered by old Turks are known, but they were very rare, isolated and always rebuffed by the authorities, military and civil.[38]

Those Arab officers in the Turkish army, like the future Mufti of Jerusalem, collaborated with the Germans. During World War II some of them remained loyal to their former allies, took refuge in Berlin, and supported the Nazis. They formed the bridges and connections from one genocide to the next.

During the two World Wars the Arab populations represented a permanent danger for the Allies. This strategic factor was the motive for the abandonment, respectively, of the Christian and Jewish victims. Through pressure and threats of reprisals on states and *dhimmi* communities, the Young Turks succeeded in isolating the Armenians. Another member of the Nili group, Alexander Aaronsohn—Aaron's younger brother—was horrified at the massacres of the Armenians. Arriving in New York in September 1915 on a mission, he wrote a report on these events and criticized the passivity of the rest of the world.

Yet the Christian nations are looking on the martyrdom of a race and they cowardly turn their eyes away. In vain does the blood of their brethren cry from earth, they close their ears and say: we are not our brothers' keepers.[39]

The abandonment of the victims by third parties is the result of one of the strategies of *jihad,* which aims to isolate the targeted people by threats and by the exacerbation of inter-*dhimmis* conflicts. The isolationist tactics of neutralizing the victim, precedes the genocide. This tactic of isolationism was practiced against the Lebanese Christians, and constantly against the Israelis.

The Armenian tragedy is not an unique phenomenon; it belongs to an immense historical cycle of dhimmitude that still operates—in Lebanon, Sudan, in the war against Israel, and in the other Muslim-Christian conflicts. This cycle has its own characteristics, linked to the principles and values of the civilizations of *jihad.* Germany has officially acknowledged the Shoah; other countries, sometimes fifty years later, took cognizance of the responsibility of their governments of the time. But Turkey, although the most civilized Muslim country, continues to deny the past and to forbid other countries—recently the United States and France—to acknowledge the events nearly a century after their occurrence. This irrational attitude is part of the historical negationism which has obliterated the whole history of dhimmitude. Like the Lebanese Christian Charbel Barakat, Armenians can say, "Not only were they abandoned by the international community, but they have no official cause recognized as such."

Inter-Religious Dialogue and Dhimmitude

Today, we can only welcome the modern tendency toward ecumenism, and the dialogue between civilizations. This very important aspect of international relations makes it possible to break down the barriers of prejudice to permit true universal brotherhood. The work of rapprochement in respect of the religion and culture of others is nonetheless fraught with problems. In fact, the relationship between the three monotheistic religions is asymmetrical in every respect. Relations between Church and Synagogue are not parallel. The Bible does not mention the Christians and advocates no specific doctrine or jurisdiction concerning them. In contrast, Christianity, born of Judaism, developed a doctrine on the basis of patristic writings which asserted that the Church—not the Jews or Jewish history—was the *True Israel* (*Verus Israel*). It imposed a legal, political, and social anti-Judaism based on religious teaching for Christendom. These elements are nonexistent in Judaism regarding Christians.

In relation to Islam, the position of Judaism and Christianity is both similar and different. The Jewish and Christian Scriptures do not mention Muslims; they are not the subject of any specific doctrine or jurisdiction. However, the Church's position toward Muslims differs from its position toward Jews. Christianity does not proclaim that it was the True Islam (*Verus Islam*); it did not drive the Muslims out of Mecca by forbidding them to reside there. Unlike Jewry, deprived of any political power, Christians and Muslims built empires that were in constant confrontation.

Islam, on the contrary, places Judaism and Christianity in an identical position. Islam is considered as the "True Judaism" and the "True Christianity." Jews and Christians are mentioned frequently in the Koran, the *sunna*, and in biographies of the Prophet. These normative writings formulate a doctrine concerning them, and a theological jurisdiction which they must be forced to abide by, as an obligation imposed on them. It is this Judeo-Christian bonding which, paradoxically, makes it impossible for Christians to achieve a reconciliation with Islam *against* Israel—reconciliation can only succeed *via* Israel, and *with* Israel. However, reconciliation with Israel involves rejecting the theologies of substitution, abandonment of *jihad*, and liberation from dhimmitude. Hence, the road to freedom for Christians is contrary to the knavery of *dhimmi* clergies.

The doctrinal position concerning the Jews and Christians, inscribed in the Islamic revelation, unlike the Bible, constitutes the major obstacle to rapprochement with Islam. No demand for different interpretations was formulated by official European political or religious organisms. Anti-Zionism and economic interests have concealed these problems which remain unresolved.

Judeo-Christian Rapprochement and anti-Zionism

Here it should be stressed that it was in European societies that diverse movements of liberation militated for the emancipation of the Jews, alongside the struggle against traditional prejudices, the abolition of slavery, and the granting of equal rights. These aims were pursued decade after decade—from the eighteenth century, and even earlier—first by Christians, and later by Jews. It was in European and in American societies that these biblically-inspired ideals were thought out by pious Christians and secular rationalists, and slowly, somewhat reluctantly, enforced by governments. Principles of human equality are alien to many cultures. The Judeo-Christian dialogue and rapprochement belongs to this ongoing process, which was started by Christians. Many books have been devoted to these aspects, but the subject is too vast to be examined in this conclusion.

The rapprochement with the Jewish people after World War II took place at two levels which the Churches deliberately separated: the theological level of Judeo-Christian relations; and the Israel/Palestine political level. It could be said that each successful advance on the first plane was immediately counterbalanced by a greater regression on the second, which canceled out the first; it was as if the two movements of the scales were perfectly adjusted and synchronized. Thus, the closer the Christian world drew toward reconciliation with Judaism, the louder grew the clamor supporting the Palestinian cause which negated Israel's existence. Much has been written on the subject of the Judeo-Christian rapprochement since *Nostra Aetate*. Each declaration, each step was analyzed and discussed. And each movement toward the Jews was contradicted by multiple assurances of support for the Palestinians. In this way, public opinion was successfully persuaded to reconcile respect for the dead victims of antisemitism with a culture of hostility for the living Israelis that questions and endangers their existential rights.

These maneuvers were denounced by many Christian historians, clergymen and intellectuals. And, first and foremost, Pope John-Paul II initiated important steps toward Jews, Judaism, and Israel, but gestures are not policies. And despite his historic pilgrimage to Jerusalem in March 2000, and the intense emotions aroused by his presence at Yad Vashem—and the moving meditation of the ailing and courageous pope at the Western Wall—the pro-Palestinian policy of the Vatican has remained constant. The body of Christendom, represented by the Palestinian *dhimmi* clergies—Catholic, Protestant, and Orthodox—deliberately chose Arafat as the acclaimed protector of Christianity's holy places. This choice of Arafat—Nobel Peace Laureate and erstwhile godfather of international terrorism, champion of *jihad,* and destroyer of Lebanese Christianity—was the culmination of anti-Zionist political choices going back to the nineteenth century. In a remarkably well-documented book on traditional Christian antisemitism and its evolution into anti-Zionism, Paul Giniewski concluded that the delegitimization of Israel perpetuated the theology of the fall and degradation: "the language, the spiteful grudge of certain Christian texts is explicable in the light of this betrayal, of this Zionist aggression against a certain theology."[40]

Of all the currents that run through the Vatican and the World Council of Churches, anti-Zionism is the most powerful, supported by the West's strategic interests in the Muslim world. For the Jubilee 2000 Christmas celebrations in Strasbourg, Europe's parliamentary capital, it was officially proposed to create, not a Judean, but a Palestinian village next to the Cathedral for the traditional Christmas market. This was in line with a common tendency in European churches to dress the Holy Family—including the Jews of Jesus's time—in anachronistic Arab Bedouin dress.

The Patriarch of Jerusalem, Michel Sabbah—a friend and admirer of Arafat—was to be the guest speaker. Following strong protests by a large number of Jews and Christians, the speech and the propaganda piece were belatedly cancelled at the end of November.

To my knowledge neither the Vatican nor the World Council of Churches has officially condemned anti-Zionism as a criminal ideology advocating the elimination of the State of Israel. European policy is automatically pro-Arab, pro-Islamic, and consequently anti-Zionist—and thus anti-Christian.

European anti-Zionism represents a medium-term program devised by dominant political and religious currents. This policy was marked by a tendency to obfuscate Israel's existence particularly during the 1980s; by a refusal to recognize even West Jerusalem as its capital, and the boycott by Europe—and the media—of the trimillennia celebrations of the "City of David". The constant denigration and condemnation by international bodies and government-controlled media and the policy aimed at isolating it internationally, has propagated a general anti-Zionist subculture, based on disinformation, ignorance, and amalgams. Worst of all, since the late 1960s at the instigation of the Arab League, a false symmetry has been mediatized between a Palestinian Arab people, representing a civilization of *jihad* and dhimmitude, and Israel's rights in its homeland, liberated from *jihad* and dhimmitude. In fact, the denial of the historical and cultural rights of the Jews in Israel is tantamount to denying the whole history of Christianity. This denial of Israel's historical rights, which is the concealed position of the ruling political circles in the European Union and the Palestinian *dhimmi* Churches, is at the origin of Europe's own self-repudiation.

All the traditional antisemitic policies which led to the Shoah are visible in this global picture. The Europe which finances the Palestinian Authority's territories, in spite of proven massive corruption, shares in the collective responsibility for the culture of genocidal hatred which is taught there in schools, universities and through the media. Thus, European taxpayers contribute unwittingly to this incitement. Here, it is important to emphasize that the principle concerning the relinquishment of land in exchange for peace and security is in accordance with the injunctions of *jihad*. Except for the Arabian peninsula, all the Arab countries consist of land yielded by Christians and others to Arab armies in exchange for the peace and security of dhimmitude.

One should not let these ambiguities overshadow the spectacular progress accomplished within the Roman Catholic and the Reformed Churches. The advance there concerns the suppression of any form of antisemitism in theology, dogma, and liturgy. These important achievements certainly represent a revolution which would have been unthinkable twenty years ago. After World War II and the trauma of the Shoah, the Judeo-Christian dialogue was established at the level of the religious hierarchies and worked to recognize Judaism in its essence. The determined efforts of many Catholics culminated in the Vatican's recognition of the State of Israel in 1993.

The Judeo-Christian reconciliation movement could be initiated and could develop due to a Christian current combining receptivity and openness. It would be a difficult task to list all the Christians, who by their struggles and their writings testified to the complementarity of the two religions and their roots in the same values. After World War II it was in this congenial soil, and through a mutual wish for rapprochement, that a dialogue germinated which allowed the Jews the possibility of expressing themselves freely, and granted Christians the moral strength and courage to confront traditional antisemitism.

It should be noted that this type of dialogue does not exist in the realm of dhimmitude. There, only servile speech is permitted. It is important, therefore, to acknowledge this major quality of self-criticism in a society, of self-examination, deeply anchored in biblical values and without which change and improvement in human relations are impossible. In dhimmitude, the victim's restricted speech can only be expressed through lies, blocking dialogue and the work of memory which transforms the individual's whole being. Consequently, the Muslim-Christian dialogue carried on by the *dhimmi* clergy was lacking, because it wished to model itself on the Judeo-Christian dialogue on the basis of a fictitious parallelism between Islam and Judaism. The Lebanese, Sudanese, and Indonesian *jihad*—to name but three: the exodus of the Christian *dhimmis;* the taking of hostages from the West; and the assassination of *harbis* by Islamists are all played out behind the soporific screen of commonplace anti-Israeli declarations.

The abrogation of the dogma of contempt for the Jews also liberates the Church from a poison that deformed its message. Moreover, it allows the Church to ask from Muslim authorities the same attitude in respect of

Christians. For their part, the Jews cannot, out of opportunism, profess a negationist version of Christian suffering in Muslim lands, because a joint testimony of dhimmitude depends on a combined effort and cannot emerge when there is contempt between the two *dhimmi* peoples. The reconciliation of the two People of the Book should encourage the Muslims to freely associate themselves in this interfaith reappraisal. The rapprochement between Israel and the Vatican constitutes a landmark along this path. The vociferous anti-Zionist hatred propagated in Europe should not overshadow the Christian rapproachement with Judaism, achieved by a motivated clergy and the general public.

The Dialogue with Islam

Because critical dialoguc with a *dhimmi* is forbidden, the movement for reform and openness toward the non-Muslim did not exist in the *umma*. The abolition of dhimmitude and slavery was imposed by Europe and this loss of superiority and privilege was felt as a humiliation. Humiliation is caused by the frustration of a self overvaluation vis-à-vis the vilified person, who henceforth becomes an equal; humiliation is felt in a relationship of equality with a scorned person. The lack of a *sui generis* openness to the Other enclosed the Muslim-Christian dialogue in the tradition of dhimmitude, that is to say, of flattery. Islamic prejudice toward the Christian faith has led Christian theologians to deform their faith by "Islamizing" or "Palestinizing" its origins. Here one might reflect on whether the Islamization of Christianity results from a revived Marcionite Christian initiative, or from the Islamic rejection of an *equality in difference*—whence the need to erase this difference by a form of "Islamization."

Another major aspect lies in the work of historical criticism, constantly operating in Western Judeo-Christian societies and nonexistent in the closed societies of *jihad* and dhimmitude, where it is replaced by the theme of *the perfection of the golden age and of the Islamic government of the shari'a*. All these elements block the development of Muslim critical thought about its relationship to the *harbis,* the non-Muslims living outside the *dar al-Islam* and not yet subjected by *jihad;* as well as to the *dhimmis,* the non-Muslims subjected by *jihad* to the *dhimma* "pact of protection."

Even the refutation of the myth of the Islamic golden age is only carried out through the Islamic prism by evoking the misfortunes of Muslim societies at specific times when the *shari'a* was not correctly applied. Never do the victories of *jihad* give rise to reflections on the sufferings of its victims. The whole work of relativizing the rights of the Arab Muslims, and of their own image, which should have been accomplished by their confrontation with the abrogated rights of the *dhimmis*, their abject exploitation, humiliation, and martyrdom was not attempted. This process was blocked by the glorification of tolerance and of Arabism, carried out by Arabists and the *dhimmi* Christian communities, and by countless Arabophile European politicians.

The demonization of an aggressive, imperialist, and colonial West strengthens religious stereotypes. The idealization of *jihad*, described as almost pacific military parades welcomed by the vanquished and the omission of indigenous cultures destroyed on Islamized lands, forge a Manichean vision of mankind. It blocks any effort to remove the sacred aura from *jihad*, and consequently obstructs awareness of the legitimacy of any other ethnoreligious group. It is, however, solely this acceptance of another's rights, which would make it possible to accept the equality of human beings and the legitimacy of the pluralism of both cultures and sovereignties.

At the cultural level, the teaching of Islamic preeminence in the cultural, scientific, and historical movement of mankind contradicts the deontological principles of knowledge in Western societies. The misconception born of this cultural imperialism, adopted—sometimes for convenience with a lapidary phrase—in some encyclopedias and history textbooks, undermines the scholarship and integrity of research which is still respected in Western academic circles. Moreover, this lip-service procedure strengthens the paranoid ravings and the rejection of the Otherness, since science and modern technology are only acceptable by the *ulema* through the medium of having had an Islamic origin.

One example will illustrate these different viewpoints. While Christians, including theologians, are foremost in acknowledging the history of Christian anti-Judaism and a host of past errors toward other groups and populations (that include Muslims), most Muslims intellectuals and scholars avoid recognizing the evils that *jihad* and dhimmitude inflicted on its victims over the centuries. Richard Neuhaus, editor-in-chief of *First Things*, consecrated a long essay to this and other themes related to *jihad* from the viewpoint of the subjected Christians and Jews. Immediately after its publication in October 1997, both he and the journal itself—published by an inter-religious, nonpartisan research and education institute—were attacked via a press release, the web and e-mail letters by Ibrahim Hooper, National Communications Director for the Council on American-Islamic Relations (CAIR), a Washington-based Islamic advocacy group, and their supporters. After this strong reaction—"and dozens and dozens of letters from as far away as Australia"—Father Neuhaus wrote a rejoinder, entitled "Islamic Encounters":[41]

"Venomous diatribe." "Hateful xenophobia." "Doing the work of Adolf Hitler." "Agitating for a new crusade." "Obviously mentally ill." Such were among the sentiments expressed in response to my review in the October 1997 issue of Bat Ye'or's important new book recently published in this country, *The Decline of Eastern Christianity under Islam. From Jihad to Dhimmitude*. In my comment I indicated the difficulties in establishing a respectful dialogue with contemporary Islam, but it really need not be *this* difficult. [. . .] The campaign obviously had the aim of intimidating into silence anyone who dares to say anything less than complementary about things Muslim. [p. 62]

And in his concluding remarks, he rightly pointed out that

the liberal democratic tradition is in largest part the product of Christianity, especially the Christian imperative of self-criticism and openness to the other [. . .] To date, there have not been similar developments in Islamic societies. This does not mean that Islam is necessarily incompatible with liberal democracy. [pp. 63–64]

Answering CAIR's diatribe, affirming an equivalence between a Judeo-Christian and a Muslim-Christian dialogue, Neuhaus commented:

There are dialogues and then there are dialogues. Some Jewish-Christian dialogues are exercises in niceness, pretending that differences make little or no difference. To such dialogues Muslims, or for that matter almost anyone else, can be invited without difficulty. Then there is dialogue in the service of truth, and the truth is that Islam is not to Christianity what Judaism is to Christianity. For starters, Islam is not, as Judaism is, an integral part of the Christian understanding of the story of salvation. [p. 64]

As far as Judeo-Christian relations are concerned, it has been shown above how the Arab League states, by their threats on the Eastern Christian communities, constituted a major factor for keeping alive the concept of the "deicide people" even though it contradicts Islam's doctrine of an unsuccessful crucifixion of Jesus. This stance contributed greatly to poisoning the climate between Jews and Christians by constantly exploiting the conflicts which they were trying to solve. Such a tendency runs the risk of extending into the future, reproducing in Europe the same inter-religious conflicts of dhimmitude.

Today, one must not conceal the basic problems, which are fundamental problems of civilization. For over fifty years they have been camouflaged under the cloak of anti-Zionism, and their discussion and analysis deliberately obfuscated.

At the theological level, the doctrinal differences have barely changed. The Koran provides its own interpretation of biblical events and gives a somewhat different version than that of the original. For Muslims, it is the Koran alone which is the original divine message, the biblical narrative being no more than a falsified Revelation. These important divergences on the subject of the persons and events described in two distinct accounts give rise to a fundamental religious conflict—contradictions which were analyzed by Heribert Busse in his *Islam, Judaism and Christianity*. The theological conflict primarily concerns the Land of Israel. Christian antisemitism had denied to the Jews historical rights by the doctrine of the fallen deicide people. For Islam, this same refusal results from a historical negationism which Islamizes all Jewish and Christian biblical history. Any Church support for Islamic negationist policy concerning Israel strengthens its own negation, which Islamic doctrine has integrated into that of Israel's origins.

The statement that Islam is at the origin of the world implies the Islamization of the history of mankind. Jews and Christians are seen as usurpers, for the biblical narrative of the history of the Israelites—and then of Christianity—in the land of Israel is not the history of the Jews and Christians, but of the Muslims. One understands why Muslim immigrants in Europe object to the expression "Judeo-Christian values." Such a term is actually meaningless for traditionalists, since all the biblical values are considered Islamic as a result of the Islamization of the Hebrew Patriarchs, Prophets, of Moses, Jesus, and his Apostles. Today, some European politicians have begun to *avoid* speaking of "Judeo-Christianity," only referring to the values of a Greco-Roman civilization in order not to offend their Muslim electorate. It is clear that acknowledgment of other peoples and cultures in their historical and religious integrality and specificity, and not as insolent usurpers of Islamic history, involves a fundamental theological change. Here, it must be emphasized that the interpretative approach of the sacred Scriptures by Jews and Christians is different from that of Muslims. As Professor Busse noted:

> According to Muslim faith, the Koran in its entirety is a divine revelation, announced to the Prophet by the angel Gabriel sentence for sentence, word for word, syllable for syllable, and letter for letter, for him to pass on to his community.[42]

One wonders whether the verses which are hostile to the Jews and Christians, those containing incitement to fight and subject them, or those which condemn them to eternal hellfire, are open to a different interpretation today. The same applies to the *hadiths*, the sacred sayings attributed to the Prophet.

At the historical level, Muslims usually deny any assertion that they were conquerors, but claim to have been liberators. As mankind is considered "Muslim," therefore Muslims were living in every country before the appearance of the Prophet. Hence, they cannot accept a sentence like, for instance, Professor Samuel Huntington's: "From its origins Islam expanded by conquest," or:

> The spread of Islam in the seventh century was accompanied by massive migrations of Arab peoples, "the scale and speed" of which were unprecedented, into the lands of the Byzantine and Sassanian empires.[43] (inverted commas in the original)

From the Muslim point of view *jihad* did not despoil the conquered peoples, it merely "restored" to the Muslims the infidels' property which Allah intended for them from the Creation. Discussion on this subject has not yet been seriously addressed. It is, however, of the greatest importance as it involves the legitimacy of the West.

At the legal level, the Western concept of human rights based on the principle that "all human beings are born free and equal in dignity and rights" (article 1 of the 1948 Universal Declaration of Human Rights) is in contradiction with the "Cairo Declaration of Human Rights in Islam" (5 August 1990), which is subject to the provisions of the *shari'a* and, thereby, perpetuates the inequality of the sexes and of religions (see p. 198 above). The earlier Universal Islamic Declaration of Human Rights (UIDHR), drafted on the initiative of the Islamic Council for Europe and proclaimed at UNESCO in Paris on 19 September 1981, defined the rights of the individual "according to the Law." The Explanatory Notes attached to the English version of the UIDHR stated that "the Law" meant the *shari'a*, which is

> the totality of ordinances derived from the Qur'an and Sunnah and any other laws that are deduced from these two sources by methods considered valid in Islamic jurisprudence.[44]

This conflict of jurisdiction, not only has repercussions at an international level, but presents an additional difficulty for the integration into Europe and elsewhere of large immigrant Muslim populations. The latter would be subject to the binding legal *shari'a* code which only acknowledges the condition of their indigenous Western compatriots as *dhimmis*. On 18 February 1994 the Sudanese delegation to the 50th session of the UN Commission on Human Rights in Geneva submitted its *Comments on the Report of the Special Rapporteur, Mr. Gaspar Biro*. It opened with the following statement:

> All Muslims are ordained by God to subject themselves to Sharia Laws and that matter could not be contested or challenged by any Special Rapporteur or other UN agencies or representatives.[45]

It is interesting to examine the arguments the Sudanese government employed to dispute Mr. Biro's report, because they explain the deep divergences between Western and Islamic conceptions of human rights. The
main criticism of the Khartoum government consisted in accusing Biro of
desiring

> the abolition of Shari'a Laws in the Sudan, and its tools are the collection of
> allegations of human rights' violations from whatever source. [. . .] At the
> outset, we would like to start these comments by expressing our clear and
> irreversible position that all references in the report, direct or indirect, to
> the abolition of Shari'a legislations [sic] in the Sudan are unacceptable
> firstly, because they are naked violations of religious freedom guaranteed by
> the main human rights conventions including Article 18 of the Universal
> Declaration of Human Rights and Article 18 of the International Covenant
> on Civil and Political Rights. (p.3, § 2–3)

On 15 February 2000, Biro gave evidence in Washington to the newly
created U.S. Commission on International Religious Freedom. The following quotations are taken from his written testimony.[46] On the subject of
the Criminal Act of 1991, the Sudanese government's 1994 document had
stressed that:

> These laws apply to Muslims and Christians alike, and Christians could not
> claim special prerogatives to defy the law just because the UN Secretary Gen-
> eral or the Special Rapporteur are of the same faith.

Biro, however, emphasized that "the situation remains confused, both
regarding the interpretation and the application of the quoted legal provisions," which provide such punishments as death, crucifixion, amputation
of the right hand and left foot, or imprisonment. For example, concerning
apostasy, the 1994 Sudanese government document stated:

> The rule of apostasy is unanimously upheld by Muslims as part of their faith.
> The government, the rapporteur and any other earthy [sic] power is power-
> less to change it. The government's interpretation of it is the most liberal
> there is on the spectrum of Muslim opinion.

Biro quoted Article 126 of the Criminal Act of 1991, still in force in the
Sudan:

> (2) Whoever commits apostasy, shall be given a chance to repent during a
> period to be determined by the court; where he insists upon apostasy, and
> not being a recent convert to Islam, [he] shall be punished with death.
> (3) The penalty provided for apostasy shall be remitted whenever the apos-
> tate recants apostasy before execution.

Biro declared that "in relation with punishments like amputation, stoning, crucifixion, or flogging, the government stated in its UN-circulated 1994 statement the following":

> Whether these forms of punishments are harsh or not , Muslims are obliged to apply them provided that all elements of the offence are satisfied. Muslims have no choice but to apply them because they form an integral part of their religion.

As regards the specific legislation on the status, rights and duties of woman in the Sudan, the government's *Comments* on the UNSR's Report stated:

> We would like the Special Rapporteur to know that [it] is part of the ordain [*sic*] of God, and as such comes under freedom of religion guaranteed by the various human rights covenants and for those reasons combined we don't tolerate any comments regarding the issue. (§ 117)

In September 2000, Khartoum's state governor issued a decree barring women from working in many public places, saying the ban would uphold Islamic law and maintain the honor of women. *Reuters* also reported that Sudan's president "refuses to sign a United Nations treaty on women's rights because it goes against family values" (14 January 2001).

These texts on Sudan are quoted because they illuminate the problems of integration and cohabitation which will arise between Western societies and Muslim immigrant populations, if the latter adhere to a religious legal code which the Western democratic societies reject. It is a fact that Islamists and the traditional Islamic current consider Islamic law as emanating from the divine will and insist that all Muslims have an obligation to conform to it. These multifarious problems concern Muslim relations with Jews and Christians—and with Judeo-Christian civilizations—which had forged the relationships of dhimmitude. As they have not been clarified by the *ulema*, they have now been imported into Western countries unchallenged where they continue to fester. The great majority of Muslim intellectuals have not fully understood that their own freedom is linked to the respect for the freedom of others, and to the rejection of any ideologies involving contempt and domination over their fellow human beings.

I have endeavored in this study to examine this particular Islamist current linked to dhimmitude, which is the overall subject of my research. However, it must be clearly stated that such dogmatic opinions cannot be attributed indiscriminately to all Muslims, but they should nonetheless be denounced by them.

It would be wrong to think that the immigrant Muslim population monolithically adheres to these principles. A large number of intellectuals, writers, artists, or ordinary citizens have risked their lives to fight obscurantism. The best known, mediatically, are Salman Rushdie and Talisman Nasrin, but there are hundreds more. In his courageous book, *Why I am not a Muslim*, Ibn Warraq criticized all religious fanaticism.[47]

Also, among theologians living mainly in the West, are to be found modern interpretations of traditional texts which initiate a fraternal openness toward other religions and cultures. To this category belongs the innovative and courageous work of Sheikh Professor Abdul Hadi Palazzi, secretary-general of the Italian Muslim Association, and imam of the Italian Islamic community. His profound knowledge of Islamic religious texts, and his deep personal faith, are combined in a fruitful research for unprejudiced interfaith and multicultural relationships. Nevertheless, these effort remain limited and are in no way representative.

The failure of democratization and the absence of freedom of opinion in a *Jihad* civilization results from the nondialogue with the Other, whose testimony, that is to say, his different opinion, was always rejected. It is because for centuries no atonement—or even regrets—were made for the humiliation of the *dhimmis,* to restore them a voice and their freedom, that Muslim intellectuals today are themselves condemned to silence in their own countries.

The Third Millennium and the Continuum of History

From early October 2000, the second Palestinian *intifada* war—waged with stones, bullets, and fire-bombs, but also via the world's media—highlighted all the perversions of Christian and European dhimmitude. During and after the Jewish New Year–Yom Kippur period, the PLO's armed *tanzim* snipers—mainly Muslims, but also some Christians—*deliberately* chose to shoot indiscriminately at *Jewish homes* in the Jerusalem suburb of Gilo, from the rooftops of *Christian houses* in Beit Sahour and Beit Jalah, just outside Bethlehem. The aim was to provoke an Israeli military response on *Christian homes*. In spite of the anti-Israeli propaganda campaigns by their leaders, scores of Christians—a tiny minority of 30,000, one percent of the three million Arab Palestinian population of Gaza and the "West Bank"—again began seeking visas to flee "Arab Palestine." The same reasons that drove hundreds of thousands of indigenous Christians and Jews to leave Middle East Arab countries during the last half century has motivated an increased Christian emigration from Arab Palestine—but not from Israel where they are about four times more numerous. Moreover, the *al-Aqsa intifada* totally destroyed the Palestinian economy, generously subsidized by the European Union and Muslim countries.

On the Christian side, the Jerusalem Latin Patriarchate seized the occasion to demonstrate its "service" to the cause. By e-mail messages—an average of one every three days—it stoked a pernicious anti-Israeli media campaign in the West. This *dhimmi Olive Branch from Jerusalem* Newsletter from the Holy Land, was initiated by Father Raed Awad Abusahlia, chancellor of the Latin Patriarchate. It aimed at convincing Western Churches and groups to influence their governments in favor of the Palestinian cause and to exert maximum pressure on Israel. Thus, Christian fears of Islamist extremism in the Holy Land was once again used to arouse Western hostility and retaliations against Israel.

On the media level, this anti-Israel campaign was typical of the manipulated media war against all peoples or minorities resisting *jihad* or the return of dhimmitude in their countries. In the case of Israel, the false mirrors technique was particularly flagrant; for instance, Palestinian children using slings—like David against Goliath. This symbol, borrowed from Jewish biblical history, does not exist in the Koran; the clash between David and Goliath mentioned in the Koran does not refer to a sling, and has nothing in common with the original biblical account.

The position of Arab Christian Palestinians was clearly explained by Fr. Abusahlia in several of his *Olive Branch* issues. On 6 November he explains that Muslim and Christian Arabs form one united bloc: "Christian presence among the Palestinian leadership is very considerable; most of the closed [*sic*] collaborators of president Arafat are Christians." He then cites PLO leaders Nayif Hawatma and George Habash as good examples. Already in the issue of 9 October he affirmed that Christians are so inseparable from the Muslims that they should not even be called a minority:

Here I would like to comment on a dominant mentality, which must be resisted, the tendency to call the Christians in the Orient "a minority" within "a majority" which is not Christian. I repeat the call for the cancellation of these words from the dictionary of our relations. The insistence here is that we are not a minority at all, for this word carries with it the complex of weakness and persecution, fear, alienation and perplexity. We are not weak, persecuted, scared, cringing minority; nor are we alien or imported or foreign.

This declaration echoes similar statements by the Uniate Patriarchs of Iraq in 1934, just after the massacres of Christians. They refused any minority rights' protection, knowing that *shari'a* law punishes by death a *dhimmi* community's reliance on foreign aid. The *al-Aqsa intifada* allowed the chancellor of the Latin Patriarchate to clarify the position of the Arab Palestinian Christians. His explanations seem to imply that their rights in the Holy Land are rooted in their Arabness, not in any Jewish history in the Holy Land. Christianity emerged from Palestinian Arabness. It is Arab Palestine which is the heir to biblical history, not the people of Israel which is constantly deprived of its identity and history. Thus, in the same issue of 9 October, Fr. Abusahlia invokes the presence of Arabs in Jerusalem during Pentecost at the time of Jesus:

> The Acts of the Apostles reminds us of the presence of Arabs among those in Jerusalem on the day of the descent of the Holy Spirit on the Feast of Pentecost, at the beginning of the Church, when the Apostles began preaching Christianity. (Acts 2:11)

The Arabs in Jerusalem at Pentecost to whom the Latin chancellor refers (Acts 2:11)—in order to root Palestine and Christianity in Arabism—are mentioned as follows in Acts 2:5:

> And there were dwelling at Jerusalem Jews, devout men, out of every nation under heaven.

The next verse (Acts 2:6) states that all these Jews—including those from Arabia—started to speak in their own distinctive languages, an image borrowed from Jewish prophetism. The nations then enumerated in Acts 2:9–11 follow an ancient astrological calendar of the time in which the peoples around the Mediterranean and beyond were attached to the signs of the Zodiac, hence the reference to Judea and Arabia, among others. Thus, in spite of Father Abusahlia's dialectics, Christianity remains rooted in Judaism, and not in Arabism or Arabia, where Christians did not exist then, and are barely tolerated even today.

Christian presence in the Holy Land is justified by the Apostles: "We are the successors of the Apostles, the heirs of the prophets and the saints," writes Raed Abusahlia. These Apostles and the biblical Prophets are no longer Jews in the Land of Israel—since the patriarch's chancellor refuses the same historical rights to the Jews in their ancestral homeland—but they are called "Palestinian Arabs." Fr. Abusahlia also stresses that: "The Arab identity of the Christians was reinforced by the Islamic conquest." This is, apparently, a *dhimmi* interpretation of the expulsions, massacres, and exile of all the Christianized Arab tribes expelled from Arabia—with the Arab Jews—by Islam soon after the Prophet's death.

To prove Christianity's deep roots in Arabia, Abusahlia refers to a "splendid article" entitled "Arabism the space of my faith," written by his colleague Fr. Rafiq Khoury, "considered one of the most important local theologians" and "brain worker of the Latin Patriarchate." According to the chancellor's description, Fr. Khoury shows how:

> Arabism is an inseparable part of the Holy Land Christian identity in Palestine and in the Arab world. It is even a part of the Christian Credo. I consider this "identity card" a piece of art and a summing up of our Christian position concerning this issue.

Fr. Khoury's credo contains, *inter alia*, the following declaration:

Arabness is the space of my faith. [. . .] My faith needs Arabness for its human depth. [. . .] Arabness has need of my faith in order for it to be Arabness. [. . .] Arabness is the space of my faith and the depth of my mission and the document of my accreditation. Thus ends the words of my "identity card" but I would add to them: Palestine is the space of my faith.

Thus Christian faith is steeped in Arabness, in Islam. This may explain Christianity's world support for conceding the protection of its Holy Places to an acknowledged initiator of international terrorism, the "Nobel Peace Laureate" and Arab Palestinian *jihad* hero, whose strategic goal remains the destruction of the State of Israel on the appropriate occasion. The birth of Jesus within the Jewish people has a salvific importance for Christianity. The repudiation of its origins, and its engagement in the war against Israel represents a parricidal act. And one can wonder at the ethic and the future of a parricide.

As Habib Malek has stressed, Palestinian voices do not represent all the opinions of Arab Christianity. Palestinian terrorism against defenseless people and diplomacy stifle the truth. Western anti-Zionist policy since the nineteenth century had inevitably led to this shameful situation, where Yasser Arafat has been delegated—on the threshold of a new millennium—as the defender of over two billion Christians against six million Israelis, among whom five million Jews, but also a million Christians, Druzes, Muslims, and others. Until April 2001, no Western government, nor any religious official body, has had the courage to deny him that honorific accreditation.

The destruction of Joseph's tomb—a Jewish shrine—by a raging Palestinian mob, followed by the savage lynching of two Israeli reservists in Ramallah (12 October 2000), seen worldwide on TV, had a negative impact on international opinion. This worried the Christian community in and around Bethlehem and the region of Hebron. Toine van Teeffelen, a Dutchman living there, described this image problem in an article published in the 23 October issue of *Olive Branch*:

At my institute for community education in Bethlehem we talk about how to present the Palestinian youth. There should be more public and media involvement of youth who do not participate in the fighting. They should register and communicate stories they communicate and hear. We are going to set up a youth group in which Palestinian youth from 15 years on reflect about what they can do. Especially girls are forced to stay inside after school, they cannot express their emotions outside the family.

Later, in his newsletter of 23 November, Fr. Abusahlia explained that van Teeffelen had received his doctorate in Discourse Analysis from the University of Amsterdam (1992), with a thesis on English language best-selling stories about the Palestine/Israel conflict. Many stories were then published in the international media, depicting the suffering of a peaceful Palestinian youth faced with Israeli military inhumanity. Hence, Palestinian mob violence on TV was counterbalanced by the peace-loving, nonaggressive Muslim-Christian Palestinian victims of Israel.

As already indicated, the different currents of the war against Israel are easily recognizable. Certain European ones endeavor to fabricate a similar Palestinian tragedy to that of European Jewry. This trend bases itself on a pathological obsession with the Shoah, nourished by a hatred of its victims (the Jews), whose tragic fate is transferred to their actual enemies (Arab Palestinians). This perverse substitution process expresses not only the frustration of European antisemitism, which instrumentalized the Palestinians in their war against Israel, but also banalizes the crimes that occurred throughout Europe by turning the victims into the guilty party. Thus, Israel becomes guilty for its survival; it should have disappeared in the aftermath of the Shoah. In spite of an astute disguise under the label "Justice and Peace," this new policy depicts the diabolic pathology of traditional antisemitism.

The Islamist anti-Israel current, however, is foreign to the European historical context, which is the *dar al-harb*. The Muslim war against Israel is a war against the infidel, conducted today in a similar *jihad*-like manner in other parts of the world. In this context, the Christians are considered as merely mercenaries—clients for the cause—who are even more despised than the Israelis themselves.

The *Olive Branch*'s propaganda campaign from Jerusalem, beamed to the West, is part and parcel of this recycled first current. The institute mentioned by van Teeffelen is the Arab Educational Institute in Bethlehem for Community Education, associated with the "Euro-Arab Dialogue from Below" project and an affiliated member organization of Pax Christi International whose international Secretariat continues to work closely with the Latin Patriarchate. Under the direction of van Teeffelen, this institute has collected written or narrated stories from young people, mainly young girls and women who were preferred for their greater sentimental effectiveness. The stories concentrated on themes that relate to Jewish experience in World War II. The themes listed below are taken from the 22 November 2000 issue of *Olive Branch*.

1) "Stories of the killing of innocent people, especially children." This theme evokes the civil Jewish population exterminated in Europe, especially the one and a half million children deported and deliberately slaughtered in a program of total extermination. Hence the importance in the

European media of the accidental death of 12-year-old Muhammed al-Dura in a shooting exchange, who is depicted as "an allegory of the larger Palestinian story of vulnerability and suffering."

2) "Humiliation stories," where "Israel soldiers are said to have become increasingly inhuman." These stories are said to portray "people's violated feelings of morality." And here, once again, the aim is clear to recall the Yad Vashem pictures showing Nazi soldiers humiliating Jews, including children.

3) "Stories of abandonment," where Palestinians feel abandoned by the whole world and "betrayed by the international community."

4) "First reactions stories," depicting people's reactions to "unexpected happenings or unexpected news," such as bombing and shootings.

5) "Stories of hiding," which describe how Palestinians "tell each other how to look for safety with friends," and to comfort each other with prayer and reading the Bible. "Some stories show that it is impossible to hide, which again shows the ever-present vulnerability."

Other themes are proposed: rescue and escape stories, travel stories, and so on.

The overall tone of those projects for "stories" is an impressionist picture of an Arab Palestinian society that mirrors the abandonment of European Jewry sixty years ago; the consensus of silence; the arrest of Jews at home, work or schools; their unwarranted deportations; their expulsions from their homes. Like the Jews in Nazi Europe, Palestinians need to hide, to look for safety with friends—as did Anne Frank; they are a hunted, vulnerable people who escape and need to be rescued. It would seem as if a professional, or a team of researchers, has very minutely examined Jewish suffering during World War II, so as to transfer the same image onto the Arab Palestinians. Countless times, Palestinian leaders have declared that they have become the Jews of Europe's injustice and are paying for Europe's crimes against the Jews. Of course, the reality is exactly the opposite. Arab Palestinians are far from being abandoned by the world. The international media concentrates an inordinate amount of time on them; they enjoy total support from the European Community, the fifty-four countries of the Organization of the Islamic Conference, and other states in the Americas, Africa, and Asia. Hundreds of millions of dollars regularly pour into the Palestinian Authority's treasury, in spite of a generalized corruption among the administration. The Palestinians have their own government, police, and autonomous territory from where they wage a terrorist *jihad*-war whose aim is Israel's destruction.

The wave of antisemitism that has spread throughout Europe and the world since October 2000—with Arafat's *intifada*—received much inspiration from the widely publicized "stories" and opinions of this Euro-Arab Institute, repeatedly reproduced throughout the world on television, radio, and in the press. This international network's efficiency raises questions as to the wide powers of this new Arab Educational Institute in Bethlehem.

In the fall of 2000 this Institute became an Affiliate Organization movement within Pax Christi International (PCI), a powerful Catholic NGO, active at the United Nations and other international bodies. PCI has always unilaterally defended and promoted "Palestinian rights" on the grounds of "justice," and the traditional replacement theology, whereby "Palestine" replaces "Israel." Since 1999 its International Secretariat has worked closely with the Latin Patriarchate in Jerusalem and the Institute of Bethlehem. The masking of a Palestinian terrorist *jihad* fighting "occupation" with the Jewish history of the Holocaust is constantly worked out and evoked in allegorical images by this Institute and its European collaborators, mostly clergy. It expresses perfectly the conception of a *redemptive* Palestine through a Christian struggle against Israel's evilness, its true face which is revealed by Palestinian suffering similar to the Holocaust. This theme is repeated in different forms, one example of which appeared in the 59th issue of the *Olive Branch* before Easter (31 March 2001).

Under the title: "The power of the weak", two American volunteers, Marthame and Elizabeth Sanders, wrote an article on the "blossoming" of "this *Intifada*'s non-violent resistance," and in

> the last few weeks peaceful Palestinian marches and demonstrations against the Occupation have been organized in Gaza, Ramallah, Bethlehem, Nablus, and Jenin.

The Israeli are represented as the strong who use "military weaponry (. . .) demonization, manipulation, propaganda, religious fervor", while "the Palestinians are weak". They concluded that:

> The power of the weak will defeat the power of the strong every time. And in its victory, all of the violence, power, terror, brutality, and cruelty will be redeemed. This is the message of the cross—that the one who accepted its fate is the one who gave redemption to those who sought to destroy him. Friends, help us to fight our battles here with the power of the weak. We shall celebrate its perfected victory together. Salaam-Shalom-Peace.

The theme of the immense Jewish Peril and its power, determined to destroy the cross—that is, the Church and Christianity—continues to flourish and to be propagated by the Roman Catholic Patriarchate. In his introduction to this 59th issue, chancellor Fr. Raed Abusahlia stressed that the conclusion to the above article "complete my above-mentioned ideas about the nonviolent choice for the Palestinian resistance" [*sic*]. He also gave a "homepage" message from his brother, a Swiss citizen—the same Dr. Sami Aldeeb Abusahlia, professor at the University of Fribourg and Lausanne, who in 1986 distinguished himself by printing a pamphlet entitled "Paix en Palestine" that reproduced an alleged speech by Benjamin Franklin from 1789, which was revealed to be a Nazi fake already in the 1930s:[48]

> There is a great danger for the United States of America. This great danger is the Jew. Gentlemen, in every land the Jews have settled, they have depressed the moral level and lowered the degree of commercial honesty. (. . .) I warn you, Gentlemen, if you do not exclude the Jews forever, your children and your children's children will curse you in their graves.

It is noteworthy that it was the Roman Catholic Community of Jerusalem which was the first to publish an Arabic translation of *The Protocols of the Elders of Zion* (see above, p. 169).

In this same Issue no. 59 of *Olive Branch*, Dr. Maria C. Khoury, a school-teacher, complained: "Our country is so destroyed," and "the American government has shut their eyes to the atrocities carried out by Israelis." She then reproduced excerpts from essays written by children from the Catholic Palestinian schools for a Writing Contest launched by the Latin Patriarchate from ten schools, about their families and the current situation in Palestine. She plunged herself into reading them until "the winning words sparkled across the pages". Here are some of those sparkles: "Since 1948, our people gave thousands and thousands of martyrs . . ."—"Every Palestinian family panics in every minute, because the Israeli soldiers shoot their innocent children in cold blood"—"The Israeli soldiers began to kill people without any mercy, they used many of their mean weapons in killing them, and they bombed their houses and their lands . . . they killed children in a very savage way."—"Every day we see the soldiers kill children and every night they bombed houses . . ."—"Several people die every day by Israeli soldiers."—"They destroy many houses and many people . . ."—". . . but the children of Israel are playing and happy."—"I'm so sad because Israelis killed hundreds of people."

The same issue published the written Statement by Pax Christi International submitted to the 57th session of the UN Commission on Human Rights (19 March—27 April 2001), issued as E/CN.4/2001/NGO/7. This statement enunciates five principles which it wants imposed as a new framework for negotiations and agreements between the Palestinians, Israel, and the European Union. Three expound the radical French interpretation of the 1967 UN Security Council Resolution 242 (based on the non-binding text in French, rather than the original English); the same interpretation of Resolution 338 (1973), and the equally non-binding UN General Assembly Resolution 194 on the return of refugees. PCI demands "that the peace process must be based on international law," and, as a measure of "peace and justice", it implicitly calls for the massive influx of five millions Arab Palestinians into Israel:

A first step in the solution of this refugee problem is the recognition by Israel that it was instrumental in creating the problem in the first place. (§2)

PCI also insists that a UN force must monitor human rights violations in Israel and in the "occupied territories".

The official policy of PCI toward the State of Israel can only be expressed with the approval of its International President, Bishop Michel Sabbah, the Patriarch of Jerusalem, who was elected in Amman in 1999. This policy of the Latin Patriarchate is clearly explained by its Chancellor in numerous *Olive Branch* issues. Some of its main principles are here summarized:

1) Christianity is born from Arabness; 2) Palestine belongs only to Christians and Muslims, while Israel occupies a land to which it has no right; 3) Palestinian Christians are one flesh and one soul with the Muslim Palestinians—this includes the *Hamas* Islamist movement. Many Palestinian Christians, well-known for their terrorist activities in which Jewish civilians were killed, are greatly honored and admired; 4) The expropriation of the Jewish people's heritage, and its martyrdom in its own country by the regime of dhimmitude, is described as a past golden age of Muslim-Christian symbiosis in a shared system of "justice." The abolition of this system by Israel's liberation in its homeland is an "injustice" that must be repaired and for which Israel should not only apologize, but also acquiesce in its own demise.

Pax Christi is represented at the top level in the Vatican. Its Arab international president is Arafat's advocate to the Christian world. Through Pax Christi International's network, the Arafat eliminationist policy has dominated the world, spreading hatred from the mosques and churches of East Jerusalem, Ramallah, and Gaza.

At a time when Muslim persecutions against Christians were on the rise in several countries of Africa and Asia, from October 2000 a relentlessly hostile media campaign against Israel helped to ignite a wave of anti-Jewish attacks in Europe fueling antisemitic tendencies. Security services had to be reinforced around synagogues, schools, and Jewish community centers—whereas no mosque needed to be guarded. The beginning of the third millennium in Europe evokes the 1930s—with hatred gaining ground and anti-Jewish terror developing, mainly in France. A constant frustration—apparently due to Israel's survival and its growing demographic and military strength, rather than its predicted fall to Arab-Muslim hostility—has shaped a violent anti-Israel campaign of disinformation.

This outburst, which certain European political groups have encouraged, could destroy the delicate process of reconciliation between Church and Synagogue. During the last fifty years, Church hierarchies obfuscated the reality of Israel, awaiting the disappearance of this vulnerable state seen as an accident of history. They did not understand that Israel's liberation was also the Churches' liberation, and that the real nature of the negotiation between Israel and its enemies was the abolition of the ideologies of hate and substitution of the *jihad* civilization, of which it too was a victim. Neither the Churches, nor Europe joined Israel in this titanic struggle, but rather they preferred to aggravate the situation, and this is why they both remain chained to it.

While public opinion is generally sympathetic to Israel, antisemitism is still commonplace at top political and economic echelons in Europe, filtering its influence through to the government and the media. Attacks on Jewish targets allowed politicians once again to condemn solemnly all xenophobia and antisemitism, although it was clear that it was mainly Muslim immigrants who were attacking Jewish civilians and symbols, following a violent politically correct anti-Israeli media campaign. Meanwhile, reports on the genocidal campaigns in the Sudan or the Moluccas—or even the almost daily massacres in Algeria, on France's doorsteps—were given sparse treatment, when even mentioned.

The fundamental position of the Arab Christians in the Holy Land has hardly changed since the nineteenth century war against the "Universal Jewish Peril," and the translation into Arabic of the worst, racist, anti-Jewish European propaganda. Because of their Arabness, it is claimed, Christians are heirs of the Apostles, although these latter were not Arabs, but Jews in the Land of Israel. Christian rights in the Holy Land are based on history and permanence. However, Jewish rights which are much more ancient and rooted in a permanent Jewish presence in the Holy Land, in spite of Christian persecution of the Jews there, are denied. Hence, "Arab Christianity in Palestine" affirms its rights within Marcionite Christianity, renewing in a new Arab supersessionism the theology of a fallen Israel, even though Roman Palestine—before and after the two severe defeats in 70 CE and 135 CE, and even after Christianity—is linked with Jewish history and identity.

The reflection in 1934 of the Rev. James Parkes, a great pioneering Christian thinker, theologian and moralist, aptly fits this situation:

> We may at first wonder why the attempt to prove the reality of the Divinity of Christ made it necessary to falsify the whole of Jewish history, as the Gentile Church undoubtedly did, but if we study their approach to the problem we see that they were led on inescapably by the method of their own argumentation from the first legitimate assumption to the last and most extravagant fabrications.[49]

Any history of dhimmitude, all its modern expressions, the entire contents from the first to the last pages of this book, are known—in one form or another—to all Western governments and diplomats, the Churches, and every knowledgable journalist.

A few examples for the year 2000 are cited merely as a reminder:

In the Philippines, Catholics and Protestants were attacked by the soldiers of the Holy War. Peasants in the village of Sumugod, in the province of South Lano, were carried off in July by a hundred soldiers of the *jihad*, taken to a mosque, tortured, and assassinated.

In Nigeria, the Church is anxious about Islamization. In February and May 2000 violent confrontations between Christians and Muslims, connected with the introduction of the *shari'a* in certain states, caused more than 2,000 deaths in the north of the country. In February 2001, nine out of thirty-six states applied the *shari'a*. The offenses of theft and adultery are punished by amputation, stoning, or corporal punishment, depending on circumstances. Islamic courts have been set up to supervise the application of Islamic law. More states envisage adopting the *shari'a*. Speaking on the BBC (6 February 2001), the Archbishop of Canterbury, George Carey, referred to the impossibility of building churches or teaching any religion other than Islam in the State of Zamfara. Christianity was declining in northern Nigeria because of the progressive introduction of the *shari'a* law.

In Indonesia—in spite of the repeated attempts by President Abdurrahman Wahid, a leading Muslim scholar, to oppose extremism and violence which he strongly condemned—the situation of Christians became desperate. In his appeal on 19 December 2000 to UN Secretary-General Kofi Annan, the Bishop of Amboina, Peter Mandagi, referred to the tragic events in the Moluccas (Spice Islands) since April:

> There have been countless acts of savagery, depravedness [*sic*] and criminality, such as torturing, raping of women and other sexual abuse, persecution, slaughtering, looting, and destroying of property [. . .] The criminals, lawbreakers and human rights violators are roaming about and undertake any mischief at leisure. So what is prevailing now is the law of the jungle, barbarism and savagery . . .

More details are provided in Appendix 6, entitled "Indonesia—East Timor and the Moluccas."

In the Sudan, the abduction of hundreds of women and children as well as deportations are regularly carried out, according to the last interim report to the General Assembly presented on 11 September 2000 by Leonardo Franco, the UN Special Rapporteur. It is the custom for the Popular Defense Forces (PDF) to gang-rape enslaved women and girls during forced marches to the Government of Sudan (GOS) territory and to execute those who cannot walk quickly enough. Sudanese slaves taken to the north are routinely subjected to beatings, sexual abuse, work without pay, and forced conversion.

In November 2000, President Omar Hasan al-Bashir facilitated more slave raiding when urging 12,000 PDF troops in the western town of Nyala to continue the *jihad* in Southern Sudan (*AFP*, Khartoum, 17 November 2000). On 20 November twenty-four children were enslaved and seven executed at Guong Nowh Community Elementary School. On 3 and 12 January 2001, 175 women and children were abducted as slaves and the International Committee of the Red Cross announced that its clinic had been looted (*Reuters*, 19 January). On 21 January, CSI's press release reported fifteen villages raided, fifty-three civilians killed, including fourteen children and twenty-three women, seventy-two women and children enslaved, tens of thousands displaced civilians, herds stolen. These attacks were conducted by the regular Sudanese army and their PDF militia. For years the GOS has declared a *jihad* against the black African communities of Southern Sudan that resist its policies of Islamization and Arabization. Father Hilary Boma, a Sudanese Catholic priest—released on 6 December 1999 after eighteen months of arbitrary detention in a Khartoum prison—declared in an interview in Rome to the Vatican agency "*Fides*" (17 May 2000):

> As long as Khartoum continues to look towards the Middle East and not at Africa, and consider itself first Arab and then African, it will be against Christianity, and its problem will never be solved.

Fr. Boma was in charge of both Church/Government relations and Church/Muslim relations.

None of the Christian or animist children deliberately enslaved, converted to Islam by force, mutilated, obliged to flee, or killed had his photograph blown up in the Western press. And none of them was mentioned, nor their fate pitied. But Muhammad al-Dura, a Muslim Palestinian child—accidentally killed in a cross-fire exchange between Palestinians who initiated it, and Israelis—became the most well-known child victim on the globe. He was an effective banner for antisemitic and revengeful frustration against Israel—for the million and a half Jewish children deliberately rounded up, deported, and killed in Europe sixty years earlier. The serious Geneva daily, *Le Temps*, chose this tragedy as the "photograph of the year" (30 December 2000).

Historical and political negationist currents contaminated every field, spreading in policies, media, and books. This comprehensive conditioning overlooked the plight of Christians in Muslim lands. As one example, the Arab League's negation of Sudanese slavery was echoed by the UN Commission on Human Rights in April 2000. The member states of the European Union, individually and collectively, as well as Canada, played a key role in the Commission's decision. These Western states have endeavored to protect their strategic and economic interests with the Islamic world by pursuing appeasement policies, including cooperating with the Government of Sudan in the cover-up of slavery. So as not to offend the Arab League, they refused to acknowledge slavery in Sudan, but referred to it obliquely as a problem of mere "abduction." The role of Europe has been crucial to the decision of the UN Commission on Human Rights to eliminate the use of the term "slavery" regarding Sudan and to replace it with the term "abduction" in all resolutions.

Dhimmitude has become a global way of relationship between Europe and Muslim countries. It has established at all levels a dissymmetry in respect of human rights, freedom of the press, of opinion and religion, as well as of democratic rights. The reason is that dhimmitude is not recognized as a crucially important page of world history. Hence the West has adopted the Islamic view of history, where *dhimmi* nations had no history, no culture, no existence. Indeed, *dhimmi* peoples have neither a cause nor history. They do not have the right to claim any reparations for the centuries of exile, deportations, spoilations, massacres and persecution. They do not even have the right to speak of this. And when they try to retrieve some of their homeland and part of their history, they are called aggressors and usurpers. However, it is precisely their testimony which could allow the injustice of dhimmitude to be recognized, opening the way to peace and reconciliation.

The present situation results from an ongoing process undertaken by the *dhimmi* clergy in collaboration with the anti-Zionist Churches of Europe in order to purify Christianity from its Jewish roots. This Marcionite current, whose most extreme and violent expression is manifested in Nazism, continued after World War II via Arabism and Palestinianism.

In September 1987 a "Colloque des Chrétiens du Monde Arabe" ("Colloquium of Christians from the Arab World") was held in Paris. The participants included Christian theologians and intellectuals from Europe and the Middle East, and the ambassador and director of the Arab League in Paris.[50]

The colloquium reexamined and refined the political themes of a Christian delegitimization of Israel within its Marcionite thematic theology, notwithstanding the prudence and the coded language in which it was presented. Thus, Mgr. Georges Khodr declared that

> fidelity to Jesus, the seal of the ancient prophecy, includes the absolute refusal of any Judaization in contemporary Christianism, and in general, of every historic fixism. (. . .) No salvific word will come from our mouth other than *in an unlimited love of the Muslim man.* (p. 28–29) [italics in the text]

The duty of Eastern Christianity is to strive for a meeting of brothers on the road which leads to what was "given to the Saints", to the suffering face of the Arab man. (p. 30) [inverted commas in the original]

In his address to the Colloquium, Abbé Youakim Moubarac called for the restoration of the Church of Antioch, which—he explained—means a Church liberated from Judaism, which is limited to the letter of the Scriptures, while this Church claimed its spirital message.

It is, therefore, a substitute for the theology called "the history of salvation" and its confinement in the "Judeo-Christian tradition," similar to a Procustean bed, what our Fathers called "the Economy of the Mystery." (p. 34) [inverted comas in the original]

Concerning the revival of an Arab Renaissance, Moubarac expressed his belief that Paris could be the ideal place

to centralize the functioning of a *Foundation* dedicated to *the Arab development of culture,* through the revitalization of the Antiochene heritage in all its fullness. (p. 37) [italics in the original]

The Antiochene heritage signifies here, in a perverted wording, Christianity's purification from its Jewish roots. Backed by the Arab League and its powerful networks, this anti-Israel passion has distilled hate in the West at all levels in the population, as well as in the political, intellectual, and media world. It was this relentless, concealed work, which is today exploding.

Dhimmitude, as we have tried to examine in this study, has many faces. As a political system, it is a living entity manifested by laws and behavior patterns. Today, it happens that Christians are its main victims, although not exclusively. Hence, some Christians have joined Muslims in questioning the motivation of those Jews who denounce it, for those Christians are convinced that *Jews must hate Christians* just because *Christians had formerly been taught to hate Jews.* Judaism is so much misrepresented that the essential meaning of the Bible, which is the liberation of man from physical and spiritual slavery, is soon forgotten. However, as Father Richard John Neuhaus has stressed, Jews and Christians share together this legacy. Many Christians have devoted their life and strength, enduring hardship and professional sacrifices, to defend persecuted Jews. Thus, it is also normal for Jews to denounce the oppression that Christians suffer, or anyone else. Moreover, dhimmitude concerns Jews and Christians in an identical manner, and it is impossible—unless one is cynical—to examine it for one community and not the other. Dhimmitude is based on the replacement theology, which affects in the same manner Jews and Christians. In the twenty-first century Palestinian replacement theology—entirely created during these last twenty years by European Churches, theologians and politicians, in order to undermine Israel—is threatening Christianity in a way that they could not have foreseen at the time, nor understand.

As I correct the copyedited pages of this book in early April 2001, defamation and anti-Zionism is growing in the press and state-controlled television in Europe. It is fed by powerful pro-Arab, antisemitic, political interests that condition public opinion to criminal hatred through the media. Pro-Israeli voices are rare or easily dismissed and drowned out by mass disinformation. Europe seems to be remembering its past only to repeat it.

Appendix 1:
Arab Feuds in Nineteenth-Century Palestine

Jerusalem, 2 May 1856

My Lord,

I regret to have to report that the loss of life has been considerable at Jeba in the district of Nablus, and that intelligence has reached me of aggressions with further loss of life on the plain of Esdraelon where Mohammed Hhussain 'Abdu'l Hady invaded the camp of the Turkomans. There he found some of the leading people of that district collecting taxes, namely Akili Aga and his brother, and Salehh Aga of Caiffa [Haifa]. These represented to him that he was out of his own territory, and within the Pashalic of Acre. Moreover that they were Agents of the Government, and so long as his Cousin remains Kaimakam of Nablus, it would be strange if he were to assail those under the immediate protection of Government— but he refused to listen, and a battle ensued, in which about 40 lives were lost. At the same time, the great Plain [of Esdraelon] was suddenly covered with camps of Abbâd and Meshalhhah Arabs from East of Jordan, who had come to his side.[1]

[. . .] the plain of Esdraelon, which swarmed with a disgusting set of Arabs such as he [the Kaimakam] had never seen before—and that there is no doubt of Mohammed Hhussain 'Abdu'l Hady having been guilty of the greatest atrocities, and massacre of women and children. Why such deeds should be done, during the governorship of his relative in Nablus, may perhaps be accounted for among the endless complications of Arab feuds, [1] but Christians and Europeans are inclined to look upon these unexpected invasions as forming part of a plan for universal disorder, and confounding of all rule and method—arising from dissatisfaction at the recent liberal innovations of Turkish Government. [*Hatt–i Humayun* Edict of 1856]

1. Palestine was frequently the scene of devastating traditional feuds between the Qays and Yaman Arab federated tribes from northern and southern Arabia. 'Abd al-Hadi claimed to be Yamani. See Maoz, *Ottoman Reform in Syria and Palestine 1840–1861*, 113–18.

FO 105/524 (No. 27, copy sent to London, extract)
James Finn, British Consul, Jerusalem, to
Viscount Stratford de Redcliffe, Ambassador at Constantinople.

Acre, 15 April 1877

M. le Consul-Général,

I have the honour to report to you that last Monday the 9th instant a fatal quarrel took place at Hader of Mount Carmel, between the Bedouins of the neighbourhood of Caiffa [Haifa], the Jews, and the Christians of Caiffa.

The quarrel began between the Bedouins and the Jews at Hader, and then the Christians interfered to protect the Jews.

They attacked each other with stones, and two Christians were wounded and one Bedouin dangerously so.

Afterwards the Mussulmans of Caiffa are said to have intended to make a demonstration against the Christians of Caiffa, but the presence of the "Torch" and a German frigate kept them quiet, and the matter was peaceably checked.

Yesterday evening news from Beyrout was circulated to the effect that war has been declared between Russia and Turkey.

Up to now the local Government is well disposed to maintain good order, but if the said news is true I am of the opinion that the presence of some European ship-of-war would be necessary to protect the tranquility of the Christians and Europeans residing in this country.

> PP (1877) (C.1806) 92. FO translation from the French. Moses d'Abraham Finzi, British Consular Agent, Acre, to George Jackson Eldridge, Consul-General, Beirut.

Appendix 2:
Destruction of the Jewish Quarter
Shiraz (Iran), 1910

On 21 May 1910 at the Alliance Israélite Universelle (AIU) school in Shiraz, a young Jewish teacher, Nissani Machallah, saw a sayyid (a Muslim dignitary) beating two elderly Jewish men with chains. Machallah asked the sayyid the reason for the blows. The sayyid responded by stabbing him to death. The Persian government, at the instigation of foreign powers, had to make material reparations to the victim's family. Orders were proclaimed enjoining respect for the lives of Jews. To avenge the criminal's three months imprisonment, the sayyid's clan had Korans thrown into the sewage of the Jewish quarter in order to provoke an uprising. They also falsely accused the Jews of killing a young Muslim girl.

Letter from Mr. Nataf, director of the AIU school in Shiraz, to the president of the AIU in Paris

Shiraz, Monday, 31 October 1910

[. . .] I heard these details in the school where I was at the time, and there first perceived the clamor of the crowd, which was gradually gathering in front of the government palace. Massed around the body of the alleged little Muslim girl found near the Jewish cemetery, they accused the Jews of having committed this heinous crime and demanded vengeance. It was subsequently established that the body was that of a young Jewish boy buried eight days ago and disinterred for the requirements of the cause, being completely putrefied and absolutely unrecognizable.

Then Cawam-el-Mulk, the acting governor, having ordered his troopers to disperse the frenzied mob, they headed for the Jewish quarter, where they arrived at the same time as the soldiers sent by Nasr-ed-Dowlet [military governor, whose task was to protect the Jewish quarter]. As if they were obeying orders, the latter were the first to break into the Jewish houses, thereby giving the signal to plunder. The carnage and destruction which then occurred for six to seven hours is beyond the capacity of any pen to describe. Having immediately understood the danger they risked, our core-

403

ligionists—as is the custom in such circumstances—buried everything of
value in underground hiding places. Objects which could resist immersion
in water were dropped into the ponds of house courtyards—a useless precaution. The most concealed places were totally emptied. The assailants
dived into the ponds to retrieve the objects thrown there.

Not a single one of the Jewish quarter's 260 houses was spared. Soldiery,
louts, *sayyids,* even women and children, driven and aroused less by religious fanaticism than by a frenetic need to plunder and appropriate the
Jews' possessions, engaged in a wild rush for the spoils. At one point, about
a hundred men from the Kashgaïs tribe who were in town to sell some livestock joined the first assailants, thereby completing the work of destruction.

The thieves formed a chain in the street. They passed along the line,
carpets, bundles of goods, bales of merchandise, gum tragacanth, opium,
dried fruits, skins; demijohns full of wine, brandy; utensils, caskets containing valuable objects, anything, in a word, which was saleable. That which
didn't have a commercial value or which, on account of its weight or size,
could not be carried off was, in a fury of vandalism, destroyed and broken.
The doors and windows of the houses were torn off their hinges and carried away, or smashed to pieces. The rooms and cellars were literally
ploughed up to see whether the substratum didn't conceal some wealth.

But these fanatics weren't satisfied to rob the Jews of their possessions.
They engaged in all sorts of violence against their persons. As soon as their
quarter was stormed, the Jews fled in all directions, some to the houses of
Muslim friends, others to the British Consulate, on to the terraces, and
even into mosques. A few remained to try and defend their property. They
paid for it with their lives or a serious injury. Twelve of them died in the
mêlée. Another fifteen were stabbed or hit with bludgeons, by bullets from
rifles or revolvers; they are in an alarming condition. A further forty sustained light injuries. An unlucky woman was wearing gold rings in her ears.
A soldier ordered her to surrender them. She made haste to comply and
had taken off one of the rings and was trying to remove the other when the
impatient madman found it more expeditious to tear off the earlobe together with the ring. Another woman was wearing around her neck a big
silk braid to which was attached a small silver case containing some amu-
lets. A lout tried to snatch it from her and, seeing that the braid held, cut
it with his knife, making at the same time a deep gash in the flesh of the
unfortunate Jewess. How many more such atrocious scenes must have occurred, of which I have not yet heard.

In short, the outcome of yesterday's events is as follows: 12 people dead
and about 50 more or less grievously injured, the five to six thousand people comprising the Shiraz community now possess nothing in the world

except the few tatters which they were wearing at the moment their quarter was invaded.

What is striking, and appears strange in these sad circumstances is the inertia of the local authorities, who seem to have done only one thing—encourage the soldiers in conjunction with the populace, to ruthlessly attack and plunder the Jewish quarter, and this despite my prayers and my entreaties to send in the Cossack horsemen to stop the pillage which had begun, despite the energetic and pressing remonstrances by Mr. Smart, the British consul, in liaison with Cawam [el-Mulk], the acting governor.

> *BAIU* 35 (1910), 182–86. See also the English translation of excerpts in Littman, "Jews under Muslim Rule: The Case of Persia," *WLB* 32, n.s. 49/50 (1979), 12–14.

Appendix 3:
S.O.S. Lebanon (1945). A Homeland for Christians of the Near East

Preface

United Nations

The task that you have adopted as your supreme ideal is the reconstruction of the world, a world in which communities would be able to live in freedom and human dignity.

Among these communities, the Eastern Christians, lost in the midst of the Muslim world, risk being forgotten in your reconstruction plan, merged into the term "Arab," which is improperly applied to all Middle Eastern people.

It would seem that the problem of the Jewish homeland, an enclave in a supposedly homogeneous Arab world, is the only problem in this region of the world.

But the problem is much more complex:

This data still contain a serious ambiguity; which *is of prime importance to resolve.* Why does one talk about "Arab countries" when the nations involved *display no ethnic homogeneity,* have nothing in common except their language, but for whom, on the other hand, Islam is the official religion—with the exception of Lebanon.

For the champions of Arabism, Arab Unity can only mean Islamic Unity, as is shown in chapters 11 and 12 below.

That being so, why should the solution of the problem continue to ignore the existence of the most ancient inhabitants of those countries, who are neither Arabs nor Muslims? The Eastern Christians deserve that their fate be the object of concern and that in tomorrow's world a secure and peaceful homeland be reserved for them, worthy of their past and their spiritual values. [pp. 5–6]

Chapter 3: The Muslim Conquest

[. . .] In the beginning in order to govern, these latter [the Arab conquerors] had to resort to the services of Christians, and for half a century

Greek remained the official language. Once conversant with the mechanisms of the administration, and having "Arabized" the language and state services, Abd al-Malik (687–705) and his successors began to apply strictly the precepts of the new religion in regard to Christians.

Tolerated by Law [*shari'a*] Christians and Jews could save their lives, retain their possessions and trade, on condition that they paid the capitation tax, the ransom in exchange for sparing their lives. "Fight against those who do not believe in Allah [. . .] until they pay the jizya off hand, *being subdued*" (Koran, 9:29).

On the other hand, as only worshippers of Islam were citizens (of Islam, a theocratic state), Christians and Jews did not have rights of citizenship and could not hold public office.

In his study of the land tax (kharaj) a contemporary Muslim financier Abu Yusuf, mentioned that the aforesaid Abd al-Malik ordered a census of non-Muslims in Iraq, Syria and Mosul, as well as of their wealth; after which he left each of them the necessities for food and clothing, the surplus having to be paid into the Public Treasury.

But this regime of humiliations must have seemed clement compared with the treatment to which the Abbasids later subjected the Christians. [pp. 12–13]

Chapter 7: The Ottoman Conquest

[. . .] Nevertheless Lebanon, the Christians' refuge, only experienced relative tranquillity amidst its Muslim neighbors as a result of constant vigilance by its armed men. Lebanon can therefore be said to have been living under a regime of armed peace during this entire period.

In all other parts of the Ottoman Empire, the Christians had to live in a state of subjection bordering on servitude. The regime of inequality between Muslims and Christians was raised to the height of an Institution in Public Law. [p. 19]

Chapter 9: The Arab Question

[. . .] In face of the almost total decadence of Arabism, aggravated by encroaching Turkish influence, the Eastern Christians who had eventually adopted the Arab language, had great difficulty in manipulating and humanizing this instrument of thought, which had become obsolete. For this, a valuable asset was the Western intellectual discipline, with which they were impregnated thanks to their Christian traditions and their contacts with Europe, never entirely broken off.

In order to fight the Turks, who had become their principal oppressors, they tried to find an element of rapprochement with the Muslims of the country in their community of language, with a view to shaking off their shared yoke.

This was how the Arab idea began to take form in the nineteenth century.

In their publications in Libya, Syria and Egypt, the Christians exhumed Arab literature, history, and traditions, long buried under centuries of debris. In this way they sought to awaken awareness of the populations subjugated by the Turks, in order to assist the disintegration of the sick man [the Ottoman Empire] from within.

At the dawn of the twentieth century, the Arab press was enriched by scores of literary and political newspapers and reviews which—before and after the 1908 Turkish revolution and up to the eve of the 1914–1918 war—fanned the flame of memory and commemorated the literary glories and the widespread radiation of Arab thought in the East on every register.

The Arab Press in the two Americas—*exclusively Christian*—called for more freedoms, more justice for its homeland.

In the same period (1880–1910), Syro-Lebanese women of letters, all Christians, participated in this intellectual renaissance, and the major social issues found a resonant echo under their energetic pens which combined grace with sensitivity.

Thus, the Arab idea, that arose from the murky depths of ancient atavisms and traditions, took shape in bold relief in the dreamy soul of the Orient, whose populations *brought together* by the conquest and *maintained under the same tyranny by terror* are united by the bond of language and by *the same common mourning for their lost freedoms.* [pp. 24–25]

Chapter 10: Islamism and Arabism

Arabism—or Panarabism—is a doctrine proclaimed throughout the world; *but no one so far has dared to define it.* [p. 26]

Then, what is Arabism?

We must repeat that, since that word was invented, no official Arab document has been able to give a clear definition of it. On the contrary, certain pundits of the new ideology, adopting the notions of Western Public Law to serve their cause, claim that Arabism is based on community of memories and aspirations. *Which brings us back to the real notion of Arabism, which is a notion of an essentially religious kind.*

Let us actually analyze these two concepts:

1) *Community of memories*

No community of memories exists between Muslims and Eastern Christians. This has been the case throughout the history of these countries since the advent of Islam. The glorious periods of Muslim domination correspond to years of misery and humiliation for the Christians. Conversely, periods of decadence are matched by a respite for the Christians and a transitory relaxation. There are still Christians alive today who have not forgotten the very recent period when they had to step off the pavement and bow their heads on meeting a Muslim.

2) *Community of aspirations*

The supreme ideal which the champions of Arabism adopt and proclaim "urbi and orbi" is the restoration of the empire of the caliph in all its splendor.

However, it is very obvious that these aspirations could not be shared by Christians and Muslims, any more than such memories are shared. Because the eventual achievement of such aspirations would re-establish the theocratic Muslim state, with the often described inequality between "believers" and "infidels". [pp. 26–28]

Chapter 11: Arabism = Islamism

This brief and decisive analysis of the "community of memories and aspirations" takes us to the very heart of the question. And we are thus justified in stating that "Arabism" and "Islam" are two inseparable corollaries and that the first is only a skilful camouflage for the second. If fuller proof were required, it would be sufficient to refer to Muslim dogma, to the testimony of History, and to the current state of affairs. In the following chapter we will quote the unequivocal declarations of eminent "Arab" personalities. [pp. 28–29]

Chapter 12: Authorized Testimonies

CONCLUSION. It emerges from the evidence of the three preceding chapters that:

1) Arabism can not be dissociated from Islamism.
2) The Arab state is governed by the Sacred Muslim Law for all rules of public life, private life and religious practice;
3) Islam, as a theocratic state, recognizes only Muslims as true citizens.
4) Freedom of conscience whereby a man is free to lead a private life in

harmony with his innermost spiritual convictions without the possibility that this could entail any inequality for him in public life or the social milieu is expressly rejected by Islam. In the Muslim theocratic state absolute equality between Muslims and non-Muslims is an intolerable shame. [pp. 40–41]

Chapter 14: Toward a Salutary Solution

[Concluding line]
The Eastern Christians ask for a *Christian homeland*: **THE LEBANON!**
[p. 47]

*These excerpts (pages indicated) are translated from the French original in the author's possession: *S.O.S. Le Liban "Foyer Chrétien" du Proche Orient*. Titles, italics, and inverted commas are in the original text. Neither the English, French nor Arabic versions could be obtained at the United Nations Library in Geneva. It is said to have been written in 1945 by the Maronite Bishop of Beirut, Monsignor Ignace Mubarak. He was helped by a committee of intellectuals from different Christian communities, among whom were the prominent Maronite historian Fuad Afram Bustany of Deir al-Kamar, and the economist and political scientist Albert Sara, a Greek Catholic from Beirut. It circulated widely in the late 1940s. See in Phares, *Lebanese Christian Nationalism*, 95–96.

Appendix 4:
Saudi Arabia: *Fatwa* for non-Muslims
(5 February 1993)

The authority of a non-Muslim over a Muslim: Is it permissible?
Question (from some workers in a company):

"We are Muslim workers in a company owned by a Muslim. The owner, however, commissioned a Christian over us and we suffer from the behavior of this Christian manager who seeks to expose us as being non-productive before the owner of the company, thereby causing us problems with that owner.

Is it permissible [in Islam] for this Muslim—the owner of the company—to give authority to a Christian over us?"

Answer:

Sheikh Mannaa K. al-Qubtan, professor of higher studies in the School of Shari'a (Canonical Law of Islam), Riyadh, issued the following *fatwa*:

"The command of a non-Muslim over a Muslim is not permissible based on the words of Allah: 'and Allah will not open to the unbelievers against the believers a way.' [4:140]

Allah Almighty has endowed the Muslims with the highest rank and authority [among all men], bestowing on them strength and might: 'Might and strength be to Allah, his prophet and the believers.'

The authority of a non-Muslim over a Muslim, therefore, is inconsistent with the text of those two holy verses [because] the Muslim [who] would be rendered submissive to whoever takes charge over him, obeying such persons since the Muslim would be inferior to him. It is inappropriate for a Muslim to accept such a situation."

Dr Saleh Al-Sadlan, professor of Shari'a at the School of Shari'a, Riyadh, provides the following *fatwa:*
"Allah Almighty proclaims: 'and Allah will not open to the unbelievers against the believers a way.' [4:140] Whether in the private or the public

411

sector, an infidel may not be, to the extent possible, permitted [to have authority] over Muslims because such an act would involve the humiliation of the Muslim and the exaltation of the infidel. An infidel might exploit his position for the degradation and subjection of the Muslims working under his authority.

The advice we give to the factory owner is to fear Allah Almighty and to authorize only a Muslim over Muslims. The Islamic injunction provides that an infidel must not be employed while the Muslim can employ a Muslim in his place. Our advice to this company owner is to change this infidel manager and replace him with a Muslim."

Under the heading, "Fear Allah and keep away from the forbidden," Dr. Fahd Al-Oseimi, professor of Islamic studies in Riyadh, advises:

"That Muslim employer who authorized a Christian over Muslims should have sought the employment of a Muslim who was better than the Christian, equal to him or well prepared to be trained. It is not permissible to appoint that Christian as manager over Muslims for all the reasons advanced [verses from the Koran are cited to support the injunction, including the same verse 4:140, cited above.] It is well known that such Christian authority would force Muslims to flatter the said infidel, and we all know the story of Umar [Umar Ibn al-Khattab, one of the companions of the Prophet Muhammad and the second caliph] who upon hearing of the appointment of a Christian clerk in a government office remarked, 'Have woman's wombs become sterile, giving birth only to that man?'

Therefore, Muslims should fear Allah in regard to the way they treat their brethren, the Muslims, providing them with training that is useful in the short and the long run. As a principle, the Muslim is honest, whereas the non-Muslim is dishonest and does not fear Allah. In those countries that are ruled by non-Muslims, the Muslim people are impoverished contrary to the other residents who receive training and education.

Muslims must keep this in mind and they should not add to the calamity but rather make things easier [for their brethren]. The Muslim who appointed the infidel must keep an eye on him never taking his direct advice but rather should listen to the two parties. The owner should not fully trust the Christian when it comes to taking care of the affairs of Muslims, and as soon as he finds a Muslim to replace him, he should immediately remove him [the Christian] from his job."

Al-Muslimoon (Arabic weekly), vol.8, no.418, Riyadh, 5 February 1993.

Appendix 5:
Security Instructions for Jews
Geneva, Switzerland

Committee of the Jewish Liberal Community of Geneva
Security instructions for the HIGH HOLY DAY
(30 September–9 October 2000)

As in preceding years, we are obliged to enforce a number of security pre-cautions. In order to facilitate the task of those who are responsible, and to ensure that the holy days pass as smoothly as possible for all concerned, we would be grateful if you could collaborate as follows:

SHOW YOUR RESERVATION CARD SPONTANEOUSLY AT THE ENTRANCE
LEAVE YOUR PERSONAL BELONGINGS IN THE CLOAKROOM
COOPERATE WHEN ASKED TO OPEN HANDBAGS, BRIEFCASES, ETC.
AFTER THE SERVICE PLEASE USE ALL OF THE AVAILABLE DOORS, INCLUDING THE EMERGENCY EXITS
DO NOT REMAIN ON THE PAVEMENT OUTSIDE THE BUILDING AND PLEASE DISPERSE AS QUICKLY AS POSSIBLE

Should it be necessary to evacuate the premises rapidly:
WALK DIRECTLY TO THE NEAREST EXIT (marked "EXIT")
DO NOT RUN
DO NOT TRY TO COLLECT YOUR PROPERTY FROM THE CLOAK-ROOM
WHEN YOU ARE OUTSIDE DISPERSE QUICKLY

Thank you for your cooperation. The Committee

HAPPY NEW YEAR

(Text in French and English. Such instructions and security arrangements have become the norm in all Jewish communities of Europe, whether or-thodox or reform.)

Appendix 6:
Indonesia 2000: East Timor, Moluccas

In 1975 the mainly Christian province of East Timor was invaded by Indonesia and annexed in 1976. Over the next twenty-four years more than 200,000 East Timorese (25 % of the population) died under Indonesian oppression and for their independence. Then Indonesia—a country neglected by the international media until the grave East Timor crisis erupted in 1999—could no longer be ignored.On 6 April 2000—at a rally in Jakarta—5,000 Islamic extremists called for a jihad *against the majority Christian population in the Moluccas [Malukus] Spice Islands. By early May 2000, at least 1,000 Laskar* Jihad *(Holy War warriors) assembled in the Moluccas. These warriors came from Indonesia, and later from Afghanistan, Pakistan, Saudi Arabia, and the Philippines.The following descriptions are taken from a reliable source. They were published in January 2001 by the Barnabas Fund (UK), under the title:* Indonesia 2000: Genocide of a Christian Minority, *and slightly updated since then. (www.barnasfund.org.)*

[In the Malukus] one by one the Christian villages were attacked in what appeared to be a well planned and co-ordinated campaign. In each village the church and houses would be set on fire, and the villagers would flee for safety. Those who could not escape in time were killed. The Christians were gradually pushed back into smaller and smaller "safe" areas, as Laskar Jihad warriors pursued their aim of cleansing the islands of Christians.

Over 1,000 people were butchered in a single raid. In another, 200 were killed and their bodies horribly mutilated. In June, some 200 Christians sheltering in a church were attacked with machetes. The church was then surrounded and set on fire. At least 100 Christians died in the blaze. In another incident three children were tied up and dragged to their deaths behind a speeding car. At Duma, Halmahera island, 135 people were killed in one attack and nearly 300 Christian women and girls were abducted. They are believed to have been taken to another island where they have been raped.

In July 2000 the Christian university in Ambon city was destroyed. By September several islands had been cleansed of all Christians, and still the attacks continued, now focusing on the island of Saparua. [. . .]

414

On 15 November 2000 Jaffar Umar Thalib, the leader of the Laskar Jihad stated : "We intend during this Ramadan [which was to start 11 days later] to . . . carry out various activities paving the way for full Shari'ah [Islamic law] at least in places that have now become exclusively Islam, such as the islands of Ternate, Tidore and Bacan." The chilling reason that these is-lands have recently become 100% Muslim is that all their Christian inhabi-tants have been killed or driven out. [. . .]

Many Christian villages had been wiped out, and an estimated 75% of Ambon island itself had been cleansed of Christians. Forty per cent of Ambon city lay in ashes. [pp. 2–3]

Forced Conversions to Islam

In November 2000 the first reports of forced conversions began to emerge. In that month, 700 Christians on Ceram island were warned that they would be killed if they did not become Muslims. Hundreds of them signed a document stating that they had become Muslims, learnt to recite parts of the Qur'an and performed Islamic prayers five times a day. News later emerged that another 5,000 Christians on the island had been forced to convert earlier in the year. Many of the women had been forcibly married to Muslim men, thus effecting their conversion to Islam, at least in the eyes of their Muslim attackers.

On Bacan island 1,150 Christian men and boys were reported to have been forcibly circumcised (as a sign of conversion to Islam). Elsewhere a whole village was captured and told that they would be released if they gave up their village elders and church leaders. The elders and leaders surrendered themselves and were beheaded. The rest of the villagers, both men and women, were forcibly circumcised. Any who resisted were killed.

On Kesui and Teor islands, at least 615 Christians have been forced to em-brace Islam. [. . .]

After the attacks, the Christian survivors were gathered into several mosques and forced on pain of death to perform conversion rituals, includ-ing ritual washing and reciting the Islamic creed. Two teachers who refused to convert were killed. On December 3 and 4, hundreds of men and women were circumcised, without painkillers or antiseptic, causing heavy bleeding and infection. [p. 6]

The Refugees

By December 2000 there were approximately 487,000 Christian refugees from the Malukus, according to the estimates of the Ambon-based human rights group, the Masariku Network, and the Maranatha Church in Ambon. Of these, some 300,000 have fled from the Malukus to other parts of Indonesia, and the rest are displaced within the Malukus region. [. . .]

On Halmahera, thousands of Christians from the island itself are now homeless and destitute. There are also on the island an estimated 70,000 Christian refugees who have fled from the religious cleansing on other islands to Halmahera. Amongst the homeless are at least 8,000 pre-school children and babies, in desperate need of milk, medication and other basics. Many of the child refugees have lost their parents in the conflict. One theological school on the island is caring for 545 orphans aged 0 to 12. [p. 7]

[On 24 December 2000] twenty-four bombs had exploded almost simultaneously outside churches in nine cities and towns across Indonesia, including the capital Jakarta, the night before as Christians gathered for Christmas Eve services. At least eighteen people were killed and more than 120 injured. A further twenty-one bombs would also have exploded but were discovered and defused by the police. Some of these had been sent gift-wrapped to church ministers.

[. . .] At least 5,000 Christians (probably many more) have been killed in the past two years, and an estimated 487,000 have been forced to flee their homes. Some 7,000 have been forcibly converted to Islam. At least 455 church buildings have been destroyed, as well as countless thousand Christian homes, shops and a Christian university. [p. 1]

Appeals for help from Christians in the Malukus have largely gone unheard and unheeded by the international community. A group of Ambonese Christian leaders came to Geneva and London in July 2000 and appealed for international help. In December the Bishop of Amboina made an impassioned "SOS appeal" to Kofi Annan, the Secretary General of the United Nations, highlighting not only the butchery and destruction but also the large-scale forced conversions. But there has been minimal interest or response. [p. 8]

Appeal of the Roman Catholic Bishop of Amboina, the Rt. Rev. Peter Mandagi, to the United Nations Secretary-General Kofi Annan (19 December 2000)

"From the very start of the conflict up to now many law violations have taken place, both violations of human rights and violations of civil law, both by the local

population and by government authorities and institutions. There have been count-less acts of savagery, depravedness [sic] and criminality, such as torturing, raping of women and other sexual abuse, persecution, slaughtering, looting and destroying of property . . . Most of the victims are just simple people, who are poor and defence-less, innocent and blameless . . .

The criminals, lawbreakers and human rights violators are roaming about and undertake any mischief at leisure. So what is prevailing now is the law of the jungle, barbarism and savagery . . .

We appeal to the international community to assist the Indonesian Government in ending the conflict in the Moluccas."

Appendix A:
Muslim Historians and Theologians

Abu HANIFA (d. 767). An-Nu'man b. Thabit b. Zuta abu Hanifa. Theologian and jurisconsult, founder of the Hanafi school of jurisprudence. He died in Baghdad.

Abu YUSUF, Ya'qub (731–98). A renowned jurist of the Hanafi school of law. Author of a basic treatise on public finance.

al-ADAWI, Ahmad ad-Dardir (eighteenth century). Egyptian theologian of the Maliki school of jurisprudence. Author of a *fatwa* against the *dhimmis* in 1772.

al-BALADHURI (d. 892). Eminent Persian historian who lived at the caliphs' court from 847 to 892. Author of *Book of Conquests*.

al-BUKHARI (d. 869). Born in Bukhara, he died in Samarkand. Author of one of the most important of the six compilations of traditions (*hadith*), being the acts and sayings attributed to the Prophet Muhammad.

al-DAMANHURI, Ahmad b. Abd al-Mun'im (1690–1778). Born in Damanhur, Gharbiya (Egypt). Theologian and head of the koranic university of al-Azhar.

al-JABARTI, Abd al-Rahman (1754–ca.1822). Egyptian historian, born in Cairo, his ancestors were from Jabart, Abyssinia. Among other works, he wrote a *Chronicle* covering the years 1688–1821, which constitutes one of the most important works concerning Arab countries under Turkish rule.

an-NAWAWI (1233–77), Shafi'i jurisconsult, born in Nawa (south of Damascus). The *Minhadj at-talibin* was completed in 1270.

GHAZI b. al-WASITI (active in 1292). Native of the town of Wasit on the Tigris (Iraq), author of a treatise on the *dhimmis*.

ibn ABDUN MUHAMMAD b. AHMAD (d. 1134). Andalusian author of an authoritative legal treatise, used in Seville during the second half of the eleventh to early twelfth century.

ibn ABI ZAYD al-QAYRAWANI (922–96). Head of the North African Maliki school at Qairuan, author of several legal works and of a compendium which ensured the adoption of the Maliki school of jurisprudence in North Africa and Spain.

ibn al-ATHIR (1160–1233). Born in Jazirat Ibn Umar on the Tigris (Iraq), lived in Mesopotamia and Palestine. Author of historical works on the Zangid dynasty of Mosul (*al-Bahir*) and of a vast corpus of *Chronicles (al-Kamil fi't-tarikh)*.

ibn BATTUTA (1304–ca.1368). Born and died in Tangiers, author of accounts describing places visited in the course of several lengthy travels throughout the Islamic world, including India and China.

ibn HANBAL (d. 855). Theologian and jurisconsult, editor of a corpus of traditions and founder of the Hanbali school of jurisprudence.

ibn HISHAM (d. 833). Born and died in Egypt. Grammarian and genealogist, famous for his later recension of ibn Ishaq's biography of the Prophet Muhammad.

ibn ISHAQ (d. 761). Author of the most famous biography of Muhammad, later edited by Ibn Hisham.

ibn KHALDUN (1332–1406). Born in Tunis, died in Cairo. Jurist, kadi (Maliki), renowned philosopher, historian, and sociologist. Author of a *History of the Berbers* and a *Universal History*, preceded by an *Introduction to History (al-Muqaddima)*.

ibn an-NAQQASH (d. 1362). Egyptian preacher, author of an important *fatwa* on the *dhimmis*.

ibn TAYMIYA, Taqi al-Din Ahmad (1263–1328). Syrian theologian and jurisconsult of the Hanbali school during the Mamluks; active in Damascus, where he died. He left a considerable body of jurisprudence. His doctrine inspired the Wahabi movement in eighteenth century Arabia.

al-MAGHILI (d.1504). North African theologian, his writings on the *dhimmis* were widely circulated in Moroccan religious circles during the late nineteenth and early twentieth centuries.

MALIK b. ANAS (710–95). Theologian and jurisconsult from Medina, founder of the Maliki school of jurisprudence. Author of *al-Muwatta*, the oldest extant treatise of Islamic law, as practiced in the Hijaz.

al-MALIKI, Abu Bakr Abd Allah (eleventh century). Tunisian historian. Author of a famous chronicle, *Riyad an-Nufus*.

al-MAQRIZI [MAKRIZI] (1364–1442). Renowned historian, born in Cairo. Author of several works, particularly on the Mamluk Sultans of Egypt.

al-MARRAKUSHI, Abd al-Wahid (d. 1224). North African historian of the Almohads.

al-MAWARDI [MAWERDI] (d. 1058). Famous Shafi'i jurist of Baghdad, author of an important law treatise, *al-ahkam as-Sultaniyya* and a treatise on morality.

MUSLIM (d. 874). Disciple of al-Bukhari and compiler of one of the most important corpus of traditions (*hadith*), being the acts and sayings attributed to the Prophet Muhammad.

al-SHAFI'I (d. 820). Theologian and jurisconsult, disciple of Malik, founder of the Shafi'i school of jurisprudence. He died in Cairo.

al-SHAYBANI (d. 805). Jurist of the Hanafi school, disciple of Abu Yusuf. Author of several authoritative works, particularly an important work on *jihad: The Islamic Law of Nations.*

al-TABARI (838–923). Born in Tabaristan, died in Baghdad. Historian, theologian and jurisconsult. Author of a monumental commentary on the Koran and a universal history.

al-WANSHARISHI (d. 1508). Born in Tlemcen (North Africa), worked mostly in Fez. An Islamic jurist, author of a large collection of *fatwas: Kitab al-My'ar,* dealing mostly with Muslims living under Christian Spanish rule.

Appendix B:
Non-Muslim Historians and Authors

ARAKEL OF TAURIZ (Tabriz) (ca.1600–ca.1670). Armenian author who, at the request of the Catholicos Philippos wrote a *Book of Histories* on the deportation of the Armenians to Persia. He continued his work in Isfahan from 1661 to 1662 at the request of the Catholicos Jacob of Julfa. His book is a valuable source of first-hand information on the condition of the Armenians and the patriarchs at that period.

THOMAS ARDZRUNI (d. early tenth century). Armenian historian and author of *History of the Ardzrunis*, in which he describes contemporary events. It was continued by others from 907 to 1226.

BAR HEBRAEUS (ABUL-FARAJ) (1226–86). Born in Melitene (Malatia in Upper Mesopotamia) of a Jewish father, hence his name. Jacobite bishop of Gubbos, Labakin and Aleppo; Maphrian of the East, he died in Maraga. Author of the *Chronography* and important historical and theological works.

DIONYSIUS OF TELL-MAHRÉ (d.845). Patriarch of the Jacobites, his *Chronicle* has disappeared but extracts from it were preserved in Michael the Syrian's twelfth-century *Chronicle*. The *Chronicle* wrongly attributed to him was completed in ca. 775, before his time. See under pseudo-Dionysius of Tell-Mahré.

GARJI [GEORGI], Mattatya (1845–1918). Born in Herat, Afghanistan; scholar and head of the Jewish community. He emigrated to Palestine in 1908 and died there.

GEDALIAH OF SIEMIATYCE (d.1716). A Polish Jew who arrived in Jerusalem with a group of Jewish immigrants on 14 October 1700. Author of *Sha'alu Shelom Yerushalayim* (Pray for the Peace of Jerusalem), which describes, *inter alia*, the fiscal extortion and oppression suffered by the Jews and Christians in Palestine, and the conditions of life there.

GHEVOND. Armenian historian of the second half of the eighth century. Author of *History of the Wars and Conquests of the Arabs in Armenia.*

JOHN OF NIKIOUS (seventh century). Coptic bishop and author of an important account of the Arab conquest of Egypt, of which only an Ethiopian translation remains.

MICHAEL THE SYRIAN. Jacobite patriarch of Antioch from 1166 to 1199. Author of a famous *Chronicle*, which reproduces earlier sources before describing contemporary events.

MORDECHAI HACOHEN (1856–1929). Born in Tripoli (Libya) to a Jewish family of Italian descent. Author of the manuscript, *Highid Mordekhai* (*The Story of Mordechai*). He aided significantly the researches undertaken by Nahum Slouschz on the Jews of Tripolitania.

OBADYAH THE PROSELYTE (Johannes). Born in Oppido (Lucano, southern Italy), son of a Norman aristocrat. A priest, he converted to Judaism in about 1102 and lived in Constantinople, Baghdad, Aleppo, and Egypt.

PSEUDO-DIONYSIUS OF TELL-MAHRÉ (eighth century). Anonymous author of a *Chronicle*, wrongly attributed to the ninth-century patriarch of the same name. It provides a valuable description of the peasant condition in Mesopotamia from personal experience.

SAWIRUS (SEVERUS) b. al-MUQAFFA. Coptic Bishop of Ashmunein (Egypt) from 955 to 987. Author of a *History of the Patriarchs of Alexandria*. After his death, it was continued from 886 to 1046 by Michael, Bishop of Tinnis; then up to the thirteenth century by other ecclesiastics.

SEPEOS (SEBEOS). Armenian bishop, active in the third quarter of the seventh century. Author of a *History of Heraclius* from the end of the fifth century to 661, he describes the events of his time.

VARDAN (thirteenth century). Armenian historian, author of a *Universal History*.

Notes

Introduction

1. Bat Ye'or, *Juifs et Chrétiens sous l'Islam. Les dhimmis face au défi intégriste* (Paris, 1994).
2. Koenraad Elst, *Negationism in India. Concealing the Record of Islam*, 2nd enlarged ed. (New Delhi, 1993). For further documentation of the background to dhimmitude in India, see Kishori Saran Lal, *Theory and Practice of Muslim State in India* (New Delhi, 1999); Sita Ram Goel, *The Story of Islamic Imperialism in India*, 2nd revised ed. (New Delhi, 1994); idem, ed., *The Calcutta Quran Petition*, 3rd enlarged ed. (New Delhi, 1999).
3. George Vajda, "Juifs et Musulmans selon le Hadit," *JA* 210 (January–March 1937): 57–127.
4. Heribert Busse, *Islam, Judaism and Christianity. Theological and Historical Affiliations,* trans. from German by Alison Brown (Princeton, 1998).
5. Moshe Sharon, *Judaism, Christianity and Islam. Interaction and Conflict* (Johannesburg, 1987).
6. Bat Ye'or, *The Decline of Eastern Christianity under Islam: From Jihad to Dhimmitude. Seventh–Twentieth Century,* trans. from French by Miriam Kochan and David Littman (Madison, NJ, London, 1996).
7. James E. Biechler, *JES* 35, no. 1 (winter, 1998): 127.

Chapter 1. The Orient on the Eve of Islam

1. Marcel Simon, *Verus Israel: A Study of the Relations between Christians and Jews in the Roman Empire (AD 135–425)*, trans. from French by H. McKeating (Oxford, 1986); James Parkes, *The Conflict of the Church and the Synagogue: A study in the origins of antisemitism* (New York, 1969); Jules Isaac, *Genèse de l'Antisémitisme* (Paris, 1956); idem, *L'Enseignement du mépris, vérité historique et mythes théologiques* (Paris, 1962).
2. When the Byzantine emperors tried to reestablish justice they were rebuffed by the Church Fathers who prevented it. Regarding the opposition to the restoration of synagogues by St. Simeon Stylite in respect of the Antioch synagogues, and by St. Ambrose to the Callinicum synagogue which had become a church, see Simon, *Verus Israel*, 226.
3. Jean Juster, "La Condition Légale des Juifs sous les Rois Visigoths," in *Etudes d'Histoire Juridique Offertes à Paul F. Girard* (Paris, 1912–1913), 289–95.
4. For the anti-Jewish laws in the Byzantine Empire, see below, chap. 3.
5. Moshe Gil, *A History of Palestine, 634–1099*, trans. from Hebrew by Ethel Broido (Cambridge/New York, 1992), 3.
6. Ibid., 65; *The History of al-Tabari (Ta'rikh al-rusul wa'l-muluk)*. Vol.12, *The Battle of al-Qadisiyyah and the Conquest of Syria and Palestine*, trans. and annot. by Yohanan Friedmann (New York, 1992), 195.
7. Gil, *A History*, 8–10; *Chronique de Michel le Syrien, patriarche jacobite d'Antioche (1166–1199)*, trans. from Syriac and ed. Jean-Baptiste Chabot (Paris, 1901), 2:414.
8. Alfred J. Butler, *The Arab Conquest of Egypt and the Last Thirty Years of the Roman Administration*, 2nd ed. by P. M. Frazer (London, 1978).
9. Ibn Ishaq (d.761), see Alfred Guillaume, *The Life of Muhammad. A Translation of Ishaq's*

'Sirat Rasul Allah,' trans. from Arabic (London/New York, 1955), 197; Hartwig Hirschfeld, "Essai sur l'Histoire des Juifs de Médine," *REJ* 7 (1883): 167–93, and 10 (1885): 10–31.

10. For extortion or protection dues established in pre-Islamic Arabia, see Fred McGraw Donner, *The Early Islamic Conquest* (Princeton, 1981), 20–49; Hugh Kennedy, *The Prophet and the Age of the Caliphates* (London/New York, 1986), 18–21.

11. The perfection of the Koran, the obligation of *jihad*, and the inferiority of infidels are recurrent themes in the Koran and the Traditions (*hadiths*). For simplification, we have omitted large numbers of references to these subjects.

12. Ibn Ishaq, *The Life of Muhammad*, 231–33; Moshe Gil, "The Constitution of Medina: A Reconsideration," *IOS* 4 (1974): 44–65; William Montgomery Watt, *Muhammad at Medina* (Oxford, 1956), 221–28.

13. Koran 4:106; 6:114; 10:38; see n.11 above.

14. Ibn Ishaq, *The Life of Muhammad*, 660.

15. al-Bokhari (d.869), *Les Traditions Islamiques (al-Sahih)*, trans. from Arabic by Octave Houdas and William Marçais (Paris, 1903–1914), 2, title 41, chap.6; title 56, chap.80:3, chap.154:2. Bokhari's compilation of words and deeds attributed to Muhammad forms one of the major pillars of Islamic jurisdiction, with the compilation by his disciple, Muslim (d.875), *Sahih. Being Traditions of the Sayings and Doings of the Prophet Muhammad as narrated by his Companions and Compiled under the title "Al-Jami-Us-Sahih,"* trans. from Arabic by Abdul Hamid Siddiqi (Lahore, 1976). The Medina Jewish community included men of learning according to Shlomo Dov Goitein in his *Jews and Arabs. Their Contacts through the Ages* (New York, 1964), 48–51.

16. Ibn Ishaq, *Life of Muhammad*, 461–69; Meir Jacob Kister, "The Massacre of the Banu Qurayza: A re-examination of a tradition," *JSAI* 8 (1986): 61–96; William Montgomery Watt, "The Condemnation of the Jews of Banu Qurayzah," *MW* 42 (1952): 160–71; idem, *Muhammad at Medina*, 207–20; idem, in Peter M. Holt, Ann K. S. Lambton, Bernard Lewis, eds., *The Cambridge History of Islam* (Cambridge, 1970), 1:39–49; Maurice Gaudefroy-Demombynes, *Mahomet* (Paris, 1969), 142–46; Michael Lecker, "On Arabs of the Banu Kilab, executed together with the Jewish Banu Qurayza," *JSAI* 19 (1994); Alfred Morabia, *Le Gihâd dans l'Islam Médiéval: Le "Combat Sacré" des origines au XIIe siècle*, preface by Roger Arnaldez (Paris, 1993), 61–63.

17. Ibn Ishaq, *Life of Muhammad*, 511; Bokhari, *Les Traditions Islamiques*, 2, title 56, chaps. 102:5 and 130; Morabia, *Le Gihâd*, 64.

18. Bokhari, *Les Traditions Islamiques*, 2, title 41, chaps. 8, 9, 11, 17; and title 57, chap. 19. See Ibn Ishaq, *Life of Muhammad*, 524–25. For the treaties between Muhammad and the Jews of Makna (near Eilat), see al-Balâdhuri (d.892), *The Origins of the Islamic State (Kitab Futûh al-Buldân)*, trans. from Arabic by Philip K. Hitti (New York, 1916), 1:93–94.

19. Gil reprints these letters in *A History*, 28–29. For Muhammad's relations with Jews and Christians, see also Busse, *Islam, Judaism and Christianity*, 36–61.

20. Bokhari, *Les Traditions Islamiques*, 2, title 57, chap.I:3, and title 58, chap.6:1; Muslim, *Sahih*, 33, chap.723 (4363). For the organization of the Medina community, see Montgomery Watt, *Muhammad at Medina*, chaps. 6 and 7, 192–260.

21. Ibn Ishaq, *Life of Muhammad*, 525; Bokhari, *Les Traditions Islamiques*, 2, title 41, chap.14; 4, title 89, chap.2; Muslim, *Sahih*, 3, chap.723 (4366); Antoine Fattal, *Le Statut Légal des Non-Musulmans en Pays d'Islam* (Beirut, 1958), 85.

22. Gil, *A History*, 71; *Histoire Nestorienne (Chronique de Séert), (fin)* ed. and trans. from Arabic by Mgr. Addai Scher, in *Patrologia Orientalis* (hereafter *Patr. Or.*), eds., Mgr.R. Graffin and François Nau (Paris, 1919), 13, fasc.4:623–24; *Chronique de Michel le Syrien*, 2:425.

23. Gil, *A History*, 16. The bishop of Aylah (Eilat) went to negotiate the Christians' tribute with Muhammad, see in Montgomery Watt, *Muhammad at Medina*, 115.

24. *Chronique de Séert*, in *Patr. Or.*, 13:601. For the Christian Arab tribes' collaboration in the Islamic conquest, see Montgomery Watt, *Muhammad at Medina*; Edmond Rabbath, *Les Chrétiens dans l'Islam des Premiers Temps: La Conquête Arabe sous les Quatre Premiers Califes (11/632–40/661)* (Beirut, 1985); Walter E. Kaegi, *Byzantium and the Early Islamic Conquests* (Cambridge, 1996), passim; Tor Andrae, *Les Origines de l'Islam et le Christianisme*, trans. from German by Jules Roche (Paris, 1955).

25. *Chronique de Séert*, in *Patr. Or.*, 13:619–20.

26. Ibid., 13:601–18. Each Eastern Christian sect preserves a copy of this document,

though there are differences between them. For the inauthenticity and rebuttal of the document, see Fattal, *Le Statut Légal,* 27–33.

27. The leader of the Monophysite Christian tribe of the Ghassanids, charged with defending the Byzantine frontier against Bedouin incursions, see Montgomery Watt, *Muhammad at Medina,* 112–114.

28. *Chronique de Séert,* in *Patr. Or.,* 13:605.

29. Ibid., 606.

30. For an analysis of the development of Islamic jurisdiction, see Emile Tyan, *Histoire de l'Organisation Judiciaire en Pays d'Islam,* preface by Edouard Lambert (Lyons, 1938–43); Joseph Schacht, *An Introduction to Islamic Law* (Oxford, 1964); William Montgomery Watt, *The Formative Period of Islamic Thought* (Edinburgh, 1973); Ignaz Goldziher, *Muslim Studies (Muhammedanische Studien),* ed., Samuel Miklos Stern, trans. from German by C. R. Barber and S. M. Stern (London, 1967/1971); idem, *Le Dogme et la Loi de l'islam. Histoire du développement dogmatique et juridique de la religion musulmane,* trans. from German by Félix Arin (Paris, 1920); Gustave E. von Grunebaum, *Medieval Islam. A Study in Cultural Orientation,* 2nd ed. (Chicago/London, 1969); idem, *Classical Islam. A History, 600–1258,* trans. from German by Katherine Watson (London, 1970); Dominique and Janine Sourdel, *La Civilisation de l'islam classique* (Paris, 1983); Hamilton Alexander Rosskeen Gibb, *Studies on the Civilization of Islam,* Stanford J. Shaw and William R. Polk, eds. (London, 1962); Reuben Levy, *The Social Structure of Islam* (Cambridge, 1969). On the *dhimmi,* see Fattal, *Le Statut Légal.*

31. Goldziher, *Le Dogme,* 44–45.

32. Gil, *A History,* 28; al-Baghawi (Abu Muhammad al-Husain) [ed., at-Tibrizi], *Mishkat al-Masabih,* trans. from Arabic by James Robson (Lahore, 1975), 2:837–38, 844.

33. *Khatt-i humayun* of 18 February 1856; Roderic H. Davidson, *Reform in the Ottoman Empire, 1856–1876* (Princeton, 1963). In the Ottoman Empire, the word "*raya*" generally denotes the *dhimmis.*

34. *Jihad* is a recurrent theme in Islamic sources; here, we will only cite: Bokhari, *Les Traditions Islamiques,* 2, chap."De la Guerre Sainte," title 56; "De la Prescription du Quint," title 57; "La Capitation," title 58; Muslim, *Sahih,* 3, chaps.704–53: "The Book of *Jihad* and Expedition"; al-Tabari, *Kitab al-Jihad* (Book of Holy War), ed. and trans. from Arabic by Joseph Schacht (Leiden, 1933); Shaybani (d.805), in Majid Khadduri, *The Islamic Law of Nations,* (Shaybani's *Siyar*), trans. from Arabic (Baltimore, 1966); al-Baghawi, *Mishkat al-Masabih,* 1:806–16 (bk.18), 2:817–66 (bk. 18); Duncan Black MacDonald, "Dar al-harb," "Dar al-Sulh," "Djihad," *EI²* (1ˢᵗ ed., 1913); idem and Armand Abel, "Dar al-Sulh," *EI²* (2ⁿᵈ ed.); Emile Tyan, "Djihad," *EI²*; Armand Abel, "Dar al-harb" and "Dar al-Islam," *EI²*; Adolphe Marie du Caurroy de la Croix, "Législation Musulmane Sunnite," rite Hanéfi, Code Civil (cont.) (bk. 4): "De l'Acquisition, par droit de premier occupant, des personnes et des biens des *Harbi,*" trans. from Arabic with a preface, *JA,* 4th series, 17 (1851): 211–55 and 568–91; 18 (1851): 290–321; 19 (1852): 519–50; 5th series, 1(1853): 39–91; 2 (1853):471–528; Majid Khadduri, *War and Peace in the Law of Islam* (Baltimore, 1955); idem, *The Islamic Conception of Justice,* foreword by R. K. Ramazani (Baltimore/London, 1984); Fattal, *Le Statut Légal,* 14–18, 372–73; Emmanuel Sivan, *L'Islam et la Croisade: Idéologie et Propagande dans les Réactions Musulmanes aux Croisades* (Paris, 1968), 209–19; Rudolph Peters, *Jihad in Classical and Modern Islam* (Princeton, 1996); idem, *Islam and Colonialism: The Doctrine of Jihad in Modern History* (Paris/New York/The Hague, 1979); Jean-Paul Charnay, *Principes de stratégie arabe* (Paris, 1984); idem, *L'Islam et la Guerre. De la guerre juste à la révolution sainte* (Paris, 1986); and Morabia, *Le Gihâd.* For the modern period: see al-Azhar University, ed., *The Fourth Conference (1968) of the Academy of Islamic Research* (Cairo, 1970), 23–250; and the theories of modern Islamic scholars in part two of this book; and D. F. Green, ed., *Arab Theologians on Jews and Israel. Extracts from the Proceedings of the Fourth Conference of the Academy of Islamic Research, 1968,* 3rd ed. (Geneva, 1976), 61–68.

35. Ibn Abi Zayd al-Qayrawânî, *La Risâla (Epître sur les éléments du dogme et de la loi de l'Islam selon le rite mâlikite),* trans. from Arabic and ed. by Léon Bercher (5th ed., Algiers, 1960), 163; see Averroes' opinions in Peters, *Jihad,* 29–42.

36. Ibn Taymiya (d.1328), in Henri Laoust, *Le Traité de droit public d'Ibn Taymiya. Traduction annotée de la 'Siyasa šar'iya'* (Beirut, 1948); Ibn Khaldun, *The Muqaddimah. An Introduction to History,* trans. from Arabic, with an introduction by Franz Rosenthal (New York, 1958), 1:473 (in Bat Ye'or, *The Decline of Eastern Christianity,* 296); an-Nawawi, *Minhadj At-Tâlibîn (Le Guide*

des Zélés Croyants, Manuel de Jurisprudence Musulmane selon le rite de Châfi'î), Arabic text with French trans, annot. by L. W. C. van den Berg (Batavia, 1883), 3:255. The scholarly interpretation of van den Berg's translation has been retained in this English adaptation. The glory of martyrs claimed by *jihad* can be found throughout the corpus of *hadiths.*

37. Ibn Taymiya, in Laoust, *Le Traité de droit public,* 36; see chap. 2, n.32 below.

38. The concept is explained in ibid., 35–36; Gaudefroy-Demombynes, *Mahomet,* 528; and Fattal, *Le Statut Légal,* 71. See also the ideas of modern Islamic scholars in later chapters.

39. Mawardi, *Les Statuts gouvernementaux (Al-ahkam as-Sultaniyya),* trans. from Arabic by Edmond Fagnan (Algiers, 1915), 91.

40. Nawawi, *Minhadj,* 3:261–64; Abu Yusuf Ya'qub, *Le Livre de l'impôt foncier (Kitâb el-harâdj),* trans. from Arabic and annot. by Edmond Fagnan (Paris, 1921). For the division of the spoils, 30–69: extracts in Bat Ye'or, *The Decline of Eastern Christianity,* 299–302; Ibn Taymiya, in Laoust, *Le Traité de droit public,* 17–29; al-Baghawi, *Mishkat al-Masabih,* 18, chap.8, division of the spoils; Mawardi, *Les Statuts,* 104–6.

41. Nawawi, *Minhadj,* 3:264–65; al-Baghawi, *Mishkat al-Masabih,* 2:840–45; the same view in Abu Yusuf, *Le Livre de l'impôt foncier.* The sources unanimously confirm the strict observance of these regulations at the time of the Arab and Turkish conquests. Mawardi, *Les Statuts,* 99–100: for male booty, 276; for women and children, 283; for the division of spoils according to koranic law, see chap.12.

42. Ibn Taymiya, in Laoust, *Le Traité de droit public,* 128–29; al-Qayrawânî, *La Risâla,* 163; same opinion in Mawardi, *Les Statuts,* 93–94.

43. Abu Yusuf, *Le Livre de l'impôt foncier,* 319–20; al-Baghawi, *Mishkat al-Masabih,* 833.

44. Nawawi, *Minhadj,* 3:288–89; Abu Yusuf, *Le Livre de l'impôt foncier,* 310–20; same opinion in Mawardi, for whom a truce should not exceed four months, in his *Les Statuts,* 93–103.

45. Abu Yusuf, *Le Livre de l'impôt foncier,* 294. The enrollment of pre-pubescent boys was permitted, Nawawi, *Minhadj,* 3:260.

46. Abu Yusuf, *Le Livre de l'impôt foncier,* 307.

47. al-Azhar University, ed., *The Fourth Conference,* 23–250, contains a summary of the opinions of the four juridical schools on the *jihad;* see the important study by Morabia, *Le Gihâd.*

48. Ibn Taymiya, in Laoust, *Le Traité de droit public,* 30–31, 47–51, 147; for the origin of the "war treasury," see Morabia, *Le Gihâd,* 78, 209–11.

49. For the process of Islamization in Anatolia and the Balkans, see Speros Vryonis Jr., *The Decline of Medieval Hellenism in Asia Minor and the Process of Islamization from the Eleventh through the Fifteenth Century* (Berkeley/Los Angeles/London, 1971), 182; Iono Mitev, "Le Peuple Bulgare sous la Domination Ottomane (1396–1878)," in Ivan Dujcev, Velizar Velkov, Iono Mitev and Lubomir Panayotov, *Histoire de la Bulgarie, des origines à nos jours,* with a preface by Georges Castellan (Roanne, 1977); Dimitar Angelov, "Certains aspects de la conquête des peuples balkaniques par les Turcs," reprint in *Les Balkans au Moyen Age: La Bulgarie des Bogomils aux Turcs* (London, 1978), 220–75 (XII).

Chapter 2. Political and Economic Aspects of Dhimmitude

1. *Chronique de Séert, in Patr. Or.,* 13:581; Judah Benzion Segal, "Syriac Chronicles as Source Material for the History of Islamic Peoples," in Bernard Lewis and Peter M. Holt, *Historians of the Middle East* (London, 1962), 246–58; Michael G. Morony, *Iraq after the Muslim Conquest* (Princeton, 1984), 381–82; Donner, *Early Islamic Conquest,* 176; François Nau, *Les Arabes Chrétiens de Mésopotamie et de Syrie du VIIe au VIIIe siècle* (Paris, 1933), 100–13. This situation is confirmed by *hadiths* and Muslim chronicles.

2. *Chronique de Séert,* in *Patr. Or.,* 13:581–82. Other contemporary Christian sources deplore the enormous destruction as well as the deportation and enslavement of whole nations, see Kaegi, *Byzantium,* 205–28.

3. Ibn al-Balkhi, in Guy Le Strange, *Description of the Province of Fars in Persia at the beginning of the fourteenth century A.D.* (London, 1912), 83. Muslim historians and Greek, Armenian, Syriac, and Coptic chroniclers confirm a similar situation.

4. *Les Miracles de Saint Ptolémée,* ed. and trans. from Arabic by L. Leroy, in *Patr. Or.*

(1910), 5, fasc.5, 784. One of the saint's miracles was to force the Arabs to return all their plunder, including the children.

5. Gil, *A History*, 20, 43, 169–70; Félix-Marie Abel, *Histoire de la Palestine, depuis la conquête d'Alexandre jusqu'à l'invasion arabe* (Paris, 1952), 2:397–99; Demetrios J. Constantelos, "The Moslem Conquest of the Near East as Revealed in the Greek Sources of the Seventh and the Eighth Centuries," *Byzantion* 42 (1972): 329–30; *Chronique de Jean, Evêque de Nikiou*, extracts trans. from Ethiopian with notes by Hermann Zotenberg (Paris, 1879).

6. Abu Yusuf, *Le Livre de l'impôt foncier*, 36–42, 216–18; Qudama b. Ja'far, *Kitab al-Kharaj*, in Abraham Ben Shemesh, *Taxation in Islam*, ed. and trans. from Arabic, with introduction and notes, and a preface by Shlomo Dov Goitein (Leiden/London, 1965), 2:24–27; al-Baghawi, *Mishkat al-Masabih*, 2:866–69.

7. Mawardi, *Les Statuts*, 267. The fetus from a mother captured in the *dar al-harb* was deemed to belong to the *fay*, ibid., 99.

8. Gil, *A History*, 16–32; *Chronique de Michel le Syrien*, 2:403–4, 413; Montgomery Watt, *Muhammad at Medina*, chap.6.

9. For contacts between the Prophet and the Christian converts in Medina and the many Christian Arab tribes, see Gil, *A History*, 18–28; Montgomery Watt, *Muhammad at Medina*, chap.4; for the Christian tribes, Tor Andrae, *Les Origines*.

10. Bat Ye'or, *The Decline of Eastern Christianity*, 98–99; for the Ottoman conquest of Thrace, Macedonia, Bulgaria, Bosnia, Serbia, Dalmatia, Albania, Greece, according to contemporary indigenous Turkish and Christian sources, see Angelov, *Les Balkans au Moyen Age*; Radovan Samardzic, *et al.*, *Le Kosovo-Metohija dans l'Histoire Serbe*, trans. from Serbo-Croat by Dejan M. Babic (Lausanne, 1990).

11. *Chronique de Jean*, 234. This expression can be found in the Koran: the enemies of the Prophet and of the Muslims are considered "enemies of Allah."

12. Sebastian Brock, "Syriac sources for seventh-century history," *Byzantine and Modern Greek Studies* 2 (Oxford, 1976): 16, reprinted in *Syriac Perspectives on Late Antiquity* (London, 1984). In the Sassanian Empire, the king chose the patriarch and imposed him on the community by royal decree, see *Chronique de Séert*, in *Patrologia Orientalis* (1911), 7, fasc.2, 149. For the investiture of the Greek Orthodox patriarch by the Ottoman sultan, see, Apostolos E. Vacalopoulos, *Histoire de la Grèce Moderne*, preface by Jean Pouilloux (Saint-Juste-la-Pendue, 1975), 18.

13. For the concept of protection in pre-Islamic Arabia, see Donner, *Early Islamic Conquest*, 20–49; Montgomery Watt, *Muhammad at Medina*, 238–49; Kennedy, *The Prophet*, 18–21.

14. Nawawi, *Minhadj*, 3:116, 123; Mawardi, *Les Statuts*, 73, 83; see ibid., 109–15 for an interesting comparison between lands of war and lands of apostasy; Fattal, *Le Statut Légal*, 71; Morabia, *Le Gihâd*, 212. The same concept denying the infidel all rights can be found in Ibn Hazm, see Roger Arnaldez, "La Guerre Sainte selon Ibn Hazm de Cordoue," in Evariste Lévi-Provençal, *Etudes d'Orientalisme dédiées à la mémoire de Lévi-Provençal* (Paris, 1962), 2:454. For the relationship with non-Muslims, see Jean-Pierre Charnay, *Sociologie religieuse de l'Islam. Préliminaires* (Paris, 1977), 137–47.

15. Abu Yusuf, *Le Livre de l'impôt foncier*, 293; Mawardi, *Les Statuts*, 267; the same opinion in the Shafi'i rite appears in Nawawi, *Minhadj*, 3:123.

16. Ibid., 271–72; du Caurroy, "Législation Musulmane," 17–19.

17. Abu Yusuf, *Le Livre de l'impôt foncier*, 316. The *amân* could be given by any adult Muslim of either sex and by a slave mercenary, but not by a Jewish or Christian *dhimmi* mercenary.

18. Meir Jacob Kister, " 'An Yadin' (Qur'an, 9:29)," *Arabica* 11(1964): 272–78.

19. Nawawi, *Minhadj*, 3:286; Mawardi, *Les Statuts*, 368–69; al-Qayrawânî, *La Risâla*, 163; Fattal, *Le Statut Légal*, 81–84.

20. Abu Yusuf, *Le Livre de l'impôt foncier*, 189. For the concept of the holy war in Ibn Taymiya, see Alfred Morabia, "Ibn Taymiyya, dernier grand théoricien du gihâd médiéval," in *Mélanges offerts à Henri Laoust* (Damascus, 1978), 2:85–100; idem, *Le Gihâd*, 335–36; Yahia b.Adam, in Ben Shemesh, *Taxation in Islam* , 1:58–59.

21. *Dhimmis* were forbidden to buy weapons of war, see Nawawi, *Minhadj*, 1:349; see Vryonis Jr., *The Decline of Medieval Hellenism*, 182. For the Bulgarians, see Mitev, "Le Peuple Bulgare," 248. Until the mid-nineteenth century in Bosnia and Kosovo, Christian *rayas* had to hide their weapons from Muslims, see Cyprien Robert, *Les Slaves de Turquie. Serbes, Montêné-*

grins, Bosniaques, Albanais et Bulgares: Leurs Ressources, Leurs Tendances et Leurs Progrès Politiques (Paris, 1844), 2:12.

22. Uskup: also called Skopje, in the Former Yugoslav Republic of Macedonia. Report by British Consul J. E. Blunt (Pristina) to Sir Henry Bulwer, British ambassador at Constantinople, 14 July 1860, see Bat Ye'or, *The Decline of Eastern Christianity*, 417–18.

23. Jovan Cvijic, *La Péninsule Balkanique, Géographie Humaine* (Paris, 1918), 388–89.

24. For the text of the prohibition in Algiers, see Ernest Mainz, "Les Juifs d'Alger sous la domination Turque," *JA* (1952): 197–217; Bat Ye'or, *The Dhimmi*, 300; for Morocco, ibid., 308, 318; for Yemen, ibid., 213, 345.

25. For the deportation of the Copts in 832 in lower Iraq, see the account by Dionysius of Tell-Mahré printed in *Chronique de Michel le Syrien*, 3:79–84; extracts in Bat Ye'or, *The Decline of Eastern Christianity*, 305–13; for the Armenians in the seventh and eighth centuries: extracts from contemporary chronicles in ibid., 276–89; Bar Hebraeus, *The Chronography* (of Gregory Abu'l-Faraj, 1225–1286), trans. from Syriac by Ernest A. Budge (Amsterdam, 1932), 1:269. For the frequent repetition of deportations, see the chronicles and historical studies for Anatolia, in Vryonis Jr., *The Decline of Medieval Hellenism*, 169; 'Displacement of population'; idem, "Nomadization and Islamization in Asia Minor," *DOP* 29 (1975): 41–71; Osman Turan, "Les Souverains Seldjoukides et leurs sujets non-musulmans," *SI* 1 (1953): 65–100; idem, "L'Islamisation dans la Turquie du Moyen Age," *SI* 10 (1959): 137–52; for the Jewish communities in the Ottoman Empire, see Joseph Hacker, "The Sürgün System and Jewish Society in the Ottoman Empire during the 15th-17th Centuries" (Hebrew), *Zion* 55/1 (1990): 27–82. See also Apostolos E. Vacalopoulos, *History of Macedonia, 1354–1833*, trans. from Greek by Peter Megann (Salonika, 1973), 103–4, 122–23; for the Islamization policy in Bulgaria, see Mitev, "Le Peuple Bulgare," 250 (serfdom and forced conversions); Angelov, *Les Balkans au Moyen Age*, 261–65 and passim (resettlements); Georges Castellan, *Histoire des Balkans, XIVe–XXe siècle* (Paris, 1991), 62, 69, 84; Samardzic, *Le Kosovo-Metohija*, 108–28.

26. For the deportation of Armenians by Shah Abbas I in 1604, see Arakel de Tauriz, *Livre d'Histoires (XVIIe siècle)*, in *Collections d'Historiens Arméniens*, trans. from Armenian by Marie Félicité Brosset (St Petersburg/Paris, 1874–76), 1:309–10, 489–96, extracts in Bat Ye'or, *The Decline of Eastern Christianity*, 362–69; for the deportation of Armenians from Ararat in 1735, idem, 375–77 (see Brosset, *Collections d'Historiens Arméniens* 2:278–79); deportation of Jews from Mashhad (1839) and Herat (1857–59), idem, 390–91; see Reuven Kashani, *Qorot ha-Zemanim (Chronicle of Afghan Judaism)* (Hebrew), in *Shevet ve-Am*, n.s. no. 1 (Jerusalem, 1970): 12–13; for another description of these events, see Nicolas de Khanikof, "Méched, la Ville Sainte, et son territoire, Extraits d'un voyage dans le Khorassan" (1858), in *Le Tour du Monde* (Paris, 1861), 2e sem., 280–82.

27. These facts appear frequently in chronicles, see Bat Ye'or, *The Decline of Eastern Christianity*, 334–37, and in descriptions by travelers and diplomatic reports. For eastern Turkey in 1845, see Xavier Hommaire de Hell, *Voyage en Turquie et en Perse exécuté par ordre du Gouvernement Français pendant les années 1846, 1847 et 1848* (Paris, 1854–56), 1, 2nd pt., 461; for Bulgaria: Mitev, "Le Peuple Bulgare," 248; in Bosnia the *rayas* were obliged to feed and lodge Muslim soldiers, see Robert, *Slaves de Turquie*, 2:11. In Greece, see Lord Broughton, *Travels in Albania and other Provinces of Turkey in 1809 & 1810* (London, 1858), 1:68, 431. In 1869, at every change of garrison at Bash-Hale (east of Turkish Armenia), the Turkish soldiers were billeted in Jewish houses, although vast barracks were available. Every year this resulted in the abduction of Jewish women and girls. For the rape of Christian women in Bosnia, Cvijic, *La Péninsule Balkanique*, 388.

28. Nawawi, *Minhadj*, 3:281–82; Mawardi, *Les Statuts*, 304–5; Abu Yusuf, *Le Livre de l'impôt foncier*, 222–23.

29. For churches in Egypt, see Abu Salih the Armenian (attributed to), *The Churches & Monasteries of Egypt and Some Neighbouring Countries*, trans. from Arabic by B. T. A. Evett, with additional notes by Alfred J. Butler (Oxford, 1895); Arthur Stanley Tritton, *The Caliphs and their Non-Muslim Subjects. A Critical Study of the Covenant of Umar* (London, 1970), chap. 3. For Kosovo and Serbia in the eighteenth century, see Samardzic et al., *Le Kosovo-Metohija*, 110–24.

30. Albert M. Hyamson, *The British Consulate in Jerusalem in Relation to the Jews of Palestine (1838–1914)*, ed. with introduction and notes (London, 1939), 1:211.

31. Fattal, *Le Statut Légal*, 293; [François-Alphonse] Belin, "Etude sur la Propriété Fonci-

ère en Pays Musulmans et spécialement en Turquie (Rite Hanéfite)," *JA* , 5th series, 18 (1861): 390–431, 477–517; and 19 (1862): 156–212, 257–358; Max van Berchem, *La Propriété territoriale et l'impôt foncier sous les premiers khalifes, Etudes sur l'impôt du kharug* (Geneva, 1886); Daniel C. Dennet, *Conversion and the Poll-Tax in Early Islam* (Cambridge, MA, 1950); Frede Løkkegaard, *Islamic Taxation in the Classical Period, with special reference to circumstances in Iraq* (Copenhagen, 1950); idem, "Fay," *EI²* (1965): 889–90; Tritton, *The Caliphs*, chap.13; Eliahu Ashtor, *A Social and Economic History of the Near East in the Middle Ages* (London, 1976), chaps. 1 and 2; Claude Cahen, "Kharadj," *EI* 4 (1978): 1062–66.

32. Ibn Taymiya, in Laoust, *Le Traité de droit public*, 35–36; Abu Yusuf, *Le Livre de l'impôt foncier*, 36–43; Morony, *Iraq*, 106–17. For the property of infidels destined to become booty, see the opinion of the Andalusian jurist Ibn Hazm (eleventh century), in Arnaldez, "La Guerre Sainte," 2:457: "God has established the infidels' ownership of their property only for the institution of booty for Muslims." The concept of *fay* is linked to war and its practices: see *Kitab al-Kharaj from Qudama b. Ja'far*, in Ben Shemesh, *Taxation in Islam*, 2:25–27: "If the Imam distributes the lands among those who captured them, they become 'ushr lands, and their previous owners become slaves. If he does not distribute the lands but leaves them in whole, as a trust to the Muslims, then the poll tax lies on the necks of their owners, who are free, while their lands are charged with *kharaj* tax. This is the view of Abu Hanifa."

33. Donner, *The Early Islamic Conquest*, 226, 231–33, 237–38, 265–66; Abu Yusuf, *Le Livre de l'impôt foncier*, 37–61; Abraham N. Poliak, "L'Arabisation de l'Orient Sémitique," *REI* 12 (1938): 35–63; Ashtor, *A Social and Economic History*, 22–26.

34. Castellan, *Histoire des Balkans*, 185; Nicoara Beldiceanu, "L'Organisation de l'Empire ottoman (XIVe-XVe siècles)," in Robert Mantran (ed.), *Histoire de l'Empire ottoman* (Paris, 1989), 117–38; for Anatolia: Vryonis Jr., *The Decline of Medieval Hellenism*, 354–59; for the Balkans: see Angelov, *Les Balkans au Moyen Age*, 231; the detailed Ottoman legislative measures to protect peasant rights are described by Antoine Dabinovic, "Les pactes d'assistance entre les gouverneurs ottomans et les grands seigneurs de Bosnie et de Croatie depuis le XVe au XVIIe siècle," in *Türk Tarih Kongresi* (V), 3rd section (Ankara, 1960), 571–91. The author convincingly explains the conflict between the central authority's laws protecting the peasant and the local situations; he writes that, despite the moderation of Ottoman rule, it had "ended up by degenerating into a formidable enterprise for seizing property and people. The countries conquered by the Ottoman forces could not fail to regard themselves as the objects of brigandage, piracy, slavery," ibid., 592. For the system of *tchiftlik* in Bosnia, see Cvijic, *La Péninsule Balkanique*.

35. Report by the British consul, William Richard Holmes, from Bosna-Serai (Sarajevo), to his ambassador, Sir Henry Bulwer in Constantinople, 21 May 1861, extract in Bat Ye'or, *The Decline of Eastern Christianity*, 427.

36. Moshe Maoz, *Ottoman Reform in Syria and Palestine, 1840–1861: The Impact of the Tanzimat on Politics and Society* (London/New York, 1968), 195.

37. Abduction for slavery or for payment of ransoms is mentioned in Jewish (the Geniza), Syriac, Armenian, and Greek *dhimmi* sources; see Vryonis Jr., *The Decline of Medieval Hellenism*, 175 (eleventh and twelfth centuries); Mitev, "Le Peuple Bulgare," 248; on the mass slavery practiced by the Ottomans in Bulgaria, see Angelov, *Les Balkans au Moyen Age*, 249–61; Eliezer Bashan, *Captivity and Ransom in Mediterranean Jewish Society (1391–1830)* (Hebrew) (Bar-Ilan, 1980); Bat Ye'or, *The Decline of Eastern Christianity*, 460, n. 69, 350 ff., 362, 372; for insecurity in Palestine and Syria in the nineteenth century, see the consular reports in Bat Ye'or, *The Dhimmi*, 241, 259–70; for the Jews of Morocco in the troubled period which preceded the French occupation in 1912, see David Littman, "Quelques Aspects de la Condition de Dhimmi: Juifs d'Afrique du Nord avant la colonisation (d'après des documents de l'AIU)," *Yod* 2, no.1 (Paris, October 1976): 23–52; idem, "Jews under Muslim Rule II: Morocco, 1903–1912," *WLB* 29, n.s. 37/38 (1976): 3–19. At the time of the deportation of the Armenians in 1915, a considerable number of women and children were abducted as slaves, see Bat Ye'or, *The Decline of Eastern Christianity*, 439.

38. Extensive documentation on slaves is provided by Arab, Syriac, Greek, Armenian, Turkish, and Serbian chroniclers, and in modern works since slavery was only abolished toward the end of the nineteenth century. For Bosnia in the sixteenth century, see André Thevet, *La Cosmographie Universelle de André Thevet cosmographe du Roy. Illustrée de diverses choses*

plus remarquables, revüs par l'Auteur et incogneuës de noz anciens et modernes (Paris, 1575), 2, book 18, fo. 818; more recently, see Nahoum Weissman, *Les Janissaires: Etude de l'Organisation Militaire des Ottomans* (Paris, 1938); Paul Wittek, "Devshirme and Shari'a," *BSOAS* 17(1955), 1:271–78; Daniel Pipes, *Slave Soldiers and Islam: The Genesis of a Military System* (New Haven/ London, 1981); Bat Ye'or, *The Decline of Eastern Christianity*, 108–15; Vryonis Jr., *The Decline of Medieval Hellenism*, 175, 182; Apostolos E. Vacalopoulos, *The Greek Nation, 1453–1669* (New Brunswick, N.J., 1976), 31–35; the *devshirme* children were recruited in Albania, Greece, the Aegean islands, Bulgaria, Serbia, Bosnia-Herzegovina, Croatia, and Hungary; idem, *History*, 70–72. For the Mamluks, see David Ayalon, *Studies on the Mamlouks of Egypt (1250–1517)* (London, 1977); idem, *The Mamlouk Military Society: Collected Studies* (London, 1979).

39. Jean de Chardin, *Voyages du Chevalier de Chardin en Perse, et autre lieux d'Orient, enrichis d'un grand nombre de belles figures en taille-douce, représentant les antiquités et les choses remarquables du pays par L. Langles* (Paris, 1811), 5:226–28, 306–8.

40. Mawardi, *Les Statuts*, 308–9.

41. Nawawi, *Minhadj*, 3:28; see Abu Yusuf, *Le Livre de l'impôt foncier*, 329–31.

42. Ibn al-Balkhi, in Le Strange, *Description of the Province of Fars in Persia*, 28. The anarchy which followed the Arab conquest created an apocalyptic literature, see Brock in "Syriac Sources," 33–36. For revolts of the Copts up to the ninth century, see Ira M. Lapidus, "The Conversion of Egypt to Islam," *IOS* (1972): 2:248–62, and Dionysius of Tell-Mahré, in *Chronique de Michel le Syrien*, 3:77–84.

43. Evariste Lévi-Provençal, *Histoire de l'Espagne Musulmane* (Paris/Leiden, 1950), 1:228; Mikel de Epalza, "Les Mozarabes: Etat de la question," trans. from Spanish by André Bazzana, *REMMM* 63–64 (1992/1–2): 39–50.

44. Lévi-Provençal, *Histoire*, 1:307.

45. Haim Ze'ev (J.W.) Hirschberg, *A History of the Jews in North Africa* (Leiden, 1974), 1:108.

46. Moshe Perlmann, "Eleventh Century Andalusian Authors on the Jews of Grenada," *PAAJR* 18 (1949): 269–70.

47. Hady Roger Idris, *La Berbérie Orientale sous les Zirides, Xe-XIIe siècles* (Paris, 1962), 2:758.

48. Edrîsî (al-Idrisi), *Description de l'Afrique et de l'Espagne*, with a trans. by Reinhart Dozy and Michael Jan de Goeje (Leiden, 1866), 129–30, 142: "the products of the earth, the population, everything had disappeared"; Ibn al-Athir, *Annales du Maghreb et de l'Espagne*, trans. from Arabic and annotated by Edmond Fagnan (Algiers, 1898), 456–60; Hirschberg, *A History of the Jews*, 1:114–15.

49. Ibn al-Athir, *Annales*, passim; Georges Vajda, *Un Recueil de textes historiques judéo-marocains*, *Hesperis* 12 (1951); Eugène Fumey, *Choix de correspondances marocaines. Pour servir à l'étude du style épistolaire administratif employé au Maroc (50 lettres officielles de la Cour chérifienne)* (Paris, 1903), 294; William Shaler, *Sketches of Algiers, Political, Historical and Civil.Containing an Account of the Geography, Population, Government* (Boston, 1826); Perceval Barton Lord, *Algiers, with Notices of the Neighbouring State of Barbary* (London, 1835), 2:138–39; Elizabeth Broughton, *Six Years Residence in Algiers* (London, 1839), 352–53; Archives *AIU* (1863–1913), see Littman, "*Quelques Aspects*"; and idem, "Jews under Muslim Rule in the late Nineteenth Century," *WLB* 28, n.s. 35/36 (1975): 65–76, and idem, "Jews under Muslim Rule, II: Morocco."

50. B. Evetts, ed., and annot., *History of the Patriarchs of the Coptic Church of Alexandria, III: Agathon to Michael I (766)* , trans. from Arabic, in *Patr. Or.* (1910), 5, fasc.1:173. Marwan had written to his soldiers to rejoin him, ordering them to pillage every town and massacre its inhabitants, ibid., 5:162.; Coptic chronicles of the Middle Ages mention the abduction of Coptic children as slaves, see *Patr. Or.*, 5:115; For the 744–45 revolt by Arab tribes whose extortions forced the *dhimmis* to flee, see Gil, *A History*, 86.

51. Tritton, *The Caliphs*, chap.9. These facts fill the pages of the Jewish, Coptic, and Syriac chronicles; extracts in Bat Ye'or, *The Decline of Eastern Christianity*, Documents, 333–446. For the tribal revolts in 792–93, 796, 807–10, 813–25 in Palestine, etc., see Gil, *A History*, 280–421; *Chroniques de Denys [pseudo-Dionysius] de Tell Mahré*, trans. from Syriac and ed. Jean-Baptiste Chabot (Paris, 1895), 108–9; *Chronique de Michel le Syrien*, 3:21–22, 52–53; Ashtor, *A Social and Economic History*, chap.2. For Mesopotamia, *Chronique de Denys*, 172 and passim.

52. Gil's *A History* is an invaluable book of information on Palestine, drawn from Jewish, Arabic, Syriac, Latin, and Greek sources. For these events, see 414–16.

53. Castellan, *Histoire des Balkans*, 254. At the fall of Missolonghi (22 April 1825) during the Greek war of independence, Ibrahim Pasha sent the heads of four to five thousand rebels to Constantinople, and three to four thousand women were sold into slavery; see the letter of 11 May 1825 by the Genevan banker Jean-Gabriel Eynard, from Zante, in Broughton, *Travels*, 1:176.

54. Haim Nahoum, ed., *Recueils de Firmans Impériaux Ottomans adressés aux Valis et aux Khedives d'Egypte 1006 H.-1322 H.(1597–1904)*, trans. from Turkish (Cairo, 1934), 109–10; Kostandinos A. Vakalopoulos, *Modern History of Macedonia (1830–1912)*, trans. from Greek by J. R. Collins-Litsas and Deborah Whitehouse (Salonika, 1988), 22. In 1821 the Christian slaves originated from Thessaloniki, Serrès, and Drama; Philip P. Argenti, ed. and introduction, *The Massacres of Chios, Described in Contemporary Diplomatic Reports* (London, 1932).

55. Nahoum, *Recueils de Firmans*, 137.

56. James Bryce, ed., *The Treatment of the Armenians in the Ottoman Empire (1915–1916)* (London, 1916); Johannes Lepsius, *Deutschland und Armenien. 1914–1918: Sammlung diplomatischer Aktenstücke* (Potsdam, 1919); André Mandelstam, *La Société des Nations et les Puissances devant le problème arménien*, 2nd ed. (Beirut, 1970); Yves Ternon, *Les Arméniens: Histoire d'un génocide* (Paris, 1977); Arthur Beylerian, *Les Grandes Puissances, l'Empire Ottoman et les Arméniens dans les archives françaises (1914–1918)*, collected documents (Paris, 1983); Vahakn N. Dadrian, *The History of the Armenian Genocide. Ethnic Conflict from the Balkans to Anatolia to the Caucasus* (Providence, R.I./Oxford, 1995).

57. Muslim, *Sahih*, 4, chap. 1107 (6423–29); Bokhari, *Traditions Islamiques*, 1, title 23; 93:3; al-Baghawi, *Mishkat al-Masabih*, 1:26.

58. Dennet, *Conversion and the Poll-Tax*; Fattal, *Le Statut Légal*, 338. See the twentieth-century discussions on the methods of the conquest of Morocco in order to determine the financial system and government of the lands, in Louis Milliot, *Introduction à l'Etude du Droit Musulman* (Paris, 1953), 502–5.

59. Extracts from Syriac, Coptic, and Armenian chronicles in Bat Ye'or, *The Decline of Eastern Christianity*, Document section: "The Peasantry's Condition," 305–28.

60. This problem is covered in Abu Yusuf, *Le Livre de l'impôt foncier*.

61. Tritton, *The Caliphs*, 127–36. In Egypt under the patriarchate of Alexander II (705–30), monks were mutilated, taxed, and their order banned, see Evetts, ed., *History of the Patriarchs*, in *Patr. Or.*, 5:51, 54; for extortions under torture, ibid., 64–78; *Chronique de Denys*, passim.

62. Abu Yusuf, *Le Livre de l'impôt foncier*, 88, 99–104, 186, 313; Yahya b. Adam, *Kitab al-kharaj*, in Ben Shemesh, *Taxation in Islam*, 1. This fiscal reform was attributed to the Caliph Umar II (717–20).

63. See the coexistence of these two trends in Yahya b. Adam, ibid., and in Abu Yusuf, *Le Livre de l'impôt foncier*. For an example of the link between religion and money in Damascus in the eighteenth century (the repeal of an order for forced conversions), see Louis Pouzet, *Damas au VIIe/XIIIe siècle. Vie et structures religieuses dans une métropole islamique* (Beirut, 1988), 316.

64. Evetts, ed., *History of the Patriarchs*, in *Patr. Or.*, 5:56–58; the fugitives were the inhabitants who were fleeing from one region to another to escape slavery or fiscal oppression. All contemporary chroniclers, Armenian, Syriac, and Jewish mention "fugitives" or "exiles." See the relevant documents in Bat Ye'or, *The Decline of Eastern Christianity*.

65. Evetts, ed., *History of the Patriarchs*, in *Patr. Or.*, 5:72.

66. Ibid. For these *hadiths*, Ben Shemesh, *Taxation in Islam*, 1:60–62.

67. The chronicler had already mentioned (page 19) the misfortunes caused by the first Arab raids from 642, renewed under the Caliph Abd al-Malik and during many campaigns in Armenia.

68. Ghevond (eighth-century Armenian vartabed), *Histoire des Guerres et des Conquêtes des Arabes en Arménie*, trans. from Armenian by Garabed V. Chahnezarian (Paris, 1856), 124, 130–32; for the peasantry's condition in the Eastern Arab world, see Ashtor, *A Social and Economic History*; Bat Ye'or, *The Decline of Eastern Christianity*, extracts from chronicles in Documents, 333–61. For Anatolia, Vryonis Jr., *The Decline of Medieval Hellenism*; for Greece, Vacalopoulos, *Histoire de la Grèce Moderne*, 42–49; for Bulgaria, Angelov, *Les Balkans au Moyen*

Age; Halil Inalcik, *The Ottoman Empire: Conquest, Organisation and Economy, Collected Studies* (London, 1978), chap. 6:235.

69. For the general insecurity and the evils of anarchy in Egypt in the ninth century, Sawirus ibn al-Mukaffa (Bishop of Al-Asmunain), *History of the Patriarchs of the Egyptian Church, Known as the History of the Holy Church,* text and docs. trans. from Arabic by Yassa Abd al-Masih, O. H. E. Burmester (Cairo 1943–70), 2, pt.2, 45–59; *Chronique de Michel le Syrien,* passim; Bar Hebraeus, *The Chronography,* 1:325–483; for Armenia (1596–1628), Arakel de Tauriz, *Livre d'Histoires,* 307–9; Bat Ye'or, *The Decline of Eastern Christianity,* 115–21. In the modern period, Nestorians in the Tauris region refused to pay the Kurds the protection tax in 1843, and devastated three of their villages. By way of reprisal 4,350 Nestorians were slaughtered, 330 to 400 women and children reduced to slavery, all their property confiscated, and all their houses and churches destroyed; see in Hommaire de Hell, *Voyage en Turquie,* 2:22–24, where it is recounted. Threatened with armed intervention by Britain, the Kurds returned the women and children. The survivors took refuge in Mosul, where the Turks offered them asylum.

70. Abu Yusuf, *Le Livre de l'impôt foncier,* 203. For the expropriation of Palestinian Jews by means of exorbitant taxation, see Gil, *A History,* 151; for the *dhimmis* in Mesopotamia, Syria and Egypt in the eighth to ninth centuries, see *Chronique de Denys,* 130, 135–36, 168; *Chronique de Michel le Syrien,* 63–64, 106–7; Evetts, ed., *History of the Patriarchs,* in *Patr. Or.,* 5:64, under the patriarchate of Michael I (744–68); for the Jews in Tripolitania at the beginning of the twentieth century, see Nahoum Slouschz, "Israélites de Tripolitaine," *BAIU* 31 (1906): 107–8; for the Serbs, Cvijic, *La Péninsule Balkanique;* John Joseph, *Muslim-Christian Relations and Inter-Christian Rivalries in the Middle East: The Case of the Jacobites in an Age of Transition* (New York, 1983), 25–26.

71. For the Ottomans' retention of Christian peasants in villages, Angelov, *Les Balkans au Moyen Age,* 231; Mitev, "Le Peuple Bulgare;" Vryonis Jr., *The Decline of Medieval Hellenism;* Vakalopoulos, *Modern History of Macedonia,* 99–104. On the seizure of lands in Asiatic Turkey by increasing taxes and humiliations, see Hommaire de Hell, *Voyage en Turquie,* 1:460; in Serbia, see Cvijic, *La Péninsule Balkanique;* Angelov, *Les Balkans au Moyen Age,* 220–75; for the colonization of the land, Samardzic, *Le Kosovo-Metohija,* 109; for brigandage and anarchy, ibid., 111–24.

72. Nawawi, *Minhadj,* 3:277; but, for Qudama b. Ja'far, whose opinion reflects general practice, only fighting men were liable for payment of the *jizya,* but not sick, blind, or disabled men or monks, see Ben Shemesh, *Taxation in Islam,* 2:42–44.

73. Brock, "Syriac Sources," 19; for the taxing of Serbian children, widows, and invalids, see Samardzic, *Le Kosovo-Metohija,* 110.

74. Tritton, *The Caliphs,* 125–35; Evetts, ed., *History of the Patriarchs,* in *Patr. Or.,* 5:69–70, particularly under the patriarchate of Alexander II, 705–30. See the letters from the Geniza bearing witness to this situation among Palestinian Jews, in Gil, *A History,* 156; Shlomo Dov Goitein, "Evidence on the Muslim Poll-Tax from non-Muslim Sources: A Geniza Study," *JESHO* 6 (1963): 278–95; idem, *A Mediterranean Society: The Jewish Communities of the Arab World as Portrayed in the Documents of the Cairo Geniza* (Berkeley/Los Angeles, 1967–1989), 2 (The Community), 132, 380–94; Alexander Scheiber, "The Origins of Obadyah the Norman Proselyte," *JJS* 5 (1954): 1:37; see reproductions of receipts for the *jizya:* two lead disks from the Abbasid period (854 and 900) and another on paper (Salonika, 1755), in Hayyim Ze'ev Hirschberg (J.W.), "Research on the History and Culture of the Jews in the Muslim East," in *Annual* (Bar Ilan University), 7–8 (Tel Aviv, 1969–70): 71, figs 1, 2, and "B"—reproduced in Bat Ye'or, *The Decline of Eastern Christianity,* 323.

75. Nawawi, *Minhadj,* 3:280–81. These practices are not mentioned by Abu Yusuf, *Le Livre de l'impôt foncier,* 101–87, 191ff., nor by other jurists.

76. Georges Vajda, "Un Traité maghrébin 'Adversus Judaeos': *Ahkam ahl al-Dhimma* du Shaykh Muhammad b.Abd al-Karim al-Maghili," in [Lévi-Provençal], *Etudes d'Orientalisme,* 1:811; Léon l'Africain, *Description de l'Afrique,* new ed., trans. from Italian by A. Epaulard (Paris, 1956), 2:436–37. The same opinion is expressed by the famous Baghdad scholar, Ibn al-Fuwati (1244–1323), see Bat Ye'or, *The Decline of Eastern Christianity,* 348–49.

77. James Riley, *Loss of the American Brig Commerce. Wrecked on the Western coast of Africa, in the month of August, 1815. With an account of Timbuctoo and of the hitherto undiscovered great city of Wassanah* (London, 1817), 2:214–18, reproduced in Bat Ye'or, *The Dhimmi,* 296–97.

78. Letter from a Marrakesh Jew, an Italian protégé, 25 February 1894, in *BAIU* (January–February 1894), see Littman, "Quelques Aspects," 45.

79. Arminius Vàmbéry, *Travels in Central Asia* (London, 1864), 372–73. For the forced conversion of Persian Jews, see chap. 3, n. 22.

80. B. Evetts, ed., *History of the Patriarchs*, in *Patr. Or.*, 5:173.

81. Chardin, *Voyages*, 10:241. See also a Jewish chronicle from Fez at the beginning of the seventeenth century, in Vajda, "Un recueil de textes." On the fiscal exploitation of the whole Egyptian population under the Mamluks, see Taki-Eddin-Ahmad Makrizi, *Histoire des Sultans Mamlouks de l'Egypte*, trans. from Arabic by Etienne Marc Quatremère (Paris, 1837/1842). In Morocco, Joseph de Léon noted that Moulay Isma'il taxed the Jews as it suited him, see Chantal de La Véronne, *Vie de Moulay Ismaïl, roi de Fès et de Maroc, d'après Joseph de Léon (1708–1728)* (Paris, 1974), fol. 251.

82. Gil, *A History*, 148–51.

83. Tudor Parfitt, *The Jews in Palestine, 1800–1882* (London, 1987), 39–48; James Finn, *Stirring Times, or Records from the Jerusalem Consular Chronicles of 1853 to 1856* (London, 1878); see letters from British Consul James Finn in Jerusalem to his ambassador at Constantinople, Sir Stratford Canning, 15 July 1851; 29 May 1852 (to Malmesbury), 8 July 1858, in Hyamson, *The British Consulate*, 1:171, 185, 260.

84. Parfitt, *The Jews in Palestine*, 54–55; Isaac b.Salomon Farhi (d.1853), *Imrey Binah (Words of Wisdom)* (Hebrew) (Salonika, 1863); Andrew A. Bonar and Robert Murray M'Cheyne, *Narrative of a Mission of Inquiry to the Jews from the Church of Scotland in 1839* (Edinburgh, 1842); Israel Joseph Benjamin, *Eight Years in Asia and Africa from 1846 to 1855 By J.J. Benjamin II* (Hanover, Germany, 1859), 24–25; John Lloyd Stephens, *Incidents of Travel in Egypt, Arabia Petrae, and the Holy Land* [1837], ed. with an introduction by Victor Wolfgang von Hagen (Norman, OK, 1970).

85. James Silk Buckingham, *Travels in Palestine* (London, 1821), 257. Buckingham, author and traveler, founded the famous London literary review, *The Athenaeum* (1828–1921).

86. Astvatzatour Ter Hovhannesiantz (Bishop), *Chronological History of Jerusalem* (Jerusalem, 1890), 2, chap. 45, 399–400.

87. Letter (8 May 1844) from the French consul at Damascus to François Guizot, Paris, Direction Politique, no.15, AE. For the exactions and depradations practiced on the Armenians at the same period in the region of Trebizond at Tauris, see Hommaire de Hell, *Voyage en Turquie*, 1:431, 458, passim.

88. Moshe Perlmann, ed., *Shaykh Damanhuri on the Churches of Cairo, 1737*, trans. from Arabic with an introduction and notes (Berkeley/Los Angeles/London, 1975); Abu Yusuf, *Le Livre de l'impôt foncier*; Ibn an-Naqqash, "Fetoua 1357–1358 relatif à la condition des zimmis et particulièrement des chrétiens en pays musulmans, depuis l'établissement de l'islamisme, jusqu'au milieu du VIIIe siècle de l'Hégire," trans. from Arabic by [François Alphonse] Belin, *JA*, 4th series 18 (1851): 417–516; 19 (1852): 97–103; Ahmed ed-Dardir el-Adaoui [al-Adawi], *Fetoua* [1772]: "Réponse à une question," trans. from Arabic by [François-Alphonse] Belin, *JA*, 4th series, 19 (1852): 103–12.

89. The Greek historian Apostolos Vacalopoulos blames renegades' connivance with the regime for the destruction of the Christian peoples. The same opinion is supported by the Serbian sociologist and geographer, Jovan Cvijic, *La Péninsule Balkanique*, 387: "It can be said that it was [Bosnian] renegades who helped to reduce the *raya* [Christian] to the lowest depths of humiliation." However, the author's opinion is qualified: while acknowledging the protection of churches procured by the Bosnian Muslims, he regarded them as having been more fanatical and violent than the Turks toward their Christian fellow citizens; see Robert, *Les Slaves de Turquie*, 2:12. Nevertheless, during periods of prosperity *dhimmi* communities from Persia to Spain were placed under the favorable protection of viziers or high *dhimmi* officials, whether renegades or not. See, specifically, the development of the twelfth century Armenian community in Egypt, in Marius Canard, "Un vizir chrétien à l'époque fatimite, l'Arménien Bahrams," *AIEO* 12 (1954), reprinted in *Miscellanea Orientalia*, preface by Charles Pellat (London, 1986), 6:84–113. The Jews leveled the same accusation at their renegades.

90. For discussion of the ability of *dhimmi* courts to arbitrate or make decisions, see Fattal, *Le Statut Légal*, 351- 65; Tritton, *The Caliphs*, 186. For Mawardi, decisions by *dhimmi* judges do not have a properly compulsory character and their judgments concern those under their

jurisdiction but are not accepted by the imam, see Mawardi, *Les Statuts*, 133. That is why the *dhimmi* courts had to have their judgments ratified by the kadi.

91. Nawawi, *Minhadj*, 3:400; al-Qayrawânî, *La Risâla*, 263; Mawardi, *Les Statuts*, 132; this is the opinion of the four orthodox rites, see Fattal, *Le Statut Légal*, 361. For the koranic sources or *hadiths* invoked, ibid., 362.

92. Nawawi, *Minhadj*, 405–6. The refusal of *dhimmi* evidence is confirmed by numerous sources. For the Ottoman Empire, Vacalopoulos, *Histoire de la Grèce Moderne*, 37. This refusal is mentioned in a letter from the British ambassador at Constantinople, William Pagett, 26 February 1700, in FO, SP 97–21, 73–74. See also some consular reports in Bat Ye'or, *The Decline of Eastern Christianity*, Document section, "The Era of Emancipation," 395–430; for the refusal to lift the ineligibility, ibid., and Bat Ye'or, *The Dhimmi*, 210, 307–8, 312; Edmondo de Amicis, *Marocco* (Milan, 1878), 319.

93. Nawawi, *Minhadj*, 2:17.

94. Karsten Niebuhr, *Travels through Arabia and Other Countries in the East*, trans. from German by Robert Heron [1761–64] (Edinburgh, 1792), 1:408. This same problem of jurisdiction motivated the arrangement of the commercial ports of the Levant, intimating to foreign traders that they should reduce their relations with Muslims to the minimum and carry out their commercial transactions with *dhimmis*. The refusal of evidence from a non-Muslim necessitated the related specific clauses in the Capitulations; François Charles-Roux, *Les Echelles de Syrie et de Palestine au XVIIIe siècle* (Paris, 1928); Francis Rey, *La Protection Diplomatique et Consulaire dans les Echelles du Levant et de Barbarie* (Paris, 1899); Bat Ye'or, *The Decline of Eastern Christianity*, 158–62; For Bulgaria, Mitev, "Le Peuple Bulgare," 248.

95. Nawawi, *Minhadj*, 3:117. For the inequality in the punishment of the *lex talionis*, see Abu Yusuf, *Le Livre de l'impôt foncier*, 35, 235, 238–39, 242–45; Ibn Taymiya, in Laoust, *Le Traité de droit public*, 153–57; al-Qayrawânî, *La Risâla*, 245.

96. al-Qayrawânî, *La Risâla*, 243.

97. Ibid., 249; Fattal, *Le Statut Légal*, 113–19.

98. al-Qayrawânî, *La Risâla*, 245: the blood of a *dhimmi* is valued at half the price of a Muslim's; if the victim is a Jew or Christian woman, the price is again cut by half, hence, a quarter of the full rate and half that of a Muslim woman. These differences between the sexes may have been linked to the male's economic role.

99. Nawawi, *Minhadj*, 3:152; al-Qayrawânî, *La Risâla*, 245; Ibn Taymiya, *Majmu'a Fatawi* (Arabic) (Cairo, 1911), 4:184, no.366.

100. Before the 1856 reforms, Christian evidence was refused in Turkey: "When a raya is in dispute with a Turk, he can only call on the evidence of a Muslim," see Hommaire de Hell, *Voyage en Turquie*, 1:462; For Morocco, see de Amicis, *Le Maroc*, French ed., trans. from Italian by Henri Belle (Paris, 1882), 275.

101. Imperial *iradé*, 12 December 1875.

102. Vice-consul Charles A. Brophy (Bourgas) to Consul-General and Judge, Sir P. Francis (Constantinople), Bourgas, 9 April 1876, FO 424/40, n° 49, ann. in n° 806, extract in Bat Ye'or, *The Decline of Eastern Christianity*, 432–33.

103. Robert Curzon, *Armenia. A Year at Erzeroom, and on the Frontiers of Russia, Turkey, and Persia* (London, 1854), 84.

104. Nawawi, *Minhadj*, 3:205–6; Mawardi, *Les Statuts*, 305; al-Qayrawânî, *La Risâla*, 251.

105. Perceval Barton Lord, *Algiers*, 2:81; see also Roland Lebel, *Les Voyageurs français du Maroc. L'exotisme marocain dans la littérature de voyage* (Paris, 1936), 125–26; Hirschberg, *A History*, 2:304; Jean Ganiage, *Les Origines du Protectorat français en Tunisie (1861–1881)* (Paris, 1959), 71–74.

106. Nawawi, *Minhadj*, 3:286. Fattal, *Le Statut Légal*, 148–49; Mawardi, *Les Statuts*, 305; Ibn 'Abdun, in Evariste Lévi-Provençal, *Séville musulmane au début du XIIe siècle. Le traité sur la vie urbaine et les corps de métiers d'Ibn 'Abdun*, trans. from Arabic with notes (Paris, 1948), 128; Abdel Magid Turki, "Situation du 'tributaire' qui insulte l'Islam, au regard de la doctrine et de la jurisprudence musulmanes," *SI* 30 (1969), reprinted in idem., *Théologiens et Juristes de l'Espagne musulmanes. Aspects Polémiques* (Paris, 1982), chap. 6, 199–232.

107. This regulation was based on the principle that a Muslim could not be subject to the authority of a non-Muslim, see Fattal, *Le Statut Légal*, 148; Ibn an-Naqqach, "Fetoua," *JA*, 4th series 18 (1851): 502. Joseph de Léon notes that the Christian slaves in Morocco incurred

capital punishment if they wrote in Arabic: de la Véronne, *Vie de Moulay Isma'il*, 70. This prohibition by the Muslim jurists obliged the Jewish and Christian *dhimmis* to write Arabic and Turkish in Hebrew or Syriac characters.

108. AIU. Maroc 4: C.11 (Tangiers), in Littman, "Quelques Aspects," 23–24; English trans.
in Littman, "Jews under Muslim Rule in the late nineteenth century." *WLB* 28, n.s. 35/36
(1975): 72.

109. Nawawi, *Minhadj*, 2:348–50.

110. Ibid., 349.

111. Harvey E. Goldberg, *The Book of Mordechai: A Study of the Jews of Libya* (Philadelphia,
1980), 74.

112. Rab. Abraham Hai Adadi (d.1874), in ibid., 76 n. 4.

113. See the discussion of this relationship, ibid., 44–45.

114. Charles de Foucaud, *Reconnaissance au Maroc. Journal de Route (1883–1884)* (Paris,
1888), 398–400; Nahum Slousch, *Travels in North Africa* (Philadelphia, 1927), 483. For the
Jabal Nafusa, see Mordechai Hakohen, *Highid Mordekhai (Mordechai's tale)* (Hebrew), sect. 91,
in Goldberg, *The Book of Mordechai*, 74.

115. Report by the acting consul for Bosnia-Herzegovina, Edward Bothamley Freeman, to
the Foreign Minister, Lord Edward Derby, London, from Bosna Serai (Sarajevo), 30 December 1876, extract in Bat Ye'or, *The Decline of Eastern Christianity*, 430–31. For the condition of
the Christians in European Turkey in the nineteenth century, see Abdolonyma Ubicini, *Lettres
sur La Turquie, ou Tableau Statistique, religieux, politique, administratif, militaire, commercial, etc. de
l'Empire ottoman depuis le Khatti Cherif de Gulkhané (1839). Accompagné de Pièces Justificatives*
(Paris, 1854), vol.2; Mantran, *Histoire de l'Empire ottoman;* Cvijic, *La Péninsule Balkanique;* Castellan, *Histoire des Balkans;* Robert, *Les Slaves de Turquie*, 2:11: every spahi could thrash the *raya*
on the *tchiftlik* (his estate).

116. MAE *Documents Diplomatiques, Affaires Arméniennes, Projets de Réformes dans l'Empire Ottoman, 1893–1897* (Paris, 1897), 6, *Arménie-Macédoine-Turquie*, letter from Paul Cambon (Constantinople) to Jean-Paul-Pierre Casimir-Perier, Minister of Foreign Affairs (Paris), Pera, 20
February 1894, 10–13.

117. Ibid., Letter to Gabriel Hanotaux, Minister of Foreign Affairs in Paris, Erzerum, 31
August 1894, 14–15.

118. Ibid., *Rapport Collectif des Délégués consulaires adjoints à la Commission d'enquête sur l'affaire
de Sassoun*, ibid., 28 July 1895, 98.

119. Robert B. Serjeant, "A Judeo-Arab House-Deed from Habban (with notes on the former Jewish Communities of the Wahidi Sultanate)," *JRAS* (October 1953): 119, repr. idem.,
Customary and Shariah Law in Arabian Society (London, 1991), 8:119. Prohibition on Jews carrying arms, in Niebuhr, *Travels through Arabia*, 2:256; see also Yomtob-David Sémach, *Une Mission de l'Alliance au Yémen* (Paris, 1910), 77, and ibid., in *BAIU* 35 (1910): 122.

120. Serjeant, "A Judeo-Arab House-Deed," 118.

Chapter 3: Religious and Social Aspects of Dhimmitude

1. Ibn an-Naqqash, "Fetoua," 18:432. For additional documentation on the subjects examined in this chapter, see Bat Ye'or, *The Dhimmi*, Index D (General), 439–44.

2. Ibn an-Naqqash, "Fetoua," 18:475.

3. Reproduced in Leonard Patrick Harvey, *Islamic Spain, 1250 to 1500* (Chicago/Lon-
don, 1990), 57.

4. Sawirus, *History of the Patriarchs*, 5:51. Syriac and Armenian chronicles describe the
same situation; Tritton, *The Caliphs*, chap. 9.

5. Mawardi, *Les Statuts*, 308–9; Moshe Perlmann, *Shaykh Damanhuri*, 20–21; Ibn an-Naqqash, "Fetoua," 513; Abu Yusuf, *Le Livre de l'impôt foncier*, 195–96; Ibn Taymiya, in Martin Schreiner, "Contributions à l'Histoire des Juifs en Egypte," *REJ* 31 (1895): 9–10, and in Bat Ye'or,
The Dhimmi, 179. For some jurists' opinions on the demolition, confiscation, and rules concerning churches and synagogues in North Africa and Spain, see Idris, "Les Tributaires."

6. Nawawi, *Minhadj*, 3:284–85. As Constantinople had been taken by force, there was a

risk of all the churches being confiscated. To save them, the defeated Greek princes, with the sultan's approval, invented a sham account of surrender by Constantin Paléologue; see Nicolas Iorga, *Byzance après Byzance*, introduction by Alexandre Paléologue (Paris, 1992), 94–96.

7. Tritton, *The Caliphs*, 49; The destruction of churches was often the result of denunciations, such as the denunciation in January 1785, which caused the demolition of two churches in Constantinople repaired after a fire; see the report by the British ambassador, Sir Robert Ainslie to the Marquis of Carmarthen (London), in Bat Ye'or, *The Decline of Eastern Christianity*, 386–89.

8. For the methods used for a strict control of restorations, see Richard James Horatio Gottheil, "*Dhimmis* and Moslems in Egypt," in *Old Testament and Semitic Studies in Memory of W. R. Harper* (Chicago, 1908), 2:353–414; for the orders for the destruction of churches in Egypt alone since 722, idem.

9. al-Adawi, *Fetoua*, 110. In the nineteenth century, synagogues in Morocco could not be public buildings; see Arthur Leared, *Morocco and the Moors, Being an Account of Travels, with a general description of the country and its people, with illustrations*, rev. and ed. by Sir Richard Burton (2nd ed., London/New York, 1891), 175–77. For a description of the Jews of Morocco in the nineteenth century, see Budgett Meakin, *The Moors* (London, 1902), 425–87; David Littman, "Mission to Morocco (1863–1864)," in Sonia and Vivian Lipman, eds., *The Century of Moses Montefiore* (London/New York, 1985), 171–229; idem, "Quelques Aspects"; idem, "Jews Under Muslim Rule"; idem, "Jews in Morocco, 1903–1912."

10. At the time of the Arab conquest of Spain almost all the churches were destroyed. For Mesopotamia, see Bar Hebraeus, *The Chronography*, passim; Jean-Maurice Fiey, *Communautés syriaques en Iran et Iraq des origines à 1552* (London, 1979), chap. 3, 257; idem, *Assyrie Chrétienne. Contribution à l'étude de l'histoire et de la géographie ecclésiastique et monastique du Nord de l'Iraq* (Beirut, 1965–1968); idem, *Mossoul Chrétienne* (Beirut, 1959). For Anatolia, see Vryonis Jr., *The Decline of Medieval Hellenism*. For the late Middle Ages, see Mouzaffal Ibn Abil-Fazaïl, *Histoire des Sultans Mamlouks*, ed., R. Graffin, François Nau, trans. from Arabic by E. Blochet, in *Patr. Or.*, 14, fasc.3, 458–59. Abu Salih, *The Churches and Monasteries of Egypt*, contains a list of churches, convents, and monasteries destroyed in Egypt alone, see Appendix: "Account of the Monasteries and Churches of the Christians of Egypt; forming the concluding sections of the *Khitat* of al-Makrîzî (died A.H. 845 = A.D. 1441)." It is impossible to assess this destruction; see Tritton, *The Caliphs*, chaps. 3 and 4; for the modern period, European travelers mention the destruction of churches and their conversion into mosques in the Ottoman Empire and Persia, see Laurent d'Arvieux, *Mémoires du Chevalier d'Arvieux. Envoyé Extraordinaire du Roy à la Porte, Consul d'Alep, d'Alger, Constantinople, dans l'Asie, la Syrie, la Palestine, l'Egypte & la Barbarie (1663–1685)*, collected by L.-B. Labat (Paris, 1735); Jean-Baptiste Tavernier, *Les six voyages en Turquie et en Perse de Jean-Baptiste Tavernier (1631–1668)* (Rouen, 1712). When he returned to San'a (Yemen) in 1905, Imam Yahya ordered the demolition of several synagogues built during the Ottoman period, see Hayyim J.Cohen, *The Jews of the Middle East 1860–1972* (New York/Jerusalem, 1973), 63.

11. Earl of Winchilsea, British ambassador at Pera (Constantinople) to the Foreign Office, London, 20 May 1662, FO, SP 97–17, 274b–275.

12. Hovhannesiantz, *Chronological History of Jerusalem*, 2:90–92.

13. Parfitt, *The Jews in Palestine*, 167; Finn, *Stirring Times*, 1:103, 118–119; for the period 634–1099, and the exaction of the same taxes from Jews, see Gil, *A History*, 148–60.

14. Fattal, *Le Statut Légal*, 203.

15. Mawardi, *Les Statuts*, 306. In Morocco, Jews had to bury their dead in great haste: de Amicis, *Le Maroc*, 319. This ordinance appeared in some legal regulations.

16. Muslim, *Sahih*, 4, chap. 1149 and also (6666); see also al-Qayrawânî, *La Risâla*, 25; Bokhari, *Les Traditions Islamiques*, 2, title 56, chap.182:1.

17. Louis Voinot, *Oujda et l'Amalat (Maroc)*, Oran (1911–1912), 99–101 and chap. 4. In Yemen, Jews were forbidden to mark their graves; see Tudor Parfitt, *The Road to Redemption: The Jews of the Yemen, 1900–1950* (Leiden/New York, 1996), 100.

18. Abraham Galanté, *Documents Officiels Turcs concernant les Juifs de Turquie, Recueil de 114 Lois, Règlements, Firmans, Bérats, Ordres et Décisions de Tribunaux*, trans. from Turkish (Istanbul, 1931), 62–65.

19. Ibid., 191–92. For the condition of the Jews in the Balkans, see Esther Benbassa and

Aron Rodrigue, *The Jews of the Balkans: The Judeo-Spanish Community, 15th to 20th centuries* (Oxford, 1995).

20. Nawawi, *Minhadj*, 1:224; Mawardi, *Les Statuts*, 306. For the condition of the Jews in the Maghreb, see André Chouraqui, *Between East and West. A history of the Jews of North Africa*, trans. from the French by Michael M. Bernet (Philadelphia, 1968); idem, *La condition juridique de l'Israélite marocain*, preface by René Cassin (Paris, 1950).

21. Nawawi, *Minhadj*, 1:224.

22. For forced conversions of Christian Arabs, see Morony, *Iraq*, 379; François Nau, *L'Expansion Nestorienne en Asie* (Paris, 1914), 106–13; *Chronique de Michel le Syrien*, 3:1; for the Copts under the patriarchate of Alexander II (705–30), see Sawirus, *History of the Patriarchs*, 2:72, and under the patriarchate of Michael I (744–68), ibid., 116; Lapidus, "The Conversion of Egypt," 248–62; Moshe Perlmann, "Notes on Anti-Christian Propaganda in the Mamluk Empire," *BSOAS* 10 (1939–42), 843–61; idem. "Asnawi's Tract against Christian Officials," in David Samuel Löwinger, Béla Somogyi, and Alexander Scheiber, eds., *Ignace Goldziher Memorial Volume* (Jerusalem, 1958), 2; Makrizi, *Histoire des Sultans Mamlouks*, 1:107 and 2:154. For forced conversions of Copts at this period, see Donald P. Little, "Coptic Conversison to Islam under the Bahri Mamluks, 692–755/1293–1354," in *BSOAS* 39 (1976), 552–69. For Anatolia, see Vryonis Jr., *The Decline of Medieval Hellenism*, 143–247; Mitev, "Le Peuple Bulgare"; Idris, "Les Tributaires," 191; Robert Brunschvig, *La Berbérie orientale sous les Hafsides, des origines à la fin du XVe siècle* (Paris, 1940), 1:397–400; Tavernier, *Six voyages*, 1:125; in Persia, Arakel de Tauriz, *Livre d'Histoires*; for the Jews of Persia in the eighteenth century, Amnon Netzer, "The Fate of the Jewish Community of Tabriz," in Moshe Sharon, ed., *Studies in Islamic History and Civilization in Honour of Professor David Ayalon* (Jerusalem/Leiden, 1986), 411–19; Nehemia Levtzion, ed., *Conversion to Islam* (New York, 1979); idem, "Conversion to Islam in Syria and Palestine and the Survival of Christian Communities," in Michael Gervers and Ramzi J. Bikhazi, eds., *Conversion and Continuity: Indigenous Christian Communities in Islamic Lands. Eighth to Eighteenth Century* (Toronto, 1990), 294; Richard W. Bulliet, *Conversion to Islam in the Medieval Period. An Essay in Quantitative History* (Cambridge, MA/London, 1979).

23. Hirschberg, *A History*, 1:123–39.

24. Islamic law ruled that it was permissible to buy their children from the inhabitants of enemy territories, and also to take them prisoner; such a purchase could also take place for the children of allied peoples, see Mawardi, *Les Statuts*, 287.

25. Parfitt, *The Road to Redemption*, 66–75. See the interview with a Yemenite couple by Bat Ye'or (*The Dhimmi*, 380–82), which seems to suggest that a Jew was deliberately killed so that his children would become orphans. A child was considered an orphan if only the father died, even if the mother was still alive.

26. For Ibn Hazm of Cordova (eleventh century), it was the *dhimmi*'s state of degradation which was the guarantee of protection; see Arnaldez, "La Guerre Sainte"; the same opinion is found with Ibn Taymiya, in Turki, "Situation du 'tributaire'," 202; all the jurists concur on this point. The honorific offices conferred on *dhimmis* caused massacres of communities; for the extermination of the Jews of Grenada (30 December 1066), see Moshe Perlmann, "Eleventh-Century Andalusian Authors on the Jews of Grenada," *PAAJR* 18 (1948/49): 269–90; for the massacre and plunder of the Jews in Persia and Iraq after the assassination of Sa'd ad-Dawla (1291), Jewish vizier and doctor of Arghun Khan, see Walter Joseph Fischel, *Jews in the Economic and Political Life of Mediaeval Islam* (London, 1937), 117; Bat Ye'or, *The Decline of Eastern Christianity*, 229, 356; for the extermination of the Jews of Fez on 7 June 1465 and of other towns, when the Jews were put to the sword, leaving no survivors, see the account by Abdalbasit b. Halil in Robert Brunschvig, ed., and trans., *Deux Récits de Voyage inédits en Afrique du Nord au XVe siècle: Abdalbasit B. Halil et Anselme Adorne* (Paris, 1936): "This was a major event, a great carnage . . ." (113); "Subsequently, the people in cities far from Fez, having learned of this fact, rose up against the Jews in their towns and did almost the same to them as the inhabitants of Fez had done to their Jews. This was a catastrophe for the Jews such as they had not experienced hitherto, there perished as many of them as God Almighty wished" (121).

27. al-Qalqashandi, *Subh al-Asha* (Cairo, 1913–1919), 2:390–91.

28. Koran 5:56; 3:27, 66; 6:151.

29. Abu Yusuf, *Le Livre de l'impôt foncier*, 196.

30. Nawawi, *Minhadj*, 3:285–86.

31. Abu Ga'far al-Tabari, "al-Mutawakkil et les Chrétiens," trans. from Arabic by André Ferré, in Maurice Borrmans, et al., ed., al-Dhimma: L'Islam et les Minorités Religieuses, PISAI, Etudes Arabes, Dossier Nos. 80–81, 1991/1–2, 97 (text in Arabic also). See also Abu Yusuf, Le Livre de l'impôt foncier, 195–96; Mawardi, Les Statuts, 305–6; Ibn Qayyim al-Jawziyya, ed., S. Salih, Sharh ash-shurut al-Umriyya (Commentary on the Pact of Umar) (Arabic) (Damascus, 1961), 81, 115, 236–37; extracts in Bat Ye'or, The Dhimmi, 196–98, and idem, The Decline of Eastern Christianity, 327–28; Scheiber, "The Origins of Obadyah," 32–37; extract in Bat Ye'or, The Decline of Eastern Christianity, 339–40.

32. Idris, "Les Tributaires," 173; Edmond Fagnan, "Le Signe distinctif des Juifs au Maghreb," REJ 28 (1894): 294–98.

33. Berber tribe allied with the Almohads (1130–1269).

34. al-Marrakushi, Histoire des Almohades (Al-mu'jib fi talkhis akhbar al-maghrib), trans. from Arabic by Edmond Fagnan (Algiers, 1893), 264–65. Anselme Adorne, a traveler from Flanders, in Tunis from 27 May until 15 June 1470, notes that if Jews did not wear distinctive clothing they would be punished by stoning, see Brunschvig, Deux Récits, 192.

35. Léon l'Africain, Description de l'Afrique, 1:234.

36. Vryonis Jr., The Decline of Medieval Hellenism, 224–27.

37. Angelo di Spoleto, Pèlerinage en Egypte (1303–1304), ed., G. Golubovich (Karachi, 1919), 3:68–71; al-Damanhuri, in Perlmann, Shaykh Damanhuri, 55–57.

38. Galanté, Documents Officiels Turcs, 115.

39. Ibid., 117.

40. Ibid.

41. Ibid., 118–19. Confirmed by the British ambassador to Constantinople, James Porter to William Pitt, Secretary of State, communication, 3 February 1758, FO, SP 97–40.

42. Ambassador James Porter to William Pitt, 3 June 1758, FO, SP 97–40 (n.p.); letter reproduced in Bat Ye'or, The Decline of Eastern Christianity, 385–86.

43. Stratford Canning, British ambassador in Constantinople, to the Foreign Office, London, 12 June 1827, FO 196–10, 161–62. Broughton notes that the difference between a Muslim and a dhimmi was more pronounced in Constantinople than anywhere else; see his Travels in Albania, 2:209: "Such is the dislike of the hat, the distinction of the Frank, that the prudent always think fit, and in our time it was absolutely necessary, in visiting the city [Constantinople], to procure the protection of a Janissary." The author comments that French ambassadors to the Porte since the duc de Fériol (1699–1711) had refused to alter their clothing and part with their weapons. They insisted that their interpretors wear European dress and that distinctive badges be abolished, ibid., 2:211.

44. Mitev, "Le Peuple Bulgare," 249.

45. Galanté, Documents Officiels Turcs, 119–20.

46. Slouschz, Travels, 351–52; see Meakin, The Moors, 434; de Amicis, Le Maroc, 319; Lord Barton, Algiers, 2:98–99; see also Littman, "Jews Under Muslim Rule"; idem, "Jews in Morocco, 1903–1912"; idem, "Quelques Aspects"; idem, "Mission to Morocco."

47. Ali Bey (Domingo Badia y Leblich), Travels of Ali Bey in Morocco, Tripoli, Cyprus, Egypt, Arabia, Syria and Turkey, between the years 1803 and 1807, written by himself (London, 1816), 2:242. The particular colors of dhimmis are mentioned by Jérôme Dandini, a priest sent by the pope to the Maronite patriarch of Lebanon in 1536: see Voyage du Mont Liban (Paris, 1675), 45–50. In 1825, a traveler passing through Damascus noted that no European could appear in the streets with European clothing and only Muslims could ride an animal in the town: in Walter Joseph Fischel, ed., Unknown Jews in Unknown Lands. The Travels of Rabbi David d'Beth Hillel (New York, 1973), 67. European dress fitted to the body seemed indecent in the dar al-Islam.

48. Joseph Wolff, Researches and Missionary Labours (1831–1834) (London, 1835), 177; Chardin, Voyages, 1:129: the Christians of Caffa (Black Sea port) attached a small piece of fabric to their caps. In Iran, Jews were forced to wear a distinctive badge until the beginning of the twentieth century. In addition to Hamadan, it was required in Teheran, Shiraz, Yazd, and elsewhere; see David Littman, "Les Juifs en Perse avant les Pahlevi," TM, 395 (June 1979), 1920–29; ibid., "Jews under Muslim Rule: The Case of Persia," WLB 32, n.s. 49/50 (1979): 7–11; Laurence D. Loeb, Outcaste: Jewish Life in Southern Iran (New York/London, 1977), 20–21. Fischel, Unknown Jews, contains information on the Christians of Persia and Azerbaijan.

For extortions from Jews and their assassination, see ibid; there, too, the governors attempted to save the victims of mass fanaticism. For additional documentation, see Index D (General): "Costume (distinctive)," in Bat Ye'or, *The Dhimmi*, 440.

49. Sémach, *Une Mission*, 72–73 (idem, *BAIU* 35 (1910): 117–18); Cohen, *Jews of the Middle East*, 65.

50. Nawawi, *Minhadj*, 3:285. This unanimously prescribed rule was always applied. It remained in force in Yemen until the Jews left for Israel in 1948, and in the Maghreb until colonization: see Parfitt, *The Road to Redemption*, 107; Leared, *Morocco and the Moors*, 175–77; letter, 16 May 1900 from J. Hoefler, Tripoli (Libya) to the president of the AIU, Paris (AIU, LIBYE I.C.12): see Littman, "Quelques Aspects" (repr., rev. and expanded, Geneva, 1977), 15–16.

51. Alexander Drummond, *Travels through different cities of Germany, Italy, Greece and Several Parts of Asia, as far as the Banks of the Euphrates, in a Series of Letters* (London, 1754), 138. Broughton notes the ban on *rayas* riding horses in Constantinople, *Travels in Albania*, 1:459.

52. al-Adawi, *Fetoua*, 108–9.

53. Perlmann, *Shaykh Damanhuri*, 55–57. Like the other jurists, the author cites the opinion of famous jurisconsults of the different schools of law on the status of the *dhimmis*. He demonstrates the consensus which emerges from the broad span of converging opinions.

54. Karsten Niebuhr, *Travels through Arabia*, 1:80–81. Prohibition on non-Muslims entering mosques is described in the extensive literature of European pilgrims and travelers to Islamic countries. See Eliezer Bashan for "The Prohibition on Non-Muslims entering Mosques in the Ottoman Empire as reflected in European Sources," in *Shofar*, 15, no. 2 (winter 1997).

55. James Silk Buckingham, *Travels in Palestine through the Countries of Bashan and Gilead, East of the river Jordan, including a visit to the cities of Geraza and Gamala in the Decapolis* (London, 1821), 457; for Iraq, see Hommaire de Hell, *Voyage en Turquie*, 1:463.

56. Letter, 16 May 1900 from J. Hoefler, Tripoli (Libya) to the president of the AIU, Paris, in Littman, "Jews Under Muslim Rule," 71; for Morocco, idem, "Quelques Aspects" (rev.), 15; Riley, *Loss of the American Brig*, 515–17, 537; d'Arvieux, *Mémoires*, 1:165. In the mid-fifteenth century, Bertrandon de la Brocquière noted the ban on Christians riding horses in Syrian towns: see Charles Schefer, ed., *Le Voyage d'outremer* (Paris, 1892), 32–33; Antoine Morison, *Relation Historique d'un Voyage Nouvellement fait au Mont de Sinai et à Jérusalem, etc.* (Paris, 1725), 155. For the prohibition on Europeans riding horses or even donkeys, required by the notables of Aleppo in 1770, see Charles-Roux, *Les Echelles de Syrie*, 86; for Morocco, de Amicis, *Le Maroc*, 319; Leared, *Morocco and the Moors*, 175–77; for Yemen, Sémach, *Une Mission*, 72 (idem, *BAIU* 35, 1910, 177).

57. Ibn an-Naqqach, "Fetoua," 432; Ibn al-Fuwati (d. 1323) attributed it to the second caliph, Umar Ibn al-Khattab, renewed by al-Mutawakkil (d. 861).

58. Koran 3:27, 114; 4:143; 5:56, 62; 60:1, 2.

59. Ibid., 3:18,19.

60. See Georges Vajda, "Juifs et Musulmans selon le Hadith," *JA* 229 (1937): 57–127; Eliahu Ashtor [Strauss], "The Social Isolation of Ahl adh-Dhimma," in *Paul Hirscher Memorial Book* (Budapest, 1949), 73–94.

61. Ibn an-Naqqach, "Fetoua," 424.

62. al-Qayrawânî, *La Risâla*, 313. The stone refers to the projectiles which Muslims threw at Jews and Christians. al-Jawziyya, *Sharh ash-shurut al-Umriyya*, extract in Bat Ye'or, *The Decline of Eastern Christianity*, 327–28; see Perlmann, *Shaykh Damanhuri*, for the jurists' opinions. Hadiths on this subject are reproduced by al-Baghawi, *Mishkat al-Masabih*, 2:969–73. European travelers mention this throwing of stones at Jews and Christians by Muslim children in Hebron, Nablus, and Jerusalem: see Bonar and M'Cheyne, *Narrative of a Mission*, 163; William Cullen Bryant, *Letters from the East* (New York, 1869), 193–95; John W. Dulles, *The Ride through Palestine* (Philadelphia, 1881), 142; for Libya, see Slouschz, *Travels*, 153; for Mosul, see report by British Vice-Consul H.E.Wilkie Young (Mosul), 28 January 1909, in n° 4, FO 195/2308, see Elie Kedourie, *Arabic Political Memoirs and other Studies* (London, 1974), 154; James Brant, British consul in Damascus (1855–60) reported that Muslim children were throwing stones at Christians and Europeans and that respectable Muslims, witnessing this abuse, did not scold

them: see Brant (Damascus) to Bulwer (Constantinople), 30 August 1860, n° 40, FO/1520, reproduced in Bat Ye'or, *The Dhimmi*, 274.

63. Perlmann, *Shaykh Damanhuri*, 55–57; Ibn Abdun, in Lévi- Provençal, *Séville musulmane*, 114.

64. Ibn an-Naqqach, "Fetoua," 510. For more of this *fatwa* in English, see Bat Ye'or, *The Decline of Eastern Christianity*, 328–29.

65. Letter, 11 November 1858 from the British Consul James Finn (Jerusalem), to Malmesbury (London), in Hyamson, *The British Consulate*, 1, 261. In Palestine, particularly in Jerusalem until 1839, Christians were pushed into the gutter by any Muslim who would swear: "turn to my left, thou dog." They were forbidden to ride on a mount in town or to wear bright clothes, see Finn, *Stirring Times*, 1:201–3; for the humiliations in the streets of Morocco, see de Amicis, *Le Maroc*, 319; Leared, *Morocco and the Moors*, 275–77; Walter Lemprière, *Tours from Gibraltar to Tangier, Sallee, Mogodore, Santa Cruz, Tarudant; and thence over Mount Atlas to Morocco, including a particular account of the Royal Haram* (2nd ed., London, 1793), 198.

66. Nawawi, *Minhadj*, 2:315.

67. Harvey, *Islamic Spain*, 57.

68. al-Baghawi, *Mishkat al-Masabih*, 2:972.

69. Nawawi, *Minhadj*, 3:285; Perlmann, *Shaykh Damanhuri*, 57; al-Adawi, *Fetoua*, 108–9; for the prohibition on decorating the outside of *dhimmi* houses: idem; see Galanté, *Documents Officiels Turcs*, for the order by Ottoman Sultan Ahmad III fixing a height of twelve pics for Muslim dwellings and nine pics for those of *dhimmis*; for Jewish houses in Yemen, see Sémach, *Une Mission*, 23 (idem, *BAIU* 35 (1910): 68).

70. Broughton, *Travels in Albania*, 1:459, 2:244; Niebuhr, *Travels through Arabia*, 1:115. For the obligation to paint the façades of *dhimmi* houses black, see Ubicini, *Lettres sur La Turquie*, 2:344. Broughton points to the restrictions imposed in northern Greece on the movements of Christian merchants who could not even take a walk in the suburbs without specifying its purpose to the Pasha, in Broughton, *Travels in Albania*, 1:62; their wives and children were retained in order to oblige the merchants to return: ibid., 1:78.

71. *The History of al-Tabari*, vol. 13, *The Conquest of Iraq, Southwestern Persia, and Egypt*, trans. from Arabic by Gautier H. A. Juynboll (New York, 1989), 13:90; al-Baghawi, *Mishkat al-Masabih*, 2:865–66. On Umar's orders the Jews were deported to Jericho.

72. Parfitt, *The Road to Redemption*, 104.

73. Edrisi (Al-Idrisi), *Description de l'Afrique*, 79–80. Ali b.Yusuf had two Jewish doctors, see Hirschberg, *A History*, 1:123.

74. Chevalier E. de Hesse-Wartegg, *Tunis, the Land and the People. With Twenty-Two Illustrations* (new ed., London, 1882). In 1827 three Jews were recognized in Qairuan and burned alive: see Brunschvig, *La Berbérie*, 299 n. 3.

75. Leared, *Morocco and the Moors*, 217.

76. Robert Kerr [agent of the Presbyterian Church of England], *Pioneering in Morocco, A record of Seven Years' Medical Mission Work in the Palace and the Hut* (London, 1894). The Jews of Yemen were subject to the same residential and travel restrictions: see Sémach, *Une mission*; Cohen, *Jews of the Middle East*, 65. In Morocco and Yemen, Jews had to return to the *mellah* (Jewish quarter) before nightfall: de Amicis, *Le Maroc*, 319; this measure was probably aimed at protecting them from aggression at night.

77. For Egypt, Sawirus, *History of the Patriarchs*, in *Patr. Or.*, 5:43, 52; see the travels of Dionysius of Tell-Mahré in Egypt, in *Chronique de Michel le Syrien*, 3:62–83; for Mesopotamia, *Chronique de Denys*, passim; for the Balkans, Cvijic, *La Péninsule Balkanique*; Castellan, *Histoire des Balkans*, 185–89.

78. Ibn al-Fuwati, in Bat Ye'or, *The Decline of Eastern Christianity*, 348–49.

79. Finn, *Stirring Times*, 1:201–3; see the letter from the French Consular Agent at Damascus, 9 December 1837, AE, n° 14.

80. Hommaire de Hell, *Voyage en Turquie*, 1:461, et passim. Benjamin, *Eight Years in Asia*, 68–75. See also "Reports by Her Majesty's Diplomatic and Consular Agents in Turkey Respecting the Condition of the Christian Subjects of the Porte (1868–75)," PP: Turkey, n°16 (1877), and the report by John George Taylor, British consul in Kurdistan (1865–74), sent from Erzerum to Sir Henry George Elliot, ambassador in Constantinople, 18 March 1869, n°13, PP, 1877 (C.1739), 92, 638–55; extracts in Bat Ye'or, *The Dhimmi*, 281–88.

81. David Cazès, *Essai sur l'Histoire des Israélites de Tunisie* (Paris, 1888), 100. Louis Frank, *Tunis. Description de cette Régence* (Paris,1862), 64–65.

82. In Morocco, soldiers stopped the first Jews they encountered and forced them to remove the brains from the decapitated heads, see in de Amicis, *Le Maroc*, 275; Voinot, *Oujda et l'Amalat*, 96. Recently published documents mention that, in Rabat and Meknes (Morocco), Jews were forced to salt the heads of dead rebels on the sabbath. Following protests from the French and British governments, Sultan Muhammad IV (1859–73) abolished these orders: see Eliezer Bashan, *Mimizrah Shemesh ad Mevo'o* (*Studies in the History of the Jews in the Orient and North Africa*) (Hebrew) (Lod, 1996), 274, 280. For Yemen, see Parfitt, *The Road to Redemption*, 86–87.

83. Paul Paquignon, "Quelques Documents sur la condition des Juifs au Maroc," *RMM* 9 (1909): 112–19. The *fatwas* listed all the humiliations imposed on the tributaries; see the ban on wearing shoes outside the *mellah*: ibid., 119–23.

84. Laurence Oliphant, *The Land of Gilead with Excursions in the Lebanon* (London, 1880), 12–13. The concept of the impurity of *dhimmis* and Europeans was particularly widespread in Persia: see Chardin, *Voyages*, 4:161. The Persians prohibited drinking from the glass of a non-Muslim; they rejected any contact with them: Hommaire de Hell, *Voyage en Turquie*, 1:514, 2:68, 348, 357.

85. Mawardi, *Les Statuts*, 299–300; this is at the very foundation of the concepts of *fay* and *jizya*; Abu Yusuf, *Le Livre de l'impôt foncier*.

86. In pre-Islamic tribal society, the life and property of an unprotected person was lawful for an Arab; this became the situation of the unprotected, non-Muslim *harbi*. The *amân* tended to alleviate this situation, but it was temporary and conditional. See du Caurroy, "Législation Musulmane," 568–91 ff. The concept of the sanctity of life and property only applied to Muslims, see al-Qayrawânî, *La Risâla*, 295. In pre-Islamic tribal society, protection (*jar*) was not accompanied by rituals similar to the compulsory religious degradation of the *dhimmi*.

87. On this conflict between law and tolerance, see the sections on the Copts and the statements by President Sadat below, p. 240.

88. See in particular, Count Constantin-François de Volney, *Voyage en Égypte et en Syrie pendant les Années 1783, 1784 et 1785, suivi de Considérations sur la Guerre des Russes et des Turcs* (Paris, 1825; 1st ed. 1788–89); Ubicini, *Lettres sur La Turquie*, examines each community separately.

89. Hommaire de Hell, *Voyage en Turquie*, 1:464.

90. Broughton, *Travels in Albania*.

91. Finn, *Stirring Times*, 1:201–3, passim.

92. Enclosed with despatch no. 4, Mosul, 28 January 1909, FO 195/2308, in Kedourie, *Arabic Political Memoirs*, 154.

93. Cvijic, *La Péninsule Balkanique*, 387–89; for the psychology of the *raya*, 264. Mimicry as a factor of Islamization is also mentioned in Samardzic, *Le Kosovo-Metohija*, 18, 109, 115.

94. *Chronique de Michel le Syrien*, 2:303–5, 402–3; *Patr. Or.*, 13:214–15, 244; Butler, *The Arab Conquest of Egypt*; Henry Bettenson, ed., *Documents of the Christian Church* (London/New York/Toronto, 1956), 65–68.

95. According to the Coptic chronicler, Patriarch Simon 1 (689–701) struggled throughout his life to prevent trouble between Christians and Muslims: Sawirus, *History of the Patriarchs*, 43. Today it is hard to imagine the violence of the reciprocal hatred felt by the patriarchs of the different Churches, and toward rivals.

96. Simon, *Verus Israel*; Parkes, *The Conflict*; idem, *Antisemitism* (London, 1963); Bernard Blumenkranz, *Juifs et Chrétiens dans le Monde Occidental, 430–1096* (Paris/Hague, 1962), 162, 208; Jules Isaac, *Genèse de l'Antisémitisme*; idem, *Jésus et Israël* (Paris, 1959); idem, *L'Antisémitisme a-t-il des racines chrétiennes?* (Paris, 1962); Léon Poliakov, *The History of Anti-Semitism, I: From Roman Times to the Court Jews*, trans. from French by Richard Howard (London, 1966); idem, *The History of Anti-Semitism, II: From Mohammed to the Marranos*, trans. from French by Natalie Gerardi (London, 1974); Robert Wistrich, *Antisemitism. The Longest Hatred* (London/New York, 1991).

97. Jean Juster, *Les Juifs dans l'Empire Romain, Leur Condition Juridique, Economique et Sociale* (Paris, 1914), 2:175; on this subject, see Marcel Simon, *Recherches d'Histoire Judéo-Chrétienne*

(Paris/Hague, 1962); idem, *Verus Israel*, 439, n.136; and the comprehensive study by William Nicholls, *Christian Antisemitism: A History of Hate* (Northvale, NJ/London, 1995).

98. Juster, *Les Juifs*, 1:368; the council of Narbonne (589), canon 9, forbade Jews to sing psalms at their funerals: see Juster, "La Condition Légale," 42; on the destruction of synagogues, see Parkes, *The Conflict*, 166–68.

99. Juster, *Les Juifs*, 471, *C.Th.* 16.8.25 (15 February 423) and *C.Th.* 16.8.27 (8 June 423). This law passed into the *dhimma* pact and is still in force in some Islamic countries. Parkes, *The Conflict*, analyzes the sources and developments of the Christian anti-Jewish legislation.

100. Juster, *Les Juifs*, 1:465, *C.Th.* 16.8.25 (15 February 423), renewed in the East on several occasions. The punishments provided by law in cases of confiscations of synagogues by Christians were much more severe than under Islam for the same infraction.

101. Ibid., 1:230, *C.J.* 1.5.12 §4 and §5.

102. Ibid., 1:233, *C.Th.* 16.8.18 (19 May 408), *C.J.* 1.9.11.

103. Ibid., 2:47, *C.Th.* 3.7.2 (14 March 388).

104. Ibid., the same provision for *dhimmis* in the Shafi'i rite.

105. Ibid., 2:114.

106. Makrizi, *Histoire des Sultans Mamlouks*, I/2:154.

107. Gottheil, "*Dhimmis* and Moslems in Egypt," 382–84.

108. For the Church's policy of supersession, see Isaac, *Genèse*, 164, 169; this subject is examined by Simon, *Verus Israel;* idem, *Recherches d'Histoire Judéo-Chrétienne;* Juster, *Les Juifs*, 1:44.

109. See the article published in Paris by S. Vailhé. "Les Juifs et la Prise de Jérusalem en 614," *EO* (1909): 12:15–17. "It is nothing new that an almost universal popular belief sees the hand of the Jew behind the great catastrophes which have stained mankind with blood; it is nothing new that this strange race is credited with an odious role in the misfortunes which befall a town or a nation": ibid., 15; and idem, 17: "Of course! the Persians were renowned for their cruelty and barbarism; and yet all the authors agree to impute the largest share of responsibility to the Jews for the outrageous misfortunes which struck the Holy City." For a discussion of the reliability of these souces written centuries after the event, see Gil, *A History*, 6–8.

110. For the welcome that the Eastern patriarchs accorded the Arabo-Muslim invaders and their collaboration with them, see Sebastian Brock, "Syriac Views of Emergent Islam," in Brock, *Syriac Perspectives*, 8:9–21. For collaboration between Byzantine and Serbian dissident princes and the conquering Turkish armies, see Dabinovic, "Les pactes d'assistance." For the denunciations and betrayals by Serbian princes and military men and the formation of a Turkophile party in Serbia, see ibid., 2:513–49; for the collaboration of the patriarchate of Constantinople, see Iorga, *Byzance après Byzance*, chap.5; in 1557, the Serbian patriarch of Pec was the brother of Mehmed Sokullu, a converted Christian, Islamized by the *devshirme*, who succeeded to the position of vizier. There is scarcely any doubt that a privileged class of Christian officials benefited from the Islamic conquest and collaborated with it.

111. Blumenkranz, *Juifs et Chrétiens*, 100. The persecution by Dagobert is thought to have occurred between 631 and 639; idem, *Les Auteurs Chrétiens Latins du Moyen-Age sur les Juifs et le judaïsme* (Paris/Hague, 1963), 217. The destruction of crosses in Jerusalem at the instigation of "a Jew" (see *Chronique de Michel le Syrien*, 2:431), belongs to this Judeophobic tradition. The chronicle of the Coptic patriarchs notes the destruction of crosses under the patriarchate of Isaac (686–89), without mention of Jews, *Patr. Or.*, 5:25. Abd al-Malik (685–705) ordered the destruction of crosses throughout the Umayyad Empire.

112. Blumenkranz, *Les Auteurs Chrétiens Latins*, 218–19; the patriarch records a detailed account of a pseudo-miracle in the Church of the Holy Sepulcher in Jerusalem, aimed at inciting the Christian kings to impose baptism on the Jews: idem, *Juifs et Chrétiens*, 102.

113. Ibid., 380–84. The Jews were accused of collusion with the Fatimid sultan al-Hakim although they were persecuted by him no less than Christians, with the result that Jews were killed in Europe as a reprisal.

114. Ibid., 384.

115. Bernard Blumenkranz, *Le Juif médiéval au miroir de l'art chrétien* (Paris, 1966); for the orientalization of iconography, idem, 36–39. Artistic representation from the fourteenth to the sixteenth century, contemporary with the Turkish conquest of eastern Europe, reflected the spread of this Asiatic influence in the clothing and individuals depicted. Many Armenian,

Greek, and Serbian painters and miniaturists fled the Turks and took refuge in Western Europe.

116. Blumenkranz, *Juifs et Chrétiens*, 318.

117. Jean-Baptiste Beaudin, French consular agent in Damascus, to Baron Roussin, ambassador of the king in Constantinople, Damascus, 19 July 1833, n° 1, AE.

118. Beaudin to Roussin, Damascus, 6 August 1835, n° 9, AE, underlined in the text.

119. Isaac b. Salomon Farhi, *Imrey Binah* (*Words of Wisdom*) (Ladino) (Belgrade, 1837).

120. Comte Gabriel de Lantivy (Jerusalem) to Prime Minister François Guizot (Paris), Jerusalem, 28 January 1844, AE, Direction Politique, 44.

121. Finn, *Stirring Times*, 1:111–12.

122. Consul Outrey (Damascus), 31 March 1858, to the French Ambassador in Constantinople, AE, Correspondance Politique Turquie, Damascus, vol.5, n° 60. (Trans. from French).

123. See Bat Ye'or, *The Dhimmi*, 278–81, for extracts from the correspondence on this subject to Sir Moses Montefiore (Ramsgate), 23 September 1869, signed by Haym Romano, David Harpi, Menahem Farchi, Jacob Halevi, Jacob Peretz, Raphael Halevi, Isaac Maimon, and Aaron Jacob (Damascus); and from Montefiore (Ramsgate) to Lord John Russell, Foreign Secretary (London), 16 October, n° 7157, and encl., in PP 1861 (2800) LXVIII.

124. Bernard Pierron, *Juifs et Chrétiens de la Grèce Moderne, Histoire des relations intercommunautaires de 1821 à 1945* (Paris, 1996).

Chapter 4: Modernity: A Time of Hope and a Time of Ashes

1. Narcisse Leven, *Cinquante Ans d'histoire: l'Alliance Israélite Universelle (1860–1910)* (Paris, 1911), I:168–70; 372-87; see also *BAIU*, 1866 (2nd sem.): 4–6; 1875 (1st sem.): 58–61; 1875 (2nd sem.): 23–27; 1876 (2nd sem.), 43; 1889, n°14:49–51; 1892, n°17:48–54; for other letters, see 1893, n°18:45–47; 1897, n° 22:75–81; 1898, n° 23:63–71; 1900, n° 25:73–75; 1907, n°32:66–67; 1908, n° 33:93–99; 1909, n° 34:77–79.

2. *BAIU.* 1910, n° 35:182.

3. Letter of 31 October 1910 from Mr. Nataf, director of the boys' school in Shiraz, to the president of the AIU (Paris), in *BAIU* 35 (1910): 182–88, repr. in Littman, "Jews under Muslim Rule: The case of Persia," 12–14. See Appendix 2 for a fuller description.

4. See Bat Ye'or, *The Decline of Eastern Christianity*, chap. 7: Nationalisms (1820–1918).

5. Vahakn N. Dadrian, *The History of the Armenian Genocide*, chap. 8.

6. MAE. *Documents Diplomatiques, Affaires Arméniennes (Supplément), 1895–1896* (Paris, 1897), 43, n° 59, letter sent from Harput, 28 November 1895.

7. Full text in Dadrian, *The History of the Armenian Genocide*, 147; the conditions whereby the protection of the *dhimmis* was abrogated conform with the opinions of the Muslim jurists cited above.

8. MAE. *Documents Diplomatiques, Affaires Arméniennes (Supplément)*, 47, n° 62, translation of a letter sent to the French consul in Aleppo by an eyewitness of the massacre, Urfa, 22 January 1896; 50, n° 63, letter of 29 January 1896 from the consul of the Portuguese nation in Aleppo, Zaicopoli, to the Italian ambassador in Constantinople, being descriptions from several witnesses. See also Dadrian, *The History of the Armenian Genocide*, 147–51. For the arrival of 42 Jews in Jerusalem (October 1896), who fled Urfa after several were killed fortuitously during the massacres, see Bat Ye'or, *The Dhimmi*, 89, 377–79 (AIU document and photograph).

9. For a discussion on estimated figures, see Dadrian, *The History of the Armenian Genocide*, 265–72.

10. MAE. *Documents Diplomatiques, Affaires Arméniennes (Supplément)*, 88, n° 123, letter from J. de La Boulinière, French chargé d'affaires in Constantinople, to Berthelot, Minister of Foreign Affairs, from Pera, 1 March 1896.

11. MAE. *Documents Diplomatiques, Affaires Arméniennes (Supplément)*, 89, n° 124, 10 March 1896.

12. Ibid., 28, n° 44, letter to French ambassador Paul Cambon in Constantinople, Diyarbakir, 18 December 1895.

13. Kedourie, *Arabic Political Memoirs*, 141–42.

14. Dadrian, *The History of the Armenian Genocide*, 183.

15. Edouard Driault and Michel L'Heritier, *Histoire diplomatique de la Grèce de 1821 à nos jours* (Paris, 1925), Vol. 1: *L'Insurrection et l'Indépendance (1821–1830)*, 287.

16. Ibid., 456.

17. There is an important literature on this subject; see, *inter alia*, Barbara W. Tuchman, *Bible and Sword. England and Palestine from the Bronze Age to Balfour* (New York, 1984); Michael J. Pragai, *Faith and Fulfilment. Christians and the Return to the Promised Land* (London, 1985).

18. Quoted by David Littman in "Mission to Morocco (1863–64)," in Lipman, eds., *The Century of Moses Montefiore*, 176.

19. Letter of 25 May 1839 from William Tanner Young, British Vice-Consul in Jerusalem, to Foreign Secretary Lord Palmerston: see Hyamson, *The British Consulate*, 1:4–7.

20. This prohibition appears frequently in different places, because the Muslim jurists identified collective prayer by Jews with the construction of a new synagogue; the position was the same for Christians. This measure still applies today in Saudi Arabia, where Christians cannot assemble for prayer, while residence for Jews is totally forbidden.

21. Driault, *Histoire diplomatique*, 2:190.

22. Jean-Baptiste Beaudin to Baron Roussin, AE, from Damascus, 2 August 1838, n° 20.

23. See Abraham J. Brawer, "Damascus Affair," *Encyclopaedia Judaica* (Jerusalem, 1971), 5:1250–52; Tudor Parfitt, "The Year of the Pride of Israel: Montefiore and the Damascus Blood Libel of 1840," in Lipman, eds., *The Century of Moses Montefiore*, 131–48; and a recent comprehensive study by Jonathan Frankel, *The Damascus Affair. 'Ritual Murder,' Politics, and the Jews in 1840* (Cambridge, 1997). For a revival of this accusation during the Gulf War at the UN Commission on Human Rights, see David Littman's detailed article, "Syria's Blood Libel Revival at the UN: 1991–2000," in *Midstream* (February–March 2000), 2–8, and oral statement to the UNCHR, 26 March 2001, for the World Union for Progressive Judaism, E/CN.4/2001/SR 13.

24. John Forsyth, Washington, to John Gliddon, Alexandria (Egypt), 14 August 1840, in Cyrus Adler and Aaron Margalith, *With Firmness in the Right: American Diplomatic Action Affecting Jews, 1840–1945* (New York, 1946), 4.

25. This article is reprinted in Achille Laurent, *Relation Historique des Affaires de Syrie depuis 1840 jusqu'en 1842, Statistique générale du Mont-Liban et Procédure complète dirigée en 1840 contre les Juifs de Damas, à la suite de la disparition du Père Thomas, publiée après les Documents recueillis en Tunisie, en Egypte et en Syrie, par Achille Laurent*, vol. 2 (Paris, 1846), 349–60. According to Jonathan Frankel (*The Damascus Affair*, 416), Achille Laurent was most probably the collective pseudonym of French Consul Ratti-Menton, Sibli Ayub—Ratti-Menton's closest adviser—and Jean-Baptiste Beaudin, interpreter and chancery head at the Damascus French consulate.

26. Hugh Rose, Beirut, to Foreign Secretary Lord Palmerston, 2 April 1847, FO, n° 19.

27. Hugh Rose, Beirut, to Henry Wellesley, Constantinople, 3 May 1847, FO, n° 14; on this question, see also Louis Loewe, ed., *Diaries of Sir Moses and Lady Montefiore* (London, 1983), 1:208–74; 2:9–17.

28. Joseph Simoni, Damascus, to Henry Wellesley, Constantinople, April 28, 1847, FO, n° 7.

29. Loewe, ed., *Diaries of Sir Moses Montefiore*, 1:287.

30. Ibid., 292–93.

31. Ibid., 1:259.

32. Ibid., 2:20. On 9 September 2000, Pope John Paul II beatified Pope Pius IX.

33. *Sud*, in Laurent, *Affaires de Syrie*, 2:358; see also Frankel, *The Damascus Affair*, passim.

34. Henry Harris Jessup, *Fifty Three Years in Syria* (New York, 1910), 2:424–25, quoted in Parfitt, "Montefiore and the Damascus Blood Libel of 1840," in Lipman, eds., *The Century of Moses Montefiore*, 145.

35. Pierre-André Taguieff, *Les Protocoles des Sages de Sion: Introduction à l'étude des Protocoles, un faux et ses usages dans le siècle* (Paris, 1992), I:160–63. Pierre Pierrard, *Juifs et Catholiques français. D'Edouard Drumont à Jacob Kaplan, 1886–1894* (Paris, 1997).

36. Norman Cohn, *Warrant for Genocide. The Myth of the Jewish World Conspiracy and the Protocols of the Elders of Zion* (London, 1967).

37. Negib Azoury, *Le Réveil de la Nation Arabe dans l'Asie Turque, en Présence des Intérêts et des Rivalités des Puissances Etrangères, de la Curie Romaine et du Patriarcat Oecuménique. Partie Asiatique*

de la Question d'Orient et Programme de la Ligue de la Patrie Arabe (Paris, 1905). Elie Kedourie provides interesting information on Azoury in *Arabic Political Memoirs and other studies* (London, 1974), 109–23. See also Eliezer Be'eri, *The Beginning of the Arab Israeli Conflict* (Hebrew) (Tel Aviv, 1985), 22–23, 119; Martin Kramer, *Arab Awakening & Islamic Revival. The Politics of Ideas in the Middle East* (New Brunswick, NJ, 1996). In his book Azoury mentions his Syrian friend 'Abdal-Rahman al-Kawakibi (d.1903) from Aleppo, author of a work, *Umm al-qura,* published anonymously in Cairo (1899), which reproduced alleged symposium proceedings of a secret society in Mecca, composed of 22 fictitious characters—representing scholars and divines from the Muslim world—who were promoting a new Caliphate for the Egyptian Khedive Abbas, to be under French protection. Between April 1902 and February 1903, the Egyptian journal, *al-Manar,* reproduced Kawakibi's book which was widely read and discussed; see Kedourie, *Arabic Political Memoirs,* 110.

38. Azoury, *Le Réveil de la Nation Arabe,* preface, III.

39. Ibid., IV.

40. Ibid., VI.

41. Ibid., VIII. In fact, Azoury was sentenced to death *in absentia* by the sultan for treason.

42. This book was never published; nor were the other two projects that were announced opposite the title as being in preparation: *La Patrie arabe. Etude approfondie de l'état actuel et de l'avenir des pays arabes asiatiques;* and, *Les Puissances étrangères et la question des sanctuaires chrétiens de Terre Sainte. Resumé historique et exposé de la situation actuelle.*

43. Eliezer Be'eri, *The Beginning,* 119.

44. Kedourie, *Arabic Political Memoirs,* 117.

45. Farid Georges Kassab, *Le Nouvel Empire Arabe, La Curie Romaine et le Prétendu Péril Juif Universel. Réponse à M. Azoury bey* (Paris, 1906), 23.

46. See above, ch. 1, n. 26.

47. Be'eri, *The Beginning,* 23.

Chapter 5: The Mandate Period (1921–1956)

1. Woodrow Wilson, *War And Peace. Presidential Messages, Addresses and Public Papers (1917–1924),* ed., Ray Stannard Baker and William E. Dodd (New York/London, 1927), 1:161–62; and Congressional Records, 680–81 (1918).

2. For an idealized description of this future Arab nation, see "An official Proclamation from the Government of Great Britain to the natives of Arabia and the Arab Provinces," dated 4 December 1914 ("almost certainly composed by [Ronald] Storrs"), FO. 141/710, file 3156, "translation," Cairo, 19 June 1916, in Elie Kedourie, *In the Anglo-Arab Labyrinth. The McMahon-Husayn Correspondence and its Interpretation, 1914–1939* (London/New York, 1976), 21–22.

3. British High Commissioner in Egypt, 1914–16; letter printed in Sylvia G. Haim, *Arab Nationalism. An Anthology* (Berkeley/Los Angeles/London, 1976), 91.

4. Kedourie, *Arabic Political Memoirs,* 130.

5. Report by Mgr. Bagratte, Prelate of the Baku Armenians, in Beylerian, *Les Grandes Puissances,* 730.

6. For a discussion of the theories denying the genocide of the Armenians and the Allies' Turkophile policy vis-à-vis the Soviet threat, see Norman Ravitch, "The Armenian Catastrophe," *Encounter* (London, December 1981): 69–84. For an analysis of the political turnaround by the historian Arnold Toynbee, see ibid., and Elie Kedourie, *The Chatham House Version and Other Middle Eastern Studies* (London, 1969), chap.12.

7. Christians of the Nestorian rite and Nestorian Uniates joined to Rome.

8. Kedourie, *Chatham House Version,* 301–16. The sovereignty of an Arab prince worried the large Baghdad Jewish community which—in 1919, and again in 1921—requested British citizenship, ibid., 300–301.

9. Report: *Question of the Frontier between Turkey and Iraq, Report submitted to the Council by the Commission instituted by the Council Resolution of September 30th, 1924,* League of Nations, Geneva, 1925 (Document C.400.M.147, 1925, vii), 79.

10. Ibid., 80.

11. Ibid., 81.

12. Ibid., 90.

13. Organized by the Decentralization Party. This movement, made up of Christian and Muslim delegates, called for administrative decentralization of the Arabic-speaking provinces of the Ottoman Empire.

14. Antoine Hokayem and Marie-Claude Bittar, *L'Empire Ottoman. Les Arabes et les Grandes Puissances, 1914–1920* (Beirut, 1981), 198.

15. Ibid., 175–80. The contradiction between the ecumenical and universalist conception of the Christian clergy and that of national political sovereignty was still to be found in Lebanon, even in 1970. See the lecture given in Paris by Abbé Youakim Moubarac on 2 June 1970: "Musulmans, chrétiens et juifs à l'épreuve de la Palestine," under the aegis of the Association de Solidarité Franco-Arabe (France-Pays-Arabes, 1970), repr. in Youakim Moubarac, *Pentalogie Islamo-Chrétienne* (Beirut, 1972–73), 5 (*Palestine et Arabité*), 145–73.

16. This report was published on 2 December 1922 by *Editor & Publisher*, New York, vol.55, n° 27, 2nd section, I to XXVIII, under the title, *First Publication of King-Crane Report on the Near East. A Suppressed Official Document of the United States Government*. An internal note (illegible signature), dated 20 January 1923, addressed to [William E.] Rappard, described the King-Crane Report as propaganda in favor of an American mandate over various Near Eastern countries. Rappard was delegate of the Swiss government to Washington, Paris, and London (1917–19), Secretary-General of League of Red Cross Societies (1919–20), and Director of the Mandates Section, 1 November 1920–26. See also Neil Caplan, *Palestine Jewry and the Arab Question, 1917–1925* (London, 1978), 35–37. In his memoirs, Ronald Storrs, appointed Military Governor of Jerusalem (28 December 1917) by the British government, recalls the not very serious methods of the King-Crane Commission; see Ronald Storrs, *Orientations* (London, 1943), 354–55.

17. Pierre-André Taguieff, *Les Protocoles des Sages de Sion*, 1:261–74; Yehoshafat Harkabi, *Arab Attitudes to Israel* (Jerusalem, 1972), 229–37, 518; Bernard Lewis, *The Jews of Islam* (Princeton, 1984), 184–87; idem, *Semites and Antisemites. An Inquiry into Conflict and Prejudice* (London, 1986), 132–39, 208–10. For the propagation in the Middle East of modern European antisemitism by Christian Arabs, see Kedourie, *Chatham House Version*, 335–42; Selim Abou, *Béchir Gemayel ou l'Esprit d'un Peuple* (Paris, 1984), 225–26.

18. See the declarations by Rashid Rida, in Neville J. Mandel, *The Arabs and Zionism before World War I* (Berkeley/Los Angeles/ London, 1976), 153.

19. For the approval by Christian leaders of an autonomous Jewish majority in Palestine, see the reports by Sami Hochberg, editor of the Constantinople newspaper *Le Jeune Turc*, in Mandel, *The Arabs and Zionism*, 154–56; see Pierre Rondot, *Les Chrétiens d'Orient* (Paris, 1955), 129, 233: he mentions that Christians collaborated with the Zionists in Palestine at the artisanal and economic levels.

20. Renée Neher-Bernheim, *La Déclaration Balfour, 1917: Création d'un foyer national juif en Palestine* (Paris, 1969), 272–76; see also Leonard Stein [secretary of the Zionist executive in London], *The Balfour Declaration* (London, 1961), 292–95; André Mandelstam describes the expulsion and plunder of Jews in Jaffa, Tel Aviv, and surrounding villages in his *Le Sort de l'Empire Ottoman* (Paris/Lausanne, 1917), 365–66.

21. Mandelstam gives the reported intervention of a Social Democrat deputy, Dr. Cohen, at the German Reichstag in mid-May 1917, concluding: "Is the [Chancellor of the Empire] ready to exercise pressure on the government of the Osmanlis, to make impossible in Palestine a repetition of the atrocities committed in Armenia." The evacuation of the Muslim population, without being pillaged, was undertaken for their protection, ibid, 366–67; see also Stein, *The Balfour Declaration*, 208–17.

22. Cohen, *The Jews of the Middle East*, 24–25.

23. Yehoshua Porath, *The Emergence of the Palestinian Arab National Movement, 1918–1929* (London, 1974), 32; for the antisemitism of the British military administration, see Storrs, *Orientations*, 361–62 ff.; [Peel Report] *Palestine Royal Commission Presented by the Secretary of State of the Colonies to Parliament*, Comd. 5479 (London, July 1937). The Peel Report stresses that Christians and Muslims, whose relationship had always been difficult, were united in their hostility to the Jews: ibid., 52.

24. ISA, R.G.2. 10/244.

25. Ibid.

26. Ibid. This was before the articles in *The Times* of London (16, 17 and 18 August 1921) by Philip Graves exposed *The Protocols* as a crude forgery.

27. ISA, R.G.2. 10/244.

28. ISA, R.G.2. 5/155.

29. Ibid., see Memorandum from the MCA to the Peace Conference in Paris (3 February 1919, after its General Assembly in Jerusalem, 27 January 1919).

30. Storrs, *Orientations*, 358.

31. Ibid., 371.

32. Porath, *The Emergence (1918–1929)*, 32.

33. Storrs, *Orientations*, 378.

34. Porath, *The Emergence (1918–1929)*, 60–62.

35. Ibid., 71, 80–81. King-Crane Commission Report, III, V, X, XI, XVIII, XXIV: "The Christians, and most other non-Moslem groups, are unanimous in the belief that a strong mandate is necessary for a considerable time, because they do not feel confidence in an Arab government, which in a country [Syria] four-fifths Moslem might be too favorable to the majority."

36. Porath, *The Emergence (1918–1929)*, 97. For the killings and assassinations of Jews, the plunder and destruction of their property, see 1937 *Peel Report*, 50 (April 1920: 5 killed, 211 injured, with women and children), 51 (May 1921: 47 killed, 146 injured), 80, 98, 100, 119, and passim, for the rampant Arab terrorism leading to the assassination of Jews and the destruction of property.

37. Stein, *Balfour Declaration*, chap.16, particularly 268–69; Kedourie, *The Chatham House Version*, 375–94; idem, *In the Anglo-Arab Labyrinth*, passim. For Toynbee's role in the anti-Zionist reversal of British policy and the mendacious propagation of agreements with the Sharif Husayn concerning Palestine: ibid., chap.7; for a critical analysis of Toynbee's method of work, see Pieter Geyl, *Debates with Historians* (London, 1955), chaps. 5, 6, 7, and 8. Toynbee summarized his viewpoint on the early Arab-Muslim conflicts with a sweeeping generalization in his BBC 1952 Reith lecture: "In the seventh century of the Christian Era the Muslim Arabs liberated from a Christian Graeco-Roman ascendancy a string of Oriental countries—from Syria right across North Africa to Spain," in Arnold Toynbee, *The World and the West* (London/New York, 1953).

38. Kedourie, *In the Anglo-Arab Labyrinth*, 309–19, describes, not without humor, the propagation of the myth and the debilitating effect on the Foreign Office of the complaisant self-blame it generated; also, *The Chatham House Version*, 390–94. For the same attitude among British civil servants in Palestine, see the *Peel Report*, 110, para. 41.

39. "British Policy in Palestine," June 1922, extracts in Peel Report, 1937, 33.

40. Joseph, *Muslim-Christian Relations*, 102.

41. Ibid., 103; see *The Times*, 11 December 1925.

42. Kedourie, *Chatham House Version*, 301–6 and 389.

43. In 1917, the British promised the Assyrians an independent homeland in their native land; for these events, see Rondot, *Les Chrétiens d'Orient*, 162–70; for the festivities which accompanied the massacres of the Assyrians, described as Christians, ibid., 166.

44. Joseph, *Muslim-Christian Relations*, 115. The fate of the Christians in Iraq, the interference by the government and its stranglehold on the communities kept the Syrian Christians' fears alive. See Rondot, *Les Chrétiens d'Orient*, 134–35.

45. Joseph, *Muslim-Christian Relations*, 108; in 1914 there were about 5,000 Armenians in Syria and Lebanon; by 1949 their numbers had risen to approximately 100,000 in Syria and 80,000 in Lebanon: see Rondot, *Les Chrétiens d'Orient*, 187.

46. Kedourie, *Chatham House Version*, chap.11, "Religion and Politics," examines the political conflicts and psychological tension connected with the crisis of identification; Rondot, *Les Chrétiens d'Orient*, 133: "except for a few individuals and politicians, the majority of Christians and the clergy found Arab nationalism somewhat disturbing." A deputy in the Syrian Chamber, Edmond Rabbath, was regarded as a "hostage" imposed by circumstances, in other words, a man who was totally deprived of freedom of opinion, ibid., 131.

47. Porath, *The Emergence (1918–1929)*, 266; Peel Report, 67- 68.

48. Yehoshua Porath, *The Palestinian Arab National Movement, 1929–1939: From Riots to Rebellion* (London, 1977), 109.

49. Porath, *The Emergence (1918–1929)*, 303.

50. Ibid.

51. Porath, *The Palestinian (1929–1939)*, 98.

52. Ibid., 268–70; for terrorism by Arab-Palestinian extremists against moderates, see the Peel Report, 135; Kamal S. Salibi, *The Modern History of Lebanon* (London, 1965), 151–87, examines the conflict in Lebanon in 1936 between independentists and pro-Syrians.

53. Porath, *The Emergence (1918–1929)*, 294–303.

54. Mordechai Nisan, *Minorities in the Middle East: A History of Struggle and Self-Expression* (Jefferson, NC/London, 1991), 195; Doris Behrens-Abouseif, "The Political Situation of the Copts, 1798–1923," in Benjamin Braude and Bernard Lewis, eds., *Christians and Jews in the Ottoman Empire. The Functioning of a Plural Society* (New York/London,1982), 2:199.

55. In Art.13; see Albert H. Hourani, *Minorities in the Arab World* (London/New York, 1947), 41.

56. Charles Issawi, *Egypt in Revolution. An Economical Analysis* (London/New York, 1965), 164.

57. Kedourie, *Chatham House Version*, 199–201; Yahudiya Masriya, "A Christian Minority: The Copts in Egypt," in *Case Studies on Human Rights and Fundamental Freedoms: A World Survey* (The Hague, 1976), 4:86–87.

58. Abou, *Béchir Gemayel*, 274.

59. Joseph, *Muslim-Christian Relations*, 101.

60. Kedourie mentions uprisings and the assassination of three Greek Orthodox men assimilated to Greeks in 1908–9, *Chatham House Version*, 454 n. 42.

61. Ibid., 318.

62. Ibid.

63. Ibid., 331- 42. See also Haim, *Arab Nationalism;* Anouar Abdel-Malek, *La pensée politique arabe contemporaine* (Paris, 1970).

64. For similar relationships between the British administration and the Copts at the beginning of the century, see Behrens-Abouseif, supra. n. 54; for Britain's abandonment of the Assyrians, see Rondot, *Les Chrétiens d'Orient,* 167- 68. Christian Arab politicians withdrew their support from the Assyrians in order to avoid jeopardizing the situation of the Christians in the whole Arab world, ibid., 167.

65. Taguieff, *Les Protocols,* 1:160–64.

66. Doreen Ingrams (compiled and annotated), *Palestine Papers 1917–1922. Seeds of Conflict* (London, 1972), 60.

67. Ibid., 168.

68. Storrs, *Orientations,* 432.

69. Cardinal Eugenio Pacelli, 17 April 1937, in C. Galassi Paluzzi, *Roma onde Christo è Romano nella parola di Pio XII* (Rome, 1943), 40 ff., quoted by Friedrich Heer, a Catholic professor at the University of Vienna, in "The Catholic Church and the Jews Today," *Midstream* (May 1971): 17, n° 5:23.

70. Ibid., 22.

71. Ibid., 23.

72. For a detailed study of the collusion between the Vatican, the German Catholic hierarchy, and the leaders of the Third Reich, see Annie Lacroix-Riz, *Le Vatican, l'Europe et le Reich de la Première Guerre mondiale à la guerre froide* (Paris, 1996). For the efforts—through clerical channels—to save Nazi criminals after the war, see 423–59.

73. Storrs, *Orientations,* 83.

74. The large body of Christian exponents of Arab anti-Zionism included Khalil Sakakini (d.1953), George Antonius (d. 1942), Alfred Roch, vice-president of *hizb al-Arabi* (the party of the Grand Mufti of Jerusalem, Haj Amin al-Husayni), Isa al-Isa, editor of *Filastin*, and so on. See Rondot, *Les Chrétiens d'Orient,* 129, "The Syro-Palestinian Committee, which is trying to stir up Europe, permanently keeps a very useful Christian member on its governing body."

75. Kedourie, *Chatham House Version*, 337. George Antonius's book, *The Arab Awakening. The Story of the Arab National Movement* (London, 1938), bears the dedication: "To CHARLES R. CRANE, aptly nicknamed Harun al-Rashid, affectionately."

76. *Israël*, Cairo, 29 April 1937.

77. See Walid Phares, *Lebanese Christian Nationalism. The Rise and Fall of an Ethnic Resistance* (Boulder, CO/London, 1995), 96, 123, 134, n. 19. See appendix 3.

78. Mgr. Arida represented 275,000 worshippers and his anger at this appointment lasted several days, see Robert Brenton Betts, *Christians in the Arab East. A Political Study* (London, 1979), 143.

79. Ibid., 144. For the Vatican's policy toward Israel, see Andrej Kreutz, *Vatican Policy on the Palestinian-Israeli Conflict: The Struggle for the Holy Land* (Westport, CT, 1990); idem, "The Vatican and the Palestinians, a Historical Overview," *Islamochristiana*, 18 (1992): 109–25; André Chouraqui, *La Reconnaissance, le Saint-Siège, les Juifs et Israël* (Paris, 1992); Henri Tincq, *L'Etoile et la Croix, Jean-Paul II—Israël: L'explication* (Paris, 1993). Storrs mentions the Vatican's opposition to Zionism and its support of Arabism from the beginning of the British mandate, in *Orientations*, 358.

80. Taguieff, *Les Protocoles*, 1, chap.7 examines the introduction of the *Protocols* into the Arab world and its reception there.

81. See Daphne Tsimhoni, "The Arab Christians and the Palestinian Arab National Movement during the Formative Stage," in Gabriel Ben-Dor, ed., *The Palestinians and the Middle East Conflict* (Ramat Gan, 1978), 79.

82. See the periodical *Israël*, Cairo, June and December 1933.

83. Robert Montagne, "Réactions Arabes Contre Le Sionisme," [Summary of the Congress of Bloudane] (September 1937), in *Entretiens Sur L'Evolution Des Pays De Civilisation Arabe*, III (meeting of July 11–13, 1938 under the auspices of L'Institut des Etudes Islamiques de l'Université de Paris et du Centre d'Etudes de Politique Etrangère) (Paris, n.d.), 42–61.

84. Lukacs Hirszowicz, *The Third Reich and the Arab East* (London/Toronto, 1966), 27. Journals financed by the Nazis included *La Nation Arabe* from 1930, edited by Shakib Arslan, published in Geneva till 1943, see Kramer *Arab-Awakening*, 105–10; and *Al-Nahar*, Beirut, see Hirszowicz, ibid., 130–31. For an exhaustive analysis of Arab-Nazi relations, see ibid.

85. Ibid., p.27.

86. Hirszowicz, *The Third Reich*, passim, examines the mufti's collaboration with the Nazis, his close contacts with Hitler and his efforts to conscript Muslim soldiers, whether Arab or not, into the Nazi forces; for the Arab troops fighting with the Nazis in Greece and the Balkans, 311–12; for the mufti's collaboration in the extermination of the Jews, ibid; also Maurice Perlman, *Mufti of Jerusalem. The Story of Haj Amin el Husseini*, (London, 1947); and Zvi Elpeleg, *The Grand Mufti Haj Amin Al-Hussaini, Founder of the Palestinian National Movement* (London/Portland, OR, 1993).

87. Abusive antisemitic articles in the Egyptian press, notably in *al-Ahram, Akhbar al-Yawm, al-Ikwan al-Muslimun, Misr al-Fatat, Mokattam, Proche-Orient*; for anti-Jewish demonstrations in Cairo and Alexandria, see, *La Tribune Juive d'Egypte*, 3 May and 1 November 1938; for incitement to hatred preached in mosques, ibid., 3 and 24 May, 12 July 1938, and many subsequent issues; for the distribution of tracts, e.g. "Every Muslim who plunges a knife into the entrails of a Jew secures a place in paradise," ibid., 8 February 1938.

88. This is the official figure, generally considered well below the real number. The late Professor Elie Kedourie, born in Iraq, refers to an Iraqi source that indicates a figure of 600 killed and a very large number injured, see *The Chatham House Version*, 307. For the British administration's laxism in these massacres and the indictment of Zionism (the same process as for the Armenians), ibid., 306–8, and idem, *Arabic Political Memoirs*, 283–314; Naim Kattan, *Adieu Babylone* (Montreal, 1975), gives an eye-witness description of these events.

89. Anwar Sadat, *Revolt on the Nile* (London, 1957), 35.

90. Ibid., 40.

Chapter 6. From the Jewish Exodus to the Christian Exodus

1. *Tribune Juive d'Egypte*, Cairo, 9 April 1945. *The Protocols* was first published in Arabic by the Roman Catholic community of Jerusalem in 1926, see above, chap. 5, n.81.

2. Ibid., 4 July and 4 and 11 November 1945; *The Jewish Chronicle*, 9, 16, 23 November

1945; Joseph Schechtman, *On Wings of Eagles: The Plight, Exodus and Homecoming of Oriental Jewry* (New York/London, 1961), 184–205; World Jewish Congress Archives, Geneva; *BAIU* (Intérieur), 1, n° 2, November 1945, 9.

3. "Anti-Jewish Riots in Tripolitania," 3–4, in Renzo De Felice, *Jews in an Arab Land. Libya, 1835–1970* (Austin, TX, 1985), 365 n.19; see also Clifton Daniel, *NYT*, 8, 13, 15 November 1945.

4. Harvey Goldberg, "Rites and Riots: The Tripolitanian Pogrom of 1945," *Plural Societies* 8, n° 1 (Spring 1977): 37.

5. This official report from the Libyan community is reprinted in extenso in De Felice, *Jews in an Arab Land,* 193–208; for the British Military Administration's responsibility in these events, ibid., 208–16.

6. Nehemia Robinson, *The Arab Countries of the Near East and their Jewish Communities* (New York, 1951), 77–78. For details, see also in Siegfried Landshut, *Jewish Communities in the Muslim Countries of the Middle East* (London, 1950).

7. *Report of the Commission of Enquiry into Disturbances in Aden in December 1947* (London, 1948).

8. Quoted in Mallory Browne, "Jews in Grave Danger in Moslem Lands," in *NYT*, 16 May 1948.

9. Richard A. Yaffe, "Arab Pogroms Endanger 800,000 Outside Palestine," in *PM*, 18 January 1948.

10. *Journal d'Egypte*, 21 June 21 and 24 July 1948; *Progrès Egyptien*, 22 June, 20 July 1948, 1; *Bourse Egyptienne*, 20 July 1948; *National Zeitung*, Basle, 10 and 13 August 1948: "Terreur au Caire"; Yahudiya Masriya, *Les Juifs en Egypte* (Geneva, 1971), 52–53.

11. Chouraqui, *Between East and West,* 181–82.

12. Ibid., 182–83; De Felice, *Jews in an Arab Land,* 223–28.

13. For Egypt, see Bat Ye'or, *Jews in Egypt* (Hebrew) (Jerusalem, 1974), 71–140; Maurice Roumani, *The Case of the Jews from Arab Countries: A Neglected Issue* (Jerusalem, 1975); Shlomo Hillel, *Operation Babylon, The Story of the Rescue of the Jews of Iraq* (New York, 1987); Mordechai Ben Porat, *To Baghdad and Back. The Miraculous 2,000 Year Homecoming of the Iraqi Jews*. Trans. from Hebrew by Marcia Grant and Kathy Akeriv (Jerusalem/Hewlett, NY, 1998).

14. For Egypt, see Masriya, *Les Juifs en Egypte*, 66–69, appendix I and 2.

15. Cohen, *The Jews of the Middle East*, 26–37; Landshut, *Jewish Communities in the Muslim Countries.*

16. Ibid., 44–45.

17. Phares, *Lebanese Christian Nationalism;* for this rapprochement between Christian Lebanese and the Zionists, see ibid., 93–97; for the 5 August 1947 letter of Archbishop Ignace Mubarak, see the UN Official Records of the Second Session of the General Assembly, *Ad Hoc* Committee on the Palestinian Question. Summary Records of Meetings: 25 September–25 November 1947, 57–59. See the long extract in Bat Ye'or, *The Dhimmi*, 401–3; also appendix 3.

18. Roumani, *The Case of the Jews*, 53.

19. Bat Ye'or, "The Dhimmi factor in the Exodus of Jews from Arab Countries," in Malka Hillel Shulewitz, ed., *The Forgotten Millions. The Modern Jewish Exodus from Arab Lands* (London/New York, 1999), 33–51. Several articles in this volume deal with different aspects of the exodus of Jews from Arab countries and their integration into Israeli society.

20. Sélim Naguib, "Les Droits de l'homme en Egypte, le cas des Coptes," doctoral thesis, Université de Droit, d'Economie et de Sciences Sociales (Paris, 2 June 1992), 229–30. See also idem, *Les Coptes dans l'Egypte d'Aujourd'hui* (Brussels, 1996).

21. Albert H. Hourani, *Arabic Thought in the Liberal Age, 1798–1939* (London/New York, 1962), 297.

22. Ibid.

23. No work on inter-*dhimmi* relationships exists. For the Eastern Christians, see the comprehensive study by Jean-Pierre Valognes (pseudonym), *Vie et Mort des Chrétiens d'Orient. Des origines à nos jours* (Paris, 1994).

24. Founded on 11 September 1951 by a lawyer, Ibrahim Fehmi Hilal, dissolved on 24 April 1954; see Naguib "Les Droits de l'homme," 312–15; for the memorandum (1 September 1953), see Sami Awad Aldeeb Abu-Sahlieh, *Non-Musulmans en Pays d'Islam, Cas de l'Egypte*

(Fribourg, 1979), appendix I (314–18); Edward Wakin, *A Lonely Minority: The Modern History of Egypt's Copts* (New York, 1963). For the situation of the Copts under Nasser, cf. Georges Henein, *L'Express*, 20–26 November 1972.

25. Naguib, "Les Droits de l'homme," 278; Rondot, *Les Chrétiens d'Orient*, 235. Four Christians died as a result of the burning of a church at Suez by Muslims. Masriya, "A Christian Minority. The Copts in Egypt," in *Case Studies on Human Rights and Fundamental Freedoms. A World Survey* (The Hague, 1976), 4:91–92, for the telegram of protest sent by the National Assembly of Coptic Churches to President Sadat (summer, 1972); for the Islamists' demands vis-à-vis the Copts concerning bells and processions, the forfeiting of the life of a Christian who takes up arms against Muslims, see Gilles Kepel, *The Prophet and Pharaoh. Muslim Extremism in Contemporary Egypt* (London/California, 1985/86), 204–8.

26. Raphael Israeli, *Man of Defiance, A Political Biography of Anwar Sadat* (London, 1985); Anwar El Sadat, *Revolt*; idem, *In Search of Identity. An Autobiography* (Glasgow, 1978); for Sadat's policy of Islamization, see Naguib, "Les Droits de l'homme," 208–13.

27. Zawya al-Hamra (Cairo), June 1981; Minya, 26 November 1988; Asyut, 24 December 1989; Upper Egypt and Cairo, 2 and 9 March 1990; Fayyum, 15 April 1990; Minya, 16 June 1991; Asyut, May 1992; Luxor, June 1992.

28. Phares, *Lebanese Christian Nationalism*; Jean-Pierre Péroncel-Hugoz, *The Raft of Mohamed* (New York, 1987); idem, *Une Croix sur le Liban* (Paris, 1984); Anne Sinai and Chaim I. Waxman (eds), "Ethnic and Religious Minorities in the Middle East," *MER*, New York (autumn 1976): 9:1, and (winter 1976/1977): 9:2.

29. Charles Malik, "The Near East: The Search for Truth," *FA* (30 January 1952), reprinted in Haïm, *Arab Nationalism*, 189–22. Charles Malik was Lebanese ambassador to the United Nations in New York and later foreign minister in the government of Camille Chamoun (Kamil Sham'un), president of Lebanon 1952–1958.

30. Youakim Moubarac, *Pentalogie*, 4, *Les Chrétiens et le Monde Arabe*, 60. Abbé Moubarac was professor at the Institut Catholique de Paris at Louvain University, and at the Institut Orthodoxe Saint-Jean de Damas. He became Secretary-General of the Council of Catholic Patriarchs of the Orient.

31. Ibid., 61.

32. Ibid., 5, 139.

33. Ibid., 203.

34. Ibid.

35. Ibid., 205.

36. Ibid., 206.

37. Ibid., 212.

38. Salibi, *The Modern History of Lebanon*, 194–202.

39. Camille Chamoun, *Crise au Liban* (Beirut, 1977), 8; for the Palestinians' identification with Islam, see ibid., 5.

40. In Abou, *Béchir Gemayel*, 304–5; quoted in *as-Safir*, 18 August 1975, see Joseph Aboujaoude, *Les partis politiques au Liban* (Kaslik, Lebanon, 1985), 96.

41. Ibid., 217; John Laffin, *The War of Desperation: Lebanon 1982–1985* (London, 1985); ibid., *The PLO Connections* (London, 1982); Jillian Becker, *The PLO: The Rise and Fall of the Palestinian Liberation Organization* (London, 1984); and the important evidence and documents in Raphael Israeli, ed., *PLO in Lebanon: Selected Documents* (London, 1983). For an analysis by a specialist in Islam, see P. J. Vatikiotis, "The Spread of Islamic Terrorism," in Benjamin Netanyahu, ed., *Terrorism: How the West Can Win* (London, 1986), 77–83.

42. Chamoun, *Crise au Liban*, 1.

43. Abou, *Béchir Gemayel*, 117.

44. Ibid., 81–82.

45. Moubarac, *Pentalogie*, 4:236.

46. Ibid., 240.

47. Ibid., 240–41.

48. Chamoun, *Crise au Liban*, 54; for a description by the survivors, see Becker, *The PLO*, 122–26; Michel Riquet, *Une minorité chrétienne: Les Maronites au Liban* (Geneva, 1977).

49. Chamoun, *Crise au Liban*, 11–89; Israeli, ed., *PLO in Lebanon*, documents seized by the Israeli army in Lebanon in 1982 from PLO military bases, 169–204.

50. Moubarac, *Pentalogie*, 5 : 141–42.
51. Chamoun, *Crise au Liban*, 6.
52. Ibid., 55.
53. Ibid., 88.
54. Speech, 8 September 1982, in Abou, *Béchir Gemayel*, 396–97.
55. Abou, *Béchir Gemayel*, 65–66.
56. Chamoun, *Crise au Liban*, 3. After the taking of hostages and the death of the Israeli athletes at the Olympic Games of Munich (1972), the European capitals hastened to open PLO offices, thereby sustaining terrorist attacks and more hostage-taking. The media competed in civility to the PLO, its enemies were described as "conservative isolationists," allied with Zionist-Nazis, against "Islamo-progressists." The Soviet-Islamic-Third World bloc was instrumental in the United Nations General Assembly's adoption on 10 November 1975 of the resolution assimilating Zionism with a form of racism. Pope John-Paul II received Arafat at the Vatican on 15 September 1982, the same day as Bashir Gemayel's funeral.
57. Ibid., 19–20, 78, 120–30, 150.
58. Ibid., 39, 59, 125; Abou, *Béchir Gemayel*, passim.
59. Nisan, *Minorities in the Middle East*, 151–55.
60. Kyriakos Mikhail, quoted in Nisan, *Minorities in the Middle East*, 124; see also Behrens-Abouseif, in Braude and Lewis, eds., *Christians and Jews in the Ottoman Empire*, 2 : 199.
61. Storrs, *Orientations*, 72–73.
62. Quoted in Naguib, "Les Droits de l'homme," 302. Father Sergios was famous for his nationalist and xenophobic speeches, cf., Rondot, *Les Chrétiens d'Orient*, 147.
63. For these memoranda, cf., Naguib, "Les Droits de l'homme," 307–25, and Aldeeb Abu Sahlieh, *Non-Musulmans en Pays d'Islam*, in the annexes section.
64. Speech by Bashir Gemayel, 29 November 1981, in Abou, *Béchir Gemayel*, 383. See Rondot, *Les Chrétiens d'Orient*, 227: "In most cases the Christian minorities in the diaspora have scarcely any hesitation in buying their tranquility by abandoning claims which would risk being judged excessive. Above all they seek compromise, as was their ancestral custom."
65. Last speech before his assassination that same afternoon on 14 September 1982, in Abou, *Béchir Gemayel*, 409.
66. Ibid., 396: in a speech of 8 September a week earlier, to the Lebanese TV company and representatives of the media.
67. Ibid., 410, this text was first published in "Notre Droit à la différence" (Discours-testament de Béchir Gemayel), *Bulletin d'Information* Union Libanaise-Suisse, Lausanne, no.1, December 1982; from this version, large extracts were translated into English and published in Bat Ye'or, *The Dhimmi*, 403–5.
68. Betts, *Christians in the Arab East*, 273–74.
69. See Youakim Moubarac's option for the great space—the Third World—against "the small reduced Lebanon," lecture, 2 June 1970, "Musulmans, chrétiens et juifs," 21.
70. Moubarac, *Pentalogie*, 5 : 86.
71. Ibid., 4 : 242.
72. Ibid., 5 : 253–56. Moubarac recommended to "de-Judaize" (*désenjuiver*)" the Church and to "de-Zionize" (*désioniser*) Judaism in order to join with Islam, ibid., 259.
73. Radio Damascus, 3 November 1954, in Betts, *Christians in the Arab East*, 214–15, 274 n.325.
74. Rondot, *Les Chrétiens d'Orient*, 235–36. In his book published in 1955, Pierre Rondot describes the feeling of insecurity and mistrust of Arab Christians, their awareness of past extortions and their widespread anxiety beneath an apparent calm, in *Les Chrétiens d'Orient*, 230.
75. Moubarac, *Pentalogie*, 5 : 28.
76. Ibid., 23.
77. Ibid., 57.
78. Ibid., 32.

Chapter 7. *Jihad* and Dhimma: Modern Formulations

1. Khurshid Ahmad (Pakistan's former minister of Planning and Development and head of the Jamaat-i-Islami), "The Nature of the Islamic Resurgence," in John L. Esposito, ed., *Voices of Resurgent Islam* (New York/Oxford, 1983), 222–25.

2. See Olivier Carré, *Mystique et Politique, lecture révolutionnaire du Coran par Sayyid Qutb, Frère musulman radical* (Paris, 1984); idem, *Le Nationalisme Arabe* (Paris, 1993); see Olivier Roy, *L'Echec de l'Islam Politique* (Paris, 1992); Panayiotis Jerassimos Vatikiotis, *Islam and the State* (London, 1987); Daniel Pipes, "Fundamentalist Muslims between America and Russia," *FA* 64, no.5 (summer 1986): 938–59; idem, "In Muslim America: A Presence and a Challenge," in *National Review*, 21 February 2000, 40–41.

3. Abul Ala Mawdudi, *Towards Understanding Islam* (London, 1980), 10. This publication uses both the word "God" and "Allah" for the divinity.

4. Ibid.

5. Hasan al-Turabi, "The Islamic State," in Esposito, *Voices*, 241. Turabi was dismissed in December 1999 by President Omar el-Bechir.

6. Mawdudi, *Towards Understanding*, 107; see also *Five Tracts of Hassan al-Banna (1906–1949). A Selection,* trans. by Charles Wendell (Berkeley, 1975), 105; and Turabi, in Esposito, *Voices*, 242. See also Justice Dr Nasin Hasan Shah, "Islamic Concept of State and its effect of Islamization of laws in Pakistan," *HI* 16, no.1 (spring 1993): 5–18.

7. Charles J. Adams, "Mawdudi and the Islamic State," in Esposito, *Voices*, 116; Yvonne Y. Haddad, "Sayyid Qutb: Ideologue of Islamic Revival," in ibid., 177; John L. Esposito, "Muhammad Iqbal and the Islamic State," in ibid., 74–80; Abdulaziz Sachedina, "Ali Shariati: Ideologue of the Iranian Revolution," in ibid., 198; Carré, *Mystique et Politique,* 170–77; Ruhollah Khomeiny, *Principes Politiques, Philosophiques, Sociaux et Religieux. Extraits de trois ouvrages majeurs de l'Ayatollah.* Texts selected and translated from the Persian by Jean-Marie Xavière (Paris, 1979); idem, *Islamic Government,* trans. by Joint Publications Research (Arlington, VA., 1979); idem, *Pithy Aphorisms, Wise Sayings, and Counsels* (Teheran, 1994).

8. Idem, *Principes Politiques,* 26–29. Sayyid Abul A'la Mawdudi [Maududi], *The Islamic Movement, Dynamics of Values, Power and Change,* new English version, ed., Khurram Murad (London, 1984); see also David Sagiv, *Fundamentalism and Intellectuals in Egypt, 1973–1993* (London, 1995). Also, Johannes J.G. Jansen, *The Neglected Duty. The Creed of Sadat's Assassins and Islamic Resurgence in the Middle East* (New York, 1986).

9. Resolution No. 49/19-P on the CDHRI, 19th Islamic Conference of Foreign Ministers, Cairo (31 July–5 August 1990).

10. See Tyan, *Histoire de l'Organisation.*

11. Mawdudi, *Towards Understanding,* 122.

12. Khursid Ahmed, in Esposito, *Voices,* 218–21.

13. Javid Iqbal (son of Muhammad Iqbal), "Democracy and the Modern Islamic State," in ibid., 258–59; Abul Ala Mawdudi, "Les droits des dimmîs dans l'état islamique" in *Al-Dimma, L'Islam et les Minorités Religieuse, PISAI,* Etudes Arabes. Dossiers no. 80–81 (Rome, 1991/1–2), 175–89.

14. Ruhollah Khomeini, Teheran, 16 August (AP), Nation Radio Broadcast Address, in "Iran Sends Forces. Kurds said to overrun City," in *IHT,* 17 August 1979.

15. Carré, *Mystique et Politique,* 128–29; see the analysis of Qutb's thought in Kepel, *The Prophet and Pharaoh,* 38–69. Qutb examines the stages leading to "the resurgence of the Muslim countries . . . followed, sooner or later, by their conquest of world domination": ibid., 45. For the Islamist theses and world conquest, see also Jansen, *The Neglected Duty.*

16. Qutb, in Carré, *Mystique et Politique,* 138–42.

17. Ibid., chap. 5; Sadiq al-Mahdi (president of Sudan from 1985 to July 1989), "Islam— Society and Change," in Esposito, *Voices,* 254; Turabi, in ibid., 242–49 and Yûsuf al-Qaradâwî, "Le Statut des Non-musulmans dans la Société Islamique" (Arabic, 1983), in *Al-Dimma,* 35–55.

18. John F. Burns, "UN Force, Once Cheered, Is Now a Target of Sarajevo Anger," *IHT (NYT),* 10 August 1992. See the statements by Turkish representatives after the massacres at the beginning of the century about the happy and tranquil life the Assyrians had enjoyed "for centuries" (see page 149), and similar statements by spokesmen of Hamas about the *dhimmis* in Palestine (see arts. 6 and 31 in the 1988 Constitution).

19. See the reports by British consuls during the nineteenth-century emancipation period, in Bat Ye'or, *The Decline of Eastern Christianity,* 81–82, 170, 177, 416–33. See Yeshayahu A. Jelinek, "Bosnia-Herzegovina at War: Relations between Moslems and Non-Moslems," *HGS* 5, no.3 (1990): 276: "In point of fact, tolerance of the kind described by the Moslems was a

myth. The Christian population, who had suffered in the past from the status of *raya* (serfs), and were virtually enslaved by the aristocratic Moslem land-owners, found it difficult to believe in Moslem toleration" (parenthesis in the text).

20. Ibid., 283. For the atrocities committed against the Orthodox Serbs, see Lacroix-Riz, *Le Vatican, l'Europe et le Reich*, 423–28.

21. Jelinek, "Bosnia-Herzegovina at War," 287.

22. John Zametica, *The Yugoslav Conflict* (London, 1992), 38–39. The same opinion is expressed by Sheikh Abu Bakr Mahmoud Goumi, former chief cadi of northern Nigeria: "When you are Muslim, you can not accept being governed by a non-Muslim, consequently if we want a viable Nigeria, we must follow a single faith." Jacques de Barrin, "Le Nigéria, fragile colosse," *Le Monde*, 18 February 1988. And "Religious Riots Halted, Nigeria Says," and "Nigeria Death Toll Rises to Hundreds," *Reuters*, 23 February; *IHT*, 25 February 2000. The same Muslim secession provoked a civil war in the south of Thailand and the Philippines. In Britain, where there is a considerable immigrant Islamic community, Kalim Siddiqui, president of the London Muslim Institute, claimed a sort of legal autonomy for Muslims based on the *shari'a* (Islamized areas); see Roy, *L'Echec de l'Islam politique*, 108, 154.

23. Burns in *IHT*, 10 August 1992.

24. Rony Brauman et al., *Populations en danger* (Paris, 1992), introduction, 9.

25. Père Hubert Barbier, Statement to the UN Commission on Human Rights (UNCHR) under the auspices of the International Fellowship for Reconciliation (E/CN.4/1993/SR.22, §19–22; and UN *verbatim* recording in French); *Vigilance Soudan* (Paris, April 1993), n° 9; Isabel Vichniac, "Khartoum est accusé d'épuration ethnique et religieuse," in *Le Monde*, 18 February 1993.

26. Barbier, Statement to the UNCHR. See also the statement by Rev. William L. Wipfler, representing the Anglican Consultative Council, and Samuel E. Ericsson, representative of the International Association for the Defence of Religious Freedom, 16 February 1993 (E/CN.4/1993/SR.22, §29–31, and 45).

27. Mgr. Macram Max Gassi, bishop of El Obeid, Sudan. Statement to UNCHR, under the auspices of Pax Romana, 3 March 1993, (E/CN.4/1993/SR.52, §85–91, and the UN *verbatim* recording in English, which is more detailed). The Sudanese government accused the United States and Europe of employing a double standard to discredit Sudan. See also its rebuttal of the report by the Special Rapporteur on Religious Intolerance of the UNCHR (E/CN.4/1993/62).

28. E/CN.4/1994/48.

29. *Tribune de Genève (AFP*, Geneva), 14 February 1994, and *AFP* (Khartoum), 14 and 22 February 1994; the 41 page document (E/CN.4/1994/122) of 1 March 1994 from the Government of Sudan. The Sudanese arguments will be examined in chap. 11 below.

30. The Report for the year 1995 by the UNSR, Gaspar Biro (E/CN.4/1996/62); all the facts about Sudan quoted below are taken from this Report. See also his Report for the year 1996 (E/CN.4/1997/58), and for the year 1997 (E/CN.4/1998/66). Dr. Biro resigned in May 1998.

31. Sheikh Yûsuf al-Qaradâwî, *Saut al-Haqq wal-huriyya*, 9 January 1998, see in *MEMRI* [The Middle East Media and Research Institute, Washington, DC], "Special Report: The Meeting between the Sheik of Al-Azhar and the Chief Rabbi of Israel" [15 December 1997], trans. from Arabic, 8 February 1998 (Reaction of the Muslim Brotherhood, 11).

32. Daphne Tsimhoni, *Christian Communities in Jerusalem and the West Bank since 1948. An Historical, Social and Political Study* (Westport, CT/London, 1993), 12–14.

33. George Emile Irani, *The Papacy and Middle East: The Role of the Holy See in the Arab-Israeli Conflict, 1962–1984* (Notre Dame, IN, 1986). See the comprehensive study by Valognes, *Vie et Mort des Chrétiens d'Orient*, 566–613. See also the declaration of Joaquim Navarro-Valls, spokesman of the Holy See, on "the old and fruitful relations" with the PLO, *L'Osservatore Romano*, 26 October 1994, and *La Documentation catholique*, no. 2104, p. 1014, in Gérald Arboit, *Le Saint-Siège et le Nouvel Ordre au Moyen-Orient. De la Guerre du Golfe à la reconnnaissance diplomatique d'Israël* (Paris, 1996), 177.

34. Jacques Frémeaux, *Le Monde Arabe et la Sécurité de la France depuis 1958* (Paris, 1995).

35. Roy, *L'Echec de l'Islam*, 14–19, 215–16; Esposito, *Introduction*: "Islam and Muslim Poli-

tics," *Voices*, 5–14; Yves Lacoste, "Editorial," *Hérodote* (Géopolitique des Islams), no.1, 4th trim., 1984, 14–15; Kepel, *The Prophet and Pharaoh*, 241.

36. Amir Tahiri, "Aliyev, Andropov's Moslem-Wooer Has His Work Cut Out," *IHT*, 30 November 1982. Aliyev was the KGB's second-in-command during the Brejnev period.

37. Ibid.; inverted commas in the text. See also Amir Taheri, *HolyTerror. Inside the World of Islamic Terrorism* (London, 1987), 218.

38. Ali Shariati, *Histoire et Destinée*, preface and presentation by Jacques Berque (1982), 2nd ed. (Teheran, 1991).

39. *L'Evénement du Jeudi*, 13–19 September 1990. The theme of "the humiliation of the Arabs" constituted a permanent concern of Western policy and rhetoric.

40. Jacques Berque, "Fait et Droit en Palestine" (February 1973), in Maxime Rodinson [Presentation of texts], *Les Palestiniens et la Crise Israélo-Arabe: Textes et Documents du Groupe de recherches et d'action pour le règlement du problème palestinien (G.R.A.P.P.), 1967–1973* (Paris, 1974), 98; see also Yves Lacoste, 'Dynamique de l'Islam d'aujourd'hui: Entretien avec Jacques Berque', *Hérodote* 36 (January–March 1985): 52.

41. Jacques Berque, *Les Arabes* (Paris, 1973), 124. Berque sets particular store by the words "internationalist" and "internationalism," when they express universal hostility to the State of Israel. Here again, the Nazi theme of a world hatred of Israel resurfaced.

42. Ibid., 123. For the opening of Soviet Communist Party archives and the granting of access to a million documents concerning the funds and weapons lavished on international—particularly Palestinian—terrorism, see *IHT*, 26 May 1992. For Third-Worldist anti-Zionist rhetoric, see Taguieff, *Les Protocoles*, 284–89.

43. Jacques Berque, "Les Nations et le Peuple Arabes devant la Palestine" (3 May 1969), in *Les Palestiniens et la Crise Israélo-Arabe*, 24–25.

44. Ibid., 31.

45. Ibid., 35. Earth has a capital letter in the text. In Nazi ideology, membership of the Jewish "race," considered an "unexpiable" crime, justified the genocide of the Jewish people.

46. HAMAS is the acronym of *Harakat Muqawama Islamiyya* (the Movement of Islamic Resistance), in Raphael Israeli, *Fundamentalist Islam and Israel: Essays in Interpretation* (USA & UK, 1993); see also idem, *Muslim Fundamentalism in Israel* (London, 1993). The development of the PLO's policy since the 1993 Oslo Peace Accord will eventually show whether the political divergences between *HAMAS* and the PLO are ideological or strategic. In December 1998, in the presence of President Clinton, the National Congress of the PLO, at a special session convened for that purpose (art. 33), amended the politicidal Palestinian National Covenant (1968). Soon after the outbreak of the second *intifada* in October 2000, the Palestinian National Authority allied itself with *HAMAS*.

47. Palestinian National Charter, art. 19, 20; *HAMAS* Constitution, art. 30, 32, etc.

48. Kepel, *The Prophet and Pharaoh*, 114.

49. Ismail R. al-Faruqi, "Islam and Zionism," in Esposito, *Voices*, 261–67 (excerpts from chap. 10 of Faruqi's book, *Islam and the Problem of Israel* , published by the Islamic Council of Europe (London).

50. Arafat has issued countless calls to *jihad* against the Israelis.

51. See Berque's article, "Les Nations," in *Les Palestiniens et la Crise Israélo-Arabe*, 35.

52. Mgr. Georges Khodr, metropolitan of Byblos and Mt. Lebanon; lecture given under the aegis of the Association de Solidarité Franco-Arabe on 2 June 1970: "L'Arabité," in *Musulmans, chrétiens et juifs à l'épreuve de la Palestine* (Paris, 1970), 42.

53. Moubarac, *Pentalogie*, 3 (*L'Islam et le Dialogue Islamo-Chrétien*): 124–25.

54. Idem, *Recherche sur la Pensée Chrétienne et l'Islam dans les Temps modernes et à l'Epoque contemporaine*, preface by Edmond Rabbath (Beirut, 1977), 176.

55. Idem, *Pentalogie*, 5: 29, 31, 36, 127, 181.

56. Ibid., 87. For totally opposing opinions by Catholic and Protestant theologians and clergymen, see Jacques Ellul, Robert Martin Achard, Michel Riquet, Roger Braun, Cardinal Joseph Ratzinger, Cardinal Albert Decourtray, Marcel Dubois, Bernard Dupuy, René Dujardin, and many others; in the United States: Reinhold Niebuhr, Alice and Roy Eckardt, Edward H. Flannery, Eugène Fisher, Eva Fleishner, Claire Huchet Bishop, Franz Mussner, Clemens Thomas, John T. Pawlikowski.

57. Moubarac, *Pentalogie*, 3: 139.

58. Idem, *Recherche sur la Pensée Chrétienne*, 507.

59. Idem, *Pentalogie*, 4: 201.

60. Ibid., *Pentalogie*, 5: 30. A considerable number of books have been published by Christians linking Christianity to Islam by concealing its Jewish roots, in accordance with the movement to Islamize human culture. An extreme example of this Islamizing trend is illustrated by Sarwat Anis al-Assiouty, *Recherches Comparées sur le Christianisme Primitif et l'Islam Premier*, 1. *Théorie des Sources, Evangiles et Corans Apocryphes, Logia et Hadiths Forgés* (1987); 2. *Jésus le Non-Juif: Culte d'Isis Précurseur du Christianisme, Classes Sociales à Rome et en Arabie* (1987); 3. *Origines Egyptiennes du Christianisme et de l'Islam: Résultat d'un siècle et demi d'archéologie, Jésus: réalités historiques. Muhammad: évolution dialectique* (Paris, 1989). The author is an Egyptian jurist and a Christian theologian.

61. Moubarac, *Pentalogie*, 5: 63, 213–14. See the Declaration of the "Islamic-Christian Conference," 2–6 March 1969, Cartigny, Switzerland, under the auspices of the World Council of Churches, in Moubarac, *Pentalogie*, 3: 305–6.

62. Idem, *Pentalogie*, 5: 304.

63. Idem, *Pentalogie*, 3: 305–6

64. Idem, *Pentalogie*, 5: 41. The involvement of Christians in nourishing, sustaining, and aggravating Islamic hatred against Judaism and Israel remains invaluable. One poisonous declaration from a Christian clergyman, converted to Islam, gives the tone; see Sheikh Ibrahim Khalil Ahmad—former professor and head of a Church in Upper Egypt—in Rivka Yadlin, *An Arrogant Oppressive Spirit. Anti-Zionism as Anti-Judaism in Egypt* (Oxford, 1989), 85.

65. Moubarac, *Pentalogie*, 5: 61. For a contrary opinion by a Protestant scholar, see Robert Martin-Achard, *Actualité d'Abraham* (Neuchâtel, 1969). See also John T. Pawlikowski (Catholic Theological Union, Chicago, IL), "Vatican II on the Jews: A Dramatic Example of Theological Development," presented to the 1999 Convention of the Catholic Theological Society of America, Miami, FL, 12 June 1999.

Chapter 8. The Return of Dhimmitude

1. See Tyan, *Histoire de l'Organisation;* Fattal, *Le Statut Légal.*

2. Ubicini, *Lettres sur la Turquie.*

3. Jean-Paul Gabus, Ali Merad, Youakim Moubarac, *Islam et Christianisme en Dialogue* (Paris, 1982), 133. From the same viewpoint, cf. Olivier Carré, *L'Islam laïque ou le retour à la Grande Tradition* (Paris, 1993).

4. Carré, *Mystique et Politique*, 103–22, 207–10; idem, *Le Nationalisme Arabe*, 88 and passim; Roy, *L'Echec;* Kepel, *The Prophet and Pharaoh.*

5. A whole file has been devoted to this subject, see Maurice Borrmans et al., eds., *Al-Dimma;* Nasim Hasan Shah, "The Concept of al-Dhimma and the Rights and Duties of Dhimmis in an Islamic State," *JIMMA* 9 (July 1988), 2:217–22; Shaykh Showkat Hussain, "Status of Non-Muslims in Islamic State," *HI* 16 (1993), 1:67–79. In the ensuing pages, we have only selected a few factors which are characteristic of dhimmitude. For a fuller report on the position of Christians in the early 1990s, see International Institute for the Study of Islam and Christianity, *The Status of the Church in the Muslim World*, Monograph No.1 (London, 1992). This publication is a valuable source till 1992, supplemented and confirmed by others. It has not been referred to extensively because our subject is not confined to the condition of the Christians alone, but is part of a much larger and more complex study.

6. Olivier Carré, *L'utopie islamique dans l'Orient arabe* (Paris, 1991), 106–7, 131–32.

7. Amnesty International, *Saudi Arabia: A secret state of suffering* (London, March 2000).

8. E/CN.4/1993/41, 28 January 1993; see also, "Concluding Observations of the Committee on Economic, Social and Cultural Rights on the subject of the initial report of the Islamic Republic of Iran to this UN treaty body" (9 June 1993, E/C.12/1993/7). For the full discussions on the second periodic Report of the Islamic Republic of Iran to the Human Rights Committee (another UN treaty body), see *Official Records of the Human Rights Committee 1992/93* (New York and Geneva, 1996), CCPR/12 (vol. 1), 5–6, 86–108, 245–53, 362–81;

CCPR/12/Add.1 (vol. 2), 72–99 contains Iran's Report (CCPR/C/28/Add. 15); see also the Human Rights Committee's *Commentaries* (CCPR/C/79/Add. 25, 3 August 1993).

9. All these regulations conform to the stipulations of Muslim jurisconsults concerning *dhimmis*. Censorship in relation to the media (radio, television, press, photographs) suppress from the public domain any cultural manifestation by those religions which are only tolerated in a humble status. See Galindo Pohl's Report for the year 1993 (E/CN.4/1994/50), 2 February 1994).

10. E/CN.4/1995/55 (16 January 1995).

11. E/CN.4/1996/59 (21 March 1996), § 44–45.

12. E/CN.4/1998/59 (28 January 1998), § 25–27.

13. E/CN.4/1999/32 (28 December 1998), § 35–39.

14. E/CN.4/2000/35 (18 January 2000).

15. E/CN.4/2000/16 (10 February 2000), § 150–53. See also E/CN.4/2000/SR.48, § 33.

16. These facts are mentioned by the UNSR on Sudan Dr. Gaspar Biro, in his detailed Reports from 1994 to 1998. See also Fr. Hubert Barbier's statement to the UNCHR, 16 February 1993 (E/CN.4/1993/SR.22, § 19–22); open letter from Archbishop Erwin Joseph Ender, Papal Pro-Nuncio, to the president of Sudan, *News Bulletin*, London, 6 October 1991; Bishop Macram Max Gassi's statement to the UNCHR, 3 March 1993, (E/CN.4/1993/SR.52 § 85–91).

17. Pedro C. Moreno (ed.), *Handbook on Religious Liberty around the World* (Charlottesville, VA, 1996), 95–110. For further details, see the written statement of the Association for World Education (AWE) to the UN Sub-Commission on Human Rights: "The Blasphemy Legislation in the Penal Code of Pakistan," E/CN.4/Sub. 2/1998/NGO/3.

18. E/CN.4/1999/NGO/31 (29 January 1999).

19. "Inaugural Address by the Chief Executive of Pakistan at the Pakistan Convention on Human Rights & Dignity," Islamabad, 21 April 2000, § 4.

20. As quoted by *AP* (*Pakistan*), 17 May 2000; see also *IHT*, 18 May 2000, p.7.

21. Naguib, "Les Droits de l'homme," 346–48; for attacks on the Copts' fundamental rights, see ibid., 325–52. In 1972 the Minister of Islamic Affairs confiscated lands in mortmain belonging to the Coptic community and reserved the revenue from it solely for the Muslim poor. In 1989 a court ordered the return of Christian property; the order has only been partly executed.

22. Ibid., 263–80.

23. *Country Reports on Human Rights Practice for 1990*, U.S. Department of State (Washington, DC, 1991); for the deterioration in the Copts' living conditions, see Naguib, "Les Droits de l'homme"; Péroncel-Hugoz, *Le Radeau; NYT* (Int. ed.), 27 July 1992; Kepel, *The Prophet and Pharaoh*, 156–69.

24. Testimony on 10 June 1997 before the U.S. Senate Foreign Relations Committee, Near East Subcommittee, by the Rev. Keith Roderick, Secretary-General of the Coalition for the Defense of Human Rights Under Islamization, in *The Copts, Christians of Egypt*, published by The American, Canadian, Australian and European Coptic Associations, vol. 25, no. 1, January 1998.

25. See the statement on 17 August 1992 by René Wadlow, main representative of the International Fellowship of Reconciliation, to the UN Sub-Commission on Human Rights (Geneva), E/CN.4/Sub.2/1992/SR.19, § 27–32; see also, Douglas Jehl, "Killings Erode Cairo's Claim to 'Control' Militants," in *NYT* (Int. ed.), 15 March 1997.

26. *Al Kiraza Magazine* (Chief Editor: Pope Shenouda III), Cairo, vol. 28, issue 3–4, 21 January 2000, p. 1. For more detailed information, see *Christians in Egypt: Church Under Siege*, Institute for Religious Minorities in the Islamic World (Zurich/London/Washington, 1993); Human Rights Watch report on "Egypt: Violations of Freedom of Religious Belief and Expression of the Christian Minority," Human Rights Watch/Middle East, vol. 6, no. 2 (New York), November 1994. See also the report of the Egyptian Organization for Human Rights (EOHR) on the "Collective punishment in Al-Kosheh village," 28 September 1998; *Egypt's Endangered Christians, A Report by the Center for Religious Freedom of Freedom House* (Washington, 1999).

27. Report on the situation of human rights in Iraq for the year 1994 by UNSR Max van der Stoel, E/CN.4/1995/56, § 34.

28. Law no.6, § 3 of 3 April 1954, reactivated in law no.7 of 1 April 1963, sect. 2.

29. For these laws, see Tsimhoni, *Christian Communities in Jerusalem*, 2, 3.

30. Ibid., 14 n. 24.

31. Interview in *La Repubblica*, Milan, 30 March 1988; see also the justification for the *intifada* in *Al-Usbu al-Jadid*, East Jerusalem weekly, 1 January 1992.

32. *JP*, 2 May 1991.

33. Statement issued by the Bethlehem Municipality, Institutions, societies and citizens of Bethlehem, 30 March 1991.

34. *Famille Chrétienne* (weekly), Paris, 26 December 1991, no. 728.

35. The press and radio have often mentioned these exoduses; for example, in F.Corley, "Christian Travails in a Muslim Land," *The Wall Street Journal* (European ed.), 11 August 1993.

36. Youssef M. Ibrahim, "Egypt Wooing Islamic Moderates, Finds They're Just Polite Extremists," *IHT* (from the *NYT*), 19 August 1993; and ibid., "Egypt's Secular Society Reels; And Fundamentalist Cultural Offensive Gains," *IHT* (from the *NYT*), 4 February 1994; for the Islamists' justification for their murderous campaigns against foreign tourists, in the wake of the World Trade Center bombing, see Thierry Desjardins, "Egypte: sur la piste du terrorisme islamique," *Le Figaro*, 6–7 March 1993, and ibid., "Egypte: l'Islamisation rampante," 8 March 1993; also, Kepel, *The Prophet and Pharaoh*.

37. Johannes J. G. Jansen, *The Dual Nature of Islamic Fundamentalism* (London, 1997), 170. Jansen translates *ifti'at* as "hostility."

38. Ibrahim, "Egypt, Wooing Islamic Moderates," in *IHT*, 19 August 1993.

39. Israeli, *Muslim Fundamentalism*, 69.

40. Ibid., 83.

41. *Al-Sirat* (*The Path*), Umm al-Fahm, Israel, November 1987, no.7, 20–23, in Israeli, *Muslim Fundamentalism*, 99 and n.46.

42. For the anti-Israel campaign waged by the Palestinian Churches, dated Jerusalem, 27 January 1988, see *JP*, 26 and 29 January 1988.

43. "Prayer for Jerusalem, Palm Sunday 1990. Christians for Peace in the Holy Land." This text aroused the indignation of many European clergymen.

44. *Al-Watan al-Arabi*, Cairo, 25 May 1990: Message of the Greek Orthodox Patriarch of Palestine and Jordan to President Saddam Hussein.

45. Poster declaration, Jerusalem, 29 January 1991.

46. *Church Times* (Church of England weekly), London, 11 June 1993. The initiative for an international conference on the condition of the Christians in the Holy Land came from the World Islam Festival Trust and was supported by Mgr. Samir Kafity, Anglican bishop of Jerusalem. The Churches' responses were cautious, modified, or favorable, like that of the Lutheran church in Jerusalem. According to the Israeli government, these maneuvers at the instigation of the World Islamic Fund aimed at torpedoing the negotiations with the Vatican. This initiative reveals the political role and manipulation of the *dhimmi* clergy: see *JP*, 4 October 1992.

47. *JP*, (Int. weekly ed.), 1 November 1997. For the Palestinian anti-Christian terror campaign, see *JP*, 1, 18, 22, and 24 July 1994.

48. See also Shawky F. Karas, *The Copts since the Arab Invasion: Strangers in their own Land* (Jersey City, NJ, 1985).

49. Aldeeb Abu-Sahlieh, *Non-Musulmans en Pays d'Islam*, 342 (Appendix 5).

50. *IHT*, 25 May 1998, p.7.

51. E/CN.4/2000/4/Add.1, Opinion N° 10/1999 (Egypt), 52–55. For the Egyptian government's incomplete response to this "Opinion," see E/CN.4/2000/4, § 27–28.

52. Offense n° 2944 for the year 1997 (in Marsa-Matrouh).

53. These appeals were forwarded to the Egyptian ambassador at the United Nations in Geneva, but no answer was ever received.

54. E/CN.4/2000/SR. 46, § 99, and 2000/SR. 48, § 33, *AFP*, 14 April 2000. Another appeal was made by Littman on 15 August in a statement to the UN Sub-Commission on Human Rights that included the case of Prof. Sa'ad Al-Din Ibrahim, director of the Ibn Khaldun Center for human rights, who, *inter alia*, had defended the Copts, E/CN.4/Sub.2/2000/SR 21 § 79–80. On 20 November 2000, the AWE appealed to the UNWGAD again as Dr. Abdel-Malek's health was deteriorating after three years in prison. The Egyptian "reply" again did not address this arbitrary detention. See AWE's written statement E/CN.4/2001/NGO/49.

55. Bashir Gemayel, *Liberté et Sécurité* (Beirut, 1983), 15.

56. Ibid., 37–38; see also Chamoun, *Crise au Liban*; and the fine article by Jacques Ellul, "Les Chrétiens et Beyrouth," in *Réforme*, Paris, 30 May 1970.

57. Gemayel, *Liberté*, 31, speech on 8 May 1980 to a delegation of the Christian Democrat European Union.

58. E/CN.4/1996/62, § 89, and E/CN.4/1997/58, § 56.

59. See the article in *Le Courrier* (Geneva), "Pakistan, Chrétiens et ahmadis sont à la merci des fondamentalistes," by Jacques Berset, 31 October 1998.

60. Nisan, *Minorities in the Middle East*, 131.

61. Naguib, "Les Droits de l'homme," passim.

62. Article in *Le Monde*, 22 March 1979, reprinted in Gemayel, *Liberté*, 17.

63. Abou, *Béchir Gemayel*, 411. This was President-elect Bashir Gemayel's last speech before his assassination on the same afternoon, 14 September 1982. The manipulation of information during Israel's 1982 military campaign in Lebanon produced a vast literature, see Julian J. Landau, *The Media, Freedom or Responsibility: The War in Lebanon, 1982, A Case Study* (Jerusalem, 1984).

64. Gemayel, *Liberté*, 17–18.

65. Ibid., 36–37.

66. "Entretien. En marge de temporaire accordé par le poète palestinien Mahmoud Darwich, l'un des plus grands poètes arabes contemporains, à Farouk Mardam-Bey et Elias Sanbar," 25 November 1983, *REP* 10 (winter, 1984): 19–20.

67. See Celestine Bohlen, "Pope Calls on Lebanon to Resume Special Role for Peace," *NYT*, 12 May 1997, A8.

68. See Frémeaux, *Le Monde Arabe*.

69. Jacques Berque has often voiced his dream consisting of endowing Europe with several Andalusias; for the Euro-Arab continent, see the article in *Hérodote*, 36 (1985): 29–30.

70. Jacques Berque in *Les Palestiniens*, 29–30.

71. Betts, *Christians in the Arab East*, 226–67.

72. Khodr, "L'Arabité", 40, reproduced in Moubarac, *Pentalogie*, 5: 185–99.

73. *Bull. de St-Julien-le-Pauvre* (Paris, 1957), quoted by Moubarac in *Pentalogie*, 4: 64.

74. Ibid., 5: 139.

75. Betts, *Christians in the Arab East*, 227.

76. *NYT*, 18 September 1989, quoted in Herbert Schlossberg, *A Fragrance of Oppression, The Church and its Persecutors* (Wheaton, IL, 1991), 191.

77. Statement by Rondot to Jesuit priest in Lyon, quoted in Abou, *Béchir Gemayel*, 368; for the hostility of the left-wing French press toward a peace treaty between Lebanon and Israel, ibid., 233.

78. Joseph, *Muslim-Christian Relations*, 113–14.

79. For an analysis of the double language of the *dhimmi* and overstating as a self-protection tactic, see Abou, *Béchir Gemayel*, 330–36. The Christian's feeling of insecurity and fear which generates the process of identifying the victim with his oppressor cannot be overemphasized.

80. *Le Monde*, 15 May 1980.

81. Mouna Naïm, "Jacques Chirac sera au Liban et en Egypte le messager d'une nouvelle politique franco-euro-arabe," *Le Monde*, 4 April 1996. The journalist William Pfaff affirmed that "Israel's creation in 1948 automatically turned the Arabs against Europe and the United States" (*IHT*, from the *Los Angeles Times*, 6 June 2000).

82. Abou, *Béchir Gemayel*, 277. The Vatican considered that Lebanon was "a pilot country for the development of Muslim-Christian relations," see in Betts, *Christians in the Arab East*, 226.

83. Abou Iyad, *Palestinien Sans Patrie, Entretiens avec Eric Rouleau* (Paris, 1978), 268–70. Abu Iyad was in charge of the PLO's Special Services.

84. Betts, *Christians in the Arab East*, 219. The same idea in Moubarac, *Pentalogie*, 3: 38.

85. Aldeeb Abu-Sahlieh, *Non-Musulmans en Pays d'Islam*, 317 (Annexe I:5).

86. Ibid., 322 (Annexe II:5); italics in the text, probably by Coptic Nation Association.

87. Moubarac ended his lecture by referring to "France's indestructable loyalty to its Muslim policy and the symbiosis of French and Arab cultures on either side of the Mediterra-

nean," Youakim Moubarac, "Musulmans, chrétiens et juifs," 29; and idem, *Pentalogie,* 5:145–74.

88. See in Abou, *Béchir Gemayel,* the condemnation of the Lebanese forces by French pro-Palestinian left-wing circles; for their rapprochement with Israel, 65–77; for Youakim Moubarac, 110.

89. John H. Watson, *Among the Copts* (Brighton, 2000), 103–13.

90. Schlossberg, *A Fragrance of Oppression,* 194.

91. *Reuters* (Cairo), "Sudan rejects Amnesty report of oil impact on war," 17 May 2000.

92. Paul Marshall with Lela Gilbert, *Their Blood Cries Out,* introduction by Michael Horowitz (Dallas, TX, 1997).

93. 1 May 1997. Witnesses: Panel 1—Congressman Frank Wolf; Panel 2—Mr. Steven Coffey, Principal Deputy Assistant Secretary of State; Panel 3—Bat Ye'or, Nina Shea, Walid Phares.

94. John Eibner, "My Career Redeeming Slaves," *MEQ* (December 1999): 3–16. Gunnar Wiebalck accompanied John Eibner on most of CSI's fact-finding visits to Sudan, undertaken with the blessing of the local chiefs.

Chapter 9. Expansion of Inter-*Dhimmi* Conflicts in the Modern Period

1. For anti-Zionism, see also Paul Giniewski, *L'Antisionisme* (Brussels, 1973); Jacques Givet, *The Anti-Zionist Complex,* introduction by Daniel Patrick Moynihan (Englewood, NJ, 1982); Léon Poliakov, *De Moscou à Beyrouth, Essai sur la Désinformation* (Paris, 1983); Robert S. Wistrich, *Hitler's Apocalypse. Jews and the Nazi Legacy* (London, 1985), chaps. 8–12; idem., *Between Redemption and Perdition. Modern Antisemitism and Jewish Identity* (London, 1990), pt. 4; idem., *Antisemitism: The Longest Hatred* (London/New York, 1991); Taguieff, *Les Protocoles,* chap.5 and bibliography.

2. Quoted in Draft Preliminary Report (Epilogue, 10). Visit to Sudan, 19–25 January 1995, CSI (Zurich).

3. *Le Monde,* 26 May 1986. In October 1971 an international congress of terrorists met on the premises of the Stensen Institute in Florence under the direction of the Jesuits. See Jean Servier, *Le Terrorisme* (Paris, 1979), 117. For the collaboration between Islamists, the extreme right, and neo-Nazis, see Edwy Plenel, "Le Flirt de l'extrême droite avec l'Iran," *Le Monde,* 13 August 1987.

4. Moubarac, *Pentalogie,* 5:58–142, 205.

5. Walter Henry Nelson and Terence C. F. Prittie, *The Economic War Against The Jews* (New York, 1977).

6. Fernand Braudel, *The Mediterranean and the Mediterranean World in the Age of Philip II* (London, 1975), 2:802. It was Léon Poliakov who informed me in 1993 that Braudel had belonged to the Camelots du Roy in the 1930s, an ultramontane, terrorist, and antisemitic organization.

7. Ibid., 802.

8. Ibid., 803.

9. Ibid., sub-heading, 811.

10. Ibid., 826.

11. Rondot, *Les Chrétiens d'Orient,* 129. In 1984 Pierre Rondot, former director of the Centre des Hautes Etudes sur l'Afrique et l'Asie Modernes (Paris), published a surprising article. After having praised Islamic tolerance, which he had previously denounced in his *Les Chrétiens d'Orient,* he concluded on a positive note calling for Muslim-Judeo-Christian coexistence: "this coexistence, traditional for so long, conforms to the spirit of the three religions, and all sincere Believers wish its prompt restoration." As this coexistence was based on the dhimmitude of Jews and Christians—ordained by the *shari'a*—was his praise for such a system tantamount to a recommendation for its future expansion to Europe in particular, and for the West in general? See his "Relations entre Musulmans, Chrétiens et Juifs: Un bref aperçu," in *AAM,* no. 142 (autumn, 1984): 3–13.

12. Betts, *Christians in the Arab East,* 264 n. 235. For the Christians' feeling of insecurity—even of abandonment when the Mandates ended—see Rondot, *Les Chrétiens d'Orient,* 130–36.

13. Haim, *Arab Nationalism,* 64; Carré, *Le nationalisme arabe,* 57.

14. Haim, *Arab Nationalism,* 243; Constantin Zurayk, first president of the University of Damascus and professor at the American University of Beirut, a Syrian and Greek Orthodox by religion, expresses the same opinion, ibid., 167–71. See Rondot, *Les Chrétiens d'Orient:* "Lebanon represents to them [the Christians], the finest but also the most adventurous opportunities," 240. For the pressure that France, still the mandatory power, put on the Christians to involve them in defending Arabism and to identifying with it, see ibid., 135–36.

15. King-Crane Commission Report.

16. Prof. Howard Bliss, principal of the Evangelical College of Beirut (later to become the American University), collaborated actively with the American delegation charged with these investigations. This same concept was taken up again and developed in the theology of Third-Worldism liberation. Thus, Youakim Moubarac criticized Westerners for "the narrowness, even chauvinism, of their withdrawal solely into the West"; in his Paris lecture of 2 June 1970, in Moubarac, "Musulmans, chrétiens et juifs," 24.

17. Moubarac, *Pentalogie,* 3:151.

18. Ibid., 152–53.

19. Ibid., 166–67.

20. Ibid., 156.

21. Idem.

22. Ibid., 158.

23. Ibid., 169. These opinions were strongly challenged by many Christian theologians.

24. Ibid., 172.

25. Ibid., 170.

26. Ibid., 173–74.

27. Betts, *Christians in the Arab East,* 158.

28. *October,* 30 April 1978, quoted and trans. from Arabic, in Ronald Nettler, *Islam and the Minorities* (Jerusalem, 1979), 16. Muslims believe that Jesus professed Islam and they refute the crucifixion. For other prior comments from 1972–75 by Anis Mansour on: the blood libel, Hitler and the Jews, Jews as wild beasts, Freud and Kafka, see the English translations from his articles from *Al Akhbar* and *Akhir Sa'ah,* in D. F. Green, ed. *Arab Theologians* (3rd ed., 1976), 92–93. In November 1975, Anis Mansour represented Egypt at the 40th International PEN Congress in Vienna. For the Egyptian campaign of hatred against Israel and Jews, see Yadlin, *An Arrogant and Oppressive Spirit.* See also Yossef Bodansky, *Islamic Anti-Semitism as a Political Instrument* (Houston, TX, 1999). The flow is constant; see 'Adel Hamooda, "A Jewish Matzah made from Arab Blood," in *Al Ahram,* 28 October 2000 (trans. from Arabic, in *MEMRI,* Special Dispatch—Egypt, no. 150, 6 November 2000); and General (Res.), Hasan Sweilen, "The Jewish Personality and the Israeli Action" (2 parts), in *October,* 3 and 10 December 2000 (trans. from Arabic, in *MEMRI,* Special Dispatch—Egypt, No. 166, 19 December 2000).

29. Carré, *Le nationalisme arabe,* 174. Reissues of his poems depict the crucified Messiah on the cover, ibid., 261. Every aspect of propaganda is examined in Jacques Ellul's study, *Propagandes* (Paris, 1990), 25: "Propaganda takes over present, but also past, literature and history which is rewritten to suit the needs of propaganda." The proportion of Christians among the Palestinians is less than five percent, a third of whom live in Israel. In France, Darwish is highly praised as a poet.

30. *Tishrîn,* February 1991, article, "Musulmans et Chrétiens, même combat contre Israël," extracts reproduced in *Courrier International,* n°16 (21–27 February 1991), 4, and quoted by Taguieff, *Les Protocoles,* 1:356; see also 255.

31. Khodr, "L'Arabité," 38.

32. Ibid., 44.

33. *JP,* 5 April 1997.

34. Khodr, "L'Arabité," 43.

35. Ibid. The psychological mechanisms leading to exoneration during the war with Lebanon, by disguising Israelis as Nazis and Palestinians as Jews, has been the object of a considerable number of studies.

36. Moubarac, *Pentalogie,* 5:36.

Notes to Chapter 9

37. For this campaign, cf., "The Anti-Israel Crusade," *JP*, 4 October 1992, editorial comment; Andrea Levin, "Encyclopedia propaganda II," *JP* (int. weekly ed.), 11 September 1993; Giniewski, *L'Antisionisme*, 202–10.

38. World Council of Churches (Statements). *The Theology of the Churches and the Jewish People. Statements by the WCC and its member churches*, with a commentary by Allan Brockway, Paul van Buren, Rolf Rendtorff and Simon Schoon (Geneva, 1988), 170.

39. Nicholls, *Christian Antisemitism*, 377.

40. Jacques Ellul, foreword, in Bat Ye'or, *The Decline of Eastern Christianity*, 18.

41. Moubarac, *Pentalogie*, 5:63–71.

42. A. Roy Eckardt, "A Tribute to Reinhold Niebuhr (1892–1971)," *Midstream*, 16 (June/July, 1971).

43. See Gérard Arboit, *Le Saint-Siège*, 34, 39, 55, and passim.

44. Ibid., 131.

45. Idem.

46. *Le Monde*, 7 March 1991. The idea that the State of Israel represents an injustice, which implies that its non-existence incarnates justice, is frequently voiced. The Eastern Churches constantly acted as a brake to diplomatic relations between the Holy See and Israel. Father Khuri, secretary to the Patriarch Michel Sabbah, declared that a "recognition of Israel by the Vatican would be premature, for it would mean consecrating the injustice which is done to us, we Christians of Jerusalem." See Veronique Grousset, *Le Figaro magazine*, 19 December 1992, in Arboit, *Le Saint-Siège*, 167.

47. Daniel Jonah Goldhagen, *Hitler's Willing Executioners. Ordinary Germans and the Holocaust* (New York, 1996), 37–38.

48. *The New Republic*, 8 April 1991.

49. Tsimhoni, *Christian Communities*, 173.

50. Naim Stifan Ateek, *Justice and Only Justice: A Palestinian Theology of Liberation* (Maryknoll, NY, 1989).

51. Ibid., 152.

52. Ibid., 159.

53. Ibid., 158.

54. Perlman, *Mufti of Jerusalem*, 51; quoted in Bat Ye'or, *The Dhimmi*, 390; see David Pryce-Jones, *The Closed Circle. An Interpretation of the Arabs* (London, 1989), 206.

55. Ateek, *Justice and only Justice*, 169.

56. Ibid., 170.

57. Ibid., 164.

58. Kenneth Cragg, *The Arab Christian: A History in the Middle East* (London, 1992).

59. See the perspicacious review of this book by Habib Malik, in *The Beirut Review* (spring, 1992): 3:109–22.

60. Cragg, *The Arab Christian*, 98.

61. Ibid., 291.

62. Haim Shapiro, "Jewish-Christian Dialogue, Root and Branch," in *JP*, 23 February 1997.

63. Cragg, *The Arab Christian*, 162.

64. Joseph Aboujaoude, *Les partis politiques au Liban* (Kaslik, Lebanon, 1985), 106.

65. Cragg, *The Arab Christian*, 242.

66. Ibid., 205.

67. Ibid., 209.

68. Ibid., 218.

69. Ibid., 210.

70. Ibid., 275.

71. For the references in Arnold Toynbee's *A Study of History* and for a discussion of this racist Judeophobic viewpoint, see Wistrich, *Hitler's Apocalypse*, chap. 11: Inversions of History, 227–28.

72. Kenneth Cragg, *Palestine. The Prize and Price of Zion* (London and Washington, 1997).

73. Habib C. Malik "The Forgotten Christians of Lebanon," in *Books & Culture* (a Christian Review), vol. 4, no. 5 (Carol Stream, IL, September/October, 1998), 42.

74. Habib C. Malik, "Christians in the Land Called Holy" in *First Things* (New York, January, 1999) 89:11–12.

75. *JP*, 4 October 1992.

76. Ibid., 23 December 1998.

77. Sheikh Muhammad Hussein Fadlallah, *JPS*, 25 (autumn 1995): 1:61–75.

78. Habib C. Malik, *Between Damascus and Jerusalem: Lebanon and Middle East Peace* (Washington DC, 1997), 8.

79. Ibid., 10.

80. Pierrard, *Juifs et Catholiques français*, 28, 124.

81. Geneviève Dermanjian, *La Crise Anti-Juive Oranaise (1895–1905). L'antisémitisme dans l'Algérie coloniale* (Paris, 1986), 206.

82. Ibid., 135.

83. Pierre Sorlin, *"La Croix" et les Juifs (1880–1899)* (Paris, 1967), 76–77.

84. Hirszowicz, *The Third Reich*, 130.

85. Ibid., 251. For Egypt, see Masriya, *Les Juifs en Egypte*, Appendix, "Nazis au Caire," 66–69.

86. Published by the Egyptian government. See extracts of these proceedings in D. F. Green, ed., *Arab Theologians*, and the introduction.

87. Abdul al-Latif Tibawi, *Second Critique of English-Speaking Orientalists and their Approach to Islam and the Arabs* (London, 1979). In his appendix 4 the author lists the university centers for Islamic studies in England which benefit from funds originating in Muslim countries. We are reprinting the author's allegations, reserving our own opinion: Cambridge (funded by several Arab countries), Oxford (the author mentions three Arab sources of finance for the years 1977–1979), and Exeter. For the United States, the author lists Harvard University, the University of Michigan, the University of Pennsylvania, and the Center of Contemporary Arab Studies at the University of Georgetown in Washington DC. Tibawi considers that the Arab contribution to the finances of these study centers in the West justifies the demand for university teaching and publications in accordance with Islamic religious and political concepts. For the United States, see Fred R. von der Mehden, "American Perceptions of Islam," in Esposito, *Voices*, 18–31; and on the Gulf War, and the pro-Iraqi, anti-Zionist and anti-American parties, see idem, "France-Irak, L'Argent de la Corruption," in *L'Evénement du Jeudi*, 13–19 September 1990.

88. Ellul, *Propagandes*, 268.

89. Ibid., 48. See Paul Giniewski, *La Croix des Juifs* (Geneva, 1994), chap.5.

90. Bruno Etienne, *La France et l'islam* (Paris, 1989), 180, without specifying place or date.

91. Muhammad Aqqad, *The Muslim Foundations of European Civilization* (Cairo, 1970).

92. Information bulletin of the permanent delegation of the League of Arab States, Geneva, 1 May 1970, n° 7, "Pour la Vérité et la Justice. La Conférence Mondiale des Chrétiens pour la Palestine," 6.

93. Ibid., 7.

94. Information bulletin of the permanent delegation of the League of Arab States, Geneva, 30 November 1970, n° 15, "Le directeur de 'Témoignage Chrétien' dénonce la propagande sioniste," 6.

95. See Daniel Pipes, *Greater Syria: The History of an Ambition* (New York/Oxford, 1990), 100–11. Kenneth Cragg devotes pages of praise to Sayigh and dedicates his book to him; see also in Taguieff, *Les Protocoles*, 326, n.17; and 316–39, for the Palestinization of European anti-Jewish stereotypes.

96. For some useful documentation on the manipulation of the United Nations during this period, see Harris Okun Schoenberg, *A Mandate for Terror. The United Nations and the PLO* (New York, 1989).

97. Groupe d'étude sur le Moyen-Orient, n° 80, December 1979.

98. Groupe d'étude sur le Moyen-Orient, n° 14, 12 September 1969, Geneva.

99. Tsimhoni, *Christian Communities*, 170.

100. Hirszowicz, *The Third Reich*, 267.

101. Ibid., 258–64.

102. Ibid., 268, from notes probably written by Etter in December 1942. For the Palestinian

Arab rapprochement with the Nazis, see Francis R. Nicosia, *The Third Reich and the Palestine Question* (London, 1985).

103. Conor Cruise O'Brien, *The Siege. The Saga of Israel and Zionism* (London, 1986), 611. This was at a time when Prime Minister Jacques Chirac repeatedly referred to Saddam Hussein as a personal friend.

104. Nicholls, *Christian Antisemitism,* 351–52.

105. Ibid., 354.

106. Taguieff, *Les Protocoles,* 1:217–50, 318, 341–63; Alain Dieckhoff, "Antisionisme et Mythe de la Conspiration Juive Mondiale," in Taguieff, *Les Protocoles,* 2:343–64.

107. Wistrich, *Hitler's Apocalypse,* 247. For a condensed analysis of French anti-Zionist policies and its pro-Arab and pro-Palestinian influence in the EEC, see in Avraham Sela, ed., *Political Encyclopedia of the Middle East* (Jerusalem, 1999), "France, French Interests and Policies," 259–62.

108. See *L'Evénement du Jeudi,* 13–19 September 1990. France's Minister of Defense, Jean-Pierre Chevènement—President of the organization France-Iraq—resigned his post before the Gulf War began in January 1991, rather than participate in the coalition against Iraq. In a letter, Odai al-Tayi, ex-counsellor to the Iraqi ambassador to Paris, urged France to renew with its traditional anti-American pro-Arab policy, see *Le Figaro,* 31 May 1993.

109. *L'Evénement du Jeudi,* "France-Irak, L'argent de la Corruption," 13–19 September 1990, Paris.

110. David Littman, "Syria's Blood Libel Revival at the UN: 1991–2000," *Midstream* (February–March 2000): 2–8. On 24 February 2001, the Cairo Weekly *Roz Al-Yussuf* reported that an Egyptian film producer, Munir Radhi, was making a film adaptation of *The Matzah of Zion* (5% of the profits would go to General, now Marshal Mustafa Tlass, Syria's Defense Minister since 1972), see in *MEMRI:* Special Dispatch-Syria/Egypt, 1 March 2001, no. 190. This matter was raised at the UNCHR on 26 March 2001 by David Littman, on behalf of the World Union for Progressive Judaism (E/CN.4/2001/SR.13).

Chapter 10. The Politics of Dhimmitude in Europe

1. *Five Tracts of Hassan al-Banna,* 93.

2. Carré, *Mystique et Politique,* 103–22.

3. al-Turabi, "The Islamic State," in Esposito, ed., *Voices,* 242.

4. al-Faruqi, "Islam and Zionism," in Esposito, ed., *Voices,* 264. This opinion is in accordance with the Islamic concept of Jews and Christians since they are only tolerated as *dhimmis.* See Borrmans, eds., *Al-Dimma, L'Islam et les Minorités;* and the command and legitimacy for the murder of infidels according to Qutb, in Carré, *Mystique et Politique,* 132.

5. al-Faruqi, "Islam and Zionism," in Esposito, ed., *Voices,* 265.

6. Trans. from Arabic, in *MEMRI,* Special Dispatch no. 41, 2 August 1999.

7. Quoted in Alain Boyer, *L'Islam en France* (Paris, 1998), 25.

8. Md. Alauddin al-Azhari, *The Theory and Sources of Islamic Law for Non-Muslims* (Dacca, 1962), 4 and 11.

9. Israeli, *Muslim Fundamentalism,* 163.

10. Ibid.

11. Elie Rekhess, "The Iranian Impact on the Islamic *Jihad* Movement in the Gaza Strip," quoted in Johannes J. G. Jansen, *The Dual Nature of Islamic Fundamentalism* (London, 1997), 68.

12. See Georges Vajda, "Juifs et Musulmans selon le Hadit," 58–127.

13. *Al-I'tisam,* reported by *Ha'aretz* and *JP,* 10 March 1989, quoted in Israeli, *Muslim Fundamentalism,* 161. The reference to monkeys (apes) and pigs relates to Jews and Christians. Islamists follow this traditional interpretation of the koranic expression in sura 2:61b ("apes") and, especially, 5:65 ("apes and swine").

14. For a similar declaration by an Islamist murderer of foreign tourists in Egypt, see *IHT,* 25 May 1998 (*supra,* page 246).

15. Abu'l A'la Mawdudi, *Islam: An Historical Perspective* (London, 1980), 3–4.

16. Mawdudi, *Towards Understanding*, 40.

17. Abbasali Amid Zanjani, *Minority Rights according to the Law of the Tribute Agreement. A Survey of some Purports of the International Rights from the Viewpoint of the Islamic Jurisprudence* (Teheran, 1997) 90–91.

18. Trans. from the Arabic in *MEMRI*, Special Dispatch no 41, 2 August 1999.

19. J.D.J. Waardenburg, "Mustashrikun" (Orientalists), *EI²* 7:736–54; Maurice Borrmans et al., ed., *Al-Mustašhriqun (Orientalistes), Textes arabes sur l'Orientalisme, PISAI*, Etudes Arabes: Dossiers, no. 83, 1992/2. This publication reproduces Arab texts on the Orientalists; Bernard Lewis, "The Question of Orientalism," *The New York Review of Books* (24 June 1982): 49–56.

20. Abd al-Latif al-Shuwayrif, "Les dangers de l'Orientalisme et notre façon de les affronter," trans. from Arabic by Michel Lagarde, in *Al-Mustašhriqun*, 34–49; Khomeiny, *Principes*, passim; on the evil doings of the Orientalists, cf. Kepel, *The Prophet and Pharaoh*, 118–19.

21. Comments reported by Nizar Qindil, "L'Histoire et les fautes des Orientalistes" (text dated April 1991), trans. from Arabic by Janine Mahfouz, in Borrmans, ed., *Al-Mustašhriqun*, 70–73.

22. In Mawdudi, *Towards Understanding*, 37, n.3.

23. Chris Hedges, *IHT*, 24–25 July 1993.

24. Tibawi, *Second Critique*, 37.

25. Mawdudi, *Towards Understanding*, 83.

26. Goldhagen, *Hitler's Willing Executioners*.

27. Georges Corm, *Le Proche-Orient éclaté 1956–1991* (expanded ed., Paris, 1991), 377–78. The crime of despising the Arabs, leveled at Western governments, constitutes a constant recrimination.

28. John L. Esposito, *Islam The Straight Path* (Oxford/New York, 1994), ix.

29. John L. Esposito, *The Islamic Threat. Myth or Reality?* (New York/Oxford, 1992), 39.

30. Ibid.

31. Ibid., 43, see the discussion on the civilizing aims of the Turkish conquest of the Balkans in Angelov, "Certains Aspects . . .", in idem, *Les Balkans au Moyen Age*, 221–22, 261 (XII).

32. Esposito, *The Islamic Threat*, 53.

33. For the legality of taking the blood of a *harbi*, see *supra*, 55; Morabia, *Le Gihâd*, 212. The same obligation to kill the infidel is found in Qutb. It is the concept of *harbi* that justifies the murder. The victim is not executed because of crimes he personally may have committed, but because he is a member of the nation of nontributary infidels. This concept eliminates legal procedure: individual accusation, proof of crime, right of defense, or due process.

34. Esposito, "Islam and Muslim Politics," 12, and the same ideas in his *The Islamic Threat*, 71, 120.

35. Bat Ye'or, *The Decline of Eastern Christianity*, chap.5; "Bat Ye'or Interviewed by Paul Giniewski," in *Midstream* (February–March 1994): 16–19; idem, "Myths and Politics. The Tolerant Pluralistic Islamic Society: Origin of a Myth." Address delivered on 31 August 1995 to a Symposium on the Balkan War (Ramada Congress Hotel, Chicago, Ill.), under the auspices of the Lord Byron Foundation for Balkan Studies and the International Strategic Studies Association (see *www.dhimmi.org*). Idem, "Jews and Christians under Islam," in *Midstream*, (February–March 1997): 9–12.

36. Extracts from Yasser Arafat's statement at the General Assembly of the United Nations (New York), 13 November 1974, in *JPS* 4(1975): 181–94. See also International Documents on Palestine (1974) (Institute of Palestine Studies, Beirut, 1977), 134–44; the two passages quoted are taken from this second source, except for the three words in square brackets which appear in the *JPS* source; larger extracts were reproduced in Bat Ye'or, *The Dhimmi*, 397–98.

37. Azoury, *Le Réveil de la Nation Arabe*, 18–19.

38. David Kushner, "Intercommunal Strife in Palestine during the late Ottoman Period," *AAS*, 18, no.2 (July 1984): 187–204.

39. Morison, *Relation Historique d'un voyage*, 245, 292, 296.

40. Edward Robinson, *Biblical Researches in Palestine and the Adjacent Regions: A Journal of Travels in the Years 1838 & 1852*, (3rd ed., London, 1867).

41. Victor Guérin, *Déscription géographique, historique et archéologique de la Palestine, accompagnée de cartes détaillées* (Paris, 1868–80), I: Judée (Préface), ii.

42. Statement by Arafat (transcription from the UN audio cassette of the English simultaneous interpretation from Arabic); see letters by David Littman, present at the press conference, in *Tribune dimanche* (Geneva), 11 September 1983; *Tribune de Genève,* 13 September 1983, and *IHT,* 4 April 1984. According to Greek Catholic Archbishop François Abu Mokh, when Arafat was received by Pope John Paul II two weeks later (15 September 1983), he told the pope that he felt at home in the Vatican, the seat of the successors to St. Peter, "the first Palestinian exile"; see François Abu Mokh, *Les Confessions d'un Arabe Catholique. Entretiens avec Joëlle Chabert et François Mourvillier* (Paris, 1991), 195. Such anecdotes betray a total ignorance of history because thousands of Jewish captives in Rome had already preceded St. Peter by a century, and the use of the term "Palestinian" is an anachronism before the year 135 of the Christian era, when the Romans changed the name "Judea" to "Palestine."

43. *JP,* 11 November 1977.

44. *Le Monde,* 25 July 1987.

45. Joseph, *Muslim-Christian Relations,* 125.

46. Nicholls, *Christian Antisemitism,* 364.

47. Permanent delegation of the Arab League, Information Bulletin, 1 May 1970, no.7.

48. United Nations, press release, GA/PAL/44.

49. "Gathered for Life: Official Report," 6th Assembly, World Council of Churches, Vancouver, Canada, 24 July–10 August 1983, cited in Nicholls, *Christian Antisemitism,* 376; see also WCC, *The Theology of the Churches and the Jewish People.*

50. Paul Cousseran, "Procès Papon: double manipulation," in *Le Figaro,* 22 October 1997.

51. An article in *Le Figaro* had pointed to the virulent antisemitism in certain Muslim circles in France: "Some pious defenders of the Koran actually read *Mein Kampf* or *the Protocols of the Elders of Zion* in their spare time"; in Thierry Oberlé, "Islamistes: la France sur la défensive," *Le Figaro,* 26–27 September 1990; Yves Lacoste, "La crise actuelle, une chance pour l'intégration," interview with Arezki Damani (president of the France-Plus Association), in *L'Occident et la Guerre des Arabes, Hérodote,* no. 60/61, 1st and 2nd trim., 1991, 28; see also Hussein Zaanoun and Alain Chery, "Dans les collèges de la banlieu nord de Paris," in ibid., 235–38.

52. John Watson has examined this schism in the Coptic communities, but it also exists among the Lebanese. This illustrates, but in a different context, the analysis by Jacques Ellul in his *La subversion du christianisme* (Paris, 1984).

53. Al-Azhar, *The Fourth Conference,* 927: C.—*On Civilization and Society:* (2) and (3).

54. Council of Europe, Parliamentary Assembly, *The Contribution of the Islamic Civilisation to European Culture* (Strasbourg, 1992), doc. 6497, 15.

55. *Q-News, The Muslim Magazine,* n° 297 (October 1998), "A new dialogue with Islam."

56. *Al-Muhajiroun, The Voice, The Eyes and The Ears of the Muslims,* London, Press release dated 21 December 1999 (www.almuhajiroun.com.).

57. Numerous books and articles have examined the development of terrorist networks in Europe; for the exceptional security measures during the Gulf War, see Yves Lacoste, "*L'Occident et la guerre des Arabes,*" in *Hérodote,* no. 60/61, 1st and 2nd trim.(1991),16; Antoine Sfeir, *Les réseaux d'Allah, Les filières islamistes en France et en Europe* (Paris, 1997).

58. Zanjani, *Minority Rights,* 326–29 and passim. Zanjani devotes his fifth chapter ("Annulment and Violation of the Tribute Agreement") to the consequences of the non-fulfillment of its commitments by the religious minorities.

59. Ibid., 251–53.

60. Alain Chevalérias, "Dialogue islamo-chrétien," in *La Nef,* no.79 (January 1998).

61. Michel Hayek, "Nouvelles approches de l'islam," *Les Conférences du Cénacle,* Beirut, 1968, No.9–10, XXII année.

62. Rondot, *Les Chrétiens d'Orient,* 263–64.

63. Samuel P. Huntington, *The Clash of Civilizations and the Remaking of World Order* (New York, 1996); and an earlier article, "The Clash of Civilizations?" in *FA* 93 (summer, 1993).

64. Huntington, *The Clash of Civilizations,* chaps. 10 and 11.

65. Alexandre Del Valle, *Guerres Contre l'Europe. Bosnie-Kosovo-Tchétchénie . . .* (Paris, 2000), 90.

66. Bloch, *Le IIIè Reich,* 432.

67. Quotation from the Protestant Pastor Martin Niemöller, in Goldhagen, *Hitler's Willing Executioners,* 160. In his remarkable study, Goldhagen highlights two major ideas in the

processes which led to the genocide: that of "intentionality" and the institutional framework of the Nazi policy of elimination.

68. Boyer, *L'Islam en France*, 44.

69. Frémeaux, *Le monde arabe*, 86.

70. Ibid., 293.

71. Huntington, *The Clash of Civilizations*, 286–91; Yosef Bodansky, *Offensive in the Balkans. The Potential for a Wider War as a Result of Foreign Intervention in Bosnia-Herzegovina* (Alexandria, VA/London, 1995).

72. For the hatred of the West felt by all the Muslim countries during the Gulf War, see Huntington, *The Clash of Civilizations*, 248–56.

73. Del Valle, *Guerres contre l'Europe*, devotes chapter 6 to the information war, its holding the Shoah hostage, its stereotypes, amalgams, and false mirrors. Del Valle particularly denounces American influence but he does not see the institutional bases of the disinformation, already created in Europe by anti-Zionist propaganda. This same anti-Jewish structure, much refined by over twenty years of disinformation, can be applied in other conflictual contexts. For the Arab appropriation of the Shoah, see ibid., 227–39.

74. Henri Boulad, "A propos de l'islamisme et de l'islam," in *Choisir* (Catholic monthly), Geneva, April 1997, 26–28.

75. Transcription from the audio cassette of the English simultaneous interpretation from Arabic. In the same statement, Mr. Ramlawi accused Israel of killing Count Bernadotte in 1948 and of trying to kill the High Commissioner for Human Rights, Mrs. Mary Robinson, during her November 2000 visit to the region. There was no official refutation of this slander either then or later, even after a full UN investigation refuted it.

76. For a description of the early destructions by Arab tribes in Byzantine Palestine, as described in the earliest sources, see Gil, *A History of Palestine*, 169–79.

Chapter 11. Conclusion

1. Edouard Engelhardt, *La Turquie et le Tanzimat ou Histoire des Réformes dans l'Empire Ottoman depuis 1826 jusqu'à nos jours* (Paris, vol. 1,1882; vol. 2, 1884).

2. Mohammed Sabry, *L'Empire Egyptien sous Mohamed-Ali et la Question d'Orient, 1811–1849* (Paris, 1930), 80–81.

3. Ibid., 70–74.

4. Ibid., 591, letter (Cairo, 5 August 1849) on the death of Muhammad Ali, from British Consul-General Charles August Murray to Foreign Secretary Lord Palmerston.

5. Serjeant, *Customary and Shariah Law in Arabian Society*, 118.

6. Ibid., 119.

7. Ibid., 121.

8. William Montgomery Watt, *The Majesty that was Islam: The Islamic World, 661–1100* (London, 1974), 47.

9. Ibid., 48. For their condition in seventh-century Arabia, see Michael Lecker, "Judaism among Kinda and the *ridda* of Kinda," *JAOS* 115 (1995): 635–50; idem, "On Arabs of the Banû Kilab executed together with the Jewish Banû Qurayza," *JSAI* 19 (1995): 66–72. Both articles reprinted in idem, *Jews and Arabs in pre- and early Islamic Arabia* (Aldershot, Hampshire, 1998), 10 and 14.

10. Watt, *The Majesty that was Islam*, 49.

11. Ibid., 257.

12. Idem, *Muhammad at Medina*, 215.

13. Mark Cohen, *Under Crescent and Cross, the Jews in the Middle Ages* (Princeton, 1994), introduction, XX.

14. For a discussion of Cohen's thesis, already expressed in "Islam and the Jews: Myth, Counter-Myth, History," *JQ*, 38 (spring 1986): 125–37, see this author's *Rejoinder*, "Islam and the 'Dhimmis" in *JQ*, 42 (spring, 1987): 83–88; for a critical review of Cohen's book, see Paul Fenton in *European Judaism*, vol. 28, n° 1 (spring 1995): 96–98.

15. Louis Gardet, *La Cité Musulmane: Vie sociale et politique. Etudes musulmanes* (Paris, 1954), 348.

16. V. Poggi S. J., "Recensiones" in *Orientalia Christiana Periodica*, 58 (1992), 2:606–7. For Fr. Neuhaus, see pp. 380–81 above.

17. British politicians acknowledged that the Armenians were sacrificed to their appeasement policy toward the Muslims of India. Regarding the Jews, British foreign policy stressed Arab and Muslim pressures for their anti-Jewish policy. In 1938 Lord Zetland, Secretary of State for India, invoked Indian Muslim hostility to "any Jewish sovereignty" in Palestine. See Martin Gilbert, *Exile and Return, The Emergence of Jewish Statehood* (London, 1978), 210; and for the situation in 1939, see 219–20.

18. Idem. See the comments (12 November 1935) to the Chief Secretary in Jerusalem by Eric Mills, senior member of the British Mandate Administration in Palestine. After a visit to Germany he referred to "the elimination of Armenians from the Turkish empire"; and added: "*The Jew is to be eliminated and the State has no regard for the manner of this elimination,*" 163.

19. For the influence of the Muslims and the Christians in Palestine on the anti-Zionism of British policy and on French hostility toward the Jewish National Home at the San Remo Conference (1920), see ibid., 129–30.

20. Ibid., 220; Bloch, *Le Troisième Reich*, 52. Gerhart M. Riegner of the World Jewish Congress—a particularly sensitive actor in the rescue of the Jews of Europe—described in his memoirs, *Ne Jamais Désespérer* (Paris, 1998), the obstruction by the allied and neutral governments to the efforts to rescue Jews. Goldhagen refers to German literature calling for the elimination of the Jews as early as the second half of the nineteenth century; see his *Hitler's Willing Executioners*, 71–79. Similar literature existed in France and throughout Europe.

21. Gilbert, *Exile and Return*, 203.

22. Ibid., 226, and the whole of chap. 17.

23. In a statement to the UN Security Council on 13 October 1999, and press release 12/99 of 13 October 1999 (Embassy of Sudan, Ottawa, Canada). For a description of these events—"a flawed decision without due process, which has stained the reputation of the United Nations in its relationship with the NGO community"—see the detailed analysis by René Wadlow, main representative of the Association for World Education (Geneva), in his two memorandums (dated 18 October and 8 November 1999), widely circulated.

24. CSI press release (New York/Zurich), 26 October 1999.

25. Zanjani, *Minority Rights*, 270–71.

26. Annie Laurent (ed.), *Vivre avec l'Islam? Reflexions chrétiennes sur la religion de Mahomet*, preface by Msg. Béchara Raï, 3rd edition, revised and corrected (Versailles, 1997). See, in particular, the article by Jean Sleiman, "Violence et Sacré dans le Coran," 35–74.

27. Alain Besançon, *Trois Tentations dans l'Eglise* (Paris, 1996), 162–63.

28. Sheikh Nadim al-Jisr, "Good Tidings About The Decisive Battle Between Muslims And Israel, In The Light Of The Holy Quran, The Prophetic Traditions, And The Fundamental Laws Of Nature And History," in *Al Azhar*, 105–26. According to al-Jisr, this law is mentioned in the Koran (2:251) and in the past has led Christians to destroy one another in order to favor Muslim interests.

29. Moubarac, *Pentalogie*, 4:235–45.

30. Boyer, *L'Islam en France*, 50.

31. 30 June 2000 (from Washington, DC). The documents contained in an e-mail dated 2 July 2000 from Free Lebanon to the World Lebanon Organization, and widely circulated.

32. Ibid. See also U.S. Congressional Record, 14 June 2000. In its winter issue 2001, *MEQ* published an entire volume on "Disappearing Christians of the Middle East." It was made available by the AWE to member states of the UNCHR (April 2001), UNSRs, and others.

33. *MEMRI*, Special Dispatch—PA, trans. from Arabic, 14 October 2000, n° 138. This passage from the Koran in Bell's translation reads: "O ye who have believed, do not choose Jews and Christians as friends; they are friends to each other; whoever makes friends with them is one of them; verily Allah doth not guide the wrong-doing people." (Koran, 5:56).

34. Goldhagen, *Hitler's Willing Executioners*, 67.

35. Pierre-André Taguieff, et al., *L'Antisemitisme de Plume 1940–1944* (Paris, 1999), 12.

36. Father P. Stéphane Joulain (M. Afr.), St. Anne's Church, Jerusalem.

37. Yair Auron, *The Banality of Indifference. Zionism and the Armenian Genocide* (New Brunswick, NJ/London, 2000).

38. Excerpt from "Pro Armenia," a report written by Aaron Aaronsohn for the British Intelligence Service, in November 1916. Aaronsohn, a Palestinian Jew living in Zichron Yaakov, was the leader of the Nili underground group working with the British. Some of the members were arrested by the Turks, tortured, and killed, including his sister Sarah. The group provided extensive information on the Armenians and tried to arouse international intervention to save them. For a detailed analysis of this subject, see Auron, *The Banality of Indifference*, excerpt p. 20. The British deleted this passage, as well as others, from the report.

39. Auron, *The Banality of Indifference*, 172.

40. Paul Giniewski, *L'Antijudaïsme Chrétien* (Paris, 2000), 330.

41. Richard John Neuhaus, "The Approaching Century of Religion," in *First Things* (Oct. 1997): 75–79; "Islamic Advocacy Group Calls on Catholic Church to Investigate Priest's Anti-Muslim Remarks," Press Releases CAIR, 16 Oct. 1997, and Ibrahim Hooper, "*First Things* Editor Owes an Apology to Muslims"; Neuhaus, "Islamic Encounters," in *First Things* (Feb. 1998), 62–65.

42. Busse, *Islam, Judaism and Christianity*, 139.

43. Huntington, *The Clash of Civilizations*, 211.

44. Ann Elizabeth Mayer, *Islam and Human Rights. Tradition and Politics* (San Francisco/London, 1991), 87.

45. *Comments by the Government of the Sudan on the Report of the Special Rapporteur, Mr. Gaspar Biro, Contained in Document E/CN.4/1994/48*, (41 pages), *dated 1 February 1994* (Geneva, 18 February 1994).

46. Gaspar Biro, *Government Sanctioned Religious Discrimination in the Sudan between 1993 and 1998*. Prepared Testimony to the U.S. Commission on International Religious Freedom. Washington DC, 15 February 2000: *http://www.uscirf.gov./hearings/15feb00/birPT.php3*

47. Ibn Warraq, *Why I am not a Muslim* (New York, 1995).

48. See Franklin Institute News, 13 (1938), 4:1–2; and Claude-Anne Lopez, "Benjamin Franklin, the Jews, and cyber-bigotry. Prophet and Loss," in *The New Republic*, 27 January 1997, 28–31.

49. Parkes, *The Conflict*, 96.

50. Georges Khodr, "Renouveau Interne, Oecuménisme et Dialogue." Lecture delivered at a Colloquium in Paris (September 1987), in *Les Chrétiens du Monde Arabe* (Colloque: 1987). Preface by Pierre Rondot (Paris, 1989), 28–32; Youakim Moubarac, "Trois Projets pour l'Orient Arabe." Lecture delivered at a Colloquium in Paris (September 1987), ibid, 33–38.

Glossary

ahl al-dhimma. The people vanquished by the Muslims and protected under the terms of their treaty of surrender.

ahl al-kitab. The People of the Book (Bible), Jews and Christians; other ethnoreligious groups were also included under this terminology, such as the Zoroastrians and Sabeans.

alim (pl. *ulama,* anglicized as *ulema).* A scholar of Islamic religious and legal studies.

amân. Safety and protection granted to the *harbi* in Muslim territory, without which his life and property were at the mercy of any aggressor; also, quarter given in battle.

Capitulations. Charters or treaties between the sultan and various European countries, stipulating commercial or religious clauses.

dar al-harb. "Domain of war": the non-Muslim world where Islamic law does not rule. See *harbi.*

dar al-Islam. "Domain of Islam": the Muslim world where Islamic law rules.

devshirme. Turkish system of recruiting Christian children from among the *dhimmi* populations in the Balkans: for conversion, slavery, and assignment in the army as janissaries or for service in the Imperial Household and the administrative duties of the Ottoman state.

dhimma. Originally a protection pact or treaty granted by the Prophet Muhammad to the Jewish and Christian populations whom he had subjected.

dhimmi (*zimmi, raya*). Indigenous Jews, Christians, and Zoroastrians who—subjected to Islamic law after the Arab or Turkish conquest—benefited from the *dhimma.*

dragoman. An interpreter with knowledge of Arabic, Turkish, and European languages.

Echelle. Commercial trading post in the Levant.

fatwa. Legal opinion issued by a jurisconsult based on the Koran and the Sunna.

fay. War booty taken from the infidels, henceforth the possession of the Islamic community (*umma*) and administered by the caliph.

firman. A decree by the sultan.

ghulam. Young male slave assigned to the sultan's service, usually of Christian origin.

hadith. Saying or action (tradition), attributed to the Prophet Muhammad.

harbi. An inhabitant of the *dar al-harb*, the domain of war, beyond the *dar al-Islam.*

ijma. Consensus of the *umma.*

imam. Religious and political head of the Muslim community (*umma*). Used also for a spiritual authority.

Jacobite. Christian belonging to the Monophysite rite: Copt, Aramaean (Syriac), Armenian, or Ethiopian.

jihad. Holy war against non-Muslims; its aims, strategy and tactics make up a theologico-legal doctrine. Also applied to a person's inner struggle to fulfill the commandments of Allah.

jizya. A fixed, obligatory koranic poll tax, paid by the *dhimmis* to the Muslim state.

kharaj. Land tax, which, in earlier times signified a general tax or tribute. It was often confused by foreigners with the *jizya* or poll tax.

mamluk. Slave assigned to military service and in government, mainly of Christian origin.

mawla (pl. *mawali*). Originally a non-Arab "client," who was often of an Arab tribe; at the time of the first conquests, they represented freed indigenous slaves.

Melchite. Christian belonging to the Greek-Orthodox rite.

millet. Ethnoreligious community.

miri land. Property belonging to the Islamic state through conquest.

Monophysite. See Jacobite.

muwallad. Neo-Muslims from Spain. Originally a non-Arab slave or a child of non-Arab converts.

Nestorian. Christian supporter of the dissident beliefs of Bishop Nestorius, Patriarch of Constantinople (428–31).

raya. See *dhimmi.*

shari'a. Islamic sacred law, based mainly on the Koran and the Sunna.

sunna. The received words and deeds attributed to the Prophet Muhammad, embodied in *hadiths.*

sürgün (exile). Deportation of populations.

tanzimat. The body of the reform and renovation of the Ottoman Empire legal system in the nineteenth century.

tshiftlik. Large agricultural domain in the Balkans.

ulema. See *alim.*

umma. The Islamic community, in its religious significance.

wali. Governor-general of a province.

waqf (pl. *awqaf*). Property devoted to an irrevocable endowment or trust, usually religious.

zimmi. See *dhimmi.*

Bibliography

Abdel-Malek, Anouar. *La Pensée politique arabe contemporaine*. Paris: Seuil, 1970.

Abel, Armand. "Dar al-harb"and "Dar al-Islam," *EI*[1].

───── and Duncan Black Macdonald "Dar al-sulh," *EI*[1].

[Abel], Salmon, Pierre, ed. *Mélanges d'Islamologie. Volume dédié à la mémoire de Armand Abel*. Leiden: Brill, 1977.

Abel, Félix-Marie. *Histoire de la Palestine depuis la conquête d'Alexandre jusqu'à l'invasion arabe*. 2 vols. Paris: Gabalda, 1952.

Abou, Selim. *Béchir Gemayel ou l'Esprit d'un Peuple*. Paris: Anthropos, 1984.

Abou Mokh, François. *Les Confessions d'un Arabe Catholique. Entretiens avec Joëlle Chabert et François Mourvillier*. Paris: Centurion, 1991.

Abu Yusuf, Ya'koub. *Le Livre de l'Impôt Foncier (Kitâb el-Kharâdj)*. Translated from Arabic and annotated by Edmond Fagnan. Paris: Paul Geuthner, 1921.

Aboujaoude, Joseph. *Les partis politiques au Liban*. Lebanon: Kaslik, 1985.

Abraham de Crète. *Mon Histoire et celle de Nadir, Chah de Perse (XVIII siècle)*. See Brosset, *Collection*, 2.

Abû Sâlih the Armenian (attributed to). *The Churches & Monasteries of Egypt and Some Neighbouring Countries*. Translated from Arabic by B. T. A. Evetts, with additional notes by Alfred J. Butler, Oxford: Clarendon Press, 1895.

Adams, Charles J. "Mawdudi and the Islamic State." In *Voices of Resurgent Islam*, 99–133, edited by John L. Esposito (1983).

[al-Adawi] el-Adaoui, Ahmad ad-Dardir. *Fetoua* [1772]: "Réponse à une question." Translated from Arabic by François-Alphonse Belin, *JA*, 4th ser., 19 (1852): 103–12.

Adler, Cyrus and Aaron Margalith. *With Firmness in the Right. American Diplomatic Action Affecting Jews. 1840–1945*. New York: The American Jewish Committee, 1946.

Ahmad, Khurshid. "The Nature of the Islamic Resurgence." In *Voices of Resurgent Islam*. 218–29, edited by John L. Esposito (1983).

Aldeeb Abu-Sahlieh, Sami Awad. *Non-Musulmans en Pays d'Islam. Cas de l'Egypte*. Fribourg: Editions Universitaire, 1979.

Alexander, Edward. *Israel Watch*: "The Nerve of Ruth Wisse." *Commentary* 95, no. 5 (May 1993): 48–52.

Ali Bey [Badia y Leblich, Domingo]. *Travels of Ali Bey in Morocco, Tripoli, Cyprus, Egypt, Syria and Turkey, between the years 1803 and 1807, written by himself*. 2 vols. London: Longman, 1816.

de Amicis, Edmondo. *Marocco*. 5th ed. Milan: Fratelli Trèves, 1878.

———. *Le Maroc*. Translated from Italian by Henri Belle, with 174 illustrations. Paris: Hachette, 1882.

Andrae, Tor. *Les Origines de l'Islam et le Christianisme*. Translated from German by Jules Roche. Paris: Maisonneuve, 1955.

Angelov, Dimitar, et al., *Histoire de la Bulgarie, des origines à nos jours*. With a preface by Georges Castellan. Roanne, France: 1977.

———. *Les Balkans au Moyen Age. La Bulgarie des Bogomils aux Turcs*. London: Variorum Reprints, 1978.

———. "Certains aspects de la conquête des peuples balkaniques par les Turcs." In idem, *Les Balkans*, 220–75 (XII).

Anis al-Assiouty, Sarwat. *Recherches comparées sur le Christianisme Primitif et l'Islâm Premier*. 1. *Théorie des Sources: Evangiles et Corans Apocryphes, Logia et Hadîts Forgés*. 2. *Jésus le Non-Juif: Culte d'Isis Précurseur du Christianisme. Classes Sociales à Rome et en Arabie*. 3. *Origines Egyptiennes du Christianisme et de l'Islam: Résultat d'un siècle et demi d'archéologie. Jésus: réalités historiques. Muhammad: évolution dialectique*. Paris: Letouzey & Ané, 1987/1987/1989.

Antonius,George. *The Arab Awakening. The Story of the Arab National Movement*. London: Hamish Hamilton, 1938.

Aqqad, Muhammad. *The Muslim Foundations of European Civilization*. Cairo, 1970.

[Arab League] Bulletin d'informations de la Délégation permanente de la Ligue des Etats Arabes, Geneva, 1 May 1970, n° 7 and n° 15, 30 November 1970.

———. Groupe d'étude sur le Moyen-Orient, n° 14, Geneva, 12 September 1969; and n° 80, December 1979.

Arafat, Yasser. Statement at the General Assembly of the United Nations (New York), 13 November 1974. In *JPS* (1975): 181–94; International Documents on Palestine (1974). Beirut: Institute of Palestine Studies, 1977, 133–44.

Arakel of Tabriz. *Livre d'Histoires*. See Brosset, *Collection d'Historiens*, vol. 1, 1874.

Arberry, Arthur John, ed. *Religion in the Middle East: Three Religions in Concord and Conflict*. 2 vols. Cambridge: Cambridge University Press, 1969. Vol. 1. *Judaism and Christianity*. Vol. 2. *Islam*.

Arboit, Gérald. *Le Saint-Siège et le Nouvel Ordre au Moyen-Orient. De la guerre du Golfe à la reconnaissance diplomatique d'Israël*. Paris: L'Harmattan, 1996.

Ardzrouni, Thomas. *Histoire des Ardzrouni (Xe siècle)*. See Brosset, *Collection d'Historiens*, vol. 1.

Argenti, Philip P., ed. *The Massacres of Chios, Described in Contemporary Diplomatic Reports*. With an Introduction. London: John Lane/The Bodley Head, 1932.

Aristarchi Bey, Grégoire. *Législation Ottomane ou Recueil des lois, règlements, ordonnances, traités, capitulations et autres documents officiels de l'Empire Ottoman*. Published by Demétrius Nicolaïdes, Constantinople: Frères Nicolaïdes, 1873.

Arnaldez, Roger. "La Guerre Sainte, selon Ibn Hazm de Cordoue." See Evariste Lévi-Provençal, *Etudes d'Orientalisme dédiées à la mémoire de Lévi-Provençal*. 2 vols. Paris: Maisonneuve & Larose, 1962, 2:445–59.

d'Arvieux, Laurent. *Mémoires du Chevalier d'Arvieux. Envoyé Extraordinaire du Roy à la Porte, Consul d'Alep, d'Alger, de Tripoli & autres Echelles du Levant, contenant ses voyages à Constantinople, dans l'Asie, la Syrie, la Palestine, l'Egypte & la Barbarie* [1663–1685], *recueillis de ses mémoires originaux, & mis en ordre, avec réflexions par le Père J.-B. Labat*. 6 vols. Paris: Le Normant, 1811 [First ed. 1735].

Ashtor [Strauss], Eliahu. "The Social Isolation of Ahl adh-Dhimma." In *Etudes orientales à la mémoire de Paul Hirschler.* Edited by O. Komlós. Budapest, 1949.

———. "Levantine Jewries in the Fifteenth Century." *BIJS* 3 (1975): 67–92.

———. *A Social and Economic History of the Near East in the Middle Ages.* London: Collins, 1976.

al-Asnawi. See Moshe Perlmann, "Asnawi's Tract against Christian Officials," and "Notes on Anti-Christian Propaganda in the Mamluk Empire."

Ateek, Naim Stifan. *Justice and only Justice. A Palestinian Theology of Liberation.* Maryknoll, NY: Orbis Books, 1989.

Auron, Yair. *The Banality of Indifference. Zionism and the Armenian Genocide.* New Brunswick, NJ/London: Transaction Publishers, 2000.

Ayalon, David. *Studies on the Mamluks of Egypt (1250–1517).* London: Variorum Reprints, 1977.

———. *The Mamluk Military Society. Collected Studies.* London: Variorum Reprints, 1979.

[Ayalon] Sharon, Moshe, ed. *Studies in Islamic History and Civilization in honour of Professor David Ayalon.* Jerusalem: Cana/Leiden: Brill, 1986.

Ayeb, Habib. "L'Egypte dans la coalition." (January 1991), *Hérodote* (*l'Occident et la Guerre des Arabes*), 1st and 2nd trim. n° 60–61 (1991): 133–46.

al-Azhar (Academy of Islamic Research), ed. *Kitab al-Mu'tamar al-Rabi'li-Majma'al-Buhuth al-Islamiyya* (Arabic). 2 vols. Cairo: General Organization for Government Printing, 1968.

———. *The Fourth Conference of the Academy of Islamic Research.* English ed. Cairo: General Organization for Government Printing, 1970. See D. F. Green.

Al-Azhari, Md. Alauddin. *The Theory and Sources of Islamic Law for Non-Muslims.* Dacca: Madrasah-I-Alia, 1962.

Azoury, Negib. *Le Réveil de la Nation Arabe dans l'Asie Turque. En Présence des Intérêts et des Rivalités des Puissances Etrangères, de la Curie Romaine et du Patriarcat Oecuménique. Partie asiatique de la Question d'Orient et programme de la Ligue de la Patrie Arabe.* Paris: Plon, 1905.

al-Baghawi, Abu Muhammad al-Husain. *Mishkat al-Masabih.* Edited by at-Tibrizi, translated from Arabic into English by James Robson. 2 vols. Lahore: Ashraf Press, 1975 [1963–65].

al-Balâdhuri. *The Origins of the Islamic State (Kitâb Futûh al-Buldân).* Translated by Philip K. Hitti. New York: Columbia University Press, 1916.

al-Banna, Hassan. *Five Tracts of Hassan al-Banna (1906–1949). A Selection [Majmu'at Rasa'il al-Imam al-Shahid Hasan al-Banna].* Translated from Arabic and annotated by Charles Wendell. Berkeley: University of California Press, 1978. [Near Eastern Studies, 20]

Bar Hebraeus, *The Chronography.* See Budge.

Barkan, Omer Lûtfi. "Les déportations comme méthode de peuplement et de colonisation dans l'Empire ottoman." *RFSE* 11 (1949–50): 67–131.

Barton Lord, Perceval. *Algiers, with Notices of the Neighbouring State of Barbary.* 2 vols. London: Whittaker, 1835.

Bashan, Eliezer. *Captivity and Ransom in Mediterranean Jewish Society (1391–1830)* (Hebrew). Ramat-Gan: Bar-Ilan University, 1980.

————. *Mimizrah Shemesh ad Mevo'o. Studies in the History of the Jews in the Orient and North Africa.* Lod: Orot Yahadut Hamaghreb, 1996.

————. "The Prohibition on Non-Muslims entering Mosques in the Ottoman Empire as reflected in European sources." *Shofar,* 15, no.2 (winter 1997), 43–56.

Bat Ye'or (pseudonym). *Yehudai Mitzraim (Jews in Egypt)* (Hebrew enlarged edition). Translated by Aharon Amir. Tel-Aviv: Maariv, 1974. See Masriya, Yahudiya (1971).

————. *The Dhimmi: Jews and Christians under Islam.* Translated [French, 1980] by David Maisel, Paul Fenton, and David Littman. Preface by Jacques Ellul. Rutherford, NJ/London: Fairleigh Dickinson University Press & Associated University Presses, 1985.

————. "Islam and the *Dhimmis*: Rejoinder" [to Mark Cohen, *JQ* 38 (1986): 125–37]. *JQ* 42 (summer, 1987): 83–88.

————. *The Decline of Eastern Christianity under Islam. From Jihad to Dhimmitude. Seventh–Twentieth Century.* Translated [French, 1991] by Miriam Kochan and David Littman. Foreword by Jacques Ellul. Cranbury, NJ/London: Fairleigh Dickinson University Press & Associated University Presses, 1996.

————."The Dhimmi factor in the Exodus of Jews from Arab Countries." In *The Forgotten Millions. The Modern Jewish Exodus from Arab Lands.* See Shulewitz.

————. "Bat Ye'or interviewed by Paul Giniewski." *Midstream* (February–March 1994): 16–19.

————. "Dhimmitude: Jews and Christians under Islam." *Midstream* 43, no. 2 (February–March 1997): 9–12.

————. "Islam, History and Taboo." *Midstream* (February–March 1998): 7.

Becker, Carl Heinrich. "Djizya." *EI*[1].

Becker, Jillian. *The PLO. The Rise and Fall of the Palestine Liberation Organization.* London: Weidenfeld & Nicolson, 1984.

Be'eri, Eliezer. *The Beginning of the Israeli-Arab Conflict* (Hebrew). Tel Aviv: Sifriat Poalim, 1985.

Behrens-Abouseif, Doris. *"The Political Situation of the Copts, 1798–1923."* In *Christians and Jews in the Ottoman Empire,* edited by Benjamin Braude and Bernard Lewis, 2: 185–205. New York/London: 1982.

Beldiceanu, Nicoara. *Le Monde Ottoman des Balkans, 1402–1566.* London: Variorum Reprints, 1976.

————. "L'Organisation de l'Empire ottoman (XIVe-XVe siècles)." See Robert Mantran.

Belin, François-Alphonse. "Etude sur la Propriété Foncière en Pays Musulmans et spécialement en Turquie (Rite Hanéfite)." *JA,* 5th ser. 18 (1861): 390–431, 477–517; 19 (1862): 156–212, 257–358.

Benbassa, Esther and Aron Rodrigue. *The Jews of the Balkans. The Judeo-Spanish Community, 15th to 20th centuries.* Oxford: Oxford University Press, 1995.

Ben Dor, Gabriel. ed., *The Palestinians and the Middle East Conflict.* Ramat Gan: Turtledove Publishing, 1978.

Ben-Porat, Mordechai. *To Baghdad and Back. The Miraculous 2,000 Year Homecoming of the Iraqi Jews.* Translated from Hebrew by Marcia Grant and Kathy Akeriv. Jerusalem: Gefen Books, 1998.

Ben Shemesh, Abraham. *Taxation in Islam.* Edited and translated from Arabic with an introduction, notes, and preface by Shlomo Dov Goitein. Leiden: Brill & London: Luzac. Vol. 1, *Yahya b. Adam's Kitab Al-Kharaj,* 1967 (2nd revised edition); vol.

2, *Qudama B. Ja'far's Kitab Al-Kharaj* (part 7), 1965; vol. 3, *Abu Yusuf's Kitab Al-Kharaj,* 1969.

Benjamin, Isaac Joseph. *Eight Years in Asia and Africa from 1846 to 1855. By J.J. Benjamin II.* Preface by Dr. Berthold Seeman. Published by the Author. Hanover [Germany], 1859.

Ben-Zvi, Itzhak. *The Exiled and the Redeemed. The Strange Jewish 'Tribes' of the Orient.* Translated from Hebrew by Isaac A. Abbady. London: Vallentine Mitchell, 1958.

Berberian, Avedis. *History of Armenians, 1772–1860 (Chronological)* (Armenian). Constantinople, 1871.

van Berchem, Max. *La Propriété territoriale et l'impôt foncier sous les premiers khalifes. Etude sur l'impôt du kharâg.* Geneva: George, 1886.

Berque, Jacques. *Les Arabes.* Paris: Sinbad, 1973.

———. "Les Nations et le Peuple Arabes devant la Palestine" (3 May 1969). [Presentation, articles by Jacques Berque, Jacques Couland, Louis-Jean Duclos, Jacqueline Hadamard and Maxime Rodinson]. In *Les Palestiniens et la Crise Israélo-Arabe. Textes et Documents du Groupe de recherches et d'action pour le règlement du problème palestinien (G.R.A.P.P.), 1967–1973.* Paris: Editions Sociales, 1974, 24–35.

———. "Fait et Droits en Palestine" (February 1973). In idem, 98–102.

———. *L'Islam au défi.* Paris: Gallimard, 1980.

———. *Entretien.* See Yves Lacoste, *Hérodote* 36 (1985).

———. *France-Irak, L'argent de la Corruption,* in *L'Evénement du Jeudi.* Paris, 13–19 September 1990.

Besançon, Alain. *Trois Tentations dans l'Eglise.* Paris: Calmann-Levy, 1996.

Bethmann, Erich W. and Mustapha Ziada, eds. *Handbook for Fellowships of Muslims and Christians.* New York/Cairo: Continuing Committee on Muslim-Christian Cooperation [1956].

Bettenson, Henry, ed. *Documents of the Christian Church.* London/New York/Toronto: Oxford University Press, 1956.

Betts, Robert Brenton. *Christians in the Arab East. A Political Study.* London: SPCK, 1979.

Beylerian, Arthur. *Les Grandes Puissances, l'Empire Ottoman et les Arméniens dans les Archives Françaises (1914–1918), recueil de documents.* Preface by Jean-Baptiste Duroselle. Paris: Publications de la Sorbonne (Series "Documents"34), 1983.

Birnbaum, Henrik and Speros Vryonis Jr., eds. *Aspects of the Balkans: Continuity and Change. (Contributions to the International Balkan Conference held at UCLA, October 23–28, 1969).* The Hague/Paris: Mouton, 1972.

Biro, Gaspar. *Government Sanctioned Religious Discrimination in the Sudan between 1993 and 1998.* Prepared Testimony to the United States Commission on International Religious Freedom. Washington DC, 15 February 2000: *http://www.uscirf.gov./hearings/15feb00/birPT.php3.*

———. See Official Documents and Reports.

Bittar, Marie-Claude and Antoine Hokayem. *L'Empire Ottoman.* See Hokayem.

Blumenkranz, Bernhard. *Juifs et Chrétiens dans le Monde Occidental, 430–1096.* Paris/The Hague: Mouton, 1960 [Etudes Juives 2].

———. *Les Auteurs Chrétiens Latins du Moyen-Age sur les Juifs et le Judaïsme.* Paris/The Hague: Mouton, 1963 [Etudes Juives 4].

———. *Le Juif médiéval au miroir de l'art chrétien.* Paris: Etudes Augustiniennes, 1966.

Bodansky, Yosef. *Offensive in the Balkans. The Potential for a Wider War as a Result of Foreign Intervention in Bosnia-Herzegovina.* Alexandria, VA/London: 1995.

————. *Islamic Anti-Semitism as a Political Instrument.* Houston, TX: Freeman Center for Strategic Studies, 1999.

al-Bokhârî. *Les Traditions islamiques (Al-Sahih).* Translated from Arabic by O. Houdas and W. Marçais, 4 vols. Paris: Ernest Leroux, 1903–14.

Bonar, Andrew A. and Robert Murray M'Cheyne. *Narrative of a Mission of Inquiry to the Jews from the Church of Scotland in 1839.* Edinburgh: William Whyte, 1845.

Borrmans, Maurice, et al., ed. *al-Dimma, L'Islam et les Minorités Religieuses. Etudes Arabes sur l'Orientalisme.* Etudes Arabes, Dossiers 80–81 *PISAI* (1991/1–2).

————. *al-Mustaŝriqun (Orientalistes), Textes Arabes sur l'Orientalisme.* Etudes Arabes, Dossier n° 83, *PISAI*, 1992–2.

Bowman, Steven B. *The Jews of Byzantium, 1204–1453.* Preface by Zvi Ankori. Tuscaloosa: University of Alabama Press, 1985.

Bowring, John. *Report on the Commercial Statistics of Syria.* New York: Arno Press, 1973 [Reprinted 1st ed. London, Her Majesty's Stationary Office, 1840.]

Boyer, Alain. *L'Islam en France.* Paris: Presses Universitaires de France, 1998.

Braude, Benjamin and Bernard Lewis, eds. *Christians and Jews in the Ottoman Empire. The Functioning of a Plural Society.* Vol. 1, *The Central Lands;* Vol. 2, *The Arabic-Speaking Lands.* New York/London: Holmes & Meier, 1982.

Braudel, Fernand. *The Mediterranean and the Mediterranean World in the Age of Philip II.* Translated from French by Siân Reynolds. London: Collins, 1975/New York: Harper/Collophon Books, 1977. 1st French ed. 1949).

Brauman, Rony, et al. (coll.). *Populations en danger, 1992.* Paris: Hachette, 1992.

Brawer, Abraham Jacob. "Damascus Affair." *EJ* 5 (1971):1249–52.

Brinner, William M. "An Egyptian Anti-Orientalist." In *Islam, Nationalism and Radicalism in Egypt and the Sudan,* 228–48, edited by G. R. Warburg and V. M.Kupferschmidt New York, 1983.

Brock, Sebastian. *Syrian Perspectives on Late Antiquity.* London: Variorum Reprints, 1984.

————. "Syriac Sources for seventh-century history." In *Byzantine and Modern Greek Studies* II. Oxford, 1976: 17–36. [Reprinted in *Syrian Perspectives on Late Antiquity.* VII].

————. "Syriac Views of Emergent Islam" [1982]. In idem VIII: 9–21 & 199–203.

Brockway, Allan. See World Council of Churches (1988).

Brocquière, Bertrandon de la. *Le voyage d'oultremer.* Edited and annotated by Charles Schefer. Paris, 1892.

Brosset, Marie Félicité. *Collection d'Historiens Arméniens.* 2 vols. Translated from Armenian and annotated by M. F. Brosset. St-Petersbourg/Riga/Leipzig & Paris: Geuthner, 1874–1876.

Broughton, Elizabeth. *Six Years Residence in Algiers.* London: Saunders & Otley, 1839.

Broughton, Lord. *Travels in Albania and other Provinces of Turkey in 1809 & 1810.* 2 vol. London: Murray, 1858.

Brunschvig, Robert, ed. and trans. *Deux récits de voyage inédits en Afrique du Nord au XVe siècle: Abdalbasit b. Halil et [Anselme] Adorne.* Paris: Larose, 1936. [Institut d'Etudes Orientales de la Faculté de lettres d'Alger, n° 7.]

————. *La Berbérie orientale sous les Hafsides, des origines à la fin du XVe siècle*, 2 vol. Paris, 1940/47. [Institut d'Etudes Orientales de la Faculté de lettres d'Alger, n° 8.]

Bryant, William Cullen. *Letters from the East*. New York: Putnam, 1869.

Bryce, James, ed. *The Treatment of the Armenians in the Ottoman Empire (1915–1916)*. London: His Majesty's Stationary Office, 1916.

Buckingham, James Silk. *Travels in Palestine through the Countries of Bashan and Gilead east of the river Jordan, including a visit to the cities of Geraza and Gamala in the Decapolis*. London: Longman, 1821.

Budge, Ernest A. Wallis. *The Chronography of Gregory Abû'l-Faraj, 1225–1286. The son of Aaron, the Hebrew physician commonly known as BAR HEBRAEUS, being the first part of his Political History of the World*. Translated from Syriac. 2 vols. London: Oxford University Press, 1932.

Bulliet, Richard W. *Conversion to Islam in the Medieval Period, An Essay in Quantative History*. Cambridge, MA/ London: Harvard University Press, 1979.

van Buren, Paul. See World Council of Churches (1988).

Busse, Heribert. *Islam, Judaism and Christianity. Theological and Historical Affiliations*. Translated from German by Alison Brown. Princeton: Markus Wiener Publishers, 1998. [Princeton Series on the Middle East].

Butler, Alfred J. *The Arab Conquest of Egypt and the Last Thirty Years of the Roman Administration*. With a critical bibliography, notes and additional documents. 2nd ed. by P. M. Frazer. London: Oxford University Press, 1978 [1st ed. 1902].

Cahen, Claude. "Dhimma." *EI²*.

————. "Djizya." *EI²*.

————. "Kharadj". *EI²*.

————. "Note sur l'accueil des Chrétiens d'Orient à l'Islam." *RHR* 2 (1964): 51–58.

Cambridge History of Islam. Vol. 1, *The Central Islamic Lands;* vol. 2, *The Further Islamic Lands. Islamic Society and Civilization*, eds. Peter M. Holt, Ann K. S. Lambton, Bernard Lewis. Cambridge: Cambridge University Press, 1970.

Cambridge. *Religion in the Middle East*. See Arberry, ed.

Campbell, Patrick. *Report* (1839). See Bowring, 1840.

Canard, Marius. *Miscellanea Orientalia*. Preface by Charles Pellat. London: Variorum Reprints, 1986.

————. "Un vizir chrétien à l'époque fâtimite, l'Arménien Bahrâm" [*AIEO* 12, 1954]. In idem, 6: 84–113.

————. "Les Relations Politiques et Sociales entre Byzance et les Arabes." *DOP* 18 (1964): 33–56. See Dumbarton Oaks (May 1963).

————. *L'Expansion arabo-islamique et ses répercussions*. London: Variorum Reprints, 1974.

Caplan, Neil. *Palestine Jewry and the Arab Question, 1917–1925*. London: Frank Cass, 1978.

Carré, Olivier. "Juifs et Chrétiens dans la Société islamique idéale d'après Sayyid Qutb." *RSPT* 68 (1984): 50–72.

————. *Mystique et Politique, lecture révolutionnaire du Coran par Sayyid Qutb, Frère musulman radical*. Paris: Le Cerf, 1984.

————. *L'utopie islamique dans l'Orient arabe*. Paris: Presses de la Fondation nationale des sciences politiques, 1991.

————. *Le nationalisme arabe*. Paris: Fayard, 1993.

————. *L'Islam laïque, ou le retour à la Grande Tradition*. Paris: Armand Colin, 1993.

Castellan, Georges. *Histoire des Balkans, XIVe-XXe siècle*. Paris: Fayard, 1991.

du Caurroy [de la Croix, Adolphe Marie]. "Législation Musulmane Sunnite, rite Hanéfi." Code Civil (cont.), bk. 4 [*Siér* ou *jihâd*]: De l'acquisition par droit de premier occupant, des personnes et des biens des *Harbi*." Translated from Arabic with a preface. *JA* 4th ser. 17 (1851): 211–55 and 568–91; 18 (1851): 290–321; 19 (1852): 519–50; 5th ser. 1 (1853): 39–91; 2 (1853): 471–528.

Cazès, David. *Essai sur l'Histoire des Israélites de Tunisie*. Paris: Darlacher, 1888.

Chabot, Jean-Baptiste. "Les Evêques Jacobites du VIIIe au XIIIe siècle d'Après la Chronique de Michel le Syrien." *ROC* 4 (1899): 443–51, 495–511; 5 (1900): 605–36; 6 (1901): 189–219. See *Chronique de Michel le Syrien*.

Chamoun, Camille. *Crise au Liban*. Beirut, 1977.

de Chardin, Jean, Chevalier. *Voyages du Chevalier de Chardin en Perse, et autres lieux d'Orient, enrichis d'un grand nombre de belles figures en taille-douce, représentant les antiquités et les choses remarquables du pays par Langles*. 10 vols. Paris: le Normand, 1811.

Charles-Roux, François. *Les Echelles de Syrie et de Palestine au XVIIIe siècle*. Paris: Paul Geuthner, 1928. [Bibliothèque archéologique et historique, vol. 10.]

Charnay, Jean-Paul. *Sociologie religieuse de l'Islam. Préliminaires*. Paris: Sindbad, 1977.

————. *Principes de Stratégie Arabe*. Paris: L'Herne, 1984.

————. *L'Islam et la Guerre. De la guerre juste à la révolution sainte*. Paris: Fayard, 1986.

Chery, Alain and Hussein Zaanoun. "Dans les collèges de la banlieu nord de Paris." *Hérodote* (L'Occident et la Guerre des Arabes), n° 60/61, 1st and 2nd trim. (1991): 235–38.

Chevalérias, Alain. "Dialogue islamo-chrétien." *La Nef* 79 (1998).

Chouraqui, André. *La Condition juridique de l'Israélite marocain*. Preface by René Cassin. Paris: Presses du Livre Français, 1950.

————. *La Reconnaissance, Le Saint-Siège, les Juifs et Israël*. Paris: Laffont, 1992.

————. *Between East and West. A History of the Jews of North Africa*. Translated from French by Michael M. Bernet. Philadelphia: The Jewish Publication Society of America, 1968.

Chronique de Denys de Tell-Mahré [pseudo-Dionysius]. 4th part published according to Ms 162 in the Vatican Library, with a translation from Syriac into French and with an introduction and historical and philological notes by Jean-Baptiste Chabot. Paris: Bouillon, 1895. [Bibliothèque de l'Ecole des Hautes Etudes]

Chronique de Jean, Evêque de Nikiou. Extracts translated from Ethiopian into French with notes by M. H. Zotenberg. Paris: Imprimerie Nationale, 1879. [Extract from *JA*.]

Chronique de Michel le Syrien. 4 vols. Edited and translated from Syriac by Jean-Baptiste Chabot. Paris: Ernest Leroux, 1899–1905.

Chronique de Séert (Histoire Nestorienne). Edited and translated from Arabic by Mgr. Addaï Scher. In *Patrologia Orientalis*. Edited by Mgr. R. Graffin and François Nau. 20 vols. Paris: Firmin-Didot, 1907–1929, 7: fasc. 2; 13: fasc. 4.

Cohen, Haim J. *The Jews of the Middle-East, 1860–1972*. New York/Toronto: Wiley & Sons/Jerusalem: Keter & Israel Universities Press, 1973.

Cohen, Mark R. *Under Crescent and Cross. The Jews in the Middle Ages*. Princeton: Princeton University Press, 1994.

Cohn, Norman. *Warrant for Genocide. The Myth of the Jewish World Conspiracy and the Protocols of the Elders of Zion.* London: Eyre and Spottiswoode, 1967.

Comnène, Anne. *Alexiade (règne de l'empereur Alexis I Comnène 1081–1118).* Edited and translated by Bernard Leib. 3 vols. Paris: 1937–45. [Byzantine Collection.]

Constantelos, Demetrios J. "The Moslem Conquest of the Near East as Revealed in the Greek Sources of the Seventh and the Eighth Centuries." *Byzantion* 42 (1972): 325–57.

Corm, Georges. *Le Proche-Orient éclaté, 1956–1991.* New expanded edition. Paris: Gallimard, 1991. [1ˢᵗ ed., La Découverte, 1983.]

Cragg, Kenneth. *The Arab Christian. A History of the Middle East.* London: Mowbray, 1992.

———. *Palestine. The Prize and Price of Zion.* London/Washington: Cassell, 1997.

Crandall, Kenneth H. *The Impact of Islam on Christianity.* Preface by Erich H. Bethmann. New York: American Friends of the Middle East, 1952.

Curzon, Robert. *Armenia. A Year at Erzeroom, and on the Frontiers of Russia, Turkey and Persia.* 3ʳᵈ ed. London: John Murray, 1854.

Cvijic, Jovan. *La Péninsule Balkanique. Géographie humaine.* Paris: Armand Colin, 1918.

Dabinovic, Antoine. "Les pactes d'assistance entre les gouverneurs ottomans et les grands seigneurs de Bosnie et de Croatie depuis le XVe au XVII siècle." In *Türk Tarih Kongresi* (5), 3ʳᵈ section. Ankara, 1960, 478–673.

Dadrian, Vahakn N. *The History of the Armenian Genocide. Ethnic Conflict from the Balkans to Anatolia to the Caucasus.* Providence, RI/Oxford: Berghahn Books, 1995.

———. "The Convergent Aspects of the Armenian and Jewish Cases of Genocide. A Reinterpretation of the Concept of Holocaust." *HGS* 3/2 (1988): 151–69.

———. *German Responsibility in the Armenian Genocide. A Review of the Historical Evidence of German Complicity.* Foreword by Roger W. Smith. Watertown, MA: Blue Crane Books, 1996.

———. *Warrant for Genocide. Key Elements of Turko-Armenian Conflict.* New Brunswick, NJ: Transaction Publishers, 1999.

al-Damanhuri. *Iqamat al Hujja al-bahira ala hadm kana'is Misr wa-l-Qahira (Presentation of the clear proof for the obligatory destruction of the churches of Old and New Cairo)* [1739]. See Moshe Perlmann, *Shaykh Damanhuri* (1975).

Dandini, Jérome. *Voyage du Mont Liban* [1536]. Paris, 1675.

Daniel, Norman. *Islam and the West.* Edinburgh: The University Press, 1980.

Darwich, Mahmoud. "En marge du transitoire. Entretien avec Farouk Mardam Bey et Elias Sanbar." *REP* 10 (winter 1984): 7–21.

Davidson, Roderic H. *Reform in the Ottoman Empire, 1856–1876.* Princeton: Princeton University Press, 1963.

Dennet, Jr., Daniel C. *Conversion and the Poll-Tax in Early Islam.* Cambridge, Mass.: Harvard University Press, 1950.

Dermanjian, Geneviève. *La Crise Anti-juive Oranaise (1895–1905). L'antisémitisme dans l'Algérie coloniale.* Paris: L'Harmattan, 1986.

Dieckhoff, Alain. "Antisionisme et Mythe de la Conspiration Juive Mondiale." See Taguieff, *Les Protocoles* (1992), 2: 343–64.

al Djabarti, Sheikh Abd-el-Rahman. *Merveilles Biographiques et Historiques, ou Chroniques.* 9 vols. Translated from Arabic by Chefik Mansour Bey, Abdulaziz Kalil Bey,

Gabriel Nicolas, Kalil Bey, and Iskender Ammoun Effendi. Cairo: Imprimerie Nationale, 1888–96.

Donner, Fred McGraw. *The Early Islamic Conquests*. Princeton: Princeton University Press, 1981.

Doutté, Edmond. *Missions au Maroc. En Tribu*. Paris: Geuthner, 1914.

Driault, Edouard and Michel L'Heritier. *Histoire Diplomatique de la Grèce de 1821 à nos jours*. Vol. 1, *L'Insurrection et l'Indépendance (1821–1830)* by Edouard Driault; vol.2, *Le Règne d'Othon. La Grande Idée (1830–1862)*, by Edouard Driault. Paris: Les Presses Universitaires de France, 1925.

Drummond, Alexander. *Travels through different cities of Germany, Italy, Greece and Several Parts of Asia as far as the Banks of the Euphrates, in a Series of Letters*. London: Strahan, 1754.

Dubois, Père Marcel Jacques. *L'Exil et la Demeure. Journal de bord d'un Chrétien en Israël (1962–1983)*. Jerusalem: L'Olivier, 1984.

Dujcev, Ivan and Velizar Velkov, Iono Mitev et Lubomir Panayotov. *Histoire de la Bulgarie, des origines à nos jours*. Preface by Georges Castellan. Roanne: Horvath, 1977.

———. "L'Epoque de la Domination Byzantine." In idem.

Dulaurier, Edouard. *Recherches sur la Chronologie Arménienne: Technique et Historique. Ouvrage formant les Prolégomènes de la Collection Intitulée: Bibliothèque Historique Arménienne*. 2 vols. Paris: Imprimerie Impériale, 1859.

Dulles, John W. *The Ride through Palestine*. Philadelphia: Presbyterian Board of Publication, 1881.

Dumbarton Oaks, Center for Byzantine Studies, Washington, D.C. (Harvard University).

———. *The Relations between Byzantium and the Arabs*. Symposium, May 1963.

———. *Prédication et propagande au moyen-âge: Islam, Byzance, Occident*. Colloquia 3, session on 20–25 October 1980. Pennsylvania & Paris, 1983.

Dussaud, René. *La pénétration des Arabes en Syrie avant l'Islam, etc*. Paris, 1955. (Institut Français d'Archéologie de Beyrouth, Bibliothèque arch. et hist. n° 59.)

de Dzar, Iohannes. *Histoire de l'Aghovanie (XVIIe siècle)*. See Brosset, 1.

Edrîsî. See al-Idrisi.

Eibner, John. "My Career Redeeming Slaves." *MEQ* (December 1999): 3–16.

Elégie sur les Malheurs de l'Arménie et le Martyre de Saint Vahan de Kogh'then. Petite Bibliothèque arménienne. See Dulaurier, *Recherches sur la Chronologie Arménienne*.

Ellul, Jacques. *Propagandes*. Paris: Economica, 1990. [1ˢᵗ ed., 1962]

———. "Les Chrétiens et Beyrouth." In *Réforme*, 30 May 1970, Paris.

———. *La parole humiliée*. Paris: Seuil, 1981.

———. *La subversion du christianisme*. Paris: Seuil, 1984.

———. *Un Chrétien pour Israël*. Monaco: Rocher, 1986.

Elpeleg, Zvi. *The Grand Mufti. Haj Amin Al-Hussaini, Founder of the Palestinian National Movement*. London/Portland, OR: Frank Cass, 1993. [Hebrew, 1988]

Elst, Koenraad. *Negationism in India. Concealing the Record of Islam*. 2ⁿᵈ expanded edition. New Delhi: Voice of India, 1993. [1ˢᵗ ed. 1992]

Engelhardt, Edouard. *La Turquie et le Tanzimat ou Histoire des Réformes dans l'Empire Ottoman depuis 1826 jusqu'à nos jours*. Paris: Librairie Cotillon & Librairie Conseil d'Etat, vol. 1,1882; vol. 2, 1884.

de Epalza, Mikel. "Les Mozarabes: Etat de la question." Translated from Spanish by André Bazzana. *REMMM* 63–64 (*Minorités Religieuses dans l'Espagne Médiévale*) (1992/1–2): 39–50.

Esposito, John L. ed. *Voices of Resurgent Islam.* New York/Oxford: Oxford University Press, 1983.

————. "Introduction: Islam and Muslim Politics," in idem, 5–13; "Muhammad Iqbal and the Islamic State", in idem, 175–90.

————. *Islam and Politics.* 2nd revised edition. New York: Syracuse University Press, 1987.

————. and James P. Piscatori. "Democratisation and Islam." *MEJ* 45/3 (summer, 1991): 427–40.

————. *The Islamic Threat. Myth or Reality?* New York/Oxford: Oxford University Press, 1992.

————. *Islam. The Straight Path.* Oxford/New York: Oxford University Press, 1994.

Etienne, Bruno. *L'Islamisme radical.* Paris: Hachette, 1987.

————. *La France et l'Islam.* Paris: Hachette, 1989.

————. and Mohamed Tozy. "Les Islamistes et la stratégie géopolitique de l'Islam contemporain." *Hérodote* (*Géopolitique des Islams, N° 1*), 4th trim. 35 (1984): 35–54.

Evans, Arthur J. *Through Bosnia and the Herzegovina on foot. During the insurrection, August and September 1875, with an historical review of Bosnia and a glance at the Croats, Slavonians, and the Ancient Republic of Ragusa.* 2nd revised and expanded edition. London: Longmans, 1877.

Evetts, B., ed. *History of the Patriarchs of the Coptic Church of Alexandria. III. Agatho to Michael I (766).* Translated from Arabic and annotated by B. Evetts. In *Patrologia Orientalis* (1910), 5, fasc. 1.

Evliya, Efendi. *Narrative of Travels in Europe Asia, and Africa in the Seventeenth Century.* Translated from Turkish by The Ritter Joseph von Hammer. 2 vols. London: Oriental Translation Fund, 1834–46.

Fadlallah, Shaykh Muhammad Hussein. *JPS.* 25 n° 1 (autumn 1995).

Fagnan, Edmond. "Le Signe distinctif des juifs au Maghreb." *REJ* 28 (1894): 294–98.

————. "Arabo-Judaïca." In *Mélanges Hartwig Derenbourg, 1844–1908.* Paris: Ernest Leroux, 1909, 103–20.

Farhi, Isaac b. Salomon. *Imrey Binah (Words of Wisdom).* (Ladino). Belgrade, 1837.

al-Faruqi, Ismail R. "Islam and Zionism." In *Voices of Resurgent Islam,* 261–67, edited by John L. Esposito (1983).

Fattal, Antoine. *Le Statut Légal des Non-Musulmans en Pays d'Islam.* Beirut: Imprimerie Catholique, 1958.

Felice, Renzo De. *Jews in an Arab Land: Libya, 1835–1970.* Translated from Italian by Judith Roumani. Austin, TX: University of Texas Press, 1985.

Fiey, Jean-Maurice. *Mossoul Chrétienne.* Beirut: Col. Recherches-Orient chrétien, 1959.

————. *Assyrie Chrétienne. Contribution à l'étude de l'histoire et de la géographie ecclésiastiques et monastiques du Nord de l'Iraq.* 3 vols. Beirut: Col. Recherches-Orient Chrétien, 1965–68.

————. *Communautés syriaques en Iran et Iraq des origines à 1552.* London: Variorum Reprints, 1979.

Finn, James. *Stirring Times, or Records from the Jerusalem Consular Chronicles of 1853 to 1856. By J. Finn. Edited and compiled by his widow* [Elizabeth Anne Finn], *with a preface by the Viscountess Strangford*. 2 vols. London: C. K. Paul, 1878.

Fischel, Walter Joseph. *Jews in the Economic and Political Life of Mediaeval Islam*. London: Royal Asiatic Society for Great Britain and Ireland [Monograph 22], 1937 [reprint, 1968].

———— ed. *Unknown Jews in Unkown Lands. The Travels of Rabbi David d'Beth Hillel (1824–1832)*. Translated and edited with introduction and notes. New York: Ktav, 1973. See d'Beth Hillel, *Travels*.

de Foucauld, Charles. *Reconnaissance au Maroc. Journal de Route (1883–1884)*. Paris: Société d'Editions Géographiques Maritimes et Coloniales, 1888. (Reprint, 1939: *Journal de Route Conforme à l'Edition de 1888 et augmenté de fragments inédits rédigés par l'auteur, pour son cousin François de Bondy*.)

Frank, Louis. *Tunis, Description de cette Régence*. In J. J. Marcel, ed. *L'Univers, Histoire et Description de Tous les Peuples: Algérie, Etats Tripolitains, Tunis*. Paris: Firmin Didot, 1862, 1–224.

Frankel, Jonathan. *The Damascus Affair. "Ritual Murder." Politics, and the Jews in 1840*. Cambridge: Cambridge University Press, 1997.

Frémeaux, Jacques. *Le Monde Arabe et la Securité de la France depuis 1958*. Paris: Presses Universitaires de France, 1995 [Politique d'Aujourd'hui].

Fumey, Eugène. *Choix de correspondances marocaines, pour servir à l'étude du style épistolaire administratif employé au Maroc (50 lettres officielles de la Cour chérifienne)*. Paris: Maisonneuve, 1903.

Gabus, Jean-Paul. See Moubarac. Youakim, *Islam* (1984).

Galanté, Abraham. *Documents Officiels Turcs concernant les Juifs de Turquie. Recueil de 114 Lois, Règlements, Firmans, Bérats, Ordres et Décisions de Tribunaux*. Translated from Turkish. Istanbul: Haim Rozio, 1931.

Ganiage, Jean. *Les Origines du Protectorat Français en Tunisie (1861–1881)*. Paris: Presses Universitaires de France, 1959. [Institut des Hautes Etudes de Tunisie.]

————. *L'Expansion Coloniale de la France sous la Troisième République (1871–1914)*. Paris: Payot, 1968.

Gardet, Louis. *La Cité Musulmane. Vie Sociale et politique. Etudes musulmanes*. Paris, 1954.

Gargi, Mattatya. *Qorot ha-Zemanim*. (Hebrew). See Kashani.

Gaudefroy-Demombynes, Maurice. *Mahomet*. 2nd ed. Paris: Albin Michel (L'évolution de l'humanité), 1969 [1st ed., 1957].

Gedaliah de Siemiatyce, *Sha'alu Shalom Yerushalayim (Pray for the Peace of Jerusalem)* (Hebrew). Berlin, 1716.

Gemayel, Bashir. "Notre Droit à la différence." (statement by Bashir Gemayel), *Bulletin d'information*. Lausanne: Union Libanaise-Suisse, 1 (December 1982).

————. *Liberté et Sécurité*. 2nd ed. Beirut: La Résistance Libanaise, 1983.

Gerber, Jane S. *The Jews of Spain. A History of the Sephardic Experience*. New York: The Free Press, 1992.

Gervers, Michael and Ramzi J. Bikhazi, eds. *Conversions and Continuity: Indigenous Christian Communities in Medieval Islamic Lands*. Toronto: Pontifical Institute of Medieval Studies, 1990 [Papers in Medieval Studies 9].

Geyl, Pieter. *Debates with Historians*. London: Batsworth, 1955.

Ghazi b. al-Wasiti. See Gottheil, "An Answer to the Dhimmis" (1921).

Ghévond. *Histoire des Guerres et des Conquêtes des Arabes en Arménie.* Translated from Armenian by Garabed V. Chahnazarian, with numerous notes. Paris: Charles Meyrueis, 1856.

Gibb, Hamilton Alexander Rosskeen and Howard Bowen. *Islamic Society and the West. A Study of the Impact of Western Civilisation on Muslim Culture in the Near East.* Vol. 1, pt. 1 and 2. *Islamic Society in the Eighteenth Century,* London/New York/Toronto: Oxford University Press, 1950/1957.

———. *Studies on the Civilization of Islam.* Edited by Stanford J. Shaw and William R. Polk. London: Routledge & Kegan Paul, 1962.

Gil, Moshe. "The Constitution of Medina. A Reconsideration." *IOS* 4 (1974): 44–65.

———. *A History of Palestine, 634–1099.* Translated from Hebrew by Ethel Broido. Revised ed. Cambridge/New York/Melbourne/Sidney: Cambridge University Press, 1992.

Gilbert, Martin. *Exile and Return. The Emergence of Jewish Statehood.* London: Weidenfeld & Nicolson, 1978.

Giniewski, Paul. *L'Antisionisme.* Brussels: Librairie Encyclopédique, 1973.

———. *La Croix des Juifs.* Geneva: MJR, 1994.

———. *L'Antijudaisme Chrétien. La Mutation.* Paris: Editions Salvator, 2000.

Givet, Jacques. *La gauche contre Israël. Essai sur le néo-antisémitisme.* Paris: Jean-Jacques Pauvert, 1968.

———. *The Anti-Zionist Complex.* Introduction by Patrick Moynihan. Englewood, NJ: SBS Publishing, 1982 [French ed. 1979].

Godard, Léon Abbé. *Le Maroc, notes d'un voyageur: 1858–1859.* Algiers, 1859.

Goitein, Shlomo Dov. "Evidence on the Muslim Poll Tax from non-Muslim Sources. A Geniza Study." *JESHO* 6 (1963): 278–95.

———. *Jews and Arabs. Their Contact through the Ages.* New York: Schocken, 1964 [1st ed., 1955.].

———. *Studies in Islamic History and Institutions.* Leiden: Brill, 1968.

———. *A Mediterranean Society: The Jewish Communities of the Arab World as Portrayed in the Documents of the Cairo Geniza.* 5 vols. Berkeley/Los Angeles: University of California, 1967–85.

———. "Changes in the Middle East (950–1150), as illustrated by the documents of the Cairo Geniza." In D. H. Richards, ed., *Islamic Civilisation: 951–1150. Papers on Islamic History III.* Oxford: Cassirer, 1973, 17–32.

Goldberg, Harvey E. *The Book of Mordechai. A Study of the Jews of Libya. Selections from the 'Highid Mordekhai' of Mordechai Hakohen.* Edited and translated from Hebrew with an introduction. Philadelphia: Institute for the Study of Human Issues, 1980. See Hakohen (1978).

———. " Rites and Riots. The Tripolitanian Pogrom of 1945." *SPS* 8/1 (1977): 35–56.

Goldhagen, Daniel Jonah. *Hitler's Willing Executioners. Ordinary Germans and the Holocaust.* New York: Alfred A. Knopf, 1996.

Goldziher, Ignaz. *Le Dogme et la Loi de l'Islam. Histoire du développement dogmatique et juridique de la religion musulmane.* Translated from German by Felix Arin. Paris: Geuthner, 1920 [reprint, 1973].

[Goldziher] *Ignace Goldziher Memorial Volume.* Edited by. David Samuel Löwinger, Béla Somogyi and Alexander Scheiber. 2 vols. Budapest-Jerusalem, 1948/58.

———. *Muslim Studies (Muhammedanische Studien).* Edited by Samuel Miklos Stern. Translated from German by C. R. Barber and S. M. Stern. 2 vols. London: George Allen & Unwin, 1967/1971.

Gorgi. See Gargi and Kashani.

Gottheil, Richard James Horatio. "An Answer to the Dhimmis." *JAOS* 41 (1921): 383–457.

———. "Dhimmis and Moslems in Egypt." In *Old Testament and Semitic Studies in Memory of W. R. Harper.* Chicago, 1908, 2:353–414.

———. "A Fetwa on the Appointment of Dhimmis to office." *ZfA* 26 (1912): 203–07.

Green, D.F. [pseudonym of David Littman and Yehoshafat Harkabi], eds. *Arab Theologians on Jews and Israel. Extracts from the Proceedings of the Fourth Conference of the Academy of Islamic Research* (1968). With an introduction. 3rd ed. Geneva: Editions de l'Avenir, 1976 [1st ed. 1971]. See al-Azhar (1970).

Grignaschi, Mario. "La Valeur du Témoignage des Sujets Non Musulmans (*Dhimmi*) dans l'Empire Ottoman." In *La Preuve*, vol. 18, pt.3. *Civilisations Archaïques, Asiatiques et Islamiques. RSJB*, Brussels: Editions de la Librairie Encyclopédique, 1963, 227–36.

Grunebaum, Gustave E. von. *Medieval Islam. A Study in Cultural Orientation.* 2nd ed. Chicago: University of Chicago Press, 1969 [1st ed. 1946].

———. *Classical Islam. A History, 600–1258.* Translated from German by Katherine Watson, London: Allen & Unwin, 1970.

Guérin, Victor. *Description géographique, historique et archéologique de la Palestine, accompagnée de cartes détaillées.* 7 vols. (Pt. 1, *Judée*, 3 vols.; pt. 2, *Samarie*, 2 vols.; pt. 3, *Galilée*, 2 vols.). Paris: Imprimerie Impériale, 1868–80.

Guillaume, Alfred. *The Life of Muhammad. A Translation of Ishaq's 'Sirat Rasul Allah'.* Translated from Arabic with an introduction and notes. London/New York/Toronto: Oxford University Press, 1955.

Hacker, Joseph. "The Sürgün System and Jewish Society in the Ottoman Empire during the 15th–17th Centuries" (Hebrew). In *Zion* 55/1 (1990): 27–82.

Haddad, Yvonne Y. "Sayyid Qutb: Ideologue of Islamic Revival." In *Voices of Resurgent Islam*, 67–98, edited by John L. Esposito, (1983).

Haim, Sylvia G., ed. *Arab Nationalism. An Anthology.* Selected and edited with an introduction. Berkeley/Los Angeles/London: University of California, 1976.

Hakohen, Mordechai. *Highid Mordekhai (The Story of Mordechai)* (Hebrew). Jerusalem: Ben-Zvi Institute, 1978. See Goldberg, *The Book of Mordechai* (1980).

Harkabi, Yehoshafat. *Arab Attitudes to Israel.* Jerusalem: Israel Universities Press, 1972.

———. *Palestinians and Israel.* Jerusalem: Keter, 1974.

———. See Green.

Harsgor, Michael. See Stroun.

Harvey, Leonard Patrick. *Islamic Spain, 1250 to 1500.* Chicago/London: University of Chicago Press, 1990 [paperback, 1992]

Hayek, Father Michel. *Nouvelles approches de l'Islam* (Lecture delivered on 6 March 1967). Beirut: Conférence du Cénacle (XXII) 9–10 (1968): 8–28.

Herr, Friedrich. "The Catholic Church and the Jews Today." *Midstream* 17, n° 5 (May 1971): 20–31.

von Hesse-Wartegg, Chevalier E. *Tunis, the Land and the People.* New ed. London: Chatto & Windus, 1882.

Hillel, David d'Beth. *The Travels of Rabbi David d'Beth Hillel from Jerusalem through Arabia, Koordistan, Part of Persia and India to Madras* [1824–1832]. Madras, 1832.

Hillel, Shlomo. *Operation Babylon. The Story of the Rescue of the Jews of Iraq.* New York: Doubleday, 1987 [1st ed. (Hebrew) Israel: Edamim, 1985].

Hirschberg, Hayyim Ze'ev [W. H.]. *A History of the Jews in North Africa.* 2 vols. Leiden: Brill, 1974/81.

———. "Research on the History and Culture of the Jews in the Muslim East." *Bar Ilan* (University) *Annual*, 7–8, Tel Aviv (1969–70).

Hirschfeld, Hartwig. "Essai sur l'histoire des Juifs de Médine." *REJ* 7 (1883): 167–93; *REJ* 10 (1885): 10–31.

Hirszowicz, Lukacs. *The Third Reich and The Arab East.* London: Routledge & Kegan Paul/Toronto: University of Toronto Press, 1966.

Hizkiya. "Elégie d'un poète judéo-persan" (*Arnes mi-Hizkiya*. Ms. 341, Elkan Adler collection). Translated by W. Bacher. *REJ* 48 (1904): 94–105. [See Bat Ye'or, *The Dhimmi* (1985), 359–61]

Hodgson, Marshall G.S. *The Venture of Islam. Conscience and History in a World Civilization.* Vol. 1, *The Classical Age of Islam.* Vol. 2, *The Expansion of Islam in the Middle Periods.* Chicago and London: The University of Chicago Press, 1974 [1st ed. 1958/1961].

Hokayem, Antoine and Marie-Claude Bittar. *L'Empire Ottoman. Les Arabes et les Grandes Puissances, 1914–1920.* Beirut: Editions Universitaires du Liban, 1981. [L'Histoire par les Documents, 6].

Hommaire de Hell, Xavier. *Voyage en Turquie et en Perse exécuté par ordre du Gouvernement Français pendant les années 1846, 1847 et 1848. Cartes d'Inscriptions, etc. et d'un Album de 100 planches dessinées d'après nature par Jules Laurens.* 4 pts. in 2 vols. Paris: Bertrand, 1854–56.

Hourani, Albert H. *Minorities in the Arab World.* London/New York/Toronto: Oxford University Press, 1947.

———. *Arabic Thought in the Liberal Age, 1798–1939.* London/New York/Toronto: Oxford University Press, 1962.

Hovhannesiantz, Astvatzatour Ter (Bishop). *Chronological History of Jerusalem.* Jerusalem: St. James' Press, 1890.

Huntington, Samuel P. *The Clash of Civilizations and the Remaking of World Order.* New York: Simon & Schuster, 1996.

Hussain, Sheikh Showkat. "Status of Non-Muslims in Islamic State." *HI* 16 (1993), n° 1: 67–79.

Hyamson, Albert M., ed. *The British Consulate in Jerusalem in Relation to the Jews of Palestine (1838–1914).* With an introduction and notes. 2 vols. London: Goldston, 1939/41 [*JHSE*].

———. "The Damascus Affair-1840." *JHSE* 16 (1945–51): 47–71.

Ibn Abd al-Hakam. *Futûh Ifrîqiya Wa'l-Andalus (Conquête de l'Afrique du Nord et de l'Espagne).* Arabic text with translation and notes by A. Gateau. 2nd ed., revised and expanded. Algiers, 1948.

Ibn 'Abdun. See Lévi-Provençal, *Séville musulmane* (1948).

Ibn Abi Zayd al-Qayrawânî, Abu Muhammad Abdallah. *La Risâla (Epître sur les éléments du dogme et de la loi de l'Islam selon le rite mâlikite)*. Translated from Arabic with a preface, notes, and index by Léon Bercher. 5th ed. Algiers, 1960 [1st ed. 1945].

Ibn Abil-Fazaïl, Moufazzal. *Histoire des Sultans Mamlouks*. Translated from Arabic by E. Blochet. In *Patrologia Orientalis*, eds. Mgr. R. Graffin and François Nau, 12: fasc. 3; 14: fasc. 3; 20: fasc. 1. Paris: Firmin-Didot, 1907–29.

Ibn al-Athîr. *Annales du Maghreb et de l'Espagne (Al-Kamil fi-ta'rikh/Grande Chronique)*. Translated from Arabic and annotated by Edmond Fagnan. Algiers: Adolphe Jourdan, 1898.

––––––. In *Byzance et les Arabes*. See Vasiliev, vols. 1 and 2.

Ibn Ishaq. See Guillaume.

Ibn al-Balkhi. See Le Strange, *Description* (1912).

Ibn al-Fuwati. *Al-Hawadit al-Jami'a . . . (Une histoire complète de Bagdad)* (Arabic). Edited by Mustafa Jawad. Bagdad, 1932.

Ibn Iyâs. *Journal d'un Bourgeois du Caire, 1500–1522 (Chronique d'Ibn Iyas: Histoire des Mamlouks . . .)*. Translated from Arabic and annotated by Gaston Wiet. 2 vols. Paris: Armand Colin, 1955 [Bibliothèque Générale de l'Ecole Pratique des Hautes Etudes: 6th sect.].

Ibn al-Idhari. See Vasiliev, *Byzance et les Arabes*, vol. 1.

Ibn Khaldun. *The Muqaddimah. An introduction to History*. Translated from Arabic, with an introduction by Franz Rosenthal. 3 vols. New York: Pantheon Books/Bollingen Foundation, 1958.

––––––. *Histoire des Berbères et des dynasties musulmanes de l'Afrique septentrionale*. Translated from Arabic by William MacGuckin, Baron de Slane. New edition by Paul Casanova, with a bibliography of Ibn Khaldun. 4 vols. Paris: Paul Geuthner, 1968–69 [1st ed. Algiers, 1852–56].

Ibn an Naqqach. "Fetoua [1357–1358] relatif à la condition des zimmis et particulièrement des Chrétiens en pays musulmans, depuis l'établissement de l'Islamisme, jusqu'au milieu du VIIIe siècle de l'Hégire." Translated from Arabic by [François Alphonse] Belin, *JA* 4th ser. 18 (1851): 417–516; 19 (1852): 97–103.

Ibn Qayyim al-Jawziyya. *Sharh ash-shurut al-Umriyya (Commentary on the Pact of Umar)* (Arabic). Edited by S. Salih. Damascus, 1961.

Ibn Taghribirdi [Taghri Birdi], Yusuf. *An-Nujum az-Zaira fi Muluk Misr wa'l-Qahira (The Brilliant Stars in the Kingdoms of Egypt and Cairo)*. See Fagnan, "Arabo-Judaïca."

Ibn Taimiya. *Majmu'a Fatawi* (Arabic). Cairo, 1911.

––––––. See Schreiner, "Contributions à l'Histoire des Juifs " (1895).

––––––. See Laoust, *Le Traité* (1948).

Ibn Warraq (pseudonym). *Why I am not a Muslim*. New York: Prometheus Books, 1995.

Idris, Hady Roger. "Contributions à l'histoire de l'Ifriqiya, d'après le *'Riyad an-Nufus'* d'Abu Bakr El-Maliki." *REI* 9 (1935): 105–77 and *REI* 10 (1936): 45–104.

––––––. *La Berbérie Orientale sous les Zirides, Xe-XIIe siècles*. 2 vols. Paris: Adrien Maisonneuve, 1959/62. [Institut d'Etudes Orientales, Algiers, 22.]

––––––. "Les Tributaires en Occident Musulman Médiéval d'après le *'Mi'yâr'* d'al-Wanšariši." In Pierre Salmon, ed. *Mélanges* (1974): 172–96. See [Abel].

al-Idrisi [Edrîsî]. *Description de l'Afrique et de l'Espagne.* Arabic text published for the first time from mss in Paris and Oxford. With a translation, notes, and glossary by Reinhart Dozy and Michael Jan de Goeje. Leiden: Brill, 1866.

Inalcik, Halil. "The Ottoman Decline and its Effects upon the *Reaya.*" In *Aspects of the Balkans,* eds. Spiros Vryonis, Jr., and Henrik Birnbaum, (1972).

———. "The Emergence of the Ottomans." In *Cambridge History of Islam* (1977), 1: 263–91.

———. "The Heyday and Decline of the Ottoman Empire." In *Cambridge History of Islam* (1977), 1:324–53.

———. *The Ottoman Empire: Conquest, Organisation and Economy. Collected Studies.* London: Variorum Reprints, 1978.

Ingrams, Doreen. *Palestine Papers 1917–1922. Seeds of Conflict.* Compiled and annotated. London: John Murray, 1972.

Iorga, Nicolas. *Byzance après Byzance.* Foreword by Alexandre Paléologue. Paris: Le Nadir & Balland, 1992.

Iqbal, Javid. "Democracy in the Modern Islamic State." In *Voices of Resurgent Islam,* 252–60, edited by John L. Esposito. (1983).

Irani, George Emile. *The Papacy and Middle East: The Role of the Holy See in the Arab-Israeli Conflict, 1962–1984.* Notre-Dame, IN: University of Notre-Dame Press, 1986.

Isaac, Jules. *Genèse de l'Antisémitisme.* Paris: Calmann-Lévy, 1956.

———. *Jésus et Israël.* Paris: Fasquelle, 1959.

———. *L'Antisémitisme a-t-il des racines chrétiennes?* Paris: Fasquelle, 1960.

———. *L'Enseignement du mépris, vérité historique et mythes théologiques.* Paris: Fasquelle, 1962.

Israeli, Raphael, ed. *PLO in Lebanon. Selected Documents.* London: Weidenfeld & Nicolson, 1983.

———. (with the collaboration of Carol Bardenstein). *Man of Defiance. A Political Biography of Anwar Sadat.* London: Weidenfeld & Nicolson, 1985.

———. *Palestinians between Israel and Jordan. Squaring the Triangle.* New York: Westport, CT and London: Praeger, 1991.

———. *Muslim Fundamentalism in Israel.* London/Washington/New York: Brassey's (UK), 1993.

———. *Fundamentalist Islam and Israel. Essays in Interpretation.* USA/UK: Milken Library of Jewish Public Affairs, 1993.

Iyad, Abou. *Palestinien Sans Patrie. Entretiens avec Eric Rouleau.* Paris: Fayolle, 1983.

Jafari, Muhammad Taqi (Ayatollah). *A Comparative Study of the Two Systems of Universal Human Rights. From the Viewpoint of Islam and the West.* Translated from Persian by the Translation and Publication Department, Islamic Culture and Relations Organization. Teheran: Alhoda International Publisher, 1999.

Jansen, Johannes J.G. *The Neglected Duty. The Creed of Sadat's Assassins and Islamic Resurgence in the Middle East.* Preface by Charles J. Adams. New York: Macmillan/ London: Collier Macmillan, 1986.

———. *The Dual Nature of Islamic Fundamentalism.* London: Hurst & Co., 1997.

Jelinek, Yeshayahu A. "Bosnia-Herzegovina at War. Relations Between Moslems and Non-Moslems." *HGS* 5/3 (1990): 275–92.

Jessup, Henry Harris. Introduction by James S. Dennis. *Fifty Three Years in Syria.* New York: Fleming H. Revell, 1910.

Joliffe, T. R. *Lettres sur La Palestine, La Syrie et L'Egypte, ou Voyage en Galilée et en Judée, Avec Une Relation Sur la Mer Morte, et Sur l'Etat Présent de Jérusalem.* Translated from English by Aubert de Vitry. Paris, 1820.

Joseph, John. *Muslim-Christian Relations and Inter-Christian Rivalries in the Middle-East. The Case of the Jacobites in an Age of Transition.* New York: State University of New York Press, 1983.

Juster, Jean. "La Condition Légale des Juifs sous les Rois Visigoths." In *Etudes d'Histoire Juridique Offertes à Paul F. Girard.* Paris, 1912–13, vol. 1:276–335.

———. *Les Juifs dans l'Empire Romain. Leur Condition Juridique, Economique et Sociale.* 2 vols. Paris: Paul Geuthner, 1914.

Kaegi, Walter E. *Byzantium and the Early Islamic Conquests.* Cambridge: Cambridge University Press, 1996 [1st edition 1992].

Karas, Shawky F. *The Copts since the Arab Invasion. Strangers in their Land.* Jersey City: American, Canadian, and Australian Coptic Associations, 1985.

Kashani, Reuven. *Qorot ha-Zamanim (The Chronicle of Afghan Jewry of Mattatya Garji)* [of Rabbi Matathias Gargi]. *Shevet ve-Am* (Hebrew). n.s., 1 (1970): 5–28.

Kassab, Farid. *Le Nouvel Empire Arabe. La Curie Romaine et Le Prétendu Péril Juif Universel. Réponse à M. N. Azoury bey.* Paris: Giard & Brière, 1906.

Kattan, Naim. *Adieu Babylone.* Montreal: Les Editions de la Presse Ltée, 1975.

Kedourie, Elie. *The Chatham House Version and other Middle-Eastern Studies.* London: Weidenfeld & Nicholson, 1969.

———. *Arabic Political Memoirs and Other Studies.* London: Frank Cass, 1974.

———. *In the Anglo-Arab Labyrinth, The McMahon-Husayn Correspondence and its Interpretation, 1914–1939.* Cambridge/London/New York/Melbourne: Cambridge University Press, 1976.

———. *Islam in the Modern World.* London: Mansell, 1980.

———. *The Crossman Confessions and other Essays in Politics, History and Religion.* London/New York: Mansell, 1984.

———. "Arnold J. Toynbee. History as Paradox." In *The Crossman Confessions,* 191–206.

———. "Religion and Politics. Arnold Toynbee and Martin Wright." In *The Crossman Confessions,* 207–18.

Kennedy, Hugh. *The Prophet and the Age of the Caliphates.* London/New York: Longman, 1986.

Kepel, Gilles. *The Prophet and Pharaoh. Muslim Extremism in Contemporary Egypt.* Preface by Bernard Lewis. Translated from French by Jon Rothschild. London: Al Saqui, 1985 [American ed., University of California Press, 1986].

Kerr, Robert. *Pioneering in Morocco. A record of Seven Years' Medical Mission Work in the Palace and the Hut.* London: Allenson, 1894.

Khadduri, Majid. *War and Peace in the Law of Islam.* Foreword by R. K. Ramazani. Baltimore: Johns Hopkins University Press, 1955.

———. *The Islamic Law of Nations* (Shaybani's *Siyar*). Baltimore: Johns Hopkins University Press, 1965.

———. *The Islamic Conception of Justice.* Foreword by R. K. Ramazani. Baltimore/London: Johns Hopkins University Press, 1984.

de Khanikof, Nicolas. "Méched, la Ville Sainte et son territoire. Extraits d'un voyage dans le Khorassan, 1858.—Texte et Dessins inédits." In *Le Tour du Monde*. Paris: Hachette, 1861, 2nd sem., 280–82.

Khodr, Georges. "L'Arabité." Lecture delivered under the aegis of the Association for Franco-Arab Solidarity in Paris on 2 June 1970. Published with lecture of Youakim Moubarac, "Musulmans, Chrétiens et Juifs à l'épreuve de la Palestine." Paris: France Pays-Arabes, 1970.

———. "Renouveau Interne, Oecuménisme et Dialogue." Lecture delivered at a Colloquium in Paris (September 1987), under the aegis of a group: Christians of the Arab World and their friends. In *Les Chrétiens du Monde Arabe (colloque: 1987)*. Preface by Pierre Rondot. Paris: Maisonneuve & Laroe, 1989, 28–32.

Khomeiny, S. Ruhollah. *Principes politiques, philosophiques, sociaux et religieux de l'Ayatollah Khomeiny. Extraits de trois ouvrages majeurs de l'Ayatollah*. Texts selected from the Persian version by Jean-Marie Xavière. With an introduction and explanatory notes. Paris: Libres-Hallier, 1979.

———. *Islamic Government*. Translated by Joint Publications Research. Arlington, VA, 1974.

———. *Pithy Aphorisms, Wise Sayings and Counsels*. Teheran: The Institute for Compilation and Publication of Imam Khomeini's Works. International Affairs Division, 1994.

King-Crane Commission. See Reports (*King-Crane Commission*).

Kister, Meir Jacob. " 'An Yadin' (Qur'an, 9/29)." *Arabica* 11 (1964): 272–78.

———. "The Massacre of the Banû Qurayza. A re-examination of a tradition." *JSAI* 8 (1986): 61–96.

Kramer, Martin. *Arab Awakening and Islamic Revival. The Politics of Ideas in the Middle East*. New Brunswick, NJ: Transaction Publishers, 1996.

Kreutz, Andrej. *Vatican Policy on the Palestinian-Israel Conflict. The Struggle for the Holy Land*. Westport, CT: Greenwood Press, 1990.

———. "The Vatican and the Palestinians: a historical overview." *ISLAMOCHRISTIANA* 18 (1992): 109–25.

Kushner, David. "Intercommunal Strife in Palestine during the late Ottoman period." Asian and African Studies, *The Institute of Middle Eastern Studies*, University of Haifa, vol. 18, n° 2 (July 1984): 187–204.

Kyrris, Costas P. "L'Importance sociale de la conversion à l'Islam (volontaire ou non) d'une section des classes dirigeantes de Chypre pendant les premiers siècles de l'occupation turque (1570-fin du XVIIe siècle)." *Actes du Premier Congrès international des Etudes balkaniques et sud-est européennes*, 3. Sofia, 1969, 437–62.

Labour, Jérôme. *Le Christianisme dans l'empire perse sous la dynastie sassanide, 224–632*. Paris: Lecoffre, 1904.

Lacoste, Yves. *Editorial*. "Géopolitique des islams," *Hérodote* (Géopolitique des Islams), n° 35, 4th trim. (1984): 3–18.

———. "Dynamique de l'Islam d'aujourd'hui. Entretien avec Jacques Berque." *Hérodote* (Les Centres de l'Islam), n° 36, 1st trim. (1985): 49–61.

———. "La crise actuelle, une chance pour l'intégration. Entretiens avec Arezki Damani (Président de l'Association France-Plus)." *Hérodote* (L'Occident et la Guerre des Arabes), no. 60/61, 1st and 2nd trim. (1991): 23–32.

———. "L'Occident et la Guerre des Arabes." *Hérodote*, no. 60/61, 1st and 2nd trim. (1991): 3–22.

Lacroix-Riz, Annie. *Le Vatican, l'Europe et le Reich de la Première Guerre mondiale à la guerre froide*. Paris: Armand Colin, 1996.

Laffin, John. *The PLO Connection*. London: Corgi, 1982.

———. *The War of Desperation. Lebanon 1982–1985*. London: Osprey, 1985.

Landau, Julian J. *The Media. Freedom of Responsibility. The War in Lebanon, 1982*. Jerusalem: B.A.L. Mass Communications, 1984.

Landshut, Siegfried. *Jewish Communities in the Muslim Countries of the Middle East*. London: Jewish Chronicle, 1950.

Laoust, Henri. *Le Traité de droit public d'Ibn Taimiya. Traduction annotée de la 'Siyasa šar'iya'*. Beirut: Institut Français de Damas, 1948.

[Laoust]. *Mélanges offerts à Henri Laoust*. 2 vols. Damascus: Institut Français, 1978 [*BEO* 30].

Lapidus, Ira M. "The Conversion of Egypt to Islam." *IOS* 2 (1972): 248–62.

Laurent, Achille. *Relation Historique des Affaires de Syrie depuis 1840 jusqu'en 1842. Statistique générale du Mont-Liban et Procédure complète dirigée en 1840 contre les Juifs de Damas, à la suite de la disparition du Père Thomas, publiées d'après les Documents recueillis en Turquie, en Egypte et en Syrie, par Achille Laurent*. Paris: Gaume Frères, 1846.

Laurent, Annie. ed., *Vivre avec l'Islam? Réflexions chrétiennes sur la religion de Mahomet*, preface by Msg. Béchara Raï. 3rd edition, revised and corrected. Versailles: Editions Saint-Paul, 1997.

de La Véronne, Chantal. *Vie de Moulay Isma'il, roi de Fès et de Maroc. D'après Joseph de Léon (1708–1728)*. Paris: Paul Geuthner, 1974.

League of Nations. See Official Documents and Reports.

Leared, Arthur. *Morocco and the Moors, being an Account of Travels, with a general description of the country and its people, with illustrations*. Revised and edited by Sir Richard Burton. 2nd ed. London: Sampson Low, Marston, Searle & Rivington/ New York: Schribner & Welford, 1891.

Lebel, A. Roland. *Les Voyageurs français du Maroc. L'exotisme marocain dans la littérature de voyage*. Paris: Librairie Coloniale et Orientaliste Larose, 1936.

Lecker, Michael. "On Arabs of the Banû Kilab executed together with the Jewish Banû Qurayza." *JSAI* 19 (1995), 66–72.

———. "Judaism among Kinda and the *ridda* of Kinda." *JAOS* 115 (1995): 635–50.

———. *Jews and Arabs in pre- and early Islamic Arabia*. Aldershot, HA: Variorum Collected Studies Series, 1998.

Lemprière, William. *Tours from Gibraltar to Tangier, Sallee, Mogodore, Santa Cruz, Tarudant and thence over Mount Atlas to Morocco, including a particular account of the Royal Harem &c*. 2 ed., London: Walter, 1793.

Léon l'Africain, Jean-Léon. *Description de l'Afrique*. New edition, translated from Italian by A. Epaulard, and annotated by A. Epaulard, Th. Monod, H. Lhote and R. Maury. 2 vols. Paris: Maisonneuve, 1956.

Lepsius, Johannes. *Deutschland und Armenian, 1914–1918: Sammlung Diplomatischer Aktenstücke*. Potsdam, 1919.

Le Strange, Guy. *The Lands of the Eastern Caliphate. Mesopotamia, Persia, and Central Asia from the Moslem conquest to the time of Timur*. London: Frank Cass, 1966 [1st ed. Cambridge, 1905].

———. *Description of the Province of Fars in Persia at the beginning of the fourteenth century*

A. D. (From the MS. of Ibn Al-Balkhi in the British Museum). London: *RAS*, 1912 [Monograph 14].

Leven, Narcisse. *Cinquante Ans d'histoire. L'Alliance Israélite Universelle, 1860–1910.* 2 vols. Paris: Felix Alcan, 1911/20.

Levin, Andrea. *Israel Watch.* "The Encyclopedias." *Commentary* 96/1 (July 1993): 47–54.

Lévi-Provençal, Evariste. *Documents Inédits d'Histoire Almohade. Fragments Manuscrits du "Legajo" 19/9 du Fonds Arabe de l'Escurial.* Translated with an introduction and notes. Paris: Paul Geuthner, 1928 [Textes Relatifs à l'Histoire de l'Occident Musulman. Vol. I].

———. *Séville musulmane au début du XIIe siècle. Le traité sur la vie urbaine et les corps de métiers d'Ibn 'Abdun.* Translated from Arabic with notes. Paris: Maisonneuve, 1948 ["Islam d'Hier et d'Aujourd'hui." Vol. 2].

———. *Islam d'Occident. Etudes d'Histoire Médiévale.* Paris: Maisonneuve, 1948 ["Islam d'Hier et d'Aujourd'hui". Vol. 7].

———. *Histoire de l'Espagne Musulmane.* Vol. 1, *La Conquête et l'Emirat Hispano-Umaiyade* (710–912). New revised and expanded edition, 1950 [1st ed. 1944]; vol. 2, *Le Caliphat Umaiyade de Cordoue* (912–1031), Paris: Maisonneuve & Larose/Leiden: Brill 1950; vol 3, *Le siècle du Califat de Cordoue,* Maisonneuve & Larose, 1967.

[Lévi-Provençal]. *Etudes d'Orientalisme dédiées à la mémoire de Lévi-Provençal.* 2 vols. Paris: Maisonneuve & Larose, 1962.

Levtzion, Nehemia, ed. *Conversion to Islam.* New York/London: Holmes & Meier, 1979.

———. "Conversion to Islam in Syria and Palestine and the Survival of Christian Communities." In Michael Gervers and Ramzi J. Bikhazi, eds., *Conversions and Continuity: Indigenous Christian Communities in Medieval Islamic Lands. Eight to Eighteenth Century.*Toronto: Pontifical Institute of Medieval Studies, 1990: 289–312 [Papers in Medieval Studies 9].

Levy, Reuben. *A Baghdad Chronicle.* Cambridge: Cambridge University Press, 1929 [reprint Philadelphia: Porcupine Press, 1977].

———. *The Social Structure of Islam.* Cambridge: Cambridge University Press, 1969.

Lewis, Bernard. *The Jews of Islam.* Princeton: Princeton University Press, 1984.

———. *Semites and Antisemites. An Inquiry into Conflict and Prejudice.* London: Weidenfeld and Nicolson, 1986.

——— and Peter M. Holt. *Historians of the Middle East.* London: Oxford University Press, 1969.

——— and Benjamin Braude, eds. *Christians and Jews.* See, Braude.

———. "The Question of Orientalism," *The New York Review of Books* (24 June 1982): 49–56.

Lipman, Sonia and Vivian David Lipman, eds. *The Century of Moses Montefiore.* London: Oxford University Press, 1985 [Littman Library of Jewish Civilization].

Little, Donald P. "Coptic Conversion to Islam under the Bahri Mamluks, 692–755/ 1293–1354." *BSOAS* 39 (1976): 552–69.

Littman, David Gerald. "Jews under Muslim Rule in the Late Nineteenth Century." *WLB* 28 n.s. 35/36 (1975): 65–76.

———. "Jews under Muslim Rule, II: Morocco 1903–1912." *WLB* 29, n.s. 37/38 (1976): 3–19.

————. "Quelques Aspects de la condition de dhimmi. Juifs d'Afrique du Nord avant la colonisation" (d'après des documents de l'AIU). *YOD* 2, n° 1, Paris, P.O.F. (1976): 22–52. [Enlarged, revised reprint with ill., Editions de l'Avenir, Geneva, 1977: 32].

————. "Les Juifs en Perse avant les Pahlevi." *TM* 34, N° 395 (1979): 1910–35. [Enlarged, revised reprint with illustrations, Editions de l'Avenir, Geneva, 1979: 28].

————."Jews under Muslim Rule: The Case of Persia." *WLB* 32, n.s. 49/50 (1979): 2–15.

————. "Mission to Morocco (1863–64)." In *The Century of Moses Montefiore*, edited by Sonia and Vivian David Lipman, 171–229.

————. "The U.N. Finds Slavery in the Sudan." *MEQ* (September 1996): 91–94.

———— and René Wadlow. "The UN Convention on Genocide of 1948 and the Palestinian-Hamas Charter of 1988." *Midstream* (September–October 1998): 8–12.

————. "Universal Human Rights and 'Human Rights in Islam'." *Midstream* (February–March 1999): 2–7.

————. "Islamism Grows Stronger at the United Nations." *MEQ* (September 1999): 59–64.

————. "Syria's Blood Libel Revival at the UN: 1991–2000." *Midstream* (February–March 2000): 2–8.

————. See Green.

Loeb, Laurence D. *Outcaste: Jewish Life in Southern Iran*. New York/London/Paris: Gordon & Breach, 1977.

Loewe, Louis and Raphael. See Montefiore.

Løkkegaard, Frede. *Islamic Taxation in the Classical Period with special reference to circumstances in Iraq*. Copenhagen: Branner & Korch, 1950.

————. "Fay." *EI*² 2 (1965) 889–90.

MacDonald, Duncan Black. "Dar al-Harb" and "Dar al-Sulh," *EI*¹. See Abel.

————. "Djihad." *EI*.

al-Maghili. *Ahkâm ahl al-Dimma (Réglementation des Dhimmis)*. See Vajda, "Un Traité."

al-Mahdi, Sadiq. "Islam—Society and Change." In *Voices of Resurgent Islam*, 230–40, edited by John L. Esposito (1983).

Mainz, Ernest. "Les Juifs d'Alger sous la domination Turque." In *JA* (1952): 197–217.

Makrizi, Taki-Eddin-Ahmad. *Histoire des Sultans Mamlouks de l'Egypte*. Translated from Arabic by Etienne Marc Quatremère. With philological, historical, and geographical notes. 4 vols. in 2 vols. Paris: Firmin Didot, 1837/42 [Oriental Translation Fund of Great Britain and Ireland].

Malik, Charles. "The Near East: The Search for Truth." *FA* 30 (January 1952).

Malik, Habib C. "The Forgotten Christians of Lebanon." *Books and Culture*. A Publication of Christianity Today. Carol Stream, IL, September/October, 1998.

————. "Christians in the Land called Holy."*First Things*, New York, 89 (January 1999).

————. *Between Damascus and Jerusalem. Lebanon and Middle East Peace*. Washington DC: The Washington Institute for Near East Policy, 1997.

al-Maliki. *Riyad an-Nufus*. See Idris.

Mandel, Neville J. *The Arabs and Zionism before World War I*. Berkeley/Los Angeles/London: University of California Press, 1976.

Mandelstam, André. *Le Sort de l'Empire Ottoman.* Paris/Lausanne: Payot, 1917.

———. *La Société des Nations et les Puissances devant le problème arménien.* Preface by Edmond Wadih Naïm. 2nd ed. Beirut: Association Libanaise des Universitaires Arméniens, 1970.

Mann, Jacob. *The Jews in Egypt and in Palestine under the Fatimid Caliphs. A Contribution to their Political and Communal History based chiefly on Geniza Material hitherto unpublished.* 2 vols. London: Oxford University Press, 1969 [1st ed. 1922].

Mantran, Robert, ed. *Histoire de l'Empire Ottoman.* Paris: Fayard, 1989.

Ma'oz, Moshe. *Ottoman Reform in Syria and Palestine, 1840–1861. The Impact of the Tanzimat on Politics and Society.* London/New York: Oxford University Press, 1968.

———. ed. *Studies on Palestine during the Ottoman Period.* Jerusalem: Magnus Press, 1975.

Margalith, Aaron. See Adler, Cyrus.

Marshall, Paul (with Lela Gilbert). *Their Blood Cries Out. The Worldwide Tragedy of Modern Christians who are dying for the faith.* Introduction by Michael Horowitz. Dallas, TX: Word Publishing, 1997.

Martin-Achard, Robert. *Actualité d'Abraham.* Neuchâtel: Delachaux & Niestlé, 1969.

Masriya, Yahudiya [Bat Ye'or]. *Les Juifs en Egypte.* Geneva: Editions de l'Avenir, 1971.

———. "A Christian Minority. The Copts in Egypt.," *Case Studies on Human Rights and Fundamental Freedoms. A World Survey.* 4 vols. The Hague: Martinus Nijhoff, 1976, 4:79–93 [French, 1973].

Maurand, Jérôme. *Itinéraire de Jérôme Maurand d'Antibes à Constantinople* [1544]. Italian texts published for the first time with an introduction and a translation by Léon Dovey. Paris: Ernest Leroux, 1901.

[Mawardi] Mawerdi, Abou 'l-Hasan 'Ali. *Les Statuts Gouvernementaux ou Règles de Droit Public et Administratif (Al-ahkam as-Sultaniyya).* Translated from Arabic and annotated by Edmond Fagnan. Algiers: Adolphe Jourdan, 1915.

Mawdudi, Abul Ala. *Toward Understanding Islam.* London: UK Islamic Mission, 1980.

———. *Islam. An Historical Perspective.* London: The Islamic Foundation, 1980 [1st ed. 1974, 2nd revised ed. 1977].

———. *The Islamic Movement, Dynamics of Values, Power and Change.* New English version edited by Khurram Murad. London: The Islamic Foundation, 1984.

———. "Les droits des dhimmis dans l'Etat islamique." In *Al-Dhimma. L'Islam et les Minorités Religieuses,* Dossier N° 80–81 (1991/1–2): 175–89. Rome: *PISAI.*

Mayer, Ann Elizabeth. *Islam & Human Rights, Tradition and Politics.* Boulder, CO: Westview Press and London: Pinter Publishers, 1991.

M'Cheyne, Robert Murray. See Bonar.

Meaken, Budgett. *The Moors. An Account of People and Customs with 132 Illustrations.* London: Swan & Sonnenschein, 1902.

Mehden, Fred R. von der. "American Perceptions of Islam." In *Voices of Resurgent Islam,* 18–31 edited by John L. Esposito (1983).

Merad, Ali. See Moubarac, Youakim, *Islam* (1984).

Merrâkechi [al-Marrakushi], Abd al-Wahid. *Al-mu'jib fi talkhis akhbar al-maghrib (Histoire des Almohades).* Translated from Arabic by Edmond Fagnan. Algiers: Adolphe Jourdan, 1893 [*Revue Africaine,* n° 202–7].

Michael the Syrian. See *Chronique de Michel le Syrien.*

Milliot, Louis. *Introduction à l'Etude du Droit Musulman.* Paris: Recueil Sirey, 1953.

Mitev, Iono. "Le Peuple Bulgare sous la Domination Ottomane (1396–1878)." See Ivan Dujcev, *Histoire de la Bugarie* (1977).

Montagne, Robert. "Réactions Arabes Contre Le Sionisme." [Summary on the Congress of Bloudane, September 1937]. In *Entretiens Sur L'Evolution Des Pays De Civilisation Arabe* (meeting of 11–13 July 1938 under the auspices of L'Institut Des Etudes Islamiques de l'Université de Paris et du Centre d'Etudes de Politique Etrangère). Paris: Paul Hartman, n.d.

Montefiore, Moses. *Diaries of Sir Moses Montefiore and Lady Montefiore.* Edited by Dr. Louis Loewe. A facsimile of the 1890 edition, introduced by Professor Raphael Loewe with a new index by Walter Schab. London: The Jewish Historical Society of England and the Jewish Museum, 1983.

Morabia, Alfred. "Ibn Taymiyya, dernier grand théoricien du Gihâd médiéval." See in Laoust, *Mélanges* (1978), 2:85–100.

―――. *Le Gihâd dans l'Islam Médiéval. Le "Combat Sacré" des origines au XIIe siècle.* Preface by Roger Arnaldez. Paris: Albin Michel, 1993.

Moreno, Pedro C. ed. *Handbook on Religious Liberty Around the World.* With a foreword by John Whitehead. Charlottesville, VA: The Rutherford Institute, 1996.

Morison, Antoine. *Relation historique d'un voyage nouvellement fait au Mont Sinaï, et à Jérusalem. On trouvera dans cette relation un détail de ce que l'auteur a vu de plus remarquable en Italie, en Egypte, en Arabie, . . . sur les côtes de Syrie et en Phoenicie; . . . aussi l'origine . . . et le gouvernement politique de l'Empire ottoman, etc.* Paris: Antoine Dezallier, 1705.

Morony, Michael G. *Iraq After The Muslim Conquest.* Princeton: Princeton University, 1984.

Moubarac, Youakim. "Vocation Islamique de Jérusalem." Lecture delivered at a conference on *Le conflit du Moyen-Orient: Justice et Paix,* Geneva (Foyer John Knox, World Council of Churches), 1968.

―――. "Musulmans, chrétiens et juifs à l'épreuve de la Palestine." Lecture delivered under the aegis of the Association de Solidarité Franco-Arabe in Paris on 2 June 1970 (published with the lecture by Mgr. Khodr, "L'Arabité"), Paris: France Pays-Arabes, 1970.

―――. *L'Islam et le Dialogue Islamo-Chrétien, Pentalogie Islamo-Chrétienne.* 5 vols. Vol. 1, *L'Oeuvre de Louis Massignon;* vol. 2, *Le Coran et la Critique occidentale;* vol. 3, *L'Islam et le Dialogue Islamo-Chrétien;* vol. 4, *Les Chrétiens et le monde arabe;* vol. 5, *Palestine et Arabité.* Beirut: Edition du Cénacle Libanais, 1972–73.

―――. *Recherches sur La Pensée Chrétienne et l'Islam dans les Temps Modernes et à l'Epoque Contemporaine.* Preface by Edmond Rabbath. Beirut: Université Libanaise, 1977.

―――. Jean-Paul Gabus and Ali Merad. *Islam et Christianisme en Dialogue.* Paris: Le Cerf, 1982 [published under the aegis of the Centre Unité Chrétienne of Lyon].

―――. "Trois Projets pour l'Orient Arabe." Lecture delivered at a Colloquium in Paris (September 1987), under the aegis of a group: Christians of the Arab World and their friends. In *Les Chretiens du Monde Arabe* (colloque: 1987). Preface by Pierre Rouodot. Paris: Maisonneuve & Larose, 1989, 33–38.

al-Muhajiroun. *The Voice, the Eyes and the Ears of the Muslims* (press release). London: 1999.

Muslim. *Al-Sahih (Being Traditions of the Sayings and Doings of the Prophet Muhammad as narrated by his Companions and Compiled under the title 'Al-Jami'-Us-Sahih').* Translated from Arabic by Abdul Hamid Siddiqi. 4 vols. Lahore: Ashraf Press, 1976.

Naguib, Sélim. *Les Droits de l' Homme en Egypte, le cas des Coptes.* Doctoral Thesis, Université de Droit, d' Economie et de Sciences Sociales, Paris, June 1992.

———. *Les Coptes Dans l'Egypte d'Aujourd'hui.* Brussels: Editions Illustra, 1996.

Nahoum, Haïm, ed. *Recueils de Firmans Impériaux Ottomans adressés aux Valis et aux Khedives d'Egypte, 1006 H.-1322 H. (1597–1904 J.-C.).* Translated from the Turkish with a foreword, summaries, tables, and notes; preface by Mohammed Zaky El-Ibrachy. Cairo: L'Institut Français d'Archéologie Orientale, 1934.

Nau, François. *L'Expansion Nestorienne en Asie.* Paris: Musée Guimet, 1914.

———. *Les Arabes Chrétiens de Mésopotamie et de Syrie du VIIe au VIIIe siècle.* Paris: Imprimerie Nationale, 1933 [Cahiers de la Société Asiatique. First Series I].

an-Nawawi. *Minhâdj At-Tâlibîn (Le Guide des Zélés Croyants: Manuel de Jurisprudence Musulmane selon le rite de Châfi'i.* Translated from Arabic and annotated by L. W. C. van den Berg. 3 vols. Batavia: Imprimerie du Gouvernement, 1882–84.

Neher-Bernheim, Renée. *La Déclaration Balfour, 1917. Création d'un Foyer National Juif en Palestine.* Paris: Julliard, 1969.

Nelson, Walter Henry and Terence C. F. Prittie. *The Economic War Against The Jews.* New York: Random House, 1977.

Netanyahu, Benjamin. *Terrorism. How the West Can Win.* London: Weidenfeld & Nicolson, 1986.

———. *A Place Among the Nations. Israel and the World.* New York/London: Bantam Books, 1993.

Nettler, Ronald L. *Islam and the Minorities* (booklet). 2nd ed. Jerusalem: Israel Academic Committee on the Middle East, 1979.

———. *Past Trials and Present Tribulations. A Muslim Fundamentalist's View of the Jews.* London: Pergamon, 1987.

Netzer, Amnon. "The Fate of the Jewish Community of Tabriz." See [Ayalon].

Nicholls, William. *Christian Antisemitism. A History of Hate.* Northvale, NJ/London: Jason Aronson Inc., 1995.

Nicosia, Francis R. *The Third Reich and the Palestine Question.* London: Tauris, 1985.

Niebuhr, Karsten. *Travels through Arabia and Other Countries in the East.* Translated from German by Robert Heron. With notes and Illustrated with Engravings and Maps. Edinburgh: Printed for R. Morison and Son, 1792.

Nisan, Mordechai. *Minorities in the Middle East. A History of Struggle and Self-Expression.* Jefferson, NC/London: McFarland, 1991.

Obadyah (the Norman). *Chronicle.* See Scheiber, "The Origins of Obadyah."

O'Brian, Conor Cruise. *The Siege. The Saga of Israel and Zionism.* London: 1986.

Official Documents and Reports: PP, FO, MAE, League of Nations, United Nations, etc.

———. PP. "Dispatches from Her Majesty's Consuls in the Levant, Respecting Past or Apprehended Disturbances in Syria: 1858–1860." 1860: 500–501.

———. PP. "Correspondence relating to the Affairs of Syria: 1860–1861." 1861.

———. PP. "Reports by Her Majesty's Diplomatic and Consular agents in Turkey Respecting the Condition of the Christian Subjects of the Porte: 1868–1875." Turkey, no. 16 (1877): 638–65 [C. 1739].

————. PP. "Further Despatch Respecting the State of Affairs in Bosnia no. 20 (1877)": 553–58 [C. 1768].

————. PP. "Further Correspondence Respecting the Affairs of Turkey. 1877" (1877): 143 [C. 1806].

————. MAE. *Documents Diplomatiques, Affaires Arméniennes, Projets de Réformes dans l'Empire Ottoman. 1893–1897.* Vol. 6, *Arménie, Macédoine, Turquie.* Paris: 1897.

————. *King-Crane Commission.* First published by *Editor & Publisher,* vol. 55, n° 27- 2nd section, pp. 1–38, New York, 2 December 1922, with the title *First Publication of King-Crane Report on the Near East. A Suppressed Official Document of the United States Government.*

————. *Question of the Frontier between Turkey and Iraq. Report submitted to the Council by the Commission instituted by the Council Resolution of September 30th,* 1924. Geneva: League of Nations, 1925 (Document C.400. M.147, vii).

————. [Peel], *Palestine Royal Commission. Presented by the Secretary of State for the Colonies to Parliament.* Cmd. 5479. London: His Majesty's Stationery Office, July 1937.

————. *Report of the Commission of Enquiry into Disturbances in Aden in December 1947.* London: His Majesty's Stationery Office, Colonial N° 233, 1948.

————. *Country Reports on Human Rights Practices for 1990.* Department of State, Washington: U.S. Government Printing House, 1991.

————. "The Contribution of the Islamic Civilisation to European Culture." Strasbourg: Council of Europe, Parliamentary Assembly, 1992, doc. 6497.

————. Report by the UN Special Rapporteur on Iran (Commission on Human Rights), Reynaldo Galindo Pohl, 28 January 1993 (E/CN.4/1993/41), 2 February 1994 (E/CN.4/1994/50), 16 January 1995 (E/CN.4/1995/55).

————. Report by the UN Special Rapporteur on Iraq (Commission on Human Rights), Max van der Stoel, 15 February 1995 (E/CN.4/1995/56).

————. Reports by the UN Special Rapporteur on Sudan (Commission on Human Rights), Gáspár Bíró; General Assembly Interim Reports (for the years 1993–97): A/48/601; A/49/539; A/50/569; A/51/490; A/52/510; UNCHR Reports (for the years 1993–97): E/CN.4/1994/48; E/CN.4/1995/58; E/CN.4/1996/62; E/CN.4/1997/58; E/CN.4/1998/66.

————. *Government Sanctioned Religious Discrimination in the Sudan between 1993 and 1998.* Prepared Testimony by Gáspár Bíró for the United States Commission on International Religious Freedom. Washington DC, 15 February 2000: *http://www.uscirf.gov./hearings/15feb00/birPT.php3.*

————. Report. *The Status of the Church in the Muslim World.* London: International Institute for the Study of Islam and Christianity, 1992 [Monograph N° 1].

Oliphant, Laurence. *The Land of Gilead, with Excursions in the Lebanon.* London: Blackwood, 1880.

Palmer, J. A. B. "The Origin of the Janissaries." *BJRL* 35 (1952–53): 448–81.

Paquignon, Paul. "Quelques Documents sur la condition des Juifs au Maroc." *RMM* 9 (1909): 112–23 [La Mission Scientifique du Maroc], Paris: Ernest Laroux, 1909.

Parfitt, Tudor. " 'The Year of the Pride of Israel': Montefiore and the Blood Libel of 1840." In *The Century,* edited by Sonia and Vivian David Lipman, 131–48. (1985).

————. *The Jews in Palestine. 1880–1882.* London: Royal Historical Society/The Boydell Press, 1987 [Studies in History, 52].

————. *The Road to Redemption. The Jews of the Yemen 1900–1950.* Leiden/New York/ Cologne: E. J. Brill, 1996.

Parkes, James. *The Conflict of the Church and the Synagogue. A Study in the Origins of Antisemitism.* New York: Atheneum, 1969. [1st ed., London, 1934].

————. *Antisemitism.* London: Valentine Mitchell, 1963.

————. *Whose Land. A History of the Peoples of Palestine.* Revised ed. London: Penguin Books, 1970. (1st ed. 1949]

Parliamentary Papers (PP). See Official Documents and Reports.

Patriarchs. See Evetts.

Patrologia Orientalis, ed. Mgr. R. Graffin and François Nau, 20 vols. Paris: Firmin-Didot, 1907–29. See *Chronique.*

Peel, Lord. *Palestine Royal Commission Report.* See Report [Peel].

Perlman, Maurice. *Mufti of Jerusalem. The Story of Haj Amin el Husseini.* London: Gollancz, 1947.

Perlmann, Moshe. "Notes on Anti-Christian Propaganda in the Mamlûk Empire." *BSOAS* 10 (1939–42): 843–61.

————. "Eleventh-Century Andalusian Authors on the Jews of Granada." *PAAJR* 18 (1948–49): 269–90.

————. "Asnawi's Tract against Christian Officials" [*Al-kalimât al-Muhimma fi Mubâsharat ahl adh-dhimma [An earnest appeal on the employment of the Dhimmis*]. In *Ignace Goldziher Memorial Volume,* edited by David Samuel Löwinger, Bela Somogyi and Alexander Scheiber, vol. 2. Jerusalem, 1958.

————. "Ghiyar." *EI*².

————. "Notes on the Position of Jewish Physicians in Medieval Muslim Countries." *IOS* 2 (1972): 315–19.

————. *Shaykh Damanhuri on the Churches of Cairo, 1739.* Edited and translated, with an introduction and notes. Berkeley/Los Angeles/London: University of California, 1975.

Péroncel-Hugoz, Jean-Pierre. *The Raft of Mohamed.* Translated from French by George Holoch. New York: Paragon House, 1987 [French ed., 1983].

————. *Une Croix sur le Liban.* Paris: Lieu Commun, 1984.

Peters, Joan. *From Time Immemorial. The Origins of the Arab-Jewish Conflict over Palestine.* New York: Harper & Row, 1984.

Peters, Rudolph. *Jihad in Classical and Modern Islam.* Princeton, NJ: Princeton Press, 1996.

————. *Islam and Colonialism. The Doctrine of Jihad in Modern History.* Paris/New York/ /The Hague: Mouton, 1979 [Religion and Society 20].

Phares, Walid. *Lebanese Christian Nationalism. The Rise and Fall of an Ethnic Resistance.* Boulder, CO/London: Lynne Rienner Publishers, 1995.

Pierrard, Pierre. *Juifs et Catholiques français. D'Edouard Drumont à Jacob Kaplan (1886–1994).* Paris: Le Cerf, 1997.

Pierron, Bernard. *Juifs et Chrétiens de la Grèce Moderne. Histoire des relations inter-communautaires de 1821 à 1945.* Preface by Haïm Vidal Séphiha. Paris: L'Harmattan, 1996 [Histoire et Perspectives Méditerranéennes].

Pipes, Daniel. *In the Path of God. Islam and Political Power.* New York: Basic Books, 1983.

499

——. *Slave Soldiers and Islam. The Genesis of a Military System.* New Haven, CT/London: Yale University Press, 1981.

——. "Fundamentalist Muslims between America and Russia." *FA* 64, n° 5 (summer 1986): 938–59.

——. *The Rushdie Affair. The Novel, the Ayatollah and the West.* New York: Birch Lane Press & Carol Publishing Group, 1990.

——. *Greater Syria. The History of an Ambition.* Oxford/New York: Oxford University Press, 1990.

——. *The Hidden Hand. Middle East Fears of Conspiracy.* New York: St. Martin's Press, 1996.

——. "In Muslim America. A Presence and a Challenge." *National Review* (21 February 2000): 40–41.

——. ed., "Disappearing Christians of the Middle East". *MEQ* (Winter 2001), entire issue.

Pitcher, Donald Edgar. *An Historical Geography of the Ottoman Empire, from earliest times to the end of the sixteenth century. With detailed maps to illustrate the expansion of the Sultanate.* Leiden: Brill, 1972.

Poggi, V. In *Orientalia Christiana Periodica.* Vol. 58, 2(1992) Recensiones: 606–07.

Poliak, Abraham N. "L'Arabisation de l'Orient Sémitique." *REI* 12 (1938): 35–63.

Poliakov, Léon. *The History of Antisemitism.* Vol.1, *From Roman Times to the Court Jews.* Translated from French by Richard Howard. London, 1966; vol.2, *From Mohammed to the Marranos.* Translated from French by Natalie Gerardi. London: Routledge & Kegan Paul, 1974 [Littman Library of Jewish Civilization].

——. *De Moscou à Beyrouth. Essai sur la Désinformation.* Paris: Calmann-Lévy, 1983.

Porath, Yehoshua. *The Emergence of the Palestinian Arab National Mouvement 1918–1929.* London: Frank Cass, 1974.

——. *The Palestinian Arab National Movement 1929–1939. From Riots to Rebellion.* London: Frank Cass, 1977.

Pouzet, Louis: *Damas au VIIe/XIIIe siècle. Vie et structures religieuses dans une métropole islamique.* Beirut: Dar el-Machriq, 1988.

Pragai, Michael J. *Faith and Fulfilment. Christians and the Return to the Promised Land.* London: Valentine Mitchell, 1985.

Prittie, Terence. See Nelson, Walter Henry.

Pryce-Jones, David. *The Closed Circle. An Interpretation of the Arabs.* London: Weidenfeld & Nicolson, 1989.

Ptolémée. *Les Miracles de Saint Ptolémée.* Arabic text translated and edited by L. Leroy. In Mgr. R. Graffin and François Nau, eds. *Patrologia Orientalis,* Paris, 1910, vol. 5, fasc. 5.

al-Qalqashandi. *Subh al-Asha.* 14 vols. Cairo, 1913–19.

al-Qaradâwî, Yûsuf. "The Status of Non-Muslims in Islamic Society" (Arabic). In *Al-Dimma,* 35–55.

——. *Saut Al-Haqq wa Al-Huriyya,* 9 January 1998. In *MEMRI,* "Special Report. The meeting between the Sheikh of Al-Azhar and the Chief Rabbi of Israel" [15 December 1997], 8 February 1998.

al-Qayrawânî. See Ibn Abi Zayd al-Qayrawânî.

Qindil, Nizar. "L'histoire . . . et les fautes des Orientalistes." Translated from Arabic

500 ISLAM AND DHIMMITUDE

by Janine Mahfouz (April 1991). In *Al-Mustašriqun (Orientalistes) PISAI* (1992/2): 70–73. See Bormanns.

Qubrusi, Khalil Iskandar. "A Call to the Arab Christians to join Islam." In Elie Kedourie, *The Chatham House Version and other Middle-Eastern Studies*, London, 1969, Appendix, pp. 343–50.

Qudama b. Ja'far. *Kitab al-Kharâj*. See Ben Shemesh.

Rabbath, Edmond. *Les Chrétiens dans l'Islam des Premiers Temps. La Conquête Arabe sous les Quatre Premiers Califes, 11/632–40/661*. 2 vols. Beirut: Université Libanaise, 1985 [Etudes Historiques XXIII].

Rahman, S. A. *Punishment of Apostasy in Islam*. Lahore: Institute of Islamic Culture, 1972.

Rance, Didier. *Chrétiens du Moyen-Orient. Témoins de la Croix*. 2nd revised ed. Paris: Aide à l'Eglise en détresse & "Bibliothèque A.E.D.," 1991.

Ravitch, Norman. "The Armenian Catastrophe: History, Murder & Sin." In *Encounter*, 69–84. London 1981.

Rendtorff, Rolf. See World Council of Churches (1988).

Reports. See Official Documents and Reports.

Rey, Francis. *La Protection Diplomatique et Consulaire dans les Echelles du Levant et de Barbarie*. Paris: Larose, 1899.

Richards, Donald Sidney, ed. *Islamic Civilisation: 951–1150*. (Papers on Islamic History III) Oxford: Cassirer, 1973.

Riegner, Gerhart M. *Ne Jamais Désespérer*. Paris: Le Cerf, 1998.

Riley, James. *Loss of the American Brig Commerce. Wrecked on the Western coast of Africa, in the month of August, 1815. With an account of Timbuctoo and of the hitherto undiscovered great city of Wassanah*. 2 vols. London: John Murray, 1817.

Riquet, Michel. *Un Chrétien face à Israël*. Paris: Laffont, 1975.

––––––. *Une minorité chrétienne au Proche-Orient: Les Maronites au Liban* (booklet). Postscript by Father Michel Hayek. Geneva: Editions de l'Avenir, 15 January 1977 [Centre d'Information et de Documentation sur le Moyen Orient].

Robert, Cyprien. *Les Slaves de Turquie. Serbes, Monténégrins, Bosniaques, Albanais et Bulgares: Leurs Ressources, Leurs Tendances et Leurs Progrès Politiques*. 2 vols. Paris: Passard & Labitte, 1844.

Robinson, Edward. *Biblical Researches in Palestine and the Adjacent Regions: A Journal of Travels in the Years 1838 & 1852*. 3rd ed., London: John Murray, 1867 [1st ed. 1841].

Robinson, Nehemia. *The Arab countries of the Near East and their Jewish Communities*. New York: Institute of Jewish Affairs & World Jewish Congress, 1951.

Rodinson, Maxime. *Les Palestiniens et la Crise Israélo-Arabe. Textes et Documents du Groupe de recherches et d'action pour le règlement du problème palestinien (G.R.A.P.P.), 1967–1973*. A collection of texts by Jacques Berque, Jacques Couland, Louis-Jean Duclos, Jacqueline Hadamard and Maxime Rodinson. Paris: Editions Sociales, 1974.

Rondot, Pierre. *Les Chrétiens d'Orient*. Paris: Peyronnet, 1955.

––––––. "Relations entre Musulmans, Chrétiens et Juifs. Un bref aperçu." *ASM* 142 (1984): 3–13.

Roumani, Maurice M. *The Case of the Jews from Arab Countries. A Neglected Issue*. Jerusalem: World Organization of Jews from Arab Countries (WOJAC), 1977.

Roy, Olivier. *L'Echec de l'Islam Politique.* Paris: Seuil, 1992.

Ruppin, Arthur. *Les Juifs Dans le Monde Moderne.* Paris: Payot, 1934.

Sabry, Mohammed. *L'Empire Egyptien sous Mohamed-Ali et la Question d'Orient. 1811–1849.* Paris: Paul Geuthner, 1930.

Sachedina, Abdulaziz. "Ali Shariati: Ideologue of the Iranian Revolution." In *Voices of Resurgent Islam,* 191–217, edited by John L. Esposito (1983).

Sadat, Anwar. *Revolt on the Nile.* London: Allan Wingate, 1957.

———. *In Search of Identity. An Autobiography.* New York: Harper & Row/Glasgow: Fontana & Collins, 1978.

Sagiv, David. "Judge Ashmawi and Militant Islam in Egypt." *MES,* 28, no. 3 (July 1992): 531–46.

———. *Fundamentalism and Intellectuals in Egypt, 1973–1993.* London: Frank Cass, 1995.

Said, Edward W. *Orientalism.* London and Henley: Routledge & Kegan Paul, 1978.

Salibi, Kamal S. *The Modern History of Lebanon.* London: Weidenfeld & Nicolson, 1965.

Samardzic, Radovan, and Sima M. Cirkovic, Olga Zirojevic, Radmila Trickovic, Dusan T. Batakovic, Veselin Djuretic, Kosta Cavoski, Atanasije Jevtic. *Le Kosovo-Metohija dans l'Histoire Serbe.* Translated from Serbo-Croat by Dejan M. Babic. Lausanne: L'Age d'Homme, 1990.

Sawirus [Severus] ibn al-Mukaffa. *History of the Patriarchs of the Egyptian Church, known as the History of the Holy Church.* Texts and documents translated from Arabic by Yassa 'Abd Al-Masih, O.H.E. Burmester and Antoine Khater. 6 pts. in 3 vols. Cairo: Société d'Archéologie Copte, 1943–1970.

Schacht, Joseph. *An Introduction to Islamic Law.* Oxford: Oxford University Press, 1964.

Schechtman, Joseph. *On Wings of Eagles. The Plight, Exodus and Homecoming of Oriental Jewry.* New York/London: Thomas Yoseloff, 1961.

Scheiber, Alexander. "The Origins of Obadyah the Norman Proselyte." *JJS* 5, no. 1 (1954): 32–37.

Schlossberg, Herbert. *A Fragance of Oppression. The Church and its Persecutors.* Wheaton, IL: Crossway, 1991.

Schoenberg, Harris Okun. *A Mandate for Terror. The United Nations and the PLO.* New York: Shapolsky Publishers, 1989.

Schoon, Simon. See World Council of Churches (1988).

Schopoff [Skopov], A. P. *Les Réformes et la Protection des Chrétiens en Turquie, 1673–1904, Firmans, Bérats, Protocols, Traités, Capitulations, Arrangements, Notes, Circulaires, Règlements, Lois, Mémorandums, etc.* Paris: Plon, 1904.

Schreiner, Martin. "Contributions à l'Histoire des Juifs en Egypte." *REJ* 31 (1895): 9–10.

Sébéos [Sépêos]. *Histoire d'Héraclius.* Translated from Armenian by Frédéric Macler. Paris: Imprimerie Nationale, 1904. See Dulaurier.

Segal, J. Benzion. "Syriac Chronicle as Source Material for the history of Islamic peoples." In Bernard and Peter M. Holt, *Historians of the Middle East,* London, 1969, pp. 246–58.

Sela, Abraham. *Political Encyclopedia of the Middle East.* Jerusalem: The Jerusalem Publishing House, 1999.

Sémach, Yomtob-David. *Une Mission de l'Alliance au Yémen.* Paris: Siège de la Société (AIU), 1910 [*BAIU* 35 (1910): 48–156].

―――― *A travers les communautés israélites d'Orient. Visites des écoles de l'Alliance Israélite.* Paris: Alliance Israélite Universelle, 1931.

Serjeant, Robert B. "A Judeo-Arab House-Deed from Habbán (with notes on the former Jewish Communities of the Wahidi Sultanate)." *JRAS* (October 1953): 113.

――――. *Customary and Shariah Law in Arabian Society.* London: Variorum Reprints, 1991, 8:119.

Servier, Jean. *Le Terrorisme.* Paris: Presses Universitaires de France, 1979 [Que Sais-je?].

Sfeir, Antoine. *Les réseaux d'Allah. Les filières islamistes en France et en Europe.* Paris: Plon, 1997.

Shah, Nasim Hasan. "Islamic Concept of State and its effect of Islamization of Laws in Pakistan." *HI* 16, no. 1 (spring 1993): 5–18.

――――. "The Concept of Al-Dhimah and the Rights and Duties of Dhimmis in an Islamic State." *Jimma* 9, no. 2 (July 1988): 217–22.

Shaler, William. *Sketches of Algiers, Political, Historical, and Civil, Containing an Account of the Geography, Population, Government.* Boston: Cummings & Hilliard, 1826.

Shariati, Ali. *Histoire et Destinée.* Preface and presentation by Jacques Berque (1982). 2nd ed. Teheran: Al Hoda, 1991.

Sharon, Moshe. *Judaism, Christianity and Islam. Interaction and Conflict.* Johannesburg: Sacks Publishing House, 1989.

――――. See [Ayalon].

Shaybani, *Siyar.* See Majid Khadduri, *The Islamic* (1965).

Shaw, Stanford J. "Ottoman Population Movements during the last years of the Empire, 1885–1914: some preliminary remarks." *JOS* 1 (1980): 191–205.

―――― and Ezel Kural Shaw. *History of the Ottoman Empire and Modern Turkey.* Vol. 1, *Empire of the Gazis. The Rise and the Decline of the Ottoman Empire, 1280–1808*; vol. 2, *Reform, Revolution, and Republic. The Rise of Modern Turkey, 1808–1975.* Cambridge/London/New York: Cambridge University Press, 1976–77.

Shea, Nina, ed. *In the Lion's Den. A Primer on Mounting Christian Persecution Around the World and How American Christians can Respond.* Afterword by Dr. Ravi Zacharias. Washington, DC: Freedom House, 1996 [Expanded edition, Broadman House, 1997].

Shulewitz, Malka Hillel, ed. *The Forgotten Millions. The Modern Jewish Exodus from Arab Lands.* London/New York: Cassell, 1999 [Paperback ed. Continuum, 2000].

al-Shuwayrif, Abd al-Latif. "Les dangers de l'Orientalisme et notre façon de les affronter." Text appeared in 1973 in Tunis.Translated from Arabic by Michel Lagarde. In *Al-Mustašriqun (Orientalistes) PISAI* (1992/2): 34–49. See Borrmans.

Simon, Marcel. *Recherches d'Histoire Judéo-Chrétienne.* Paris/The Hague: Mouton, 1962.

――――. *Verus Israel. A Study of the Relations between Christians and Jews in the Roman Empire (AD 135–425).* Translated from French by H. McKeating. Oxford: Oxford University Press, 1986 [Littman Library of Jewish Civilization] [French ed., 1964].

Sinai, Anne and Chaim I. Waxman, eds. "Ethnic and Religious Minorities in the Middle East." Part 1 (9 articles) and part 2 (9 articles). *MER*, vol. 9, n° 1 (autumn 1976) and vol. 9, n° 2 (winter 1976/77).

Sivan, Emmanuel. *L'Islam et la Croisade: Idéologie et Propagande dans les Réactions Musulmanes aux Croisades*. Paris: Maisonneuve, 1968.

———— *Radical Islam*. New Haven/London: Yale University Press, 1985.

Slouschz, Nahoum. "Israélites de Tripolitaine." *BAIU* 31 (1906): 103–09.

————. *Travels in North Africa*. Philadelphia: Jewish Publication Society of America, 1927.

Smith, William Cantwell. *Islam in the Modern World*. Princeton, NJ: Princeton University Press, 1957.

Sorlin, Pierre. *"La Croix" et les Juifs (1880–1899)*. Paris: Grasset, 1967.

Sourdel, Dominique and Janine. *La Civilisation de l'Islam Classique*. Paris: Arthaud, 1983.

di Spoleto, Angelo. *Pèlerinage en Egypte (1303–1304)*. Edited by G. Golubovitch. 3 vols. Karachi, 1919.

Stein, Leonard. *The Balfour Declaration*. London: Valentine, Mitchell, 1961.

Stephens, John Lloyd. *Incidents of Travel in Egypt, Arabia Petrae, and the Holy Land*. Edited with an introduction by Victor Wolfgand von Hagen. Norman, OK: University of Oklahoma, 1970 [1ˢᵗ ed. 1837].

Stillman, Norman. *The Jews of Arab Lands. A History and Source Book*. Philadelphia: The Jewish Publication Society of America, 1979.

————. *The Jews of Arab Lands in Modern Times*. Philadelphia/New York: The Jewish Publication Society of America, 1991.

Storrs, Sir Ronald. *Orientations*. London: Nicholson & Watson, 1943 [1ˢᵗ ed. 1937].

Strauss, Eliahu. See Ashtor-Strauss, Eliahu.

Stroun, Maurice and Michael Harsgor. *Le refus d'assumer son passé historique ou L'Imbroglio israélo-palestinien*. Geneva: Ed. Metropolis, 1991.

Sultân, S. Abd al-Hamid Sultân. "Les mobiles qui inspirent l'Orientalisme" (1990). Translated from Arabic by Maurice Borrmans. In *Al-Mustašriqun (Orientalistes)*, *PISAI* (1992/2): 50–67. See Borrmans.

al-Tabari. *Kitab al-Jihad (Book of Holy War)*. Edited and translated from the Arabic by Joseph Schacht. Leiden: Brill, 1933.

————. "Al-Mutawakkil et les Chrétiens." Translated from Arabic by André Ferré. See *al-Dimma*, (1991/1–2): 96–103.

————. *The History of al-Tabari (Ta'rikh al-rusul wa'l-muluk)*. Vol. 12, *The Battle of al-Qadisiyyah and the Conquest of Syria and Palestine*. Translated and annotated by Yohanan Friedmann; vol. 13, *The Conquest of Iraq, Southwestern Persia, and Egypt*. Translated and annotated by Gautier H. A. Juynboll. New York: State University of New York Press, 1992.

Taguieff, Pierre-André. *La force du préjugé. Essai sur le racisme et ses doubles*. Paris: tel gallimard, 1990 [1ˢᵗ ed. La Découverte, 1987].

————. *Les Protocoles des Sages de Sion*. Vol. 1, *Introduction à l'étude des Protocoles, un faux et ses usages dans le siècle*; vol. 2, *Etudes et documents*. Paris: Berg International, 1992.

————. ed. *L'Antisémitisme de Plume 1940–1944. Etudes et documents*. Paris: Berg International, 1999.

Taheri, Amir. *Holy Terror. Inside the World of Islamic Terrorism*. New York/London: Adler & Adler, 1987.

Tavernier, Jean-Baptiste. *Les six voyages en Turquie et en Perse de Jean Baptiste Tavernier*

[1630–1632 & 1663–1669]. New revised and corrected edition. 6 vols. Rouen: 1712 [1ˢᵗ ed.1676].

Ternon, Yves. *Les Arméniens, histoire d'un génocide*. Paris: Seuil, 1977.

Thevet d'Angoulesme, André. *La Cosmographie universelle de André Thevet cosmographe du Roy. Illustrée de diverses figures des choses plus remarquables, revüs par l'auteur et incogneuës de noz anciens et modernes*. 2 vols. Paris: P. L'Huilier, 1575.

Tibawi, Abdul al-Latif. *Second Critique of English-Speaking Orientalists and their approach to Islam and the Arabs*. London: The Islamic Cultural Centre, 1979.

Tincq, Henri. *L'Etoile et la Croix. Jean-Paul II—Israël: l'explication*. Paris: Lattès, 1993.

Tritton, Arthur Stanley. "Islam and the Protected Religions." *JRAS* (1931): 311–38.

———. *The Caliphs and their Non-Muslim Subjects. A Critical Study of the Covenant of Umar*. London: Frank Cass, 1970 [1ˢᵗ ed. 1930].

Tsimhoni, D. "The Arab Christians and the Palestinian Arab National Movement during the Formative Stage." In *The Palestinians and the Middle East Conflict*, edited by Gabriel Ben-Dor, 73–98.

———. *Christian Communities in Jerusalem and the West Bank since 1948. An Historical, Social and Political Study*. Westport, CT./London: Praeger, 1993.

Tuchman, Barbara W. *Bible and Sword. England and Palestine from the Bronze Age to Balfour*. New York: Ballantine Books, 1984. [1st ed., 1956]

al-Turabi, Hassan. "The Islamic State." In *Voices of Resurgent Islam*, 241–51, edited by John L. Esposito (1983).

Turan, Osman. "Les Souverains Seldjoukides et leurs sujets non-musulmans." *SI* 1 (1953): 65–100.

———. "L'Islamisation dans la Turquie du Moyen Age." *SI* 1 (1959): 137–52.

Turki, Abdel Magid. *Théologiens et Juristes de l'Espagne Musulmane. Aspects Polémiques*. Paris: Maisonneuve & Larose, 1982 ["Islam d'Hier et d'Aujourd'hui." Vol. 16].

———. "Situation du 'tributaire' qui insulte l'Islam, au regard de la doctrine et de la jurisprudence musulmanes." *SI* 30 (1969). In idem, 199–232.

Tyan, Emile. *Histoire de l'Organisation Judiciaire en Pays d'Islam*. Preface by Edouard Lambert. 3 vols. Lyons: Annales de l'Université de Lyon, Paris, 1938–1943.

———. "Djihad." *EI*² 2 (1965): 551–53.

Ubicini, Abdolonyma. *Lettres sur la Turquie, ou Tableau Statistique, religieux, politique, administratif, militaire, commercial, etc. de l'Empire ottoman depuis le Khatti-Cherif de Gulkhané (1839). Accompagné de Pièces Justificatives*. 2 vols. Paris: Librairie Militaire de J. Dumaine, 1853–54.

Vacalopoulos, Apostolos E. *History of Macedonia, 1354–1833*. Translated from Greek by Peter Megann. Salonika: Institute for Balkan Studies, 1973.

———. *Histoire de la Grèce Moderne*. Preface by Jean Pouilloux. French edition adapted by Pierre Dieudouné and Gaston Rochas. Saint-Juste-la-Pendue: Horvath, 1975.

———. *The Greek Nation, 1453–1669*. New Brunswick, NJ: Rutgers University Press, 1976.

Vaïlhé, S. "Les Juifs et la Prise de Jérusalem en 614." *EO* (1909), 12:15–17.

Vajda, Georges. "Juifs et Musulmans selon le Hadit." *JA* 219 (January–March 1937): 57–127.

———. *Un Recueil de Textes Historiques Judéo-Marocains. Hesperis* 12. (Paris): Larose, 1951.

————. "Ahl al-Kitab." *EI²*.

————. "Un Traité maghrébin 'Adversus Judaeos': Ahkâm ahl al-<u>D</u>imma du Shaykh Muhammad b. Abd al-Karim al-Maghili." In *Etudes d'Orientalisme dédiées à la mémoire de Lévi-Provençal*, 2:805–13. Paris: Maisonneuve & Larose, 1962.

————. "L'Image du Juif dans la tradition islamique." *NC* 13–14 (1968): 2–7.

Vakalopoulos, Kostandinos. A. *Modern History of Macedonia (1830–1912)*. Preface by Apostolos E. Vacalopoulos. Translated from Greek by J.R. Collins-Litsas and Deborah Whitehouse. Salonika: Barbounakis, 1988.

Valognes, Jean-Pierre (pseudonym). *Vie et Mort des Chrétiens d'Orient. Des Origines à nos jours*. Paris: Fayard, 1994.

del Valle, Alexandre (pseudonym). *Islamisme et Etats-Unis. Une Alliance contre l'Europe*. Preface by General Pierre-Marie Gallois, Postscript by Jean-Pierre Péroncel-Hugoz. Lausanne: L'Age d'Homme, 1997.

————. *Guerres Contre l'Europe. Bosnie-Kosovo-Tchétchénie . . .* Paris: Editions des Syrtes, 2000.

Vámbéry, Arminius. *Travels in Central Asia, being the account of a journey from Teheran across the Turkoman Desert on the Eastern Shore of the Caspian to Kheva, Bokhara, and Samarcand, performed in 1863, etc.* London: 1864.

Vasiliev, Alexandrovich Alexander. *History of the Byzantine Empire*, Vol. 1, *From Constantine the Great to the Epoch of the Crusade (A.D.1081)*; vol. 2, *From the Crusades to the Fall of the Empire (A.D.1453)*. Madison and Milwaukee: University of Wisconsin, 1928–29.

————. *Byzance et les Arabes*. Vol. 1, *La Dynastie d'Amorium (820–867)*. French edition prepared by Henri Grégoire and Marius Canard with the help of C. Nallino, E. Honigmann, and Claude Backvis; vol. 2, *La Dynastie macédonnienne (867–959)*. French edition prepared by Henri Grégoire and Marius Canard; vol. 3, *Die Ostgrenze des Byzantinischen Reiches (363–1071)*. Brussels: Editions de l'Institut de Philologie et d'Histoire Orientales, 1935/50/68.

Vatikiotis, Panayiotis Jerassimos. *Islam and the State*. London: Croom Helm, 1987.

————. "The Spread of Islamic Terrorism." In *Terrorism. How the West Can Win*, edited by Benjamin Netanyahu.

Voinot, Louis. *Oujda et l'Amalat (Maroc)*. Oran [Extract from the *Bulletin de la Société de Géographie et d'Archéologie de la Province d' Oran* (1911–12)].

Volney, Comte Constantin-François. *Voyage en Egypte et en Syrie, pendant les années 1783, 1784 et 1785, suivi de considérations sur la guerre des Russes et des Turks*. 2 vols. Paris: Parmentier & Froment, 1825 [1ˢᵗ ed. 1788–89].

Vryonis, Jr., Speros. *The Decline of Medieval Hellenism in Asia Minor and the Process of Islamization from the Eleventh through the Fifteenth Century*. Berkeley/Los Angeles/London: University of California, 1971.

————. "Nomadization and Islamization in Asia Minor." *DOP* 29 (1975): 41–71. See Dumbarton Oaks, May 1963.

————. ed. *Islam and Cultural Change in the Middle Ages*. Wiesbaden, 1975.

————. "Religious Change and Continuity in the Balkans and Anatolia from the 14th through the 16th Century." In idem, *Islam* (1975): 127–40.

———— and Henrik Birnbaum ed. *Aspects of the Balkans: Continuity and Change. Contributions to the International Balkan Conference held at UCLA, October 23–28, 1969*. The Hague/Paris: Mouton, 1972.

Waardenburg, J.D.J. "al-Mustashrikûn (Orientalistes)." *EI* ² 7 (1992): 736–54.

Wakin, Edward. *A Lonely Minority. The Modern History of Egypt's Copts.* New York: William Morrow, 1963.

Wadlow, René and David Littman. See, Littman, *Midstream* (1998).

al-Waqidi. *Kitab al-Maghazi* (The Book of Expeditions) (Arabic). 2 vols. Edited and translated from Arabic by M. Jones. London, 1966.

Watson, John H. *Among the Copts.* Brighton: Sussex Academic Press, 2000.

Watt, William Montgomery. "The Condemnation of the Jews of Banû Qurayzah." *MW* 42 (1952): 160–71.

———. *Muhammad at Mecca.* Oxford: Clarendon Press, 1953.

———. *Muhammad at Medina.* Oxford: Clarendon Press, 1956.

———. "Muhammad." In *The Cambridge History of Islam* (1970), 1 : 39–49.

———. *The Formative Period of Islamic Thought.* Edinburgh: Edinburgh University Press, 1973.

———. *The Majesty That Was Islam. The Islamic World, 661–1100.* London: Sidgwick & Jackson, 1974.

———. *Islamic Fundamentalism and Modernity.* London/New York: Routledge, 1988.

———. *Muslim-Christian Encounters. Perceptions and Misconceptions.* London/New York: Routledge, 1991.

Weissman, Nahoum. *Les Janissaires. Etude de l'Organisation Militaire des Ottomans.* Doctoral thesis. Paris:University of Paris, 1938.

Wendell, Charles. See al-Banna.

Wilkie Young, H. E. "Notes on the City of Mosul." Appendix in n° 4, 28 January 1909, FO 195/2308. In Elie Kedourie, ed., *MES* 7, 2 (May 1971): 229–35.

Wistrich, Robert S. *Hitler's Apocalypse. Jews and the Nazi Legacy.* London: Weidenfeld & Nicolson, 1985.

———. *Between Redemption and Perdition. Modern Anntisemitism and Jewish Identity.* London/New York: Routledge, 1990.

———. *Antisemitism. The Longest Hatred.* London: Thames Methuen & New York: Pantheon Books, 1991.

Wittek, Paul. "Devshirme and Shari'a." *BSOAS* 17(1955): 271–78.

Wilson, Woodrow. *War and Peace. Presidential Messages, Addresses and Public Papers (1917–1924) by Woodrow Wilson.* Edited by Ray Stannard Baker and William E. Dodd. New York/London: Harper & Brothers, 1927.

Wolff, Joseph. *Narrative of a Mission to Bokhara in the Years 1843–1845 to ascertain the fate of Colonel Stoddart and Captain Conolly.* 7th ed., abridged from the original. 2 vols. Edinburgh: William Blackwood, 1852 [1st ed. 1845].

———. *Researches and Missionary Labours among the Jews, Mohammedans and other sects, by the Rev. Joseph Wolff during his travels between the years 1831 and 1834, from Malta to Egypt, Constantinople, Armenia, Persia (1831–1834).* 2nd ed. London: 1835.

World Council of Churches. *The Theology of the Churches and the Jewish People. Statements by the World Council of Churches and its member churches. With a commentary by Allan Brockway, Paul van Buren, Rolf Rendtorff, Simon Schoon.* Geneva: WCC Publications, 1988.

———. "Gathered for Life: Official Report." 6th Assembly, World Council of Churches. Vancouver, Canada, 24 July–10 August 1983.

Yadlin, Rivka. *An Arrogant Oppressive Spirit. Anti-Zionism as Anti-Judaism in Egypt.* Oxford/New York: Pergamon Press, 1989 [Vidal Sassoon International Center for the Study of Antisemitism, Hebrew University of Jerusalem].

Yahya ibn Adam. *Kitab Al-Kharaj*. See Ben Shemesh.

Zaanoun, Hussein and Alain Chery. "Dans les collèges de la banlieu nord de Paris." *Hérodote* (L'Occident et la Guerre des Arabes), n° 60/61, 1st and 2nd trim. (1991): 235–38.

Zametica, John. *The Yugoslav Conflict. An analysis of the causes of the Yugoslav war, the policies of the republic and the regional and international implications of the conflict* (May 1992). London: International Institute for Strategic Studies (Adelphi Paper 270), Brassey's, 1992.

Zanjani, Abbasali Amid. *Minority Rights According to the Law of the Tribute Agreement. A Survey of some Purports of the International Rights From the Viewpoint of the Islamic Jurisprudence.* Teheran International Publishing Co., 1997.

Ziada, Mustapha. See Bethmann.

General Index